"If They Move . . . Kill 'Em!"

Sam Peckinpah
'If They Move...Kill 'Em!'

David Weddle

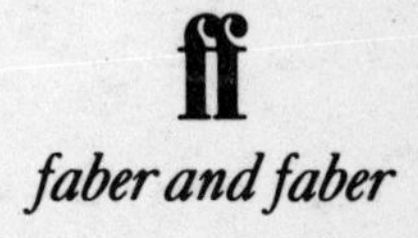

faber and faber

First published in the USA in 1994
by Grove Press
841 Broadway
New York, New York 10003
U.S.A.

First published in Great Britain in 1996
by Faber and Faber Limited
3 Queen Square London WC1N 3AU

Printed in England by Clays Ltd, St Ives plc

A CIP record for this book
is available from the British Library

ISBN 0-571-17884-7

10 9 8 7 6 5 4 3 2 1

To my mother and father,

who made it all possible

Acknowledgments

This book has been distilled from over 500 hours of interviews and a first-draft manuscript of over 2,300 pages. That amorphous mass of research would never have been sculpted into a readable book without the assistance of several people. First I must thank Jesse Graham, who talked me into writing it in the first place and spent many late-night hours on the phone offering emotional support and feedback. Jesse pushed me constantly to probe deeper, to leave no stone unturned, and made crucial contributions to the final round of editing. Howard Libes is the one living human to have read every page of the original manuscript. He helped me throughout the editing process, by suggesting ways not only to cut and tighten but to improve the structure, character development, and prose. Writers like to complain that there are no editors in New York who actually edit anymore, but Anton Mueller at Grove Press put that myth to rest. Anton laid out the groundwork that enabled me to finally bring the manuscript down to a practical length, and showed enormous patience as he waited and waited and waited for me to produce a final draft. The copy editor, Marc Romano, also made a significant contribution with his sharp eye for detail and hundreds of suggestions for tightening and improving sentence structure.

My agent, Kristine Dahl, believed in this book when no one else did; without her efforts it would not exist. She demolished another cliché, that of the money-hungry agent who cares only about the deal. The time and effort that she expended couldn't even begin to be compensated for by the meager financial returns. Her assistants Gordon Kato and Dorothea Herrey were equally generous with their advice and support.

I'd also like to thank Greg Critser for introducing me to Dahl, and Ann Godoff, who originally bought the book for Atlantic Monthly Press and provided me with guidance in its formative stages that helped shape the final product.

I will never find enough words to express my gratitude to the Peckinpah family—Walter and Fern Lea Peter; Kristen, Melissa, and Mathew Peckinpah; Marie Selland—for allowing me into their lives, for enduring hours and hours of questions, for their willingness to delve into a past that was often painful . . . for trusting me. A special thanks to Gill Dennis, who propped me up in my darkest hours, and Max Evans, whose letters and phone calls and passionate belief in this project helped me maintain the faith. And then there is Jim Silke, whom I am so grateful to for finally trusting me, for the insights, the prodding, and the support.

The Sam Peckinpah collection at the Margaret Herrick Library at the Academy of Motion Picture Arts and Sciences in Los Angeles contains every production file, screenplay, and scrap of professional and personal correspondence that Peckinpah accumulated over his fifty-nine years. I spent six months combing through those files, with the guidance of Val Almendarez, Howard Prouty, and the rest of the library staff. All of my interview tapes and the "uncut" manuscript for this book will be donated to the library and become part of the Peckinpah collection for future scholars to draw upon.

Of all the books on Peckinpah that preceded this one, two stand out as outstanding pieces of scholarship: *Peckinpah: The*

Western Films by Paul Seydor, and *Peckinpah: A Portrait in Montage* by Garner Simmons. They form the foundation upon which this book is built, and have influenced it in countless ways. Seydor's is the most thorough critical examination of Peckinpah's work ever done, and Simmons still gives the most complete accounting of the making of each Peckinpah television show and feature film. Both men generously donated their time, advice, and research materials to me.

I would also like to thank Laura Larsen and Don Jordan for valuable assistance with some of my computer files; Nick Redman for research materials; Frank Kowalski for his great storytelling ability, which planted the seeds of fascination from which this sprouted; Jeff Slater for rare film footage; Paul Joyce for setting up interviews and valuable financial support; my brother James Weddle, who came in at the eleventh hour and helped me push through to the finish line; Don Shay, for interview material with deceased members of the Peckinpah Bunch; and my UCLA interns who worked for no money and with great enthusiasm—Josh Lobel, Shelly McCrory, Sandy Nang, Jill Le Ger, Maggie Guinn, Emily Love, and Jason Shankel, who offered valuable insights on Peckinpah's contributions to the screenplay of *Straw Dogs*.

Don't make me out no saint,

but don't put me down too deep.

The Ballad of Cable Hogue

Contents

Prologue
"What Is Going On in My Heart?"

On May 1, 1969, 1,000 people filed into the Royal Theater in Kansas City to see what the Warner Bros. publicity department had advertised as "The First in the World Public Showing of One of the Year's Biggest Movies!" Response to the ad in the local paper was so great that another 500 people had to be turned away at the door. Few noticed the film's director standing with a phalanx of dark-suited studio executives in the outer lobby, looking uncomfortable and out of place in faded Levi's, worn cowboy boots, and a tan leather jacket that matched the complexion of his deeply lined face. Even fewer would have recognized his name, or cared that he'd been hailed in Europe as one of the most talented of a new generation of American filmmakers.

It was a Midwestern crowd with little appetite for highbrow critical theories. They'd come to see a good old-fashioned shoot-'em-up western with plenty of action and thrills and predictable good guys and bad guys. With stars like William Holden and Ernest Borgnine and a title like *The Wild Bunch*, this looked like a picture that could deliver the goods.

But when the lights lowered and velvet curtains parted that night, the good citizens of Kansas City got more than they bargained for, much more. Uneasy shifting began with the very first scene.

William Holden, leading his outlaw band into the withered fringes of a dust-choked town, comes upon a group of giggling children squatting barefoot and ragged in the dirt. As his horse pulls abreast of them, Holden glances down at the object of their mirth and the camera catches a wink of horror and premonition in his stoic gaze. The children grin tauntingly as he spurs his horse onward, then return to the miniature arena they've constructed out of sticks and dried mud. Inside it, several scorpions writhe on a teeming anthill. "Turn 'em over!" one of the boys giggles. A poking stick flips the scorpions, their stingers twitching spasmodically at thousands of tiny red tormentors. A haunting melody slips beneath the heavy percussion soundtrack, tying an eerie connection between the scorpions succumbing to a sea of red and the destiny of Holden and his men.

If anyone in the audience still thought this movie might stay within the comfortable boundaries of a conventional western, those hopes disappeared in the gunfight that followed.

While robbing a railroad office in the parched town square, Holden's gang is ambushed by a posse of bounty hunters. But who are the good guys and who are the bad? The bounty hunters are every bit as sleazy and ruthless as the outlaws, neither group displaying a glimmer of guilt as they blow away innocent bystanders caught in the crossfire. The 70mm picture seems to explode beyond the confines of the screen. The action is shot from a dizzying variety of angles, some filmed in slow motion, others at normal speed, cut together in an alternating rhythm so that time seems to compress and then expand. Bullets smash into chests, shoulders, limbs, and faces like incoming mortar shells, spraying fountains of blood and flesh; bodies jerk and twist; glass windows shatter lethargically, the sparkling shards raining down like ice crystals; horses and riders tumble to earth with balletic grace.

No, this was no ordinary western. This was like no western, no movie, anyone had ever seen before.

Thirty people bolted up the aisle and out of the theater, some to vomit in the adjoining alley. But most remained pinned to their seats, horrified yet transfixed. "I saw the picture with one eye at times, from behind arms and fingers spread in fright," Phyllis Jiles, a woman in her early twenties, recalled afterward. "But I must admit, I was excited, repulsed, and at the same time drawn to what I saw on the screen."

Another found the violence "unreal, yet too real."

But the opening shootout was only an appetizer, a spring picnic, compared to the battle some two hours later, when Holden and his bunch plunge into suicidal combat with an entire Mexican army.

Armed to the teeth, William Holden, Ernest Borgnine, Ben Johnson, and Warren Oates come to a poised halt beneath an adobe archway, the entrance to General Mapache's lair.

"Ah!" the drunken general grunts as he wheels around on unsteady legs. *"Los gringos otra vez."*

A moment of stillness, the air vibrating like a guitar string stretched to the breaking point.

"What you want?!" Mapache bellows, waving his big sloppy arms.

Holden's reply is quiet, measured. "We want Angel."

"You want Angel, no?" Mapache's fat sweaty cheeks spread away from a row of gleaming white teeth, the face of evil grinning back at them. "All right, I am going to give it to you."

Like a loving father gently coaxing his infant son to take his first steps, Mapache helps the Bunch's fallen comrade to his feet. After being dragged around the village square by an automobile for almost a day, his face is lacerated and blistered, his eyes glassy and reeling. Mapache coos soft encouragement—"Angelito"—and uses a long, stained knife to cut the ropes that bind his hands. Angel's eyes manage to focus on his friends standing ten feet in front of him; his arms raise up stiffly, like Jesus on the cross. He takes a tentative step, but in a wicked flash Mapache's knife slashes across Angel's neck and the blood fountains out of his open throat.

The Bunch's reaction is instantaneous: their guns roar, bullets ripping through Mapache's chest and blossoming red out of his back.

He falls to earth, his last breath grunting from his body, and then there is another unbearable pause. Two hundred Mexican soldiers stare at their fallen leader in disbelief, the hands of some half-raised in tenuous surrender.

"Hee! Hee!" Borgnine titters, grinning like a jack-o'-lantern, eyes burning into Holden, silently goading him to take them over the edge into the abyss.

With great deliberation Holden pivots, takes aim at the Mexicans' German military adviser in all his Prussian regalia, and fires. The German goes down, the spell is broken, two hundred Mexicans go for their guns, and the courtyard is engulfed in a maelstrom of flying lead.

Bodies pile on top of bodies, careening earthward in slow motion and fast, arcing upward on mushroom clouds of tossed grenades. Images flash, one after another in an accelerating dance of death, repulsive and erotic, depraved yet strangely beautiful. Warren Oates grabs a machine gun and whirls on a line of soldiers filing through a narrow doorway: "YEEEAAAAAAH!" he shrieks, unhinged, agonized, perversely transcendent, as bullets smash into him and spray out of his gun.

A woman, the lover of one of the Mexican soldiers, shoots Holden in the back. He grimaces, turns, and spits out "Bitch!" before unloading his shotgun into her belly.

Oates falls backward away from the machine gun, dead. Holden grabs it and rips forth another burst, hitting stockpiles of explosives that blow the entire courtyard skyward with thundering booms.

"Give 'em hell, Pike!" Borgnine screams exultantly, just as a Mexican boy raises a rifle to shoot Holden, fatally this time, in the back.

In the audience, Phyllis Jiles found the Bunch's headlong rush into death "strangely exhilarating . . . I felt something of a mental orgasm."

"I want to get the hell out of this place!" someone cried a few rows away. Another woman screamed, sprang from her seat, and ran out of the theater.

In the lobby, a man vented his outrage on the bewildered theater manager while an enormously obese woman screamed into a pay phone: "Get down here, and bring the church sisters with you! We're going to run these people out of town on a rail!"

"Only a madman could call this creation!" one livid patron scribbled furiously on the reaction card that the clammy-palmed publicity man from Warner Bros. had handed out. "It's not art! It's not cinema! It's pure wasted insanity!"

"You ought to be shot for making it!" several other outraged pacifists wrote.

Up near the very top of the cavernous theater, next to the projection-booth door, the madman who'd made the movie, Sam Peckinpah, stood quietly observing the chaos. Beside him the film's editor, Lou Lombardo, paled at boos and hisses rising up from the ocean of people beneath them. He leaned close to Peckinpah's ear and whispered urgently: "Sam, we've got to get out of here! They're getting ready to kick the shit out of us!"

The director's brown-gray beard parted into the enigmatic half-grin, half-grimace that Lombardo had come to know so well during countless hours in the editing room over the past year. "Leave now?" Peckinpah said in a raspy whisper, his hazel eyes shining brightly. "Hell, partner, I think we've got 'em on the run!"

Peckinpah viewed the anger of those who had sat through the entire movie with irony. He suspected the real target of their rage was not him, but themselves. "They want to walk out, but they can't," he would say later. "They can't turn their faces away and that makes them mad."

Not everyone hated the film. About a quarter of the audience loved it passionately. One young man approached the director afterward and confessed that in the final shootout he had thoughtlessly started to cheer. "Then I was ashamed," the man said, "because I realized there was no justification at all for my cheering."

"You see," said Peckinpah, "people begin to see the violence within them, the violence just below the surface. It's in all of us, as the film shows, whether we be criminals, lawmen, children (who imitate their elders, although they are violent naturally), or old men. . . . Violence usually begins with a reason, with some principle to be defended. The real motivation, however, is a primitive thirst for blood, and as the fighting continues reasons or principles are forgotten and men fight for the sake of fighting."

Many in that Kansas City audience saw parallels between the wholesale slaughter in the movie and the war in Vietnam, which was roaring full-tilt in the summer of 1969. For others it evoked the riots in Watts, Detroit, Chicago, on college campuses across the United States, and the recent assassinations of Bobby Kennedy and Martin Luther King, Jr. "To me," one wrote on his preview card, "it showed up nothing but the fact that we are not the peace loving anti-war Americans we think we are."

Nearly two months later, *The Wild Bunch* was shown to the international press for the first time in the Bahamas. Warner Bros. had organized an international film festival on Grand Bahama Island to promote its most prestigious summer releases. Five hundred journalists were flown in from all over the world to see six films over the period of one week. Luchino Visconti's *The Damned* and Francis Ford Coppola's *The Rain People* were among those shown, but it was *The Wild Bunch,* screened at the end of the festival, that ignited a brushfire of controversy.

"The audience reaction was extreme," Roger Ebert, critic for the *Chicago Sun-Times,* recalls. "Some people walked out. Others closed their eyes. When the lights went up, the applause was matched by boos and hisses. And then the arguments started."

"I never thought," one woman complained to Ebert, "that I'd live long enough to see William Holden shoot a woman."

But others, Ebert among them, had been captivated. "It was a visceral experience," he recalls. "I thought it was beautiful, I thought it was artistic, I thought it was grand in its vision. I really did love it."

At the press conference the next morning the movie's stars and producer, Phil Feldman, faced a bristling audience without the support of their director. Peckinpah had not shown up.

Furious journalists began firing salvos. "I have only one question to ask," said Virginia Kelly of *Reader's Digest. "Why was this film made?"*

"Why did everyone bleed so much?" another writer wanted to know.

"Lady," Ernest Borgnine responded impatiently, "did you ever see anyone shot by a gun without bleeding?"

"I just can't get over the reaction here," said a perturbed William Holden. "Are people surprised that violence really exists in the world? Just turn on your TV set any night. The viewer sees the Vietnam war, cities burning, campus riots. He sees plenty of violence."

"Both Borgnine and Holden seemed to be rather dazed by the film themselves," Roger Ebert recalls. "This was not the kind of movie Hollywood would have made five or ten years earlier. Certainly there's nothing like it elsewhere in Holden's earlier career. Holden had worked with unconventional directors like Billy Wilder and he had done some pretty inventive acting in nonconventional roles, but he'd never done anything like this."

A half-hour into the press conference Peckinpah finally appeared, wearing a dilapidated Stetson, a pair of mirrored sunglasses dangling from his neck, and a camera slung around his shoulder like a sidearm.

"Why did you make this film?" Stuart Byron of *Variety* asked. "What does it say? Why all the violence?"

Peckinpah shrugged. "I have nothing to say. The film speaks for itself."

"Then why are we holding this press conference?" Rex Reed stridently demanded.

Peckinpah shrugged again. "That's a good question."

Finally, Roger Ebert had heard enough. He rose to his feet. "I suppose all of you up there are getting the impression that this film has no defenders. That's not true. A lot of us think *The Wild Bunch* is a great film. It's hard to ask questions about a film you like, easy about one you hate. I just wanted it said: to a lot of people, this film is a masterpiece."

"Hear! Hear!" cried another critic. There was a burst of applause, and nods of appreciation from the actors and director.

The widely polarized reactions continued as reviews of *The Wild Bunch* came out over the weeks that followed.

"There is little justification for discussing this ugly, pointless, disgusting bloody film," wrote critic William Wolf.

Judith Crist of *New York* magazine advised: "If you want to see *The Wild Bunch,* be sure and take along a barf bag."

But critics for *The New York Times, The Los Angeles Times,* and *The New Yorker* praised the film's brilliance, and Richard Schickel of *Life* agreed with Ebert's assertion that it was a masterpiece.

"Sam Peckinpah is a film-maker dedicated to telling truths and still preserving the legend of the American West," said *Time.* "*The Wild Bunch* is Peckinpah's most complex inquiry into the metamorphosis of man into myth. Not incidentally, it is also a raucous, violent, powerful feat of American film-making. . . . *The Wild Bunch* contains faults and mistakes, but its accomplishments are more than sufficient to confirm that Peckinpah, along with Stanley Kubrick and Arthur Penn, belongs with the best of the newer generation of American film-makers."

Americans have never quite known what to do about Sam Peckinpah. Even at the peak of his career in the late sixties and early seventies, when many critics hailed him as one of the most brilliant filmmakers of his generation, an equal number condemned him as a misogynist, sadist, even a fascist. (For the record, he actively supported liberal Democratic politicians.) In the late seventies, when both his life and art spiraled into a nihilistic abyss, the critics and public found little to admire in his films, and even his most ardent defenders abandoned him.

Yet as much as we may want to turn away from Peckinpah, shrug him off, forget him, we cannot. Like traumatic visions from our collective unconscious, his films keep springing back at us, sinking their teeth in, refusing to let go.

The first sparks of the great Peckinpah revival started in the early 1980s, shortly before Sam died. They were struck by a fanatic handful of film directors, academics, and critics who insisted that this rude delinquent was the most important American director of the last fifty years. In the decade that followed, these passionate disciples managed to fan the flames into a worldwide conflagration.

Seven books have already been published on Peckinpah's life and movies, and another two or three besides this one are presently in the works. In 1993 the BBC produced a feature-length documentary on him, and his films continue to play to packed houses in revival theaters and on college campuses, where professors have devoted entire courses to the study of his work.

In November of 1993 the Amiens Film Festival, in France, held a nine-day Peckinpah retrospective in which the entire body of his work—everything from his first crude kinescope, *Portrait of a Madonna,* to the Julian Lennon rock videos that he directed just before he died—was shown. The rediscovery of Peckinpah's early television shows came as a revelation, and the breadth and depth of his artistic output left audiences awestruck.

Even American critics have had to admit that Peckinpah looms large on the cinematic landscape. While it is still impossible to see his versions of *The Wild Bunch* and *Pat Garrett and Billy the Kid* in his own country, they, along with *Ride the High Country,* are now widely recognized as masterpieces and have become yardsticks by which every new American western is now measured.

His editing style—much imitated but never equaled—was the most revolutionary since Sergei Eisenstein's use of montage in *The Battleship Potemkin.* "No one, even today, has mastered the art of multicamera, multispeed editing [like Peckinpah has]," says Paul Schrader. "He would have five or six cameras going, all at different speeds and in his mind he had figured out which camera had to be at which speed—which one is running at 32 frames [per second] and 24, and 96, and 48, and how they're going to cut together." *The Wild Bunch* changed forever the way movies would be made and left its mark on an entire generation of film directors: Francis Ford Coppola, Oliver Stone, Michael Cimino, Walter Hill, Alex Cox, and John Milius, to name only a few.

"There is no doubt when seeing his films that you are looking at one of the great masters of American cinema," says Martin Scorsese.

Revival screenings of *Major Dundee, The Ballad of Cable Hogue, Straw Dogs, Junior Bonner, The Getaway, Bring Me the Head of Alfredo Garcia,* and *Cross of Iron* reveal that Peckinpah offered more than brilliant technique. He had an intensely personal vision, filled with recurring themes and imagery that have obsessed a long line of American artists.

"There are other, older friends in whose anachronistic company Sam Peckinpah should feel at home: Melville, Hawthorne, Twain, Hemingway, Faulkner," Kathleen Murphy wrote in *Film Comment* shortly after the director's death in 1984. "They all fished dark waters, from Moby Dick's domain to the Mississippi to the Big Two-Hearted River. . . . Our most native sons are outlaws all, men obsessed by whatever dream is violated or diminished, as it must always be—by a white whale or war, by unmanning bureaucracy or changing times—these fractured souls convulse in outrage. Such wars are waged inside us all, but American fiction itches to turn them out of doors, relocating them on whaling ships and river rafts, in Spanish villages and Southern Gothic mansions, in westerns. But style is content. These books and films are voiced and visualized as hallucinatory dramas that could only be played out in that ultimate theater in the round, the artist's mind and imagination."

Sam Peckinpah projected his hallucinatory dramas, his inner wars, onto the landscape of the American Southwest: an existential no-man's-land along the Texas-Mexico border where right and wrong, good and bad, depended on which end of the gun you were standing on, or how much gold was at stake. In this stark wilderness his protagonists embarked—or were pushed, kicked, and shoved—on quests for vengeance, riches, self-definition, self-destruction, and, occasionally, redemption. If they managed to claw the latter out of the hot sand, it came at a terrible price, on their own terms, and along a path of their own choosing. God, if he was hiding in the infinite recesses of the bleached sky above them, spoke no words of guidance and sent no burning bushes to light the way.

The eroticized violence in Peckinpah's films, the constant juxtaposition of romantic idealism with love of savagery, reflects America's own vacillation between utopian aspirations and a fetish for brutality—a dichotomy stitched deep in the fabric of its own Wild West mythology. Peckinpah used the framework of the western to explore the conflicting polarities within the American psyche and within himself. The last great director of western films, Peckinpah had himself been raised in the fading remnants of that Wild West. He grew up to see it smothered beneath the asphalt lava flow of civilization, and as a filmmaker he would make its death throes his most potent theme.

"*The Wild Bunch* is a powerful film because it comes from the gut of America, and from a man who is trying to get America out of his gut," film director Paul Schrader has written. "The trauma of expatriotism is a common theme in American art, but nowhere is the pain quite so evident as in the life of Sam Peckinpah. *The Wild Bunch* is the agony of a Westerner who stayed too long, and it is the agony of America."

Peckinpah made his films not with the cool detachment of an intellectual commentator observing events from up high, but as one of the writhing sufferers trying to clamor out of the pit. His are not the neatly structured, politically correct movies of Stanley Kramer, Richard Brooks, Alan Parker, or Kevin Costner, with their prepackaged characters and neatly devised plots and resolutions that leave an audience with the smug assurance that the social or psychological "problem" examined has been solved or at least explained. Peckinpah's films are filled with jagged edges, abrupt shifts in tone, and embarrassing moments of self-revelation in which the director lays naked some of his most neurotic and misguided obsessions for all to see.

The river of fiction that he navigated was admittedly narrow. Don't look for women protagonists in his films; there aren't any. Though they aren't all whores who enjoy a good rape, and most have far more dimension than his detractors ever gave him credit for, his women play supporting roles. Peckinpah's perspective is resolutely male. His women provide conflict and motivation for his men, serve as objects to be loved or hated (or most frequently *hated and loved*), or function as a Greek chorus that critiques the self-destructive shortcomings of male camaraderie, combat, and codes of honor. Don't look to his films for a portrait of a healthy, mutually nurturing marriage; he was much more convincing when dramatizing the failure of love than depicting its triumph.

Don't look for portrayals of whole and happy families either; most of his drifters and misfits have lost faith in that dream years before we meet them—as Peckinpah, by the time he reached the zenith of his art, had as well.

But if his river ran narrow, it also ran deep. Right to the core. "What makes Peckinpah an important director is his willingness to test himself," Stephen Farber wrote in his review of *Straw Dogs* for *Cinema* magazine. "[He] is committed to traditional ideals of masculinity—the myth of the Westerner—but he does not refrain from boldly questioning the masculine mystique. That self-questioning makes *Straw Dogs* more painful and pertinent and involving than a detached liberal discourse on the subject of male chauvinism could possibly be. Peckinpah is a man smashing his own defenses through his art, and perhaps his films inevitably generate more emotion than they seem able to contain. In *Straw Dogs* Peckinpah's personal obsessions intersect with a subject of special contemporary interest—the disintegration of traditional concepts of sexual role and identity. And that is why, for all of its flaws and confusions, *Straw Dogs* is a major work and a seminal film of the 70's."

Paul Schrader says that the most valuable lesson he learned from Peckinpah's work was "to go into your neuroses, to go into those things about yourself that you fear, not to cover them up, but to open them up."

"I'm defining my own problems; obviously, I'm up on the screen," Peckinpah admitted to an interviewer late one night, when booze and fatigue lowered his defenses enough for a rare moment of candor. "In a film, you lay yourself out, whoever you are. The one nice thing is that my own problems seem to involve other people as well. . . . *Straw Dogs* is about a guy who finds out a few nasty secrets about himself, about his marriage, about where he is, about the world around him. . . . It's about the violence within all of us. The violence which is reflecting on the political condition of the world today. It serves as a cathartic effect. Someone may feel a strange sick exultation at the violence, but he should then ask himself: 'What is going on in my heart?' "

There are few answers to be found in Peckinpah's work, few

resolutions, for he found none for himself in life. In fact, his personal life, as we will see, was often the very antithesis of a model for adjustment. There are no grand conclusions offered in his films about man's longing for heaven while running full tilt for hell, no solutions for mankind's fallen state, no roadmaps instructing us how we might enter our own house justified. We will have to find the way there by ourselves.

What Peckinpah's films offer is a chance to engage in the struggle. His movies draw viewers into intense psychodramas, giving them a chance to struggle *with him*, and perhaps make some discoveries.

"I always felt he was making movies about things he couldn't explain," says screenwriter Gill Dennis, who married Peckinpah's daughter Kristen. "He was making movies about things that people wouldn't acknowledge were there. It was like he was saying, 'See that? What do you think of that? How does that fit into your scheme of things?' "

Ken Kesey, the author of *One Flew Over the Cuckoo's Nest* and *Sometimes a Great Notion*, advises young writers not to write what they know, but what they don't know. "Don't look for the answer. The answer is usually dull. Look for the mystery."

Perched high atop a camera crane in filthy jeans and weathered cowboy boots with a sweaty bandanna knotted around his leathery head, like a half-mad Ahab, Peckinpah loved nothing better than to lead a company of actors and technicians deep into the heart of primitive Mexico on a fevered search for the movie they were making, to capture on film a fleeting glimpse of his own personal truth.

When Gill Dennis asked the director what epitaph he'd like to have on his tombstone, Peckinpah replied: "I suppose the fact that I never stopped looking . . . searching."

1

"Oh, Another Black Peckinpah!"

In his later years, Sam Peckinpah liked to give interviewers the impression that his childhood was a page right out of a Louis L'Amour western. He expounded on the rigors of growing up on a cattle ranch in central California in the 1930s. He told tales of herding, roping, and branding steer, of riding bucking broncos, of hunting deer and running a trap line in the High Sierras, of crossing streams with names like Coarsegold, where grizzled old prospectors still panned for the elusive yellow powder, of saloons in wild and woolly frontier towns like North Fork, where men knocked back shots of rotgut and still drew six-guns to settle their misunderstandings.

A rough, uncouth, yet fantastically exciting boyhood, he described. But only partially true.

Sam Peckinpah was the son of one of the most prominent attorneys in Fresno, California. He grew up in a sprawling suburban-style ranch house, with twenty-four acres of exquisitely landscaped property for his playground. During the Great Depression, while thousands of dispossessed families camped under trees along roadsides, young Sam lacked for no material possessions. He had his own bedroom, crammed with every toy his heart desired. He attended an exclusive grade school, and when he entered public high school he stood out as "the rich kid" who had his own Model A Ford and wore stylish new clothes while his peers made do with hand-me-downs.

Yet the tall tales he later spun for journalists were not complete fabrications either. The genteel middle-class lifestyle he was born into was only a recent development for the Peckinpahs. Just a generation earlier, Sam's grandfather, Charlie Peckinpah, had crossed the Great Plains with his parents in a covered wagon. The Peckinpahs forded rivers, slogged across deserts and swamps, climbed over treacherous mountain passes, and persevered through confrontations with Indians and bandits.

In the 1870s, Charlie lay claim to a 6,000-foot mountain in the High Sierras, just south of Yosemite, California. He and his brothers set up the Peckinpah Lumber Company in a meadow on top of the peak and by 1885 were hauling more than a million board feet of timber off the mountain each year.

Sam's maternal relatives, the Churches, were equally hardy pioneers. Moses J. Church—Sam's great-uncle—dug the first major irrigation canal in central California. The Fancher Channel carried water from the Kings River in the Sierra foothills to the flatlands sixteen miles south, and transformed a desert into productive farmland. As homesteaders converged on Fresno, cattle barons who wanted to preserve the open range counterattacked with hired guns. They tried to shoot Moses Church three times, but in each instance he successfully evaded his assailants.

The assassination attempts didn't much bother Moses; he knew they were the death throes of dinosaurs. The cattle barons were as doomed as the Mono Indians who'd occupied the land before them. Moses had discovered a weapon infinitely more powerful than the six-gun or Winchester: water. He brought it to where it wasn't. By the 1880s more than a thousand miles of canals had transformed the valley into wheat fields, groves of fig, peach, and walnut trees, and vineyards. Moses had fathered the greatest irrigation system in the world.

Sam Peckinpah grew up listening to the many larger-than-life tales of his ancestors. Through them a grand romantic vision of the Wild West unfolded in his imagination—a mythic realm that he longed to be a part of but that time had withdrawn forever out of reach.

His maternal grandfather, Denver Church, lived through the frontier's demise at the turn of the century, but changed with the changing times and flourished. In his youth he had been a hunter and trapper, a cattleman and part-time prospector, but in 1895 he put himself through law school and joined the burgeoning ranks of the professional class. He became a district attorney, a Superior Court judge, and finally a United States Congressman for a district that included Fresno County.

Yet Denver recalled with longing and regret the days of his youth, when a man could gaze from a mountaintop out at the great rolling expanse of a continent still untethered by fences and telegraph wires. So he bought a cattle ranch in the foothills of the Sierra Nevada, barely beyond the shadow of Peckinpah Mountain. Forty-one hundred acres of rolling grassland—the old Dunlap Ranch, everyone called it, and the name would stick. It became Denver's retreat, his escape hatch from the twentieth century, a dusty time capsule where the past almost seemed to live and breathe again. He stayed there for weeks and months at a time between stints in Washington—hunting, trapping, and tending to a couple hundred head of cattle.

Sam Peckinpah also stayed there, almost every summer of his youth and on many weekends. His grandfather, father, and older brother taught him to hunt, ride, and herd cattle. He got the chance to live out his fantasies, to have a taste of the long-lost world that the older men talked about. And there he discovered the cruel realities that hid behind the romantic mythology. His ancestors had been brutal men. They had to be to carve out a place for themselves in a wilderness. If one of his boys did something that Charlie Peckinpah disapproved of, he thought nothing of knocking him to the ground with the back of his hand. If a dog stuck his wet nose in Denver Church's face while he was otherwise occupied, he taught the animal a lesson by sticking a lighted cigarette on its snout. "That'll learn him."

The disparity between the romantic myth and the reality of the Wild West provoked complex reactions in the young Sam Peckinpah. His deeply conflicted feelings toward both would later give his westerns an incredible emotional charge.

Sam's mother, Fern, was born to Denver and Louise Church in 1893. She grew into a full-figured girl with her mother's round face and long thick auburn hair. The congressman's daughter had many eager suitors, and her teenage years were a whirlwind of dinners, dances, and picnics. She filled her diary with lengthy descriptions of the clothes she wore to these events and assessments of her various male admirers.

But behind the gay façade she was, from the beginning, a troubled girl. Her mother almost died giving birth to her, and while Louise was recovering Denver nursed his infant daughter with a bottle, changed her diapers, and rocked her to sleep in his arms. An intense bond formed between them. Through all the years that followed, Denver doted and fretted over his precious "Daught." His passionate devotion spoiled the girl. She developed an overwhelming need to be the center of attention at all times, an obsession that would imprison her for her entire life. Denver's image of Fern's fragility became her own; her parents' diaries and early letters contain constant references to Fern's headaches and sick spells.

When Fern was nineteen she fell madly in love with a pharmacist from Long Beach, Bob Nichols. Denver took an instant dislike to the pill-peddling city slicker. Anyone who didn't ride and hunt and love it was weak in Denver's eyes, and Denver hated nothing more than weakness in a man. He treated his own son, Earl, with coolness and at times even open hostility because he thought the boy too timid.

In a long letter to his daughter, Denver tried to dissuade her from marrying Nichols, yet promised he would let Fern make the final decision. "I have always been opposed to parents trying to choose companions for their children—am of the opinion the less they do about it the better."

But he lied. According to Fern's surviving children, her father went behind her back and either paid the young suitor off or threatened him, or most likely both. Whatever the method, Bob Nichols, the love of Fern's life, suddenly vanished one day, never to return. After the initial shock wore off, Fern tried to put on a happy face and proclaim to everyone that it had all worked out for the best, that maybe she and Bob weren't meant for each other after all. But forty-five years later she admitted her real feelings in her diary: "I loved my Dad dearly. We had a wonderful closeness and understanding. Then he double-crossed me about Bob, which I never got over. I never got over the hurt of Dad going back on me and the loss of my sweetheart besides. I wrote and told him I forgave him, but the hurt was always deep inside. . . . Dad broke Bob and me up—he completely dominated me, so I have never felt I could win an argument or fight. I just get heartbroken and revert to tears and teenage bewilderment."

Two years later she married David Peckinpah, who at the time drove a stagecoach between the towns of North Fork and South Fork, which were halfway between Peckinpah Mountain and Dunlap's Ranch. The middle of Charlie Peckinpah's three sons, David was quieter and more introspective than his brothers but warm and supportive to family and friends. With his gangly six-foot-one frame, open smile, dark Irish features, and Victorian sense of ethics, David reminded many of the youthful Abraham Lincoln—his greatest hero.

Denver Church took an instant liking to his new son-in-law. "Physically that boy is well nigh a perfect specimen of young manhood," he wrote in a letter to his wife.

It didn't take Denver Church long to convince his new son-in-law to follow in his footsteps and pursue a career in law. The American Dream had changed with the coming of the new century. The frontier to be conquered was no longer without, but within. If a man could set fire to his ambition and pursue his goals with unshakable resolve there were no limits to what he might achieve, nothing to stop him from climbing to the very top of those skyscrapers that now reached up toward the heavens in cities all across the land. Nothing to stop a lumberjack's son, if he applied himself diligently, from winning a seat in the United States Congress—or even, someday, the White House.

When Denver left for Washington, D.C. in November of 1916 to begin his third congressional term, David, Fern, and their newborn son Denny followed. David attended law school at National University and supported himself by working as a doorkeeper at the House of Representatives.

On January 29, 1917, Denver Church announced he would retire at the end of his third term. David graduated from law school in 1919, passed the bar exam shortly afterward, and joined Denver's law firm in Fresno. But Denver didn't last long in private practice; politics was in his blood whether he liked it or not, and soon he was off to run again for assistant district attorney. David teamed up with another lawyer, Raymond Carter. By the mid-1920s he had a thriving practice as a civil and criminal defense attorney.

But by that time he had discovered that behind his wife's brightly animated affectations stirred dark and troubling waters. She was fiercely jealous of any threat to her position in the spotlight, and the biggest threat was David's mother, Isabelle, whom Fern saw as secretly plotting the destruction of their marriage.

"We went over to the Peckinpahs' last night," Fern wrote in her diary. "Mrs. P came out to meet us. She kissed P. D., then me, and last and *longest*, Dave. She and Dave always act as though they were acting on stage and had to make an everlasting impression. Well, it surely does on me every time I see them. If he was just a boy it wouldn't look so funny, or if she were a poor little old lady. But she is so big and healthy looking and seems like she was just trying to make skinny Dave hollow. She wraps her arms around him so tight and gives me a look that always says 'Miss Church—See? He is all mine and you certainly belong in the background' etc."

Soon they weren't going to visit David's parents anymore, nor any of his brothers. When his brothers came to visit David, Fern would rub her head, claim she wasn't feeling well, and disappear into her bedroom. To avoid conflicts David began seeing his mother on the sly, as if visiting a mistress—either during lunch, or by leaving the office early so Fern wouldn't know about it. His brothers fell into the habit of telephoning him at his office instead of at home and visiting him there too. David's mother was almost never mentioned in his own house. The skeleton was stuffed in the closet along with Denver's betrayal of Fern, and everyone assumed the best possible face and carried on.

There were other disquieting tensions, like Fern's reluctance to act as a full-time mother to their son Denny. That she loved the boy there can be no doubt. Her diary entries and letters from his first few years gush with descriptions of Fern's little darling. But in the baby's less endearing moments, when he cried or threw a tantrum, Fern would abandon him to David or her mother and retire to her bedroom, claiming to feel ill.

"My mother loved babies," Fern Lea Peckinpah, her adopted daughter, recalls. "But she treated them like they were dolls. When they fussed, she couldn't take it."

The task of raising the boy was left almost entirely to Louise and Denver. Denny stayed at his grandparents' ranch for long stretches at a time. He was even left once at the home of one of the ranch hands, Carl Bushman, for a couple of months. "Bushman had married a Mono Indian," Denny himself recalls. "By the time they picked me up I was speaking Mono."

Louise Church was not oblivious to her daughter's difficulty in adjusting to married life. Though Louise had been raised in the Episcopal Church, she converted to Christian Science in the 1920s and convinced David and Fern to join the faith as well. Louise and David hoped Christian Science would help Fern overcome her many "illnesses." She responded with great zeal, and the pages of her diaries are filled with purple praise for the Lord and his teachings. But the new faith only served to fix Fern, like fly in amber, as a helpless little girl dependent on her Almighty Father in Heaven for salvation. Deep below her cheerful façade, rage rumbled.

More than eight years passed between Denny's birth and Fern's second pregnancy. By 1924 her longing for a little girl overcame her dread of childbearing. Morning sickness struck in the spring of that year, and she stayed in bed almost the entire nine months, too overcome with nausea and back pains to rise. Lying in the damp sheets, she kept her spirits up by dreaming of the little girl who soon would be hers to hold, praying for her Heavenly

Father to deliver that one gift to her, a little girl she could treasure as her father had treasured her.

Fern went into a difficult labor on February 21, 1925. She was exhausted, breathing shallowly, only dimly aware of her surroundings, when the nurse opened the door and came forward with the wrapped bundle. When she saw the light-olive skin and brown hair, the mark of the dark Irish all over him, she exclaimed, "Oh, another black Peckinpah!"

But when the nurse forced the child into Fern's arms she saw something was different about this one, very different. The eyes. Big and bright as Hudson headlights. They seemed to stare at her with a strange knowingness, feminine yet strong. They triggered in her an outpouring of love that she had never known before.

A picture of Fern with her second son, David Samuel Peckinpah, taken a year later shows her in a big floppy white hat and lace blouse, her face fuller, her hair longer. Grinning from the cradle of her arms is a face almost as round as hers, with huge luminescent eyes and fuzzy brown hair. On the back is an inscription in Fern's handwriting: "Our dear baby is one year old today! My, oh my, what a wonderful thing it has been to have our darling a whole year. It seems such a tiny while ago since they brought him to me all wrapped up in a pink blanket and his little rose bud mouth. If I had known how much happiness the little chap was going to bring me, I couldn't have found one tear for my baby girl that I wanted so very, very much."

In 1931 Fern adopted the little girl she'd prayed for—she couldn't stand the stress of another pregnancy—and named the blue-eyed blonde Fern Lea. But her precious "D. Sammy," as she liked to call him, remained her favorite. The attachment between them was profound. They bathed together until he reached the age of four. When Fern put a stop to the practice the boy rebelled by stealing some jewelry from her bedroom and burying it in the garden. It took them weeks to find it.

"He has the most beautiful eyes a child ever had," Fern wrote in her diary in 1932, when D. Sammy was seven years old. "They are never the same color—sometimes a deep blue-green or green-blue and sometimes they are nearly soft brown. . . . He is love itself just bubbling over and so much understanding and sympathy. The tears roll from those big eyes over anyone's troubles. . . . I sometimes don't feel worthy of being the little fellow's mommie. I want so much to do the very best thing for him always. I love him better than life itself. God gave me a treasure to have and to hold."

When the family went for rides in the car, Fern insisted that D. Sammy sit between her and David while Fern Lea took the backseat. As time went on it became clear the boy was filling a gap, both physically and emotionally, that was growing between Fern and her husband, who was spending more and more time away from home working late at the office and attending meetings of the various civic organizations that he now belonged to.

On February 21, 1939, she wrote in her diary: "Today is my little boy's birthday—fourteen little short years I've had my precious little boy. Somehow, now that Denny Boy is married and away at school, I hate to think of D. Sam growing up much more than I did Denny. But it's just no joke when they are so far from home—so I want my little boy little for a long, long time. We're going to sleep together tonight. Always do on birthday nights, you know. Went to town till after noon and did I have to hustle to get two lemon pies baked (beautiful) and just the kind of chicken dinner cooked that he wanted. Didn't want any [other] boys—just the family. The little sweetheart always wants just his own family."

In the early years D. Sammy blossomed under all her attention. His mother passed on to him her deep, sensual appreciation for nature and all things of the earth, and her strong visual intuition. Fern's mother had taught her to love gardening, but her own gardens far surpassed the neat rows of roses and pansies that Louise planted around the ranch house at Dunlap's. "She [Fern] could touch a stick of wood and tomorrow you would find it blooming," Sam recalled in 1972. "There are trees she planted that are 150 feet tall now in front of houses all over Fresno." By watching her and working with her in her gardens, young Sam developed his mother's eye for color and composition.

"Mother, fortunately and unfortunately, was the most powerful figure in his life," says Fern Lea. "He got his creativity from her, though I'm certain he would have denied it. Sam was basically a woman, emotionally. I think of a man as being systematic in his reasoning, to come to a certain point. Sam would get to the answer emotionally—the way he felt about it, the way he visualized it. I think he was embarrassed by it because in our family, 'By God, the men are men!' I don't think he ever worried about being homosexual, that was never it, but he didn't want that side of him to show."

By 1937 David Peckinpah had built a reputation as one of the top two or three attorneys in Fresno. In the midst of the Great Depression—while refugees from the Dust Bowl flocked to California in search of migrant farm work, camping beneath oak trees, along roadsides, and in vacant fields across the state; while storefronts in downtown Fresno were boarded up and those who managed to scrape by wondered if they could survive another year of hard times—David built the family house on land he bought northeast of Fresno. There were almond, apricot, and orange trees, pastures for half a dozen horses, and a large barn.

Here Fern Peckinpah built her most elaborate garden. An artificial brook, powered by a water pump, weaved its way among the roses, irises, lilacs, pansies, and petunias. There were miniature waterfalls, tiny bridges, and castles. In this fairyland, Eden before the bitten apple, the shimmering red and yellow and blue flower petals held the dark undercurrents and disturbing ambiguities of Fern's life at bay.

As a child, D. Sammy also spent much of his time in a world of his own devising. His bedroom was his retreat. Its ceiling was cratered with lead—the result of one of his experiments with his chemistry set. (A more successful formula—principally equal parts vinegar and soda—bubbled eerily and served as an efficient ant killer; this he knew because he'd tested the product over and over again on local populations.) The built-in shelves along one wall held his prized collection of "Big-Little Books," more than thirty volumes supported on either end by bookends modeled after Walt Disney's Goofy. Moby-Dick, the Three Musketeers, Hercules, Aladdin and his magic lamp, Paul Bunyan, Pecos Bill,

Icarus, Jason and the Golden Fleece, King Arthur and the Knights of the Round Table—classic tales told in an easy-to-read juvenile prose. He pored over them for hours, reveling in the magic worlds they described, the gallant heroes and their fantastic adventures. When tired of reading, he reenacted the stories with wooden soldiers, or by envisioning himself as Hercules, D'Artagnan, Tarzan, or Wyatt Earp taking on hordes of evil assailants at once.

"When I was six or seven, I learned the poem by Tennyson, 'The Charge of the Light Brigade,' by heart," Sam Peckinpah recalled in 1970. "From that point on I started staging it. By the time I was eleven we must have had fifty kids weekly re-enacting that famous battle. We used to charge at each other with rubber [band] guns and swords. We stormed the heights of Balaclava time and time again. I possibly haven't stopped yet."

Each year right after Christmas Sam and his friends would gather up all the discarded trees from the neighborhood, arrange them into elaborate fortresses in the backyard, and fight desperate pitched battles with rubber-band guns. "They shot cut-up sections of inner tube; they really hurt if they hit you!" Fern Lea recalls. The action was always choreographed by Sam. "Follow me, men, onward to victory!"

Most often it was Fern Lea—he called her "Spuddy" because she loved potatoes—who shared the make-believe world of his early years. Sometimes he'd trick her, like the time they'd been filling water balloons at their father's office and dropping them off the back landing. Sam was fascinated by the lethargic grace with which they fell, almost like time and gravity slowed to a crawl, then sped up again when they exploded across the pavement. "Spuddy, tell you what, why don't you go down and see if you can catch one?"

Standing soaking wet in the alley a minute later, shards of red rubber dangling from her outstretched fingers, and looking up at him, doubled over with laughter there on the landing, she realized that his large hazel eyes and sonorous voice were not to be trusted.

But he could be wonderful too. When she fell sick with a stomach ache he'd stay in the room with her, entertaining her with imitations, funny faces, and distorted voices. "I would start laughing and the pain would ease up a great deal," Fern Lea recalls. "There was a really sweet side to him then, a very tender side."

At night the two of them would gather around the radio. Their parents would be in the other room, David reading a story from *The Saturday Evening Post* out loud to Fern. Sam tuned in their favorite program: Arch Oboler's "Lights Out!" "Lights out! Lights out!" he'd cackle in a high, giddy voice, scampering around the room knocking out all the light switches until it was just the two of them there in the dark staring at the dull glow of the radio dial, entranced by "The Chicken Heart that Ate New York City!" or the "Inside-out Cloud!" that sucked the guts out of its helpless victims.

"What's that, Doc, there on the floor?!"

"It's a man . . . a man, I tell you . . . and he'd been turned *inside-out!!!* Skin on the inside, raw organs on the outside!"

"AAAAAAHHHH!!!" Sam would suddenly scream in Fern Lea's ear, sending her airborne.

Every Christmas David or Denny would take the pickup truck into the mountains, cut a pine from the snowy Sierra slopes, and bring it back to the house. Once erected under the high-beamed ceiling, it would be Sam and Fern Lea's task to decorate it. Sam directed the operation imperiously. Every light bulb, every ball, every trinket and bauble had to be placed in a particular spot picked by his discerning eye. "God damn it, Spuddy, not like that!" he reprimanded when she tried to throw angel hair on by the handful. It had to be applied one strand at a time, he insisted, to achieve a well-balanced effect.

They'd dig David's extra-long hunting stockings out of his dresser and hang them over the fireplace to assure a maximum take, and would be up at the crack of dawn on Christmas day to empty the bulging contents out on their beds: cashews, rock candy, and windup toys tumbled out on their sheets, always accompanied by an onion or clove of garlic—a reminder from their father that their behavior always left room for improvement.

When their parents got up they had breakfast: bacon, eggs,

and, if Fern was up to making it, sweet moist graham bread or thick cinnamon rolls. It was the best time of year for all of them. They almost always managed to put aside the growing tensions that plagued them the rest of the year. Yet as Sam grew older he became aware of the trouble between his parents.

"They loved each other," says Fern Lea. "My father took care of my mother. I don't think my mother ever paid a bill. He was very good to her. But looking back on it now I felt it was not an equal partnership. He took care of her and I took care of my mother too. My mother didn't drive and when she did it made her very nervous and she told me the reason she didn't drive anymore was that I made her too nervous. . . . Emotionally she didn't grow up, nobody helped her grow up, certainly not my father . . . and I think the same thing happened to Sam; he never grew up either."

By the mid-thirties David was in high demand at the Exchange Club, the Elks, and the other civic organizations he belonged to. "It was wonderful watching the people respond to him," says Susan Peckinpah, who was adopted by David and Fern in 1943. "He really was a very dynamic, charismatic man. He had a very clear, succinct set of values, but it came out in such a folksy manner that it didn't offend people."

Fern found playing second fiddle at such functions to be torture. Eventually she refused to go, yet resented David for going without her. "Oh dear me, he isn't mine anymore," she wrote in her diary. "I count every second that we are together, but they are not his Rosary. . . . I stay home and watch for him and get blue and cross. Last night he stayed in town to catch up with his work, but when I phoned at 7:00 and 7:30 he wasn't there. At 8:00 he called me and said he was just leaving for the lodge."

"My mother turned harmless things into something morally wrong," says Fern Lea. "Most of it revolved around her need for attention. Sam turned out to be the same way when he grew up."

To get what she craved Fern used what she'd always used: her illnesses. There were the backaches, the throbbing feet and hands, the "heart attacks" that her doctors found no medical evidence of. And the headaches, always the headaches, paralyzing her with skull-splitting pain. But instead of retiring to her room,

Fern often insisted on lying on the living room couch with a damp washcloth over her forehead and all the curtains drawn, forcing everyone else in the house to sit still and quiet so as not to disturb her. If Sam or Fern Lea made the slightest whisper within hearing range, her pale face would crane sharply upward. "What was that you said?" she'd demand with a serrated edge to her voice. "It was terrible, terrible!" says Fern Lea.

When the sick spells struck, David responded dutifully—rubbing his wife's aching hands or temples, reading stories to her from *The Saturday Evening Post* to try to take her mind off the pain. "My mother wanted things her way and most of the time she got them," says Fern Lea. "When she didn't, she got her headaches."

"She was a very, very powerful person," says Susan Peckinpah, "but didn't perceive herself as such. She saw the men as having all the power, but it wasn't allowed then for women to assert power directly."

Sam Peckinpah inherited his mother's talent for manipulating others. As an adult he developed a genius for it, but in his adolescent years he grew to detest his mother's grim dictatorship.

Fern Lea remembers her mother following Sam into the hallway once when he was twelve or thirteen. She was berating him for some transgression and, as was often her habit, beating him on the back. Fern Lea caught a glimpse of the expression on her brother's face as he passed her and thought, *She better stop; if she hits him once more . . .*

But young Sam never vented his anger to his mother's face; neither did anyone else in the family, for one very good reason: David Peckinpah strictly forbade it. And if defied, amiable, likable David Peckinpah unleashed a fearsome temper that easily rivaled that of his father, Charlie.

"I remember one time that precipitated it with me," Denny Peckinpah recalls. The family had headed up to the mountains for the weekend in their Nash touring car. David, Fern, and Sam—who was four or five years old at the time—were going all the way up to their cabin in Crane Valley, but they were dropping Denny off at Dunlap's Ranch so he could spend some time with his grandparents. "They were going to drop me at the front gate, which is four miles from the Dunlap house, but I was old enough in those days to walk that with no problem. I was a teenager. So they stopped at the gate to let me out and I was sitting in the back-seat. I was probably thirteen or fourteen, something like that. My mother said something about being careful when I was walking up the road and I made some smart remark about how I was old enough to take care of myself. The old man reached over there and caught me by the collarbone, jerked me out that back window, and caught me on the way down with that backhand. He says: 'Don't ever let me hear you speak to your mother that way again!' Believe me, I didn't."

Sam, who'd witnessed the beating, learned the lesson too—learned it and obeyed it till the day his mother died over fifty years later.

If Sam and Fern Lea bickered—and they often did—or failed to carry out one of his orders, David would hiss: "Go out and cut yourself a switch!" And they'd have to make the long, lonely, trembling journey out onto the ranch-house grounds to find a switch for him to beat them with. If they failed to come back with a healthy specimen, they knew their father would make good his promise to "go and get one myself! And believe me, you won't like the one I pick!"

"I got backhanded a few times," says Fern Lea. Sometimes the marks remained visible for days. "My father had a temper when he was angry. Once he let go it was horrible. . . . His anger, when he got going, was almost as bad as being drunk. I mean, I guess he did lose it and he didn't often, but it was horrible."

Denny would simply stand up and take his blows, but Sam, it seems, had a flair for the dramatic. "The old man hit him, there was no question about that—backhanded him—and Sam just flew backwards and crashed into the wall," Denny laughs, "like he'd really been hit and he hadn't, of course, see. My mother heard the commotion and came charging in and said: 'Oh, Dave, you killed him! You killed him!' Sam was lying there on the floor, loving it."

He learned to employ theatrics also as a safe way of striking back at his mother. Once a month Fern held an afternoon tea at her house for the Friday Club, a female counterpart to the Elks and

Masons. Young Sam and Fern Lea dreaded the periodic invasion of the big-bosomed women with their dyed hair and brittle curls, reeking of talcum powder, waving their lace handkerchiefs, and cooing like overfed pigeons.

Finally, when Sam was fourteen and Fern Lea eight, he drew her into his room and revealed his plan for a counterattack. Sworn to secrecy, she helped him gather the necessary wardrobe and props. Then, just before the women were due to arrive, they assembled it in the hall that led off of the large screened-in porch. They had to work fast: a pair of David's Levi's and a plaid shirt stuffed with newspaper, a wide-brimmed hat and an overripe gourd for a head, and a long, fierce butcher knife plunged deep in the shirt's breast with a bottle of ketchup sprinkled liberally over it for the final grisly effect. "He was very careful about the details," Fern Lea recalls, "the scarf around the collar, the hat pulled down just right, the boots a certain way. The details were very important to him."

D. Sam stood back to survey the final product, nodding sagely: yes, that would do fine.

At the sounds of the first club members arriving, they snapped the hall light out and retreated to Sam's room, leaving his door open just a crack and waiting in giggly, cold-sweat anticipation for the inevitable moment when their mother would lead the new guests on a tour of the house.

"Oh, what elegant flagstone, Fern!" one of the women said as they drew closer to the booby trap.

"And here's Fern Lea's room." The group was just beyond the door to the hallway now. Sam and Fern Lea huddled close to each other, suppressing an urge to laugh out loud.

"Oh, it's lovely, Fern! Just Lovely!"

"And in here is where D. Sammy—"

A click of the knob turning, the door creaking open, and gray light spreading over the hideous stricken form. "AHHHH! Oh! Oh, my lord!"

The two children scampered back into the darkness of Sam's room, rolling on the floor, so breathless with laughter they nearly peed their pants.

Young Sam longed to leave his mother's protective orbit and enter the world of his father, his older brother, and his grandfather, Denver Church. Dunlap's Ranch—for D. Sam, who consumed pulp westerns at a voracious rate, it offered a vision of paradise. He watched the older men working the cattle in their leather boots and chaps and weathered Stetsons; smelled the wood smoke, sweat, and dust; watched the lariats whirling slow and weightless in the air, then flicking out around the head of a steer and pulling taut and vibrating. He drank in the rough, raw sensuousness of it all.

At night around the big fireplace in his grandfather's cabin—where a huge pot of beans, onions, potatoes, and venison was always bubbling—he listened to the tales the men told of the old days. How the Peckinpahs and Churches crossed the plains and carved their kingdoms out of the new land. How Denver's family had hunted deer Indian fashion: teams of hollerers drove the deer to lines of riflemen, who passed the carcasses on to those who gutted and cleaned them. They had killed as many as a hundred deer a day that way.

He sat enthralled in the billowing orange-and-yellow light of the fire while Denver's hired hands—Wild Bill Baker, Bill Dillon, and Ed Klippert—told stories of cattle stampedes, desperate horseback rescues in mountain snowstorms, river crossings, prizefights and wrestling matches (Baker had battled the infamous Strangler Lewis in the ring and had the cauliflower ears to prove it). Listened to their stories of elaborate practical jokes, like the time Dillon found himself working with a half-wit helper who dragged his ass if you didn't ride him every minute of the day. So Dillon took the glass eye out of his left socket and put it on a fence post right in front of the kid and said: "I'm gonna be keepin' my eye on you today." And that boy worked like a son of a bitch till sundown. He heard the way they talked about guns—caliber, barrel length, and make—lovingly, reverently, almost erotically.

And he listened to *how* these men—smelling of garlic, tobacco, horse sweat, and whiskey—told their stories, drinking in their peculiar poetic idioms, rhythms, and metaphors: "Coon Dog Benson was the talkin'est man you ever saw." "Well, kiss my sister's black cat's ass!" "That boy smelled bad enough to gag a dog off a gut wagon!"

And as he listened, a vision of the American West formed in his mind. Not the West as it had been, but the West these older men reinvented—their memories and imaginations sifted away all the hours of tedium, fruitless struggles, failure, and despair until all that remained were brilliant nuggets of hilarity, suspense, and high adventure. A West where men rode free on galloping steeds, unrestricted by clinging sisters, wives, or neurotic mothers. A big land where men could breathe deep and drink the magic elixir of liberation—whiskey—that sent them off brawling and whoring and howling for more. A land where life was embraced at its most dangerous, its most extreme; when he saw this masculine Eden before his eyes he wanted desperately to be a part of it.

But wedging his way through the garden gate and bridging the gap between fantasy and reality proved no easy trick, as he discovered almost from the very first moment that the dream formulated in his mind.

He was just five, maybe six, when he was allowed to watch his first spring roundup at Dunlap's. All 300 head of cattle had been crammed into the corrals for branding and ear clipping. D. Sammy stood up on the top rail of the main corral, his face flushed and eyes glowing as the irons hissed against the steers' left hips, filling the air with the odor of singed hair and burning hide.

He swung his fist excitedly, tottering for balance as Bill Dillon wrestled a steer's ear toward the long blade of his clipping knife. "Cut his ears off, Bill! Cut his ears off!" the boy cried jubilantly. Dillon pressed the blade home, the steer moaned, and blood shot out in D. Sammy's direction. The boy turned chalk-white and toppled backward like a felled tree. Some sixty years later his brother Denny still laughs over the memory. "That killed his appetite for branding for a while."

"There seemed to be an unspoken agreement between my parents from the beginning," says Fern Lea, "that Denny was my father's child and Sam was my mother's. Sam was my mother's favorite, but the sad thing was he didn't want to be my mother's favorite, he wanted to be my father's."

Fern herself noted the unspoken alliances in an entry in her diary:

Denny all business.
David nearly all business.
Sammy most all sentiment,
and me most all sentiment and feelings.
These are the qualities that control us.

Because Denny had been more or less raised by his grandparents, he had fallen under Denver Church's influence almost completely. By the time the boy was seven Denver had him reciting passages from the writings of Robert Ingersoll, the Bible, or Denver's own political speeches. He'd critique Denny's diction, delivery, gestures, and posture. Though Denny harbored fantasies of becoming an architect, a writer, or a photographer, his fate was essentially decided by his grandfather and father before he finished grade school. He would join the family law firm, go into politics, and add yet another list of credits to the clan. By the time D. Sammy was four, Denny was thirteen, riding, roping and herding cattle, and hunting deer with the rest of the men in the hills above Dunlap's.

But the men didn't quite know what to make of Sam's fine brown hair, long eyelashes, delicate, almost pretty features, and large hazel eyes that stared at you with such quiet intensity. "There's something about the little fellow," David admitted uneasily to his wife, "that makes you want to shield him from the world." Denver Church was troubled by no such inclination. He read introspection as passivity and pronounced sensitivity as weakness. And, as he had with his own son, he responded to both with contempt.

Betty Peckinpah, a Palo Alto girl who married Denny in 1937, discovered this for herself on her first visit to Dunlap's. Denver Church led her on an expedition into the surrounding hills and showed her how to lay a trap line, just as his father had taught him. The next day he handed her a .22-caliber rifle and told her to go check her traps. When she came upon a live raccoon still struggling to free itself from a set of steel teeth, she dropped the rifle and fled down the hill in tears. "I was never forgiven for that," she says bitterly, noting that the old man had made no effort to prepare her for what she might find.

She saw the same venom turned on young Sam. "He [Denver] used to take it out on Sam quite frequently because Sam liked to read. He always loved to read. Denver's attitude was, if you were a real boy you were outside riding horses, hiking, and doing things like that. I always felt so sorry for Sam when he'd get a tongue-lashing about not being outside when he could be in the mountains. Denver had a devastating sarcasm. He was one of the most sarcastic men I ever met. He had a tongue like an adder, and both Denny and Sam inherited it."

But D. Sammy had something Denver's own son Earl had lacked: coupled with his sensitivity was a fierce combativeness. From the very beginning he rose to meet his grandfather's challenging barbs, determined to elbow out a place for himself among the giants.

Once, up at Crane Valley, where the Churches owned a set of cabins, D. Sammy had been given a rake to help the rest of the men clean up some fallen leaves. He was three years old. When Denver unleashed his adder's tongue on the boy for working too slowly, D. Sammy flew into a rage of his own. His face bright-red, he grabbed a nearby pitchfork, almost longer than he was, and charged, forcing his grandfather to beat a hasty retreat. David and Denny interceded, finally wrestling the fork away. Sam won a victory of sorts that day, for though his grandfather still treated him with healthy doses of sarcasm in the years to come, he also granted D. Sammy a measure of grudging respect.

In later years Sam Peckinpah loved to give interviewers the impression that he'd done a lot of hard cowboying in his teenage years. In truth his experience amounted to occasionally herding a few head of cattle from one fenced-in field to another, and an ill-fated entry in a junior rodeo at Bass Lake. He got thrown by two bull calves, landing on the same patch of hard dirt each time. "I got up and said, 'Okay, I got the message!' " he admitted to Garner Simmons. He could ride well enough, but never had a true affinity for horses and cattle.

It was hunting that he loved. He threw himself into it with a passion, and under Denver Church's stern supervision he would learn to track and shoot like an Indian.

He started with rats. "Big fat ones," Fern Lea recalls. Sam stalked these on his own in his grandfather's barn and feedbins, forcing his sister to hold the flashlight while he aimed the .22 and fired. He developed a cool, detached eye and learned to lead the fleeing rodents before he squeezed the trigger.

Then came the trout in Fine Gold Creek. Denver showed him the deep holes they hid in, and how to tease them into striking a lure. One day D. Sammy returned with thirteen or fourteen, beaming proudly. Denver frowned. "Well, I hope you like to eat them." Sam ate trout for a week and learned his lesson: you kill to feed your stomach, not your ego.

Then came the quail. Denver sent the boy out with a shotgun and two shells and told him, "Come back with two quail or don't come back." Sam learned to "ground sluice" the birds—spraying a load of buckshot into a flock before it had a chance to get airborne, thus killing two or three at a time. Denver had learned this as a dirt-poor Napa boy when hunting had been a matter of necessity, not sport.

Then came rabbits, raccoons, foxes, and bobcats. "I remember my grandfather always forcing me to be observant," Sam told Simmons. " 'Where did you go? What did you see? Where did you cross the fence? Describe what you saw there. . . . He made me tell all these things because when you were hunting by yourself in the High Country that was the difference between making it back to camp and starving in the woods. He made me tell him everything, and if I couldn't he'd give me a kick in the ass. One good boot from the judge was all you needed."

The same prodigious memory that enabled Denver to recite long passages of Scripture also allowed him to form an incredibly detailed mental map of the 4,100 acres he owned at Dunlap's. He literally knew the location of every tree, stump, sapling, and rock on his property. He knew where the deer hid and what direction they'd flee in if you flushed them from a certain thicket. "Most amazing," says Ed Klippert. As foreman of the ranch in the late thirties, he witnessed Denver's photographic memory in action on countless occasions. "It was almost unbelievable."

The coon hunts were the grisliest. Once the dogs treed a coon, one of the hunters would climb up and shake it loose from the branches. If a dog was a "scrapper," like Denver's old Tom, a vicious fight followed. In a stream or pond a coon could gain the upper hand, scramble up on the dog's head, even drown it. But most of the time the dog finally got it by the belly and shook it to death, fur and blood flying everywhere. The transformation in the hounds from affectionate pets craving love and approval to eye-rolling beasts, oblivious to all but the taste of the blood in their mouths, fascinated young Sam. He eventually sent back to Kentucky for a black-and-tan hound that he trained himself.

Then, finally, came the deer. The biggest quarry and a rite of passage. Sam was fourteen when Denny took him up into the Sierras near "the old Chetwood place." Sam had his mother's .32 Winchester carbine that carried a heavy slug and kicked like a mule. Late in the afternoon Denny led him up a steep ridge and told him where to position himself. He left Sam tightly gripping his rifle and moved on up through the trees. Five minutes later Denny flushed a big buck and fired over its head. It kicked up its heels and leaped stiff-legged down the mountain toward Sam. Denny waited for the shot. And waited and waited. Nothing but the thin cool wind rushing through the pine needles. At last he started down the grade. He found Sam where he'd left him, wide-eyed and breathing fast. "What happened?" Denny asked.

"I don't know," Sam answered, the words spilling out all over one another. "I emptied my gun at him, but he didn't go down!"

Denny looked to the ground at his brother's feet. There lay the scattered cartridges, all of them unfired. He shook his head. Buck fever. In his excitement D. Sam had levered the shells in and out of the gun without firing them, not even realizing that he hadn't been pulling the trigger.

But later that day, coming down to camp, they flushed another buck. This time D. Sam's finger found the trigger and the deer jerked and thudded to the ground. The next day, as light was fast disappearing over the rocky peaks and the snow falling heavily from the sky, he got another. When the carbine's heavy slug ripped out the other side of the animal, it sprayed a crimson blossom across the crystalline snowpack. Eerie yet strangely beautiful, the image would haunt him for a long, long time.

On the next hunt, his third deer brought yet another perspective, as Sam later told Garner Simmons: "He was at the edge of a bluff, maybe a hundred yards off. It was snowing. I was walking. I snuck around a tamarack and shot him in the neck. When I circled around to where he was, he was hanging half over the edge but still alive. As I approached him he watched me with this mixture of fear and resignation, and I wanted to say, 'I'm sorry,' because I really didn't mean to kill him. I got caught up in the chase. But there was nothing I could do except pull his hindquarters away from the edge and put a bullet through his head to end his suffering. When that was done, I knelt beside the carcass in the snow to gut it and found myself unable to control my tears. I had such incredible communication with that animal. I would have done anything to have seen him run again. But when you're really hunting there is a relationship between a man and what he kills to eat that is absolutely locked. It's hard to explain to people who think that meat comes from their local grocery store, or to those cats who come out and shoot anything that moves for trophies. But I cried for that deer with more anguish than any other time in my life. It was dusk, and the snow was coming down harder. It was one of the most extraordinarily moving moments in my life."

It was a reaction that Denver Church would probably have had little sympathy for. "If you're going to cry, get out of here right now!" he had barked at Fern Lea when she wept at the sight of the cattle getting their ears clipped. He'd been forced to quell such sentiments within himself long ago in order to survive. David Peckinpah too would have been an uneasy witness to such an outpouring of emotion. D. Sammy had completed his rite of passage, won tacit approval from the men who'd towered over him, but in so doing he had had to learn to conceal such signs of "weakness." As an adult he would display little tolerance for it in others, and its unpleasant reflection on the face of an employee or offspring often transformed him into a merciless bully. He'd won his place among men, but the price had been stiff.

Decades later, Sam Peckinpah would talk nostalgically about his early years. "It was the finest time of my life," he told Garner Simmons in 1973. "There will never be another time like that again." But in more private moments he often revealed a different attitude. Camille Fielding, a close friend of Sam's for many years, remembers a gathering in the early 1970s at The Broken Bit, a restaurant Denny owned in the mountain town of Oakhurst, just fourteen miles from the old Dunlap spread. She and Sam found themselves alone at a table at one point, looking out at the fields of wild lupine. "It must have been wonderful to grow up here as a child," Camille said dreamily.

"No, it wasn't," Sam snapped, startling her with the sharpness of his reply. After a moment's hesitation, he poured forth his feelings.

"He was so sad, talking about being a little boy, learning to ride," Camille recalls. "What you're expected to be to survive in that environment. You couldn't fall down and be hurt, you had to get up and go on. Not like any childhood I knew. You fell down and wanted to cry and your dad wouldn't let you. Hit you if you cried. It's a nightmare thing, and I heard this coming out of him. It hurts when you fall off a horse and nobody gets up to help you. 'Get back on!' A little kid. Not to be able to cry, to show pain. I think a lot of his rage stems from that."

"They never accepted Sam the way they had accepted Denny," Betty Peckinpah says of the older men in the family. "David was not so openly hostile, but he never understood Sam's theatrical ambitions, his writing. For me, the tragedy of Sam was that he spent his life trying to find acceptance from that family. The macho posturing . . . that wasn't Sam. It was, but it wasn't. That was him trying to win approval from his family. He spent his life trying to do that and it tore him apart inside. He never did get acceptance. It made him one of the saddest people I ever knew."

It was the best of times and the worst. As Peckinpah often said himself, "Things are always mixed." His radically different remembrances of his childhood reflect a deep ambivalency in which his feelings of attraction and repulsion for both his mother's world and that of his father and grandfather created an internal tug-of-war that he would struggle to resolve throughout his life. It's what drove him to the theater and films, and gave his work its deadly charge.

The pugnaciousness with which D. Sammy took on his family elders also made itself felt early in Fresno's public schools. Joe Bernhard met Sam on the grammar-school playground when he was six and Sam nine. "I was getting the shit kicked out of me by the second biggest guy in the class, when I hear this voice say softly, 'All right, that's enough.' It was Sam. He pulled the guy off of me."

Soon Joe was taking boxing lessons from the older boy—Sam passing on tips he'd learned from H. W. Waddle, a private detective who worked for his father; a former highway patrolman, Waddle had boxed in the police's amateur league. "You gotta plant your feet when you place the hard blows," Sam told Bernhard with an air of great authority.

"Sam was a little guy for his age," says Bernhard. "He'd been picked on and beat up too."

Don Levy remembers attending the first day of football practice at Fresno High. He, Sam, and a bunch of other skinny, gawky sophomores had decided to try out for the team.

The broad-shouldered coach blew his whistle sharply. "All right, men!" he shouted at the newcomers. "You're going to run the gauntlet!"

Like a flock of nervous chicks, the pencil-limbed lower classmen bunched together. They didn't know exactly what running the gauntlet meant, but from the way the neanderthal seniors leered and giggled, they knew it wouldn't be a truckload of laughs.

"Peckinpah, get up here!"

The skinniest of the whole bunch stepped forward in a torn and grass-stained uniform.

A dozen mammoth seniors had lined up at spaced intervals along the length of field before him, grinning like saber-toothed tigers.

The coach shoved a pigskin into the boy's gut. "See that far goalpost? I want you to try and make it there. Let's see how far you get. Ready?"

The shrill whistle sounded again and the ragged, skinny kid took off like a slug from his mother's mule-kick carbine, head tucked down, leather helmet extended before him like a battering ram, straight into the gut of the first hulking giant. The senior bent like a jackknife and crumpled to the ground minus most of his breath. The rest of the varsity players gaped in disbelief as the coach bellowed: "God damn it, Peckinpah, you aren't supposed to tackle *him!* You're the one with the ball!"

Sam kicked at the grass with a split-seamed shoe, playing dumb—"Oh, I get it, sorry"—while Levy and the rest of the little guys tried to conceal their grins. He struck a blow of victory for the runts that day, and learned the value of the sucker punch—a great equalizer that he would employ frequently in the years to come.

"He was fearless to the point of stupidity," Bernhard remembers. "Sam would fight anybody. I remember once he fought a guy who was bigger than him. He had Sam pinned down. Then, suddenly, Sam got this burst of strength and got free and kicked the shit out of the guy. He told me later he'd thought the guy had spit on him. What really happened was the guy's nose was bleeding. He was bleeding on Sam."

The girls who went to school with him have distinctly different memories. "Dear Sam," Doris Roullard wrote in his fifth-grade autograph book. "If all the girls lived across the sea, oh what a swimmer you would be!"

One female former classmate remembers D. Sam as a very handsome, big-eyed boy who always dressed well. He was the rich kid, but not a snob. He roller skated with the other kids and played kick the can on warm summer nights. "He liked to draw, airplanes mostly, and write stories. They were very scary, full of the most horrible bloody descriptions. We'd squeal and run away, but he'd call us back to hear more. He was very descriptive."

But still, the other kids noticed something different about their companion. A sense of apartness, inner solitude, that they couldn't penetrate. When not performing for them, he often withdrew. At high school pep rallies he frequently sat alone and he seldom went to parties. Joe Bernhard remembers Sam going through an entire "Hell Week" of hazing to join a high school fraternity. But as soon as he won acceptance, he quit.

"He was a very sensitive boy," says a female former classmate. "He kept to himself. He never had close friends like the rest of us. He was always going out to that ranch. His father made him work out there. They kept him busy."

The movies became his sanctuary. Saturday nights in downtown Fresno at the Kinema and State theaters, he reveled in the wondrous worlds that unreeled on the giant white screen. There were Errol Flynn's swashbuckling epics: *Captain Blood, The Charge of the Light Brigade, They Died with Their Boots On,* and *Robin Hood,* with director Michael Curtiz's sweeping crane shots, mythic shadows, and the flashing swordplay peppered with glib wisecracks.

And of course the westerns, always the westerns. Harry Carey, Tim McCoy, Ken Maynard, Buck Jones, William Boyd—fearless, straight-shootin', hard-ridin' hombres all. Sam's cousin Earlene Heafey remembers him practicing his Tom Mix mount on old Nellie, the family horse, up at the cabin in Crane Valley. He'd jump off a nearby rock onto Nellie's back and dig in his heels for a fast getaway.

At age eleven he saw *The Plainsman* and fell in love with Jean Arthur's incarnation of Calamity Jane. His grandmother brutally shredded this fantasy by casually remarking that she and Denver had met the real Calamity during their tour of the Great Plains in the 1890s. What was she like? D. Sam eagerly asked. "She was a dirty drunken woman and she smelled bad . . . and your grandfather spent too much time with her."

In his junior year of high school he discovered that he need not remain a member of the audience, a passive observer of that elusive fantasy realm, but could actually step inside it. Sam tried out for a part in a school play and got it. Cast as a newspaper editor in a mystery/melodrama, *The Late Christopher Bean,* he even got to stage a fight and helped choreograph the tumbles and falls. The teacher liked him well enough to put him in another production, *Out of the Frying Pan into the Fire.*

His family didn't know quite what to make of this. His father had been pressing for him to join the debating club, the Fresno High School Senate, as both he and Denny had done. It was good preparation for law school.

"What is that you're wearing . . . makeup?" Fern Lea asked, aghast when he returned home one day after rehearsals. But he hardly seemed to notice her question; his eyes gazed inward with a strange excitement.

Tom Mullins, Sam's closest friend from high school, recalls: "He was into the dramatics early. We had a Spanish teacher named Miss Gunderson. Sam came into class one day with a prop gun that he'd gotten from the theater department. He held it to his head and shouted: 'I'm tired of it all!' He pulls the trigger and—POW!—falls down on the floor. I'll tell you, she damn near died of a heart attack!"

He developed a flair for something else that junior year: girls. Marie Selland, a freshman at the time, remembers seeing him at the attendance office one morning. He was late, like the rest of them gathered there, but somehow Sam managed to charm the secretary behind the counter into giving him a pass. "He had a story. It was like a little performance. I was standing back thinking: God, he's really cute!" But it would be another five years before she'd have her first date with him, for he was in demand. The girls went for this dreamy-eyed lawyer's son with his soft brown hair, sharp clothes, and Model A Ford (bought for him by David) in which he raced up and down the streets of Fresno.

"He could strike up a conversation with a gal at a drive-in, the drugstore, anywhere, and within a few hours he'd have them out in the backseat of his car," marvels Tom Mullins. "I sure could never do it. He had them all. By the time he got to college he was a hell of a cocksman, that's all I can say."

Observing this latest development in his son's life, David Peckinpah thought it prudent to introduce a cautionary note, and so ordered D. Sam to attend the trial of another teenage boy whom he was defending. The charge was statutory rape. "The kid got convicted," Denny recalls. "Then he didn't want to pay Dad his eight-hundred-dollar fee. He said it was too high, and besides, he lost. . . . Dad said: 'You should have thought of that before you climbed into the backseat to get between her legs.' "

At the time, Fresno was still a relatively small farm town with conservative Midwestern values. Many of Sam's schoolmates found it shocking that a father would force his son to sit through a rape case, even statutory rape. "People thought it was a little harsh for a person that young," Walter Harpain, a former neighbor, recalls.

When Sam talked about the experience with Garner Simmons years later, his tone was philosophical: "He [David Peckinpah] thought I would better understand the complexities of trying to establish the truth and keep out of trouble."

But one of his girlfriends at the time claims it had a traumatic impact. "That hit him really bad. He had nightmares. It really shook him up. He was a very sensitive boy."

It could have been more theatrics to win her sympathy, but it is interesting to note how often rape scenes recur in his work as a director—always traumatic and disturbing, and usually with a passive male observer present, either physically or psychologically, who is helpless to stop the event.

David may have had another motive for dragging his youngest son into the courtroom. He still hoped, despite all the signs to the contrary, that D. Sam would go to law school and join the family firm. D. Sam attended several of his father's trials and followed the proceedings with great interest, but the lessons he gleaned were not quite what his father had in mind.

"My father," Sam later recalled, "believed in the Bible as literature, and in the law. He was an *authority*, and we all grew up thinking he could never, ever be wrong about anything."

But sitting there in the courtroom, D. Sam saw how his father used his folksy Honest Abe charm and a skillful manipulation of the facts to convince a jury of something that substantially wasn't true, how David smelled out the prejudices of individual jury members and then played to them. Once he signed on clients David would fight for them, no matter what the odds, right to the wall if necessary—even if the clients were guilty, which sometimes they were. He'd pull every courtroom trick he knew to win for them. Loyalty was admirable, yes, but didn't it matter who you gave your loyalty to? "I just sat there listening," Sam later recalled, "and then I started to question . . . Is there such a thing as a good that leads to evil?"

David Peckinpah's courtroom performances were famous throughout Fresno. Friends and relatives came to watch his trials for the sheer entertainment. By employing a variety of subtle dramatic techniques—hand gestures, inflections, pregnant pauses, and meaningful glances—he created an air of suspense that kept a jury on the edge of its seats. He employed old standbys—such as firing an inflammatory question at a witness and getting him to answer before the opposing attorney could object—with smooth expertise.

"In the full intensity of conflict he could be devastating, and never more so than when he thrust the knife with a smile and a quip," a former colleague recalled. "Standing quietly before the jury box, before saying something that would blow his adversary off balance with a gale of laughter, he'd swipe the heel of his hand across his chin slowly and by the time the gesture was complete he would be in character and let go, bringing the house down."

D. Sam's sessions in court did little to curb his growing wild streak. "He was not a real soft, laid-back person," says Walter Harpain. "He needed action. He needed something going. He was no person to stand back and let the world go by. No way. When there was something going on, he wanted to be involved."

Routinely now, he'd cut out of school at lunch and head for Stillman's Drugstore in his Model A. There, he'd buy a soda, read magazines, and watch girls for the rest of the afternoon. But sodas weren't enough to quench his thirst.

Finally, it came time for another rite of passage. For years he'd listened to the cowboys at Dunlap's talk about their epic drunks—three-day, four-day, even week-long benders. Bill Dillon got so drunk in local saloons that bartenders kept in shape by loading his inert form into the back of his buckboard. They'd give the horses a slap and the team would trot him on back to his cabin. Sam listened to the way the old men talked about "the brown"; a strange passion inflamed their voices, and when they described the crazy frenzies of fighting and whoring, singing and laughing that this liquid sent them off on, he sensed something powerful, even mystical, at work.

One weekend Sam and two of his buddies hiked up to an old abandoned cabin on the Dunlap spread to camp out. In their bedrolls were every kind of liquor bottle they'd been able to swipe. Sam had let Ed Klippert, the ranch foreman, in on their scheme. "Listen, don't tell the folks, but we're going up to Charlie DeLong's old cabin to get drunk! I've never been drunk in my life!"

"I went by there," Klippert recalls. "Man, they had everything under the sun! They mixed it up and went crazy as a bunch of Comanches! Sam fell in the fireplace, like to burn himself up. Man, I'm tellin' you, you never saw such a mess. I'll never forget it. That was the first time old Sam got drunk, and he threw a wingding, I'll tell you. But he learned to like it."

Sam's evenings were spent at the local drive-in. Pearl Harbor had exploded in flames, the war had come, but it still seemed distant and exciting, like all those Errol Flynn movies. It had ended the Depression, and people had money in their pockets again. The kids who weren't old enough to be drafted or sign up to make the world safe for democracy had nothing but time on their hands. There were no more mountains to cross, rivers to ford, no more soil to till or trees to fell, no material wealth to strive for that they didn't already have. So they found their adventure by drag racing on black-topped roads in the middle of the night, playing chicken, making backseat conquests along the banks of the irrigation canals and drinking Coke spiked with a little of the old man's booze, or hammering it down straight from a bottle scored for them by a college kid.

But it all came to an abrupt stop one night—the night D. Sam was caught doing doughnuts in his father's Hudson pickup in a nearby field. For months he'd been sneaking it out of the garage after his parents went to bed. It had more power than his Model A and he wanted, above everything else, to go faster.

David Peckinpah concluded that the time had come for drastic action. D. Sam was grounded for a month. His grades had been slipping badly and he'd shown none of the ambition and discipline of his older brother. It was decided that D. Sam would be sent away for his senior year to San Rafael Military Academy, a spit-and-polish prep school north of San Francisco where upper-middle-class families sent troublesome or unwanted kids. A change of environment and a dose of martial discipline would straighten the boy out, his father hoped.

The academy put on an impressive show for the parents on visiting day. There were barracks divided into individual bedrooms for each student, classrooms, a gym, a mess hall, tennis courts, a football field, and a parade ground. The facilities were clean, the grass neatly trimmed, and the kids' uniforms bright and gleaming as they marched past the review stand in precisely ordered platoons.

But behind the façade, the school was a joke—all show and no substance.

"Our commandant, Major Nichols, didn't have much of a background," John Breed, an alumni of San Rafael, recalls. "He was a former chauffeur who'd been commissioned as a major in the National Guard. One teacher was an ex-used car dealer, another an ex-con from San Quentin. The music teacher was a drunk; another was a homosexual who got kicked out after he threw a party for the boys and tried to pick one up."

The academy's instructors were good at one thing: making rules. The cadets learned the basics of marching, saluting, addressing officers, and military etiquette. There was no smoking in the rooms at night, except for seniors. No liquor, and no girls allowed.

"Sam hated going there," remembers Marie Selland, his first wife. "And yet he told me it had been good for him. That used to drive me crazy, this idea he had that these terribly unpleasant experiences were somehow good for you."

It was a concept David Peckinpah had stressed over and over

again: adversity builds character. By enduring hardship, rising to the challenges life throws at you, you grow stronger—he had preached to his children, often using the story of Job, his favorite passage from the Bible, as illustration.

Sam may have thought the restrictions at San Rafael were good for him, but that didn't stop him from rebelling against them. He valued authority, but didn't respect it.

"Sam wasn't exactly the military type," Breed recalls. "He made fun of the military conventions, wearing the uniforms, etc. They had a large field there. If you broke the rules you had to march in the afternoons around this field with a rifle. You could end up walking around the field for quite a few days. I remember Peckinpah used to be marching there. I was right behind him a lot of the time. I don't think the owners of the school particularly liked him. You could usually tell those that were in favor and those that were out. The kids that were in favor received commissions as lieutenants and captains. Peckinpah never got past PFC. He just wouldn't put up with all the bullshit that went on there." By the time he graduated Sam would have the dubious honor of earning more demerits in a single year than any other cadet in the history of the academy.

At night, after lights-out, they'd slip out the windows of their rooms and zigzag through the shrubbery and across the damp grassy fields, and make their way into the small town of San Rafael. They might score some beer, flirt with the local girls, or maybe take in a show at one of the two movie theaters.

It was probably during one of these nocturnal expeditions that he first saw *The Ox-Bow Incident*. Fern Lea remembers him bubbling over with excitement about it on one of his visits home. Here, for the first time, was a different kind of western. None of the phony Tom Mix highjinks that he'd now grown tired of. No forty-gallon hats, silver six-guns, or horses that did every trick but bring their master his evening paper. Here were a couple of real cowboys—Henry Fonda and Henry Morgan—in faded frayed clothes, riding into a stark and sunbaked cow town. And the story—there was a real story, not just a random collection of chases and shootouts. It cut deeper. It's easy to see why the film appealed to young Peckinpah. A hunger for death lurks beneath the bored citizens of the backwater town. Aroused by a rumored murder, they turn into a rabid lynch mob that hangs three innocent men. The central conflict, between the martinet father who leads the mob and the weak quiet son who is forced to participate, spoke to Sam's innermost struggles.

"You'll do it!" The father orders when his son balks at whipping the horses out from beneath the noosed men. "I'll have no female boys bearing my name. You'll do your part."

And then afterward they discover the men they've lynched were innocent, and the father locks the son out of his house. The boy yells through the closed door at a man he now hates: "I saw your face! It was the face of a depraved, murderous beast! . . . Aren't you glad you made me go, Father? Weren't you proud of me? How does it feel to have begot a weakling, Major Tetly? Does it make you afraid that there may be some weakness in you too that other men might discover and whisper about? Open the door, Major, I want to see your face! I want to know how you feel now!"

And his father's answer from behind the door that separates them: the crash of a gunshot.

Here was a western that was more than a western, that spoke to something deep and inarticulate within Sam. He drank it all in, in the darkness of the theater. Did Fern Lea notice, he asked her after she'd seen it also, how Henry Fonda's face was hidden by another guy's hat brim when he read the letter by one of the hanged men? How it kept the scene from getting too mushy and weepy-eyed? And how the dog crosses the town's dusty street from left to right in the opening shot, when Fonda and Morgan ride into town, then crosses right to left when they ride out again in the final shot? How that kind of put a ribbon around the whole story, tied it together in a way?

In the eyes of the United States Government D. Sammy was no longer Fern's precious little boy but a fully grown man, old enough to die for his country. At San Rafael, the boys sat up nights listening to the news broadcasts about the battles raging in Europe and the South Pacific. They wondered aloud how they'd hold up under enemy fire, worried secretly that they might turn yellow and run. But the question still seemed hypothetical. They knew they might die, but death seemed distant and abstract. "No one really thought about the brutality of it," says John Breed, "because of the propaganda. According to the newsreels, everyone was a hero."

Far stronger than the fear was the great gut-rush of excitement. Now at last there was somewhere to go, new worlds to discover beyond the shores of the Pacific that had thwarted their ancestors nearly a century before.

Another memory about one of Sam's visits home that last year stands out for Fern Lea. She found herself alone in the living room one day with her brother, who at 5′10″ stood as tall as he ever would. He looked at her with those big hazel eyes and suddenly began reciting a poem by Edna St. Vincent Millay:

My candle burns at both ends;
It will not last the night;
But ah, my foes, and oh, my friends—
It gives a lovely light!

"That's me, Spuddy," he said, almost in a whisper. "That's going to be me."

By 1943 the American war machine had cranked into high gear. Never before in history had such awesome power been unleashed by a single nation. There were fifteen million men and women in the armed services. Assembly lines in Michigan, California, Pennsylvania, Mississippi, and New England rolled out 29,497 tanks that year, 85,898 aircraft and a total ship tonnage of sixteen million. The industrial output of the United States was more than double that of all the Axis powers combined. In less than two and a half years America's gleaming juggernaut would smash Adolf Hitler's thousand-year Reich and Hirohito's Empire of the Rising Sun to smithereens.

Antiwar sentiment had been strong before Pearl Harbor. Most Americans felt they had been suckered into the First World

War, on whose battlefields 116,516 of our boys had been killed, 204,002 wounded—many came back minus arms or legs, or so badly blinded and lung-scorched by mustard gas that they would spend the rest of their lives in the grim wards of VA hospitals. And after it was all over, most people had to admit they'd never understood the cause of the war in the first place.

But this staunch isolationism evaporated with the billowing smoke of eight stricken battleships and three destroyers sinking into the waters of Pearl Harbor. The surprise attack by Japan triggered American bloodlust. Here at last was a just cause, a "Good War" against appropriately evil and "inhuman" enemies: Nazi stormtroopers, the yellow peril. Savages like those faced at the Washita River and Little Bighorn.

There was only one vote in congress against a declaration of war after the Japanese attack. By 1942 all able-bodied men—Republicans and Democrats, Klan members and card-carrying communists, sharecroppers and stockbrokers' sons—were rushing down to the recruiting stations to sign up.

Denny Peckinpah, recently graduated from law school, joined the Navy. David Peckinpah wanted to join up too, but at forty-eight he was too old. He did his part by inviting servicemen from local bases to spend holidays and weekends at his home. Two days before his eighteenth birthday Sam outdid both his father and brother by volunteering for the United States Marine Corps, the fiercest fighting force his country had to offer. "Sam felt he was the runt of the family," Fern Lea explains. "He wanted to prove himself. Going into the marines was the way to do that."

He first went to Flagstaff, Arizona, under an early version of the ROTC, then to boot camp at Parris Island, South Carolina. If he had found the military discipline at San Rafael overbearing, his arrival on the island must have come as a grave shock. Gay Paree it was not.

"The way they set things up psychologically at Parris Island was fascinating," says Craig Carter, a former marine who served in Sam's battalion during approximately the same period of time.

For troublemakers like Peckinpah, the drill instructors had devised many innovative behavior-modification techniques.

A favorite was to load two field packs on the "wiseguy" and make him run circles around the platoon. If you started to dog it, the DI's size-eleven boot would remotivate your ass. Run and run and run in circles until you finally dropped. Equally effective was to have the "numb-nuts" stand with his ten-pound rifle held over his head until he finally staggered and lowered it; he couldn't drop it on the ground, though, or he'd be in deep shit. The DI might tell you to climb a tree and chant, "I'm a horse's ass from Yemassee! I'm the biggest damn ass you ever did see!" Meanwhile the rest of your platoon threw rocks at you.

They marched for hours in cadence. *What makes the grass grow? Blood! Blood! Blood!* If a recruit tripped and fell no one stopped; they marched right over him. If platoon members failed to slap their rifle straps smartly when presenting arms, the DI would march them over to a paved area and bark: "All right, you ladies can't hit the straps, let's see how you do on concrete!" And they'd pound the cement for fifteen minutes or more, until their fists were bruised and cut. If all else failed, there was always the "piss and punk"—thirty days in the brig on bread and water.

And so it went, from the crack of dawn to ten at night for ten eternal weeks. Some couldn't take it. Some had psychotic breaks and bolted up from their bunks in the middle of the night screaming passages from the Bible. Others went catatonic, staring trancelike into space. Those who survived the tearing-down process were then gradually rebuilt into new men; the civilians died and were reborn as marines.

"Sometimes the homesickness, loneliness, will become almost unbearable," Sam Peckinpah wrote in a letter to his son, when Mathew also joined the marines nearly forty years later. "The Corps is not a finishing school. It is not a game. It is a way of life—and its basic purpose is to maintain the fact that a combat Marine is the best fighting soldier in the world. Your non-coms and your commissioned officers will have what amounts to almost absolute power over you. They will try and break you, but as they try and break you, they will be teaching you—how to save your ass and your buddy's, how to kill with efficiency; *how to learn.* When you come out you will know the pride of being a Marine . . ."

Sam's ten weeks had passed. The final day had come. "The drill instructors came into the barracks and said, 'All right, you maggots, out in the street!' " Craig Carter recalls. "So we fell out in three minutes out in the street. No weapons, no belts. They came along—there were seventy-eight of us—and the three drill instructors had a box. A ceremony that goes back to the goddamned Romans! They came up and gave us our Marine Corps emblems. We took off these little khaki caps—'piss-cutters,' they called them—and put the emblem in the hole there. The DI said: 'You can call yourselves marines.' They let us stand there at ease and they let that soak in. Each one of the seventy-eight of us accepted this information in his own way. It was the first chance we'd been given to be an individual."

Marching out of Parris Island, they came upon a group of new recruits with long hair and still wearing their civilian clothes. "I thought to myself: I looked like *that?*" Carter recalls. "The whole psychological plan had worked on me. I *belonged.* I'd take the gates off hell if they told me to do it."

From Parris Island Sam went to officer candidate school at Camp Lejeune, North Carolina. A thyroid imbalance—a condition he'd suffered from since childhood—caused him to fall asleep during classes, but doubtless he found the curriculum of military tactics, strategy, and command structure less than stimulating. The Marine Corps reached the belated conclusion that he was not officer material. He was washed out of OCS and sent to Camp Pendleton in the summer of 1945, where he would ship out for the Far East. The Peckinpah men must have wondered if D. Sam would ever amount to anything, and he probably wondered that himself.

By the summer of 1945 America was steeling itself for the last great battle of the war: the invasion of Japan. A total of 767,000 men were slated for taking the first island, Kyushu. If they suffered the same 35 percent casualty rate inflicted on Americans in Okinawa, 268,000 of them would end up dead or wounded. To take all four main islands, as many as one million Americans were expected to die. But then, a monstrous miracle. On August 6 and 9, the U.S. planted two breathtaking, radioactive blossoms on Hiroshima and Nagasaki. In a couple of eye-blinks over 120,000 people perished. Five days after the second bomb was dropped, Japan surrendered.

When Private Sam Peckinpah shipped out of San Diego harbor in September 1945, it was not for the beaches of Kyushu, Shikoku, Honshu and Hokkaido, but for China, where the First Marine Division had been assigned the task of disarming 630,000 Japanese soldiers and civilians and shipping them home.

Twenty days later the troopship pulled into Taku harbor in the East China Sea. It was as if they'd landed on a strange and distant planet; few of the marines had ever been farther than a couple hundred miles away from their hometowns.

Craig Carter remembers leaning over the railing of the boat as it pulled into Taku. Hundreds of sampans rushed out from the shore to meet them, their pilots chattering in a strange high-pitched dialect that sounded like records playing backward, and holding up goods—bracelets, silk kimonos, brass bowls—for the marines to buy.

At Taku they boarded a procession of LCT landing craft that took them inland, up the Hai Ho River to Tangku. Throngs of Chinese cheered them all along the way. At Tangku they boarded trains that took them eighty miles inland to Tientsin. A city of then about three and a half million people, roughly the same size as Chicago at the time, Tientsin straddled the banks of the Hai Ho and several railroads converged there, making it the hub of north China.

Peckinpah's battalion (the Second) was billeted in an old Japanese school on the outskirts of the city. By railroad and truck convoy through Tientsin and then by LST troopships from Taku harbor, over 600,000 Japanese would be evacuated during the next three months.

Marines who served with Sam Peckinpah in China remember him as an easygoing and likable guy. He was thin, wiry, his boyish face now offset by a heavy mustache. He was a friendly but subdued companion who tended to hang back from the boisterous clowning around in the barracks. "He was a quiet guy," says Leo Cardarelli. "Used to watch us crazies. He seemed to be a studious-type guy. We used to kid him about his name: 'Pick a peck of pickled Peckinpah's.' "

He read a lot—*Time* magazine and books the rest of them had never heard of. "He was reading books I didn't even know about," says Mike Fitzgerald. "I didn't even know who [F. Scott] Fitzgerald was. He was telling me he had read most of his books."

But once you got to know him better, Sam revealed a more assertive side. Fitzgerald killed many an idle hour debating the politics of postwar China with Sam. "He was very bright. Very argumentative. He had a lot of good arguments." In the heat of one of their disagreements, Sam suddenly pulled a piece of paper out from his footlocker, stood up and read from it as if it were an official proclamation. "Fitzgerald, you know *nothing!*" He announced, then dramatically crumpled the page.

Most marines avoided KP duty like the plague; the long hot hours in a greasy kitchen made the boredom of guard duty look appealing. But Sam lobbied hard for a job cleaning the ovens and giant fuel ranges. The position had its perks, but they were of his own making. "I had my own black market," he later explained. "I was selling white gas to the cooks in [Tientsin] restaurants. White gas and cigarettes."

Though their official mission was to disarm and repatriate the Japanese, it soon became clear to the marines that their government was also using them to prop up Chiang Kai-shek's Nationalist regime. When the Japanese had invaded China in 1937, the Nationalists and Mao Tse-tung's communists joined forces against them. But now, with the invaders defeated, the two factions had begun to fight again. The ink on the armistice treaties had barely dried before the Cold War was on. Russia and America were carefully positioning their chess pieces in Third World theaters. And the U.S. could not afford, Washington decided, to let the communists seize control of the world's most populous nation.

Marines were posted on strategic bridges and along the major rail lines linking Tientsin, Peiping, and Chinwangtao, and around coal mines that were vital to China's economy. The marines virtually occupied the port city of Tsingtao and held the communists at bay until Nationalist troops could be funneled in. Large stores of captured Japanese weapons and munitions were turned over to Chiang's forces, and all the while America attempted to pose as a disinterested neutral power in the conflict between the two Chinese factions. At first the plan appeared to be working; the Nationalists consolidated their hold on North China.

It was fitting that marines were billeted in the old British legations in Tientsin and Peiping. For over a hundred years the British, French, Germans, and Japanese had vied for preeminence in China, either through strategic "spheres of influence" or outright conquest. Now, with the French and British exhausted, it looked like America might have the entire pie to itself. If the Nationalists won it would be possible to return to the good old days when foreign powers controlled Chinese commerce through a series of proxies—local warlords, merchants, and politicians. Only this time Uncle Sam would be pulling all the strings.

Back in the United States the news media portrayed the brewing civil war as a battle between Mao Tse-tung's godless red hordes and Chiang Kai-shek's noble freedom fighters. But for the marines in China, the realities were not nearly so clearly delineated. "We had the Nationalists all around us," Craig Carter recalls. "We saw the way the officers were treating their enlisted men. The Nationalist officers were living in town. They didn't even go into the field with their troops. They were living like warlords." Hundreds of thousands of Chinese peasants had been forced to join the Nationalist army, but few wanted to fight. While their generals skimmed money and pilfered supplies, they were ill-equipped and underfed.

"We were attacked on a motorized patrol en route from Tientsin to Peiping," Carter recalls. "*The New York Times* wrote it up as a communist attack. Actually, they were starving Nationalists. They wanted to steal our guns and gas and sell them for food."

The communists were just as short on supplies, but they possessed in abundance a crucial element the Nationalists lacked: idealism, a dream of a better world.

In 1945 and 1946 many of the battles were over the caches of ammunition, food, fuel, and arms desposited in hundreds of locations around North China. Some of these had been left behind by the Japanese; others were new shipments courtesy of the United Nations and the Marshall Plan. The marines ended up guarding much of it and so found themselves under attack, most frequently from the communists. There were a few nasty skirmishes, but never more than a half-dozen marines killed in any single action. Usually the communists withdrew at the first signs of strong resistance. "Most were probing actions," says Carter, "they were just testing us. It's the old military rule of never losing contact with your enemy."

The marines were hard pressed to secure all the railroad lines and ammo dumps during their first months in China; ironically, they had to call upon the Japanese for help. Japanese garrisons were asked to remain armed and to maintain their control over rail centers and strategic towns to keep them from falling into the hands of the communists, and Japanese soldiers were put on guard duty side-by-side with marines. "It was strange," says Mike Zownir, a marine who'd fought on Okinawa.

Sam Peckinpah did guard duty on many of the trains running between Tientsin and Peiping. Most of the trips were uneventful—long, slow, hot journeys, Chinese peasants and their luggage crammed into every available inch of space, some even perched on the roofs of the cars.

Occasionally the communists, or some other faction, would take a shot at the passing train and a bullet would smash through a window, buzz across the car, and pass out the other side. Sometimes the marines would fire back aimlessly, unable to sight their attackers in the tangled countryside. Most times the communists were not seriously trying to stop the train; it was like a game, two bored armies taking potshots at each other. But the game could have deadly consequences, as Sam discovered the day a bullet tore through a window and into a nearby Chinese passenger, killing him immediately. Peckinpah later called it "one of the longest split-seconds" in his life. When another bullet crashed through the car, everyone threw themselves to the floor. "I remember falling down, and it was so long . . ." Sam later recalled. "I noticed that time slowed down." He had discovered the eternal instant. It fascinated him, the way a moment of trauma stretched itself, every sensory detail heightened and every motion elongated—how at the very edge of death one felt life most keenly, even with a strange elation.

But such engagements were rare during the marines' first

months in China, the exception rather than the rule, and liberty in Tientsin and Peiping offered ample compensations. For a while it seemed like the return of that golden era before the war, when China duty was considered the choicest assignment a marine could draw.

Hundreds of saloons lined the narrow, winding streets of Tientsin and Peiping. They ranged from American-style cocktail lounges to crude holes-in-the-wall in which an unfurnished plank laid across a couple of barrels served as the bar. Five Star Beer was the most popular brew. There was also champagne and plenty of Russian vodka. In the dives you risked ingesting lethal home-brewed concoctions. "Some of it was aged four days," says Craig Carter. "Some of it was raw wood alcohol colored with creosote or tobacco juice to make it look like American whiskey. The alcohol would make you drunk and could kill you. The adulterators that the Chinese put in this stuff to make it look like American whiskey, which was spelled 'Wysky,' would certainly kill you."

Almost as abundant and easy to purchase were women. The desperate poverty after years of war made it simple. "Guys were trading cigarettes for blow jobs," says Carter. "Any bartender, any cop could get you a woman," Tom Dowlearn says. "They were all over the place."

There were White Russian women, statuesque Manchurians, olive-skinned Eurasians, and an abundant supply of fifteen- and sixteen-year-olds, smooth and slender and firmly curved.

Virtually all types could be found in Tientsin's awe-inspiring flesh emporium, "The House of 10,000 Assholes"—so nicknamed by the marines after the Summer Palace's "Temple of 10,000 Buddhas." If the establishment had a real name, the Americans never knew it. The cracked and decaying seven-story building had served a succession of conquering armies—the Japanese, the French, the British. For all anybody knew, it might have dated back to the Mongols.

"You'd walk in the place and look up the stairs and see girls with no pants on," Tom Dowlearn recalls. The halls were dimly lit by small flickering bulbs and reeked of sulfurous coal smoke; plaster bubbled and flaked off the walls and ceilings.

Peckinpah thrived on the bars and brothels of Tientsin. Here was the masculine paradise he'd longed for while sitting in front of his grandfather's fireplace as a kid—all the drinking and whoring and brawling a man could want. But his fascination was fueled by more than the opportunity to let his id off its leash. In those dilapidated saloons and those cramped bedrooms lurked something dark and desperate, a vision of life at the frazzled end of the rope. Amid the strangled carnal moans, the naked groping, seeping in through the grate with the coal smoke, was the stench of death. Not even the smooth slender limbs of a sixteen-year-old could shield you from it, and by 1946 the smell was growing stronger.

"Peckinpah and I were in a whorehouse one time when the Nationalists started pounding on the door," Mike Fitzgerald recalls. "The Nationalist troops would tear through these places with machine guns and kick down doors. We were in this room, they kicked on the door, we opened it. They were looking for spies."

The civil war was heating up, and as it did the gap between the *Stars and Stripes* image of the Nationalists as defenders of democracy and the reality most marines witnessed continued to widen. Public executions and torturing of "spies" became a common sight.

"They'd execute them on Saturday morning," Fitzgerald recalls. "They'd tie these guys up with rope and shoot them."

Leo Cardarelli witnessed a public beheading. "Chiang Kai-shek and his soldiers used to do that quite a bit. They'd behead them for thievery, anything. This one was done in a compound. I happened to be there, a bunch of other guys were there. I got very upset about it. They just knelt the guy down and hit him with a goddamned big sword . . . I never want to see one of them again. They were bastards. Chiang Kai-shek was nothing but a dictator."

Most disturbing was the effect this moral chaos had on some of their fellow marines. Chinese lives became as devaluated as their currency, and in some of the Americans a latent savagery rose quickly to the surface. "We had idiots aboard trains, believe it or not," says Dowlearn, "that would take their rifles and see how close they could come to hitting these poor coolies working out in the fields."

Peckinpah told an interviewer from *Life* magazine in 1972: "Another Marine told me—boasted to me—that he'd thrown a Chinese woman down on a concrete platform and raped her, hit her head against the pavement, and after he was done she didn't move. I'd been practically adopted by a Chinese family. I actually decided I was going to kill him. I went out and stole a gun, a Russian gun, and offered to sell it to him. You know, the souvenir mentality. When I sold it to him, I was going to kill him. Put the barrel of the gun right up under his chin and pull the trigger. The night before our meeting, I saw him standing there, completely blind. He'd drunk some bad whiskey. If it hadn't been for that, I might be in prison today."

Provoked by an act of barbarity, he'd come within a hair of committing the ultimate barbarity. Should he have felt guilty for not having killed the torturer, or for wanting to? The moral certainties his father had preached to him over the family dinner table, the simple choices between right and wrong, had ceased to apply. The Good War had turned bad and nobody quite knew how or why.

When Sam Peckinpah's battalion moved to Peiping in the spring of 1946, he soon ceased accompanying his comrades on their drinking and whoring expeditions. He'd begun to dabble in Zen and had taken up with a Chinese girl from a good family. Her English name was Helen. "He met her just before he left to come back to America," says Marie Selland, Sam's first wife. "She was a young communist. She was very much into politics. He really fell in love with her. He hated to leave her. [Servicemen were forbidden to marry Chinese. Sam requested a discharge in Peiping, but was refused.] She spoke English very well. They had a lot to talk about. He had a picture of her; it wasn't at all the picture of what you might think of Sam's women looking like. This young, beautiful Chinese woman, but with big glasses and a big heavy sweater, looking very serious."

She talked about the Marxist vision of the people taking over from their oppressors, of doing away with all the emperors and warlords, about a land where everyone would live in harmony and brotherhood. She did not convert him. He had been too deeply inculcated by the rugged individualist creed of the American West to ever cherish becoming an anonymous member of a collective, and had already seen too much of the dark side of human nature to genuinely believe that a utopia could come from the hands of man. But the dream, the desperate longing for a better world, that he understood.

From the House of 10,000 Assholes to the arms of a Marxist madonna, from the warlords and death squads to the Communists with their dream of redeeming the human race to the peasants who asked for nothing more than a chance to survive . . . Sam Peckinpah left China at the end of 1946 with no notches on his gun, no medals on his chest, and only the rank of corporal on his sleeve. But he came home to Fresno with a vision that had expanded far beyond the boundaries of Peckinpah Mountain and Dunlap's ranch, and vexed by the perplexing dualities within himself and his fellow men.

2

The Prodigious Interloper

Sam Peckinpah had left for China in the fall of 1945 a boy; he returned a year later a man. But like the five million other servicemen who came home that year, he still had no idea what he wanted to do with his life. He knew what he didn't want to do: go to law school and then into practice with his father and brother.

But within a few months a quirk of fate, or rather a pair of shapely legs, would lead him to his life's work. The legs belonged to a striking young blonde, Marie Selland. She would become the first great love of his life. But his second love soon proved an irresistible rival: the director's chair.

He entered his profession at the dawn of the most innovative and exciting era in Hollywood since the birth of silent movies. A little electronic box sparked the revolution. It shattered the Hollywood power structure and allowed a whole new generation of directors to storm through the cracks. A decade later they would redefine the American cinema.

When D. Sammy came home in 1946, the mood in his family was, at first, ecstatic. On November 28, Fern wrote in her diary: "It's nearly midnight of the first Thanksgiving since the war and my heart is full of joy and gratitude and I feel very humble and grateful. It was wonderful to look at all the smiling faces when we were gathered at the table just waiting for David to start carving the 20-lb turkey. Sammy . . . was a happy guy there at the far end of the table between his two good looking girl cousins. All three girls were pretty and oh! it was a *wonderful day!!*"

But after the initial euphoria wore off, readjustment proved difficult for Sam. After all he'd seen and been through, it was difficult to return to the quiet confines of domestic life. His mother and father forbade smoking and drinking in the house. He and Denny had acquired large appetites for both in the service, and Sam began following his older brother up the falls near Bass Lake, where friends of Denny's—the Williams brothers—owned a nightclub, The Timber Room. It offered plenty of booze, slot machines, and the kind of action a China marine longed for. "Babe Williams ran the place," Denny recalls. "He had a baby face, but he was tough. I remember there was a fight one night out on the stairs leading into the club. Babe took this guy's head and started slamming it on the concrete steps. He was slamming the guy's head and yelling: 'I'm the manager, you son of a bitch! I'm the manager!' "

Needless to say, Fern Peckinpah did not approve. On New Year's Eve, 1947, she wrote in her diary: "Before he went away he had no use for the Falls and all that it stands for, but now he's all *mixed up*, poor little boy! . . . Four years ago when he went away from home, he was one of the finest boys in the land, with such a fine high standard in every way. . . . I'm not feeling sorry for myself but trying to understand and keep a smile. That's a hard job at times 'cause I can't help remembering seeing those beautiful eyes all cloudy with drink, his step uncertain and him crying and his speech mixed up. Of all my loved ones Sammy is the last one in all the world that I can believe I'd ever see like that. You just can't hardly take it!"

That winter Fresno State College put on a fund-raising carnival. There was a midway with dart booths, fortune tellers, apple-bobbing contests, and a Gay-Nineties revue produced by members of the college drama department. Instead of going to the Falls that night, Sam wandered down the midway and into the show. A stout, auburn-haired girl pounded a Tin Pan Alley tune out of an upright piano, while another—with long blond hair piled high on her head and even longer legs clad in black silk—sang "She May Have Seen Better Days."

The singer had sharp angular features and high cheekbones. Her large hazel eyes were warm and melancholy, with a sad intelligence that stretched far beyond her years; yet at the same time they seemed remote, like some strange animal that you could stare and stare at but never really fathom. Her long thin arms and fingers waved about in the air as she sang, the movements contrived and artificial yet somehow mesmerizing. But in the end it was those legs—those slender, firmly curved calves and thighs stretching up into the short frills of her dress—that won his heart and glands.

"Marie had a body," Marian Dysinger, the girl at the upright piano, recalls. "Sam took one look at those killer legs. He said later he never really appreciated Marie until he saw her in that show, and that he just had to get better acquainted with a pair of legs like that."

They'd known of each other for years, had attended Fresno High together, but had never exchanged more than passing nods in the halls. Marie Selland also came from a prominent Fresno family. Her father, Art Selland, was a successful stockbroker, a member of the Exchange Club and the school board, and later would become the city's mayor. The family lived in a handsome two-story colonial house just a few blocks away from the college campus.

Like Sam, Marie had acted in high school plays. But hers was no mere flirtation with the theater, it was a head-over-heels love affair. She started acting in the fourth grade. They'd been studying China in school and each student had to turn in a project on the subject—topographical maps, written or oral reports, pie graphs, etc. Marie and her friends decided to make up a play about an American family visiting China. Her friends played the Americans while Marie portrayed all the Chinese, from a shy little peasant girl to a foot-bound old woman.

From there on acting was an obsession for her. She and her friends spent countless hours on the playground making up plays based on Greek myths and other historical subjects they were studying at the time. In junior high she took her first formal drama class. She not only acted in most of the school plays, but organized a drama club with her fellow students. They met in one another's homes after school and planned and staged their own productions.

In high school she took up smoking and practiced inhaling with the bent-wrist sophistication of Bette Davis, her latest idol. She played a German house mother in *Letters from Lucerne,* a play about a Swiss girls' school during World War II, and she was Kitty Duval, the prostitute with deluded dreams, in William Saroyan's *The Time of Your Life.*

The theater offered Marie freedom from the intense shyness and self-judgment that often inhibited her in social situations; freedom to express all the emotions she normally kept hidden from her peers, to slip into the skin of another person and see the world through different eyes.

She toured with a stock company in Massachusetts after graduating from high school in the summer of 1945, then enrolled at Fresno State in the fall, where a small theater department flourished under the direction of John W. Wright.

Her father supported her theatrical ambitions, but her mother, Cecilia, thought her daughter was wasting her time. "You know you're going to marry and have children, so why bother?"

"No!" Marie would reply in a fury. "I'll never do that!"

Years later, while reading her mother's diaries, Marie discovered Cecilia also had played leading roles in high school plays and been quite enthusiastic about acting, until she'd gotten pregnant and, as a result, married. "Her dreams died," Marie says. "So maybe she was trying to keep me from being disappointed like she had been. There was no place for dreams like becoming an actress in my mother's world."

But it was a different world now, or so it seemed. During the war millions of women had gone to work in factories and offices on the home front, and into uniform overseas. They had proved they could do as well as men, if not better, and the rigidly defined sex roles seemed to be breaking down, opening up all kinds of new possibilities. *Why not become an actress if that's what you wanted to be? Who said you were doomed from birth to a life of changing diapers, cooking and cleaning?*

Marie rapidly established herself as a star at Fresno State—a talented, versatile actress capable of carrying a leading role or taking on an almost limitless range of character parts. "We all thought Marie was something special," says former classmate T. Elton Foreman. "She was *the* actress at Fresno State—the kind of person who doesn't make any impression on you in a social situation, but then you see her on stage and she comes to life."

"She had a great deal of concentration and intensity," says one of her college instructors, Howard Campbell. "She would get involved with the character and actually become the character while she was on stage."

Offstage she was "lofty, ethereal, you know, Desdemona," says another former student, Jim Baker. "She was a pre-hippie, with long blond hair that she kept in braids. She wore Mother Hubbard dresses, a pre-beatnik even."

"She was a bohemian," says former classmate Dick Lewis. "She didn't care about material things at all. She would go around barefoot at Fresno State. Sam was the same way. If any two belonged together, it was Sam and Marie."

Marie had just broken up with a boyfriend when Sam saw her in the Gay-Nineties revue. A few days later a girl whom Sam was going out with at the time suggested Marie double-date with them and a friend of Sam's who'd just gotten out of the service. It doesn't take much guesswork to figure out who instigated the proposal. Marie agreed and the four went out to one of the local college hangouts for dinner. The chemistry was powerful and instantaneous.

"Sam and I struck up a conversation," Marie recalls, and, much to the consternation of their respective dates, "it continued all evening long. We talked about poetry and books. He was incredibly well read. God, it was so unusual to meet somebody like that. We talked about Rupert Brooke, a poet who wrote poems about World War One. We talked about Steinbeck. Sam liked him a lot." She fell quickly under his spell. His hair had darkened and he'd had it cut short so it lay smoothly along the handsome contours of his head. The mustache he'd grown in China had been whittled down to an elegant Clark Gable line above his upper lip.

"He was one of the most beautiful men I'd ever seen. He had the look of a poet. I loved his feelings about the mountains and nature. I guess I refused to see the deep inner conflicts he had, I refused to see them for a long time."

From that night on they were inseparable. Sam may have read more literature, but Marie knew the theater. Through her he rediscovered the seeds of his own fascination, planted during those high school plays and half-forgotten with the onrush of San Rafael Military Academy, the marines, and China. She talked incessantly about acting and her favorite playwrights. As the excitement animated her voice and gestures, he felt his own pulse quickening and began to entertain thoughts he'd never allowed himself to take seriously before.

"Their courtship was a real college love affair," says former classmate George Zenovich. "They were always together. She influenced him tremendously."

"They just glowed when they were together," Fern Lea recalls. "They were always holding hands, touching one another. It was obvious they were very much in love."

When Marie went back to Fresno State in February to start the next semester, Sam followed her. He enrolled as a history major—a concession to his father, who still hoped he'd go to law school. He'd made a concession to his mother too. He promised her he would stop drinking. "I'm just bubbling over with happiness and I want to remember this day forever," Fern wrote in her diary. "There have been some pretty tough times to face in the last five months, but they are all over *now.* I believe in him 100%." It was the first link in a chain of broken promises that would extend over the entire length of his life.

For the moment, though, his parents were pleased, and when

he arrived for the first day of classes at Fresno State it was in a secondhand Jeep that his father had bought for him.

But instead of going after history courses, he lobbied for admittance to a class on directing for the theater that was taught by Howard Campbell—a young, progressive instructor whom Marie had been raving about. "They didn't want to let him in," she recalls. "He'd had no classes in drama and it was an upper-division class. But he had a lot of college credits [from classes taken at Arizona State while in the Marine Corps] so they finally let him in, but all the other students looked down on him."

"At one time or another each of us guys were sweet on Marie," says Dave Parker, a former member of the drama department at Fresno. "Then along comes this interloper, not even a drama major, and Marie falls in love with him. We all looked at him cynically. Obviously he couldn't have any talent."

For the first couple of weeks Sam sat back and observed, rarely contributing to the group discussions. Some of his classmates read this reticence as apathy. He seemed to be playing it cool, almost disinterested. But beneath the facade, a mind worked furiously, taking in the instructor's words, turning over all the possibilities that they suggested. "Howard Campbell was very intellectual, very cerebral," Marie remembers, "but very interesting. He was one of those rare teachers that really turn you on to new ideas. He introduced us to a lot of playwrights we hadn't read before, the French and Italians—Pirandello was a major one. He got us to think about more than just saying our lines and giving a performance. He got us to explore the character. We read Stanislavsky, Boleslavsky. He taught us to search for the character, to search for the truth in a play."

For their first assignment, each student was to direct a short scene. Sam recruited two actors and began working on an excerpt from the stage version of *Of Mice and Men.* It took place in a barn. Lennie, the retarded giant, has accidentally killed a puppy and is trying to bury it in a pile of hay when he is discovered by the seductive but dangerous daughter-in-law of the ranch owner. As the scene progresses, the girl encourages Lennie to stroke her long blond hair: "Here—feel right here. Feel right aroun' there an' see how soft it is." Unable to control his confused onrush of passion, Lennie winds up strangling her.

Lennie would be the first of many such murderous innocents to appear in Peckinpah's work as a writer and director. In television and movie scripts they appear again and again: child-men, unable to comprehend or fit into the complex and corrupt world that surrounds them, yet they themselves also carry the demon seed of violence. "I think that's how Sam felt about himself," says Marie. "That he didn't fit in, that he wasn't quite 'right' somehow, that he stood apart. He was always very alone as a person, even around other people."

William Walsh, the actor who played Lennie, vividly recalls Peckinpah's direction. "Up until that time at Fresno State they had taught acting by pure mechanical rote. We were all taught to perform a given part with the exact same delivery, pacing, and vocal intonations, so everybody came out sounding and acting exactly alike." But Peckinpah had listened carefully to Campbell's espousal of a new approach and was eager to try it out for himself.

"My experience with Sam was completely different from anything I'd done before," says Walsh. "He gave you leeway. I could have done that scene different every rehearsal and he wouldn't have cared, he encouraged you to. I remember his direction being so free-flowing. My puppy was my own knotted-up yellow sweater. We had started using it a couple of days before we did the scene for the class. I kept saying: 'We've got to find something better than this. Doesn't somebody have a plush animal, something . . .' Sam just kept saying, 'Don't worry about it, if we get the scene set up all right, when you pull that yellow sweater out nobody's gonna laugh.' "

Something in Peckinpah's penetrating eyes silenced Walsh's protests; something in the hypnotic cadence of his low voice made it terribly important, all of sudden, to please this man.

"I don't know how he did it. The way he had me lead up to it. He just kept telling me that he and I knew it was a sweater, but Lennie didn't know it. Lennie knew it was this little animal, and if Lennie knew it the audience would too. I had indicated it by stroking it out of sight of the audience and looking at it. When I eventually brought it around onto my lap so they could see it, they already knew it was an animal and they reacted as if they'd seen the broken body of a little puppy. I mean, it worked. It was a moment, and I just thought: my God, how did we get to do that?"

"It was remarkable," Marie says. "People were knocked over. He not only got the emotions from the actors, he used the light from two windows at the back of this little stage area. In the late afternoon you'd get a light through one of these windows when the sun hit a certain point. Sam used that light in such a striking way. There were just a couple of chairs there on the bare stage, but I saw the barn where they were, I saw the little puppy. I was *there.* It was one of those remarkable moments in theater. It was just a class exercise, he'd had no training. That was what was so amazing, and irritated the hell out of us, especially the men."

He was ecstatic afterward, reviewing every nuance of the scene over and over again. The infatuation was instantaneous, and would last until the day he died.

He began reading plays with a vengeance, following the recommendations of Marie, Howard Campbell, and his fellow students: Chekhov, Brecht, Shaw, Saroyan, and, most important, Williams. The young playwright's work came as a revelation to him. *The Glass Menagerie* had premiered in Chicago just the year before. Like Arthur Miller, who would unleash *Death of a Salesman* on Broadway two years later, Williams belonged to a new generation of playwrights who had moved beyond the stark realism of Eugene O'Neill. Williams' bold combination of expressionistic staging, lyrical dialogue, and acute psychological detail created a poetic hyperrealism that triggered the adrenaline of Peckinpah's imagination.

And, of course, the subject matter and characters of *Menagerie* struck home. The manipulative and controlling mother, Amanda; her son, Tom, who longs to escape the suffocating confines of their home, yet is tortured by guilt over his disloyalty to his family; and Laura, emotionally stricken, crippled Laura, too delicate, too different to find a place for herself in this world. "He very much identified with Tom," Marie says, "haunted by the past . . . his rootless wandering . . . the relationship with the mother." Tom was in a way a sophisticated and complex reworking of the western hero: a loner who embodied the contrary impulses of the American male, pulled toward the security of home and family yet simultaneously repulsed by it and yearning to escape.

While the other students in his directing class were content to do informal run-throughs of short scenes, for his next project Sam set about editing and rewriting *Menagerie* so that it could be staged as a one-act on the drama department's main stage. "I guess I've learned more from Williams than anyone," he later said. "He's easily America's greatest playwright. I've always felt strongly moved by him. . . . I think I learned more about writing from having to cut *Glass Menagerie* than anything I've done since."

Taking a piece of existing material and reworking it would become his real genius as a writer. In his career in television and feature films he would originate very few stories himself, but instead displayed a knack for transforming a piece of mediocre material into something extraordinary. He would reshape the characters and dialogue and subtly alter the scenes and structure until the vision and style, and finally the story, were his own. This began with *Menagerie.*

The final product once again floored his classmates. "It was obvious in an instant that he was a major talent," says Dave Parker. "His blocking was stunning. He had a feel for stagecraft and getting performances out of actors—a Broadway-class talent."

Suddenly the semester was over. It had passed in one breathless rush and now he was faced with three idle months of living at home. The prospect bred an intolerable sense of claustrophobia. When a couple of his friends told him they were heading south to attend a summer session at the National University of Mexico in Mexico City, he jumped at the opportunity to go with them and offered to drive them there in his Jeep. "He found it hard living at home after the Marine Corps," says Fern Lea. "He found all the rules and restrictions difficult to deal with. Mexico was an opportunity to escape."

He'd barely arrived before his friends abandoned him to

pursue other adventures and he found himself alone in the teeming plateau-top city, equipped with only a smattering of half-forgotten high school Spanish. Yet, as in China, he had no trouble meeting and getting close to the people.

Sam immediately saw striking similarities between the peasants who lived in the labyrinths of shanties surrounding Mexico City and those of Tientsin and Peiping. The Mexicans also had endured a long succession of conquerors—from the Aztecs to the Spanish to the French to the Americans to their own *Federales.* It was here that Sam read John Reed's saga of the Mexican revolution, *Insurgent Mexico,* for the first time. Reed had a journalist's sharpness for detail and a poet's passion. He vividly contrasted the pastoral dreams of Pancho Villa with his bloody actions; he eloquently depicted the simple savagery and capricious cruelty of both sides in the war, and the warm comradeship and romantic idealism that bound the rebels together and eventually propelled them to victory.

Peckinpah became as fascinated with the revolution as Reed himself had been. Ultimately Mexico was as doomed as China, but for a few short years it had looked as though the chain of tyranny had been broken; for a brief span people believed it was actually possible to change the world, to alter the nature of man and save the human race from itself. People had laid down their lives by the thousands for this dream. The fact that the dream had been unattainable made the sacrifice all the more noble, from Peckinpah's cynical/romantic point of view. Mexico and its battle for redemption would weave its way in and out of his television shows and movies, and would serve as the major backdrop for his screenplay *Villa Rides,* and his films *Major Dundee, The Wild Bunch,* and *Bring Me the Head of Alfredo Garcia.*

Peckinpah thrived in this land of eroded Aztec pyramids and crumbling Spanish haciendas, ornate Catholic churches and whorehouses both elegant and shabby. This was a land of irresistible extremes. Its people embraced life spontaneously. They danced, drank, fought, made love, and killed with a frenzy, their quicksilver emotions changing in an instant from tears and tenderness to murderous rage. This south-of-the-border land had long served as a mecca for writers. Ambrose Bierce disappeared forever into its depths during the revolution that Reed chronicled. The Beat generation—Jack Kerouac, William Burroughs, Allen Ginsberg, and Neal Cassady—all made pilgrimages there at roughly the same time as Peckinpah; Malcolm Lowry's masterpiece, *Under the Volcano,* was published that same year.

"Mexico has always meant something special to me," Sam would say later. "My Mexican experience is never over."

The classes he took at the University were inconsequential, and he found his most significant educational experiences on his own. After Reed's book he set about reading most of Shakespeare's major plays. He developed a great affinity for the Englishman's towering but much-flawed heroes. Haunted by guilt, torn between impulses noble and base, fated to tragic ends—and when they finally fell there was a grandeur to their descent. The tales often ended in orgies of bloodshed and destruction, bodies littering the stage, yet you felt oddly uplifted, exalted.

Toward the latter part of the summer he joined an independent theater company and worked as the assistant to the director on a production of Maxwell Anderson's *Joan of Lorraine.* "He loved the experience," says Marie. "Sam's desire for a career in the theater really solidified there. He became *very, very* interested in pursuing it."

When he returned to Fresno that fall, he finally gathered up the courage to face his father with the truth: he wasn't going to law school, he was changing his major, he wanted a life in the theater.

The news couldn't have pleased David Peckinpah, but he took it well. Sam later recalled: "He broke out one of the copies of the [Robert] Ingersoll collection he had. I remember his quoting it. Ingersoll's quote on the theater as a career: 'Shakespeare is the intellectual ocean that touches the shores of all knowledge.' My father said, 'You want to go with that?' and I said, 'Yeah, that's where I'm going.' He said, 'Well go.' He encouraged me and helped support me. He said he thought it would be nice to have a legal education as a backstop [a line he'd used to seduce Denny away from dreams of becoming a writer]. But I had spent too many years listening to conversations about the law—right and wrong—I was beginning to get my own ideas."

David Peckinpah's support for his youngest son never wavered, but he also never really understood his odd yearnings. It was, at least, an improvement. At least D. Sam had a focus now; at least he'd finally stopped drifting. "Dad thought Sam would end up teaching theater at a high school or college somewhere," says Fern Lea. "He could at least earn a living. Nobody thought Sam would end up in films."

Sam had not yet finished springing surprises on his parents. When driving back up from Mexico that September, his Jeep had broken down. He left it in a gas station in Arizona to be repaired and came back to Fresno by train. When it came time to go pick the Jeep up again a couple of weeks later, he asked Marie to accompany him. "My mother was away with my sisters at the beach. She would never have let me go," Marie recalls. "I was home alone with Dad. He said, 'Well, it's all right, I guess. But write your mother a note and explain it to her.' " The young couple left by train, picked Sam's Jeep up in Arizona, and, without telling anyone, headed for Las Vegas to get married. "We honeymooned at a motor lodge in Cucamonga and ate hamburgers for our honeymoon dinner," Marie recalls. "He gave me a polished silver band he'd gotten in Mexico as a wedding ring; later he had it set with an emerald and two small diamonds. He designed the setting himself."

When they returned to Fresno they kept the marriage a secret. Both the Peckinpahs and the Sellands could see that matrimony was in the wind, but neither family suspected it had already occurred. It was deliciously romantic for the young couple, sneaking off for rendezvous, bound together by a secret union. "Sam was my first lover," Marie says with palpable wistfulness these many decades later, "and he was wonderful in that way."

One would have expected big trouble between Marie and Fern Peckinpah; after all, the young willowy blonde had stolen Fern's precious D. Sammy. But Marie succeeded in charming Mrs. Peckinpah from the very beginning. "Mom wanted to dislike Marie, but she couldn't," Fern Lea explains. "Marie was so warm and kind to her. She'd sit for hours and listen to my mother rattle on. Mom couldn't help but like her."

Marie did notice tensions in the Peckinpah house. She noted the unusual closeness between Sam and his mother despite the mounting tensions of recent years. Often the two would disappear into another room for an hour or more for one of their "heart-to-heart" talks, a ritual that continued for several more years.

Their secret marriage lasted for five days. But then the Sellands, giving in to the inevitable, began to talk about throwing a big wedding for the couple. Marie recalls: "Sam got nervous, so we decided we had to tell them. We waited till a family gathering at the Peckinpah's. David cooked one of his breakfasts: lamb chops, sausage, eggs, pancakes. Endless food. Sam and I hid a note among the lamb chops. Mother asked for another and out came the note. The sisters [Marie's and Sam's] were all happy, the parents were shocked. My father was secretly relieved—no expensive wedding to pay for now. The only disappointment for him was he'd been dying to see me walk down the stairs of our house in my wedding dress."

That very afternoon Marie packed up her bedroom set, and the couple moved into the small cabin on the far end of the Peckinpah's twenty-four-acre spread. (It had been rented to hired hands in the past.) There were two rooms: a kitchen/living room with a woodburning stove, and a bedroom with an apricot tree outside the window. There was a porch with a washtub on it and a view of the nearby vineyards. They would live there together throughout their remaining year at Fresno State, Sam's bedside table growing higher and higher with volcanic mounds of books. Conrad, Hemingway, Thoreau, Faulkner, Dickens, science books, volumes of history on China and ancient Greece. Aristotle's *Poetics* gave him the foundations for dramatic writing, and he became a strong believer in the philosopher's theory that great drama provides an audience with a catharsis through which they can purge their own pain, rage, and fear.

After the Greeks came the French: Albert Camus' *The Stranger* and *The Plague*, Jean-Paul Sartre's *No Exit*, *The Flies*, and *The Wall*. Out of the rubble of postwar Paris had come a new philosophy, existentialism, that jettisoned all notions of God, Heaven, and any preexisting code of conduct or morality. There is no a priori right and wrong, no good and evil, Camus and Sartre contended. The universe is absurd and meaningless, a spiritual wasteland out of which each man must carve his own meaning and morality. The Frenchmen articulated feelings that had been evolving within Sam since he first attended his father's court trials as a kid, feelings that had solidified in China and Mexico.

Alongside such heady material were scores of cheap detective novels and westerns. "Sam was an insatiable reader," says Marie. "Our whole life was reading books and talking about them, exchanging plays, seeing movies, talking about what worked and what didn't, what plays we'd like to do. I was going to be a famous actress and he was going to be a famous director."

Back at Fresno State that fall, Sam was acting in plays as well as directing them. He had a half a dozen supporting roles in productions on the college's main stage. He played a conveener in Thornton Wilder's *The Skin of Our Teeth,* and Chick Clark, the newspaper reporter in *My Sister Eileen.*

He'd been accepted as one of the gang now. He and Marie joined the other students often at Pancho's, a favorite hangout near campus. Or they'd pile as many as they could fit in Sam's Jeep and take off on a Saturday to go skiing at Badger Pass, or, as summer drew near, to Kings River to swim, lounge in the sun, and drink beer.

Sunday mornings they'd all converge on the college radio station to broadcast the "Fresno Bee Comic Strip of the Air!" Huddled around the studio microphones, they distorted their voices to bring Dick Tracy, Dagwood and Blondie, and Little Orphan Annie to life. There were sound effects, music cues; gradually this led to full-scale productions of original suspense stories, mysteries, and situation comedies. "Of course we'd go out partying a lot on Saturday night and not be in the best of shape on Sunday morning," former drama student Wanda Dove recalls. "I can remember Sam, particularly, at times being really hung over. He'd lie on the floor with the microphone, doing his dialogue, you know: 'Leapin' Lizards!' "

He, of course, had not kept his vow of abstinence for very long. "We all drank in those days," says Marie. "It seemed natural, it was the thing to do. Nobody thought anything of it."

But his friends did notice Sam's moodiness. He could suddenly withdraw behind those hypnotic hazel eyes and nobody was ever sure quite what he was thinking. When Dave Parker started to razz him backstage once before a performance of *Elizabeth the Queen,* Sam's eyes turned to ice. "I wouldn't talk like that to me, Dave," he said through clenched teeth. Startled by the sudden ferocity, Parker backed off.

"Sam was an enigma to everybody, no matter how long or well you knew him," says Marian Dysinger. "He was like a kaleidoscope. It just depended on when you put the tube up to your eye, what you might see. There seemed to be a lot of warring factions in Sam."

"When he drank he got crazier than a bedbug," says Jim Baker. "One time, I remember, it was a really hot day and we'd spent it around the pool of a hotel there in Fresno. We'd been doing a lot of drinking. We were talking, then he stood up and threw me in the pool. It was funny, but there was a sense of danger when he was drunk. Sam only weighed about 145 pounds, but he was wiry and very strong, explosively strong, the way wiry people can get. He would grab things and pick them up and you'd think: Jesus, I wonder if he can do that! I've seen him lift stuff that you wouldn't think a guy his weight would be able to lift."

As an actor Peckinpah had an unpolished charisma, and many of his former classmates recall that he was a shameless scene-stealer. But directing continued to be Sam's main focus. He didn't want to be stuck on stage following someone else's instructions. He wanted to be the one in control, the one bringing his vision to the stage, rather than helping someone else realize theirs.

For the advanced directing class, Howard Campbell came up with an innovative idea: why not mount a production of a full-length play and allow a different student to direct each of the individual scenes? "I always felt that if you were going to have a university theater, you should give the students experience in acting *and* directing," the former instructor explains.

Campbell picked Williams' *A Streetcar Named Desire* for the project. It had caused a sensation on Broadway that very year, blazing new frontiers with its frank approach to sexuality, particularly homosexuality. Williams had opened up a whole range of subject matter that had previously been considered taboo.

It opened on Broadway, but not quite in Fresno. J. W. Wright, the gray-haired patriarch of the drama department, had okayed the project without ever reading the play. Despite the nationwide publicity it had received, he was unaware of its content. One day shortly before the production was to premiere, Wright strolled in to the theater to watch a rehearsal. Minutes later he was stomping out again, face red with outrage.

Wright tried to cancel the production. He'd never liked this young Campbell with his psychological-method mumbo-jumbo anyhow. But Campbell, with the students solidly behind him, pressed Wright into a compromise. The production was banished to the basement Lab Theater for a private instead of public performance, and some of the more explicit passages were removed. It was only the first in a long line of battles that Sam Peckinpah would fight against administrators who wanted to castrate a script or film.

Nevertheless, Campbell continued to push for more directing opportunities for students. He argued that they should be given the chance to direct some of the plays produced on the departments' main stage. Up until that time all main-stage productions had been directed by instructors. There could be no greater learning experience, Campbell reasoned, than to allow the most talented students the opportunity to mount a full-scale production before the general public.

Wright finally gave in. Students would be allowed to direct two out of the four main-stage productions that year. As soon as the plan was announced, the undergrads began scrambling to find plays they could submit. Marie Peckinpah was one of them. "I wanted to direct an English play about two male friends who had an unusually close relationship, so close something seemed wrong," Marie says. "But Campbell turned me down because there was no way Wright would ever approve it. Then I vacillated over what I wanted to do instead and meanwhile Sam got approval to go ahead with his production."

Sam made a politically safe choice: *Guest in the House* by Hagar Wilde and Dale Eunson, a palatable psychological thriller that had been a hit on Broadway in 1942. The plot concerned a young girl who is taken in by a happy, all-American family. But beneath the girl's cheery surface lurks a psychopath. She begins poisoning the minds of the different family members, pitting them against one another; by the play's end harmony has been shattered and the household reduced to chaos. Certainly the subversiveness of the story appealed to Peckinpah, but the plot and characters never rose above the level of melodrama.

Sam got the go-ahead to start rehearsals in November 1947. When the show premiered in the second week of December, he became the first student in the history of Fresno State to direct a play on the college's main stage. All of the department's facilities had been placed at his disposal, and he used them well. The production scored highly with the Midwestern sensibilities of Fresno audiences.

"It was a very good show," says Marian Dysinger, who acted in the play. "Sam was a very good director . . . not an easy director. He pushed you so you couldn't just cruise. He had very strong feelings about how he wanted the character and was meticulous about sticking with something until he got it the way he wanted it."

"He had a good eye," says the production's technical director, Merlyn Burriss. "You rarely see an undergraduate given this responsibility. He had a good sense of timing and theatrical blocking. He knew how to make pictures [within the proscenium]. If you stopped the action at any given moment, the composition would be very good. It's not a natural thing to see in a lot of directors."

Sam followed this effort up in the spring with a more personal production in the smaller Lab Theater. *Dutch Courage* was an original play he'd found, written by a war veteran. Never before produced, it centered on a group of American soldiers pulling duty in the ruins of postwar Europe. It strongly echoed Sam's own China experiences and was the first of his many explorations into the psychology and society of professional soldiers.

Don Levy was the other directorial star at Fresno State. Thin and gawky, with a knack for comedy, he became the second student to direct a play, *My Sister Eileen*, on the main stage. Levy had seen *Guest in the House* and thought it was "all right." But *Dutch Courage* knocked his socks off. "It was done hard. No fooling around. The lead, Jack Grady, had never acted before. He played a sergeant in the play and he was a mean little bastard. I saw it and thought: this Peckinpah's good!"

Levy cast Sam as Chick Clark in *My Sister Eileen*, and over the course of the production they became friends. Levy planned to go to USC in the fall to get a master's degree. They had a good drama department there run by William de Mille—Cecil's brother—who had directed plays on Broadway and films in Hollywood during the silent-movie days. An M.A. in drama could secure you a teaching career; with a De Mille as your mentor, the Hollywood studios just might throw open their gates.

"Sam was so good in theater, it never really dawned on me that he would go into movies," says Marie. "But movies were always on his mind; he was very interested in movies."

He and Marie went to the latest Hollywood releases in downtown Fresno almost every weekend. There were three pictures in particular during his first two years back from China that had a strong and lasting impact on him: *My Darling Clementine*, *Red River*, and *The Treasure of the Sierra Madre*. *The Ox-Bow Incident* had sparked the first awakening that westerns could be much more than white-hatted heroes, swarthy villains, and dime-novel plots. Now he began to see that his country's legendary cowboys, cattle barons, outlaws, mountain men, Indian war chiefs, and cavalry officers had the makings of a genuine American mythology, one with all the grandeur and complexity of the Greek and Shakespearean tragedies, every bit as fertile ground for exploring the mysteries of human experience.

John Ford, director of *My Darling Clementine*, had already forged a mythic vision that reflected the mainstream mood of the times. His camera framed classical compositions of white men and women crossing the awesome, barren landscape of the West. His stories told how these settlers conquered the threats posed by Indians, outlaws, and their own selfish passions to colonize the badlands. His films embodied the idealism of postwar America. Flushed with its victory in the Good War, the country was now eager to carry its manifest destiny overseas to Korea, and later Vietnam. America spreading the gospel of democracy to the heathens, bringing civilization to the wilderness.

In *Red River,* Howard Hawks mixed *Mutiny on the Bounty* with Oedipus and came up with a much darker vision of the winning of the West. John Wayne—bland, tall-in-the-saddle hero of hundreds of cheap Republic programmers—was transformed into a figure of warped ambition and ego, pitted against slouching, sensitive, method-reeking Montgomery Clift. A beatnik cowpoke takes on the genre's archetypal hero and exposes the twisted pathology beneath his square-jawed façade.

And finally, John Huston's vision of Americans adrift south of the border, *The Treasure of the Sierra Madre.* Not the typically phony backlot Hollywood version of Mexico, the movie had actually been shot down there. Huston really caught the feel of it. You could almost smell the refried beans, the sweet sticky hair tonic plastered to Bogart's head after a visit to the barber shop, the stale urine and sweat in the flophouses. And the fight in the barroom involving Bogart, Tim Holt, and Barton MacLane was no weightless ballet of careening bottles, shattered chairs, and gracefully executed punches and falls. The blows were clumsy and labored and only half-connecting, mixed with undignified knees to the groin and labored gasps for air. The "heroes" ganged up on MacLane, fought dirty, fought to win, and displayed not a twinge of remorse. It was the details, the little authentic details that Huston caught with his cameras that brought film vividly to life, that sucked you into the screen and let you roam around in the characters' world for a while.

Movies were definitely on Sam's mind. But if he had any concrete plans for a career in Hollywood at this point, he never spoke of them. Maybe he was afraid of rolling eyes and exasperated sighs from family and friends; maybe he was afraid to suppose out loud that a runty kid from Fresno could ever make it big in Lotus Land. Whatever his unspoken hopes were, he packed them up along with his mountains of books and plays. In the fall of 1948 he and Marie left the small cabin on his parents' property, left Fresno for good this time, and headed for Los Angeles.

They got an apartment on Rimpau Boulevard, not far from Crenshaw, for thirty-five dollars a month. Built on top of a garage, it was small but airy and had hardwood floors. They filled it with secondhand furniture and a table and chairs that had once belonged to Denver and Louise Church. Marie took a job at the May Company in downtown Los Angeles. Between her earnings, Sam's veteran benefits, and the checks from his father, they got by.

When Sam began attending classes at USC in September, Marie did not go with him. A subtle shift had occurred when her play had been turned down for the main stage at Fresno State and Sam had gone ahead with *Guest in the House.* Initially his teacher, then an equal partner, she had now slipped into the role of follower. Without ever coming to a definite decision to do so, she'd become the loyal, supporting wife, the very thing she'd sworn to her mother she would never be. It seemed okay at first; she wasn't even consciously aware that it had happened. Whatever seeds of disquietude existed were deeply buried and slow in sprouting.

In November Marie discovered that she was pregnant. "I really wanted children," says Marie. "I always had, even when I was thinking about being the world's greatest actress. Sam wanted children too. He was wonderful throughout the pregnancy. All the times I was pregnant he was very, very caring and tried to be helpful. He was a husband who really appreciated the look. He never failed to tell me that I was very beautiful. He was just as loving and affectionate physically as always."

Sam had traded his Jeep in for a two-door Buick, which he drove down to USC every morning and parked in front of a campus boardinghouse where Don Levy and another Fresno State grad, George Pappas, shared a room. The three attended morning classes together, repaired to Levy and Pappas' room for lunch, then returned to classes in the afternoon. "Marie made lunches for all of us," Levy recalls. "That girl could make a great cucumber and bell-pepper sandwich."

Between huge bites they dealt hands of poker—"We played for pennies; Sam took it seriously, like everything else," says Pappas—and bitched about the shortcomings of the USC drama department. It was not quite what they had expected. The university was located in the old West Adams section of Los Angeles—once the city's posh west side, its voluminous Victorian mansions were already decaying and subdividing into rooming houses as the rich departed for the greener pastures of Beverly Hills and Brentwood. USC had been a small, almost obscure private college before the war. But millions of returning veterans eager to reap the benefits of the G.I. Bill changed all that. College, once the exclusive privilege of the rich, was suddenly available to the middle class. Campuses across the country were flooded with more than a million new students (college enrollment nationwide grew from 1,155,000 in 1944 to 2,616,000 in 1948). At USC enrollment more than doubled in just two years, from 8,500 in 1944 to 19,034 in 1946.

Ill-prepared for this stampede, USC jammed the new students into a variety of makeshift quarters. The infant cinema department was stuck in some old horse stables, and the theater department crammed into "The Old College"—a hoary Victorian mansion that had housed the entire university when it was first founded in 1880. A couple of big stage productions were launched each year in Bovard Auditorium, built in 1921, which seated an audience of 1,600 and had relatively modern lighting and sound systems.

But the vast majority of drama department shows were mounted in Touchstone, a 150-seat theater that had been Old College's original auditorium. "It was a strange old building," says Rory Guy, a former classmate of Sam's at USC. "Support columns came down right in the middle of the audience, blocking the view of the stage, which was very narrow." The wooden floor had ripples in it, the backstage area was minuscule, and the light boards were run by old dial dimmers. Budgets for shows were slim to nonexistent, and the scene dock was located in an old warehouse on another part of the campus.

The head of the department, William de Mille, had followed

his brother Cecil to California in 1914. He'd been moderately successful in silent movies, directing small, intimate, psychologically acute dramas that were the antithesis of Cecil's baroque spectacles. But grotesque spectacles sold better than painful truths on the Hollywood market, and William de Mille never fully emerged from his brother's shadow. When talkies arrived his career went into decline, and by the late forties his position as head of USC's drama department was the last stop on the road to obscurity.

De Mille brought to his students a great storehouse of knowledge about the practicalities of theater production and a highly professional attitude that he demanded from them in return. But aesthetically he belonged to a bygone era. His approach to acting was analytical. He believed the actor's job was to convey the playwright's intentions through precisely calculated gestures, vocal intonations, and stage business. The idea that anything be left to chance, that there be any room for spontaneity, or that the actors might bring whole new layers of complexity and meaning to a playwright's characters through their performances—as the method actors fervently believed—was foreign if not outright abhorrent to "Poppa" de Mille.

The plays he chose to direct for the department's big productions in Bovard Auditorium were less than stunning and innovative: *Dear Ruth, End of Summer, State of the Union.* "We did *Watch on the Rhine* after the Nazi threat had ceased to exist," says Rory Guy. "We did *Joan of Lorraine* by Maxwell Anderson. De Mille would try to do something fairly recent off Broadway. Very little classic material was done. I don't think one Shakespeare play was done the whole time I was there."

Nor did De Mille have much use for the new playwrights who so impressed Levy and Peckinpah. "Mr. de Mille liked plays with a clear-cut story, a beginning, a middle, and an end," says another former USC student, Marvin Kaplan. "Lillian Hellman's *Little Foxes* was one of his favorite plays. The forces of good and evil were very black and white; it's very clear who's the good guy and who's the bad guy. Mr. de Mille wasn't much for the grays."

"He [Sam] was upset by De Mille because De Mille didn't like Saroyan, didn't think Williams was a playwright in any sense of the word," another USC drama professor, James Butler, told Paul Seydor in 1977. "So Sam was always bucking and fighting for that."

De Mille directed virtually all of the department's big productions himself. All of the students in the department worked under him, either in the cast or as part of the stage crew. "De Mille knew everyone in his class," says Adele Cook, "and how to direct each one according to that person's personality."

Peckinpah did learn a few things from the old man, such as stage composition and the importance of giving every actor, no matter how small their role, a fully realized characterization so the world within the proscenium had the texture of reality. But Sam also picked up some of De Mille's less admirable traits. "De Mille was very caustic, very sarcastic, and incredibly witty," says Adele Cook. "He would select someone who was not of great consequence to him and destroy them to show everybody else that he could do that, and then everybody else would shape up right away so they wouldn't be the next one." The whipping-boy syndrome. Allen Schneider, John Ford, William Wyler, and Henry Hathaway were expert practitioners of this torture. In time, Sam Peckinpah would apply it with equal skill.

But in 1948 and 1949 he held his tongue and jumped like everyone else when De Mille hollered. He hung lights, hammered flats into position, set props, applied makeup, and gave the actors their cues. Laboring under a taskmaster like De Mille gave Sam a hard professional edge that he'd lacked at easygoing Fresno State.

There were other teachers as well. De Mille had brought Reginald Lawrence, a New York writer who'd had a few successes on Broadway, into the department to teach playwriting. Lawrence emphasized the nuts and bolts of dramaturgy: the three-act structure, the need for a strong protagonist to drive the action and rising conflict that leads to a crisis and finally a climax.

Sam's interest in writing continued to grow, but it didn't come easy. Locking himself up alone in a room and facing the glare of all that empty white paper seemed to bleach the creativity out of his brain. He could not, like some of his fellow students—Jack Gariss, Art Buchwald, and Rory Guy—complete an entire play from start to finish. But as he had done with *Glass Menagerie,* he edited and wrote additional material for the plays he directed, subtly altering them until the vision became as much his as the playwright's.

The teacher Sam found a real rapport with was James Butler, a younger man and graduate of USC himself. He'd become an instructor only a couple of years earlier, but had already instigated enormous changes. Butler's major innovation was the founding of the Experimental Theater at USC, which allowed the students themselves to select plays and produce them in the dilapidated Old College theater. The strangled budgets dictated minimalistic lighting and set design, but in return the students were given freedom to try virtually everything and anything. It was seat-of-your-pants theater, and exciting as hell. The number of productions soared, as did the students' enthusiasm.

The shows included Chekhov's *A Marriage Proposal,* Noël Coward's *Ways and Means, Oedipus the King,* and a slew of original plays by students. "Butler turned us loose in Experimental Theater," says Marvin Kaplan. "I remember Phil Goodman did *From Morn' till Midnight,* an impressionistic play. What we did scared the shit out of Butler, but he let us go ahead; we turned the whole department around." The raw energy of the shows rapidly gained popularity with the student body, and lines at the Old College theater grew longer and longer; soon there were sellouts and hundreds of people being turned away at the door.

Amid this creative frenzy, Sam Peckinpah was not the star that he had been at Fresno State. He was overshadowed by boisterous actors like Kaplan and Joe Flynn, and student playwrights like Art Buchwald—who wrote *No Love Atoll,* a hilarious parody of *South Pacific.* The prodigy at USC was Jack Gariss, an erudite pipe-smoker with an encyclopedic knowledge of literature and the theater. "Jack was expansive and the most well-read man I've ever known," says Rory Guy. "He was a rapid reader, just look at a page and he had it, the most dense material, he could finish a very heavy tome in an hour. Incredible."

Gariss wrote and directed a number of his own plays for the Experimental Theater and became a creative hub around which other students orbited. Sam developed a close relationship with Gariss but, if anything, he appeared to be more of a protégé of Gariss than the other way around. "Gariss was the head of everything," says another former student, Don Stoutenborough. "The student leader of the discussion groups. He was the cream at the top, was gonna get the Nobel Prize by the time he was thirty-five."

Sam, on the other hand, observed more than he participated in class debates, withheld his comments while other students clamored for attention, and was content to remain in the background at social gatherings the few times he attended them.

But those who worked with him in the plays that he directed at the Experimental Theater quickly realized there was more to this thin, boyishly handsome introvert than first met the eye. "Fascinating guy, very interesting," says Don Stoutenborough, who played an Italian bon vivant in a production of Pirandello's *Cece* that Peckinpah directed. "He was enigmatic, there was always something a little remote about him, you never knew exactly where you were with him. I told everyone: 'Hey, there's something going on here, this is a real director if you like to act.' And I did, I was passionate about it. He plumbed the emotions and got you to. I've worked with a lot of directors and nobody has that touch. He had a probing and sensitive, yet very masculine way. He would speak in strange tones. He could say the inscrutable thing and an actor would say, 'Yeah! Hey!' They'd see brilliance, like some sort of religion."

"If he looked at you, everything else in the world disappeared because the eyes swallowed you," says Adele Cook, who worked with Peckinpah at USC. "They didn't even have pupils; it was all just one great big pool. And when he did look at you and you were talking to him he had absolute focus. The world just dropped away; nothing else existed except the ridiculous things you were saying at that very moment. It was a very exhilarating feeling."

James Butler was impressed by the young director's work. "He was one of those fellows who had a burning ambition to go into the theater," Butler told Paul Seydor in 1977. "Once in a while you get students like that. . . . He was as hungry and driven as any man I've ever known. Most of the talk was about Williams and Saroyan. He was hung up."

Peckinpah and Levy lobbied heatedly for a chance to put on an evening of Saroyan one-acts for the Experimental Theater. Butler went to bat for them and finally overcame De Mille's objections to the playwright. "Saroyan spoke to us then," Levy recalls, "like no other writer except Williams. William de Mille didn't dig Saroyan at all. 'No plots! . . . Crazy!' But we persevered. Sam did *Hello Out There,* the greatest one-act play of all time, and I did *My Heart's in the Highlands,* and played the lead myself."

By this time Sam and Don Levy had become the closest of friends. It would be the only relationship from Sam's college years that he would maintain to the very end of his life. They were an odd couple in a way: Levy, ultra-intellectual, physically awkward, and morally conservative, and Sam, the deer-hunting, hard-drinking ex-marine who operated more from the gut than the head. But in another way it wasn't an odd match at all.

"I think Sam knew I cared, that I genuinely liked him, that I was genuinely proud of him," Levy says. "There was a bond between us. I was kind of like the nerd brother. I thought he was a fantastic director, one of the best there's ever been. *Ever been!* He thought I was the greatest actor in the world . . . an opinion that seems to have died with him. . . . I think Sam liked to play the tough guy, that mask he was always wearing, but I saw through the pretense and he saw my insecurities. We both saw one another's insecurities. Sam saw himself as an outsider. He knew that I was aware that he was searching, always searching . . ."

That year at USC there was a festival of Charlie Chaplin films, all the great silent features: *The Kid, The Gold Rush, The Circus, City Lights, Modern Times.* Sam, Marie, and Levy saw them all. Chaplin's archetypal outsider—this odd white-faced alien in a battered derby, slap shoes, and threadbare baggy pants, always searching for a place in this strange and hostile world, always searching on that metaphorical road and never finding it—Peckinpah could relate to him in spades. *City Lights* left him stunned. Chaplin's daringly ambiguous ending, where the tramp again meets the blind girl whose sight he restored with money he had stolen for an operation. She laughs at the pathetic spectacle of him shuffling along the street past her flower shop, not recognizing him until she offers him a handout—a coin and a rose for his lapel—and feels the familiar touch of his fingers. "You?" she asks, stunned. He is not the handsome young millionaire she always fantasized about. He nods, knowing at that moment he's lost her forever, yet hoping he hasn't. "You can see now." "Yes," she nods, "I can see." That final agonized close-up of him, one crooked finger raised to his lips like a frightened child, eyes shining like a cat's in the dark as the image fades into black.

Sam sat there afterward, unable to move when the lights came up. It was more than a movie, more than art; Chaplin had given him a beautiful and horrible glimpse at the truth, at the human soul. "I feel there must be a separation between church and state," he would later say of Chaplin's work. "His vision is so unique and so splendid it would be ridiculous to list him with film-makers who I feel work in another world."

He had turned his back on his parents' religion, Christian Science. To many who knew him he seemed cynical about life and his fellow man, and to a large degree he was. But beneath the cynicism the old yearning still burned; he had replaced one faith with another. The theater, his art, had become more than a professional calling; it had taken on the quality of a spiritual quest, and his devotion to it was almost religious. Despite all the hedonistic excesses in the years that followed, in an odd way he remained chastely devoted to his new faith and would give his life to it.

But this new fanatical edge was not immediately apparent in the summer of 1949, after he completed his first year at USC. Life appeared light, almost carefree at the airy apartment on Rimpau Boulevard. Sam and Levy practiced their imitations of Chaplin—the duck-footed shuffle, the twirling cane—and cooked up slapstick routines that had Marie laughing so hard she held her stomach and gasped for breath. She was big now and when Sam pressed his palm against her bare belly he could feel the baby moving.

The day she went into labor—July 30, 1949—Sam was anything but calm and collected. "He was freaking out," says Marie. "He really, really, really had a hard time with things that were physically painful. They let him come in occasionally while I was in labor, but most of the time he was in the waiting room. There was another guy there who kept opening the door to check on his wife. Sam could hear the moaning and crying. He just freaked out. He told the guy to 'shut the goddamned door!' He just couldn't stand it."

It was a girl. After seeing her for the first time in the glassed-in nursery, Sam came into Marie's room, beaming. "Well, she's the most beautiful baby in the nursery, everybody says so!"

They named her Sharon. Five days later they finally brought her home to their tiny apartment. "The first time he ever had her by himself was when she was about three weeks old," says Marie. "I went out to the market. When I came back, I could hear her crying as I came up the stairs. I opened the door and he was sitting in this chair right opposite the door looking like he was almost ready for suicide. He was holding her, and she was in this diaper—he had tried to change her diaper—this diaper that was unbelievable! It was the weirdest-looking thing! I had showed him how to change her, but I don't think he'd ever done it before. I grabbed her and he said, 'Oh my God!' "

Sharon's arrival added a new weight of responsibility onto Sam's shoulders. He abandoned the idea of completing his master's thesis that fall and began anxiously looking for work.

Jack Gariss had already left school and landed a job with Cecil B. DeMille as a writer on *The Ten Commandments.* He lived in Huntington Park, just southeast of L.A., near a small community theater that put on plays in a high school auditorium. The facilities were far from awe-inspiring, but the theater had a good reputation and had won some awards and many enthusiastic reviews for its productions. The director-in-residence had recently departed, Gariss told Sam, and the theater's board was looking for a replacement. Here was a chance to work as a professional. Sam applied for the job and, thanks to glowing recommendations from Butler and Gariss, was hired, beating out forty-one other applicants, including several from Harvard and Yale.

The Peckinpahs packed up their meager belongings and moved to Whittier—once a small town, it was fast expanding as mile upon mile of subdivisions replaced the sweet-smelling orange groves on the city outskirts. Cheap houses to meet the unprecedented demand of the postwar boom, one after another hammered and stuccoed together, each with only a slightly different floor plan or a token piece of cutie-pie window dressing to differentiate it from its neighbors.

Like many home buyers, the Peckinpahs applied for a loan under the G.I. Bill, which allowed them to purchase their "dream house" for no money down and very little per month. The American Dream was now affordable to all who had fought in the Good War. It was a nice house. A trio of orange trees had been spared for landscaping purposes, one in the front yard and two in the back, where there was a big lawn. There were three bedrooms and a large "View Window" (the latest luxury feature) in the "Dining Area" that afforded them a scenic panorama of the neighbors' backyard barely a hundred feet away. Marie revolted against the bleak uniformity of all the manicured lawns and precisely shaped shrubbery by refusing to do any gardening, a policy Sam was more than happy to follow. Soon an impressive variety of hairy weeds were sprouting out of control, providing a lush jungle habitat for many species of insect, reptile, and rodent life. To their disconcerted neighbors it looked like the Addams Family had moved in, but to Sam and Marie the house had a loose, warm, "lived-in" feel.

Sam didn't have much time for yardwork anyway. He was working sixteen to eighteen-hour days at the theater as a one-man producer/director. He'd been contracted by the Huntington Park Civic Theater to direct five plays that year at a salary of $300 a play. Since that was still not enough for them to live on, he continued to accept occasional checks from his father to make ends meet.

Sam drew up a list of plays he wanted to direct and submitted them to the theater's board for approval. The board, in turn, had some ideas of its own. The theater had always opened the season with a corny old melodrama like *The Drunkard,* in which the actors deliberately overacted for laughs; and Broadway musicals were also a big favorite with audiences. Would Mr. Peckinpah mind coming up with some selections along those lines? The process grated on Sam, but he gritted his teeth and haggled, accepting some of their choices and gaining approval for some of his own.

He gave them *South Pacific* and they gave him *Menagerie.* During his two years there he also directed *Our Town, The Man Who Came to Dinner, The Silver Cord,* and *Arsenic and Old Lace:* More directing than he'd done at Fresno State and USC combined, packed into five back-to-back shows the first year and again the second. He supervised the construction of the sets, the hanging of the lights, selected the actors and crew, laid out the production schedules, and oversaw the printing of the programs and the advertising and promotion. For talent both on and behind the stage, he drew on many of his former colleagues from Fresno State and USC. Soon he had a lean but fiercely dedicated repertory company working long hours for not a dime of salary.

"He really had the capability for creating this atmosphere where people *really* wanted to work for him," says Marie. "He learned a lot at Huntington Park. Although the choice of plays was done by committee, what he did with the plays was his. He had a really original mind: the way he looked at the material that he was given. He did really nice work on all those plays. He did [Kaufman and Hart's] *The Man Who Came to Dinner.* Even though there have been a billion productions of that, what he managed to do with it was really fun."

Among Sam's favorite productions was a comedy about a youthful impostor who enters an old-folks' home disguised as a septuagenarian. Through a series of antics and provocations, he manages to revivify the geriatric population. Sam hired elderly amateurs from Huntington Park to play many of the roles and employed a bit of comic business that Lola Owensby, a friend at the time, remembers well. "These old guys were sitting on a bench drinking from a bottle. He had them passing that bottle down the line of two or three guys and it turned into a slapstick thing. Each of them was taking a sip out of this bottle and then the next one was to get it. It was passed from one to the other and back up to the first one, but the last guy kept waiting and reaching for it, but he didn't get it until the others had drained it dry. It was very funny." The bottle routine would become a famous bit of comic relief in *The Wild Bunch*, with Warren Oates as the hapless outlaw who never gets his share.

The final production that year, *Arsenic and Old Lace*, was one of the most successful. But it didn't look that way when rehearsals first started. Sam thought he had a bomb on his hands. The female star of the show, a determined virgin, was about as sexy as a frozen mackerel. Finally, one night after rehearsal, Peckinpah sidled up to his leading man, Rory Guy, and growled, "This is just not working, she's too cold! So here's the plan: you've got to seduce this girl. You've got to do it with her. I'm going to offer you both a ride home tonight. Halfway there I'm going to run out of gas, and leave the two of you alone while I walk to a service station. . . . When I come back I don't want her to be a virgin anymore!"

"I knew I could never seduce this girl; she was an iron virgin if ever there was one," says Guy. "But she wasn't adverse to a little kissing and cuddling."

"You two sit in the back," Peckinpah said, hopping behind the wheel. About halfway to the girl's house the car began to sputter. "Damn!" Sam cursed as he pulled over to the curb. "I can't believe it; Marie forgot to put gas in it today!" He marched off into the night to find a gas station, leaving the couple in the car.

"I bet we kissed and cuddled for three minutes," says Guy, "at most five, when Sam was back! He made like he put some gas in, then got in the car. I was dumbfounded! I thought he was going to be gone fifteen or twenty minutes, or half an hour. Off we went."

As soon as they dropped the girl off, Peckinpah turned and stared pointedly at his actor. "Well?"

"*Well?* You were gone three minutes!"

"Well?" Peckinpah repeated, still staring.

"Sam, did you ever hear of foreplay?"

The exercise must have worked, for the show won a rave review in the local paper and was the season's smash.

"He handled farce well," says Marie. "It kills me. He got into this thing with westerns later on and that definitely was somewhere in his dream life. Obviously it was something really important to him, that part of your life that you hold dear. But he did good work in so many other kinds of plays, he was capable of so much more."

Between productions, life at the house in Whittier was good. Sam was a gentle, attentive father to Sharon most of the time, though there were occasional flashes of the fearsome temper he'd inherited from his father and grandfather. The sparsely furnished home was adorned by only a few exotic touches: a white porcelain kabuki dancer and a collection of Japanese woodcut prints that a friend had given to them.

"Sam, in those days, was good-looking, thin and energetic," Lola Owensby recalls. "He dressed casually, but well. He wore slacks most of the time. Marie had long blond hair and a very beautiful, open, broad smile. She had a raw-boned look and she was a free spirit. I remember they had a playground at the end of the block and a sidewalk that went through it. The wind would blow and it would be a beautiful day and she would come running down that sidewalk and there was a tree there with a branch that stuck out and she'd have to quickly duck to miss it. She was like that, very free."

Another friend, Nanette Flynn, remembers spending Thanksgiving with the Peckinpahs at the little tract house. "We went over there and I thought: well, we're eating dinner a little bit early but two o'clock's just fine. We got over there; they hadn't even started to cook the turkey! We ate about ten or eleven that night. I've never been so hungry in my life! I think they were just naive and didn't realize that it was going to take more than thirty minutes. Sam was like a relaxed tennis player: sprawling and young and enthusiastic and full of ideas and very much in love with his wife. Marie was like an early flower child. I thought: gee, they're just so free and easy with each other, isn't that great? It didn't bother them a bit that it took us nine hours to get to eat. He accepted it with great grace. I would have been a nervous wreck. We ate up all the celery and talked a lot and laughed a lot."

That summer Sam went to Albuquerque to direct summer stock, then returned in the fall for a second year at Huntington

Park, his salary now a whopping $500 a show. With an annual income of $2,500 he was almost able to support himself, but by the next summer he was ready to move on. His father and brother urged him to stay at Huntington Park, which had offered him yet another raise, but he'd set his sights on a new frontier: television.

Along with the Buicks, Chryslers, Chevies, and Fords that rolled off assembly lines in the years that followed World War II, came fifteen million tube-filled boxes that brought moving images into American homes for the first time. It began as a trickle. At first only the local bar or the wealthiest family on the block had one. Neighbors gathered around the tiny bluish glow of these boxes to see the opening of the Eightieth Congress, President Truman's state of the union address, and the World Series.

The mighty motion-picture studios that had dominated American entertainment for almost half a century shrugged the "gimmick" off as a fad that would fade in a year, maybe two. By 1951 streets across the country suddenly emptied on Saturday nights because everyone was rushing home to watch Sid Caesar in "Your Show of Shows"; movie attendance was down 20 percent to 40 percent in cities with TV stations, and over 380 movie theaters had closed across the country. It had become obvious to even the pale and sweating movie moguls that TV was hear to stay.

For the writers, directors, and actors getting in on the ground floor, it was like the days of silent movies all over again. Corporate leviathans had not yet strangled the new medium with tentacles of bureaucracy and assembly-line production methods. Many of the early television studios were run by independent entrepreneurs. Because no one quite understood TV's potential, no standardized system had yet been imposed on those creating the "product." This was before the invention of videotape, and most shows were broadcast live. Like the Experimental Theater productions at USC, it was ad hoc entertainment. Production values were scrawny, the camera work crude, but creative energy blazed.

Young writers like Paddy Chayevsky, Rod Serling, and Reginald Rose who hadn't been able to break into Hollywood or onto Broadway found fresh and fertile soil in which their talents could bloom. And leaping in with them was a new generation of directors. They stumbled and cursed over the primitive equipment, blanched in horror at the mistakes their actors made live in front of an audience of millions, but grew to love the spontaneity and excitement of the medium. They developed a boldness, a willingness to throw caution and convention to the wind. John Frankenheimer, Arthur Penn, Martin Ritt, Franklin Schaffner, George Roy Hill, Stanley Kubrick, Robert Altman, John Cassavetes (first as an actor, then a director), and (a little later) Bob Rafelson—all would cut their teeth on the new medium. In fifteen years these young turks would be making some of the most dazzling and provocative feature films ever to come out of Hollywood.

Joining their ranks in 1951 was Sam Peckinpah. In a decade he would prove himself one of the most distinguished members of this remarkable generation, but it's unlikely that even Sam himself dared to fantasize such a future when he applied for a position as a page at ABC's Los Angeles affiliate in the fall of 1951. He was turned down, but soon afterward landed a job—with the help of his old Fresno State friend, Jim Baker—as a stagehand at KLAC-TV in L.A., one of 108 TV stations that had popped up across the country in the preceding three years.

The atmosphere among the employees at the station was electric. They were pioneers on a new frontier and everything seemed possible. "The mix of people that worked there was curious," says Rudy Behlmer, a former KLAC staff member. "There were people from the stage, from film, from all walks of life. You would never find that kind of stage crew today. They saw it as an opportunity. You went in knowing that if you did start out just handling scenery, if you had anything to offer and were eager, you would be able to move up."

"People did several jobs," says Jerry Tamblyn, a former art director for the station. "It wasn't unusual for an assistant director or prop man to take over a show if the director quit. It was very loose. Everyone went out to lunch or dinner together after the shows; it was like a family."

It would be another year before a coaxial cable was strung across the country, making national broadcasts possible for the first time. Until then the big New York shows—Milton Berle's "Texaco Star Theater," Sid Caesar's "Your Show of Shows," Ed Sullivan's "Toast of the Town"—had to be recorded on kinescopes and shipped to California for viewing days later. Kinescopes were film cameras that shot the image off a television monitor; the quality varied from bad to horrible. This left a niche in local markets for independent stations that could provide good live programming. Rather than simply playing faded prints of old B-movies and tired reruns, as they would a decade later, independent stations produced an impressive spectrum of original programs. Sophisticated demographic studies and ratings systems had yet to be developed, so if an idea seemed halfway entertaining, station managers would throw it on the air and see if it took off. As in the old Mack Sennett days, camera crews were rushed out to cover exciting local events. The result was a wacky grab-bag of vaudeville broadcast live into living rooms all over Los Angeles every evening between six P.M. and midnight. (The station lay dormant the rest of the hours, not even broadcasting a test pattern.)

In the years that Sam worked there, KLAC's menu of entertainment included variety shows like "Family Night with Horace Heidt" and "Hollywood Palladium," featuring popular big bands; musical programs like "The Liberace Show," "Leo Carillo's Dude Ranch," "Tex Ritter's Western Cavalcade," and "Piano Playhouse"; situation comedies like "Life with Elizabeth," starring Betty White; a quiz show produced by Irwin Allen, later to win fame for his star-bloated disaster epics like *The Towering Inferno;* and a plethora of half-hour crime shows, mysteries, soap operas, and dramatic anthologies starring Jane Wyatt, the young Natalie Wood, Sam's childhood prince of darkness Arch Oboler, and a menagerie of other Hollywood personalities on their way up or down the slippery ladder of success.

"It was an incredible time because it was like live theater, but intimate theater; you could have the cameras move right in," says Jerry Tamblyn. "It was different than film. They hired actors who could do it in one take and make mistakes look like they weren't mistakes. In film you set the scene up and shoot it and do it over and over and over again. Because I came from the theater, I thought television was much more exciting."

"We were not hampered by the unions, as we were later on," says Don Forbes, the former program manager at KLAC who actually hired Sam Peckinpah. "If I decided I wanted to do something, I could do almost anything; I was free to experiment with lighting, with the way I shot something. One Christmas show I wrote, produced, and did the narration, which you wouldn't often get today."

KLAC was on the cutting edge of technical innovation. Cameramen at the Cahuenga Boulevard studio adapted an old hand-cranked 35mm silent movie camera into a kinescope, slapping huge 12,000-foot magazines onto the ancient machine so they could record half-hour and hour-long shows without reloading. "The magazines were three feet in diameter," former KLAC employee Jim Hobson recalls. "The film was so heavy, it weighed several hundred pounds; they had to put a motor on the take-up and a motor on the feed and a motor on the camera." As a result, KLAC had the first 35mm kinescope in the country, capable of much higher image resolution than the 16mm kinescopes the networks first used. "KLAC had the first motion-picture lighting of any television studio in the country," says Hobson. "Everybody else was using bird's eyes and fluorescents. The studio was rigged with lighting bridges and motion-picture lamps."

Fresh out of college themselves, Behlmer, Hobson, and Baker were so excited to break into the new medium, even as stagehands, that they could hardly sleep nights. Which it why is was disconcerting for Baker, once he'd gotten Peckinpah a job, to discover that his friend didn't share quite the same enthusiasm.

"He didn't give a shit," Baker says. "When it came time to move some heavy scenery, you never could find him. He'd always be hiding back in the scene shop. In fact, I got in a little bit of trouble. They said to me, 'You're the one who brought that asshole in here!' I'd find him back in some corner, writing, or he'd be on the phone."

The possibilities of television interested Sam, but pushing a broom and lugging flats around for $22.50 a week after running his own show at Huntington Park for two years did not. His mind needed creative engagement, so instead of trying to impress his superiors with a zeal for manual labor, he stole every moment he could to be alone with a pencil and yellow legal pad.

"He was teaching himself to write," says another former KLAC employee, John Langdon. "He wrote with a pencil, printed. It was just guts. He had lots of intestinal fortitude. He would *grind* it out. I never got the sense that he would have an inspiration and could hardly write fast enough. I got the feeling that he used craftsmanship and constructed his scripts. He would cut up action/cowboy novels, paperbacks, to break down the elements of the story. There's a story about Beethoven who, when found having cut up another musician's music, said, 'That's the way I always write.' Sam said it was his way of learning."

Novelist William Burroughs would later popularize this technique. By cutting up the individual scenes of a standard narrative, it was possible to rejuggle and juxtapose them and discover more dynamic ways of telling the same tale. As a filmmaker, Peckinpah would use this approach again and again with his editors, constantly pushing them to "take it a step further," to discover unorthodox, non-chronological approaches to sequences. Under his supervision they would intercut scenes and characters and separate pieces of action within a sequence to create an intense level of parallel action so that three, six, even a dozen things seemed to be happening at the same time. His first rudimentary steps toward his signature style were taken in the hidden corners of KLAC's scene shop.

Not all of the stagehand work was tedious for Sam. Pushing the springed seat of a buckboard up and down, just out of camera range, so Tennessee Ernie Ford actually looked like he was riding somewhere while he crooned his corny cowboy tunes was worth a few laughs. So was sitting ringside at "Wrestling Workout." He gave the cues for the commercial breaks—"and now for a word from our sponsor, Thytol Vitamin Supplement!"—and tried not to crack up at the muscle-bound ballets of such pituitary freaks as "Dr. Lee Gable, the Wrestling Hypnotist!" who rendered his opponents helpless with his "Mind-Numbing Zombie Trance!"

And if a work assignment required any creativity, Peckinpah's attitude changed dramatically. Don Forbes used Sam as an assistant on a couple of shows that he directed at the station. "He was very, very creative—his ideas, his approaches, his suggestions for how we carried out the show, the staging, the direction, the whole thing." Forbes was impressed enough to put Peckinpah in charge of props on several shows and raise his salary to $87.50 a week. John Langdon remembers Sam was "very organized" as a prop man.

But most of his energy still went into writing and trying to set up independent productions that would showcase his talent to Hollywood power brokers. The telephone calls he made in the back of the scene shop were not social. "He was always interested in doing something other than what he was hired to do, which was hauling scenery," says Rudy Behlmer. "He always had something he was preparing for or doing or working on or hoping to sell or interest people in. He had a lot of ability to get things off the ground. He was driven in his relatively quiet way. He was not at that time a flamboyant character at all; he wasn't full of himself, you never got that feeling. In whatever hustling he did, you never got the feeling that he was overwhelming everybody with verbal pyrotechnics. He had to do it in a soft-spoken way."

"Every person he got a lead on, an entree to, he would always try to figure how that person could be used," says Jim Baker.

One of the deals Sam swung was to get access to the Music Hall theater in West Los Angeles. He talked KLAC management, which leased the facility for "The Liberace Show," into giving it to him on a dark night for a stage production of two Tennessee Williams one-acts, *27 Wagons Full of Cotton* and *Hello from Bertha*.

The show attracted an audience of about a hundred—friends from USC and KLAC. "It went over very, very well," says John Langdon. But no one extended a fat studio contract for Sam to sign.

Meanwhile, other ambitious KLAC employees were launching projects of their own. Since the studio's two sound stages were active only about six hours every day and dormant the other eighteen, program manager Don Forbes generously gave aspiring directors a chance to use the facilities and equipment, free of charge, in the off-hours. Jim Hobson, John Langdon, Rudy Behlmer, and Jim Baker all began experimenting. It was a golden opportunity, as Peckinpah quickly recognized. He assisted the others with their projects; watching, asking questions, slowly developing a working knowledge of the new medium. By using the studio's multiple cameras and the switcher in the control booth, which shifted the picture from one camera to another at the director's command, it was possible to shoot a half-hour show in one continuous take. Pre-planned camera positions caught the action in long shots, medium shots, and close-ups, and at the end of a single run-through you had a fully edited kinescope.

Jim Hobson was forever playing with technical innovations, pushing and pulling, exploring new possibilities. He designed a piece—shot directly on film—in which the studio cameras, lights, and microphones moved to classical music, swooping and dipping and pirouetting in a "ballet" of animated objects. "Rudy Behlmer played the conductor in it," Hobson recalls. "Rudy, at one point, gives a great big upbeat and a huge light bulb falls out of its socket in slow motion and crashes to the floor, and breaks and bounces about four feet in a million pieces."

Sam's eyes lit up when he saw the footage. "How the hell did you do that?" He wanted to know what speed Hobson had shot it at, and they discussed at length the effects that could be achieved by filming at different frame rates.

It didn't take him long to come up with a film project of his own, one that would take care of some unfinished business at USC. To fulfill his neglected master's thesis, Sam proposed to produce and direct a one-act play for the stage at USC, then perform the same piece for the television cameras at KLAC. The purpose, Peckinpah told his faculty advisors, was to prove the viability of such productions for educational television, which was still in its infancy. Butler saw a more self-centered motivation. "I honestly think he did it to get into the film business," he later told Paul Seydor. Nevertheless, Butler approved the project and by the summer of 1953 Sam had thrown himself into it full tilt.

For material he chose another play by Tennessee Williams,

Portrait of a Madonna. He and Don Levy had seen it performed a couple of years earlier at the Las Palmas Playhouse with Jessica Tandy in the leading role, supported by Vincent Price. Orson Welles, Rita Hayworth, and Edmond O'Brien had been among the stars in the audience that night, but their presence paled under the spell of Tandy's performance, which earned a standing ovation at final curtain.

The play focused on a mad Southern spinster, on the day when doctors from the state mental hospital arrive to remove her from her dusty little apartment because her delusional rantings have been disturbing the other tenants in the building. Lucretia Collins is torn between her deep Christian-fundamentalist beliefs and her subconscious sexual desires. This conflict manifests itself in her hallucinatory memories of a young man whom she once loved but who married another. Like *Menagerie*'s Amanda Wingfield, Lucretia Collins bore many parallels to Sam's mother, who mourned her long-lost love, Bob Nichols, a ghost who became more idealized with every passing year.

And then there is Lucretia's inner war between fidelity to the chaste ideals of her church and her own carnal impulses. Fern Peckinpah once told her daughter Susan that when her own breasts began to develop during puberty she had wanted to cut them off. Yet on her visits to Sam in Hollywood she was fascinated by the libertine sexual practices of the natives. Susan remembers her flushed description of a pair of homosexual males that Sam pointed out in a local restaurant. "Sammy said one plays the female and the other plays the male. Just imagine that!"

Like a chameleon, the image of Fern Peckinpah would continue to reappear in Sam's work, each time bearing a slightly different shade, but the skeleton beneath always the same. As Amanda Wingfield, and in her other incarnations, she is manipulative, menacing, and culpable. But here for the first and last time he lavished her with unreserved pity, allowed himself to feel the full "personal tragedy," to gaze unblinkingly at the squashed "beauty and potential" of her life.

They rehearsed the play in the first week of July at the Stop Gap Theater at USC. A new performance space created out of an old garage on campus, it was barely more adequate than the facility in Old College.

William C. White, now an associate professor at the USC School of Theater, designed the lighting for the show, and remembers Sam directing the rehearsals: "He was always on his feet; he was not one of those directors who sit back in the seats. He stood right in front of the stage with his arms folded, extremely focused. He kept wanting to rework it. The most important thing for him was that there was something happening every second on the stage emotionally. The lighting was very carefully textured. The set was very detailed, everything in its place. He'd done a lot of research. We had great faith that he was going to do something, you could just tell by his interest in the art."

Marie played the part of Lucretia. In the past when they'd worked together it hadn't gone that well. Sam, who gave so much freedom to the other actors, allowing them to explore the nuances of their characters, became anxious with Marie and directed her every gesture and inflection. But this time he backed off and gave her some slack. "We were in tune with the ideas involved," says Marie. "It was a great experience, very exciting for both me and Sam because it was Sam's first time shooting anything."

On July 27, after performing the play before a live audience at the Stop Gap, Peckinpah moved the entire production, sets and all, to KLAC. When the station signed off the air at one A.M., Sam and his actors and crew—recruited from USC and KLAC—hauled the props and scenery into one of the station's two sound stages and began to set up the lighting. It took until nine A.M. to get everything in place. The actors were put into costume and makeup and checked beneath the lights, and microphones were tested for sound levels.

Sam had carefully planned out every camera move and staged the actors' blocking to fit the shots rather than the other way around. In the control booth Rudy Behlmer would operate the switcher, shifting from one camera to another at the preplanned cues so the entire play could be kinescoped in a single run-through. Peckinpah's detailed description in his thesis paper of the camera shots and lenses used, and the lighting design and blocking, illustrates how meticulously he had mapped out the production and how much technical expertise he had acquired from working at KLAC.

They had to have the actors, sets, and props cleared off of the stage by one P.M., when the station began its broadcast day again. This allowed barely enough time for two run-throughs before the actual shooting, which began at 11:45 A.M. and was completed by 12:06 P.M. "The time restriction was incredible," Rudy Behlmer recalls. "The only reason KLAC let Sam do this was he'd get in and get out. His major preoccupation was just getting it done."

The final result was a disappointment, but a highly educational one. Marie's performance, which had proved so effective before a live audience at the Stop Gap, came off as mannered and melodramatic under the intimate gaze of the cameras. It was a problem that had plagued stage actors since the beginning of movies, but it was the first time Sam had encountered it, and he took the blame himself. He wrote in his thesis: "If the acting in general—and that of Miss Collins [Marie] in particular—seems a little large for the television screen, it is because of the director's failure to adequately change the shades of the performances when they made the transition from stage to television."

He also discovered that his carefully planned camera positions had given the film lead-footed pacing. "The selection of shots was over cautious. Numerous opportunities for effective coverage from cameras two and three were passed up. This was because of two factors. The first reason was that all shots were pre-selected during rehearsals. The director placed much value in the theory of pre-selection. However, it was evident that on viewing the film far too much stage technique motivated the shot selection. Most of the shots indicated an accentuated stage business in stage tempo. Consequently, the rhythm and tempo of the television production was slow and therefore not as effective as the stage production. In general, each shot was effective, but the intimacy of the television screen with its tremendously reduced viewing space called for a more varied and imaginative use of the camera."

In the coming years he would apply these lessons with a vengeance. By the time Peckinpah graduated to feature films he rarely laid his shots out in advance. He walked on the set with only a general notion of how he might shoot a scene. Like John Huston, he let his actors rehearse until the scene began to take shape, *then* he decided where he would place his cameras. And rather than come up short, he would obsessively shoot angles of almost every detail within the scene to give himself as many elements to play with in the editing room as he possibly could. This approach would send schedule-brained producers into apoplexy and have his editors drowning in a sea of celluloid, clawing for solid ground. But it brought to his films a dense and incredibly layered and dynamic style, recognizable in an instant and different from that of any other director.

Viewed today, over forty years after its making, the kinescope of *Portrait* is indeed slow, crude, and overacted—and yet startlingly moving. Of course much of the credit must go to Williams; the play would have a strong impact if simply read by deadpan amateurs around a kitchen table. But it's more than Williams' words. A chord of genuine torment pierces through Marie's exaggerated gestures and intonations, and Peckinpah's camera isolates her in long extended close-ups that evoke her alienation from those around her.

In later interviews Peckinpah would orate rhapsodically about the books of Robert Ardrey, encouraging journalists to paint him as a dogmatic Darwinist who celebrated man's lust for brutal domination, and in a way he was. But again and again his own camera pauses to look at those who fail to successfully compete in "a society that has no room for the weak."

"If this world's all about winners, what's for the losers?" Robert Preston asks in *Junior Bonner.* Part of Peckinpah thrilled at the rough competitive nature of life and celebrated those who threw themselves fully into the struggle. But another part of him was perplexed and horrified by the pitiless reality of the human animal and could never reconcile it with the Christian ideals he'd rejected but couldn't quite rid his blood of.

"Sam was an idealist," says Don Levy. "I've never known an idealist who wasn't hurting."

Portrait won Peckinpah some legitimacy as a director. After its completion he shot and edited a film segment for "The Betty White Show," and a twelve-minute pilot for a children's series that dramatized classic fairy tales. In the latter, the use of expressionistic sets and lighting and more sophisticated editing—the close-ups and long shots were smoothly integrated, and there was even a montage sequence—demonstrated that his craft had grown significantly since *Madonna*.

The next project was a one-act play about Michelangelo written by Sam's former USC classmate, Jack Gariss. Sam rehearsed and staged a performance of it in an empty section of the scene shop at KLAC, hoping to entice management into broadcasting it as a half-hour drama. "Sam had it all lined up and ready to go," Don Stoutenborough, one of the cast members, recalls. "He had all the camera angles figured out, he got the performances, and we thought: this is gonna be great! This stuff is gonna be super, can't wait till we get this on film!"

But when Peckinpah finally persuaded the KLAC producer he'd been courting to watch a performance of the play, the man gave it a thumbs-down. The defeat really grated on Sam. "He was struggling to impress this guy who he didn't respect in any way," says Stoutenborough. "This guy was a little officer in the running of this game show. Sam was dismissive of the guy completely except that he had to impress him. Sam was angry. He said, 'This is great! Here we are, the talent, and here is this *nothing* out here that we have to impress!' " J. W. Wrights, he'd discovered, were not limited to Fresno State, not by a long shot.

The experience soured him on KLAC. Sam told Garner Simmons that he had an argument with an executive at the station who told him he was not being paid to think, but to do as he was told. "So I told him," Peckinpah recalled, "that if that was the case, he could take the goddamned job and shove it up his ass!"

But at other times in his later years Sam told interviewers he'd been fired from the station for refusing to wear a tie while working on the set of "The Liberace Show."

And there is a third, even more colorful anecdote about his departure from the station that is told by Peckinpah's brother-in-law, Walter Peter, who married Fern Lea in 1954. As Walter tells it, Sam had been directing the commercials for a local used-car dealer. "Folks, come on down and see old H. J. Caruso! Here at Caruso Motors our motto is *friendly* service and low, *low* prices!" The commercials were fed live and it was Sam's job to cue Caruso when he came on the air. During the lulls between commercials, H. J. Caruso's effusive piano grin turned to a saber-toothed snarl, and he amused himself by verbally lacerating members of the crew.

"Sam hated his guts," Walter recalls. "So he finally decided: fuck it! When it came time to cue the guy that he was on the air live, Sam just stood there like a Buddha for thirty seconds. So here's this dealer standing there before millions of viewers, scratching his nuts and yelling at the crew: 'You lazy fucks! I told you to move your butts!' Sam finally cued him, thirty seconds late. The next day he walked in to work and the car dealer said, 'You're fired! You're out of here!' "

It's possible that one or even all of the above stories are true. Certainly, as we will see, Sam Peckinpah committed even more outrageous acts of rebellion over the course of his career. KLAC had so many shows and commercials being shot at various locations around the city that Sam could easily have been taken off of "The Liberace Show" or banned from H. J Caruso's car lot and gone on working for other programs.

It's equally possible that none of the above stories are true. Once in the spotlight of international fame, Peckinpah fabricated many heroic anecdotes that fed his own legend of the fierce Wild West maverick who dared to buck the Hollywood system. It made for great copy, so few magazine writers bothered to question the veracity of such tales—a profitable arrangement for all concerned.

None of the former KLAC employees interviewed recall the above incidents. Marie remembers that Sam's work at the station gradually tapered off as he found jobs elsewhere and that it did not end in a dramatic confrontation.

But Jim Baker does remember that Sam was perceived as having an attitude problem, and remembers trying to convince him to keep his job with KLAC. "I said that he should straighten up and fly right because this television was going to be the coming thing. He didn't give a shit and to me it was a golden opportunity. He wanted to go into films and I thought he was completely crazy. The feeling at that time was that films were doomed and here's a wide-open thing that we've got and we're young guys and we can do anything we want. The motion-picture industry was a closed shop controlled by a handful of people. But Sam felt that film was the story-telling medium and television never would be. I now believe he was right."

And the kinds of stories that movies were telling had begun to change, due to an influx of radically different foreign pictures, mostly from Europe and Japan, made by a new generation of filmmakers who weren't afraid to approach movies as an art form and to take risks with rough-edged, innovative styles and taboo subjects.

From the tattered ruins of postwar Italy and France came stark, black-and-white pieces of neorealism like *Shoe Shine, The Bicycle Thief,* and *Forbidden Games.* Simple films about common people and their struggle to survive, stripped of all the makeup, gauze filters, lush background music, and three layers of Technicolor; simple elemental tales of survival.

And then there were the filmmakers who had their own strikingly idiosyncratic styles—Akira Kurosawa, Federico Fellini, Ingmar Bergman—whom younger French critics were beginning to call "auteurs": film authors, as worthy of serious artistic consideration as novelists, painters, and composers. American movie moguls at first found the theory laughable, then maddening when it began to gain currency in their own country over the coming decade.

Sam and Marie went to see all the new foreign films; he drank them in voraciously. Kurosawa's *Rashomon*—the tale of a rape and murder told from four different points of view. It exposed all the mendacity, betrayal, and self-deception of the human race, and yet held out a candle of hope at the end, when a woodcutter finds an abandoned baby and, in deciding to adopt it, discovers his own capacity for mercy and selfless love. A little, intimate film that captured the entire range of human experience within its slender boundaries. Peckinpah later told an interviewer it was "the finest picture ever made."

Kurosawa followed it up with *The Seven Samurai*, a stunning epic that borrowed from the mythology of American westerns and Shakespeare's tragedies and filtered it all back through the director's own unique vision. Kurosawa's editing of the battle sequences was breathtaking. In some of the swordfights the skewered samurai fell to the ground in slow motion. It brought an eerie poetry to their deaths, like Hobson's falling light bulb, yet the effect was jarring. The slow motion had been abruptly cut into the action, not integrated. Like Eisenstein scrutinizing D. W. Griffith's first uses of close-ups and parallel action, the gears inside Peckinpah's head began to turn. Was there a more effective way to cut together film shot at variable speeds so that the slow motion and normal footage flowed together in one dynamic continuum?

But it wasn't just Kurosawa's technique that fascinated Sam. In *Samurai*, a group of mercenaries agree to save a village of peasant farmers from raiding bandits. They win the battle, but as the bloody survivors watch the farmers returning to their fields, already forgetting both their tormentors and their saviors, they realize that the peasants are the only real victors. Day after day they plant and harvest their crops, birth their children, bury their dead; they endure, outlasting each wave of conquerers, who are sooner or later vanquished by the next.

It was an observation that Sam had made firsthand, years earlier in China and Mexico. *Samurai* caused his mind to whirl with new possibilities. "I'd like to be able to make a western like Kurosawa makes westerns," Sam would later tell an interviewer.

The European films, and the plays of Tennessee Williams and Arthur Miller, even began to change the face of Hollywood movies. Young new directors like Elia Kazan and Fred Zinnemann brought hard-edged, socially conscious dramas like *The Men, From Here to Eternity, On the Waterfront,* and Williams' *Streetcar Named Desire* to the big screen, along with a repertory company of mumbly, shifty-eyed method actors who wore their neuroses on the sleeves of their stained T-shirts and scuffed leather jackets.

Even the westerns had begun to change. Before John Ford had a chance to complete his classic cavalry trilogy, a new subgenre had appeared: the adult western. *The Gunfighter, High Noon, The Naked Spur, Johnny Guitar*—movies that used the horse opera as a vehicle for critiquing contemporary American society, for probing the neurotic and even psychopathic impulses that beat rapidly beneath the idealism and fanatic wholesomeness of the 1950s.

Sam's favorite among these was *Shane*. In George Stevens' direction he saw an epic vision that approached but failed to match Kurosawa's. One scene in particular riveted him.

"I'm sayin' that Stonewall Jackson was trash himself. Him, Lee, and all the rest of them rebs . . . You too." Black-clad Jack Palance hisses at sodbuster Elisha Cook, Jr., with a cobra's grin.

Cook goes for the bait. "You're a no-good lyin' Yankee!"

"Prove it," Palance whispers through his white teeth.

Cook paws clumsily for his gun. Palance's pearl-handled six-shooter clears its holster in an instant. He pauses for a moment, still grinning, savoring it and allowing Cook to absorb the full horror before he pulls the trigger. BOOM!—it cracks like Satan's whip across the prairie. Cook jerks into the air and flies backward, shoulders crashing and sliding in a puddle of black horseshit and mud. No sooner does his corpse come to a stop—now indistinguishable from the muck over which he'd just stood—than a bird calls out in a song, high and sweet.

"Killing used to be fun and games in Apacheland," Peckinpah later said. "Violence wasn't shown well. You fired a shot and three Indians fell down. But when Jack Palance shot Elisha Cook, Jr. . . . things started to change."

Sam's break into films came not from the brass at KLAC or some Hollywood bigwig who'd seen one of his plays or experimental films, but, appropriately, from Fresno—from his older brother, Denny, who was still practicing law with their father downtown in the Brix Building. Denny explains: "I had been the campaign manager for Pat Brown in Fresno County during his campaign for state attorney general. He won by a higher percentage in Fresno than in any other county in the state. I had made a point of telling him about Sam and his ambitions. Pat said, 'Well, when he's ready, let me know and I'll see what I can do to help him out in the picture business.' . . . Sam finally felt he'd learned all he could from working at KLAC, so I arranged for us all to meet at Santa Barbara. Pat was attending a district attorneys' convention there. Sam brought his resume and all that bullshit. Pat took him into the bedroom of his hotel suite and they talked for about forty-five minutes. Then Pat came out and called Walter Wanger on the phone."

One of the more colorful characters in Hollywood, Wanger had worked as a producer or production executive at Paramount, Columbia, Universal, RKO, and MGM. He'd produced John Ford's *Stagecoach* and *The Long Voyage Home,* and Alfred Hitchcock's *Foreign Correspondent.* Then he shot his wife's agent in the groin. He'd caught the two (Jennings Lang and Joan Bennett) in a not-so-Platonic embrace. Wanger served nearly four months in prison. Now out again, he wanted to capture his experience on film and make a comeback by producing *Riot on Cell Block 11* for Allied Artists (formally Monogram), a Poverty Row studio that specialized in pumping out cheap exploitation pictures.

When Wanger came on the line, Brown said, "Walter, you know you were talking about that picture you wanted to shoot at Folsom Prison? I think we can arrange that, no problem. Listen, I have a young friend here by the name of Sam Peckinpah who would like to get involved in the motion-picture business. If you can find a position for him in your production I'm sure he'll work very hard for you . . . Okay, wonderful, I'll tell him." Brown hung up, turned to Sam and said, "Well, you're in. You'll make a few hundred bucks, you'll get a screen credit and that's it. From there on you'll have to make it on your own ability."

3

"You Can't Kill a Memory That Way"

If ever a man was in the right place at the right time, it was Sam Peckinpah. He would follow a circuitous path from feature films back into television and finally back into features again, but it was as if each step were preordained to be taken at exactly the right moment. The first put him under the guidance of a mentor with a temperament that dovetailed perfectly with his own. The next took him back into television just as the greatest western boom in history created a voracious demand for writers who could pen authentic dialogue and were thoroughly steeped in the mythology of the Wild West.

If the gods handed him this incredible chain of lucky breaks, it wasn't charity. There was a price to be paid, a high one. Sam, dizzied by the rocket ride straight to the top, would not notice it for a number of years. But Marie did, right from the beginning, though she was as helpless as he to reverse the momentum once it gained speed.

While Sam's career arched slowly upward, his father David saw his own thwarted. In thirty years of private practice he'd built an unimpeachable reputation as one of Fresno's leading attorneys. He was a Republican, not a Democrat as his father-in-law Denver Church had been, but like Denver he was popular with both the big-money interests and the common citizens. A prominent member of the city's best civic organizations, with friends in city hall and among the big agricultural interests that controlled politics in the San Joaquin Valley, he knew where all the strings were and how to pull them.

So when the Republican party began looking for candidates who would help them capture a congressional majority in 1952 it didn't take long to zero in on the tall, lanky, Honest Abe visage of David Peckinpah. "He [David] got a call from President Eisenhower," Sam later recalled, "a personal call to run for Congress."

David's mind may have flashed back to Washington, D.C. in 1917, to that day he stood before the newly erected Lincoln Memorial, contemplating just how far a lumberjack's son could go if he had enough drive and perseverance. Here it was at last, an opportunity to follow in old Denver's footsteps and—who could tell—maybe even surpass him. At fifty-seven he was no spring chicken anymore, but he still had a good fifteen to twenty years, plenty of time.

He rushed home from the office early that day, eager to break the news to Fern. Perhaps he never even stopped to consider how his wife would react. His own excitement was so overwhelming that it was inconceivable that she wouldn't share it. But as the words rushed out of his mouth in a tangled jumble, he saw his mistake at once in the stiffening muscles of her round face, in the long-fingered hands that fluttered nervously to her temples, in the sudden flash of fear and anger in her eyes.

"My mother was the most selfish person I've ever known," says Fern Lea. "She could never get away from herself and her needs. She never stopped to consider what my father wanted." Already distraught over the hours David spent at his office, in court and with various civic organizations, Fern saw this new opportunity as a dire threat. It triggered all her worst fears of abandonment.

"We had a family meeting," Sam recalled, "and she [Fern] said [to David], 'If you do [run for Congress], I'll leave you.' So he didn't, and he regretted it."

David accepted the setback with tight-lipped stoicism. He had vowed before God to remain loyal to his wife in sickness and in health, good times and bad, for as long as they both should live. He would not, could not, break that commitment. But beneath the impassive mask the decision ate at him. In the middle of an argument one night, Fern Lea said to her father, "I don't think you really love Mom."

David came unglued. "How dare you! Don't you ever say that to me again!" he yelled, striking his daughter's upraised arms again and again, leaving them black-and-blue for days afterwards.

Sam's childhood hero had been humbled. He resented his mother's power play and the tension between them continued to build. His drinking increased both in frequency and quantity. Marie blinded herself to the alarming signs. When a friend asked her what she was going to do about her husband's drinking problem, she blinked in astonishment and replied: "What problem?"

Fern, of course, strongly disapproved, and still tried to exert authority over D. Sammy. While visiting the house in Whittier once she saw Marie use some cooking wine in the kitchen and blew up, threatening to cut off the money she and David had been sending to help support the young couple. In her diary, Fern later recalled telling Sam: "I'd rather buy milk for a little child overseas, instead of what you're spending my money for!"

The outburst was followed by apologies and a promise of abstinence by Sam, which he of course had no intention of keeping. On a visit to Fresno a few years later, Sharon—then six years old and exhibiting the same precociousness her father had at that age—walked up to Fern and asked brightly: "Do you drink whiskey?"

"No," her grandmother replied rigidly.

"My dad drinks whiskey."

Fern smiled icily. "No he doesn't."

Sharon nodded with equal obstinacy. "Yes he does."

"No he doesn't."

After they left, Sam—who had remained silent during the exchange—whirled on his daughter and hissed: "You told my mom I drink!" When Sharon reacted with shock and confusion he shook his head, eyes glaring. "You knew what you were doing!"

The relationship grew even more strained with the death of Denver Church. The old hunter had had a series of strokes beginning in the early forties, after Denny and Sam had left for the war. The first left one arm partially paralyzed, and he and Louise were forced to sell all their cattle and move off Dunlap's Ranch into a little apartment in Fresno, on Chestnut Avenue. But Denver wasn't going to give up the High Country without a fight. Even though his license had been revoked, he'd still sneak out in his old pickup truck and take off for the hills, usually with David, Denny, or Ed Klippert riding shotgun because the ex-congressman's steering was none too steady anymore.

But by 1950 even walking had become a challenge, and the trips to Dunlap's were no longer possible. "He moved very carefully," Marie recalls. "I remember he went to get out of the car one day and he was having trouble. Sam tried to help him and he shoved Sam away, violently. Sam laughed it off, but I could see it hurt him. Denver never allowed himself to accept help."

The more his health declined, the greater the old man's rage became. By the end, bedridden and unable to walk, he had nothing but rage left. "They built a cage around his bed," Ed Klippert recalls. "He got vicious. He didn't have any mind anymore, his mind was completely gone. They had a nurse with him twenty-four hours a day, but Mrs. Church [Louise] didn't dare get too close. He'd get ahold of her clothing or anything and he wouldn't let go. He ripped her clothes off, nearly, a time or two. He was like a wild animal."

Old Denver put up a fierce fight, but death finally won in February 1952. His extensive land holdings in Fresno and Madera counties were divided among his three children, but it was Fern who inherited Dunlap's Ranch. "I didn't think Denver would leave it to her," says Ed Klippert, who had managed the ranch in the final years. "I thought he was going to leave it to those two boys, I really did. I really believed that Sam and Denny would wind up with that place."

Perhaps Denver had assumed that in time Fern would pass the land on to his grandsons. After all, both boys had virtually grown up there, learning to ride, track, and shoot as well as their grandfather. Sam may have had many mixed feelings about those rolling hills of grass and oak trees, but he had caught his first trout there in Fine Gold Creek, shot his first deer there, and formed his first vivid associations with the American West that would permeate his life and work as a filmmaker. It was, in a sense, sacred ground.

Which is why it came as such a blow when Fern turned around and sold the ranch to an outsider without even giving Denny and Sam a chance to buy it themselves. "They were trying to raise the money, so she hurried the sale along so they couldn't buy it," says Ed Klippert.

Fern claimed she wanted to get rid of the ranch because there were too many painful memories attached to it now that her father had passed on. But her children suspected that, as always, there were darker hidden motives. Perhaps it was her way of finally getting even with her father, now that he was safely in his grave, for Bob Nichols. Betrayal for betrayal. Perhaps she was striking out at Denny, whom she viewed, with increasing distrust and animosity, as an ally with David against her and as a rival who had usurped her position as her father's favorite. In those last bedridden months Denver had called constantly for his "Denny-boy," the only person he seemed to recognize anymore. Perhaps she was lashing out at all of them, all the men by whom Fern felt cheated, betrayed, and controlled. She had found the soft spot and hit them where it hurt.

"I remember Sam on the phone for hours with Denny, talking about it," says Marie. "He was just stunned and very, very hurt. He couldn't understand how she could have done it."

A close friend of Sam's remembers him talking about the loss of Dunlap's years later. "It was a place that he had loved as a child and when it was sold it was like taking half his life away from him. He was very bitter about the way his mother handled it."

Things would never be the same again between Fern and her precious D. Sammy. Their private heart-to-heart talks came to an end and the wall she felt her son erecting ever since his return from China grew so high now that she could not even sneak a look over the top anymore. "I think it's a situation where you're supposed to love somebody, and in fact you do," Susan Peckinpah says of her brother's relationship with his mother. "But you can't stand what they are. I think those were the elements, and they were pretty brutalizing."

Within a year of Denver's death, Louise—the iron-willed pioneer woman who rode, herded cattle, shot a rifle, and backed down for no animal—withered and died also. The people and land that had provided Sam Peckinpah with a living connection to the American frontier were gone; the last remaining link was invisible, hidden deep in the pupils of his large eyes.

In 1934 Denver Church had scribbled a poem about his High Country home in a family album. It was an eerie premonition of the events that would follow some two decades later.

Let me linger on this hillside—
To my heart fond memories call;
On the quiet air of evening
I can hear the waterfall.

But the change my spirit saddens;
House and hearthstones are no more—
Nevermore that happy family
In and out the Old Home door.
Home of youth & joy & beauty,
You are in my heart today;
Tear the house down
Wreck the stable—
You can't kill a memory that way.

Each has gone where Duty calls him
Lives his life in shade or sun;

Gone the horses, dogs & cattle—
Beached canoe and rusty gun.

As of old the twilight deepens
Over all a radiance shines,
Glowing from the western hilltops,
From the moon caught in the pines.

Back in Los Angeles, Walter Wanger did not seem all that eager to give Sam Peckinpah the promised job on his new picture. Sam showed up at Wanger's office, a shabby bungalow on the Allied Artists lot in the sleazy wilderness of East Hollywood. "And there I had to wait—for three days, eight hours a day," Sam told Garner Simmons. "I think he hoped I'd go away. I finally outwaited him because I was determined to get a job in film." It was another phone call from Attorney General Brown, probably more than Sam's persistence, that finally got him in for an interview. "By that time I had memorized his [Wanger's] honorary degree from Dartmouth that was hanging on the wall, which was interesting since I was reading Budd Schulberg's *The Disenchanted* while I waited."

Wanger passed Peckinpah on to the film's director, Don Siegel, with the recommendation that he be hired as a production assistant. Now Sam found himself in an even shabbier waiting room, trying to concentrate on his dog-earred novel but reading the same sentence over and over again. Mr. Siegel was out but due back any moment. Every set of footsteps outside the door made the hairs on the back of his neck rise.

Don Siegel had come up through the ranks at Warner Bros., where he became head of the editorial department and crafted montage sequences for two of Sam's biggest idols, action directors Michael Curtiz and Raoul Walsh. Now, at age forty-two, he was directing movies for AA on fifteen and twenty-day shooting schedules. Siegel had a knack for turning tight budgets and schedules to his advantage. By using real locations, extras and bit players picked up off the streets, and minimalistic lighting, he brought a stark reality to his films. Because he'd been an editor,

Siegel knew how to shoot economically, and how to cut what he'd shot into breathless action sequences that leapt off the screen. Within a few years he would win a large following among European critics, who dubbed him a genuine auteur. Siegel's films inevitably revolved around loners and outcasts who were at odds with American society; Siegel viewed the loners with sympathy, but saw the society they battled as riddled with pathological hostility. Aesthetically and temperamentally Sam Peckinpah could not have asked for a more perfect mentor. When Siegel finally arrived and invited Sam into his office, a rapport clicked between the two almost instantly.

"I studied him," Siegel later recalled, "observed his excitement, his sense of fun . . . I liked his politeness, and I liked his burning ambition."

After twenty minutes of conversation, Siegel shrugged and said, "I've never worked with a gofer before."

"What does that mean?" Sam asked.

"Well, a gofer is a fellow that goes for things. You know, toothpicks, coffee, girls, anything."

"Girls?" Peckinpah's eyes brightened. "That's the job for me!"

He was hired as a dialogue director—a euphemism for the director's personal assistant—at a hundred dollars a week. A few days later he found himself standing, along with the rest of the *Riot in Cell Block 11* crew, in the office of Warden Heinze in Folsom Prison. Warner Bros. had just finished shooting a movie there that ran eleven days over schedule, so the warden was less than overjoyed to see another crowd from Hollywood before him. When Siegel told him they would shoot all their scenes in sixteen days, the warden said, without looking up from his paperwork, "You're full of shit!"

Siegel tried to recover from this awkward beginning by introducing the rest of his crew—cinematographer, art director, assistant director, prop master, and very last, his skinny dialogue director. The warden, who had gone right on signing papers, suddenly looked up at Sam, his expression lightening. "Are you related to the Peckinpahs in Fresno?"

"Yes, sir," Sam answered with quiet pride, "they're my family."

"Are they the judges and lawyers?"

"Yes, sir."

"Have you ever been up on Peckinpah Mountain?"

"I've hunted there ever since I've been a kid."

The warden's beefy face broke into a broad grin. He got up, came around the desk, and offered Sam his hand. "It's a great pleasure to meet you, Mr. Peckinpah." He nodded curtly at Siegel and his crew. "Can we depend on these people?"

"Yes, sir."

The warden slid a fatherly arm around Sam's shoulder and walked him past the others, out of the office, and into the hall. "Now, if you get into any trouble, or you need any help, or you want any advice, be sure to see me personally."

"We were stunned," Siegel later recalled. "We'd never been exposed before to the mystic name of Peckinpah. I decided that I was going to find out what it all meant."

Siegel tested his young assistant's mettle by putting him in charge of casting small parts and extras. "Sam, I'd like you to go out and get twenty-five hard-bitten, rough, tough men who will be the core of our prisoners. We'll be able to use them at any time that we want to. Remember now, they've got to look like prisoners. Go for it."

"I'll be back tomorrow morning with the group of men," Peckinpah said with a quick nod.

"And the next day I went out [on the set]," Siegel recalled, "and lo and behold, there was the roughest, toughest, terrible-looking [group of] men I've ever seen in my life. I thought: they make the Folsom prisoners look like sissies."

Sam learned his first lesson well. In the future he would pepper his own films with people taken right off the streets of the towns and remote locations he shot in. The weathered faces, bleak eyes, and stoic monotone voices gave the movies a palpable texture of reality conspicuously absent from studio-bound productions.

Siegel was a hard taskmaster on the set, but Sam was used to hard taskmasters; he'd lived in the shadow of them all his life and thrived on the dynamics. By the time the sixteen days were over the relationship between him and Siegel was more than that of employer and employee. As Denver Church had been in the High Country, Siegel became Sam's teacher and guide in an exciting new landscape, prodding and enticing the younger man into extending himself to the full measure of his abilities.

They would do four more features together over the next two and a half years: *Private Hell 36, The Annapolis Story, Invasion of the Body Snatchers,* and *Crime in the Streets.* "I thought Peckinpah was very bright and that he had a great deal of insight," Siegel told Garner Simmons. "So I used to trap him into doing things that I knew would cause him problems because I knew he would learn by having to find his way out. And it never took him very long. Then I told him to read the script and figure out how he would do it, then watch what I did. I told him that at first he would think that my way was better but that pretty soon just the reverse would happen."

Peckinpah later said that from Siegel he learned: "Everything. What to do, what not to do . . . I ended up learning how little I knew about pictures, human nature and survival. . . . Brutally honest, he would haul me to the office of a complaining production manager and then find the truth of the matter and proceed to chew ass—usually mine. Don has a great anger, a great sense of irony and a great warm sense of humor. (I know about the first, I have heard about the latter qualities.) But I must say that usually he was kind enough not to laugh openly while watching me run about with both feet in my mouth and my thumb up my ass (this is not easy) . . . A dedicated, painstaking craftsman, he was maniacal in his continuing battle against stupid studio authority. He was and is constantly amazed by the idiocy of our industry while still being delighted by its competence and professionalism."

Traits that Sam would later mirror. Former crew members on the Siegel films recall how Sam began to show up on the set in the same quasi-Western attire that his director favored. Siegel's deceptive soft-spoken manner concealed a straight-edged razor of sarcasm that he employed with devastating effect on negligent crew members and interfering producers. Allied Artists executives quickly learned to keep their distance from this subtly intimidating man, leaving Siegel free to shoot pictures his way, not theirs. His worshipful, watchful dialogue director saw that this was a style of command that suited his own reticent nature, and earmarked it for future reference.

The pupil was learning fast. "He was my 'patron'," Peckinpah said. "He made me work and made me mad and made me think. Finally [one day] he asked me what his next [camera] set-up was and for once I was ready and he used it."

On another day Peckinpah stopped Siegel on the set and asked him to look at a scene he was scheduled to shoot the next day. Siegel did and saw why Sam had pointed it out. The dialogue was flat, the dramatic tension nonexistent—it didn't work at all. "Sam," Siegel said, "why don't you play around with the sequence and when you're satisfied with it, then let me read it."

Peckinpah flipped past the scene to a new batch of pages. "I've already fooled around with it, sir."

"So I read it," Siegel later recalled. "It was excellent. It had tension, it had meaning, it made sense, and it had humor. So I thanked Sam and I told him to get it right out and put it on blue pages. And he turned around and went on his way. And I thought: you know, he's not going to be with me very long, because this young man is destined to be a director, a damn good director."

The second-to-last film that Peckinpah worked on with Siegel, in 1956, *Invasion of the Body Snatchers,* became an instant sci-fi classic and established the director's international reputation. A surreal allegory about an individual's struggle to resist the conformist pressures of the society that engulfs him, it predated Eugène Ionesco's strikingly similar *Rhinoceros* by a good two years. Siegel played the low-budget restrictions to his advantage with a sparse, elliptical style that heightened the nightmarish intensity. The small, sleepy town of Santa Mira is transformed into a nightmarish vision of 1950s America in which the inhabitants—infected by "alien" pods—all begin walking and talking like Muzak-brained I-like-Ike zombies.

Sam was the dialogue director and played several small parts in the film. "Peckinpah, man of a thousand faces," he later recalled. "I was also stunt man on the picture. Let me think. I was a meter reader, a pod man, and a member of the posse." And he managed to snag a small part for Marie as the pod-infected wife of a gas station owner.

Just what, if any, rewriting Sam did on *Invasion* has become a minor controversy in recent years. When thrust into the limelight after the release of *The Wild Bunch,* Peckinpah told several interviewers that he'd gotten his first official writing job on the film; Siegel gave him two weeks to polish up the script. This claim provoked an outraged protest from the picture's credited screenwriter, Daniel Mainwaring, who said that Peckinpah was taking bows for work he hadn't done.

Over the years Siegel would vacillate between backing up Peckinpah's version of events, then Mainwaring's. But a letter written by Marie to Sam's sister Fern Lea on April 6, 1955, shortly after the shooting began, confirms that Peckinpah did do extensive rewriting: "He [Sam] received the script of the next film he was to work on [which is clearly explained to be *Body Snatchers* later in the letter]—this directed by Don Siegel (our "guardian angel"). We both read the script, loved the idea, but hated the script itself. So Sam writes a fairly detailed criticism and takes it into Don. STRAIN!! He not only tells Don what he thinks of the script, he tells the producer (Wanger). COOL RECEPTION!! However, to make a long story short: He eventually talked Don into letting him try some re-writing, and was finally hired the last ten days before production started to re-write quite a bit of the script. Needless to say, we were really thrilled about his being hired as a writer. So, we were quite busy at home writing & typing & writing & typing. . . ."

Siegel raved about Peckinpah to other directors at Allied Artists, and Sam soon found his services in high demand. He later claimed he worked on fifteen pictures as a dialogue director over a three-year period—an astronomical figure, but not inconceivable given the short shooting schedules of most AA productions.

Besides the five he did for Siegel, there are three other features that Sam definitely worked on during those three years:

Wichita (1955) and *Great Day in the Morning* (1956), both directed by Jacques Tourneur, and *Seven Angry Men*, directed by Charles Marquis Warren. The latter—starring Raymond Massey as the messianic/maniacal abolitionist, John Brown—was AA's first attempt to break into class-A productions.

Warren was immediately impressed by his new assistant, as he recalled shortly before he died in 1990: "Sam would rehearse with the actors while I was laying out the shots with the cameraman. I noticed he'd done an excellent job with them, sometimes too excellent. We would shoot a scene and I'd say 'cut,' and before I could say that it was good or that it was bad, Raymond Massey would turn and say, 'How was that, Sam?' Here I was the big-shot director, but instead of asking, 'How was that, Mr. Warren?' they're turning to him!"

He was getting invited to his first Hollywood parties now, gatherings at Warren's hilltop house where Alan Ladd and Susan Hayward and other glamorous guests sat around a grand piano while Warren spun out an endless repertoire of classical pieces, swing numbers, and Broadway show tunes. Heady stuff for a kid from Fresno. "He would just sit there in the corner, listening," says Warren. "Quiet, meek little Sam. I'd say, 'Don't you want to dance? Everyone else is.' He'd say, 'No, I'm quite happy.' "

Rubbing elbows with the stars and those who pulled their strings was having its effect on him. He caught the first intoxicating whiffs of power, and more than ever knew that he wanted to sit in the chair Warren, Tourneur, and Siegel now occupied. The pursuit and attainment of that goal would change him in ways he couldn't begin to anticipate.

At home though, life seemed as loose and unpretentious as ever. The biggest change was the location. He and Marie had had enough of Whittier's suburban dry-rot. While still working at KLAC, he had sold their tract house and bought a piece of land with a Quonset hut on it, high in the hills above Malibu, for $6,000. It was no San Simeon, just an unpainted cylinder of sheet metal with a mass of wild sumac bushes by way of landscaping. But the surprisingly spacious interior was subdivided into three bedrooms, a living room, and a kitchen, and there was electricity and running water drawn from a well. Visitors were often startled by its primitiveness, but Sam and Marie felt they'd found their little patch of heaven, a blissful escape hatch from the cookie-cutter culture of L.A.

Around back there was a large yard—if you could call it that, for as long as he lived there Sam planted not a single blade of grass. In front, a large L-shaped wooden deck overlooked the gentle contours of the grassy hills rolling down to the sparkling blue Pacific. In those years before the hordes of real estate agents devoured it, Malibu really was a paradise, almost as untouched as when the Chumash Indians had dwelled there a century before. Deer grazed on the surrounding hillsides in the morning, and packs of coyotes yapped and howled like demons in the night. Hiking up the brushy canyons, Sam and Marie discovered surreal rock formations, bubbling streams, and even a waterfall or two. It was the High Country with an ocean view.

The town of Malibu itself consisted of little more than a fishing pier and a scattering of motor courts and restaurants (the Sea Lion with its pen of yelping mascots being the most popular). There was the Colony, a cluster of moldy beachfront houses adjacent to a tiny lagoon where Malibu Creek emptied out of the Santa Monica Mountains into the churning surf. Once it had been an exclusive getaway for silent-movie stars and L.A.'s idle rich; there had been a plan in the twenties to dredge the lagoon and build a marina beside the houses. The crash of '29 killed the scheme, and the Colony had since fallen into termite-gnawed decline. Sam fell in love with Malibu's funky, sun-drenched atmosphere and would remain tied to the community, through a series of beach homes and finally a banged-up trailer, to the very end of his life.

Two more daughters had joined the family—Kristen in November 1953 and Melissa in 1956. Strong traces of both parents were, of course, evident in all three girls. Sharon and Melissa most closely resembled their mother; Kristen's thin face bore striking resemblance to Sam's. Sharon was headstrong and quick to challenge authority, so like her father in this regard that the two would lock horns again and again in the years to come. Kristen appeared quieter, but had her father's penetrating eyes and intellect. Melissa was the sweet one who took on Marie's ethereal demeanor.

At the Quonset hut the family began acquiring pets. Before long it was Peckinpah's Wild Animal Park, with a total of five dogs (including Sam's weimaraner, Rita, whom he hunted with), thirteen cats (including a homosexual one and a "slow" one that kept banging its head against the back door, trying to enter through a cat door that had long since been removed), and a goat. When visitors pulled into the drive, the entire menagerie rushed up, barking, meowing, and baaing their greetings.

Sam decided a fence was needed to contain the herd. When he spotted a leftover pile of lumber up on Rambla Pacifico, he and a neighbor staged an early-morning raid. Soon the Great Wall of Peckinpah was under way. "Sam didn't know how to do any kind of handiwork, so building that fence was something he was very proud of, because he built it with his own hands," says Marie. "But it was a monstrosity! You never saw such thing in all your life!"

As for the interior of the hut, there was little danger they would be besieged by platoons of photographers from *Better Homes and Gardens*. Sam's sister, Fern Lea, had married Walter Peter, a Pennsylvania boy, in 1954. Six feet, five inches tall, with 210 pounds of oak-hard muscle, Walter harbored an insatiable appetite for classical music, liquor, and "crazy nonsense." He worked in Los Angeles as a fledgling stockbroker, and earned enough, barely, for the small apartment he and Fern Lea shared in Santa Monica.

Walter and Sam took to each other immediately; he and Fern Lea were up at the Quonset hut almost every weekend, but he still remembers his shock the first time he stepped inside: "It was a mess! Piles of books, clothes, whatever, all over the living room, the bedrooms. And the kitchen: unwashed dishes a day or two or three days old. . . . Books all over the place; Sam always had a lot of books, all kinds, scripts, all over in a big jumble."

In the summer, Sharon and Kristen would spend hours making mud patties in a "mud pool" that their parents had made for them. Every so often Sam would clean the leaves and dead branches out from under the sumac bushes, and they'd construct giant forts out of blankets and poles.

When Christmas rolled around, Sam and Marie combined forces to bring the holiday to life for their daughters. The tree wouldn't be decorated until Christmas Eve, after the girls had gone to bed. Then Sam and Marie would stay up all night covering it with ornaments and angel hair and frosting the windows with artificial snow. By dawn the Quonset hut would be transformed into a winter wonderland.

On Christmas Eve, 1955, Sam enlisted his brother-in-law Walter Peter's aid for a special project. The two of them rigged a set of sleigh bells above the roof of the Quonset hut and connected them to a hidden pulley. After Christmas dinner, Sam casually suggested they all go outside to look at the stars. In the cool night air, he rested one hand gently on six-year-old Sharon's shoulder and with the other pointed out the Big Dipper, the constellation of Orion, and other celestial wonders. As he did so, Walter slyly reached up and tugged on the pulley. Sam's eyes widened, frantically searching the heavens. "What's that? Do you hear that? Sleigh bells!! Look, look, there he is, can you see the sleigh? See the reindeer?"

"Sam was so tickled afterwards that he'd really had her believing it," Walter says. "He was so excited, like a little kid himself."

Friends from Sam's USC days—Jack and Jeanette Gariss, Mike and Nancy Galloway—would drive up to the Quonset hut on the weekends, along with new friends from Allied Artists, like script supervisor Frank Kowalski and his wife. They'd play bridge and drink cheap wine or beer while Miles Davis blasted "Kind of Blue" from the blond-wood cabinet that housed the phonograph.

But there were times now, when the bottle of wine was empty, that Sam's big pupils went hard and flat and he became as venomous as old Denver Church. Fern Lea was shocked the first time she witnessed one of these episodes. "He was loud, insulting, vicious. I'd never seen him like that before. He was so nasty to me, I cried. We left right away. He called the next morning to apologize, he was very remorseful. He said, 'I guess I was a little out of line.' I said, 'Sam, what are you doing to yourself? It's what you're doing to yourself that's disturbing, not what you did to me.' If he'd had any sense he would have stopped drinking then."

Sam still got together with some of his old KLAC friends for occasional poker games in town. One night they played for four hours straight, Sam drinking steadily the whole time. He didn't appear drunk, but he suddenly took offense to a remark by Rudy Behlmer and sprang to his feet spewing curses. "Sam went after Rudy," John Langdon recalls. "I and another guy grabbed Sam, we could hardly restrain him he was so wiry and strong. He yelled at Rudy, 'Come on, I'm ready for you!' Rudy just looked at him and said, 'Are you for real?' "

But in the Quonset hut years, with so many possibilities still ahead, the good times far outweighed the bad. At night, after dinner, drinking, and a Monopoly game, they'd drag the scratched-up armchairs out of the living room on to the wood deck and bask in the silver-blue sheen of the moon, drinking in the warm, salt-seasoned air washing up through the sage and foxtail in the hills. Far below, the pregnant expanse of the Pacific shimmered like mercury, and along the wide white stretch of sand one could make out the dim yellow lights of the Colony.

One night, while sitting there with his old Fresno State pal, George Zenovich, Sam nodded toward the Colony's lights and said, "Someday I'm going to have a house down there, Zeno."

In 1955 CBS decided to move its hit radio series "Gunsmoke" to television. Looking for a producer/director to oversee the series, they made an offer to Don Siegel. But Siegel wanted to stay in feature films and, after taking a long look, turned them down. The network then turned to another Allied Artists director, Charles Marquis Warren. Siegel thought the show had potential; he passed some of the radio scripts that had been given to him on to Sam with the suggestion that he try to write one for the series. Peckinpah settled down on the deck of the Quonset hut one afternoon to read the radio plays; an hour later he was up and pacing, excitedly relating the stories he'd read to

Marie. Here was something he could really do, a series set in Dodge City in the heart of the Old West—a town of saloons, dance-hall girls, rowdy drunken cowboys, and deadly gunslingers. If Peckinpah couldn't write a script for this show, he just couldn't write!

"Gunsmoke" had been the brainchild of writer John Meston, a doctor of languages from Oxford University (with degrees from Dartmouth and Harvard as well) who'd written most of the radio shows. Meston's scripts offered a dark, ironic vision of the American West. The good citizens of Dodge City were often bigoted, greedy, and quick to brutalize the weak and "different."

This bleak portrait of the American frontier was made palatable for a mass audience by the show's hero, Marshal Matt Dillon, a cardboard cutout plastered with all the traditional B-movie clichés: Dillon was a tall-standin', straight-shootin' crusader for truth, justice, and the American way. Rarely the center of the early "Gunsmoke" stories, Dillon usually disappeared on "out-of-town business" at the beginning of the show, and stayed away long enough for the conflict among the degenerate town folk to reach a crisis. Then he reappeared just in time to blast the villains with his long-barreled .45 and to deliver an easily digestible bromide that reaffirmed all American values—values that almost none of Dodge City's residents embraced except when the marshal held a gun to their heads. This gave each show the reassuring appearance of a happy ending, though the device was as cynical as the vision of humanity that it disguised.

Before "Gunsmoke" premiered in the fall of 1955, television westerns had offered only the creaky clichés of B-movies. Roy Rogers, Gene Autry, Hopalong Cassidy, the Lone Ranger, and the Cisco Kid pranced across the tiny screens in twenty-gallon hats and sequined outfits, engaging in the same mindless horse chases and gunfights that had dominated the genre since the days of Tom Mix. "Gunsmoke" changed all that. The "adult" western came to the small screen. The series focused on serious subjects: racial prejudice, unrequited love, self-destructive vengeance, obsessive jealousy, and greed. Every week a social or psychological problem was introduced by special guest stars, brought to a violent climax, then explained or reflected on by Dillon or the Greek chorus of series regulars—deputy Chester Goode; Kitty Russell, the comely hostess at the Longbranch Saloon; and crotchety Doc Adams.

Compared to the other TV-western fare, the show appeared fresh and sophisticated, and audiences responded enthusiastically. The week of its premiere "Gunsmoke" came in forty-second in the Nielsen ratings; the second week it jumped to twenty-second, and by the third week it had skyrocketed to number one.

Peckinpah was still on good terms with Charles Marquis Warren, and so immediately made an appointment to see the producer/director at the show's new production facilities on Melrose Boulevard, across from Paramount Studios. "Sam came to me and said, 'Boss, can I have a crack at writing one of these?' " Warren recalled. "I said, 'You can if you write it on spec.' " Which meant on speculation. If Warren didn't like the finished product he could reject it without giving Peckinpah so much as one thin dime for his labors. Sam eagerly agreed and Warren handed him three of John Meston's radio scripts, instructing him to write an adaptation of the one he liked best. Almost all of the scripts produced that season were adaptations of Meston scripts. Meston himself was available for this, but CBS feared he could only write radio dialogue—"Well, if that isn't Miss Kitty coming out of the Longbranch! Look at the bright red shawl she's wearin'!"—so screenwriters were being hired to transform the dialogue of the radio plays into action, the words into images.

For his first attempt Sam chose to adapt a Meston script called *Queue*, about a Chinese immigrant who is bullied by a trio of Dodge City bigots; it gave him a chance to exploit his intimate knowledge of both the Old West and China. He converted a tiny basement laundry room at the Quonset hut into a makeshift office and locked himself away from family and friends. It was the first complete script he'd ever tried to write. He'd gained a lot of experience on the Siegel films, but it still didn't come easy.

"It was hell, because I hate writing," Sam later said. "I suffer the tortures of the damned. I can't sleep and it feels like I'm going to die any minute. Eventually, I lock myself away somewhere out of reach of a gun and get it on in one big push. I'd always been around writers and had friends who were writers, but I'd never realized what a lot of goddamn anguish is involved. But it was a way to break in." It took three months of cursing, desk-pounding, paper-tearing, and pencil-smashing, but he finally emerged from his burrow with a completed script (or, rather, a pile of scribbled pages that Fern Lea typed up for him)—good enough, he hoped, to make the grade.

Charles Marquis Warren was putting in eighteen-hour days—"the pressure was unbelievable"—and so when Sam turned in his script, he passed it on to his secretary. "Peggy, read it for me, will you? If it's got anything, let me know." When he returned to the office the next morning his secretary was holding the script in her hand. "Well," he asked, "what did you think?"

"Mr. Warren, read it."

"Will I like it?"

"*Read it.*"

So he did. "Goddamn, it was well written," Warren recalled. "I'd been getting scripts from all these guys who prided themselves on being authentic western writers. Most of them had never even been near a horse. They'd try to write in dialect, 'Howday padna!' God they were awful! But Sam's dialogue was crisp and clean and filled with original little phrases. And he knew so much about the Old West, little details like the kind of carpenter's tools they used in those days. I had told him to work those things in, not by having the characters give a lecture but by working them into the body of a scene. He gave his scripts a real authentic feel. He learned fast. I never had to teach him twice, and sometimes he taught me."

From the beginning Peckinpah grasped that television, like film, was primarily a visual medium. Wherever possible he used action rather than dialogue to make a story point, so his scenes were dynamic instead of static. When the characters did talk, the words sounded fresh, idiosyncratic . . . real. Scattered throughout even this first script were lines of dialogue that Sam would become famous for: "You're about as humble as a turpentined cat!" The villain of the piece was a blueprint for a character that would reappear throughout Peckinpah's work: the deranged preacher who raves about the evils of sin and the rapture of serving Jesus, but is driven into a profuse sweat by his own animal lusts for sex and blood.

Warren bought Sam's script for $900 and directed the episode himself.

The show has dated badly in the thirty-eight years since it first aired. The plot is formulaic and predictable. Warren's by-the-numbers direction doesn't help. But it was as good as, if not better than, the scripts turned in by other writers that first season. Peckinpah soon sold another script, then another and another. From 1955 through 1957 he would sell about ten "Gunsmoke" episodes at $900 a crack, almost double the rate some other series were paying. All were adaptations of John Meston radio scripts; Warren gave Sam his pick from the incredible backlog that Meston had churned out in the early fifties.

The writing began to come easier and faster. "By the end I was able to knock one out in about eight hours," Peckinpah later said. "Eight hours, that is, after twenty straight hours of lying awake getting my ideas together."

He didn't type. Instead, he'd scribble away on any sheets of paper that came handy—sometimes right on the back of the pages of Meston's radio scripts—in his almost indecipherable chicken scratch that, with its backward Y's and horrific misspellings, might have resembled the penmanship of the semiliterate cowboys who populated his stories. Then he'd race the disheveled pages to one of several typists now in his employ—Fern Lea, or old USC friends like Adele Cook, Nancy Galloway, and Gay Hayden.

"Then he discovered the Dictaphone and life became wonderful for Sam because he could talk all night long," says Hayden. "He'd dictate as if he were reading the script—camera shots, the whole thing. This was very rough, really long and rambling. He overwrote, of course, in the beginning because he didn't want to stop and go back; that's not the way he thought. It came out stream of consciousness. Then he would cut. He rewrote everything. He couldn't keep his sticky fingers off of it. He would have worked forever if people hadn't taken the script away from him."

"Editing was one of Sam's greatest talents, both on film and on paper," says Nancy Galloway. "Very interesting to watch him go through a script and cut. He could be ruthless in editing his own material and someone else's. It was always interesting to see how he fleshed out and pared down a script."

The money was great; so was the prestige of writing for one of the highest-rated shows on television. But there were also frustrations. Peckinpah packed his teleplays with authentic detail. Many read like short stories. But the "Gunsmoke" producers routinely rewrote the drafts he turned in to make them more palatable to a wide audience. Many of the details that illustrated the harshness and casual brutality of frontier life, and the disconcerting incongruities and antisocial edges of his characters, were sanded away before the show made it to the screen. But along with their rough edges the characters also lost much of their humanity. The pabulumized final product was guaranteed to offend no one, but it was rarely as moving or powerful as Sam's original script.

The depiction of violence on "Gunsmoke," in particular, undercut the verisimilitude of the drama. Shot once, twice, even three times, the victims leaked not a pinprick of blood; they did not writhe in agony, they didn't even pop a shirt button. They simply fell to the ground as if the thunder of Dillon's six-gun had caused them to fall peacefully asleep.

Granted, the show's producers had to contend with the network's censors, who constantly pressured for the violence to be as bloodless and absent of brutality as possible. Nonviolent violence. *Shane* may have changed the face of violence on the big screen, but on the small glowing boxes in living rooms across the country it was still "fun and games in Apacheland."

It was maddening for Sam to watch or be forced to make these "improvements" in his work. He'd started writing because he saw it as a stepping-stone to directing; his experience on "Gunsmoke" convinced him more than ever that the director's chair was the real creative hub of filmmaking. He hung around on the set to watch the shooting of most of his scripts, observing how the directors worked with the actors, the art director, costume designer, where they put the camera, how they lit the sets and blocked the action. He noted what they did right and, at least as often, what they did wrong.

Peckinpah chose to adapt several Meston scripts that featured characters who were "not quite right" in the head. Crazy, retarded, tormented by delusions—a gallery of ragged, unshaven outsiders wandering helplessly through a world that has no place for them. The most successful of these was "Cooter."

Cooter is the name of a simpleton who wanders the streets of Dodge City, doing odd jobs for handouts. His mental impairment is the result of a traumatic act of violence. In the script he has a long scar on the side of his head from an old bullet wound. "He knows he's different from other people," says Doc Adams, "but he doesn't know what to do about it."

A local gambler hires Cooter as a bodyguard in an attempt to intimidate Marshal Dillon, who suspects the cardsharp of cheating local cowboys out of their hard-earned wages. The gambler, Sissle, gives Cooter a gunbelt and a loaded .45, and soon the little man is swaggering around Dodge City like a boy playing gunfighter. But it's a deadly game. Peckinpah suggests that the mere possession of a weapon can awaken violent instincts, even within a child/man like Cooter.

In the script, Peckinpah describes Cooter's conversation with Dillon the first time the marshal, Doc, and Chester spot him wearing the gun:

> Cooter: "I killed that old gray dog this morning. First shot too. I got real close. The gray one that's always laughing at me." Cooter grins like a dog at the three men, and moves across the street.

This scene was eliminated from the final show as the producers once again strove to make Cooter more "sympathetic"—a simple innocent who is manipulated by the corrupt gambler. But this time the intensity of Peckinpah's teleplay was retained, thanks largely to the young actor hired to play the part, Strother Martin. Martin caught not only the character's pathos—his loneliness and need to belong, and heartbreaking naiveté—but also the perverse streak of violence that lurks beneath his childlike surface.

Eventually Cooter turns on the gambler who armed him and shoots and kills him. Unable to fully comprehend what he has done, Cooter unbuckles the gunbelt and lays it and the pistol on the back of the gambler's corpse. "You better keep your gun, Mr. Sissle. You see, I'm not gonna work for ya anymore." And off he wanders with the shuffling, arm-hanging gait of a five-year-old, down the night-dark street.

"Ain't ya gonna go after him, Mr. Dillon?" Chester asks.

Dillon shakes his head. "No, he won't go far, Chester . . . I'll pick him up pretty soon. I think we've done enough to Cooter for one day."

Directed by John Stevenson, it was a first-rate show, the best of all Sam's "Gunsmoke" episodes, and very nearly equal to some he would direct for "The Westerner" a few years later.

Strother Martin liked the episode so much that he ordered a personal print of it for private screenings. Sam in turn was so impressed by the actor's performance that he invited him up to the Quonset hut for dinner. He had, without yet knowing it, recruited the first member of his repertory company, Sam Peckinpah's Wild Bunch.

The fantastic success of "Gunsmoke" and another adult western series that debuted on television the same year, "The Life and Legend of Wyatt Earp," started a genre stampede. In 1954 there had been seventeen western shows on the air; by 1959 the number had shot up to forty-eight. No other genre in history, except the situation comedy, has dominated the public airwaves as the western did in the late fifties. "Wagon Train," "Cheyenne," "Have Gun Will Travel," "Tales of Wells Fargo," "Bat Masterson"—all shooting thirty-nine episodes a year on Hollywood sound stages and on movie ranches in the Santa Monica Mountains just inland from Malibu. The grassy hills and wooded canyons surrounding Sam's Quonset hut crackled with gunfire and shook under the hooves of stampeding horses and cattle.

The big movie studios, which had at first spurned "the idiot box," now decided "if you can't beat it, join it!" and began cranking out shows to satisfy the ravenous appetite of their bastard child. Series shot on film quickly supplanted those shot live or on videotape; the image quality was better, the editing easier and more precise, the results slicker. It was like the twenties and thirties, when Hollywood produced thousands of two-reel (twenty-minute) westerns, all over again. And the new television shows were shot on the same back-breaking, low-budget schedules as the old two-reelers. Most were filmed in just three days, some in two and a half. Universal, Warner Bros., and 20th Century–Fox all applied tried-and-true assembly-line methods for pumping out the "product."

For millions of baby boom boys—then nine, ten, and eleven years old—this was television's golden era. Clad in Leatherette vests, lavishly embroidered cowboy boots, and felt Stetsons, they crouched behind living room sofas with cap pistols, exchanging shots with the bad guys on the Zenith's bluish screen. It was a golden age too for actors who could ride, wear a gunbelt, and fire a six-gun or Winchester with easy sensuality. Steve McQueen, Clint Eastwood, Richard Boone, James Garner, Robert Culp, Charles Bronson, and James Coburn were just a few of those who shot their way into the limelight during these years.

In the space of one television season Sam was catapulted from the position of an obscure dialogue director to one of the hottest young writers in television. By the late fifties he was writing for a number of other shows, including "Trackdown," "Tales of Wells Fargo," "Have Gun Will Travel," "Tombstone Territory," "Boots and Saddles," and "Man with a Gun." For "The 20th Century–Fox Hour" he did an adaptation of Henry King's adult western classic, "The Gunfighter," that was nominated for the best western of the 1956–57 season by the Writers Guild of America. His services were so much in demand that he even began subcontracting some of the scripts out to ghost writers—old USC and Fresno State pals, Don Levy among them.

One of the shows that Peckinpah wrote for was "Broken Arrow"; he sold five scripts to its producers in 1957 and 1958. The series was based on the 1950 feature film of the same name, which in turn was based on Elliott Arnold's novel, *Blood Brother.* It was a noble attempt to reverse the clichéd image of Indians as screaming red devils, and to document the many sufferings inflicted on them by the white man. But the television show was fatally flawed by 20th Century–Fox's low budgets and inspiration-crushing production schedules. Each show was shot in two and a half to three days, and the studio pressed both cast and crew to finish one and a half to two shows a week.

Peckinpah's scripts for this series were nowhere near as good as those he wrote for "Gunsmoke." They had a cranked-out quality. But in 1958 the show served as another vital steppingstone in his career. After two years and seventy-two episodes "Broken Arrow" was going off the air, and Peckinpah had been hired to write the final show, "The Transfer." (Sam repeatedly told interviewers it was "The Knife Fighter," but that in fact was an earlier script.) In the last episode, Jeffords bids farewell to his "blood brother," Cochise, and rides off to help "pacify" the Utes, another tribe that has gone on the warpath.

After Peckinpah completed the teleplay, the show's co-producer, Elliott Arnold, asked if he would like to direct it. "Christ, they knew I was dying to direct," Sam later recalled. "They didn't have to ask me a second time."

Because it was the last episode, neither he nor the producers had much to lose. But for Sam this was the big moment, his first professional job as a director. His writing, in his eyes, had only been a means to this end. Its importance to him was evident when he arrived on the set for the first day of shooting and was confronted with more than a hundred actors and technicians, all standing and staring vacantly, waiting for him to tell them what to do. Very matter-of-factly, he laid out the first three shots, then excused himself, strolled over to the men's room, and puked his guts out.

Michael Ansara, who played Cochise, recalls: "Sam depended on John Lupton and myself a lot. He would ask us things and we would help him all we could. I'd pull on his little goatee [Sam grew beards then shaved them off again throughout his life] and I'd say, 'Don't worry, little Sam! You'll be fine!' And he was. He did a beautiful job."

Beautiful by "Broken Arrow" standards. About the best that can be said for Peckinpah's first professional effort is that it is no worse than the other episodes in the series. When Jeffords leaves his post as Indian agent, he is replaced with a by-the-book authoritarian and the Chiricahua soon revolt. Sam displayed a knack for camera placement in the action sequences, and in a scene where the Apache raid the agency a tarp is pulled off a stockpile of supplies to reveal a Gatling gun and team of Union soldiers manning it. It was a rough—very rough—sketch for the confrontation between Pike Bishop's gang and General Mapache's soldiers in *The Wild Bunch,* which Sam would shoot some ten years later. And in the final scene, when Cochise and Jeffords go their separate ways, Peckinpah managed to elicit the barest glimmer of true emotion from his two stars.

But most of the battle scenes are badly marred by the blatant mismatch between the Union troops firing from behind rocks in the searing sunlight of a real canyon and the Apache crouched behind papier-maché boulders in a diffusely lit studio. It was about as phony-baloney as you could get. No meteoric talent blazed out from the nation's TV screens when the show aired that spring, no visible signs of an incubating genius.

Still, he was a director now, as well as a writer, with an agent—Peter Sabiston—and a business manager—Bob Schiller—to handle his burgeoning finances.

In the 1950s three independent producers—Jules Levy, Arthur Gardner, and Arnold Laven—joined forces, set up their own company, and signed a deal with United Artists to make low-budget pictures for UA to distribute. The films—*Vice Squad,* starring Edward G. Robinson; *Down Three Dark Streets,* with Broderick Crawford, and *The Rack,* featuring Paul Newman in his first screen appearance—were each shot in fifteen to twenty days at a cost of $350,000 to $400,000. They usually earned twice that at the box office.

"I was very, very close to Levy, Gardner, Laven," says Joe

Mazzuca. "They started me out in the mail room, then made me a script supervisor, and finally a director. Spending money with Levy, Gardner, Laven was a capital crime. They liked to keep the budget tight, real, real tight. They were not out to educate the public or give messages, they just knew what people would buy tickets for. They really had an uncanny ability to do that. It was strictly a business to them. Jules Levy was the wheeler-dealer in the group; he'd make the deals with agents for properties, etc. Arthur Gardner was a very, very good close-to-the-vest administrator, and Arnold Laven was the creative force. He directed all of their features."

Wheeler-dealer Levy had a fast-buck technique for developing "hot" properties: he came up with the title of a movie first, something with enough zing to grab people and yank them into the theater. Like every good huckster, Levy knew that Joe Public did in fact judge a book by its cover and a product by its slogan. In 1956, he came up with one that he knew would hit big: *Custer's Last Stand.*

Levy registered the title with the Writers Guild, as he'd done with dozens of others waiting in his files for screenplays that would one day fulfill their potential. As luck would have it, a novel, *The Dice of God,* was published shortly thereafter; it focused on the events leading up to Custer's fateful battle, concentrating more on the men under his command than on the general himself. Levy quickly snapped up the screen rights and Arnold Laven began shopping for a writer to do the adaptation.

Sam's agent submitted some of his "Gunsmoke" scripts. Laven read them, was impressed, and scheduled an interview with the thirty-one-year-old writer. "I remember meeting Sam," Laven recalls. "There was something about him, the fire in his eyes, the manner. He had a charisma about him, it was a ballsy, macho charisma, a very manly, together kind of guy with an appreciation for good material." Laven liked what Peckinpah had to say about the book and how he would go about adapting it, what he would change and what he wouldn't. On November 5, 1956, Peckinpah was hired to write the screenplay at a salary of $500 a week.

Sam's work on the script extended over a four-and-a-half-month period, interrupted sporadically by television scripts that he continued to hammer out on the side. Jules Levy and Arthur Gardner kept their distance while Arnold Laven, who would eventually direct the film, worked closely with Sam as the finished pages trickled into their production office at the old Hal Roach Studios in Culver City.

"It was clear that we'd made the right choice," says Laven. "The book was a very modestly written book, but we were getting first-rate writing from Sam. He wrote slowly, but the writing had some marvelous stuff that has now set a tone for a lot of westerns: that lean, unkempt, unbathed feeling."

Peckinpah's 154-page screenplay, completed on March 20, 1957, is the work of a young writer grappling to mold complex themes and characters into the framework of an epic tragedy. Already on display is an interest in how the passions, obsessions, and ambitions of individuals can affect the shape of history. But the script also demonstrates that Peckinpah still had a lot of growing up to do. He had already mastered the half-hour show, but was not nearly so adept at constructing a full-length script, though many of the screenplay's weaknesses may have been concessions to the demands of his producers.

The first two-thirds of the screenplay unreel with the predictability of a standard cavalry picture. But in the script's final third the elements that really interest Peckinpah come into sharp focus: the action pulls taut, the interplay among the characters is charged. While Custer is not the protagonist, he is a pivotal character who sets events into motion, and the other characters pause repeatedly to speculate on his motives, morality, and potential madness. Custer fascinated Sam: a Wild West Ahab, leading a band of half-breeds, misfits, and three-time losers on a perilous journey to their own Armageddon; a vain, self-centered glory seeker who wraps himself in the flag, but in reality seeks to liberate nobody and nothing but his own ego.

Peckinpah portrays Custer's elated assault on the Indian village at Little Bighorn as the act of a megalomaniac, yet at the same time he tries to capture the strange thrill of battle that caused the

Seventh Cavalry to follow Custer into the abyss. Peckinpah knew only too well, from his time in the Marine Corps, the many paradoxes of the professional soldier. He too felt a dark attraction for life at the edge of disaster, for it was here that one experienced life at its most extreme, that one lived most intensely. He couldn't help but admire men who rode to their doom with such panache, characters who, as he wrote in his master's thesis, "meet their fate with courage and dignity." *The Dice of God* was the first stumbling exploration of themes that he would return to with far greater refinement and skill in *Major Dundee, The Wild Bunch,* and *Cross of Iron.* (After hiring Peckinpah, Levy discovered that the rights to his original title, *Custer's Last Stand,* were already owned by another production company. *The Dice of God* would eventually be released as the movie *The Glory Guys.*)

The screenplay had not come easy. Sam had sweated and cursed his way through every one of the 154 pages. It had taken him two months to scratch out the first fifty, and then all of his hard work nearly went up in flames.

It was the day before Christmas, 1956, that Sam and Marie looked out the window of the Quonset hut and spotted smoke and then the yellow rippling flames on a distant hilltop. Brushfires were common in the Santa Monica Mountains, especially after the hot Santa Ana winds blasted in from the Mojave Desert in the fall, scorching the high grass and chaparral to brittle kindling. But this one looked small and faraway, and with all the usual excitement of preparing for the magic day it was easy to push concern to the back of their minds.

The writing assignments had fattened Sam's bank account considerably, and for the first time he and Marie had enough money to really do it right. On Christmas Eve Sam splurged on a giant pine tree, so tall he had to trim five feet off the top to get it into the hut.

The next morning Kristen and Sharon awoke to find the towering tree covered with ornaments of every shape and size, and mounds of presents stuffed beneath its branches. After years of living the low-rent life while brother Denny bought himself a sprawling ranch house, complete with swimming pool and pastures for riding horses, it finally looked like little D. Sammy was coming into his own. The girls tittered with delight as they emptied stockings and decimated the wrapping on their presents.

Hot, dry winds blew hard that day. They had local firefighters worried; it had been fourteen years since the last major fire in the Santa Monica Mountains, so there was plenty of dead wood and overgrowth. One carelessly tossed cigarette and those hills would flame up like stack of lighter-fluid-soaked charcoal.

Everyone's worst fears were realized at two A.M. on December 26, when a fire broke out in Newton Canyon. The sixty-miles-per-hour winds funneling through the canyon quickly fanned the flames as high as 250 feet. By dawn they'd burned four miles straight to the sea. Sparks and burning embers floated across Pacific Coast Highway, igniting several houses in the Broad Beach Colony. Firefighters scrambled to mobilize their forces, but by now the fire's draft was so great that it sucked it forward at a tremendous speed, and they were helpless to stop or divert its path; tentacles of flame spread through the adjoining hills and canyons, and Governor Goodwin Knight was forced to declare Malibu a disaster area.

On the morning of December 27, Sam looked out the window of the Quonset hut; to the north, flames were visible just one hill away, licking angrily at the withered grass and shrubs. "If it breaks over that ridge, we're out of here," he said.

But as the day wore on it looked as if the winds and the firefighters had kept the fire from turning toward them. Sam and Marie breathed a tentative sigh of relief. In the mid-afternoon Sam was down in his little basement office, scribbling away on the battered old desk beneath a naked bulb, taking General Custer page by page closer to destruction. Marie didn't feel well and was lying down in her bedroom; Kristen also was taking a nap. Sharon was alone in the living room when she thought she heard a car honk. As was her habit, she leaped up on the bathroom counter to peer out the window at the driveway. She couldn't find her voice. Like strange yellow liquid, the flames rippled and rolled down the ridge of the nearest hill . . . right toward the house. Coming from the south, not the north, where they had been watching for them. "Dad! Dad! Come quick! The fire!" she yelled.

Sam burst out of the basement door, which opened into the yard, and was greeted by smoke already thickening the air around the hut. His eyes snapped to the propane tank he'd been meaning to move away from the house, and then to the jungle of sumac running all along the north wall. They were sitting on a keg of dynamite and in a few minutes the fire would block their escape.

The rest of it played like a movie at high speed. Marie, half-dressed, grabbed Kristen, who wore only underpants. As her mother pounded down the steps toward their station wagon, the three-year-old wiped the sleep from her eyes, then popped wide awake at the sight of fire everywhere. They all piled into the car. Sam and Marie looked at each other, the same thought hitting simultaneously: *Melissa!* Then they remembered that she was spending the night at Walter and Fern Lea's in Santa Monica.

Sam gunned the station wagon up the drive to Rambla Pacifico and headed for Malibu Canyon. "Simbo's puppies!" Sharon shouted. But he kept his foot on the accelerator and turned down Malibu Canyon toward the ocean, assuring his daughter that the animals knew how to survive in a fire.

They made it down to the Malibu General Store, where other families that had been forced to abandon their homes had gathered. They stood together and watched helplessly as the hills above them blazed away. It was only then that Sam remembered the script—two months of agony up in smoke. "Wait here, I've got to go back!" he told Marie through clenched teeth as he leaped back into the wagon. "Don't forget Simbo's puppies, and the cats!" Sharon called after him.

It took him over half an hour to get back up to the Quonset hut. Sheriff's deputies and firefighters were closing down roads, so Sam was forced to take a long circuitous route. By the time he got to the hut the smoke was thick, the flames ripping along through the grass toward the sumac. He burst through the basement door, grabbed the screenplay and an armload of his television scripts. Then, in the hallucinatory chemistry of panic, he thought of Marie standing back at the general store, half-dressed, and sprinted to their bedroom and yanked from the closet the green silk evening dress he'd been able to buy with his recent prosperity. "I wore that dress for a week!" Marie recalls.

Simbo, the family's mutt, and Rita, Sam's weimaraner, had come running up the drive to greet his car, and they were waiting beside it as he hustled out of the hut. He opened the car doors and threw in the scripts and dress. The dogs leaped in after them.

Only on the way down Malibu Canyon did he remember the puppies.

The family spent the next couple of days at Jack Gariss' house in Reseda, waiting for the fire to burn itself out. When it was finally over the flames had decimated sixty-five homes and turned 200 square miles of grassy hills into a tar-black wasteland. Sam sent Marie and the kids up to her parents' house in Fresno, and David Peckinpah—always there in a crisis—drove down with Harold Waddle, a private detective who worked for him on court cases. They drove up Rambla Pacifico with Sam to assess the damage.

It didn't take a trained eye to do that. All that sumac and propane had turned the Quonset hut into an incinerator. They toed their way through the collapsed structure, looking for salvageable remains, but everything was gone. "The only things left were melted down blobs of silverware and glass," says Fern Lea.

The worst for Sharon was the animals. All of the cats except one either ran away or perished. The sole survivor emerged from the blistered landscape, but its feet were so badly burned that it died a few days later. They found the bones of Simbo's puppies all grouped together right where their whelping box had been.

Dad had lied to her; he'd grabbed his scripts instead.

Fortunately Sam had a business manager now to help reassemble the pieces. Malibu had been declared a disaster area, which qualified Sam for a low-interest loan; with that and his growing income he could build a real house on the site of the Quonset hut, or sell that property and move into something closer to the water. Meanwhile he rented a small house on the beach, close to the Malibu Sea Lion.

Sam and Marie threw a "book party" a week or so after they moved in. Friends from Fresno, USC, KLAC, and Sam's film and television work packed into the small house, each arriving with a book, everything from Tolstoy to Zane Grey. It didn't come close to replacing the old collection, but it was a healthy start; besides, at the rate Sam acquired books the family would be buried in them again in no time.

The work continued to pour in. While he was still pounding out TV scripts, another screenwriting assignment fell into Sam's lap. "The word was going around that I was a pretty hot writer," Peckinpah told Garner Simmons. "So Frank Rosenberg, a very good friend of mine and an enormously talented guy himself, gave me this book to read, *The Authentic Death of Hendry Jones*, by a writer named Charles Neider. I loved the book and was then approached to write the screenplay. I did and they paid me, I think, $3,000 [the actual figure was $4,000], which was scale at that time. It took me six months to write it. Most of the time was just getting the thing together. I wrote the last ninety pages in nine days."

Neider's novel was a fictionalized reworking of the final days of Billy the Kid, with William Bonney renamed Hendry Jones and the action set in Northern California instead of the Territory of New Mexico. In retelling the familiar story, Neider explored the gap between reality and myth, and attempted to show the gunfighter's life as it really was: emotionally desolate, wasteful, a path that inevitably led to a bloody dead end.

Peckinpah was fascinated by the book—as he had long been by the Billy the Kid legend itself—and most impressed by the way Neider's prose stretched out the moment of a simple shooting, capturing every detail and nuance of perception and thought on the part of the dying man to explore the horror and ultimate mystery of death. But Peckinpah's adaptation of the novel into a screenplay reveals that his main focus differed sharply from Neider's. He restructured the plot and invented many new scenes that reshaped the narrative into his own interpretation of the Billy the Kid story.

When he became a film director, Peckinpah was often praised (and just as often damned) by critics for demythologizing the American western. This is, in fact, a gross misinterpretation of his work. Clearly Neider's purpose was to demythologize one of the linchpin legends of the Wild West. In his adaptation, Peckinpah kept many of the novel's grim details, but then injected new mythic elements into the story. He used a wealth of realistic detail to bring his fictional universe to life. But his greatest westerns—*Ride the High Country, The Wild Bunch,* and *Pat Garrett and Billy the Kid*—though dark, complex, and intensely disturbing, would all be mythic tragedies.

In his adaptation of *Hendry Jones,* he molded the Kid and the Pat Garrett character—called Dad Longworth by Neider—into archetypes that reflected the conflicting polarities within the American male. The Kid is the embodiment of wild youth, reckless in his pursuit of instant gratification, and oblivious to the pain he inflicts on others and on himself. Dad is that youth grown to middle age, realizing the need for stability, to become part of a family and hold down a respectable job. But giving up the hormone-flushed joys of youth for the confining comforts of domesticity is not easy for most American men.

When Dad kills the Kid at the end of the story, it is his own youth he is murdering, and the power of the tale comes from the recognition by male audience members that they have had or will have to do the same in order to enter a life of stability and maturity. The difference between the book and Sam's adaptation is that Neider plays down these themes and instead focuses on the seedy reality behind the myth; Peckinpah expands and explores the themes, but retains many of Neider's brutal details to give the myth a hard edge of authenticity.

Completed on October 3, 1957, Sam's adaptation of *The Authentic Death of Hendry Jones* demonstrates a remarkable leap in craftsmanship since *The Dice of God* screenplay he completed just six months earlier. Long passages of back story scattered throughout Neider's novel are skillfully converted into tight scenes and moved up earlier in the plot to clarify character relationships and set up the central conflicts. On just his second effort, Peckinpah had mastered the full-length screenplay. Frank Rosenberg loved the finished product and submitted it to Marlon Brando to see if he would be interested in playing the part of the Kid.

A couple of weeks later Peckinpah got a call at home. Brando had read the script and loved it, Rosenberg explained, and he wanted to meet to discuss further rewrites. Sam hung up, his head buzzing like a busy signal—Brando, *the* Marlon Brando, had loved his script!

For about three weeks Peckinpah met with Brando on almost a daily basis. They would talk for hours about the script, and screen westerns together. "Sam was high as a kite," says Marie. "He really thought Brando could do a fantastic job with the character."

One night Brando called the house and invited Marie to a screening—they were going to run another western. Thinking it was Sam doing his imitation, she joshed back, "Well, you know, I've got all these kids here to take care of, it's awful difficult. If I had somebody to help me take care of them, maybe I could." Then she hung up on him.

She laughed and apologized when Sam later told her it had really been Marlon on the phone. It was funny and yet it wasn't, for the incident was the first warning sign of growing tension between them. Marie found herself now left at home to look after the kids while Sam raced off to Marlon's house or Rosenberg's office. He was having an incredible creative experience, seeing his wildest dreams come true, while she was drowning in a sea of diapers. No longer his creative partner, she had fallen somehow into the role of maid and babysitter. In the beginning she hadn't minded giving up her acting to have children, but now she began to miss it terribly and, as she reflected on the course of her marriage, came to realize there had been another reason for backing away from a career of her own. "I think on some level I realized very early on that competing with Sam wasn't safe, that he needed to be the preeminent light."

Brando told Sam he'd found the ideal director for the project, a twenty-nine-year-old filmmaker named Stanley Kubrick who'd worked as a second-unit director on the prestigious television series "Omnibus," and won widespread critical acclaim for a taut crime drama, *The Killing*, in 1956, and a blistering antiwar film, *Paths of Glory*, that had just been released. Peckinpah agreed that Kubrick was an exciting choice and his morale soared to even greater heights when the director signed on to the project. "One night we were home and Sam got a telephone call," says Marie. "His voice was very excited because it was Marlon. I went out of the room and came back a little while later and Sam was just sitting there on the bed, staring into space. I asked him what was wrong and he said Kubrick had wanted to bring his own writer onto the project to do a rewrite of the script. Sam had been fired, just like that it was over. He was devastated."

Hendry Jones had been about one old friend betraying another; now Brando had given Sam his first taste of Hollywood back-stabbing. Kubrick would eventually be fired by Brando and a succession of six other directors and seven writers would come and go before Brando directed the film, *One-Eyed Jacks,* himself. Hardly a trace of Peckinpah's original script remains in the final product. (In Brando's version, the Kid kills Dad Longworth and wins the girl.) "I think there's two sequences of mine in the picture, and I did not receive credit for it," Sam later recalled. In fact, he was denied the opportunity to even read the final script. "Marlon screwed it up," Sam later said. "He's a hell of an actor, but in those days he had to end up as a hero and that's not the point of the story. Billy the Kid was no hero. He was a gunfighter, a real killer."

Peckinpah would have to wait another fifteen years before he'd get another crack at the legend of Billy the Kid. In the meantime, Levy, Gardner, Laven had called. They were having trouble lining up financing for *The Dice of God,* but wanted to talk to him about a pilot for a new western television series. He drove into their production offices in Culver City and listened intently while Jules Levy explained the concept. He'd come up with another sure-fire idea for a hit series; they were going to call it "The Rifleman." What did Sam think? Peckinpah cleared his throat and shifted uneasily. It sounded promising, he said, but what was the story line?

That was the problem, Levy explained. They had hired first one writer, then another, to come up with a teleplay that matched Levy's title. But both scripts stank. Weaker producers might have thrown in the towel; not Jules Levy. He knew he had a big winner with "The Rifleman" and that it was just a matter of finding a writer who could deliver.

"Wait a minute," Sam said, "I've got a story . . . I've got a story at home I wrote a while back, I think it might just work."

"Okay," Levy said, "bring it in."

The script Peckinpah brought in was called "The Sharpshooter." It told the story of an expert marksman who rides into a strange town and enters a shooting contest to earn some extra money. Some of the townspeople recognize him, since he is famous throughout the territory for his skill. They bet all their money on him, but the corrupt saloon keeper who controls the town has bet his money on one of his hired gunmen. Just before the sharpshooter is to take his turn at the target, the saloon keeper gestures to his group of armed henchmen and suggests to the expert that it would be better for his health if he missed. Knowing he cannot outgun them all, the marksman misses the target on the final round, and rides out of town, his head hung in shame.

"That was the end of the story," says Arnold Laven. "Not unlike the kind of story Sam would do on "The Westerner," the cynicism and the reality placed against the romantic image of the West. We loved the writing, but the ending, you just couldn't get that sponsored in 1958. I don't know if you could get it sponsored today, to tell you the truth—a guy who doesn't have the courage of the West, to stand up for what is right."

So Laven came up with way to make the pilot more commercial. "If you inject a boy, give the rifleman a son, and give him a reason for being in the contest—say he wants to use the prize money for a down payment on a ranch for him and his boy—then if the threat is made against the boy's life instead of the rifleman's, I dare anybody in television to say that he should risk his son's life in the interest of putting the bad guys in place. His decision to throw the contest is completely justified."

Peckinpah responded to the proposed revision with enthusiasm—at least outwardly. "That's a hell of an idea!" he said, and quickly set about rewriting his script.

Undoubtedly at Laven's suggestion, he also added a climactic shootout in which, unable to live with the shame of having thrown the match, the rifleman, Lucas McCain, marches down the main street of the town, twirling his Winchester into the ready position, and pushes through the swinging doors of the Last Chance Saloon for a final shootout with the gang of bad guys. He dispatches all six without receiving so much as a scratch in return. It was pure Zane Grey melodrama, with the sentimental strain of a boy's love for his Pa thrown in to soften the mayhem. Levy, Gardner, Laven knew it would sell big in Middle America, and Sam had to admit to himself that he had a genuine flair for such hokum. The boy who had thrilled to the antics of Tom Mix and Ken Maynard in Fresno's downtown movie theaters was still alive and well within him.

But what makes the pilot of "The Rifleman" unique and fascinating is the way Peckinpah managed to infuse the story with highly personal references that give it a strong and genuine emotional undercurrent. Take, for instance, the very opening scene:

Lucas McCain and his son, Mark, ride over the crest of a grassy hill and down into the shade of a sprawling oak. They gaze into the valley below, where a scattering of cattle are grazing. It is the landscape of Sam Peckinpah's youth, the rolling hills of central California, just south of Yosemite.

"Well," McCain says, "it's new and mighty fine country, son."

The boy turns to glance back at the hill behind them.

"There's no lookin' back," McCain says, "we've come too far."

Mark drops his eyes to his saddle horn. "I wasn't really lookin' back, I was just rememberin' back."

McCain expresses something painful but long-unspoken on his stoic face, then quickly subdues it. "What do you say we start from here?"

Mark smiles, relieved. "Fine!"

They ride down into the valley and come upon an empty white farmhouse with a creek-stone chimney and a dilapidated picket fence. Beside it stands a sign:

For Sale
Dunlap Ranch
4100 Acres
See Judge Hanavan
North Fork

McCain dismounts, pulls up a fistful of the long-stemmed grass, and smells it. "How does the spread look to you?" he calls over to Mark.

Mark, running some stray cattle out of the front yard with his pony, calls back, "Looks good!"

McCain smiles warmly. "It looks good to me too. All right then, I guess we've come far enough."

The boy smiles too, and hollers, "All right!"

Sam was regaining in fiction what was lost to him forever in fact. And this time the troubling presence of a woman who might one day sell the ranch had been expunged—though not without a backward glance of regret. Now it was just the two of them, father and son, in their cowboy paradise. But Lucas McCain would turn out to be a strangely schizophrenic creation; one moment an idealistic fantasy father—strong, resilient, a patient teacher, a wise and comforting guide in times of crisis—the next moment a bloodthirsty murderer. When "pushed to the brink" (which happened every show), he unleashed a one-man Armageddon that stacked bodies faster than a Central American firing squad. It was a caricature vision of the polarities within Sam's own father, David, polarities Sam himself had inherited.

"It was a terrific script," says Arnold Laven, "head and shoulders above anything else on the market."

The William Morris Agency, which represented Levy, Gardner, and Laven and pioneered the strategy of packaging movie and television projects out of its own talent pool, took the pilot script for "The Rifleman" to another client, Dick Powell, head of Four Star Productions. Four Star—founded by Powell, Charles Boyer, and David Niven and with Ida Lupino as a host—produced dramatic anthology series such as "Four Star Playhouse" and "Zane Grey Theater," which featured a new half-hour western every week.

Powell took "The Rifleman" script to Tom MacDermott, an executive with Benton and Bowles, one of the most powerful advertising agencies in New York. This was still the era when a single sponsor would buy all the commercial time for a particular show, essentially financing the production. Most major sponsors relied on advertising firms like Benton and Bowles to pick a winning series—which made the ad agencies, not the networks, the real power in television.

A high-level advertising executive like MacDermott (who had lined up a sponsor for "Make Room for Daddy") could get a new program on the air in a remarkably short period of time. In the case of "The Rifleman," it took less than a month. MacDermott read the script, loved it, lined up Procter and Gamble as the sponsor, and three weeks later Arnold Laven was directing the pilot for Four Star's "Zane Grey Theater." Before the pilot had even aired, MacDermott had bought the show as a regular series. Today, with the Kafkaesque layers of bureaucracy that choke the decision-making process at the major networks, it is unimaginable that a show could move from initial conception to the public airways in so short a time. "The history of 'The Rifleman' is probably as remarkable as anything else that had occurred before or since in television," says Arnold Laven.

Laven cast Chuck Connors—a former baseball player—as the tall and strong-jawed lead, and Johnny Crawford as his son, Mark. Laven also came up with a special gimmick for the Rifleman's Winchester: a notch on the cocking lever that would allow him to cock and fire the weapon almost simultaneously, slamming bullets out faster than a submachine gun.

"The Rifleman" shot its way to the number-two spot in the Nielsen ratings and hovered there for most of its first season. All across America, kids dragged reluctant parents into toy stores and forced them to fork over greenbacks for a genuine Lucas McCain Winchester, complete with the automatic firing notch on the cocking lever.

"I remember Sam calling me into his office once," says Robert Heverly, a writer who would work on Peckinpah's next series, "The Westerner." "He said, 'Bob, I wrote a "Rifleman" that aired last week . . . It was number one in the country . . . number one in the whole *world!'* "

Now the money really started rolling in. Sam had been paid $1,900 for the pilot and his deal with Levy, Gardner, Laven that first season was to write scripts—a total of six, averaging $1,500 apiece, depending on whether or not he worked with a collaborator—and to act as a story consultant, which meant developing scripts with other writers. For his hand in creating the show, he would get 7.5 percent of the net profits, plus $125 for every episode produced whether he wrote them or not.

Suddenly he found himself thrust into the round-the-clock hell schedule of a weekly television series. Forty episodes were produced the first season. Sam lost no time recruiting a stable of writers; among them two of his old Fresno Staters, Don Levy and Jack Curtis, and a new discovery, Bruce Geller, a Yale graduate who had sold a few television scripts before coming into Sam's orbit.

During the first season, in which Peckinpah played a major creative role, "The Rifleman" episodes unfolded like chapters in an ongoing story. Characters grew and relationships continued to evolve; events in early episodes affected developments in later ones. This runs contrary to the formula for most episodic television shows, in which conflicts are introduced at the opening and then neatly resolved a half-hour or hour later when the segment ends, never to be referred to again. Making each show a self-contained unit enables stations to rerun them in any reshuffled order with no loss of continuity, but the result is that the series' regular characters become static stereotypes with a numbingly predictable set of mannerisms and responses to any given situation.

Peckinpah pushed for a more daring approach. He envisioned the show continuously unfolding the "story of a boy [Mark] who grows to manhood learning what it's all about." But Levy, Gardner, Laven pushed just as strongly in the opposite direction. They wanted the show to stay within the boundaries of a standard television western. At first Sam settled for partial victories: getting a subtle touch in here, an ironic nuance there. But in time the continual compromises would begin to rub him raw.

The scripts Sam wrote himself are peppered with the same personal references that had helped the pilot transcend its melodrama: the nearest town is named North Fork; McCain's farmhouse is burned to the ground by the gunmen of a land-hungry cattle baron, echoing the life experiences of Moses Church; McCain rallies his son's spirits by telling a Wild West version of the story of Job, one of David Peckinpah's favorite passages from the Bible, which he often recited to his children in times of crisis; Mark spends a night alone in the wilderness, just as Denver Church had forced a young D. Sammy to do, and the boy conquers his fear of the dark and the creatures that rustle in it.

And there are many examples of classic Peckinpah dialogue: "You're going to have to get a lot closer to make that scattergun pay for its freight"; "You can't buy it for money, marbles, or chalk"; "If those boys went to sleep and let the herd scatter, I'll pin their hides to the wall usin' their teeth for nails!"

Present also are the Peckinpah archetypes, slowly fleshing out into living and breathing human beings. The half-mad preacher reappears in "The Baby Sitter," this time under the name of Wood Bartell, a giant fanatic who roams the West preaching abstinence, forbearance, and the glory of transcending the tawdry pleasures of the flesh. But in his fat right hand he carries a long phallic bullwhip that he snaps deep into the diseased flesh of the "wicked." (He's particularly fond of snapping half-naked dance-hall girls.)

In another episode, "The Marshal," we are introduced to the Shelton brothers, the first of many such rabid jackals—the Hammond and Gorch brothers, T. C. and Coffer, Taggart and Bowen, Hedden, Venner, and Scutt—who would trot through Peckinpah's landscape in search of fresh meat. When a hotel clerk asks the Sheltons to sign the register, Andrew sneers, "We ain't spellin' men!" Before McCain blows them away at the show's climax, they manage to reduce the town's saloon to kindling and shattered glass *twice*, by brawling not with strangers but each other.

Peckinpah was fascinated by the perverse vitality of such characters, and lavished on them much more attention and humanity than he ever did to the steel-girder figure of Lucas

McCain. He had begun to break down the stereotypes of TV westerns by introducing villains who were more complex, interesting, even sympathetic than the clench-jawed heroes who gunned them down.

Sam pushed Levy, Gardner, Laven hard for a chance to direct some of "The Rifleman" shows himself. His only professional directing credit was the one hideous episode of "Broken Arrow." To show them what he was capable of, he ran the kinescope of *Portrait of a Madonna* at the studio screening room; "The Pep Boys," as Sam was now fond of calling them behind their backs, were impressed enough to give him a chance.

Arnold Laven offered to help Peckinpah prepare for his first show. Laven was no artist, but he was an accomplished craftsman. His "Rifleman" episodes, with their dynamic camera angles and editing, moved like greased lightning and made "Gunsmoke" look feeble and arthritic. "We talked about [camera] coverage and ways to attack a scene, how the first shot is always the lead-in to how to move with a scene," says Laven. "The idea was to give him a facility and visual pattern, scene by scene, so that he could get the day's work done by having had a mental preparation for what he wanted to accomplish. In television there's no time to let the actors explore a scene before you pick your camera angles. You have to pick your camera angles out ahead of time, then direct the actors' movements to the camera. I sensed as I was saying these things that they filtered through Sam's sensibility. He didn't follow my suggestions verbatim, because he obviously had his own ideas."

The first "Rifleman" Peckinpah directed was "The Marshal," which introduced the Paul Fix character as a series regular, and featured R. G. Armstrong, Warren Oates, and James Drury in supporting roles. Oates, a former marine, had been born in a Kentucky coal-mining town; Armstrong was raised on a farm in Alabama; Drury came from a ranch in Oregon. All, like Peckinpah himself, had strong personal links to rural America. They knew the people who lived on America's ranches and farms, from the owners to the hired hands—how they walked, talked, ate, hated, and loved. They brought to their roles an authenticity and raw emotionalism that Sam expertly wove into the fabric of his films. Peckinpah's stock company was beginning to solidify; Armstrong and Oates would appear again in "The Westerner" and in four Peckinpah features, and Drury would join both actors in *Ride the High Country.*

Sam's growth as a director by just his second television show was remarkable. He had obviously studied Laven's suggestions carefully; "The Marshal" has all the tightly paced assurance of his teacher's work, plus a distinctive style that is immediately recognizable. "Sam's 'Rifleman' shows had an inherent underlying violence," says Laven. "Every episode of the show was filled with violence, guys shooting everybody in sight, but it was normally done in a way that was so typical to TV westerns that it wasn't street violence, it wasn't real violence. There was something unreal when the Rifleman would shoot three guys, there was a pattern it stayed within. But Sam made it much more deadly, much more palpable, much more real. It was a little unsettling for 'The Rifleman,' that was really not the quality of the show."

Most TV directors were content to shoot an episode of a series and move on to the next assignment without so much as a glance back at the editing room, but Peckinpah followed his shows through the entire post-production process. He'd worked briefly as an assistant editor at CBS in the early fifties, when he was trying to make the break from KLAC, so he had some familiarity with Moviolas and slicing tape. He watched the editors put his "Rifleman" episodes together, noted the choices they made and why, asked judicious questions, and made a few suggestions of his own.

"Sam seemed to be a very determined person, very, very knowledgeable for someone new to the business," says Mike Klein, who worked as an assistant editor on "The Rifleman" and later on many of the Peckinpah features. "When I saw some of his work as a director I really felt that he was very talented and could go a long way in the business. I really liked the way he used the camera, especially. The directors on 'The Rifleman' were just starting to use the zoom lens; in fact the whole business was starting to get into the zoom lens. Sam used it very well when he really wanted to put a stinger on something; he'd zoom right into a close-up of Chuck Connors. You could really see the difference in Sam's shows. He was an extremely creative man."

The money from "The Rifleman," along with payments from the insurance company and the low-interest disaster-assistance loan after the Quonset hut fire and the proceeds from the sale of the property the hut sat on, finally provided Sam with enough cash to make a down payment on a $40,000 house in the Malibu Colony. It might have been sun-weathered, wind-beaten, termite-infested, but he'd gotten his house on the beach at last. The back doors of Number Ninety-seven in the Colony opened onto a wide white beach and an expanse of blue water that glistened on a sunny day like polished chrome. The corrosive effects of smog, sewage, and toxic runoff were still two decades away; the Peckinpahs were now living smack in the middle of the California paradise.

Like most of the other houses, Number Ninety-seven had been built in the thirties. After three decades of sun, wind, and salty air, it looked like a medium-sized earthquake would bring it tumbling to the ground. But after the Quonset hut the house seemed positively palatial. There was a fireplace in the living room and French windows that looked out on the beach, a built-in barbecue and a small guest house that Sam converted into an office. He would hole up in there for days at a time, sweating out scripts, Marie bringing him his meals and keeping the distractions of the outside world at bay.

For the kids, at first, the Colony was heaven on earth. They spent the long sun-drenched afternoons daring one another to higher and higher leaps off the lifeguard towers, carving tunnels into the sandstone bluffs, and constructing labyrinthian "towel houses" out of beach blankets and deck chairs.

The Colony was a paradise for the adults too, at first. Sam wasted no time throwing himself into water sports. First came bodysurfing, then he bought a ten-foot-long balsawood surfboard and paddled awkwardly out through the churning foam to take on the worst the ocean could throw at him. Afterward he would rhapsodize to Walter Peter about the thrills of hanging ten, riding the shoulder, doing a 360, "the Paul Stroud," and "getting inside the green room."

"Only trouble was," says Walter Peter, "I'd just seen him floundering around out there a couple of minutes before and it didn't exactly mesh with what he was describing to me."

Then Sam discovered scuba diving, and a whole new universe of hunting opened up to him. Instead of a rifle he carried a spear gun; instead of deer, he now stalked rock cod, halibut, and moray eels. The emerald waters off Malibu were teeming with life in those years—tuna, golden garibaldi, hundreds of anchovies swimming together like schools of switchblades, barracuda, bonito, dolphins, seals and sea lions, blue sharks, leopard sharks, and an occasional great white or gray whale. Sam, Walter, and Norman Powell, a production manager at Four Star, took scuba lessons from a stuntman, Paul Stader, who doubled for Lloyd Bridges on the hit TV series, "Sea Hunt." "Sam was fearless, but he wasn't a good diver," says Stader. "He was adequate, but you wouldn't want him in deep water; he wasn't a strong enough swimmer."

"I remember walking along the beach there in the Colony," says actor Brian Keith, "and I saw this house, and there's Marie out in front with another lady, getting a fire ready, and there was Sam coming in out of the water with a big lobster in his hand." Marie barbecued the fish and lobster, pounding the abalone into steaks or chowder, or sliced it thin and marinated it with vinegar and onions. Memories of those meals on the beach still make the Peckinpah girls' mouths water.

But as time wore on, their picture-postcard life began to yellow and curl up around the corners. Sam was drinking almost every night now, and getting seriously drunk most weekends. Walter Peter, Frank Kowalski, Norman Powell, and other guests congregated there on Saturdays and Sundays, and alcohol provided the rocket-propellant for their dizzy flights of "crazy nonsense." Sam bought one of the first stereos to come on the hi-fi market, and with it a sound-effects record. He insisted on turning the record up to full volume so it seemed as if a freight train, jet airliner, or the Indianapolis 500 were roaring through the living room. "He played it constantly, over and over and over," says Marie. "He insisted that every new guest experience the full effect. I was going crazy!"

Walter was the chief rocket scientist, steadfast at the launching pad: the kitchen blender. He cranked the blades into a high whine and poured forth into eagerly extended glasses high-octane strawberry, banana, and peach margaritas. The blender's blades cut deep into the early-morning hours until the body count scattered across the living room was truly appalling. When all of the "flotsam and jetsam" had been cleared away, there was often only three of them left. Sam, Walter, and Frank slouched in deck chairs around the barbecue out back. Walter doing imitations of transvestite German generals, letting loose high-pitched whistles and his battle cry, "I think we're gaining on them!" just before he burst into a chorus of glass-rattling opera. Meanwhile Sam and Frank honed their Bela Lugosi imitations to a fine edge, repeating their favorite line from *Dracula* over and over again like a mantra: "Lisssten to them! Childrrren of the night! Vat music zey make!"

But more and more often now there were the ferocious outbursts of rage that left all who witnessed them in a state of trembling bewilderment.

Melissa, then four years old, had already learned to sense the atmosphere the instant her father entered the room. If he was in a bad mood she knew to either leave or blend in with the furniture. "I found his shouting not nearly as frightening as when he got quietly angry and talked through his teeth," she says. "That always seemed more ominous to me, 'cause you could feel all the rage building up inside him, but it wasn't coming out."

Melissa hated to cut her nails, because her fingertips tingled afterward and gave her goose bumps. So Marie let her grow them long, which infuriated Sam. He kept threatening to cut her nails off with a knife, and one day he grabbed her hand and yelled, "All right, Marie, get me the knife!" Melissa burst into tears. He cut them off with a pair of scissors instead, but she sobbed all the way through it.

He never did worse than spank his daughters, open-handedly across the butt, but there were some close calls. "He started to get violent once with one of the girls while disciplining her," says Marie. "I can't remember which one it was. I intervened and he stopped immediately. I think it scared him. He quit drinking for a few days and was apologetic, but then he started to drink again."

At one of the beach barbecues the "crazy nonsense" took an abruptly disturbing turn. The blender had been revving in high gear since early afternoon and now it was dusk, the stars just beginning to pop out over the stretch of sand behind the house and the foamy crash of waves beyond it. Walter and Frank Kowalski targeted Sam for one of the oldest high school pranks in the book: Frank engaged Sam in conversation while Walter snuck around and got on his hands and knees behind him. Without warning, Frank gave Sam a shove. His feet flew out from under him and he landed hard. Frank and Walter cackled with glee until Sam leapt up, spitting sand. Eyes white all around, he plowed into Kowalski with both fists swinging.

The two men fought and wrestled backward across the sand, crashing into the side of the house and breaking a window. Glass flew everywhere. Robert Culp, who was there that day, came upon the two just as the fight broke up. "Sam, who had blood all over him, was walking back into the house and Frank was following him, saying, 'Sam, come on, don't you understand, I love you, man, I love you!' Sam cussed him out and went off to his bedroom and Marie went with him, and I guess my wife and I beat a hasty retreat. Suffice it to say that the booze did flow that evening and none of us were feeling any pain, I guess, except Sam."

But Sam's drinking wasn't the sole source of tension. It had been three years since Marie last worked as an actress, in a two-minute scene with a couple of lines in *Invasion of the Body Snatchers.* Sam was happy to throw her an occasional bone—he would give her a couple of bit parts on "The Westerner"—but he discouraged any thoughts of seriously pursuing a career. Little by little, Marie felt, he had manipulated her into the role of a domestic servant. Despite all his reading and artistic sensitivity and sophistication, he still believed—as his father and grandfathers had—that a woman's place was in the home, making her husband happy and looking after the kids.

When Sam took off on one of his ten-day hunting trips, he forbade Marie to go out to dinner or other social events, explaining that he would "worry about her." Fern Lea found his hypocrisy outrageous. "Sam would, I'm sure, deny it, but the way he was with Marie was just like my mother was with our father: controlling, possessive. Mom didn't know how to give and take in a marriage, how to sit down and talk about each other's needs and work things out. She never learned how, and neither did Sam. Neither did Marie, for that matter."

Sam had always ridiculed Hollywood's phony glamour and garish pretensions, and he still claimed to feel contempt for "the industry" and the society it fostered. He was in it for the art, not a Beverly Hills mansion with a private screening room, tennis courts, and a swimming pool. He wanted to make films, not movies, he cared about the quality of his work, not the dinners at Chasen's, the breakfasts at the Polo Lounge or the parties up on Mulholland Drive.

But Marie had noticed how, little by little, the town had changed him. First with the parties at Charles Marquis Warren's home, then Brando's, and now at the homes of dozens of people she didn't even know. People who were eager to meet the hot young writer who had created "The Rifleman." A crowd of glittering strangers who turned on neon smiles as if by flicking a switch inside their heads. Smiles they switched off again the minute they discovered you weren't "in the business," but were just a nobody, a housewife who used to act in college at Fresno State; they flicked off the charm and saved the wattage for someone worth expending it on, and politely excused themselves to go "freshen up" their martinis. Marie dreaded such affairs, but Sam insisted they go since he needed to make the contacts—contacts were how you got your next job, heard about a hot property, met someone who might give you a hand up to the next rung on the ladder.

Suddenly it became very important that Marie wear the right thing when they went out—no more Mother Hubbard dresses—

and when they drove home from the parties he had nothing but criticism for her. "You never mingle. For chrissake, why can't you talk to people?"

"But Sam, I didn't know a single person there."

"So? Start up a conversation. Talk about a movie you liked, talk about the goddamned weather, just get a conversation started. Is that too much to ask?"

Finally she did manage to sustain a conversation at one of the parties. She talked with a prominent screenwriter for nearly two hours. But instead of the praise she'd hoped for on the ride home, she got: "What the hell did you stand there talking to him all night for? Don't you know how to mix? Walk around, talk to different people. It's called mingling."

"He was so eager to impress these people," Marie says with a dry laugh. "I found it . . . disgusting."

Marie took the same lax approach to housecleaning that she had had at the Quonset hut. Periodically she would go on a manic cleaning spree and afterward the place would gleam for about a week before it made another slow descent into its natural state of dishevelment. Sam had never seemed to mind this when they were living in the Quonset hut, but at the Colony, with Robert Culp, Brian Keith, Chuck Connors, Levy, Gardner, Laven, and other Hollywoodites dropping by for dinner, he began to complain bitterly. He was tired of coming home to a pigsty. Was it too much to ask, after spending sixteen hours at the studio, that when he came home there would at least be some goddamned ice in the freezer? Just what the hell was she doing with herself all day anyway?

Marie's response, it seemed to friends, was passive-aggressive. The more Sam complained, the more she slacked off on the cleaning. When they first moved in, Marie had started to redecorate the house. She redid the living room, but then the project petered out. The hallway never got wallpaper, the sceptic tank for the guest house was never repaired. It seemed symbolic in a way. The home was never completed, and soon after they moved in things started to disintegrate.

Sharon missed the Quonset hut. She'd been happy there. At

one point she said to her father, "Isn't it sad the hut had to burn down?"

Sam dismissed the thought with a curt response. "Oh, the grass is always greener on the other side."

When Melissa was eighteen months old, Marie noticed her daughter had grown lethargic and that her lymph glands were swollen. She took her to an eyes, ears, nose and throat specialist, who discovered that the child's head was bulging in several spots. Could be a brain tumor, could be leukemia, he speculated, and sent Melissa to Santa Monica Hospital for tests. Eventually her illness was diagnosed as a rare bone disease that inhibited the plates of the skull from growing together properly. The doctors worried at first that it might be fatal, then decided that it wasn't, and Melissa was put on cortisone treatments to arrest the disease's development. Over the next two years she would go into the hospital three times for stays ranging from five days to three weeks.

Marie would visit her daughter every day, consulting with the doctors, sitting by Melissa's bedside reading stories, taking her for rides through the halls on a wheelchair, and settling her down for the night with her special blanket and a few favorite toys. "The worst was when I would first arrive," says Marie, "she would immediately start crying, and cry and cry and cry, for about an hour. I think she was angry at having to be there."

But Sam never went to visit his youngest daughter, not once.

When Marie arrived home from her visits, he would grill her. "What did the doctor say, what's the prognosis? Did you ask him if there are any other treatments we could try?"

Finally Marie would blow up. "Why don't you go there yourself if you want to know?"

He'd avert his eyes and mumble, "I can't face it."

"She's asking for you. What am I supposed to tell her?"

"I can't go. I couldn't stand to see her like that."

"When Melissa came home from the hospital he would welcome her very warmly," says Marie, "but then ignore her. When she had to go back in again, he gave me a book by Mary Baker Eddy, the Christian Scientist, and insisted I sit down and read it. I read a few pages and got so mad I threw it at him. He didn't blow up; instead he reacted sheepishly. That surprised me."

The marriage was strangling both of them, and both began to look for relief elsewhere. Marie turned to her neighbors—the Taylors, the Littlejohns, and the Kleins. They'd meet for barbecues on the beach, parties for the kids, or, more and more often, for dinners at Marie's house. "Sam would come home late from the studio, exhausted," says Fern Lea, "and there would be a house full of people. There was no opportunity for him to just relax and unwind." After bearing three children, Marie had put on some weight and her blond hair had darkened, but her legs were still shapely and her large hazel eyes and warm manner attracted a number of men, both married and unmarried. She took scuba-diving lessons from one of her neighbors—Sam would never teach her—and the fact that she could master the sport injected a new sense of confidence into her veins. She wasn't completely helpless after all. There were no sexual infidelities, but for the first time the possibility raised its head.

As the creator of a hit television series with his own office on the Four Star lot, Sam Peckinpah had no trouble finding attractive young starlets who were eager to hop into bed with him. Women really went for this young writer-director with the elegant little mustache and strangely penetrating eyes. As in grade school, he stood out as a dapper dresser. He smoked with a long black-lacquered cigarette holder and could wear an ascot or a beret without looking the slightest bit foolish. There was a strong aura of masculinity about him, the unmistakable odor of a man on his way to the top. Money, mansions, fast cars, and sexual conquests—these were the measurements of manhood in Hollywood, just as shooting a four-point buck or bulldogging a steer had been at Dunlap's.

"One time Sam and I were driving around L.A.," says Don Levy, "and he said to me, 'You know, Don, I've never been unfaithful to Marie when she's been in town.' I thought: my God, what kind of a weird rationalization is that?"

Nancy Galloway, one of Peckinpah's string of typists in those days, recalls: "We were working alone together at the studio on a

'Rifleman' script one Saturday morning. Probably Sam had had way too much to drink the night before, because he suddenly started shaking uncontrollably. I got very concerned that I was going to have to call the hospital. He said, 'It's all the guilt coming home to roost.' He got past it, but it was a terrible moment. I really thought he was going to collapse on me. We had some fruit and that seemed to help him, and he never mentioned it again."

Hunting up in the High Country offered the only real sustained relief from his domestic entanglements: a chance to blow the pipes out, to leave all the complications and frustrations of home and Hollywood far behind. Every fall he took off for the High Sierras with the "Walker River Boys"—his dad, brother Denny, and a group of lawyers and judges from Fresno and Madera counties, so named because they began hunting as a group along the east fork of the Walker River in the Sweetwater Mountains of northeastern California. By the mid-fifties their preferred hunting grounds were the Shell Creek Mountains outside of Ely in eastern Nevada. (The hills around the old Dunlap spread had been hunted out long before.) For the next twenty years the Walker River Boys would leave civilization behind for a week or ten days every fall; it became a treasured ritual, Sam's one great obsession outside of filmmaking.

Walter Peter was initiated into the tribe shortly after marrying Fern Lea. Working as a stockbroker in Los Angeles, Walter was still struggling to make ends meet, so for the first several years Sam paid for all of his expenses on the trips. "Obviously the trips meant a hell of a lot to Sam," says Peter. "He would start talking about the trip in the middle of summer. 'Think you will be able to make the trip this year?' Hell, the trip wasn't until either October or November. Sam and I hunted together on my first trip. He took me under his wing because I was a pea-green rookie."

They left their base camp at 5,000 feet and moved another 5,000 feet up to stalk the deer through the highest peaks. Walter watched the way Sam moved with such patient stealth through the timber, his big eyes moving constantly back and forth across the terrain. Sam, as Ben Johnson puts it, "hunted like an Indian."

"Sam pointed out something that his grandfather had taught

him," says Peter. "He said to me, 'Do you realize that with every step you take your perspective changes? You take one step, you look, you take another step and your point of view changes.' "

Radical shifts in perspective, the same event viewed from a dizzying variety of camera angles—this would become Peckinpah's signature style as a director.

Late that first day, as the sun was setting behind the nearest peaks, Walter flushed a three-point buck and Sam plugged him. By the time they finished gutting the animal and hoisting it up in a tree for retrieval the next day, it was dark and they still had a couple of miles to hike back to camp. It took them forty-five minutes, and by the time they arrived it was pitch-black.

"Sam's happy, got a nice big buck," says Peter. "But when we get there, the old man, Dave Peckinpah, is furious. 'You took this green rookie and you kept him after sunset! He could have broken a leg and you could have . . .' He really let Sam have it for at least twenty minutes, maybe half an hour. He took off the first layer of skin and he took off the second layer of skin. He wasn't using swear words. He would say: 'I didn't raise you this way!' Sam knew that what he had done wasn't smart, and he never said one bloody word. His head was down and he just took it. I can't think of any other time where I saw Sam's head drop. When Dave was finished that was it. Nothing else was ever said."

Sam stalked more than deer in the badlands of Nevada. Equally as mouth-watering was the opportunity to hit every backwater saloon and whorehouse that dotted the two black-topped lanes of Highway 6 as it sliced its way across the state. These establishments catered to truck drivers and local cowboys and were, says Walter Peter, "Cruddy, dirty, dark. But they had a charm, they really did." Wood floors, low pressed-tin ceilings, oilcloths on the tables, the bare walls devoid of decor except for perhaps a tacked-up mimeograph of the local high school football schedule, or faded photos of forgotten riders in long-ago rodeos. With enough whiskey you could almost believe you'd stepped back into the Wild West.

Here the muscles finally unknotted in Sam's chest and shoulders; he could breath deeper, more easily, freer. Marie, the kids and Hollywood were a thousand miles and a hundred years away. He was lost, blissfully lost. Often these stops "for ammo" lasted days. They'd crank up the jukebox if the little joint had one, play poker, and swap tall tales with the old timers. They'd take turns passing out, sprawled across a table or right on the floor; waking up hours later, they'd stagger back to the bar and start right in drinking again.

If David Peckinpah accompanied them to any of the bars, it was only for a single drink before heading back to California. But he no longer reprimanded his sons for imbibing. Having given up hope of curbing their appetite for liquor and low living long ago, he now dismissed it with a "boys-will-be-boys" attitude. But the whorehouses—the Green Lantern, the Big Four, Bobby's Buckeye—he would never go near. "I'm not in need of their services," David would say stiffly, parting company with the rest as they enthusiastically stormed the front doors.

"We got to know the people well," says Walter Peter. "They knew us and trusted us 'cause we came through there every year for almost twenty years. You got in there and you felt comfortable and you wanted to party and, boy, we did many times. Many times this would happen: we'd come in around one A.M. and they were feeling pretty good and they'd shut the joint down. Nobody else could come in; they turned the whole place over to the Walker River Boys."

David Peckinpah took his last hunting trip in the fall of 1960. Now sixty-five but still as lean as he was in his twenties, he had recently been appointed a Superior Court judge in Madera County. After they got their deer that year, Sam and Denny were finally able to persuade their father to venture into the Green Lantern. "Just come in and have a drink, you'll get a kick out of it!"

"All right, I'll have a drink, but that's *it.*"

Inside, they all bellied up to the bar. Denny and Sam introduced one of the girls to David and told her he was a Superior Court judge. Her mascara-ringed eyes popped wide. "Are you really?"

"Yes, ma'am," David replied, embarrassed but titillated.

"Well, goddamn!" the girl exclaimed, walking around the

bar and plopping right down in his lap. "This is the first time I've ever been on the same side of the bar with a judge, with an honest-to-goodness judge!"

"David laughed, he loved it," says Peter. "He had maybe one hard drink and a ginger ale or something. He never got drunk, but he loved the camaraderie."

It was a sweet moment. Even the old man was able to free himself of constrictions in these high-mountain saloons. For the first time ever, perhaps, David seemed more like friend than an authority figure, someone you could joke with, look directly at instead of up to, love instead of respect and fear.

4

The Bastard Son of John Ford

Sam Peckinpah now had that house in the Colony that he used to fantasize about. The creator of a hit series, he was regarded by the industry as one of the most talented writer-directors in television. The money and offers were rolling in. He had nowhere to go but up.

But no sooner did he grab hold of his dreams than they began to slip through his fingers. Far greater professional triumphs waited for him in the coming decade, but never again would he know the naive optimism and zeal of the late fifties, when his career first began to take off. In later years every triumph would be stained by a personal catastrophe, by the memories of all he'd lost along the way.

Yet, ironically, it was the piling up of personal tragedies over the next three years that gave him the raw material to make the transition from a talented craftsman to a genuine artist. This was the beginning of a fascinating and often chilling dance between his life and art that would accelerate over time, until the two partners became indistinguishable.

By the spring of 1959, Peckinpah's relationship with the producers of "The Rifleman" had become severely strained. The compromises that he had made eagerly during the early development of the series frustrated and angered him now that the show's ratings and his own reputation had soared.

The conflict really began to escalate when Sam started to direct some episodes himself. "Sam's main problem was taking too long to create little ideas that he had," says Jules Levy. "He spent hours setting up complicated camera angles for scenes that should have taken much less time to shoot. We had to bring the shows in on a budget of $38,500 per show, and Sam consistently went over budget. That was the cause of all our arguments with him."

Even Sam's relationship with Arnold Laven—the most benign of the "Pep Boys"—began to turn sour when Laven continued to insist on sanding all the rough edges off the scripts to keep them within the comfortable confines of TV melodrama. "A lot of the things that Sam wrote were a little unsettling for 'The Rifleman,' " says Laven. "They were really not right for the show. There was an oil-and-water mix between him and my partners, in personality, in a number of ways. As much as my partners admired [him] and knew Sam was a great talent, they didn't necessarily admire or go along with Sam's singular philosophic point of view. He saw the show as more cynical than my partners did."

Peckinpah later told Garner Simmons: "I walked from the series because Jules Levy and that group had taken over my initial concept and perverted it into pap. They wouldn't let Johnny [Crawford, who played McCain's son] grow up. They refused to let it be the story of a boy who grows to manhood learning what it's all about."

Walking away from a hit series might have seemed rash, but Peckinpah was being courted by Dick Powell, the head of Four Star. Powell offered to set Sam up with his own office and staff to produce more pilots for "Zane Grey Theater." If one of them caught on, Sam could have a series of his own. This time he would be his own producer, calling all the shots, with no Jules Levy or Arnold Laven peering over his shoulder. Success or failure would rest entirely on him, and the prospect was both thrilling and terrifying. He accepted Powell's offer, resigned from his position as story consultant on "The Rifleman," and moved into an office on Four Star's new lot in the San Fernando Valley, formally the old Republic Studios, which had ground out hundreds of B-westerns in the thirties and forties starring John Wayne, Gene Autry, Bill Elliott, and Roy Rogers.

What kind of a show did Sam want to do? Obviously Powell was expecting another western from him. There were a total of forty-eight western series on the air in 1959, all of them featuring superhuman gunfighters—Matt Dillon, Lucas McCain, Wyatt Earp, Bat Masterson, Paladin—who could draw faster and shoot straighter than any outlaw alive, who always got their man, arrived in the nick of time, and saved the day. They could slug it out or shoot it out with six bad guys at once and whip them all while sustaining little more than a cut lip or a graze from a bullet.

It wasn't just Levy, Gardner, Laven—all of television was gearing its product for ten-year-olds. What if somebody did a show about the West as it really was, a show about a saddle tramp instead of a gunman, a painfully human drifter moving from one cattle outfit to the next? Like Bill Dillon and Bill Baker and the other cowboys Sam had grown up around at Dunlap's. Men who never thought farther ahead than tomorrow, simple men who liked working cattle, sleeping under the stars, getting drunk, and chasing girls, but who in the deepest recesses of their hearts were nagged by a melancholy that expressed itself occasionally in vague remarks about getting a place of their own and settling down someday. Men who talked about it but never took any action to make it happen. (Dillon died a lonely bachelor in a tiny rented room in North Fork, crippled by too many mule kicks and horse falls and alcoholism. He hadn't been able to ride for years.)

The possibilities fired Sam's synapses—a half-dozen story ideas began to formulate. His new show would not be about another gunfighter, but that quintessential American archetype: the cowboy. He would capture both the exhilarating freedom of that life and the despair that often lurked beneath all the hooting and hollering.

If the fifties western boom was the perfect time for Sam Peckinpah to break into television, Four Star Productions proved to be the perfect place. Under Dick Powell's guidance the company's stable grew from one wobbly-legged anthology series—"Four Star Playhouse"—in 1952 to a total of thirteen weekly network series on prime time in 1960. By using the anthology series as showcases for new pilots, Powell was able to test-run shows and line up sponsors for them. His new programs sold faster than hot dogs at a ballpark: "Trackdown," "Johnny Ringo," "Wanted Dead or Alive," "The Law and Mrs. Jones," "The Detectives." In just a few years Powell's small independent production company had come to rival the big studios—20th Century–Fox, Warner Bros., and Universal—in the race to pump out TV "product."

But Four Star was much different from the big studios. "Dick Powell was a very honorable guy," says Frank Baur, vice president in charge of production at the time. "He gave a lot of fellows chances, like myself, Aaron Spelling, and Sam Peckinpah and others. Dick loved that company with a passion, it was his little baby. He was a hardworking son of a gun. We hired crew people that knew what they were doing and we had their interest at heart and took care of them, treated them decently and gave them opportunities. Lots of guys were moved up from assistant directors to associate producers or given a chance to direct. We had a wonderful, happy, productive organization."

The budgets for Four Star's programs ran a little higher than the industry average—$38,000–$40,000 per episode. The shows were shot in three days instead of two and a half, and were allowed a full day of rehearsal before shooting started. Extra time was allotted for last-minute refinements in dubbing and editing as well. "We treated our shows like major motion pictures," says Herschel Burke Gilbert, who composed the music for most of the Four Star programs.

As a result, the company was able to attract top-of-the-line feature editors like Bernard Burton and Desmond Marquette, cinematographers like Lucien Ballard, and actors like June Allyson, Robert Taylor, and Gig Young into its fold. It was in this rich creative compost that Peckinpah's talent really began to flower, and it would be one of the few amiable longterm relationships he maintained with a studio over the course of his stormy career. "It was great," Sam recalled in 1978. "Working with Mr. Powell unfortunately left its mark on me. We had the best crews, the best staff. I've never been able to find people like that since."

Four Star had had great success with shows about gunfighters with a gimmick: McCain's notch-levered, rapid-fire rifle; Steve McQueen's sawed-off Winchester, which he drew and fired from a holster in "Wanted Dead or Alive"; Johnny Ringo's Peacemaker, which featured a second barrel loaded with buckshot. Operating under the Jules Levy theory, Dick Powell had now come up with the title for a new series: "Winchester." If Peckinpah could write a script to match the title, Powell was confident he could sell it as a series.

It was like "The Rifleman" all over again, only this time Sam would be given free rein to write and direct the pilot as he saw fit. While he struggled to come up with a story, Brian Keith was suggested as the lead for the new show. Peckinpah met with the actor and the alchemy was instantaneous. The son of character actor and writer Robert Keith, Brian had a tall, broad-shouldered, granite-muscled physique and a head of wild curly hair. He had appeared on Broadway in *Mister Roberts* as well as in a number of feature films, including such westerns as *The Violent Men, Arrowhead, Hell Canyon Outlaws,* and in a television series, "The Crusader."

As they spent time together—at Sam's office, at each other's houses, and in various bars scattered around Los Angeles—Peckinpah and Keith discovered they had a lot in common. Both had served in the marines in World War II—Keith's stint was rougher by far, three years, 1942–1945, during the height of the Pacific campaign—and both had grown up around cattle ranches and been fascinated by the men who worked on them.

"When I was a kid, nine or ten in 1928–29," says Keith, "we were living on this ranch in Montana near Fort Benton. About half the hands there were Blackfoot Crow Indians, and the others were guys that were just born there—they were thirty-dollars-a-month cowboys. You get to know a lot as a kid 'cause you're around all the time, you're out there in the morning when they're saddling up. You learn about the clothes and the equipment and the language and the humor, the deadpan ribbing that they do. So watching them and listening to their tales about the old days driving cattle got me fascinated."

Sam told Keith about growing up on Dunlap's, about how he wished he could have lived in the days of the Wild West, the mythical masculine paradise that had retreated into the past beyond his grasp. Soon the informal socializing between the two slipped seamlessly into a friendship, then a creative collaboration.

Keith's character would be a simple saddletramp like the ones he and Sam had known as kids—wandering from one job to the next, talking about settling down someday, but never saving enough money to make it happen. Sam named their drifter Dave Blassingame, after his father and a rancher who'd lived in Fresno County when Sam was growing up. He would have only one companion in life—his dog, Brown.

Throughout the series, Brown would fail time and time again to live up to the heroic tradition of Lassie and Rin Tin Tin. Example: Blassingame is tied up and left alone in a cabin by a pair of inbred cutthroats who will return shortly. He whistles for Brown, who's outside the cabin. The dog's ears perk up, he jumps to his feet, runs and leaps valiantly through the cabin window, glass spraying everywhere. Dave holds out his tightly bound hands. "Go on, bite the rope!" But instead, Brown saunters past him to the more appealing leftovers on the kitchen table. "You're gonna make a beautiful saddle blanket for somebody!" Blassingame sneers in disgust. Unlike his master, Brown displays not a shred of regret over his shortcomings. "That's Brown," Blassingame would later say of his "no-account" companion. "He just wakes up ta eat. Just a bunch of skin wrapped around an appetite."

The pilot for the series, "Trouble at Tres Cruces," was shot in the spring of 1959, and aired on "Zane Grey Theater" on March 26 of that year. Because it defied the mold of the typical half-hour TV western, no sponsor swooped in to snatch it up, and Sam was forced to pick up other work in the months that followed. He did two more episodes for "Zane Grey"—the best by far was a stunning little piece co-written with Robert Heverly, "Miss Jenny"—and a couple of shows for an NBC series, "Klondike."

While working on the latter, Peckinpah struck up a friendship with David Levy, head of programming for NBC. Sam screened "Tres Cruces" for Levy and described the series he and Keith envisioned. Levy loved the concept and decided to put the series on the air. He sold the show to NBC's programming board while network president Robert E. Kintner was out of the country, and made a commitment for thirteen episodes. Levy and Dick Powell gave Sam creative carte blanche to develop the series as he saw fit. There was only one small glitch: Four Star's lawyers had discovered that they did not in fact own the rights to the "Winchester" title. Sam was asked to come up with another and did: "The Westerner."

Sam would hire the writers, directors, actors, and key crew members; he would have complete control over the writing, editing, dubbing, and musical scoring of every episode. At last he was in a position to show Hollywood what he could do when not interfered with. His throat grew dry and tight with fear, the familiar wave of nausea swelled up in him—if the show fell on its ass he would have no one to blame but himself. Then the fear was washed over by a tremendous surge of excitement. The time had come, as he would later be fond of saying, to "get it on."

He moved back to a second-floor office in the Four Star administration building—a long, thick-walled, Spanish-tiled structure that had been there since the Republic days—and began assembling his writing team. Jack Gariss (once revered by his USC classmates as the next Orson Welles) was hired as story editor and associate producer. Gariss' extensive written critiques and suggestions helped craft the series' weaker scripts into solid drama. Bruce Geller, whom Sam hired to write a script for "The Rifleman," became a quasi-staff member, creating four original "Westerner" episodes himself and rewriting several others. Robert Heverly, who had co-written "Miss Jenny" with Sam, also became a regular. He would co-write two episodes of the show with Peckinpah and do uncredited rewrites on a couple more. Jack Curtis, an old Fresno Stater who'd written a "Rifleman" and a "Zane Grey" episode for Sam, hammered out a script for the show, as did Tom Gries, an extremely talented writer-director who'd made a name for himself on "Rawhide." E. Jack Neuman—

who had written for "Playhouse 90" and the pilots for several other series, including "The Line Up"—also contributed an original script.

Peckinpah would arrive at the studio early in the morning and work late into the night rewriting scripts; then, when the show went into production, checking the sets, watching dailies, supervising the editing and dubbing, the musical scoring, casting, and conferring with the show's other directors. "His health was completely shot, even back then," says Heverly. "His secretary, Bobby Smith, would plead with him to get some sleep. I used to wonder sometimes what the hell held him up."

He was beginning to have the anxiety attacks that would plague him for the rest of his life. "He'd get so goddamned tense he'd hyperventilate," says Heverly. Bobby Smith kept a paper bag in her desk drawer so Sam could breath into it and regain control of himself.

But the work was splendid. The drafts of the "The Westerner" scripts in Sam's files are filled with his handwritten revisions, proving that he did extensive dialogue rewrites on almost all the episodes. His own idiosyncratic style permeated the series:

"I caught a couple slugs in my appetite"; "You thin-gutted, mink-livered, sidewindin', backstabbin' buzzard!"; "You ain't the law, you're a meat-hookin' jay-birder!"; "That was the most deep-dyed-in-the-wool, fancy-gaited, copper-collar job of fast talkin' I ever heard in all my born days!"; "Burgundy Smith, you egg-swallowin', dog-stealin', chicken-livered bottom-dealer! . . . You steal my dog, I'm gonna feed you your ears!"; "I don't like you, Ritchie, or that rat's litter you call family!"

Intensely personal themes that would reverberate throughout the body of Peckinpah's work can be found in every episode of "The Westerner." His disillusionment with marriage and romantic love are evident in "Jeff" and in the comedies where Blassingame meets up with golden-tongued bunco artist Burgundy Smith. In the latter, the two invariably compete for the attentions of a young woman, but their ardor turns queasy at the first sign that the lady wants something more permanent than a roll in the hay. "Blassingame, think!" Burgundy warns when Dave falls under the spell of a local beauty and announces his intention to marry her. "No more the joy of dollar liquor tricklin' down your parched throat. She'll put a stop to that. No more the joy of thrusting yourself into the maw of chance! She'll have you tied, boy, apron-stringed and plowin'. She'll make you quit everything you enjoy, even other women!"

Man's salivating urge for violence is the subject of "School Days," in which a mob almost lynches Blassingame for a murder he didn't commit. Betrayal—a wife turning on her husband, a husband on his wife, one friend against another, or a man against his dog—crisscrosses through "The Westerner" like fat through a cheap piece of beef. Silver, gold, American greenbacks, the price a man is willing to accept in exchange for his soul—this is perhaps the most dominant theme in "The Westerner" and in all of Peckinpah's work. On his travels through the Texas/Mexico wasteland, Dave Blassingame is confronted again and again with hard moral choices—choices between money and loyalty to a friend, money and human life, money and the letter of the law, money and the sanctity of a grave.

Peckinpah often told interviewers that all his dramas were morality plays. But his films and television shows were not simpleminded lectures on right and wrong or good and evil, for he knew that such comforting black-and-white demarcations were an illusion. Instead they were open-ended existential inquiries, a search for morality in a land where it appears to have evaporated. In each episode Blassingame is confronted with a difficult, ambiguous situation that calls for tough decisions without the presence of God or a set of tangible social laws or values to guide him. He must choose who he is, what he stands for, what he can live with and what he can't, and through the decisions he makes he defines himself.

Peckinpah directed five of the thirteen episodes of "The Westerner." The other segments were farmed out to leading television directors, such as Tom Gries, Ted Post, and Elliot Silverstein (they would all go on to direct feature films). Peckinpah's growth as a director from "Broken Arrow" to "The Rifleman" had been astounding; from "The Rifleman" to "The Westerner" he made another quantum leap. Only Gries proved a serious rival; Peckinpah's command of the medium by this time was breathtakingly self-assured—all the more so when one considers the fact that "The Westerner" shows were shot in three days. Sam's episodes don't look like television shows at all, but like highly polished little movies.

The authentic look of "The Westerner" was achieved by putting Four Star's art directors, costume designers, and camera, editing, and post-production crews into a full-court press. Peckinpah challenged, needled, and threw tantrums to push his team beyond the standards of average television. He demanded that art directors and property masters overdress the sets with many more props and atmospheric details than could be used so that he could then walk through and begin removing items one by one until he had "edited" the set down to the look that he wanted. It was the same basic approach he took toward writing and film editing: gather as much raw material as possible, provide yourself with as many choices as possible, then gradually chip away at the material until you have your finished sculpture.

He insisted that the actors' clothing be convincingly aged and grungy. Blassingame would not be riding into town after crossing a hundred miles of desert in a neatly pressed outfit. The saloons he frequented would not be the generic Hollywood mockups of every other TV western; they would be *real*, so real the people at home could smell the stale beer on the floorboards, the sour stench of tobacco juice in the spittoons.

The gritty feel of reality on the sets also filtered into the actors' performances. Most remarkable is Brian Keith's portrayal of Blassingame in all thirteen episodes of the show. In video pabulum like "Family Affair" and "Hardcastle and McCormick," Keith stumbles through his scenes as if he's been rudely awakened from a long nap. But his performance in "The Westerner" is a revelation. He displays startling range and subtlety: heartbreak and disillusionment in "Jeff," a man torn between his best and worst impulses in "Mrs. Kennedy," and childlike naiveté when he falls in love with Libby Lorraine in "The Courtship of Libby." In all its subtle nuances, its intriguing combination of brute strength, emotional fragility, and a haunting inner melancholy, Keith's performance reveals a talent as potent as Brando's, a talent that was unfortunately wasted on a parade of mediocre projects after the series folded.

The months of camaraderie between Peckinpah and Keith had worked a subtle magic, but it was more than camaraderie that nudged Keith past his usual somnambulistic state. "A lot of times Sam got the performance out of Brian by intimidation," says Norman Powell, a production manager on several of the shows. "I would see the two of them screaming at each other. They'd go off and really yell at each other. Brian is a tough guy too. What Brian would do was try and bully Sam. Sam would go just so far and then start yammering back at him."

For all their layered detail, Peckinpah's "Westerner" episodes do not recreate the Old West "as it really was," but instead as he reimagined it. These television shows and his later films are mythic or allegorical narratives, often surreal in style. The dense and dusty detail makes their self-enclosed world vibrantly believable, but it is Peckinpah's world, not the real one.

"Jeff"—directed by Peckinpah from a script he wrote with Robert Heverly—unfolds like a dream, the images cloaked in half-concealing shadows. Dave Blassingame rides into a filthy border town to rescue a young woman, Jeff, whom he knew years before when she was just "a tow-headed whelp" who had a crush on him. But the years leave their mark on people. Jeff has become a prostitute in a rathole saloon, caught up in a sadomasochistic relationship with a domineering pimp who alternates between playing her protector and tormentor. Blassingame beats the pimp in a brutal fight and wins his permission to take Jeff away with him. "You're a fool," the pimp gasps. "So am I. Take her and get out."

But when Blassingame goes back to Jeff's seamy room and tells her to gather up her things, she says she can't go, her place is here. The perverse relationship with the pimp fulfills needs that Dave is unable to fathom. "You want something that isn't here," Jeff tells him with melting wax eyes. "You want something that maybe never was."

When Blassingame turns to leave, Jeff shuffles after him and takes his arm. He turns to look at her and she leans forward to plant a tender, chaste kiss on his stubbled cheek. He runs a callused hand gently along the side of her pale face, but she turns it away from him. "Yeah, you're right," he murmurs, "why should I worry about you?" His big hand moves to delicately untie the thin ribbon that holds her blond hair. He folds it carefully in his palm—the action denying his words, revealing the slow acid burn of love forever lost.

Jim Silke, who would later become Peckinpah's most frequent and closest screenplay collaborator, observes: "The whole concept of the female in 'Jeff' is Sam's. He met dozens of girls like that in whorehouses in China, Mexico, and Nevada. This one was probably based on one of the first, I have no doubt about that. The theme is that love is great, but not enough sometimes. Sam's whole concept of the world as he portrayed it in his films was: it's not the way you think it's going to be, it's not the way you thought it was."

A man's romantic illusion hopelessly shattered—like a cold-sweat nightmare, "Jeff" gives voice through its images to Sam Peckinpah's inner despair over the disintegration of his marriage. Marie herself actually appears in the show as a fanatic Christian who emerges from the town's lacerated shadows when Blassingame first rides in on his mission of mercy. She wears filthy rags, her face haggard and big eyes ablaze as she urges the cowboy to come to God—her identity mingling with that of Sam's mother, Fern.

At the end of the show, as Blassingame rides out of town, broken and slump-shouldered, Marie again emerges from the darkness and accosts him. "Have you found salvation, brother?" she wants to know.

Blassingame's face is gaunt; shadows cling to its hollows. He shakes his head and looks out at the void of wilderness that waits ahead of him. "Have you?"

"Yes," Marie nods with large, feverish eyes. "I have." From the brothel behind them a whore's laugh echoes mockingly. He glances back in its direction then spurs his horse on into the night, and on an adobe wall that he passes a fanatic has painted the words:

Tonight a soul is lost
He wanders the wide Earth
But he finds only emptiness

Brilliantly crafted, haunting, bleeding like an open wound—"Jeff" is a minor masterpiece, easily the finest episode in the series.

As the program's producer, Peckinpah for the first time oversaw every aspect of the series, from pre-production to air dates. He supervised the budgets, shooting schedules, casting, crew selection, editing, dubbing, musical scoring, and timing of the final prints for proper exposure and contrast. It was on "The Westerner" that he began assembling the actors and crew members who would work with him throughout his career: actors Dub Taylor, Warren Oates, Slim Pickens, and R. G. Armstrong, stuntman Whitey Hughes, assistant editor Mike Klein, and cinematographer Lucien Ballard.

Lucien Ballard was the cinematographer on three of "The Westerner" shows. His shadowy dreamscape images in "Jeff" and hard-edged compositions in "Line Camp" made them two of the most visually striking episodes in the series. Sam wrote to Ballard on April 16, 1960: "First, as a producer, I'd like to tell you how much I appreciate the contribution you have made to 'The Westerner.' Second, as a director, I would like you to know that 'The Courtship of Libby' and 'Jeff' were by far the two best things I have ever done, and I hold you directly responsible. I would like us to get together as soon as possible to discuss future projects."

Ballard, who got his start as an associate cinematographer to Josef von Sternberg in the 1930s, and in the fifties shot one of Budd Boetticher's westerns, would go on to shoot five feature films for Peckinpah.

"The Westerner" was Sam's walk through the fire. He went into the flames as a writer who had directed a few television episodes, and came out a filmmaker. The show easily qualifies as the best half-hour western series in the history of television. No other contender even comes close. Peckinpah, who had gotten his start on TV's first adult western, "Gunsmoke," had now taken the genre from pretentious melodrama into the lofty realm of art—and he'd done it in just four years.

But the show did not receive cries of adulation from all corners when it premiered on September 30, 1960, not by any means. Television audiences had, quite simply, never seen anything like it before: a program that focused week after week on prostitution, rape, adultery, grisly murders; on a "hero" who faltered at the critical moment, made wrong decisions, went on drunken sprees, cursed, seemed a stranger to ambition and held few moral convictions . . . a hero who wasn't a hero at all.

The NBC censor, Lorne Williamson, constantly tried to push the show back within the boundaries of a conventional western. Memos from Williamson warned Peckinpah that the "excessive" drunkenness, sex, rough language, and brutality of "The Westerner" would not be tolerated.

Fortunately Dave Levy and Dick Powell went to bat for Peckinpah and the show retained a remarkably hard edge—guns thundered with real charges, bullets splintered posts and walls with visceral force; when shot, men careened backward from the impact and their wounds bled real-looking blood. The opening show, "Jeff," even had the word "damn" in it, one of the first times it had been spoken on network television.

Unfortunately NBC president Robert Kintner did not like "The Westerner" and resented the fact that Dave Levy had put it into production without his approval. As a result it got very little publicity and was shoved into a poor time slot: 8:30 P.M. on Fridays, which was considered "the children's hour." Its competition was a new animated show from Hanna-Barbera, "The Flintstones," and one of the new hour-long programs that were just beginning to appear on TV, "Route 66."

When it premiered with the "Jeff" episode, the series provoked highly polarized responses, as would most of Peckinpah's work from this point on. The reviewer for *Weekly Variety* wondered if Sam Peckinpah had gone "shock happy to win success in a crowded field." The critic acknowledged that the show displayed a lot of talent both in front and behind the camera, and that the writing was skilled and the directing polished and inventive.

But, he wrote: " 'Tis a pity such talents have been wasted to find expression in such a sordid story." The same issue praised the newest episodes of "Leave It to Beaver" and "Ozzie and Harriet" for their "wholesome" and "clean-cut" comedy, and said the first "Rifleman" show of the season was "right on target."

But James Powers of the *Hollywood Reporter* wrote: " 'The Westerner' is made by people who know that time has nothing to do with breathless theater; a half-hour is just as good in the right hands as three hours. It is made by people more interested in telling a story than aping a formula in the naive hope that guiltless plagiary will make them rich. It shows again that TV's whine of 'no time' is just another way of saying 'no talent.' 'The Westerner' is a great show, a stand-out series, and its strongest competition in the weeks ahead will be its own standards. . . . It was, you may be surprised to know, a moving poetic drama (not melodrama, drama), written with expert economy and directed and acted the same."

Because of Robert Kintner's antipathy toward it, NBC had ordered only thirteen episodes of the series. (Prior to that time networks had usually bought a minimum of twenty-six, which gave an unusual show a chance to start out slow and build an audience.) "The Westerner" proved no match for the one-dimensional high jinks of "The Flintstones," or "Route 66." Its ratings never crept higher than 12.4 percent of U.S. TV households. "The Flintstones" came in at 22.5, "Route 66" at 22.0. "Gunsmoke," still the top show in television, pulled a whopping 40.3. No surprise that "The Westerner" was canceled about halfway through its run.

"Robert Kintner couldn't wait to cancel it," says Levy. "I knew it was pointless to argue. It didn't have the ratings. Ratings were already becoming paramount. I was against ratings. I was for nursing a show along, particularly if I felt I had the right creative team. I never wanted to hit them with numbers and sales figures. I wanted to stay with them because I believed in the creative side. I said, 'This will win an audience if we stay with it.' "

But Levy's approach was fast becoming obsolete. The make-it-up-as-you-go days of TV were coming to a close. Television was now a multimillion-dollar, corporation-dominated "industry" where ratings, demographic charts, and the bottom line, not writers and directors, dictated creative decisions. The day that NBC announced cancellation of "The Westerner," it also named its replacement, a situation comedy, "Yes, Yes, Nanette," starring Nanette Fabray.

Peckinpah later claimed that over 1,000 letters of protest poured in to the network following the announcement of the show's cancellation. Two bulging folders of them survive in Sam's files—hundreds of letters from viewers across the country bristling with indignation.

USC film students, who had been conducting lively classroom discussions about the show, wrote a joint letter of protest, and a group of the top writers in television—James Lee Barrett, Bruce Geller, Tom Gries, Christopher Knopf, Ellis Marcus, and Gene Roddenberry—took out ads in *Variety* and *The Hollywood Reporter* to mourn the show's passing. And Cecil Smith, an entertainment writer for *The Los Angeles Times,* would make a personal crusade of seeing that "The Westerner" was not forgotten. Over the next twenty years he would mention it again and again in his column as one of the greatest weekly series ever to hit television.

But "The Westerner" did get a chance for a second life. "So much fuss was raised when we went off the air that CBS came running with an offer to put 'The Westerner' back on," Brian Keith later recalled. "We found out they wanted us to stretch it to an hour and put it on at 7:00 at night. That meant that we'd have to cut the realism and make it for kids—in other words, cut everything out of it that made it good."

Peckinpah and Keith excused themselves from the meeting for a moment and stepped out into the hall to confer. "What do you think, Brian?" Sam asked.

"Tell them to shove it up their ass."

Sam chuckled. "I feel the same way."

Actor L. Q. Jones, a friend of both Peckinpah and Keith, observes: "If that show had gone on to run for five years, they each would have made a couple of million dollars. When somebody says, 'Here's two million dollars, all you have to do is soften your approach.' And you say, 'Shove it up your ass!' you've got to believe what you say. You have to take your hat off to Sam and Brian, both of them said it."

"It was a successful failure," Sam himself said. "Win, lose, or draw, I am proud of my work."

Sam undoubtedly realized that it was just as well the series had been canceled. The pressure of having to produce thirty-nine episodes year after year would have inevitably eroded the show's quality. The dissipation could already be seen in the series' last episode, "The Painting," written by Bruce Geller and directed by Peckinpah. The first two Burgundy Smith–Dave Blassingame comedies—"Brown" and "The Courtship of Libby"—had been daring and fresh. By the third installment the creative juices had begun to coagulate. There were still some wonderful moments, but the plot was contrived and filled with retreaded scenes from "Libby."

In truth, Peckinpah was not cut out to be the next Dick Powell; that he would leave to Aaron Spelling. Years earlier he had set his sights much higher than on becoming a TV mogul. It was time to move on to the big canvas, where the big stories were told. "The Westerner" would make this possible, for although it had been a commercial failure it had caught the attention of many in the industry. Here was a fresh and original talent, one that—if properly controlled and molded—could put a new "topspin" on tired Hollywood vehicles. Controlling Peckinpah would turn out to be much more problematic than any of the studio executives could have guessed, and just who was molding whom would become a difficult question to answer. But "The Westerner" kept producers coming back for more long after Peckinpah had earned a reputation as the industry's most maddening enfant terrible since Erich von Stroheim.

The half-hour television western was already going the way of the buffalo when "The Westerner" was canceled in the winter of 1960. The influx of new hour-long shows like "Route 66" and audience burnout from too many horse chases and shootouts caused a radical drop in popularity. The tide receded as quickly as it had risen. In 1960 there were forty-six westerns on the air; by 1964 there would be only eleven. Peckinpah got out just in time.

Sam's income in 1960 was a far cry from the millions he might have made if "The Westerner" had been a hit. For his services as a writer, producer, and director on "The Westerner," "Klondike," and "Zane Grey Theater," he had grossed about $40,000 between the fall of 1959 and the end of 1960. Still, that was a substantial sum at the time; Brian Keith had been paid $28,000 for the pilot and the thirteen episodes of the series. In addition, Peckinpah owned 15 percent of the net profits on "The Westerner" and 7 percent on "The Rifleman." His business manager, Bob Schiller, had set up Latigo Productions (named after the canyon in Malibu where Fern Lea and Walter Peter had recently bought a home), which employed Sam and sold his services to Four Star. This allowed him to set up health and pension funds into which he would sock away hundreds of thousands of tax-deferred dollars over the next eighteen years.

The increase in cash flow should have brought stability to his life at last, but by the time "The Westerner" episodes were going into production, the strain between Sam and Marie had become intolerable. The crisis occurred when writer Jack Curtis came down from Big Sur to stay at Sam's house while working on a script for the show.

Curtis had attended Fresno State with Sam and Marie and wanted to write serious novels; Sam had lured him into his stable on "The Rifleman." Red-haired, five feet ten inches tall, Curtis despised TV but saw it as a way to finance his fiction writing. He set up quarters in the guest house out back, and became a regular fixture at the Peckinpah dinner table each night. Curtis was drawn to Marie's warm manner, her large sympathetic eyes, and keen intelligence. Obviously this was no ordinary housewife but a well-read woman with an impressive understanding of the theater and literature. Marie, for her part, found Curtis' company a welcome relief. Sam was drinking heavily every night now—when he was home—and, at least around her, seemed to be angry all the time.

"One night we were all in the kitchen there, Jack, me, and Sam," says Marie. "Sam was drunk, talking with Jack about script ideas. Sam started getting vicious as he critiqued Jack's stories—ridiculing them, really, really going for the throat. I intervened and said, 'Sam, stop it! What are you doing?' And he blew up. He yelled, 'Well, if you like him so much, you can have him!' and marched out of the house. I went after him and followed him out to the driveway, saying, 'Sam, come on, don't leave, come on back inside.' But he wouldn't. He got in the car and drove off. So Jack and I stayed and finished cooking dinner. Jack kept saying, 'It's all right. He'll come back.' "

"Sam told me much later," says Joe Bernhard, "that he went to the Malibu Inn and had a few drinks, thought it over, and decided maybe he'd been wrong. So he got back in his car and drove back to the Colony."

In the kitchen of Number Ninety-seven, Marie was pouring her heart out to Jack, recounting all of the frustrations, hurts, and angers of the last months as she continued to work over the stove. Suddenly, Jack's hands gripped her shoulders and applied gentle pressure. She allowed them to turn her toward his face. Like in a crazy dream his mouth descended to hers. Then, like a crazy, terrible nightmare, came the sound of the kitchen door crashing open. A blurred figure rushed forward.

Sam hit Marie and swung on Jack too; blood gushed from the writer's nose. "That's it! I'm leaving!" Jack shouted while Marie lay on her back on the floor, trying to breathe.

"It was so strange, the whole thing," Marie says, looking back on it. "Sam coming in the back door like that . . . it was almost like a setup."

Marie kicked Sam out of the house later that night. He was still angry when he left, but also shocked by what he had done. He returned the next day, apologetic, but she refused to take him back, so he gathered up some of his possessions and moved in with Joe Bernhard, who had a basement apartment in Laurel Canyon in the Hollywood hills. Sam stayed there, and off booze, for three weeks.

He called Marie again and again and again to tell her he was sober and to promise that things would be different if she would just take him back. She did, at last, let him move back into the house, but when the Fourth of July weekend came a few days later, she left with the girls to visit her parents in Fresno and take stock of their fractured marriage. Sam, alone and still on the wagon at the Colony, filled the hours with long, soul-searching letters to Marie in which he begged for forgiveness and gushed about how much he missed her and his daughters. "Can we talk, you and I, sometime when I won't see the fear and uncertainty in your eyes, in your love? I want to fight that fear. I want to build that certainty. I want us to be part of each other in a way and with an understanding and patience and respect more and better than we have ever had. . . . We have got to quit being strangers. The time is long past—You must talk to me for I have learned how to listen."

Marie gave in. She came back to Number Ninety-seven with the girls and they became a family again. It was too hard to turn her back on all that they'd been through together, too frightening to consider how a divorce would affect the children, impossible to forget all they had shared at Fresno State, USC, the little house in Whittier, the Quonset hut.

The barbecues on the weekends resumed and it wasn't long before Sam slipped back into the booze. It was all right to have a few drinks now and then, he told himself, as long as he didn't let it get out of control like before. He'd learned his lesson. He had to pace himself, know when to stop so he didn't get so thoroughly sloshed he couldn't think straight. But that didn't mean he couldn't have a few belts on the weekend, or maybe one or two when he came home at night. With the long hours and the pressure, he had to unwind once in a while.

So the sound-effects records, the jazz, the mariachi music and the high-pitched whine of the blender started up again. Life resumed its familiar rhythm and things were back to the way they'd been before that terrible night.

But not really. Something had changed; both he and Marie felt it, though neither could bring themselves to speak of it. They never sat down to have those soul-searching talks Sam spoke of in his letters. Both were too afraid of what they might find.

They had passed through a one-way door that night with Jack Curtis, and there was no going back. At the barbecues Marie still glowed beatifically, still the warm and welcoming Earth

Mother to all her guests. But deep inside her she had gone cold. Inside her was a block of ice that Sam would never melt, not with all the bouquets and apologies in the world. So they threw parties that lasted all weekend long. Local teenagers made a habit of cruising the stretch of sand behind the Peckinpahs' house because they could always find an iced keg of beer there among a throng of adults too blitzed to notice if they snuck a few glasses for themselves. Neither Sam nor Marie minded the constant crowds now—they made them feel safe.

During times of crisis in the past Sam had always been able to turn to his father for advice and emotional support. True to form, David Peckinpah took the train down from Fresno and met with Sam and Marie separately to see if he could act as a mediator. It must have been a difficult role to play, especially since his own marriage had become unstable by this time.

In September 1959, Governor Edmund Brown decided to reward David for the help he'd given him on an important San Joaquin Valley irrigation case. Peckinpah had argued the case before the Supreme Court and won for the State of California, and now Brown wanted to appoint David as a Superior Court judge in Madera County. For years, the missed opportunity to run for Congress had lain heavily in David's gut. Now, at age sixty-two, came another opportunity, probably the last, for him to be something more than just another lawyer. Perhaps he could eventually move on up to the court of appeals. It was a new challenge and an exciting one. He knew what Fern's reaction would be, but this time she wouldn't stop him.

Fern Lea happened to be visiting her parents the day David came home and broke the news of the governor's offer. "He said he'd been asked to take the judgeship, then he said, 'But I would never think of doing it,' " says Fern Lea. "He was lying to my mother right then. He was setting it up, easing her into it, but in a terrible way. He was always afraid to face her on issues."

Fern Peckinpah wrote in her diary on September 30, 1959: "I felt the world had dropped out from under me when I got an idea of what was going on. Weeks ago Dave and I discussed the judgeship in Madera—yes, he really talked about it to me. He brought up the disadvantages and the love of our own home [the judgeship would require that he establish a residence in nearby Madera County] and left me fully convinced he was not interested after long consideration. Then bang the world fell! First time in years he did not bring the paper home. By chance I heard of the article in the paper."

The article revealed that David had accepted the judgeship. It described him as "jubilant," and quoted him saying that he considered the new job "a great honor."

For Fern it was her father scuttling the engagement to Bob Nichols all over again. David had promised one thing while all the while planning to do the exact opposite, as if her needs didn't matter at all. It hammered home once again the utter powerlessness of her male-dependent life.

Fern threatened to divorce David, but didn't. Instead she moped around the house, bitter and recriminating. "She refused to attend his swearing in," says Fern Lea. "She was hateful to him." Yet she couldn't give up the hope that David would eventually "come to his senses," resign, and rejoin her at home so that things could "be like they used to be." David took a small apartment in Madera County to satisfy the residency requirement, and commuted back and forth between it and Fresno. Fern found herself alone with Susan in the sprawling ranch house for days at a time. When David did return home they fought bitterly.

Fern wrote in her diary: "After the bitter talk I went down on the creek alone and had hysteria worse than ever in my life. I could not stop screaming and crying for oh so, so long. I've been exhausted all day. [Her handwriting becomes blurry.] Something is the matter with my eyesight so I see the words all double. . . . I can't go on this way. I can't walk either."

And in another entry she wrote: "Dave went all to pieces and told me just what he thinks of me. His eyes were black, oh! so black and said something like I was the meanest person he'd ever known, dirty stinking, self-centered, morbid etc. Had everything to be happy about but wouldn't be happy and didn't want anybody else to be. That I had already maybe (about) caused him to have one heart attack already and that I just wanted to get him down and I was sure doing it. He said I hated everyone and when I asked him what he meant, he said he was sure I hate him. He was crazy mad and at last said he didn't want to talk anymore and went out of the house. Lots of swear words were used. . . . We're not going on this way. . . . I can't possibly see how this has happened to us. Oh dear! Oh dear, oh dear!"

But they did go on that way. The two were barely on speaking terms, could hardly stand to be in the same room anymore, but neither had the courage to bring a clean end to it.

The same seemed to be true of Sam and Marie. By this time Sam was "playing around" with a couple of starlets, most notably Mary Murphy, who had appeared opposite Marlon Brando in *The Wild One* and played a dance hall girl in the "Going Home" episode of "The Westerner." At home he was drinking more heavily than ever and picking Marie out as a frequent target for verbal abuse. No matter what she said or did, it always seemed to be the wrong thing.

Says one friend who knew the family well: "I wonder if Sam wasn't trying to drive Marie away on purpose, to push her into proving that she didn't love him."

Finally, the terrible thing that everyone could see coming, but never dared admit, happened. "I had a crush on somebody," Marie says simply. It was a neighbor; they began an affair. Looking back more than three decades later, she can see that she might have used it as a way to finally get out of the marriage, for she knew it would be the ultimate, unforgivable sin in Sam's eyes. It was the passive way out. She couldn't sit down with Sam face-to-face and admit that it was over.

Robert Heverly remembers Peckinpah calling him into his office one day and saying, abruptly, "Bob, my wife's fucking somebody else."

"Oh?" was all Heverly could think to reply.

"Yeah," Sam said matter-of-factly. "I'm trying to get the goods on her."

He also told Brian Keith of his intention to "get the goods" on Marie. Keith couldn't understand why on earth Sam would want to. What did it matter? If the marriage was over, it was over.

Why put himself through something as horrible as that, what purpose would it serve?

But some dark and primal urge compelled him to it. The details of the final confrontation would hurt too many people still living. Although it was not violent, suffice it to say it was an ugly scene. "It was," says Marie, "a terrible, terrible ending."

It would take her twenty years to put the memory of that final confrontation to rest, but at least she finally did. Sam never managed to. It was a wound he could not, would not allow to heal. He would pick at it with morbid fascination until his dying day. With all his own infidelities, he of course had no right to feel victimized. It was the hypocrisy of a chauvinist, a hypocrisy he and generations of American men both before and after him shared.

From this point onward, betrayal would become the dominant theme in Peckinpah's work. Often it is cloaked in masculine garb: Gil Westrum plans to turn on his old partner, Steve Judd, in *Ride the High Country;* Captain Ben Tyreen plots vengeance against his old comrade in arms, Amos Dundee, in *Major Dundee;* outlaw Pike Bishop is on the run from a former member of his gang, Deke Thorton, now turned bounty hunter in *The Wild Bunch;* Pat Garrett kills his best friend and surrogate son in *Pat Garrett and Billy the Kid;* intelligence agent Mike Locken is shot by his partner, George Hansen, who's gone over to "the other side" in *The Killer Elite.* More than one perceptive reviewer has noted that, for all their macho bravado, these tales of male bonding turned sour unfold with the gushing sentiment of tragic love stories.

And then there are the other scenes, the ones in which a wife or girlfriend betrays her man, almost always sexually. They run through Peckinpah's films like a recurring nightmare, a traumatic memory that couldn't be shaken off or washed away no matter how many cases of whiskey Sam consumed. The "Mon Petit Chow" episode of "Route 66" that Peckinpah directed (it starred Lee Marvin), *That Lady Is My Wife, The Wild Bunch, Straw Dogs, The Getaway, Bring Me the Head of Alfredo Garcia,* and *Cross of Iron*—in all of them Sam would recreate the trauma with slightly different variations. These scenes would earn him everlasting infamy with the women's liberation movement. His critics called him an arrogant, condescending chauvinist; some even said he was a fascist. What most failed to recognize was that these sequences sprang out of profound personal pain. Peckinpah knew they were politically incorrect, and that by putting them on film he would make an open target of himself, but he couldn't apply the brakes. He had to do it; he didn't have any choice. It was this ruthless honesty that gave the scenes their disturbing and mesmerizing power, and what made them art.

While he could be startlingly frank on a movie screen, he found it impossible to be so in real life. In interviews he would never reveal his personal connection to the sequences, but instead rationalized them with abstract half-baked philosophy that only fed more ammo to his enemies.

For a candid explanation of this obsession one has to turn to his films, specifically to a short exchange of dialogue in *The Ballad of Cable Hogue:*

David Warner sits beside Jason Robards in the desert, staring out at mile after mile of rock, sand, and sun. Not a burning bush or a star of Bethlehem in sight, just the two of them in the overwhelming silence. "Funny thing," says Warner. "Doesn't matter how much or how little you've wandered around, how many women you've been with . . . every once in a while one of them cuts right through you, right straight into you."

Robards cocks his head toward his companion. "What do you do about it?"

"I suppose, maybe, when you die you get over it . . ."

Melissa was four years old the day her dad moved out of the house forever. She didn't know it was for keeps, but she saw how tense and brusque he was when he said good-bye, and sensed that somehow this was different from all the other times he left for work. All three of the girls had heard the muffled arguments coming from their parents' bedroom at night, but Mom and Dad rarely fought in front of them so it was easy to tell themselves it was no big deal, that the storm would soon pass and everything would be like the old days again.

After Sam left that morning, Marie called Kristen and Melissa into her dressing room. "Your father and I just can't get along anymore, it happens sometimes," she explained. "We're going to get a divorce, but it's going to be okay, you'll see him as much as you ever did."

That was that.

The two girls shuffled out into the hall. "What's a divorce?" Melissa asked.

"It means Dad's not going to live with us anymore," Kristen replied.

Melissa's face reddened. "You're lying!" She ran back down the hall to her mother's room.

Sam moved into the Holiday House, a small hotel with a bar and swimming pool a few miles up the coast. Kristen remembers visiting him there a short time after he left home. As they sat together on a couch in his darkened room, her father suddenly confessed. "Your mother and I have gotten a divorce . . . Your mother will probably get married again, but I don't think I will. I couldn't go through that again." He began to cry.

"I felt very uncomfortable," says Kristen. "I knew he was very lonely, but I didn't know how to fix it for him, what I could do to make him feel better."

Fern Lea also visited the Holiday House shortly after the breakup and witnessed an outpouring of grief. "He sat there crying on the sofa, saying, 'I'm so lonely, I am *so* lonely!' Tears just streaming down his face. He was devastated."

It wasn't a cut-and-dried ending; it couldn't be after all Sam and Marie had been through together. In fact another child—Sam's only son, Mathew—was conceived after he moved out of the Colony house. When Melissa realized her mother was pregnant again she hoped it meant her father was coming back to live with them, but by that time Sam and Marie had stopped sleeping with each other and would never do so again. Number Ninety-seven was sold, Marie and the kids moved into a big converted red barn at the base of the Malibu hills, and Sam rented a house on Bird View Drive in Point Dume, which everyone would come to refer to as "The Bird House."

In October, David Peckinpah had a major heart attack and was hospitalized. Sam and Fern Lea flew up from Fresno on a Saturday to see him. He seemed stable, and they flew back to L.A. the following day. Then, on October 30, a week later, a blood clot broke loose in one of David's arteries and his condition became critical. Sam and Fern Lea rushed to the airport to catch another flight to Fresno. They missed it, so Sam called the hospital to inform his brother. Denny told him not to rush, their father had died. While waiting for the plane and during the flight, Sam was calm, controlled, and consoling toward Fern Lea, who fell apart—he was being strong for his little sister the way the old man had been strong for them. The Peckinpah code.

When they walked into their parents' house in Fresno, Fern burst into tears. Fern Lea and Sam both hugged and kissed her, but the embraces were awkward and uncomfortable. Who's going to take care of her now? Fern Lea wondered. *Not me!* The sound of her mother's weeping and helpless mutterings—"Oh, Dave's gone!"—filled her with pity and hate. *Goddamn it, be strong for once!* Fern hadn't been sleeping, so they got a doctor to prescribe a very powerful sedative, but she still only slept a couple of hours at a time.

After Fern finally went to bed that night, Sam and Fern Lea sat up together in the living room. Sam had gone out to his father's cabin and found a bottle of Dewar's scotch that had been given to David by a client almost twenty years before. When Denny and Sam returned from the war the old man had broken it out, poured three shots, then neatly recapped it. It hadn't been opened since. That evening Sam and Fern Lea finished it off. They talked about those long-ago summers at Dunlap's and Bass Lake, the raft their father had helped them build out of lashed logs, their terror when he'd growl through his teeth, "Go cut me a switch!" the delight of rifling through his dresser drawer for a pair of hunting socks to hang over the fireplace on Christmas Eve, the breakfasts he cooked, filling the kitchen with the warm thick sizzling smell of eggs, ham, bacon, lamb chops and pancakes. "Sam seemed so cool about it all," says Fern Lea, "so in control."

Finally they decided to stagger off to bed. Fern Lea retired to her sister's bathroom to brush her teeth. Her parents' bathroom was adjacent, and from it she suddenly heard a torrent of invective. It was Sam—"Goddamn you, you son-of-a-bitch!"—hurling curses at his father.

"He was yelling at Dad for dying on him," says Fern Lea.

Just a few weeks before, David had come down to Los Angeles to see a screening of one of "The Westerner" shows. "After it was all over," Sam told Garner Simmons, "the Boss came up to me and said, 'A little rough, but—' And he gave me a nod and a smile and I knew that I had made it." David Peckinpah was not a demonstrative man, but he had finally let his youngest son know that he approved of the path he had chosen.

Despite his ambivalences toward his father—and they were many and deep—there is no question that Sam suffered from the loss. David had stood as a pillar of authority and integrity throughout the years of his childhood; when Sam needed money during college and the lean years immediately afterward, David had provided it without hesitation; when Marie had had a difficult childbirth, when the Quonset hut burned down, when Sam's marriage took a nosedive, all it took was one phone call and David was on the train to L.A. to lend whatever support he could. "He had great hands," Sam said years later. "I have good hands, but he had great hands. To hold somebody and tell them it's okay."

With his father dead there was no one left to set limits for him. There would be no other bosses to tell him that he had gone too far or needed to shape up—none he respected enough to listen to, anyway. "I wonder how Sam would have turned out if Dad had lived longer," says Fern Lea. "Dad would have kicked Sam's ass if he found out Sam was using dope."

Fern objected to a big funeral because Christian Science discouraged it. "My mother refused to let the information of his funeral go out—what time it was going to be—except for six or seven members of the family," Sam later said.

But Fern's children suspected the real reason was a lingering rage toward her husband. "When my father died, my mother wanted to have an autopsy done," says Fern Lea. "She was convinced that my father had had a major heart attack years before and that it had done something to his brain and that's why he took the judgeship and had done all these things that she didn't want him to do."

Now, even in death, she wanted to keep her husband to herself. But the children overruled her and got the word about the funeral out to the community. "Well, they had closed the courts of Fresno and 3,000 people were there," Sam recalled. "He was well-loved. Well-hated too, I guess."

Fern, looking tired and shriveled behind the black shroud the funeral director had set up to one side of the casket, babbled inane small talk throughout the entire service.

"Sam used to laugh and say, 'Mom had all the animals fixed on the ranch. It's a wonder we got away from there without being fixed ourselves!' " Fern Lea recalls.

Beneath the joke lay anger. The selling of Dunlap's, the thwarted congressional campaign, the grief given to his father over the judgeship, and now this, the final straw. Sam began telling friends that his mother had killed his father, driven him into an early grave with her constant harassment. "When she dies," he repeated over and over again in the decades that followed, "I'll piss on her grave."

He saw his mother very rarely over the remaining twenty-three years of her life. When she called him at home or at the office, those present noticed how Sam's voice became high and nervous, and how after hanging up he would be tight-lipped and agitated. He usually visited her after one of the Peckinpah family reunions that took place on top of Peckinpah Mountain every two or three years.

Sam's cousin Bob Peckinpah recalls: "Sam stayed an extra half-day up there with us one year. Then he had his driver, Chalo, take him down to Fresno. After he left, Denny's wife, Betty, was lamenting, 'How could a woman do that to these kids?' What Sam was doing was screwing up the courage to go visit her. What a horrible thing to do to kids, to mark them, to mar them for life. That's what happened."

Those, like Chalo Gonzalez, who accompanied Sam on those long, long drives to see his mother remember how he held on to the car's armrest with a white-knuckled grip, how he'd sit in the car in front of her house for a long time before finally working up the guts to go knock on her door.

Yet when that door opened, a remarkable transformation took place. Peckinpah's third wife, Joie Gould, remembers going with him to visit his mother in the early seventies. All the way during the drive to Fresno from L.A., Sam talked about Fern—what a bitch she was, the terrible, mean things she did. "She'll act very sweet," he warned, "but she's not sweet, she's not sweet at all, she's very dangerous!" He raged almost until the moment his mother opened her door. Then, like a nightclub comic switching from one character to another, Sam's whole demeanor changed. He threw open his arms, hugged and kissed her, and warmly introduced Joie. "We sat in this little parlor," says Joie, "with all the furniture and little knickknacks all perfectly arranged, this prissy little room, and Sam was wonderful to her—dutiful, polite, courtly. It was so phony it almost seemed surreal."

When they left he didn't revert instantly to hostility, but instead seemed to be on a high from the experience. It was only as they got nearer to his brother Denny's house that his anxiety returned.

Denny had an even more antagonistic relationship with his mother than Sam. Because he was a partner in his father's law firm, Fern had come to view Denny with suspicion and hostility, as an ally of David's and an enemy to her. When they arrived at Denny's, he and Sam went out to a bar together, leaving Joie to visit with Denny's wife, Betty. Afterward, on the drive back to L.A., Sam began lambasting his mother once more: "She's a bitch, she's evil, when she dies I'll piss on her grave . . ." Was he being phony with his mother, or phony with Denny? Joie couldn't tell.

In the span of one year, 1960, Sam Peckinpah saw his marriage disintegrate, as well as his parents'; he lost the home in the Colony that he had worked so hard for, lost his kids, lost his father. The whole foundation had been ripped out from under him in one violent jerk, and he would never regain his equilibrium. It was, to say the least, a year of profound disillusionment.

"If it could only be like what they told us it would be like when we were kids," Sam said to a *Life* magazine reporter in 1972.

"Like what?" the journalist asked.

"Oh, you know what I mean . . ." His voice trailed away.

The pain was too overwhelming for words. People had failed him, and he had failed them. *You can't trust anybody, not even yourself! People stop loving you, you stop loving them, people die on you, betray you, you betray yourself . . .*

His work was all he had now, his talent the only thing he could trust. So he threw himself into the breach with the fire of a fanatic.

In the fall of 1961 a messenger from MGM arrived at Peckinpah's doorstep with a screenplay. He winced when he saw the title: *Guns in the Afternoon.*

His leap from television to the big screen had not been as easy as he had hoped. After "The Westerner" folded, he had directed the "Mon Petit Chow" episode of "Route 66." Then, thanks to Brian Keith, he got his first crack at a feature film. Keith had just starred in a Disney romp, *The Parent Trap,* with Maureen O'Hara and Hayley Mills. The chronically "wholesome," "zany" comedy cleaned up at the box office. Hoping to cash in on its popularity, O'Hara's brother, Charles FitzSimons, approached Keith with a script for a low-budget western that would reteam Keith and O'Hara as hero and heroine.

"The script was pretty bad," says Keith. "It was the kind of thing John Ford would do under duress, if they bribed him with three other projects he really wanted to do." But Keith agreed to do the picture if, and only if, FitzSimons would hire Peckinpah to direct it. "I knew Sam could do the rewrites and get the visuals that would make you forget about how shitty it was."

Unfortunately FitzSimons had spent three years working on the screenplay with a writer, and he believed he had come up with the blueprint for a masterpiece. He hired Peckinpah so he could get Keith, and thus financing, but when Sam approached him with his first twenty pages of rewrites, FitzSimons dumped them in a trash can without giving them even a glance. "Sam," he said, "you've been hired to direct the picture, not rewrite it."

The relationship between the producer and director went downhill from there. *The Deadly Companions* was shot in twenty-one days in Old Tucson, Arizona, in January 1961, on a skimpy budget of $530,000. FitzSimons stood beside Peckinpah on the set every day, telling him how to stage and shoot the scenes, and forbidding him to give direction to his sister Maureen. After shooting was completed, the producer kicked Sam out of the editing room and recut the picture himself.

The result was a stilted melodrama filled with contrived plot twists, unbelievable situations, cardboard characterizations, and bad acting. The extraordinary talent that had burned so brightly in "The Westerner" flickered only fitfully here and there in little throwaway touches that Sam was able to stick in when FitzSimons wasn't looking. The picture was dumped into second-run movie houses and quickly disappeared, though, ironically, Peckinpah won some favorable reviews. Critics who had been bowled over by "The Westerner" gave him the benefit of the doubt and said that he had taken a piece of wretched material and at least made it interesting. James Powers of the *Hollywood Reporter* even went so far as to call it an "auspicious debut." Sam made sure to send a thank-you note to Powers and the others who had praised him.

Now he held in his hands the script for another B-western. But this time it had been sent by a young producer at a major studio who genuinely admired his talent.

Richard Lyons had nursed *Guns in the Afternoon* through two drafts with two different writers, N. B. Stone, Jr., and William Roberts. When he finally had a solid screenplay he began looking around for a director. Sylvia Hersh of the literary department at MGM told him about Peckinpah and urged him to look at some of the episodes of "The Westerner." Lyons ran one in a screening room at Metro and was stunned. "I had never been so thrilled in my life at the work that I saw in a half-hour," he later recalled.

By the time Sam finished reading the script for *Guns in the Afternoon,* he too was excited. The plot was barely distinguishable from hundreds of other horse operas. Steve Judd, a once-famous lawman fallen on hard times, agrees to take a job transporting gold from a mining town on the crest of the High Sierras down to a bank in the lowlands. Six guards have been killed by bandits on previous shipments, so Judd hires a former deputy, Gil Westrum, and his young sidekick, Heck Longtree, for additional firepower. But Westrum has also fallen on hard times and, unbeknownst to Judd, he and Heck plan to rob the gold themselves somewhere along the trail. Westrum's plan fails. Judd catches him and Heck trying to sneak out of camp with the paydirt in the middle of the night, and ties both of them up. Westrum escapes after Judd falls asleep, but, nagged by guilt, he follows his former partner from a distance on the trail the next day. When Judd is ambushed by an evil quintet of would-be miners—the Hammond brothers—who are also after the gold, Westrum has a change of heart and gallops back into the fray, six-guns blazing. He is hit by one of the Hammonds' bullets and dies, but his valiant charge saves Judd and the gold shipment and redeems his own honor.

What made the project intriguing was that it was set in the early years of the twentieth century, when automobiles were replacing horses and faceless uniformed police taking over from the swaggering ten-gallon-hatted lawmen who had tamed the Wild West. "The days of the forty-niners have passed and the days of the steady businessmen have arrived," a mole-faced banker informs Judd in one of the opening scenes. The heroes were aging gunfighters well past their prime and out of place in a world that no longer needed them. It was a theme that fascinated Peckinpah, one he would return to again and again in future films.

Lyons had already signed Joel McCrea and Randolph Scott to play Judd and Westrum—two towering but gray and brittle veterans of countless westerns, whose fortunes at the box office had sagged in recent years as younger audiences turned to younger heroes; their kind of old-fashioned western just didn't sell anymore. The parallels between the stars and the characters they would play were perfect; a clever director could exploit these obsolete icons to great effect.

Lyons received a call from Peckinpah the morning after he sent over the screenplay. "I've been reading and rereading this script all night," Sam said. "It is the finest script I have ever read in my life. What do I have to do to direct it?"

Sam was offered a paltry $12,000 for the job, but he snapped it up without hesitation. The ink had barely dried on his contract when he approached Lyons with a proposal. It may have been the finest script he'd ever read, but that didn't mean it couldn't be improved. He wanted to put a polish on it—no major structural changes, just clean up the dialogue a little. This time he had a producer who was willing to accommodate him.

For the next four weeks Peckinpah labored over the script. True to his word, he did not alter the basic framework of the story, for he recognized that the tight structure was its major strength. Instead, he began the intensive process of going over the scenes and reworking the dialogue, again and again, pushing for those extra layers of dimension, those unexpected nuances that would make the story real and personal to him.

"That was a complete rewrite," says Gay Hayden, who typed up Sam's revisions. "He rewrote the dialogue completely. I can't imagine that there's a word left from the original screenplay." Sam's copy of the final shooting script attests to this; it's a mass of yellow, blue, and pink pages that indicate whole scenes that have been rewritten. Only a scattering of white pages from the original screenplay survive.

As with "The Rifleman," Sam peppered the story with obscure personal references that few outside of his own family would recognize. The film would open with a small-town carnival, featuring a race between a horse and a camel down the main street. Sam had eagerly attended such events as a kid in Bass Lake and North Fork. Names like Madera County and Paul Staniford (a close friend of David Peckinpah's) popped up throughout the dialogue, and Sam named the mining town at the crest of the Sierras "Coarsegold," after a community just over the mountain from Dunlap's that really had once been a mining camp (but not in Sam's lifetime, despite his claims to the contrary in many interviews). Coarsegold's most prominent establishment became "Kate's Place," a whorehouse where the famous wedding sequence would occur. Sam knew "Kate's Place" and its inebriated inhabitants—including the syphilitic Hammond brothers—only too well from his travels in China, Mexico, and Nevada.

Litters of mad-dog brothers had begun appearing in "The Rifleman" and "The Westerner," and they would reappear in many a Peckinpah film after this. But it was in this picture, with the Hammonds, that the archetype came into full and hideous bloom.

Inbred, lice-infested, slavering, they nevertheless possessed two qualities that Peckinpah felt *almost* redeemed their many shortcomings: a surprising sense of family honor and a wild vitality. These were men who had yet to be tamed, broken, and harnessed to the plow and blinders of civilization; men who were rebelliously, if also repulsively, alive.

As for Steve Judd, Peckinpah painstakingly reworked the dialogue until the character had been fashioned into a mythic vision of his own father. Mythic because it was David Peckinpah with all his many flaws and inconsistencies sanded away and polished to the gleaming, tall, and broad-shouldered father/god of Sam's youth, the ideal image that David himself aspired to when he had stood before the Lincoln Memorial for the first time in 1917. Judd is a man of iron conviction, incorruptible integrity, a principled defender of law and justice, and a man still big enough to make his word stick.

Throughout their ride up the mountain to get the gold and back down again with it, Westrum laments about how little he and Judd have to show for all their years of honest service to the cause of law and order. They've been stomped on, shot at, wounded, laid up in the hospital for months at a time. They helped make the West safe—as the liturgy in John Ford's westerns goes—for women and children, for schools and churches and towns where decent folks could settle down and raise their families. And now they are no longer of use to all those fine, decent people. Time has passed them by, their clothes are frayed, their boot soles riddled with holes.

The purpose behind Westrum's nonstop monologue is to try to ease Judd into the idea of taking off with the gold so that Westrum won't have to take it from his former partner by force. But his verbal barrage makes not the slightest dent in Judd's rock-hard values. Judd never expected special treatment or rewards for the work he did; all he's ever wanted is an honest wage and to keep his self-respect.

"Partner, you know what's on the back of a poor man when

he dies?" Westrum says in one last effort to crack Judd's moral fiber. "The clothes of pride. And they're not a bit warmer to him dead than they were when he was alive. Is that all you want, Steve?"

Judd reins his horse to a halt, regards Westrum thoughtfully, then replies quietly, "All I want is to enter my house justified."

"That line . . . was paraphrasing a biblical verse I learned from my father," Sam later said. "He was a great student of the Bible, and this is one of the things I remember from my childhood."

About halfway up the mountain, Judd, Westrum, and Heck Longtree stop to spend the night at the isolated farm of a widower, Joshua Knudsen. Knudsen, a Christian fundamentalist, lives there with his daughter, Elsa, isolated from the outside world he despises as wicked and corrupt. An obsessed moralist, he wastes no opportunity to force harsh judgments and passages of Scripture on both his visitors and his frustrated daughter.

Knudsen is repressive of both his own physical desires and Elsa's. When he catches his daughter and Heck spooning in the barnyard after supper, he grabs the boy by the collar and pants, heaves him in the direction of the barn, and orders Elsa back into the house.

"Won't you ever learn any decency?" he asks as he follows her through the front door, slamming it behind him.

"We were only going to talk!" she spits back bitterly.

"The likes of him don't stop at talkin' . . . I'm your father, I've got to keep the dirt away, protect you from the wrong kind of men."

"That means everyone, doesn't it?" Elsa yells. "Every single man is the wrong kind of man, except you!"

In a flash of rage, Knudsen slashes the back of his hand across the girl's face.

Like that of Fern Peckinpah, Knudsen's possessiveness actually drives the loved one he seeks to control away. When Judd, Westrum, and Heck ride out, Elsa sneaks off on a horse and follows; she rides along with them to Coarsegold, where she hopes to find freedom by marrying Billy Hammond, the only handsome—but no less depraved—member of the Hammond clan.

The two-headed coin of Judd and Knudsen formed a Gestalt of the still-festering conflicts and ambivalences of Peckinpah's childhood.

"My father says there's only right and wrong, good and evil, nothin' in between," Elsa says to Judd at one point. "It isn't that simple, is it?"

"No," he admits, "it isn't. It should be, but it isn't."

Sam made only one structural change in the script, but it was crucial. Instead of Westrum getting killed in the final gunbattle, he switched things around; Judd would die and Westrum would survive. It was an inspired move, not only because it flew in the face of the genre's conventions (the villain must always die for his sins), but because it threw the story's theme into sharp focus.

With a few quick strokes of the pen, Peckinpah had made Westrum the protagonist and the upstanding Judd the antagonist. The film's central dramatic conflict now centered on Westrum, who in the opening of the story has already fallen from grace. Broke and disillusioned, he has forsaken the values he once held unshakable. When Judd first finds him he is fleecing rubes in a traveling carnival's crooked sharpshooting booth, making a mockery of his old identity. Posing as "The Oregon Kid . . . The Frontier Lawman," he wears phony long-haired Wild Bill Hickok wig and whiskers. On the journey with the incorruptible Judd he is forced to reexamine the ethics and code of honor that once gave his life meaning. When he betrays Judd by trying to steal the gold, it is himself he is really betraying.

"It all pointed this way," Judd says bitterly in the confrontation with his former partner, "all that talk about old Doc Franklin, ungrateful citizens, what we had coming but never got paid. I knew in my bones what you were aiming for, but I wouldn't believe it. I kept telling myself you were a good man, you were my friend."

Westrum attempts to rationalize. "This is bank money, not yours."

"And what they don't know won't hurt them," Judd yells. "Not them, only *me!*" He strikes Westrum twice, open-handed, across the face, then challenges him to draw. But Westrum won't. He unbuckles his gunbelt and lets it drop to the ground. Humiliated, naked before Judd's hard gaze, Westrum is forced to see just how far he has fallen. It is the turning point, setting in motion a change of heart that eventually sends Westrum riding back to Judd's side in the climactic shootout.

When the smoke of the gunfire clears, Judd is lying on the ground, blood spilling from the three slugs the Hammonds put into him. Kneeling beside him, Westrum says softly, "Don't worry about anything. I'll take care of it, just like you would have."

Judd squints at him, all the affection for his old friend flooding back. "Hell, I know that, I always did. You just forgot it for a while, that's all."

Judd's death is the instrument of Westrum's salvation. It is—as other critics have noted—a profoundly Catholic tragedy weaved from the fabric of Western myth. The theme, as Paul Seydor has so succinctly and perceptively written, is: "What does it profit a man to gain the world if he loses his soul?"

This would be the dominating theme of *The Wild Bunch, Pat Garrett and Billy the Kid*, and *Bring Me the Head of Alfredo Garcia* as well—a point missed by many reviewers who labeled Peckinpah a nihilist.

By the time Peckinpah turned in his blue, pink, and yellow-paged screenplay to Lyons, McCrea, and Scott, he had also changed the title from *Guns in the Afternoon* to *Ride the High Country*. It signified the dramatic shift in tone and content, but Sam was tight-lipped about his aspirations for the piece. "If I'd tried to talk to MGM about the basic theme," he later said, "which was about salvation and loneliness, they'd have fired me on the spot."

They didn't, for both the producer and the stars loved the new script. "He [Peckinpah] was handed a gem," Lyons told Garner Simmons, "but he knew how to cut it to really bring out its brilliance. Strange as it may seem, most people don't know what to do with a diamond in the rough." McCrea would play Steve Judd, it was decided after some haggling, and Scott would be Westrum.

When he moved into his tiny office on the MGM lot in the fall of 1961, Sam had good reason to be nervous. The owner of "more stars than there are in heaven," the glitzy, gaudy Grand Hotel of movie studios was proud of its assembly-line approach to filmmaking. It was a movie factory where "the system" was exalted, not the individual; idiosyncratic talents were molded to mesh with the gears of the machine, and if they refused to bend they were crushed and consigned to the scrap heap. Erich von Stroheim, F. Scott Fitzgerald, Buster Keaton, and the Marx Brothers were just a few of those shredded by Leo the Lion's fangs.

The lion may have been graying a bit by 1960 and losing a few teeth, but he still had a deadly bite. Riding high on $12.5 million in profits, reaped mostly from *Ben-Hur* and a rerelease of *Gone With the Wind,* the studio was in hot pursuit of another blockbuster. It poured $19 million into a remake of *Mutiny on the Bounty* with Marlon Brando and Trevor Howard, and millions more into a Cinerama extravaganza, *How the West Was Won* that featured, well, more stars than there are . . .

High Country was allotted a minuscule $800,000 budget and a twenty-four-day shooting schedule, which ranked it very near the bottom of the twenty-eight films the studio produced that year—strictly double-bill fare for the drive-ins in redneck country, where a few dollars could still be wrung out of the fading stars, McCrea and Scott.

Sam, of course, took a different view of the picture's potential.

Louis B. Mayer and Irving Thalberg were long gone, but they had their modern counterparts: the company president, Joseph Vogel, who ran its business affairs, mostly out of New York; production chief Sol Siegel, who, like Thalberg, possessed a more sophisticated understanding of the filmmaking process. Fortunately, Siegel was sympathetic toward the project, and Peckinpah had a strong ally in Lyons, who also felt that *High Country* had the potential to be more than just another B-movie. Thus Sam was given nearly a free hand in choosing his cast and the key members of his crew.

He immediately hired Lucien Ballard as the cinematographer. Ballard had worked under tight budgets before on Budd Boetticher's *Buchanan Rides Alone* and with Peckinpah on "The

Westerner." Sam knew Ballard could give the picture the majestic look he wanted; after some hard lobbying, Peckinpah and Ballard won approval to shoot it in color and Cinemascope.

For an art director, Sam was fortunate to secure the services of a wily scrounger, Leroy Coleman, who would collaborate with him again eight years later on *The Ballad of Cable Hogue.* "We stole the picture," Sam later said. "Leroy Coleman literally went out into the warehouse and stole *Mutiny on the Bounty* [sail] canvas to build our mining camp [a tent city]. They [MGM] charged seventy dollars a shirt out of wardrobe, so we went out and bought Goodwill things for two dollars and a half, so we kept the budget down."

With *Ride the High Country* Sam's stock company of actors solidified. John Anderson, James Drury, Warren Oates, L. Q. Jones, and John Davis Chandler would play the Hammond brothers, and R. G. Armstrong would be Joshua Knudsen. All but Chandler and Jones had worked with Peckinpah in television.

The studio pressured Sam to cast one of their platinum-blond starlets in the part of Elsa, but he refused. Instead he went with a newcomer: redheaded, freckle-faced Mariette Hartley. Just twenty-one years old, with a fresh, cornfed look, Hartley had recently hacked most of her hair off for a stage production of *Saint Joan.* She still remembers vividly the day she stepped trepidatiously into Peckinpah's office at MGM. He had already begun the process of reinventing himself. Gone were the berets, ascots, herringbone suits, and long cigarette holders of his Four Star days. Hartley found a man leaning back in his chair with a pair of well-worn cowboy boots propped up on his desktop and a wide-brimmed Stetson tilted down over the bridge of his nose—like Gary Cooper taking a snooze in the sheriff's office before duty called him into action again.

Hartley's Norman Rockwell appearance was an illusion. Her father and mother had both been alcoholics and now she was trapped in a terribly abusive marriage with a neurotically jealous husband who beat her regularly and brutally. The dynamics were a perfect match for Elsa Knudsen, and though Sam knew none of this, he seemed to sense it immediately. "There was something palpable about the connection that we had the minute I walked in the door," Hartley recalls. "Sam seemed like a part of my family; it was like coming home. There are those moments in your life where there is a spiritual, psychic connection that you can cut with a knife, and I certainly felt that with Sam."

Peckinpah gave her a scene to read, and when she finished he tilted his hat back on his forehead and said with almost childlike openness, "Gee, I think you're wonderful!" After calling her back for some screen tests, he signed her.

Sam rehearsed with the principals for four days—reading and rereading the script aloud, discussing characters, motivations, subtext, possible pieces of business—before the company moved by bus to the Inyo National Forest in the High Sierras, around Mammoth Lakes, just a few peaks east of the old Dunlap Ranch and Peckinpah Mountain . . . the pristine High Country of Sam's youth.

In the first four days of principal photography the company captured some stunning shots of McCrea, Scott, Ron Starr, and Hartley riding both up and down the mountain past sky-blue lakes and through shimmering groves of quaking aspen and glistening green strands of sugar pine. Lucien Ballard had insisted on bringing a Chapman crane along, and they used it to great effect in shots that slide sideways and then glide upward to follow the riders up the ridge lines.

The weather for the first few days couldn't have been better for filming. The mid-October sky was clear and blue, the sunlight fell thin and bright across the wooded mountains, but the air was freezing. "Talk about cold," says Cleo Anton, the script supervisor on the picture, "everybody had their parkas on. But not Sam. He had a serape from Mexico and that's all that guy had on. He was rugged, for as small and wiry as he was."

Peckinpah was too ecstatic to feel the cold. The footage they were getting was fantastic. On the fourth day they completed the first gunfight with the Hammonds on a windswept ridge line with great swells of pine-treed peaks in the background. But as dusk approached a thick layer of charcoal clouds crowded the sky and snow began to fall.

Sam was determined to wait the storm out, even if it meant losing several days of shooting. When the weather cleared, the white-capped peaks would provide a breathtaking backdrop. But production manager Hal Polaire worried. An MGM staff man, his ass was on the line, and his loyalty was to the brass back in the Thalberg Building, not to a fledgling director who would move on to another studio after this picture was in the can. Polaire placed a call to MGM and told them of the situation. He recommended the company be brought back to L.A. and the balance of the picture be shot in the Santa Monica Mountains. The risk of runaway costs from inclement weather was too great. It didn't take management long to come to a decision: bring the company home tomorrow.

Peckinpah's spirits plummeted. He refused to take the car the studio had provided and instead rode down the mountain in the bus with the actors. Five miles down the road the storm cleared, the sun broke through the clouds, and his despair boiled slowly into outrage.

He brooded for the entire six-hour ride back to L.A., drinking tequila and playing poker with the actors. The more he drank the angrier he became. "He was greatly tempted to tell them to shove it," says L. Q. Jones, "but we talked him out of it." When the bus pulled in to the parking lot at MGM in Culver City, Jones poured Sam into his Corvette and drove him home. "If I hadn't, he would have driven off a cliff because Sam never knew when to quit drinking, even then."

Once the initial blow had been absorbed and he sobered up, Peckinpah's commitment to the picture returned. He set about finding new locations in the Santa Monica Mountains and the Hollywood Hills that could be intercut with the Mammoth footage. Bronson Canyon in Griffith Park would serve as the sight for Coarsegold and soapsuds sprayed over the hillsides and miners' tents would simulate snow. The substitution grated on him, but his determination hardened. He would make it work, and this time he would not be castrated as he had been on *The Deadly Companions*. "If it hair-lipped the governor, he was going to make the picture his way," says Jones.

When shooting resumed, Peckinpah exhibited a ferocity that

threw the cast and crew into a confused panic. They were filming the arrival of the Hammond brothers in Coarsegold and the scene in which the brothers force Warren Oates to take a bath. "Sam berated the crew, he screamed at the actors, he cursed the transportation people, mouthed off about the horses that were in the background," says Jones. "Nothing worked. We talked about it, or rather, we listened to Sam scream. We went back and we shot it again and again and again and again, and he was trying to determine whether it was going to be easier to set fire to the actors or the camera." A sound man was canned on the spot for allowing the microphone boom to drop into a shot. That shocked the crew, all of whom were MGM lifers. To most, Peckinpah seemed to have gone insane, but Jones, who would work with the director on six more productions, detected a method in Sam's madness.

"That was his way of spending MGM's money, asserting his influence and power and getting the crew under his thumb. I saw him do it on picture after picture. It was almost always the third day before we really got down to shooting. The first day he gets everybody dissected from what they normally would do, so that now people are confused, they're uncomfortable. Then the next day he'd heighten that separation a little bit more so that actors were snipping at the production crew and production couldn't put up with the actors—everybody was in a snit. And the third day Sam would start to put it back together with Sam as the father figure so you always look to Sam to solve your problems. He's gonna give them to you, but at the same time he was going to solve them for you. So then everything would settle down and you'd get down to it. That was a very conscious applied psychology that Sam used." And one that he had learned from the United States Marine Corps. He tore the people down, then built them up again so that they were no longer MGM's men, but now his own—a hardened fighting unit ready to tear the gates off Hell if Sam Peckinpah told them to.

Though he was hard on the actors, they were almost unanimously devoted to him. Sam made James Drury, Warren Oates, L. Q. Jones, John Davis Chandler, and John Anderson eat and room together, and told them he wanted them to stay in character both on and off the set. "You are the Hammonds," he solemnly instructed, "you hate everybody here!" It worked beautifully. In the finished film, the actors don't seem to be performing at all, but instead have crawled inside the Hammonds' scaly skins.

When Mariette Hartley developed a crush on Sam, he used it to manipulate the appropriate emotions out of her for the love scenes. Soon Hartley hardly felt like she was acting at all. The lines between her "real" life and role in the film seemed to blend together effortlessly.

R. G. Armstrong, who played Elsa's Bible-fixated father, also found the dividing line between his personal life and the part he was playing murky to nonexistent. It's no accident that Armstrong kept reappearing in Peckinpah's films as a religious psychopath. It was a role that he was literally born for. He was raised on a small farm outside of Birmingham, Alabama; R.G.'s mother indoctrinated him with fundamentalist Christianity from the day he was born. "My mother prayed over me," says Armstrong. "I was redheaded. That was a sign to her. She'd had three redheaded uncles who were preachers. I heard her praying over me; she dedicated me to God."

When he grew to manhood, however, he rejected his mother's faith. "It just broke my heart. I just couldn't buy the orthodoxy and she couldn't answer my questions. 'You've got to take it on faith. Faith, Son! God works his wonders in mysterious ways!' " He became an actor and playwright instead, and approached his art with the same fervor he once held for the Bible; like Peckinpah, he had traded his mother's chosen faith for another. "It's a mystical thing when I hit the stage or step in front of the camera, it's a heightened state of being. I'm not aware of acting."

Yet in all the years that followed, he was haunted by his mother's Biblical mumblings and by the violent realities of his boyhood that dramatically contradicted them. "My brother Kenneth was two years younger than me. Daddy was mean to him. When I was four years old I watched Daddy beat him with a limb off a peach tree while Kevin was sitting in his high chair. It was Kenneth's birthday and he wanted a piece of his cake before he finished his supper. When Daddy said no, he swept his plate off of his high chair. Daddy went right outside to the peach tree, broke off a limb, and stripped the leaves off. I saw the whole thing. For years I thought I had dreamed it."

R.G. appeared in the pilot for "The Rifleman"; in the first episode of the show that Sam directed, "The Marshal"; and in a segment of "The Westerner." When shooting wrapped at the end of the day at Four Star, the actors and crews from the various shows would congregate across the street at the Stage Door bar to drink and gossip about the industry. R.G. joined them. After four or five beers, an old familiar fire raced through his veins and all of a sudden he'd find himself up on a tabletop preaching to the crowd—quoting Scripture, warning of the evils of the devil's brew, and exhorting the congregation to turn away from sin and toward the glory of Jesus. It was all in fun, just cutting up for the crowd—but Peckinpah, sitting at a nearby table, saw the flame in R.G.'s eyes and recognized it only too well.

"Sam saw the depth of my repressed hostility," says Armstrong. "I was so psychotically, traumatically encased, I was cut off from life. Sam said, 'You're a real killer.' He recognized the struggle I had with my religion, and the violence I held within myself. I think Sam and I had a kinship because we both felt like aliens in this world. We didn't know how to relate to people. He got the whole feeling; he said I was a jackleg preacher, I mean, a real potential killer who probably got religion. And that's what Sam started playing me as."

In the final confrontation between Knudsen and his daughter—when Elsa yells, "Every single man is the wrong kind of man, except you!"—the private demons of Peckinpah, Hartley, and Armstrong intersected in a flash of frightening violence. Armstrong's eyes popped out of his round face, his thick mouth bit into itself, and his huge hand lashed out and smashed Hartley hard across the face, for real. The actress fell to her knees, weeping uncontrollably. It was a chilling moment on the set.

"I had to call on that buried hostility and it finally just erupted," says Armstrong.

Remarkable too were the performances Peckinpah elicited

from his two aging stars, Randolph Scott and Joel McCrea. *High Country* would be their last hurrah; as in the final shootout itself, their last flash of glory.

Peckinpah never came out and said that the role of Steve Judd was patterned after David Peckinpah, but he kept bringing his father up obliquely in conversations—casually relating anecdotes, things that his dad had said, what he had stood for, what he'd meant to Sam. McCrea got the message; much of David Peckinpah seeped into his performance.

In the scene where Judd catches Westrum trying to sneak away with the gold, McCrea summons forth all the awesome wrath-of-God righteousness of "the Boss" himself. His lips white and quivering, eyes flat and bright when he tells his former partner: "And what they don't know won't hurt them. Not them, only *me!*"

In other scenes he captures the vulnerable underbelly of the character with the same facility. Having to scurry aside on his horse as an automobile races down the main street of a town, trying to hide his frayed shirt cuffs and farsightedness from the bankers who hire him, and to conceal his loneliness when Scott reminisces about an old girlfriend—he stirs subtle undercurrents of melancholy in the aging gunfighter.

By mid-November the production approached its final week of shooting. All that remained was the confrontation between Judd, Westrum, and the Hammond brothers. Howard Hawks or John Ford would have filmed the shootout from a dozen camera angles at most; their method was to carefully choreograph the action within classically composed long shots. This reflected a more traditional and conservative sensibility, but it was also a defense tactic. By giving the studio editors a minimum of camera angles to work with, the directors forced their producers to cut the sequences as they envisioned them and left little opportunity for butchery. But Peckinpah, who'd earned his bones in the quick-cutting medium of television, was of a new breed. He shot the gunfight from a multitude of angles, creating more, not less, choices in the cutting room—thousands of them, as many choices as he could.

"The footage I shoot is just a chunk of marble," he was fond of saying. "I start sculpting my statue when I get in the editing room." Perhaps wet clay would have been an even better metaphor, for Peckinpah understood, more clearly than any other director, the plasticity of the medium. Time could be stretched out or shrunk, the chronology of events reshuffled, the action reshaped again and again until finally it reached a form that satisfied him.

There were over 150 camera setups for the final gunfight—most made with an old blimplike Panavision camera, though an Arriflex was brought in for some of the close-ups. Long shots, crane shots, zooms from medium shots to close-ups, tracking shots of each of the seven combatants, extreme close-ups of guns firing, of each of the principals getting hit and falling. What an old-time director like W. S. "One Take" Van Dyke, or even Sam's hero, Michael Curtiz, might have shot in a couple of days, took Peckinpah six.

The final scene in the picture was Scott's farewell to McCrea, who is wounded and dying. For it Peckinpah chose an unusually low camera angle—eye-level with McCrea, who was barely holding himself up with one arm.

"Oh," McCrea grimaces when he sees Ron Starr and Mariette Hartley approaching. "I don't want them to see this . . . I'll go it alone."

Scott waves the young couple off, then rises to his feet, blinking rapidly. McCrea looks up at him, squinting against the pain. "So long, partner."

"I'll see you later," Scott says awkwardly, then turns and walks off.

Alone now in the barnyard, McCrea collapses slowly to the ground, revealing the towering peaks of the High Country in the background.

"Cut," Sam said in a dry quiet voice at the end of the first take. Getting up from his chair, he shuffled over to McCrea, his hazel eyes turned in on themselves intently. "Let's try it one more time. Only this time, before you die, turn and take a look back at those mountains."

McCrea nodded. He and Scott resumed their start positions and they did the scene again. Afterward, McCrea lay facedown in the dirt, waiting for Sam to call cut. Waiting and waiting and waiting. Had he missed it? Should he hold position? Then he became aware of a gentle rustling by his side. He glanced up and there stood Peckinpah, right beside him. "That was it," he whispered. The words like a cold wind raised the hairs on the back of McCrea's neck. "You got it."

The power of it was apparent to everyone on the set that day. "I looked up at the tears streaming down Randy Scott's face," Mariette Hartley recalls. "I was awestruck. I had never seen that kind of acting."

But it wasn't until they saw it in the theater months later that the cast and crew experienced the full impact of the composition Sam had chosen. McCrea looking up one last time at that jutting mass of rocks and trees, reaching up into the very thinnest realm of blue sky above; one last glance at the rocky wooded peaks that he and others like him had driven themselves across; one last time at the once-limitless expanse of seething wilderness, now fenced in, shrinking and dying with him as he lowers himself to the ground. "McCrea's glorification was explicit, unsubtle and shattering," Paul Schrader has written of that final, indelible image.

It was an inspired choice, but not one that Peckinpah drew out of thin air. Fern Lea remembers a photograph (later lost in the endless series of moves made over the course of Sam's later nomadic existence) taken of David Peckinpah on his last hunting trip into the High Country, just weeks before he died. In it, his back was to the camera, his expression concealed as he gazed up at the snowy crest of the Sierra Nevada.

The production finished four days over schedule and $52,000 over budget. Not bad at all, considering the fiasco in Mammoth. But there was no opportunity to breathe a sigh of relief, for Margaret Booth—the legendary, hardnosed head of MGM's editorial department—had screened all of the raw footage as it came back to the studio and hated it. Booth particularly detested the crazy camera angles of the final shootout. To her it looked like the product of a chaotic mind. She told her superiors that the film was uncuttable. (This was the first, but certainly not the last time the allegation would be made about Sam's coverage.)

Fortunately, Lyons and Peckinpah still had an ally in Sol Siegel. At the time it was still common practice for studios to take the raw footage away from a director and assign their own staff editors, who would cut it to management's specifications. But because of Booth's disaffection and Peckinpah's fervid belief in the film, Siegel decided to give the young director a crack at cutting the footage himself, with an editor of his own choosing.

Sam selected Frank Santillo, an MGM staff man, but one who had worked for years with Slavko Vorkapich, the legendary editorial genius who had constructed montage sequences for *The Good Earth, Boys' Town, Mr. Smith Goes to Washington,* and hundreds of other American films.

Peckinpah and Santillo went to work in a cramped little editing room buried among hundreds of others in a barracks-like building on the MGM lot. They ran thousands of feet of raw film through the moviola and began to painstakingly cut and splice it together. "Sam spent thirteen weeks in the cutting room," Richard Lyons later recalled. "He never left; Saturdays, Sundays, he just stayed there and cut every frame of this picture."

Santillo was not the least bit daunted by Peckinpah's superabundant coverage of the final shootout; in fact it excited him, since he understood that the sequence could be molded thousands of different ways. Instead of pasting together whole takes from the various camera angles, he used fragments of shots and wove the gun battle into an expressionistic montage.

"I knew that even with a one-frame cut the audience could retain something of what was on the screen," Santillo told Garner Simmons. "When a guy is shooting, you don't have to show him first standing there, then aiming, then firing. You've got to imply a lot. Boom!—he fires. Boom!—somebody's hit. Boom!—somebody else is hit. You make the sequence move by allowing the audience to fill in the gaps. Consequently, I cut the sequence and some of the shots were only six frames long [a quarter of a second], and I said to Sam that even at that length some of them would appear to be too long on the screen. And he said, 'Oh, no.' I could tell that he was afraid that maybe I'd cut them too short already. So we went to the screening room and looked at what I'd cut, and after the sequence was over Sam looked at me, smiled, and said, 'You know, you're right.' And then we went back, trimmed the sequence down until it was exactly the way Sam wanted it, and some of the shots were only two frames long. Sam has always given me credit for teaching him how to 'flash cut' like that."

The rapid crosscutting between camera angles sucked the viewer inside the action. Instead of watching the confrontation from a stately aesthetic distance, as they would in a Ford or Hawks movie, the audience found itself caught in the crossfire. The finished sequence had a breathtaking, kinetic power.

In the first week of January 1962, Sol Siegel screened a rough cut that Peckinpah and Santillo had prepared. Sam couldn't watch it with him. Instead he waited in the cutting room in a nervous sweat. When the picture was over, Siegel called from the screening room. "You gambled with that funny style of yours—and you've won," said the production chief. "I like it. Go ahead and make the final cut." Elated, Peckinpah and Santillo went back to work, sanding the picture to a fine edge.

Unfortunately, before they could finish, Siegel—long at odds with MGM's president, Joseph Vogel—left the studio. Vogel decided to take over the production reins himself and came out to Los Angeles to look at the movies that were almost ready for release. Vogel was a species of Hollywood dinosaur fast on the road to extinction: the old-fashioned movie mogul. Autocratic, disdainful of intellectual pretensions, conventionally Midwestern in taste and values, he was not in the best of moods the afternoon he settled into his plush screening-room chair to watch *Ride the High Country*. He'd already sat through two other MGM movies that morning, both excruciatingly bad, and he dreaded the prospect of a cheap western with a couple of has-been stars. A big expense account lunch lay in his stomach like freshly poured concrete as the lights dimmed and the film rolled out onto the screen.

Peckinpah and Richard Lyons huddled a few rows behind, hanging on the president's every twitch for a clue of the movie's effect on him. They soon had their answer. A long snarling sound reverberated through the room. Sam jabbed Lyons in the ribs and hissed, "What the hell is that noise?"

"That's the president of the company," Lyons replied, "snoring."

Sam peered at Vogel's iron-gray head now fallen limply backward in his seat and muttered, "I'll be a son of a bitch!"

Vogel managed to regain consciousness in time for the wedding in the whorehouse. His assistants had led him to believe this would be a wholesome family picture, something Disney might do. He blinked his eyes at the vision of an incredibly obese woman in purple plumes and kabuki makeup, her giant spiked breasts looming out of the screen as she laughed like an amphetamined coyote. "Welcome to Coarsegold!"

"The lights went on," Lyons later recalled. "He [Vogel] was completely white. He looked at me and said, 'Kid, you've disgraced me. This is the worst film that's ever been perpetrated on the American public.' " It was so bad, Vogel went on, he might not even release it.

"I stood up," Sam later recalled, "and said I'd be delighted to go and find financing and buy the picture . . . within three days, and he wouldn't have to release it. I was thereupon barred from the lot."

Fortunately the editing was nearly completed and Vogel, needing product even if he thought it abominable, gave Lyons the go-ahead to dub and score the picture for theatrical release. Lyons was secretly relieved to have Peckinpah locked out of the cutting room; even he was beginning to weary of the way Sam kept tearing apart finished sequences and recutting them in a ceaseless effort to "take it one step further."

"If he had his way," Lyons told an interviewer in 1975, "Peckinpah'd still be cutting that show this week."

But Lyons continued to consult with his exiled director, and even played the sound reels, after they'd been dubbed, over the telephone for Sam's approval. Peckinpah didn't get a chance to supervise the musical score, and it turned out—in Lyons' hands—to be one of the film's major weaknesses. While the main theme was richly evocative of the story's epic tragedy, the score on the whole was over-orchestrated. Almost every single scene had blaring music behind it to tell the audience what it was supposed to be feeling. This overkill marred some of the most powerful moments, such as the confrontation between Knudsen and his daughter, Elsa.

Still, Peckinpah was proud of the final product. Very proud. When MGM held a screening for the cast and crew, Sam was allowed to attend it and to invite some guests of his own, like his sister Fern Lea, her husband Walter, and Gay Hayden, who had typed up Sam's revisions on the screenplay. When the lights came up after the final shot of McCrea sinking out of frame, the applause rumbled through the theater like an earthquake. There were cheers, some people were on their feet. Fern Lea, then pregnant with her third daughter, ran to the ladies room, where she burst into tears. She had, of course, seen her father in McCrea's every word and gesture.

"Sam was very excited about the picture," says Hayden. "He was excited about the promise of it, the reception of it. He looked like a happy human being, which he didn't a lot. I don't think I ever saw him that happy again. After that, I think, when things worked and when things were good . . . then it was as if he'd won another battle and, you know, he'd beaten the bastards. But that night he didn't know the wars he was going to fight."

MGM gave the picture one public preview in a Los Angeles theater. Out of an audience of 255, 201 rated the film from very good to outstanding, seventeen rated it fair, and only one thought it was poor. But this did not restore the studio's faith in the production. *Ride the High Country* was dumped on the market in May 1962 as the bottom half of a double-bill. The A-feature it played with was *The Tartars*, a turgid pseudo-epic shot in Italy and Yugoslavia, starring Orson Welles and Victor Mature. The newspaper ads for it promised: "Hordes storm fortress! Tartars abduct Viking Beauty! Orgy celebrates conquest!" The ads for *High Country* were almost nonexistent.

It's hard to imagine a more vivid illustration of the MGM mindset: epics, any epics, even bad ones, are better than low-budget character studies. Vogel had orchestrated a self-fulfilling prophecy. He had pronounced *High Country* a bomb, and now the studio's poor distribution of it nearly assured that it would be.

Nearly. There was a wild card: the New York critics.

"The reviews the next day came out," Richard Lyons later said, "and of course we got four stars in the *News*, and the *Times* raved about it. All of the critics were talking about this little gem that was made by a major studio and they didn't know what they had. The theater managers—all these Loew's theaters—were up on ladders the next morning reversing the billing."

Life, the *New York Herald-Tribune*, and the *Hollywood Reporter* also wrote glowing reviews. *Newsweek* named it best film of the year, and *Time* placed it on its best-ten list. It won Mexico's *Diosa de Plata* (Silver Goddess) award for best foreign film, the Paris critics' award, the Silver Leaf award in Sweden, and the Grand Prix at the Belgium International Film Festival, where it beat, among other competitors, Federico Fellini's *8½*. At thirty-seven years old, Peckinpah had come a long way from that first directing class at Fresno State, where he and William Walsh had used a rolled-up sweater to simulate Lennie's dead puppy.

Ride the High Country marked a turning point not only in Sam Peckinpah's career, but also in Hollywood and America. In 1961 and 1962 two new novels exploded onto the bestseller lists, *Catch-22* and *One Flew Over the Cuckoo's Nest.* The first, by Joseph Heller, savagely ridiculed the my-country-right-or-wrong bullheadedness that had dominated American culture for the last two decades.

Catch-22 questioned the morality of war—any war, no matter what flag or values were being fought for—while America was gearing up for one of its most horrific and pointless in a seemingly endless series of wars. By 1961, the U.S. had 16,000 military advisers in Southeast Asia. The first American soldier was killed in action in Vietnam that same year. Over 50,000 more would follow him to their graves over the next decade. The years 1961 and 1962 also brought the Bay of Pigs disaster, the face-off of American and Soviet tanks in Berlin, and the Cuban Missile Crisis, which brought the entire planet to the brink of nuclear annihilation.

Heller's absurdist rejection of his patriotic duty was beginning to look like the only sane position to take.

Cuckoo's Nest, by Ken Kesey, featured a hard-drinking, hard-fighting, smooth-gambling, cowboy-style hero, Randle Patrick McMurphy. McMurphy strides into an allegorical mental ward, like a gunfighter into a saloon, to take on "Big Nurse," a personification of "the combine," the military-industrial complex that had steamrollered an entire generation into the bland conformity of sheet metal. The two novels were clarion calls for the turbulent social revolution to come.

And American westerns were changing with the times. *High Country*'s theme of aging cowboys caught in the death throes of the Wild West would become a Peckinpah favorite. He would extend and refine it in later films, most brilliantly in his masterpiece at the decade's end. But it was by no means unique to him.

A cluster of westerns with remarkably similar concerns appeared almost simultaneously with *High Country: The Misfits,* 1961, written by Arthur Miller and directed by John Huston; *Lonely Are the Brave,* 1962, written by Dalton Trumbo and directed by David Miller; and *The Man Who Shot Liberty Valance,* written by James Warner Bellan and Willis Goldbeck, and directed by John Ford. And a major western novel—*Monte Walsh* by Jack Schaefer, the author of *Shane*—appeared in September 1963. All dealt with graying cowboys who were unable to change with the times while barbed wire, telephone and power lines, automobiles and paved roads strangled a once-limitless and untamed frontier. And all displayed a profound ambivalence about the "progress" that civilization had brought to the West. The fifties were over. In November 1963 John F. Kennedy would be assassinated in Dallas, Texas, and the sparkling illusion of Camelot would crumble into dust.

It was as if these westerns anticipated the event, as if their creators somehow sensed that the era of unlimited possibilities and untainted ideals was swiftly drawing to a close, and that the traditional mythology of the Wild West had already begun to lose its relevance.

The Man Who Shot Liberty Valance, though embarrassingly corny at times, is undoubtedly the best of the three movies mentioned above. John Ford—once the poetic proselytizer of America's manifest destiny, celebrator of the white man's quest to conquer and "civilize" the frontier—had been making increasingly dark and ambivalent movies since the mid-fifties that betrayed cracks in the aging director's once-solid convictions. Like *High Country*, *Valance* starts in a West that is no longer wild, but tamed, tethered, and housebroken. The survivors from the old days, those who fought to make the land safe for decent folk, are forgotten and disillusioned and riddled with regrets.

Liberty Valance was a towering work, a final masterpiece by an old maestro. But there lay the crucial difference between it and *High Country*. Ford's film was an endpoint, the fading, cataract-shrouded vision of the old guard. Peckinpah's film was a departure point. *High Country* struck sparks because Sam had taken his personal tragedy—the death of his father—and injected it into the larger framework of a western myth. Thus it was no longer a story about the death of David Peckinpah, but about the death of an entire generation of men and the mythology that they had lived by, a mythology that Sam Peckinpah and his generation could no longer believe in, no matter how much they might have yearned to. It was the last traditional western Peckinpah would ever make. From this point on he paddled into deeper and darker waters.

High Country was a strange hybrid. It seemed like an old-fashioned western with tall-in-the-saddle heroes and traditional situations: an innocent girl who must be protected, a fast but foolish boy who learns the right values from the trail-hardened veteran, a final stand-up, fair-draw shootout. The dialogue was reminiscent of hundreds of westerns that had come before it: "Let's meet 'em head-on, halfway, just like always." "I don't want them to see this. I'll go it alone." "So long, partner."

And yet it wasn't old-fashioned at all. The fast, almost subliminal cutting in the final shootout, the gritty realism of Coarsegold, the bizarre surrealism of Kate's Place, the black-humored affection that the filmmaker lavished on his villains—all seemed to place Peckinpah with the thoroughly modern young directors (Stanley Kubrick, John Frankenheimer, Arthur Penn) who were beginning to take over the medium. Peckinpah was a man standing with one foot in the past and one in the future, his work became the link between the two, embodying what America had been and what it was becoming. This is why *High Country*, more than any of its competitors, captivated audiences in 1962, and why he became perhaps the single most important filmmaker of his time.

It was probably shortly after the movie's release that Peckinpah actually met the old master, John Ford, for the first and only time, on the steps to the Thalberg Building at MGM. "We were introduced by mutual friends," Sam told Garner Simmons. If Ford admired Peckinpah's work, he did a good job of concealing it. He responded to Sam's handshake and compliments with only a few grunted monosyllables. It couldn't have been easy for the old auteur, for he must have sensed that more than a handshake had been exchanged. The baton had been passed from one generation to the next, and the new decade would belong to the younger man.

5

Moby-Dick on Horseback

Sam Peckinpah had taken a wild rocket ride—from television writer to internationally acclaimed filmmaker in just three years. But the next three years would slam him back to earth again. At last he would be given the chance to direct big-budget, star-studded Hollywood productions, but his dream turned into a nightmare. He discovered that J. W. Wright and William de Mille had scores of counterparts at the movie studios. With millions of dollars at stake on the pictures he was directing, his conflicts with them escalated into all-out wars. The producers regarded Peckinpah's obsessive perfectionism as madness; he saw their bottom-line mentality as idiotically short-sighted.

By the time the smoke cleared from the battlefield, Peckinpah's career would lie in ruins. The bitterness of the experience fostered an antagonism toward the moneymen that would never leave him and eventually crippled his ability to make films.

But Sam didn't yet guess what lay ahead. In the spring of 1963 life was good; he was coming back out into the sunlight, leaving the darkness of 1960 behind. He had moved out of the Holiday House and rented the Bird View house overlooking the ocean at Point Dume, just a few miles north of the Colony. It was a fifties-style tract house with big black sea gulls painted on the garage door, a pool, a large kitchen, a stone fireplace, and a separate guest house beneath the main floor. The decor was haphazard: Danish furniture that one of Sam's secretaries picked out; a charcoal sketch of a delicate Indian girl fingering the strands of her long black hair; a rusty branding iron and a few other authentic cowboy artifacts. That was about it. The houses, condominiums, hotel rooms, cabins, and trailers Sam occupied from this point to the end of his life all had a cluttered, chaotic appearance, as if he'd only just unpacked his things, hadn't had time to arrange them, and didn't plan on staying long—and usually he didn't. The atmosphere was the opposite of the carefully decorated home he'd grown up in. There were no bowls of wax fruit, no ruffled drapes; the dishevelment of where he lived was an open revolt against the suffocating tastes he had grown up amid.

He had bought himself a gray Corvette convertible, just like the one in which Martin Milner and George Maharis roared across the country in "Route 66." He was living the life of a swinging Malibu bachelor. John Kennedy was still alive; America had a glamorous playboy in the Oval Office. Frank Sinatra and Dean Martin, Ian Fleming's James Bond (Kennedy's favorite literary character) were the ultracool, martini-sipping, ladykiller icons that all red-blooded men hoped to emulate. For an up-and-coming director in Hollywood, the opportunities for living out the fantasy were legion. (In a note to Peckinpah around this time, actor James Drury passed on the phone number of an ample and available starlet—"Cherokee Betty"—with the advice "Swing! Swing! Swing!")

The parade of women that passed through his bedroom at Bird View was truly awe-inspiring. Sam had a telescope set up in the window at Bird View, not for whale-watching, but for spotting young women strolling on the white sand beach below. When a pair of prospects were spotted, he and a co-conspirator would grab a couple of vodka tonics and swoop down from the eagle's nest to intercept them. "He was fantastic in bed," says one woman who slept with Sam at this time. "I mean the *best!* And believe me, I've had them all!"

The kids came to visit most weekends. Sam bought a Water Wiggle, a thin length of rubber tubing with a goofy face on one end and a nozzle on the other that attached to a regular garden hose. When one turned the water on the Wiggle flew into the air, writhing like a stuck snake and spraying water in all directions. The girls played with it for hours and practiced diving off the pool's low board, emerging at the end of the day like a trio of chlorinated prunes.

Some weekends Sam would putter around in the garden with the girls, as he had once done with his mother. He loved planting things, pulling weeds; during these afternoons with no crowds of friends around, he seemed almost serene. But then the phone would ring, a call from a producer or a writer about a project he was working on, and when he returned from the conversation his demeanor would have changed. Suddenly he was angry, yelling at the children for not pulling the weeds the right way, not working fast enough—whatever excuse was most handy.

The hostility that Sam had once targeted on Marie now was directed more and more often at his daughters. In the midst of his rages he would tell Sharon, "You're just like your mother!"

The greatest source of his irritation was the way Marie was raising the children. She took a laissez-faire approach to discipline, a cavalier attitude toward how they were doing in school, and imposed few restrictions or demands on them. It was completely opposite from the way Sam had been raised. Sam himself, frequently preoccupied with work or his drinking companions, provided even less guidance. But every once in a while he would be seized by the need to assert himself as an authority figure. Then he often overreacted—almost like a caricature of his own father—and the sudden switch from benign disinterest to dictatorial rage both terrified and confused his kids.

Sharon, the oldest, caught the worst of it. "Sharon was rebellious, so Sam was roughest on her," says Fern Lea. "He was really nasty. I remember she was eating some food and she dropped it on the floor and Sam said, 'Pick that up! Is that what you do at home at your house?' He was nasty to her in front of other people." Nor were the younger daughters completely immune to their father's anger; both got their shares of screaming and spankings.

But then there were the other times, when he could be wonderful. Like the day Kristen caught her thumb in the door of his Corvette. They were dropping Sharon off at a friend's house on Point Dume. Sharon hopped out and ran up the path to the front door. Eager to get to their next stop—the market, where her father always bought her the junk food her mother forbade—Kristen slammed the car door right on her thumb. She screamed. Sam fumbled with his seatbelt, unable to unlock it for a moment. He finally freed himself, ran around to the other side, and got the door open. Her thumb was lacerated and bleeding. The model of cool authority, Sam wrapped it up in Sharon's nightie, which had been left in the car, and drove quickly but safely to a local doctor's office. "Let's just have him take a look at it to make sure it's all right," he said casually, obeying his father's edict that you must always be strong for your children in a crisis.

The doctor put Kristen up on an examination table and quickly determined she'd need some stitches. "Don't look at it, look away," Sam counseled her as the doctor went to work. Unfortunately he failed to follow his own advice, and the sight of the needle and thread weaving in and out of his daughter's flesh sent him reeling. The nurse, seeing he was about to faint, slid a chair under him just in the nick of time.

Fans of the later films of "Bloody Sam," the "Picasso of Violence," might find it hard to believe that he could be incapacitated by the sight of a cut thumb. But Kristen sees no incongruity. "I think it's often the case that you portray in your art what frightens you most in life."

In January of 1962 Sam had a fourth child—a son, Mathew Peckinpah—conceived after he had moved out of the Colony house. Nearly a year later, Sam wrote on a sheet of yellow legal paper: "Whatever agony of loss I once enjoyed I now forgo this day. How privileged I—to have my children, four in hand, and be in love. Frightened—worried—full of sweet delight—astonished. Sees point far west, one short look, from one hand so small and fine (beyond description) that reaching out takes mine, and confident and sure, loads both of us through opening doors into the light. Brown-eyed laughing boy—11 months of love, I call him son, and thank the Gods who took the time to smile again on me."

It was during this period that Sam began to donate to the Save the Children Federation, a nonprofit organization that provided financial aid to poverty-stricken children around the world. Over a sixteen-year period Peckinpah bought sponsorships for a total of eighteen children—South Koreans, Mexicans, and American Indians. The money ($180 for each kid) helped buy food, clothing, medical care, and school supplies. Sam "adopted" four of the kids, which meant he continued to pay fifteen dollars a month for each of them until they finished high school. The children wrote to their benefactor regularly, addressing him as "Father," "Foster Father," "Uncle," or "Sam." They thanked him for his help, told him what they had bought with his donations, recounted the day-to-day events in their lives, and asked about life in America, or England, or Mexico, or Yugoslavia, or wherever else Sam happened to be making a film at the time. A few even managed to see some of his movies and wrote to tell him how much they enjoyed them, which delighted their American father to no end.

And Sam wrote back to them, faithfully, about his own nomadic life, his children, his hunting trips, the pictures he was making and what he was trying to say with them.

On January 16, 1971, Sam wrote from London to a young Korean girl, Un Kyong Lee: "We had some snow this Christmas and my son, who came over to see me from America, also did some sleighing, which he loved. In America, where I come from, we hardly see any snow, so it was a great experience for him. I wish I could have tasted the delicious rice cakes that you had over Thanksgiving, they must have been marvelous. We also had a big party on Thanksgiving, but we didn't have any rice cakes."

On September 19, 1974, he wrote to Lee again: "I am sorry to hear your brother's not well. Please let me know if there's anything I can do to get him a good doctor. . . . Keep up with basketball, but don't forget that school always comes first. Education is the most important thing in life, and what you don't learn now you will regret for the rest of your life."

When Un Kyong Lee's brother fell ill, Sam sent $400 to pay for an operation he needed. When one of his adopted children stopped writing, Sam fired a letter off to the Federation, worried that something had happened to the child and asking them to make an inquiry.

As his career escalated in the late sixties and early seventies, and his relationships with his own children continued to deteriorate, he sponsored more and more impoverished children. When friends or associates died, he bought sponsorships in their names for the surviving relatives. Felicia Balzaretti, widow of Juan Balzaretti, received this note from Sam's secretary on July 9, 1975: "Enclosed please find a letter from Gung Doe Soo, the child that Sam is sponsoring for you in memory of Juan. It would be nice if you could write back to her, but if this is not possible please let me know so that we can start a correspondence with the child, as it means so much to them."

Apparently Balzaretti did not have the time to write to the little girl, because Sam began doing so shortly afterward.

By the time the cash flow dried up in 1979, he had donated over $15,000 to the organization. In 1968, the federation gave him its Humanitarian Fellowship Award in recognition of his generous contributions. Sam wrote in response: "I was delighted to receive the . . . award, however, I feel it was hardly deserved. It is more for the sponsors to send our deep gratitude and appreciation for your superb organization, which enables us to be of assistance to needy children throughout the world. The Federation is doing a magnificent job and I am happy to be a small part of it."

It was not false modesty. At $180 a pop, the sponsorships were a bargain, considering what they offered Sam in return: a chance to be the ideal father, generous, attentive, loving, and free of all the inconsistencies and shortcomings that scarred his relationships with his own children.

In 1963 the awards for *High Country* finally began rolling in, and the Hollywood power brokers at last took notice of the young director.

Jerry Bresler—a balding, pear-shaped man in his early fifties—had produced a series of predictable action vehicles *(The Vikings),* tired soap operas (*Diamond Head,* starring Charlton Heston), and lame comedies *(Gidget Goes Hawaiian* and *Gidget Goes to Rome).* In 1963 he landed a multipicture deal with Columbia Pictures. Heston and Bresler enjoyed an amicable relationship on *Diamond Head,* so the producer began to nose around for another vehicle for the star.

He came upon a thirty-seven-page treatment by Harry Julian Fink (who would later write *Dirty Harry*) called *And Then Came the Tiger!* It told the story of a Union cavalry officer, Major Amos Charles Dundee, who is banished to a remote outpost in New Mexico during the closing days of the Civil War to look after a prison full of captured Confederate soldiers. When a rampaging Apache war chief, Sierra Charriba, wipes out an entire company from Dundee's regiment, the major decides he's tired of being a jailkeeper. He throws together a makeshift army of Union regulars, Confederate prisoners, and local cutthroats and thieves, and takes off after the Indians. Dundee becomes so obsessed with his quest for vengeance that he leads his men across the Rio Grande on a 2,400-mile trek over the mountains and deserts of Mexico, which is embroiled in one of its many revolutions. The Juaristas are battling the 70,000 French troops that have occupied their country, and Dundee soon finds he must also fight the French, who consider his incursion a violation of international law. By the time he leads a ragged group of survivors back across the Rio Grande ten months later, he has not only caught and killed the Apache, but met and beaten Europe's finest on the field of battle, and carved his name in history.

Bresler gave the treatment to Heston, who read it and agreed it had potential. Heston was interested in the idea of a group of Union and Confederate soldiers being forced by circumstances to work and fight as a unit. He had always wanted to do a movie about the Civil War. By using Dundee's regiment as a microcosm, one could probe the dynamics of the single most traumatic event in American history. But to do that one would need a strong guiding hand, an exceptional director with the vision to develop Fink's sketchy treatment into a richly textured screenplay. If Bresler could find that man, Heston would commit to the project. The executives at Columbia responded with even greater enthusiasm. They were talking about making this a *big* picture, maybe even a road-show release.

John Ford would have been the perfect director for *Dundee,* but Ford was already engaged by Warner Bros. to make a sprawling epic of his own, *Cheyenne Autumn.* But it didn't take Bresler long to hit upon the next best choice: the young turk who, according to the critics, was taking the western beyond Ford and into new and exciting territory. Bresler screened *Ride the High Country* for Heston at the studio. When the lights came up after the end credits, Heston turned to the producer and said, "Let's use him."

So the thirty-seven-page treatment arrived at the door of the Bird View house via messenger, and Sam sat down at the long bar and read it straight through. A story about a renegade cavalry officer charging into the middle of a Mexican revolution triggered his adrenaline. He saw here another chance to tackle the Custer character. In Sam's hands Dundee would become a man who, like Custer, changed the course of history and went down in textbooks as a hero. But in reality the major would be driven not by any sense of justice or ideals, but by his own ruthless ambition and corrosive demons. Sam understood that kind of man only too well.

But Fink's treatment lacked this complexity. The writer's convoluted plot ran, literally, all over the map. His dialogue was strictly Louis L'Amour, and he displayed an adolescent fascination for grotesque violence so over-the-top that it often became funny rather than horrifying, or disgusting rather than illuminating. But Sam was confident he could coax, prod, and bully Fink into realizing the story's full potential.

Sam signed on for $50,000—over four times his fee for *High Country.* After initial story conferences with Bresler and Heston, he began to supervise Fink's work on a first-draft screenplay in June 1963.

Peckinpah wanted to bring Lucien Ballard on board as the cinematographer, but Bresler overruled him, insisting that he use Sam Leavitt, who had shot *Diamond Head* as well as *Anatomy of a Murder* and *Pork Chop Hill.* Likewise, most of the other key production personnel—including first assistant director John Veitch, script supervisor John Dutton, costume designer Tom Dawson, and art director Al Ybarra—were chosen by the studio, not Peckinpah, and most had long-term contracts with Columbia. Sam was grateful to have such talent at his disposal, but the realization that the studio controlled most of the strings caused the first subtle strains of tension.

In the first week of July, Peckinpah left for Mexico with his key crew members to scout locations for the film. Jerry Bresler had to go into the hospital for surgery and was unable to come along—a fact he would later deeply regret.

After nailing down contracts with Churubusco Studios in Mexico City, Sam plunged into the country's interior to search for locations for the picture. Normally locations are chosen in closely grouped clusters that offer a wide variety of terrain, thus minimizing the number of times the company has to make a major move. A production of this size would require hundreds of crew members, actors, extras, horses and mules, and trucks full of props, costumes, and equipment. Transporting such a mammoth operation from one far-flung location to another would add costly days to the shooting schedule and send the budget skyrocketing.

But this seemed of little concern to Sam while he selected a series of remote spots strung out across the length of Central Mexico, from the mining town of Durango in the north to the sizzling Guerrero Desert southwest of Mexico City and the tepid waters of the Rio Balsas, where Sam decided the final battle with the French cavalry would take place.

"Sam, like all directors, they get caught up in the excitement of the story they're going to tell," says John Veitch, who had served as an assistant director to both John Ford and George Stevens. "Sam, being a perfectionist, wanted different terrain for each scene. There was a passage of time [in the story] and he felt that he and the actors would feel more comfortable in a different terrain and really feel it if they moved deeper and deeper into Mexico."

When Peckinpah returned to the Columbia studios and laid out the locations he'd selected, Jerry Bresler was aghast. But, reluctant to antagonize a strong-willed director who had already won the confidence of his star, Bresler agreed to Sam's plan. Peckinpah had cut his teeth in television and low-budget features. He knew how to work fast; maybe he could make up the time lost during all those moves. Besides, even Bresler had to admit the sketches that artist Jim Silke had made of the locations looked fantastic.

Then the first of a long series of crises struck. Harry Julian Fink turned in the script pages that he had pounded out while Sam was away. An average screenplay runs anywhere from 110 to 140 pages, each page being roughly equivalent to a minute of screen time. Fink's script, which covered only the first third of the plot outline that he and Peckinpah had developed, ran 163 pages.

As he read through Fink's tome, Sam's dismay boiled into outrage. On September 13, 1963, he wrote to Fink: "To put it bluntly I am appalled . . . no company or director would or can shoot your script . . . I want no part of it."

Shooting was scheduled to begin December 1. The company had a star, its key crew members, the locations, but nothing that even resembled a workable screenplay. Time for drastic action. First, Bresler got the start date pushed back to February 6, the latest they could possibly go because Heston was committed to begin *The Agony and the Ecstasy* immediately after *Dundee.* Any more delays and they'd lose their star and financing for the picture. Next, Bresler brought in a new writer, Oscar Saul, who had written the screen adaptation of Williams' *A Streetcar Named Desire.* Peckinpah and Saul would sift through Fink's material and try to cobble together a script.

Columbia's research department had provided an eleven-volume encyclopedia on the Civil War. Peckinpah and Saul pored over it as well as a file full of quotes from various philosophers on the nature and meaning of war. One by Immanuel Kant provided the primary underlying theme for *Dundee.* "War requires no particular motive; it appears grafted onto human nature; it passes even for an act of greatness, to which the love of glory alone, without any other motive, impels."

"Once you go into battle the ideals are all forgotten," Saul elaborates. "There were a lot of things in the script which we later took about how much easier it is for men to go to war, rather than to take on real responsibility, like building a home and raising a family. What Sam was trying to show in *Dundee,* and what he did show so successfully in *The Wild Bunch,* was the death wish behind this whole Western myth. Because these guys were just as ready to die as they were to have a beer."

The concept for the film began to come into tighter focus: as Dundee leads his men deeper and deeper into Mexico in pursuit of the Apache, their civilized veneer is shredded; eventually they become indistinguishable from the savages they chase.

Months later, when Peckinpah sent a copy of the finished script to R. G. Armstrong (who would play yet another demented preacher in the film, thundering through the battle scenes with a shotgun and Bible in hand, yelling, "Mighty is the arm of the Lord!"), the actor called him up and said, "Sam, this is *Moby-Dick* on horseback!"

"Goddamn it, R.G.," Sam growled, "you and Oscar Saul are the only ones who realize that!"

The script was nothing less than an all-out assault on John Ford's romantic cavalry epics. Time after time in Ford's films, the disparate personalities in an army regiment are drawn together behind a set of shared ideals, a common vision. But Dundee's troopers are at one another's throats at every bend in the trail: playful knife fights turn into deadly duels; a Southern bigot insults a black soldier, which polarizes the rest of the men and almost causes the unit to massacre itself; and Dundee and his second in command, Captain Tyreen, are never more than a hair away from shooting each other.

But although Peckinpah and Saul were able to develop a rich mix of characters, scenes, and thematic elements, they were unable to pull them together into a solidly crafted story. The first half of the script put all of the balls into motion with incredible style and skill, but then the plot began to flounder, falling back on superficial complications—predictable love affairs, digressive battles with French troops—that brought the narrative to a screeching halt and failed to explore the dramatic conflicts that had been so deftly set up.

Saul knew they were in trouble and tried to convince Peckinpah of that. But Sam—weak on story structure, and overwhelmed with the production's sprawling logistics—simply shook his head and replied, "It's gonna work, you're worrying for nothing."

"Sam was so instinctual, if it wasn't there on the page he figured he would strike gold on the set," says Saul. "Sometimes you do, most often you don't. This was the beginning of the trouble between Sam and Bresler. Jerry was a hands-on producer, a very good one. But Jerry was a studio producer, by which I mean he had his eye on the budget and his eye on a straight-line story. He was not looking to pioneer, because you go pioneering and suddenly you're on the edge of a cliff and there's no place to go but over. That happens to pioneers."

Meanwhile, with the February 6 start date looming, Peckinpah had a myriad other problems to contend with, like filling in the rest of the cast. Richard Harris was signed to play Heston's second in command, a Confederate officer and former classmate at West Point, Captain Benjamin Tyreen. Jim Hutton, James Coburn, Michael Anderson, Warren Oates, Ben Johnson, L. Q. Jones, Slim Pickens, John Davis Chandler, and Dub Taylor filled in the other key parts.

Then, just two days before the company was to move to Mexico and begin shooting, disaster struck. Bresler called, his voice tight and high: he had some bad news. Sol Schwartz, head of production at Columbia, had just been replaced by Mike Frankovich. After reviewing its position on *Dundee,* the new administration decided that the project did not merit a lavish budget or a roadshow release. The picture would be downgraded to a standard western, its $4.5 million budget cut back to $3 million. To do this, fifteen days would have to be shaved off of the seventy-five-day shooting schedule.

Gordon Stulberg, the studio's chief administrative officer at the time, explains the reasoning behind Columbia's sudden about-face: "If you look at the statistics in the industry, you will find that the middle sixties were the nadir of the film business in terms of [box office] admissions. If you begin about 1954 and trace the business right through to about 1969, the number of theaters in the United States dropped from about 28,000 to 21,000—that's about a 30 percent drop. And, more importantly, admissions dropped from about 1.1 billion a year to 900 million. You're talking about almost a 12.5 percent decline in the number of tickets sold. The business was being rocked by what was happening to admissions. Every company in those years was taking a very hard look at what it was spending on features."

Even John Ford's epic *Cheyenne Autumn* was affected. Warner Bros. downgraded it too from a road-show release to a standard feature. But Sam Peckinpah, oblivious to such larger economic forces, took the budget cut as a personal betrayal of the first magnitude.

Bresler, caught in the middle, tried to reassure both the studio brass and his hothead director. To Peckinpah he said, "Leave it to me, I'll take care of it"—implying that once shooting was under way he'd get Columbia to cut them some slack. To Frankovich he cooed: "No problem, look, I'll get Sam to cut the script while we're shooting. It needs to be tightened up anyway. We'll cut scenes, we'll simplify, and we'll eliminate shooting days that way."

So the production moved forward with both Columbia's executives and the picture's director operating under clouds of self-delusion. Already beginning to distrust his producer, Peckinpah had come to a decision on his own. He figured once he started shooting and the Columbia brass saw his footage, they'd change their minds in a hurry and pump the extra money back into the film. It was, he later admitted, a dangerously naive assumption. The wiser course would have been to "tell them all in no uncertain terms . . . what sort of film I was after, rather than taking it for granted they would let me have my way."

When filming began on February 6 in Durango, Mexico, Peckinpah went on the offensive, employing the same Parris Island tear-the-crew-down-and-rebuild-them strategy that he'd used on *High Country.*

Jim Silke, a writer and graphic artist who had befriended Sam after interviewing him for *Cinema* magazine, found himself drafted for the campaign. Before the company left for Mexico, Sam had Silke sketch the progressive deterioration of each character's wardrobe as they chased the Apache deeper into Mexico. Then, just days before shooting began, the artist received a frantic phone call from Durango. Sam hated the wardrobe, was firing "rag pickers" right and left, and wanted Silke to fly down immediately to fill the gaps. Hours later he found himself on an airplane, streaking south. Silke later told Garner Simmons: "My problem was to rebuild the wardrobe for the Mexican extras. The guy in charge was good—or at least I thought he was—but he wasn't a worker."

Gordon Dawson, the twenty-six-year-old son of the head of Columbia's wardrobe department, was another reinforcement shipped south of the border. He had started on the production as a lowly assistant, working in the studio's basement aging the stars' costumes before they were shipped off to Mexico. For most this work would have been torturously tedious, but young Dawson found it strangely exhilarating. He became obsessed with his task, working around the clock. "I really got into it and invented a lot of ways to age things with blow torches and glue and sewing."

When Peckinpah saw the end result, he said, "Get the person who did this down here."

"I was scared to death of Peckinpah," says Dawson, "and I certainly wasn't alone—everybody was scared to death 'cause he was firing people right and left. The gunsmiths didn't bring enough blank ammo, the guns weren't right, they'd misfire. Sam would fire full loads all the time, in rehearsals and everything. Sound was in trouble because the guy cut the camera on him once because the sound wasn't good, so that guy got chewed up for the rest of the picture. Sam rattled a camera operator named George Nogle so bad on that show that the guy never operated after that. He got the shakes so bad he could never operate again. Sam was screaming and yelling, he was really blistering on the set, just terrible. He didn't need to yell though, he could cut you to ribbons with a goddamn whisper, and make you lean in to hear it."

When George Stevens later heard about all of the people Peckinpah fired from *Dundee* (a total of fifteen), he commented dryly, "Sounds like he was trying to make a good movie." But watching Peckinpah direct for the first time, Jim Silke realized that Sam's bellowing drill-sergeant manner was just a façade. Beneath it the man was scared to death. "He was overwhelmed and lost and terrified, absolutely terrified. He got very drunk before we started shooting and he grabbed me and told me I was the only guy on the set that he trusted. Then he grabbed Mario Adorf [one of the actors] and told him the same thing. That's how we started." Peckinpah would continue to drink heavily almost every night after shooting.

Because of the chaos Sam had thrown the company into and his perfectionistic obsession with detail, the first week of shooting proceeded slowly. This would become a familiar pattern on most subsequent Peckinpah productions: Sam always started slowly, groping for the right tone, struggling to bring each of the characters, their relationships, and their conflicts into focus.

Jerry Bresler was producing another picture at the same time in Acapulco—a saccharine soap opera, *Love Has Many Faces* (or *Love Has Many Feces*, as the battle-hardened members of the *Dundee* company would come to call it). He was forced to shuttle back and forth between the two productions and so missed *Dundee*'s first few days of filming. When Bresler finally arrived in Durango and saw how little progress had been made, he panicked and began hanging nervously on Peckinpah's shoulder, questioning his staging and camera angles.

Sam turned two high-voltage eyes on his producer. Bresler presented a comical sight, standing there in a three-piece suit in the middle of the desolate Mexican desert—a balding penguin lost and far from home. "Jerry," Sam murmured in a voice as dry as a rock-strewn arroyo, "I'm not going to shoot another foot of film until you leave this set."

With thousands of dollars lost with every wasted second, Bresler had no choice but to comply.

Peckinpah had won an important skirmish, but when the company moved to its next Durango location a week later to begin shooting the sequence where Dundee and his soldiers occupy a Mexican village, the director clearly began to flounder. Movies, of course, are filmed out of sequence, and the village scenes took place midway through the story, precisely at the point where the script slipped out of focus. Peckinpah finally realized this, and began feverishly rewriting dialogue with the help of Charlton Heston, Richard Harris, and Jim Silke. He shot and reshot scenes, hoping to somehow pull them together.

"Sam got into the village sequence and he just shot and shot and shot," says Silke. "We didn't know what we were doing. None of it's in the finished movie, to speak of. But he did the same thing on *Wild Bunch.* The village scene in *The Wild Bunch* went on for forty-five minutes in the rough cut, and then he cut it and cut, cut until he got down to the version as it exists now. That's the search. He doesn't really know what he's looking for until he finds it. Sam would always get lost in the second act and not know what it's about. And that's okay because you've got to get lost to find your way, which is a very real thing when you get into storytelling. It just costs you millions of dollars when you're making a movie. Coppola did it with *Apocalypse Now* and it cost thirty-one million dollars."

Jerry Bresler didn't give a shit about the spiritual fine points of the creative quest. From his point of view he had a madman at the wheel of a runaway production. Bresler later explained his side of the story to Garner Simmons: "I became concerned on several levels: cost via length, the character relationship between Dundee and Tyreen, and tempo. I met and talked with Sam at the end of a day's shooting . . . The meeting ended with my ultimatum: unless he agreed to change his methods, I would have to recommend a change in directors. From this point on we were completely at opposite ends."

Unfortunately for Bresler, the executives at Columbia failed to back up his threat. "Columbia had a strange attitude," Bresler told Simmons. "Columbia was excited by the selected master takes they had seen of the film shot. However, this is a trap—they fell into it. It is essential to view the individual scenes as part of the whole and not just a scene. They became so intrigued, one of the executives began talking about releasing the picture in 70mm."

Another reason for the studio's "strange" attitude was that Bresler's nervous, henpecking manner irritated the Columbia brass almost as much as it did Peckinpah.

"Jerry Bresler was a dedicated, overconscientious worrywart, not just on *Dundee*, on every picture he did," says Gordon Stulberg. "The story that spread all over the studio was that Jerry got into such a confrontation with Peckinpah he fainted. He literally dropped into a dead faint at Peckinpah's feet!"

The offices and hallways at the Gower Street studio echoed with laughter as the story was repeated in loving and ever more colorful detail. But in a few more weeks the laughter sank into morbid silence. By that time, one month into shooting, Sam was running ten days over schedule and $600,000 over budget. Even the studio brass was forced to admit it had a real problem on its hands.

A succession of Columbia executives flew down to Mexico and nervously threaded their way through the prickly cacti to the spot where Peckinpah had set up his cameras—their faces red and beaded above choking silk neckties, sand filling their tailored pant cuffs, rocks slashing their polished Italian shoes. Coming to an awkward halt on the periphery of the set, squinting up at that shirtless, bandanna-headed figure perched high upon a camera crane barking orders to the scurrying crew below, the executives mopped their brows with monogrammed handkerchiefs and wondered how best to throw a lasso around this enfant terrible.

Peckinpah listened to their veiled and then blatant threats with the same indifference he'd shown Bresler, then mumbled, making them lean in to hear it: "Gentlemen, if you want this goddamned movie finished, why don't you let me get back to work and stay the hell out of my way."

Charlton Heston was impressed by Peckinpah's nerve but questioned his judgment. "I worked with Orson Welles, with whom Sam has a great deal in common, primarily their mutual antipathy towards office people, which in a sense destroyed them both," says Heston. "They shared this almost pathological antipathy towards anyone who had a big office above the ground floor. I have no idea why. My relationship with both men was very intense, but short in time. Orson could charm the birds out of the bloody trees. He must have known that the main people you've got to charm are the people that have *the money,* 'cause if they don't give you the money you can't make the picture. He must have known this, of course he knew it, a child would know it. But he stubbornly refused to act on it. He would disdain them publicly. I mean, that's no good. And Sam, lacking Orson's charm, of course was in even deeper poop."

Finally, Arthur Kramer, vice president of creative affairs for Columbia, showed up on the set. He'd been sent down by Frankovich with the order to relieve Peckinpah of his command. But the studio found itself checkmated when Heston intervened, as the star later recalled in his book *The Actor's Life:* "I thought this was an absolutely lousy idea. Aside from Sam's talent, the adage about horses in midstream applied."

If Peckinpah was off the picture, so was Heston. The rest of the cast fell in behind the star: Richard Harris, L. Q. Jones, R. G. Armstrong, Warren Oates, Ben Johnson, and Slim Pickens all threatened to walk if Peckinpah was fired. With two-thirds of the movie already in the can, Columbia found itself outflanked: it could either kiss the two million dollars it had sunk into the film good-bye, or roll the hard six and hope Peckinpah came back from Mexico with a marketable product. There was really no choice.

A steadfast team player, Heston felt overwhelmed with guilt for having pulled the kind of power play he normally abhorred. As an act of atonement he offered to forfeit his $200,000 salary to Columbia. The studio leapt at the opportunity, and so the star ended up making the movie for nothing. Heston wasn't alone. Sam also agreed to defer $35,000 of his $50,000 salary under the mistaken assumption that this would buy him more control over editing and post-production.

At first their victory over "the suits" sent a thrilling rush of energy through the cast and crew. They'd whipped Columbia's ass! Then reality set in and sickening lumps formed in their guts. For now they had put themselves in Peckinpah's hands.

Peckinpah never gave the actors much direction. When a scene displeased him he'd tell them to do it again and "make it different this time." Instead of intellectualizing about character motivation and development, the actors began to realize, Peckinpah forged a reality that paralleled that of the story. Like Dundee, he had become obsessed with his quest, and like Dundee's men they followed him.

Durango had been bad enough. They were there for one long month, shooting six days a week from sunrise to sundown and sometimes all through the freezing nights.

The site of one of the largest maximum-security prisons in Mexico, the town had a drug trade that was rapidly expanding to meet the voracious demands of America at the dawn of the swinging sixties. The men who walked the streets and crowded into the bars and whorehouses all carried guns, or at the very least knives. "There was somebody knifed every night on the streets," says Forrest Wood, a dialogue coach on the picture. One of the Mexican wranglers hired to look after the company's horses was shot one night. A quarrel over a woman was the cause of it, they were told by the locals. Two more Mexican crew members got shot in one of the brothels, and Peckinpah and cinematographer Sam Leavitt hightailed it out of a bar one night when more shooting erupted.

From Durango the caravan of trucks and trailers snaked south (4,000 gallons of diesel fuel would be consumed on the journey), past Mexico City to sugar-cane country, where ashes from the burning canefields rained out of blackened skies, then further still to the skillet-hot desert of Guerrero, where even the cacti shriveled beneath the beating sun.

The rivers, the Tehuixtla and Rio Balsas, were cooler, but so polluted with sewage the actors and stuntmen had to have their ears and noses flushed out by nurses after taking falls in the water. And there were the bugs: thousands of welt-inflicting gnats and mosquitoes as big as vampire bats. Only the Yaqui Indian extras and Peckinpah seemed oblivious to the bloodsuckers.

Little by little, the movie and reality were becoming eerily intertwined. The company was no longer playing the parts of cavalry soldiers; it *was* those soldiers. And just like the characters in the film, one by one the crew began to crack under the strain of this journey without end. "Those primitive conditions, the heat and long hours, strip all the masks off and the egos and neuroses really come out," says Gordon Dawson. And, as in the movie, the most frequent targets for their pent-up rage were one another.

Jim Hutton was screwing around on his horse one afternoon and came too close to Peckinpah. Sam leaped up, grabbed a pistol loaded with blanks that he kept in a holster on his director's chair, and fired a round off at the ground and then in the air. Hutton's horse reared and threw him off.

At the end of another day the cast and crew scrambled to grab a sunset shot. Perched atop a camera crane, Sam told Heston to lead the cavalry troops down a hill toward him at a trot. Heston did so, and at the end of the take turned and asked, "How was that, Sam?"

Peckinpah glowered at him. "That was shit! Jesus Christ, you came too slow!"

"Sam, you told me to bring them down at a trot," Heston said, already leading the troops back up the hill, knowing they only had time for one more take.

"The fuck I did!" Peckinpah yelled at his retreating back. "You goddamned liar!"

With a surge of adrenaline, Heston wheeled his horse around, drew his saber, and charged at his tormentor.

Peckinpah yelled at the crane operator, "Crank it up! Crank it up! For chrissakes crank it up!" When Heston's horse thundered beneath him, the seat of Sam's pants cleared the saber by a hair.

"I don't really think I would have ridden, let alone sabered him down," says Heston, "but I was fucking pissed off. But see, he got what he wanted. He had that kind of nagging, berating manner as a director. I got on with him, but . . . I suppose it's like being with a girl that you just can't stand, but she's very attractive. You know, you say, 'What am I doing with this bitch? Why am I here at three o'clock in the morning?' "

By the time they reached the river battle, Peckinpah's pace had accelerated to breakneck speed. Sam gave the twenty-five stuntmen assigned to the picture all the action they could handle.

The logging operation on Peckinpah Mountain in the 1890s

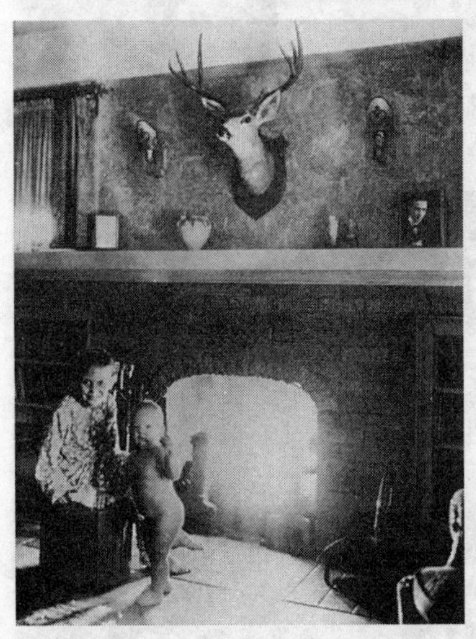

D. Sammy and Fern Lea in the Peckinpahs' living room in 1931 (portrait of David Peckinpah on the mantel)

The Fresno State production of *My Sister Eileen* (1948). Peckinpah is draped over the actor's shoulder on the right; Marie Selland is at extreme right.

The Peckinpah family in the 1940s. Susan is on David's knee; Sammy, Fern, and Fern Lea are standing.

Hunting in the Sierras in the early 1960s

Sam and Marine Corps buddies home on leave in the mid-1940s. Fern Peckinpah, center; Sam, second from right.

Directing Brian Keith in "The Westerner" (1959)

Lining up a shot for *Ride the High Country* (1962)

Courting Begonia Palacios on the set of *Major Dundee* (1965). "La Duena" is on the right.

On the set of *Noon Wine* with Jason Robards (1966)

In the center of the *Straw Dogs* psychodrama with Dustin Hoffman and Susan George (1971)

On the set of *Junior Bonner* (1972) with Sharon Peckinpah, center, and Melissa Peckinpah, left

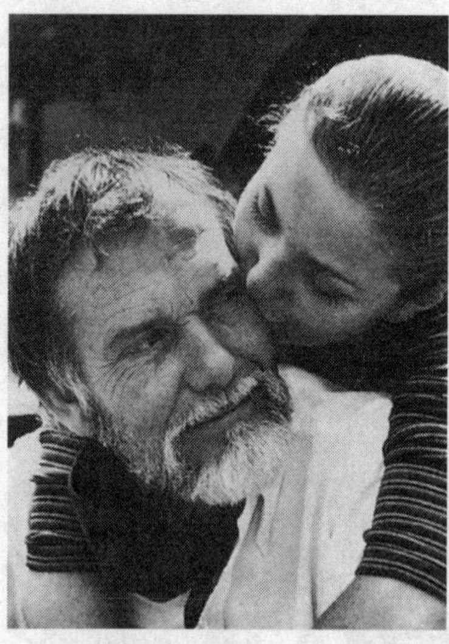

On the set of *The Getaway* (1972) with Joie Gould

Peckinpah and his alter ego, James Coburn, contemplate killing "the Kid," in *Pat Garrett and Billy the Kid* (1973)

With Katy Haber on the set of *Bring Me the Head of Alfredo Garcia* (1974)

With Mathew Peckinpah on the set of *The Killer Elite* (1975)

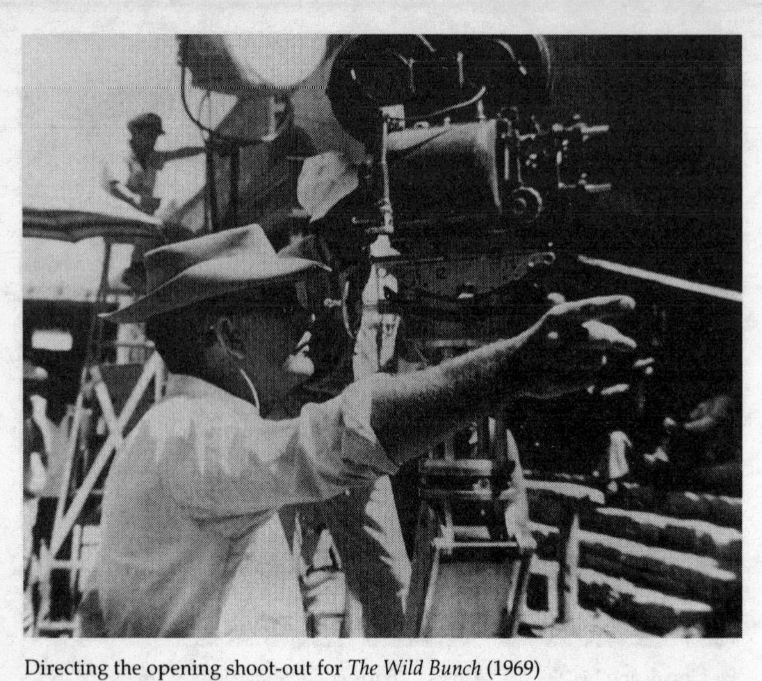

Directing the opening shoot-out for *The Wild Bunch* (1969)

Peckinpah in dialogue with Pike Bishop (William Holden) on the set of *The Wild Bunch*

Peckinpah struggles with director's block while shooting "The Battle of Bloody Porch" for *The Wild Bunch*

Peckinpah and Jason Robards inspect one of the rattlesnakes that they will dump on the heads of Strother Martin and L. Q. Jones in *The Ballad of Cable Hogue* (1970)

As soon as they could climb out of the river and change into new uniforms they were back on a horse and taking another fall, logging eight and nine stunts a day.

Peckinpah filmed the combat with multiple cameras, some running at high speed to capture the action in slow motion. Kurosawa had used slow-motion shots in *The Seven Samurai,* and so had H. G. Clouzot in *The Wages of Fear;* now Sam wanted to go beyond simply inserting slow shots in between the normal-speed action. He wanted to integrate the slow motion into the very fabric of the sequence. Exactly how, he wasn't quite sure, so he simply shot thousands of feet of slow-motion action, hoping he would discover a way to weave it into the sequence during editing. Again and again the stuntmen careened off their saddles into the dirt of the riverbank, tumbled into the sewage-laden river, charged their horses into the blast of preset explosions that flung both rider and animal to the ground. But nobody complained.

The stuntmen made and Columbia shelled out a small fortune in the five days that it took to shoot the battle. The French cavalry charge across the river, just twenty seconds of film, cost $13,000.

As he continued to shoot stunt after stunt, with all twenty-five men taking falls in some shots, many so far in the background they couldn't be seen, it became obvious that Sam was using the sequence as a drain to pour the studio's money down.

"Sam held the studio's feet to the fire," says L. Q. Jones. "He'd won the battle with them and now he wanted to have his spoils, and part of that was standing on Bresler's neck. But you cannot beat a studio because they've got you right where it smarts, and that's in the final cut, in distribution. Sam knew the most important people to charm were the money men, and that's exactly why he didn't charm them. And they knew he knew that."

Jones tried to reason with his friend. "I understand why you want to fuck Columbia over," he said, "that doesn't escape me for a second. But you're not fucking Columbia over, you're fucking Sam Peckinpah over! Can't you see that?"

Sam nodded curtly and spoke through gritted teeth, "Yeah, but I'll get Bresler, that cocksucker!"

On April 30, 1964, the cameras ground to a halt. *Major Dundee* completed photography fifteen days over schedule and $1.5 million over budget. It had come in almost exactly at the original road-show budget and schedule. Had Peckinpah planned it that way? Had there been a method behind his madness all along? No one but the director knew for sure.

There was no wrap party, no sentimental farewells, as at the end of most Hollywood productions. The haggard survivors of Peckinpah's Purgatory scattered and broke for the border without looking back. Heston had his civilian clothes ready and waiting on the set and "leaped out of my wardrobe and into them before the dust from the last shot settled." He raced off to the airport and was on a plane to Los Angeles within hours.

James Coburn made a break for it also—*quick! before Sam decides he wants to reshoot something!*—mumbling to Peckinpah as he hustled into a waiting car: "See you later, motherfucker!"

Only one among them showed no eagerness to return to the land of fast-food burgers, freeways, shopping malls, and sprawling subdivisions. For, unknown to all but a few on the production, Sam Peckinpah had been nurturing another passion of late, one almost as fierce and volatile as he held for *Dundee.*

We all dream of being a child again, even the worst of us . . . perhaps the worst most of all . . .

Nineteen-year-old Begonia Palacios was already an established star in Mexico when her agent, Lanca Becker, asked her to go on an audition for a part in *Major Dundee.* She had begun her career as a flamenco dancer at age thirteen. A year later she was touring the world with Carmen Amaya's flamenco dance troupe. Her huge dark eyes, slender upturned nose, classic Castilian features, and amply rounded figure quickly singled her out from the other girls in the company. She soon moved on to the movies and starred in several Mexican films. So Begonia was quite miffed when she read the *Dundee* script and saw how small her part was. (She would play the village girl that a young trooper, Ryan, who comes of age over the course of the story, falls in love with.) But Becker and Begonia's mother battered down her resistance. This would be a big American picture with a cast of international stars. Even though the part was small, the exposure would be fantastic for her career. "Sam Peckinpah's a very big American director," said Becker, adding with nudging smile, "and he's handsome too!"

When she arrived at Peckinpah's office at Churubusco Studios, Begonia found the waiting room packed with other young actresses auditioning for the same part. Another slap at her pride; her blood temperature began to rise.

Finally, she was ushered in to see him. Sitting at a big desk, doodling on a pad of paper, he didn't even bother to look up as she entered, and said abruptly. "What's your name?" She told him. With eyes still on his scribbling, he asked, "How's your English?"

"I don't speak English very good."

"Very *well*," he corrected without looking up.

Her blood boiled. She marched out of his office a few minutes later, threading her way through the other actresses who clogged the waiting room. That man, she hated him!

And so she was completely shocked a couple of weeks later when her agent informed her that Peckinpah wanted her for the part. He'd never even so much as looked at her during the interview. But once again Becker and her mother prevailed: it was the right career move, a chance to become a Hollywood star.

During her first days on the set Begonia watched him, high up on his camera crane barking orders at the crew below. "Come on, move it, you goddamned son of a bitch!" She watched the sad, potbellied producer make awkward suggestions and heard Peckinpah's response: "Fuck you! Get the hell off my set!"

She didn't like him. He was mean, unforgiving, a little dictator.

Then he started in on her hair. He didn't like its color, it wasn't the look he envisioned for her character. So the hairdresser dyed it one shade, then another and another. He didn't like any of them. She had her hair dyed three times in one day and each time he sent them back to try again. Finally she could stand it no more. She marched up to him, slouched like a lizard in his director's chair, and let him have it. "Look, Mr. Peckinpah, you decide what color hair you want! No more dyeing, you're burning my roots out!"

His thin lips broke into a strange half-grimace, half-grin. Angry or amused, she couldn't tell. "Okay," he said, gazing off to some far point on the horizon. "I'll think about it."

Every weekend there was a party. The cast and members of the crew would gather at Sam's rented house or at a local restaurant; there would be a lot of joking and laughing, and little Julio Corona was always on hand with his Cheshire Cat grin and oversized guitar.

"There were these long tables," says Jim Silke's wife, Lyn, who visited the location. "Lydia and Chuck Heston were there, and a lot of other people. Sam turned to Begonia—I don't think he knew her well then, but she was a Spanish dancer—and he said, 'You go dance for them.' And she put on this incredible Spanish dance on top of the table with her skirt up and these gorgeous legs kicking and flying and everybody's cheering. Sam *loved* it, he loved the innocence and the fire."

Suddenly Begonia noticed a dramatic shift in Peckinpah's attitude toward her. Whenever she came on to the set, he always had a special chair there waiting for her. He was courtly, attentive. "Do you need anything? A soda? Something to eat? Let me know if you get thirsty." Now every morning when she stepped into her trailer there was a fresh batch of flowers there, but no card. It amazed her, because no flowers grew in Durango.

But she still didn't like him.

Then, one afternoon on a remote location, her stomach churned with hunger. Not hungry enough to eat the caterer's food; she preferred starvation to botulism. Then she saw some local peasant children dressed in dusty rags and chewing contentedly on some bulging burritos. They looked delicious. She went up to one and asked where they had gotten them. *"El Señor Peckinpah nos lo compro'!"* the boy answered with a greasy grin.

That made her stop and think, for the first time, about this weatherbeaten dictator hovering above her on his camera crane. On the first day of shooting he had worn a beautiful serape to the set. When someone complimented him on it, he told them, with proud shining eyes, that it had belonged to his father. She later heard from one of the other crew members that he had given it away to a young peasant boy. That really floored her. There was more to this man than first met the eye, much more.

He began asking her out to dinner with him in the evening. Begonia's aunt had come with her on location to protect her reputation and ward off unsavory influences. "That aunt was hard as nails," says Jim Silke. "She'd come along to look after Begonia. Begonia was the big moneymaker in their family, a valuable property."

Every night when they went out, Sam would beg Begonia's aunt to let him see the girl alone. "For just a few minutes, please."

The woman shook her head. "No, Señor Peckinpah, I cannot."

"Sam was like a sick calf, for chrissakes," says L. Q. Jones. "It was very peculiar. Sam would speak his mind, say anything to anybody without the slightest fear of embarrassment. But with Begonia I don't think he could say hello without stuttering. He would think up excuses for Warren Oates and himself, or me and him to go talk to Begonia about her part. What are we talking to her about her part for? We're not even in any of the sequences that she's in! He just wanted to be around her and talk at her, and wouldn't do it without someone to help protect him when she jumped on him, so there we were."

"Everybody could see the unhappy ending coming, when he fell in love with her," says Senta Berger. "What he, in my eyes, would have needed was not a warm sincere girl, which Begonia was. He would have needed somebody who could keep up with him, understand his profession, understand his fears, understand his stubborn personality; somebody strong, somebody with their own life, an artist."

Then one weekend Sam invited Begonia to a party at the house he was renting on their current location. Nearly all of the cast and crew was there. Julio played his guitar and everyone sang along, crying and laughing, arms around one another. Suddenly Sam turned to her and took hold of her hands, squeezing so hard she almost cried out, his eyes shining like some nighttime animal's. "His eyes," she recalls nearly thirty years after that moment, trying to find words to express their effect. "They looked beyond, into your head, into your mind, like he was reading my thoughts." Without warning, he leaned forward and kissed her, quickly, chastely on the lips, then let go of her and turned back to Julio and the others.

When she finished all her scenes in the movie he asked her to stay on; he had another scene he was writing into the script for her. When she told him she couldn't, that she had signed a contract for another feature that was to start right away, he got extremely upset. "You're not very professional!"

"Sam," she explained, "I have this other show to do, this is how I make my living!"

"All right!" he waved her off. "Go then! Go ahead! Go ahead! Go!"

And so she left. Then, one day weeks later, while she was still working on the other picture in Mexico City, there was a knock on her hotel-room door. She opened it and there he was. She felt a sudden thrill and knew then that she had missed him. "Bego," he said softly, his slumped shoulders betraying his anxiety despite a massive effort to appear at ease, "I just came to tell you I'm leaving Mexico. I finished my picture, I'm going back to America." His eyes dropped for a moment then rose to meet hers again. "I'm going to miss you. I want you to come visit me in California. I want you to see my house in Malibu. I want you to see how I live."

And so, when she finished her picture, she went—bringing her aunt along with her, of course. She saw the Bird View house with its spectacular view of Zuma Beach, the expanse of silver, green, and blue ocean, and islands hovering on the horizon like purple thunderheads. They went out to eat at a local restaurant in the late afternoon, and again Sam begged her aunt for a chance to be alone with Begonia. Finally, cradling her big homely head in her hands, the woman relented. "All right, twenty minutes. But if you're not back in twenty minutes, I'm going to the police!"

Like a kid let out for summer vacation, Sam grabbed Begonia's hand and led her out to his new silver Porsche. He drove her up into the hills to a dry grassy bluff overlooking an even bigger horizon of ocean, the water reflecting the sunlight like a thousand blinking lights. Sat her up on the hood of the car, took her hands again into that crushing grip, fixed her with his big-pupiled eyes, and said softly, "Bego, will you marry me?"

It sounded like someone else's voice rising up out of her throat, someone else taking control of her mouth: "Yes . . . yes, I will."

And then he kissed her for the second time.

Back at the Columbia lot in Hollywood, Sam's war with Jerry Bresler entered its second phase, and this time the studio, not Peckinpah, held all the cards.

Charlton Heston noted in his journal on May 4, 1964: "I wandered over to Columbia and got a vivid post-mortem on *Dundee* from [Arthur] Kramer. I get the feeling Bresler would almost be willing to have the film fail, if only to justify his misgivings about Sam."

Columbia assigned its top editor, William Lyon—winner of two Academy Awards, he'd cut *From Here to Eternity, Picnic,* and been a consultant on *The Bridge on the River Kwai*—and two other staff editors, Don Starling and Howard Kunin, to wade through the 400,000 feet of film Sam had shot in Mexico. Although highly professional, these men had been selected without Peckinpah's approval and were loyal to the studio, not him. A more diplomatic director might have tried to seduce the editors into his camp, but Peckinpah felt he'd been betrayed again and an atmosphere of antagonism prevailed from the outset.

"Bill Lyon was ready to quit every single day," says Howard Kunin. "Sam couldn't stand the fact that Bill was an older editor with white hair, although Bill could cut circles around him. It didn't look like he was expending much effort, but he really had a great grasp of timing and dialogue."

Kunin found Peckinpah to be an impossible bully—demanding, temperamental, and abusive. But he had to admit that the man had talent. Sam pushed for rapid cutting in some scenes—such as Dundee's execution of a deserter, O. W. Hadley—and the results were surprisingly effective. But Peckinpah's attempt to integrate the slow-motion footage into the battle sequences proved less successful.

"Sam used slow motion extremely well in his later films, but by then he had conceived how to make it work; he had shot it with a conception of how it would work," says Howard Kunin. "On *Dundee* he just shot it wild, there was no concept at all of how it would be used. Sam tried many, many things to make it work. We even once did a whole slow-motion version of the French battle, of the hand-to-hand fighting. Sam hated it too. It just didn't work."

Bresler and Peckinpah clashed most vehemently over the battle sequences. The graphic shots of men taking bullets and the profusion of blood were too much for the producer of *Gidget Goes Hawaiian.* Peckinpah wanted to suck the audience into the film, to take it on a forced march with Dundee and his men, to make it experience with the soldiers on the screen not only the horror of war but also its perverse excitement. To Bresler it looked like the product of a sick and sadistic mind, one that he'd had more than enough exposure to in Mexico.

Peckinpah's contract guaranteed him the right to make a first cut of the film and to screen it at two public previews. After that the studio could take the picture away from him and recut it any way it pleased. Sam placed all his hopes on the previews. The audience reactions would vindicate him; once the studio realized his version worked, it would call off Bresler and he'd emerge victorious—*if* the audiences liked it.

He pruned the movie down to two hours and forty-one minutes, but felt he'd been overzealous with some cuts and wanted to put ten minutes of film back in. If the previews went well enough, Columbia might reconsider the possibility of releasing the picture as a road-show. The hardest work behind him, he began to think about the musical score—the present cut lacked both music and final sound effects.

Then it landed, the next *Dundee* bombshell: without Sam's knowledge, Bresler took the rough cut of the film to New York and screened it for a group of exhibitors (owners of theater chains). The verdict, Bresler explained to his stunned director upon his return to Hollywood, was thumbs down. The film's too long, said Bresler, it needs to be cut down to at least two hours. So now he, Bresler, and the editors would "carefully and judiciously" do just that. What about his two public screenings, Peckinpah asked, his pulse pounding. They'd just had a screening, Bresler responded, dropping his eyes, and it told them everything they needed to know.

On September 3, 1964, Sam fired off a letter to Mike Frankovich, head of production, and Arthur Kramer, vice president of creative affairs for Columbia: "I believe very strongly the picture should be previewed at this length with cuts and added shots I requested included. If they don't work—if they don't play to an audience, we have obviously no choice but to remove them. But to remove them first, to say that we might be able to put them in the second preview doesn't quite make sense to me."

When Sam drove to the studio with Begonia a few days later, the guard at the front gate stopped him. "I'm sorry, Mr. Peckinpah, but I can't let you through," he said stiffly. Sam was no longer an employee of Columbia Pictures. The name on his parking space had already been painted over; all the personal belongings from his office were there on the floor of the gatehouse in a cardboard box.

There was nothing to do but sit back and wait while Bresler and the editors performed radical surgery. Whole scenes and sequences—mostly those that lingered on the subtleties of Dundee, the demons that drove him, and his inner conflicts—were ripped out of the film; others remained in but were severely pruned, particularly the battle sequences. Gone were all the slow-motion shots, and nearly all of the graphic bullet, arrow, and saber wounds. "They cut 80 percent of the violence out and made it very attractive and exciting," Sam later recalled. "But the real, bloody, awful things that happen to men in war were cut out of the picture, which I thought was *unforgivable.*"

Altogether, twenty minutes of footage were removed (the Columbia brass would later take out another seven minutes). Bresler himself later estimated that the film on the cutting-room floor amounted to around $500,000 in production costs. The final result was hopelessly fragmented and at times incoherent. Characters seemed to act without motivation, conflicts, relationships, and plot points were set into motion but never brought to fruition; in its last half-hour the story collapsed like a house of cards into a jumble of arbitrary scenes.

Even Bresler recognized that he'd ripped holes the size of sound stages in the narrative, and he tried to plug them up by adding a narration track. Reverting to Harry Julian Fink's initial concept that the story would unfold as a series of diary entries, trooper Ryan became the audience's guide through the twisted wreckage of *Dundee.* The device was pitifully inadequate. Huge plot gaps and major character motivations were summed up in three and four-sentence paragraphs that only added to the confusion.

Peckinpah did not see the devastating results until the film's first public screening at the Egyptian Theater on Hollywood Boulevard on February 5, 1965. Charlton Heston, James Coburn, Jim Silke, and many others from the cast and crew snuck into the back rows to see what their three months of agony south of the border had amounted to. Jerry Bresler, conveniently, was out of town at the time. The screening was a disaster. By the last half hour the incoherent plot twists and incongruent music were provoking laughter from the audience.

"We came out of the Egyptian and Sam was absolutely rigid," says James Coburn. "He reached in his pocket for this pint of whiskey and he was shaking so much he dropped it and broke it on the sidewalk. My wife put her hand on his shoulder and said, 'Sam, Sam, easy baby, it's just, just, it's just a movie. I know, we all feel that way, but Jesus, don't let it hurt you.' She calmed him down a little bit, but he was . . . If Jerry Bresler had been there at that moment he would have fucking killed him."

But it must be said that *Dundee,* even in its fragmented state, was not an utter failure. The cinematography (despite some poor color matches that probably would have been eliminated if Peckinpah could have supervised the post-production) is often stunning. Leavitt's camera captures the vast existential wasteland of the border country with panoramas of dry grassy plains, jagged cactus deserts, and boulder-littered mountains, and breath-taking shots of Dundee's regiment riding silhouetted across ridge lines and through shimmering silver dust storms.

The richness of detail that Sam pushed so hard for is evident throughout—the smell of unbathed men, lathered horse flesh, frying pork fat and beans wafts off the screen.

The performances are, with the exception of Senta Berger, excellent. And the first half of the film in particular is peppered with powerfully realized scenes. But despite these bursts of brilliance, the film was a mangled mess.

Peckinpah later said: "*Dundee* was one of the most painful things that ever happened in my life. Making a picture is . . . I don't know . . . you become in love with it. It's part of your life and when you see it being mutilated and cut to pieces it's like losing a child or something."

Columbia still hoped that all its misgivings about the production would prove wrong. The studio treated *Major Dundee* as its most prestigious release for the spring of 1965. But the hundreds of thousands of dollars spent on publicity and advertising proved futile. The reviews of the picture were devastating. Sam's reputation with the critics—whom he had painstakingly courted with thank-you notes and flattering letters since "The Westerner" through *The Deadly Companions* to *Ride the High Country*—now unraveled before his eyes.

Newsweek, which had declared *High Country* the best American film of 1962, showed no mercy toward *Dundee:* "Think of Yosemite Falls or suicides from the top of the Empire State Building, or streaking meteorites downward toward the earth and you'll get some idea of the decline in the career of Sam Peckinpah. *Major Dundee,* his third film, is a disaster."

The golden boy had turned to tarnished brass. His attempt to redefine the cavalry picture and turn the set pieces of the genre inside out had fallen flat on its face. *Dundee* grossed a disastrous $1.6 million in its first year of release; Columbia optimistically predicted it would eventually pull in $2.5 million, but even if that figure were reached the studio would recoup only a little more than half its expenditures.

Sam didn't just lie down and take his licks. He methodically wrote letters to every major reviewer and explained his side of the story. His campaign had some effect, particularly by the time *Dundee* made it over to Europe. Already familiar with how Columbia had mutilated the film, English critics gave Peckinpah the benefit of the doubt and pronounced *Dundee* a brilliant if fatally damaged film.

Initially, *Major Dundee* was a serious setback in Sam Peckinpah's career; just how serious would soon become evident. But over the long haul, Sam was able to turn this defeat to his advantage. In the years that followed, he would tell interviewers that before Columbia cut it to pieces, "*Dundee* was a fine film, possibly the best picture I've ever made in my life." It was the kind of tale auteurist film critics eagerly gobbled up: another sensitive artist crushed by the Hollywood machine. Like Von Stroheim's *Greed* and Welles' *Magnificent Ambersons, Major Dundee* became one of the cinema's legendary lost masterpieces.

With *Major Dundee,* Peckinpah made the subtle but critical transition from a promising young talent to a living legend—the enfant terrible, riding straight out of the Wild West to take on the Hollywood power structure; the erratic genius who managed to land a few good punches before they yanked his work of art away and mangled it. It made great magazine and newspaper copy and helped Peckinpah to become one of those rare directors—like Alfred Hitchcock and Orson Welles—who were as well known to the public as any of the stars who appeared in their films.

But in truth *Dundee* would not have been Peckinpah's masterpiece, not even a great film, if Columbia had given him final cut. Saul and Peckinpah's screenplay lays out the complete story as Sam shot it. It is brilliant in patches—particularly in the first half—but it never reaches its full potential, falls apart in the final third, and remains far inferior to *Ride the High Country, The Wild Bunch,* and several of his other films.

But in a way, Peckinpah was not deluding himself when he said *Dundee* could have been a masterpiece, for he could feel such a film inside him, burning to get out. He had tried to bring it to the screen with *Dundee* and failed. The shape was still amorphous, he hadn't quite gotten a handle on it yet. But he would one day.

By the time Sam was barred from the Columbia lot in the fall of 1964, he had already signed a lucrative multipicture deal back at MGM. His first assignment was to direct *The Cincinnati Kid* for producer Martin Ransohoff. Based on the novel by Richard Jessup, the story was pretty thin—a transparent reworking of *The Hustler* with five-card stud poker replacing the pool tables. Steve McQueen would take up Paul Newman's part as the young turk who challenges the old master, and Spencer Tracy would replace Jackie Gleason as the aging champ who accepts the kid's challenge and whips him soundly in the final reel.

Ransohoff, who put the package together, belonged to a new breed of independent producer that had emerged out of the wreckage of the old movie factories. With the changes in the industry, the studios were shedding the last vestiges of the mass-production system. Most of the old-time moguls were gone—Harry Cohn's reign of terror at Columbia ended with his death in 1958; Jack Warner still presided over his lot in Burbank, but he would be gone within a couple of years. As production shrank from thirty to fifty feature films a year per studio to around a dozen, the payroll for contract actors, writers, directors, and technicians was pared away. Talent was hired on smaller multipicture contracts or on a picture-by-picture basis. Instead of one executive developing an entire lineup of films for a given year, much of the product was supplied by independent producers like Ransohoff, who bought properties, packaged the talent, and oversaw the productions, which were then released under the studio's banner.

The new independent producers were not loyal company men; they were fast-talking deal-makers, energetic entrepreneurs. Ransohoff got his start producing television commercials in New York with his own company, Filmways. Fantastically successful, he moved his operation to California, where he hit the motherlode with a new television show, "The Beverly Hillbillies," and a number of spinoff series, which lead to a deal to produce features for MGM.

Ransohoff may have known little about the artistic fine points of filmmaking (or even the basics), but his huckster's savvy told him movies had to offer something new and startling were they to lure the public out of its well-upholstered TV rooms. For over a decade the movie studios had been battling that little electronic box. They had introduced a wide array of miracle weapons into the war—Panavision, Vistavision, Cinemascope, Cinerama, stereo sound, 3-D, even Smell-O-Rama—but had continued to lose ground at the box office. By 1965 their position had deteriorated from a retreat to an all-out rout. Some newspaper columnists had even begun to speculate that movies might go the way of vaudeville and die out altogether.

Wily new entrepreneurs like Ransohoff took a look at the marketplace and began to come up with new strategies. While box-office attendance for American films had been dropping steadily since 1945, the percentage of tickets sold for foreign films had grown to 5 percent of the overall receipts. Most of the foreign films were in the old narrow-screen format, in black and white with hard-to-read subtitles. What was their appeal? Not all the artsy-fartsy camera angles and bullshit symbolism, the new generation of producers concluded—it's the sex, the graphic violence, frank language, and adult situations. Look at all the wanton orgies in Fellini's *La Dolce Vita,* the brutally explicit rape scene in Bergman's *The Virgin Spring,* the exuberant debauchery in Tony Richardson's *Tom Jones.* These movies made American pictures look about as exciting as a Sunday-school lecture.

Irma la Douce, The Prize, Of Human Bondage, A Shot in the Dark, Cleopatra, and *The Carpetbaggers* were just a few of the mid-sixties movies that challenged the standards of decency set by the production code of the Motion Picture Association of America (MPAA). In the thirties and forties the MPAA had forbidden open-mouthed kissing, married couples kissing—even fully clothed—on a double bed, and strictly limited the inches of cleavage that could be exposed. It had fought to restrict the sexual content of American movies throughout the fifties (eliminating, for instance, all references to homosexuality in the screen adaptations of Tennessee Williams' *A Streetcar Named Desire* and *Cat on a Hot Tin Roof*). But toward the end of the decade the association began to lose its control as producers realized they could reap great publicity by battling the MPAA over the racy content of their pictures.

Whether the nude scenes stayed in or eventually were cut, the controversy guaranteed millions would flock to the theaters in hope of catching a glimpse of Elizabeth Taylor or Richard Burton unclothed.

Ransohoff leaped eagerly into the fray with his 1963 production, *The Americanization of Emily*, a World War II service comedy written by Paddy Chayefsky and directed by Arthur Hiller. The production earned headlines in *Variety* when the MPAA tried to block the filming of four nude scenes. (The women who disrobed in the movie were referred to in the script as "naked nameless broads one, two and three.")

Ransohoff told the *Variety* reporter: "The code is antiquated in today's industry. We are losing our market because we allow foreign pictures full of nudity done in an artistic manner to play our top houses, but we can't get into them because the code robs us of our artistic creativity. . . . I'd rather have a good film that makes $5 million, than a lousy film that makes $11 million. I'm preoccupied with the creative integrity of my pictures."

This champion of fine art then had press releases printed up about the fracas and mailed them to newspapers across the country, leading *The New York Times* to conclude: "In Hollywood, there is widespread belief that Mr. Ransohoff has attacked the code to get publicity for his movie, and because he feels nudity will help the box office appeal of his picture." The *Times* article, of course, provided just the publicity Ransohoff was seeking. Before *The Americanization of Emily*'s release, he compromised with the MPAA and trimmed some footage out of one of the scenes.

When Ransohoff began looking around for a director for *Cincinnati Kid*, his co-producer, John Calley, urged him to screen *Ride the High Country*. He did and was impressed. "I thought that *The Cincinnati Kid* had the feel of a western," says Ransohoff, "and felt that Sam would give that kind of feel to it. I was interested in doing a gunfight with a deck of cards; *The Cincinnati Kid* was almost a romantic western."

Sam had no illusions about the material. It wasn't Shakespeare or Tolstoy, but the money was great—$67,750—and he needed it after forfeiting most of his salary on *Dundee*. If he could make a solid commercial hit out of *Kid* it would buy him the opportunity to make a film of his own.

But when Sam settled into one of the plush bungalows on the MGM lot—formerly reserved for such stars as Clark Gable, Greta Garbo, and Buster Keaton—he began to have second thoughts about *The Cincinnati Kid.* It looked like he had signed on as captain of the Titanic.

There was no screenplay, only a ninety-seven-page treatment by Paddy Chayefsky, which Sam disliked. A series of writers—Frank Gilroy, Ring Lardner, Jr., and Charles Eastman—were hired to flesh it out to a script, but each delivered half-baked drafts filled with contrived plot twists and cardboard characters. Ransohoff never seemed to be in town for more than a few days at a time before taking off again for New York or Paris or some other far corner of the globe in pursuit of yet another hot deal. Peckinpah ended up cutting the best sequences out of the various drafts and pasting them together to come up with a workable screenplay.

Martin Ransohoff thought the center of the story was the soap-opera love triangle that the other writers had constructed under his supervision. (The Kid is torn between the love of a "good" woman and his lust for a "bad" one.) But much to his consternation, Peckinpah began to turn the focus away from that and concentrate more on the harsh landscape the Kid inhabited (New Orleans during the Depression), on the cold-bloodedness of his profession and its effect on his personality. He even told his producer that he wanted to shoot it in black and white. "I had warned him that I didn't want total realism, I wanted something that would be a licorice stick, popcorn," says Ransohoff. "It was supposed to be a gunfight with a deck of cards, with great characters in a terrific setting."

Sam, for his part, found Ransohoff's suggestions for plot twists, character developments, and dialogue "absurd, immature, and senseless," and told him so.

The conflict increased when they began casting the other major roles. Spencer Tracy withdrew from the project because MGM balked at paying his asking price, so Edward G. Robinson was brought in to replace him. Sam agreed that Robinson was a good substitute, but was disappointed to lose Tracy. Then Ransohoff came up with his suggestions for the two female leads: Sharon Tate—a young starlet he had under contract and under his bed sheets—and Ann-Margret. The two voluptuous, swinging-sixties fantasy girls were perfect for the "popsicle" movie that Ransohoff wanted to make, but hideously wrong for the film Peckinpah envisioned.

Sam voiced his objections to both actresses with lacerating sarcasm. Ransohoff backed off on Tate, agreeing to cast Tuesday Weld—a marginally better choice—instead. But he refused to give up Ann-Margret.

The relationship between the producer and director rapidly deteriorated. Now whenever the two men were in the same room together the tension condensed on the walls and ceiling. And as the first day of shooting drew closer, Peckinpah grew increasingly agitated over the incomplete script (Terry Southern had been brought in for yet more frantic rewrites) and the confused state of the production.

Sam wasn't the only one getting nervous. Ransohoff and Calley were beginning to have serious doubts about Peckinpah's emotional equilibrium. Ransohoff had received repeated phone calls from Jerry Bresler, who filled his ear with *Dundee* horror stories and urged him not to hand the reins of his picture over to this madman.

Filming began on November 30. On the fourth day the company moved to a hotel-room set on an MGM sound stage to shoot a scene that Terry Southern had written under Ransohoff's supervision. In it a gambler, played by Rip Torn, was to make arrangements over the telephone for a big poker game. The script explicitly described how during this conversation Torn was to massage the rear end of "a half-clad cutie, who lies stretched across the bed reading a book called *The Power of Surrender.*" Finally the girl was to cry out, "Oh gosh, I can't stand it!"

Peckinpah began shooting the scene at six P.M., and worked late into the night running the actors through the action and dialogue again and again. Gradually he began to strip the extraneous elements away. First the vibrator was taken out, then the baton, then all of the girl's dialogue, then finally her underwear, leaving her stark naked beneath a fur coat.

Ransohoff was in northern California at the time, overseeing another film he had in production there, *The Sandpiper*. John Calley was on *The Cincinnati Kid* set, watching the store for his partner, and he didn't like what he was seeing. Calley was disappointed at the loss of the vibrator, alarmed at the amount of time Sam was taking to shoot a simple expository scene, and disturbed by the shift in tone that it was undergoing. "We went to eleven or twelve o'clock at night," Calley recalls. "Sam was shooting the scene over and over again and screwing around with this weird adjunctive aspect to the film. The film made no sense that he was shooting."

Sam kept purring to the girl in a soft, hypnotic voice as they rehearsed the action. The camera, ultimately, was placed not in front of the girl but behind her; when she took the coat off and slipped into bed, her nakedness was sensed more than really seen. "Sam started to get something out of her that was very sad," says Jim Silke, who was on the set that night. "She didn't do anything. She didn't say anything. She was just there . . . Sam knew what he wanted. The story was not her nudity, but in Rip Torn's face. He just didn't care about her. He'd picked her up for a good time, he'd used her, and now he was done with her."

Peckinpah finished at around midnight, satisfied he'd caught something extraordinary on film. "I thought it was some astonishingly good footage," he later recalled. He had found the right tone, and felt he had a handle on the movie at last.

Meanwhile, John Calley had returned to his office and called Ransohoff in northern California. "You'd better get your ass back here!" Calley said. "We're in big trouble."

The next day Sam shot a chase through the trainyards of downtown Los Angeles that would take place in the opening of the finished film: the Kid flees from a pair of card players who think he cheated them. Peckinpah added to the background of the chase itself a railroad workers' strike that escalated into an all-out riot.

L. Q. Jones, who played one of the pursuers, recalls: "That riot had 200 people in it. We did in one afternoon what it would normally take a good director on a big picture at least a week to do. It was really gorgeous. Fights, fires, cars turning over, motorcycles sliding—it wasn't gratuitous, it was to reinforce the time period, the Great Depression."

At the end of the day Sam rode back to the studio with his cinematographer, Philip Lathrop. "Well, I think we got enough," he said after a long, thoughtful silence. "We'll go on the back lot later and put together a couple of walls and get some close-ups."

When they arrived at the studio, Peckinpah got out of the car and said, "I'll see you Monday."

Lathrop nodded and walked over to the studio's camera department. As he stepped in the door the head of the department came over to him and said, "You're not working Monday."

"You mean I got fired?" Lathrop asked.

"No, the director did."

While Sam had been up on a camera crane in the trainyards, Ransohoff and Calley had been in a screening room at MGM, looking at the rushes from the first four days.

Ransohoff was aghast at what he saw. "It was dour, it was gray and bleak. Here I was trying to make an upscale movie. This movie was supposed to be a popsicle. MGM had a very clear vision, we knew what we wanted to make, and they were paying me and relying on me to make it, and I didn't think Sam was making it. Shutting down meant losing $500,000. We had an all-star cast, and now no director. Believe me, it was not done lightly. I was really disappointed because I had really gone out on a hook for Sam. It was very embarrassing for me."

"I did three pictures with Marty Ransohoff and found him to be a pain in the ass on all of them," says writer-producer E. Jack Neuman. "He wouldn't know if the rushes on *Cincinnati Kid* were good or bad. He just doesn't know how to look at film."

The following Monday Peckinpah and his agent were called into Ransohoff's office. Shortly before the appointed time, Calley ran down to the MGM prop department and got an Everlast boxing headguard. Slipping into Ransohoff's office minutes before Sam was due to arrive, he presented it to the producer, saying, "Here, Marty, I think you'd better put this on." Ransohoff laughed uneasily. Both had heard of a recent incident on the MGM lot: Sam had sucker-punched his friend Frank Kowalski in the middle of a heated argument and sent him to the hospital. When Ransohoff's secretary announced Sam's arrival over the intercom, the producer slipped the headguard into the bottom drawer of his desk and said, "Tell him to come on in."

To the two producers' surprise and relief, the meeting went very smoothly. "It was a five-minute meeting," says Ransohoff. "I said, 'Sam, I just plain don't like the film. This is not the picture that I want to make.' It was nothing personal, I wasn't mad at the guy. I was disappointed. I had gone out on a limb for him. I've had to replace a director three or four times over a forty-five-picture career. It happens, and it's not a lot of fun. There was no big psychodrama, it was simply that we wanted to make a change."

"Sam was really classy," says co-producer John Calley. "He got up, shook hands all around, and walked out of the room."

But the worst was yet to come. Ransohoff went to the trade papers and sanctimoniously announced the reasons for Peckinpah's removal from the picture. The result was an article in the December 9 issue of *Variety* that read, in part: "Peckinpah's problems apparently stemmed from his filming a nude scene which wasn't called for in the script, but which the director wrote in on his own. Last Friday he reportedly excused the featured cast and began to lens the nudie scene using an extra from the cast."

Sam's jaw fell when he read it. Ransohoff's audacity was unbelievable. Here was a man who'd promoted his last production based on the nude scenes venting outrage with the moral authority of a Billy Graham. And the brain-dead reporters seemed to be buying it.

Columnist Sheilah Graham wrote: "I agree with Marty Ransohoff's decision to replace director Sam Peckinpah in *The Cincinnati Kid*. Nudity is certainly going too far when a director, Sam, films a nude scene for his own amusement. In the first place, he should share the wealth, in the second, he has no right to waste the boss's money."

No one on the set the night Sam shot the hotel-room scene—not cinematographer Philip Lathrop, not dialogue director Jim Silke, not unit production manager Austen Jewell—remembers the scene as the shocking piece of pornography that Ransohoff to this day describes. All corroborate Peckinpah's claim that although the girl was in fact naked beneath her fur coat, the bare skin actually captured on film was fleeting, and the eroticism implied rather than explicit.

When Sam's business manager, Bob Schiller, met with Ransohoff to see about getting Peckinpah's salary paid in full, the motive for the charges of an outrageous nude scene became clear. "I said to Ransohoff, 'All right, what are we going to do? What about the payoff here? You're into the film and now you're yanking him off. What's your intention as far as his compensation?' Ransohoff said, 'Well, we're studying that.' I said, 'What do you mean, studying it?' He said, 'We're studying as to whether he violated the moral turpitude term in the contract.' "

Schiller and Peckinpah's lawyers refused to be cowed, and Sam was eventually paid his full salary. Norman Jewison took over as director and two weeks later started shooting the picture from scratch. It was now being filmed in color, with Tuesday Weld and Ann-Margret wandering through a tasteful pastel-shaded vision of Depression-era New Orleans with voluptuous sixties-style manes of blond and red hair.

Sam would hold on to his bungalow at MGM for another year, thanks to a lucrative development deal set up before *The Cincinnati Kid* catastrophe. But the studio refused to come up with the financing for any of the scripts he had hammered out with Jim Silke. When his contract expired he was out on the street. The phone stopped ringing, his own calls went unreturned. He couldn't even get past the front gate at some studios. The *Dundee* disaster followed by the firing and Ransohoff's public condemnation had destroyed his credibility. His soaring reputation took a nosedive straight into the rocks. *Newsweek* wrote in its stinging obituary for Peckinpah's career: "As comic characters yell while falling over cliffs: 'Yeoow!' "

"Sam's reputation as a rebel started to grow," says John Veitch, who would later become head of production for Columbia

Studios. "He did nothing to dispel it. I think a lot of people got concerned that he was a problem. They used to call me to ask about him and I'd say, 'It's not true.' Once you get a reputation as being difficult, the unfortunate thing about it is that it grows and everybody runs scared. It'll start maybe with the head of the studio saying, 'Well, we don't want to take a chance with him.' Or some actor saying, 'Well, I understand he's been a problem, I don't know if I want to work with him.' Or an agent trying to push one of [his] own clients says, 'Well, you know, I've got a director who makes the schedule, he doesn't cause any problems. Why do you need this headache?' All those people all the way down the line are afraid they're going to be involved with him, and his reputation grows, and a lot of times it's very unfair."

To casual acquaintances Sam seemed to take his professional banishment "like a man." He shrugged it off philosophically and kept banging out screenplays, hoping that one would be hot enough to serve as his ticket back into the big time.

But those closer to him knew he'd been hit hard. "It totally destroyed him for a long time," says L. Q. Jones. "The thing that really destroyed him was the word went around town that Sam makes lewd pictures, that he can't be trusted. Nobody would hire him, so he couldn't make movies. Well, that's like telling a preacher that he can't go to church. That's Sam's church. So what do you do? You go to pieces, which is what he did."

6

On the Beach

At the dawn of one of the most exciting eras in American cinema, Sam Peckinpah found himself sitting on the sidelines. Most of his contemporaries were finally getting their big breaks, and in the late sixties this new generation of directors burst forth with some of the most daring and innovative films ever to come out of Hollywood.

There were a number of converging factors that spawned this second golden age, the most important being the upheaval taking place within American society.

The Vietnam War had turned into one ugly open wound. President Lyndon Johnson had won his first elected term in office by painting Republican opponent Barry Goldwater as a dangerous hawk who wanted to massively expand America's military role in Southeast Asia. After the election, when South Vietnam seemed about to cave in to the North, Johnson boosted U.S. combat troops from 16,000 to 464,000 by 1967. The war was now costing taxpayers $2 billion a month, yet corruption in the South

Vietnamese government was siphoning off 40 percent of the American aid. U.S. bombers now pulverized villages and napalmed jungles in South Vietnam and along the Cambodian border. B-52s unloaded their bomb-bay doors over Haiphong Harbor, the military installations surrounding Hanoi, and finally over the city and its suburbs, inflicting terrible casualties on civilian populations. Television crews were out in the thick of the firefights and every night on the six o'clock news Americans were treated to the sights and sounds of the bleeding, the burned, the maimed, and the dying. The benign "Leave It to Beaver" utopia of the fifties, and Americans' image of themselves as the white-hatted good guys standing tall for freedom, truth, and justice among the world's nations, was completely and irretrievably shattered.

Antiwar demonstrations broke out at induction centers, on college campuses, and the White House lawn. In March 1966, 20,000 antiwar protesters paraded down Fifth Avenue in New York City while thousands of others marched in Washington, the Midwest, and California. In October 1967, 50,000 antiwar activists gathered around the Lincoln Memorial, then marched across the Potomac and stormed the Pentagon, yelling obscenities as they rushed lines of soldiers and federal marshals guarding the building with fixed bayonets. Demonstrators were smashed over the head with gun butts and nightsticks, and 250 were arrested, including novelist Norman Mailer.

The war wasn't the only issue sparking mass protests and riots on the home front. Black civil rights leaders were tired of seeing their followers clubbed, tear gassed, and shot in the Deep South, and frustrated with the continued wide disparities between white and black America. More militant leaders like Stokely Carmichael had emerged, urging open revolution against whitey. "They taught us to kill [in Vietnam]," said Carmichael. "Now the struggle is in the United States. We have no alternative but to use aggressive armed violence in order to own land, houses and stores inside our communities, and to control the politics of those communities."

And by 1966 and 1967 it looked like that revolution was only one lit match away from catching fire. In Watts, a black slum in south-central Los Angeles, widespread rioting resulted in two dead and twenty-five injured. Riots also rocked Chicago, New York, Cleveland, Boston, and Buffalo. Four thousand National Guardsmen had to be called into Chicago to put down unrest; federal troops had to be deployed in Mississippi as well, and 4,700 paratroopers were rushed in to Detroit by President Johnson to stop black rioting that had racked up thirty-eight deaths and $150 million in property damage. "It looks like Berlin in 1945," Detroit mayor Jerome P. Cavanagh said afterward. Something had gone horribly wrong with America, and nobody quite knew how it had happened.

As the old American Dream gave its last death kicks, a new group of visionaries stepped into the vacuum with a kaleidoscopic alternative. Ken Kesey and his band of Merry Pranksters careened across the nation in a mandala-splashed schoolbus, spitting sparks that started a psychedelic grassfire from coast to coast, and a former Harvard psychology professor, Timothy Leary, established his International Foundation for Internal Freedom for the research and promotion of LSD. Leary urged the younger generation to "Turn on, tune in and drop out."

In San Francisco, Kesey's Acid Tests—wild multimedia events where both performers and participants expanded their consciousness by chugging LSD-laced Kool-Aid—turned Haight-Ashbury into the freaked-out, turned-on, flower-power vortex of the burgeoning counterculture. Thousands of youths flocked to San Francisco in '67 for the "Summer of Love." Ten thousand hippies congregated for a Be-In in New York's Central Park, and 50,000 swarmed into Monterey for the Pop Festival of July 1967, which featured a whole new generation of acid-rock musicians: Jimi Hendrix, The Jefferson Airplane, The Grateful Dead, The Who, Janis Joplin.

Hollywood's writers and directors couldn't help but react to the tempest of conflict and confusion that had engulfed the country and their own lives; in fact they were ready and eager to plunge right into the eye of the storm. And the breakdown of the old studio system made it possible. When the New Hollywood producers embarked on their quest to inject more "adult" subject matter into American movies—whether their motives were exploitive or sincere—they opened the door for a period of unprecedented experimentation both in the style and content of Hollywood films. And, fortunately, the economics of the time were favorable for it.

"You could do a film for so much less money," says Martin Baum, who would become head of ABC Pictures, one of the most daring production companies of that era. "Failure didn't mean as much. You failed on a two-and-a-half-million-dollar picture, how bad was it? You sold it to television for almost a million dollars, you got foreign rights on it, and you broke even. Prints [of the movie for the theaters] and advertising were a couple of million dollars at most. So your costs were manageable, and you could try things and do interesting things. Life wasn't going to end if your picture didn't become a blockbuster."

The new generation of Hollywood directors wasted no time in demanding that producers back up their pontificating about the "art of the cinema" with action by giving them the control over their films that their European counterparts enjoyed.

Elliot Silverstein, director of *Cat Ballou* (1965) and *A Man Called Horse* (1970), spearheaded the creative-rights movement for directors. In 1965 the Directors Guild of America negotiated a basic agreement with the major studios that gave directors the right to supervise the editing of their movies. Directors were now guaranteed at least one public screening of their cut of a film before the studio could step in and take it away from them.

"That's why editing began to change in the sixties and became so much more experimental," Silverstein explains. "Directors had some hope that at least they could present the film in the way they saw it, and therefore they could shoot it without worrying as much about how it looked in dailies because they knew how they wanted the footage to be cut later. That's why montage became more popular. The old directors like Ford and Hawks would shoot scenes in long takes with a few setups; they'd camera-cut so there would be only one way the editors could put it together. Now we didn't have to do that."

Like kids turned loose in a toy store, American directors ran wild, trying out all the new techniques they'd been enviously watching the Europeans play with. Paddling out in uncharted waters, searching for new ways to shoot scenes, tell stories, breaking as many of the old rules as they could to see what new discoveries would be made.

"It was an exciting time, it was a wonderful time," says Reza Badiyi, who worked as a second unit director during those years. "It was a very aware time, no other era was like that. It was madness!"

Sidney Lumet's *The Pawnbroker* (1965) was one of the first of the American art films. A character study of a concentration-camp survivor (Rod Steiger) living in contemporary New York City, the movie was shot in black-and-white and utilized the flash-cuts of Resnais' *Hiroshima Mon Amour* to evoke the anguished death-camp memories impinging on Steiger's present life. There were graphic nude scenes and violence, and dialogue laced with obscenities that all but obliterated the MPAA production code. Its grim ending avoided any message-happy moral conclusions and left many questions about the tortured protagonist unanswered.

A product of live television, Lumet had already stacked up an impressive list of film credits by the time he directed *The Pawnbroker*. Not so with Mike Nichols, who burst onto American screens after spectacular success as a stand-up comic (with partner Elaine May) and as a stage director on Broadway. Nichols became one of the golden-boy auteurs with his very first film, an adaptation of Edward Albee's *Who's Afraid of Virginia Woolf?* (1966). Also shot in black-and-white and riddled with four-letter words and lascivious dialogue, Albee's play laid naked all of the twisted, self-lacerating neuroses that hid behind the American middle-class façade. Behind the tightly closed doors of their perfectly landscaped suburban homes, Ozzie and Harriet were locked in a cannibalistic feeding frenzy. Beneath the Lucite coat of normalcy lay a pathological patchwork of stunted ambitions, self-loathing, and desperate delusions.

Nichols turned around a year later and rendered a more comic but no less scathing portrait of the middle class and the "generation gap" in *The Graduate*. Adultery, alcoholism, and vacuous materialism ran rampant, and the image of Dustin Hoffman floating in the blue-gray void of his backyard swimming pool in the scuba-diving outfit his father forced him to try on for the guests distilled the alienation of an entire generation. Nichols employed jump cuts for slick narrative transitions and edited whole sequences to the rhythms of Simon and Garfunkel's sound track, making *The Graduate* sophisticated and arty yet slickly commercial.

Another American auteur who began to peak in 1967 was Arthur Penn, also a veteran director of Broadway and live TV. Penn had already made several powerful films, including a version of the Billy the Kid legend, *The Left-Handed Gun* (1958), which portrayed the Kid as a fifties antihero: confused, angry, but longing for normalcy. The violence in *Left-Handed Gun* was abrupt, cruel, and stripped of any trace of romanticism, and Penn anticipated (or perhaps inspired, for Sam was very familiar with the film) Peckinpah's use of children in *The Wild Bunch.* In one scene a little girl runs out in the street to stare at the Kid's freshest kill. She points at the man's dislodged boot and laughs, until her mother yanks her away and slaps her.

But it was with *Bonnie and Clyde* (1967) that Penn took the lead as the preeminent American director. He—and screenwriters David Newman and Robert Benton—mythologized the mad-dog bank-robbing killers into sixties-style rebels striking back at the system. The action took place in the Depression at a time when banks were foreclosing on debt-burdened farmers, but in the context of the sixties there was a double meaning, for the banks were helping to finance the Vietnam war machine.

In the film's final scene, Bonnie and Clyde are ambushed by sheriff's deputies and riddled with bullets. Faye Dunaway and Warren Beatty had been rigged with hundreds of squibs—tiny capsules of black powder and condoms full of red dye placed beneath their clothing. When triggered electronically the squibs exploded gaping holes in Beatty's shirt and pants and Dunaway's dress and splattered the dye in all directions. As a kicker, Penn shot the action in slow motion. Beatty and Dunaway jerked spastically as bullet holes erupted across their torsos.

Audiences in 1967 sat in shell-shocked silence afterward. No one had seen anything like it before.

It appeared that Penn had beaten Peckinpah to the summit—the combination of squibs and slow motion achieved the visceral horror Sam had been reaching for but unable to grasp on *Major Dundee*. Yet, after chewing it over, Peckinpah realized it could still be taken a step further—in fact several steps. Penn had simply shifted into slow motion at the climax and then out of it again when the outlaws were both dead. The squibs had jacked up the impact tenfold, but the use of slow motion had been essentially no different than Kurosawa's in *The Seven Samurai*. Editorially it was static. The weaving of slow motion into the very fabric of a sequence—cutting into it, cutting out, then back in again as he'd attempted on *Dundee*—had still to be achieved. But it wouldn't be long before Penn or someone else took that next step.

And where was Peckinpah during these years? Out at his house in Malibu, pounding out scripts, hoping to come up with one that would serve as his ticket back into the big time.

"He wrote and wrote and wrote," says L. Q. Jones. "That period of time after *Cincinnati Kid* was by far the most productive, as far as output of scripts and ideas."

Sam's most frequent writing partner during these years was Jim Silke. Silke first met Peckinpah in 1963 when he interviewed him for *Cinema* magazine, which Jim had started while still the executive art director at Capital Records. Peckinpah recognized almost immediately that this tall, bespectacled young man shared his own obsessive passion for movies and the history and folklore of the Old West. A strong friendship soon formed between them.

Silke had done no screenwriting before meeting Peckinpah, but he was hungry to learn, so Sam became his drill instructor, coaching, pushing, and bullying him through basic training. It began with some minor rewrite chores on *Dundee* and *Cincinnati Kid*, then intensified when Sam decided to collaborate with Silke on an adaptation of a James Michener novel, *Caravans*—another of the author's cinderblock-size melodrama-adventures. They started working on it while *Cincinnati Kid* was in preproduction, and continued to after Sam was fired. At the same time they hammered out another action-thriller, *Ready for the Tiger.* MGM eventually canceled both productions, and when Sam's development deal with the studio expired he was forced to begin working out of his home again, strictly on spec. Silke worked with him.

Peckinpah had bought the screen rights to two slender novels that he desperately wanted to make into movies. They became twin obsessions, and for the rest of his life he would try to maneuver, hustle, and seduce producers into financing them. The first was *The Hi Lo Country* by Max Evans. As gritty and rough-edged as the high desert mesas that served as its backdrop, *Hi Lo* told the story of Big Boy Matson, an awesome totem pole of a man. Born in the larger-than-life era of the Wild West, Matson returns to New Mexico after World War II to find himself defiantly at odds with the newly rich landowners who have changed ranching from a way of life into big business.

The second book was *Castaway,* a bizarre psychodrama by James Gould Cozzens. It started off like a piece of Ray Bradbury science fiction. When an unspecified catastrophe overtakes New York, the sole survivor, Mr. Lecky, takes refuge in a cavernous department store, which has also escaped destruction. There he finds everything he needs to live out his days in luxury—until he discovers that he is not alone. An intruder, a monstrous apelike creature, stalks the product-cluttered aisles bent on, Lecky is convinced, killing him so that it can take possession of the store's vast spoils.

In a panic, Lecky races to the gun department, arms himself, and hunts down and shoots his adversary. But here, with dreamlike logic, the drama turns into an eerie Gestalt. Bleeding and dying, the creature becomes pitiful, whimpering like a lost child. After it has finally died, Lecky works up the courage to approach the corpse and turn its face to the light, and is shocked by what he sees. Cozzens writes: "Mr. Lecky knew why he had never seen a man with this face. He knew who had been pursued and cruelly killed, who was now dead and would never climb more stairs. He knew why Mr. Lecky could never have for his own the stock of this great store." It was himself he had shot; *he* was the monster.

One thinks immediately of the young D. Sammy, the skinny,

big-eyed quiet boy who loved nothing better than to hide away in his room with his Big Little Books, who faced relentless ridicule from his grandfather for his sensitive nature, who in order to win the approval of the family's men had had to kill his "feminine" childlike side. "It's certainly Sam's point of view," Silke says of *Castaway*. "It's about what we do to ourselves."

Peckinpah and Silke talked and struggled and fought, wrote and rewrote for almost two years until they finally completed screenplays for both *The Hi Lo Country* and *Castaway*. By this time their collaboration had settled into the routine of an old married couple. Silke was out at Peckinpah's house almost every day, and many nights, scribbling away until the wee hours of the morning. Every other week Sam and Jim would go shopping together at the local Mayfair Market ("May Farket," Sam called it). Sam would buy the meats, Jim the bread and peanut butter; always they ended their mission hovering over the white mist of the ice cream freezer, fighting over what flavor to buy.

"He always wanted a fancy-flavored ice cream and I wanted plain vanilla," says Silke. "It was something that I was hard and fast on and I would never give up that argument. That became a bone of contention. 'Dumb fuckin' Silke, he wants vanilla.' He'd go on about how that goes with my personality, the whole thing, he'd build it into a novel. He'd pick over the fancy flavors for twenty minutes. It'd drive me crazy. It was a delaying tactic, to avoid writing. Sam had hundreds of delay tactics, anything to not do it. That's why he'd delay on the ice cream, and he also pissed me off. I mean, that's part of the game."

Then it was back to the house, where they'd lock themselves up in the office, Sam barking roughly at Begonia whenever she dared interrupt them. Now the painful process of pulling characters and scenes apart and putting them back together again began. They probed each other with questions, looking inward for their own demons, their most private obsessions, fears, the nasty secrets kept hidden from even their own eyes—for this is where the real material would be found.

For Silke, the two years following *Cincinnati Kid* were creatively exhilarating, the most exciting time of his life. "Sam was at his best when he was down," says Silke, who had witnessed many of Peckinpah's neurotic excesses on *Dundee*. "When he's down, all of a sudden he's tough, he was just marvelous. He was really resilient. We produced like you couldn't believe. We were always working, and on spec. I was on call twenty-four hours a day."

Economically it was a lean time, but not as desperate as Sam later liked to paint it. He used the money he got from *Cincinnati Kid* and his development deal at MGM to buy a house on Broad Beach, at the very northern end of Malibu, and a small and funky cattle ranch—consisting of "two hundred acres of sagebrush," Sam later said, a rundown ranch house, and a few scattered steer—near his favorite hunting grounds in Ely, Nevada. Residuals from his television shows continued to trickle in, allowing him to maintain both properties through this fallow period. But as his savings dwindled he was forced to sell his profit percentages of both "The Rifleman" and "The Westerner" for $10,000 each. Sam later expressed great regret over this, but his business manager, Bob Schiller, claims the creative accounting of television production companies made it unlikely that he would have ever seen big money.

For the first time in years he did not have the pressure of a major production hanging over his head, and so had time to enjoy the good life on the glimmering sands of Broad Beach. It was a renascence of the early days at the Colony.

While no seaside mansion, the new house was the biggest Sam had owned yet. A beige two-story square-shaped structure, its living room had an atrium with indoor plants, a twenty-foot ceiling, and high windows admitting bright California sunlight during the day and fine blue moonlight at night. There were three bedrooms; the master bedroom had a balcony overlooking the beach. Sam's office was located directly below it, with a giant picture window that also looked out on the white sand and blue water. "There could be absolutely no noise anywhere near it when Dad was working in there," Melissa recalls. There was a kitchen with a counter that served as the bar and a prime vortex at parties, a small dining area, and, out back, a large gray-painted deck with glass windbreaks and steps leading down to the rolling sand dunes.

Weekends, of course, were a nonstop party. A couple dozen of Begonia's Los Angeles relatives would converge there with platters of Mexican food like paella (chicken cooked with rice, corn, red and green peppers, crabmeat, shrimp, and clams) and pica de gallo (chicken, the sweet root *jicama*, hot peppers, onions, and oranges).

Sam was delighted by the invasion; Mexico was now coming to him every Saturday and Sunday. Often he could be found out back, barbecuing. There was no built-in barbecue at this house, so he would simply dig a pit in the sand, fill it with coals, and when they were rippling yellow-red he would lay the meat right on them. "He'd burn the hot dogs until they were black," Melissa recalls. "They'd be shriveled and full of sand, but we'd put this relish on them that he made with fresh-cut onions." When cooking beef or pork or chicken, he marinated the meat with the latest batch of "boongow" he and Walter Peter had mixed up. After devouring one of his steaks, Lyn Silke came back and asked, "Sam, what's in this sauce? It's delicious!"

He stared at her, smiled enigmatically, and shook the ash of his cigarette into the boongow bowl. "What isn't in it?"

He loved to prepare mystery hors d'oeuvres for his guests. His assistant on these special projects was usually his son, Mathew, now three years old going on four. Skinny as a Mexican village dog, hazel eyes half hidden by an unruly mop of blond hair, Mathew spent most of his weekends running around the Broad Beach house stark naked. One day his father took him aside. "This is gonna be our secret project, partner, just between you and me." He handed the boy a bucket and told him to go around the garden and gather up every snail he could find. Mathew returned a half-hour later, the bucket brimming with mucusy mollusks. He watched with wide-eyed fascination as his father soaked them in water and table salt, slipped their slick curly bodies out of their shells, then stuck them on the barbecue and slathered them with boongow. Sam then plated them up and, with a wink, sent Mathew around to offer them to the guests. "Sam, what is this stuff?" someone finally inquired.

Mathew recalls that when he told them, one person vomited.

"Dad loved to play games," says Mathew, "like stealing food

off of your plate when you weren't looking. He was really good at it. You'd be eating dinner and he'd look out at the beach like something had really caught his eye, and say, 'Mathew, what in the hell is that?' You'd look and he'd grab your potato, and *laugh.* He really got a big kick out of it."

Recalling those long-ago days, Jim Silke says wistfully: "We would have the time of our lives. I don't drink, and I was drunker than any of them."

But the dark side always lurked, ready to spring out unexpectedly. Fern Lea saw it one night when she and Sam found themselves sitting alone at the kitchen counter. He looked at her with a strangely naked expression and said that he knew he wouldn't live very long. Her mind leaped back to that day when he'd quoted the Edna St. Vincent Millay poem on one of his visits home from the San Rafael Military Academy. There was no romantic bravado this time, but instead a weariness, a sad fatalism that Fern Lea hadn't ever seen before. Sam dropped such remarks so cryptically, out of nowhere, that she never knew how to respond.

His kids saw the dark side far more often than the other visitors—far more often than they wanted to. Resentments between Sam and Marie still festered, and they found expression in conflicts over which set of values the kids were to be raised by, hers or his. As pawns in the battle, the kids took most of the hits.

Sam lived in terror of some terrible calamity claiming his children's lives. Whenever they would come to visit him on movie locations in the years that followed, he would insist they fly on separate airplanes. That way if a plane crashed he wouldn't lose all of them. "My father took it upon himself to instill fear in us," says Kristen. "But it wasn't altogether unreasonable. The world is a dangerous place."

Marie's father was killed in an automobile accident a few years after she and Sam divorced. Art Selland, then mayor of Fresno, had been just a few miles away from home when a truck struck the car he was riding in with a group of associates. Catapulted from the car, Art died almost instantly. The tragedy converted Sam into a seatbelt fanatic. Many a new acquaintance would be shocked to climb into a car with the legendary wildman, "super macho" movie director, only to have him bitterly admonish them for not buckling up.

The issue became a major focal point in the ongoing battle between Sam and Marie. Sam insisted the kids wear their belts even on the shortest of trips. Marie countered that safety belts were silly and a nuisance. After living with their mother all week, the kids would climb into the car with their father, forget the new groundrules, and receive a stinging reprimand. "Goddamn it, how many times do I have to tell you?" They found themselves on slippery and treacherous ground; keeping their footing was no simple task.

All of the kids liked Begonia. She was beautiful, dark, exotic, vivacious, much like a kid herself. She taught the girls flamenco dancing and made a great playmate on the beach.

Begonia wanted desperately to bear a child but kept having miscarriages. Family members suspected the rigors of flamenco dancing were the cause—she had pounded her body with hard stomping since her early teens. One morning Kristen, Melissa, and a friend were playing noisily downstairs while Begonia was trying to rest in the bedroom upstairs. Sam came down a couple of times and told them to be quiet. "But like most kids," Kristen recalls, "it didn't really register. We were too busy having fun." Until Sam came down the third time, yelling. He told them that they'd caused Begonia's last miscarriage. "It's your fault that baby died!"

Kristen felt a confusing mixture of guilt and anger—guilt because part of her feared her father was telling the truth, and anger because another part of her knew he was talking nonsense.

Young Mathew got the worst of Sam's rages. "Because he was a boy, Dad came down on him awfully hard," says Kristen.

Marie was vehemently opposed to war toys and wouldn't allow them in her house, so Sam went out and bought a division's worth of toy guns, knives, grenades, and soldiers for Mathew to play with at Broad Beach. One weekend he took him into the swirling surf to teach him to snorkle, but the boy balked. Scared by the turbulence, the cold, and the massive expanse of ocean, he refused to stick his face down into the water. Sam coached him gently for a few minutes, but when Mathew continued to resist he lost patience, grabbed his son's head, and pushed it under the water.

Sharon Peckinpah, then seventeen, had had enough of it. The oldest child, and headstrong, she received some of the worst verbal lashings from Sam. He would rip into her over the most trivial transgressions—for setting the table wrong, or for using a hostile tone of voice. When Sharon argued back, he'd say with disgust, "You're just like your mother!"

Sharon finally told Marie that she was afraid of her father and didn't want to visit him anymore. She started seeing a psychiatrist, who advised Marie not to send the girl over to her father's house against her will. Sam tried to coax Sharon back. He told her how much he missed her and wanted to spend time with her, but she would not give in, and eventually left the area altogether to attend a private boarding school in Ojai, sixty miles north of Los Angeles.

Sam started seeing a psychiatrist himself during this time. Robert Culp recommended a man whom he had been seeing, Dr. Charles Wahl, a professor at UCLA who also had a private practice. Sam went to see Wahl sporadically over a four-year period, hoping that the sessions would help him cut down on his drinking and come to terms with his rapidly multiplying demons. But the sessions became testy when Wahl's word-association exercises and probing questions edged their way closer to the many unresolved conflicts from Sam's childhood. Finally one day, when Wahl stuck his scalpel into a fresh wound, Sam leapt to his feet and spat out: "Why the hell should I listen to you? You're fat and you smoke too much!" And then stormed out of the office.

Despite his harshness, Sam always came through for his kids in a crisis. One weekend at Broad Beach, the house jammed with the usual crowd, Sam stood at the stove pouring boiling water into the cone filter of a coffee maker as he shot the shit with Norman Powell. Mathew, yearning for some attention, hung at his father's side trying to interject a question. Distracted, Sam accidentally let the filter overflow and the entire coffee maker toppled, spilling boiling water on his son's shirt and chest.

"The first thing I was worried about was that I'd screwed up and Dad would get pissed at me," says Mathew. "Dad grabbed me and lifted me up and popped my shirt off, popped all the buttons right off. He's lifting me up and he puts me in the sink. I was really embarrassed, upside-down with cold water running on me. There were no words. I was in the sink and the next thing I knew we were in the car."

Norman Powell took the wheel while Sam held his boy, wrapped in a towel, in the passenger seat. "I drove him fast but safely to the hospital," Powell recalls. "Sam later on said to me how much he appreciated the way that I drove, not wasting any time, but not getting out there and endangering them by going too quickly."

"I was in shock," says Mathew. "I remember saying, 'Turn off the sun.' I thought the heater was on. I think Dad was just as shocked and scared. It aged him about ten years in about ten minutes. We were going down the hill past Malibu Canyon and he kept saying it was okay, it was going to be okay. I thought maybe the sun was coming through the windows. My skin kind of sloughed off. We went to the emergency room and Dad went in with me and I got wrapped up."

"Sam was very, very concerned. He held it in, but you could tell he was extraordinarily concerned," says Powell.

Mathew had second- and third-degree burns on his chest, back, and stomach, but when they healed he was left with only a slight scar. "After that, Dad became an ultra-safety freak about anything being around the stove," says Mathew.

"The thing is," says Kristen, "Dad really did love us, all of his kids. We always knew he loved us intensely, despite all the weird ways he expressed it."

Daniel Melnick was another of the new Hollywood producers. Thirty-four years old, lean, dark-haired, and devoutly hip, Melnick was a partner with David Susskind and Leonard Stern in Talent Associates, a production company with two prime-time television series on the air: the comedy smash "Get Smart" and the stylishly produced but poorly rated "Run Buddy Run." TA had also sold some dramatic specials to the networks and had a number of others in development. Like Ransohoff, Melnick professed a desire to make shows with real artistic merit. The difference was that Melnick meant it. If put to the test he could prove he'd actually read *Catch-22* and *One Flew Over the Cuckoo's Nest*—the books, not a reader's one-page synopsis—and could come up with an in-the-ballpark definition of existentialism.

He supervised "Run Buddy Run" for TA and developed "high-class" dramatic specials such as a television production of *Death of a Salesman* starring Lee J. Cobb, George Segal, and James Farentino and directed in an exquisitely haunting, expressionistic style by Alex Segal. The show would win Melnick an Emmy in 1966.

In the fall of that year ABC launched a new hour-long dramatic anthology series, "ABC Stage 67," that the network hoped would revive the golden age of TV drama, when "Playhouse 90," "Kraft Television Theatre," "Philco Playhouse," and "Studio One" had dominated the airwaves. ABC did not produce the individual shows for the series, but instead bought them from a variety of independent producers. Melnick saw a chance to realize one of his most burning artistic ambitions: to produce an adaptation of Katherine Anne Porter's dark and disturbing novella *Noon Wine.* A stark but powerful and flawlessly crafted story, it was hardly the kind of sugary pabulum that then monopolized network programming. It was a courageous, audacious, and anything but commercial choice, but if anyone had the charm and sophistication to sell it to ABC, it was Melnick. He flew to Maryland, met with the seventy-six-year-old author, and secured the screen rights to the story, with the provision that Porter would have final approval over the teleplay.

Now he had to find a writer of extraordinary skill to do the adaptation, someone with a strong feel for southern Texas, where the story takes place. His associate producer on "Run Buddy Run," Lois O'Connor, had been at Filmways when Peckinpah was preparing to shoot *The Cincinnati Kid.* O'Connor felt Sam had been sacked unfairly and believed in his talent, and so suggested him as a strong candidate for both writing and directing *Noon Wine.*

The idea clicked immediately with Melnick. He had seen both *Ride the High Country* and "The Westerner," and loved them. He got hold of Peckinpah through his agent and asked him to come in to the office to discuss the project.

The two hit it off immediately. Sam spoke so softly that the producer had to lean in to hear him, but the man's hazel eyes burned intensely. Of course he knew the story, Peckinpah said—it had been one of his favorites for years. In fact, he already knew exactly how he would shoot it.

A bit of an exaggeration, but only a bit. Sam's first job offer in a year and a half turned out to be a long slow softball lobbed right over home plate. Porter's story took place in the middle of his own favorite fictional landscape: the sun-fried western wasteland at the turn of the century.

The fortunes of a poor and lethargic farmer—Royal Earle Thompson, who is more adept with a bottle of whiskey than a plow—change dramatically one day when a mysterious stranger shows up at the broken front gate of his farmhouse, looking for work. Speaking in clipped cryptic sentences, with eyes like burnt-out light bulbs that rarely make contact with others, the Swedish child-man agrees to work for Thompson for a paltry seven dollars a week, plus room and board. The Swede, Olaf Helton, may not be much of a talker, but he turns out to be a dynamo when it comes to farming. With manic energy and practiced skill, he transforms Thompson's ramshackle spread over a nine-year period into one of the region's most profitable farms, and Thompson himself into a comfortable middle-class landowner.

But the idyll is shattered one day when a bounty hunter, Homer T. Hatch, shows up at Thompson's now-mended front gate looking for Helton. The big Swede, he informs the farmer, escaped from a booby hatch in North Dakota years before, where he'd been kept in a straitjacket after running his own brother through with a pitchfork. His prosperity in jeopardy, Thompson tries to explain to the bounty hunter that Helton hasn't acted crazy at all these past nine years. Sure, he don't talk much and keeps to himself in his off hours, playing those harmonicas of his that he guards so jealously, but he works hard and saves his money and hasn't harmed a hair on anybody's head. In fact, he's practically one of the family now.

But Hatch is not moved by this appeal. "Point is, I'm for law and order! I do not like law breakers or escaped lunatics!" When he pulls out a pair of handcuffs and asks Thompson to help him subdue Helton, the farmer erupts, threatening to throw Hatch off his place if he doesn't leave right now. Hatch pulls a large bowie knife and says, "Try it, try it, go ahead!"

Hearing the commotion, Helton comes running in from the field at that moment and attempts to intercede. Instead of backing down, Hatch—as Thompson sees it—lunges at the Swede with his bowie knife. Before his mind can quite catch up with his actions, Thompson has picked up a nearby ax and rammed the blade into Hatch's head. The skull caves in like a dented beer can and out leaks a stream of oily blood.

Thompson goes to get the local sheriff and tells him the entire story: how Hatch stabbed Helton in the belly and how he himself killed the bounty hunter in an attempt to save Helton's life, and how the Swede had fled into the hills afterward like an animal running off to die.

But when the sheriff's posse tracks Helton down in the surrounding countryside, they find him unmarked by any knife wounds and strong enough to fight like a mad dog, until one of the posse men smashes his head in with a fallen tree branch.

The fact that Helton hadn't been stabbed throws suspicion on Thompson's version of the events, and he is tried for murder. The jury acquits him, but the cold looks he receives from the sheriff, his neighbors, even his own wife and two sons tell Thompson that no one really believes his version of the truth. In their eyes he is and will always remain a killer.

Nevertheless, he forces his wife, Ellie, to ride around to all their neighbors' farms so he can tell his side of the story again. He forces Ellie to lie and say she saw the confrontation and that he's telling the truth. But the Thompsons are met with indifference and subtle ridicule. In the end Thompson succeeds only in further alienating his own wife and sons.

At night he tosses in sweat-soaked sheets, mind knotting itself up over the details of that fateful moment. Had Hatch really tried to stab Helton, or had he just seen it that way? Could he have stopped Hatch without killing him, could he have saved Helton's life without becoming a murderer himself? The image of Hatch's fat laughing face fills him with rage again, and before he knows it he has leapt from his bed screaming and reenacting the swing of that ax all over again. Ellie awakens to the sight and howls, "Stop! Stop!" Her two boys rush in and the eldest wheels upon his father. "She's scared, she's scared to death. What did you do to her? You touch her again and I'll blow your heart out!"

But Royal Earle Thompson's heart is already blown out. He slinks from of the bedroom, away from his farmhouse, a double-barreled shotgun in hand, out to the farthest corner of his land, where he pencils a note—one last futile attempt to explain his side of the story—then points the barrel of the gun at his head and removes one shoe so he can work the trigger with his big toe.

A man forced by an arbitrary chain of events to confront his own capacity for brutality—a flash of sudden violence that cannot be called back, repaired, or repented, a momentary monstrous impulse that destroys his life. Sam knew where the black heart of this story lay, and was eager and ready to drive a stake through it.

Melnick knew by the end of his meeting with Peckinpah that he'd found the right man for the job. Melnick recalls: "Sam said, 'I've got to tell you something. I'm blacklisted, there's going to be a lot of pressure on you not to use me.' Well, because of my neurotic personality, the moment I was told that there was pressure not to use someone, that was guaranteeing that I was going to fight to the death to use them. This was shortly after the McCarthy era and I felt strongly against blacklisting. What I didn't know was that Sam wasn't blacklisted for political reasons; he got blacklisted because of his personality!"

Melnick learned the true circumstances when the trade papers announced that Talent Associates had hired Peckinpah for the project. Within twenty-four hours the producer received a dozen phone calls from industry power brokers urging him not to use Sam. Not only did Charles FitzSimons, Jerry Bresler, and Martin Ransohoff log in with their horror stories, but there were also calls, Sam later recalled, "from people who not only had never worked with me, but who didn't even know me. They all tried to warn him off me."

"You're going to work with Peckinpah, are you crazy?" the callers exclaimed. "He's going to ruin you! The man's a drunk, unstable, he's gonna run your budget right up to the sky!"

"Melnick wasn't as cocky as he'd been at first," says Reza Badiyi, second unit director on "Run Buddy Run." "He started saying, 'What have we got ourselves into?' "

But the producer's stubborn, maverick side made him stick with his choice. "Give Mr. Melnick that credit," Sam later said. "As far as my career, whatever it's worth, he's the man." Sam began hearing scuttlebutt of his own once he signed on with the producer. "People told me he [Melnick] was really a miserable son of a bitch. I found him to be one of the toughest, best, intelligent, you know, really groovy cats I ever worked with in my life. I would say that we made the picture, not me."

Melnick, in turn, was pleasantly surprised by the collaboration. "It turned out to be one of the most satisfying and stimulating creative experiences I've ever had. Sam probably had never been, before or after, as meticulously responsible, because Sam had a very, very, unique, very special to himself, very profound sense of honor. Part of that honor was not letting someone like me, who had taken that kind of chance with him, down."

Peckinpah first offered the part of Roy Earle Thompson to Charlton Heston, but Heston turned him down. Then Melnick suggested Jason Robards. The son of a silent-movie actor, Robards had studied at the American Academy of Dramatic Arts, then gone on to win acclaim in several stage revivals of Eugene O'Neill plays—*The Iceman Cometh* and *Long Day's Journey into Night*—that almost singlehandedly restored the playwright's fading reputation. Robards had become a mid-level film star in the screen adaptations of *Long Day's Journey* and Herb Gardner's *A Thousand Clowns*. Peckinpah agreed to the choice at once: if they could land an actor of Robards' caliber for the lead, they'd be halfway home.

Robards had heard of Peckinpah. A year earlier he had been visiting Spencer Tracy and Katharine Hepburn in California. Hepburn said, "A guy lives down the beach here that you should meet, you'd get along very well with him. His name's Sam Peckinpah."

"I don't know him," Robards said.

"Well, I like him. Spencer's going to do *Cincinnati Kid* with him."

Now Peckinpah and Melnick arrived at the house Robards was renting in Malibu to discuss *Noon Wine*. "We just sat around and drank beer and talked," says Robards. "I think I was probably preconditioned to like him. Spence and Katy were very good friends and they were very straightforward people; if they said something I listened to it. What Sam and I talked about, I don't know. We didn't talk about the story, because he hadn't finished the script yet. We talked about the service. 'Where were you in the war?' Blah, blah, blah. About the beach, and L.A., and that he went to USC Drama School. It was one of those conversations. And then he left with Danny, leaving me with my agent, John Foreman, and I said, 'John, set it up, tell them it's okay. I'll do it, I'd love to work with him.' Just based on Sam, based on meeting him and sitting and talking with him."

Now came the Chinese water torture: writing the script. Sam began by diving as deep as he could into Porter's world. "He went down Maryland to see Katherine Anne Porter and spent some time," says Robards. "They got drunk on bourbon and branch water, and he came back, and then he really went to work."

He began by poring over Porter's novella and an essay she wrote twenty years after it called *Noon Wine: The Sources*. In it Porter broke down the components of the narrative and explained their origins in the memories, fantasies, and family anecdotes of her childhood, then described how they had been combined into one lean, smooth-flowing story.

Certainly he saw his mother in Royal Thompson's wife, Ellie. Lying alone in her dark, airless bedroom, crippled by recurring headaches, shrinking from the least bit of stress, possessed by a rigid Puritanism, intolerant of alcohol, coarse language, and her husband's many human frailties. And he saw his father in Roy Thompson's inability to stand up to his wife and his volcanic outbursts of rage toward his sons.

But more fascinating still was the thematic complexity of the piece. Who ultimately was responsible for the tragedy at Thompson's farm? Porter concluded in her essay that there was no simple answer. "Everyone in this story contributes, one way or another, directly or indirectly, to murder, or death by violence." The bounty hunter, Hatch, contributes by provoking a violent confrontation, Thompson by killing Hatch when he might have stopped him by peaceful means, and Thompson's wife and sons contribute to his suicide by refusing to forgive him for a murder he hadn't meant to commit. In their own unintentional, misguided ways, both Thompson and his wife betray each other.

By the time he'd read the last sentence of Porter's essay, Sam knew what the story meant to him: the failure of love. Roy Thompson fails his wife and sons and they fail him, just as David Peckinpah failed Fern and she him, as Sam had failed Marie and vice versa.

Finally he applied himself to the nuts and bolts of the adaptation. Sam's copy of Porter's story, with its underlined passages and notes in the margins, reveals how he began strategizing the structure of his script. Much of the narrative was revealed through a series of flashbacks from the points of view of Ellie and then Roy Thompson—an ingenious fictional device, but simply too cumbersome and time-consuming for a one-hour television show. So Peckinpah simply took the events described in the flashbacks, reshuffled them into a straight chronological order, and fleshed them out into full-fledged scenes. He did this with incredible precision and economy, his new dialogue matching seamlessly with Porter's, demonstrating how keen his ear was for the dialect of the rural Southwest.

With all the plot points now in place, he then went through the story from beginning to end, expanding some pieces of expositional prose into scenes, and elsewhere pruning Porter's dialogue to eliminate digressions, condense the action, and accelerate the drive of the story. He performed this with the skill of a neurosurgeon, leaving most of the character nuances, thematic intricacies, and atmospheric details intact.

Peckinpah even enriched the emotional depth of the piece at several junctures by adding small scenes: intimate details from his parents' relationship were slipped into the exchanges between Roy and Ellie Thompson to magnify the tragedy of a rapidly failing marriage.

Olaf Helton's scenes, which Sam added, were particularly poignant. From Lennie in the first scene he directed at Fresno State to Cooter and Weed Pindle in his "Gunsmoke" scripts to this latest creation, Peckinpah had an uncanny feel for these murderous child-men—strangers in a strange land, to paraphrase Ellie Thompson's description of the Swede.

Sam's most critical alteration of the story went unnoticed by most, including Porter when they read the first draft of his script. Instead of Thompson taking his shotgun all the way out to the farthest corner of his land to end his life, Peckinpah made a decision early in his writing—as a note in the margin of his copy of the story indicates—to have Thompson merely walk across the farmyard to the barn to blow his brains out. To Melnick and others on the production team it seemed like a purely tactical decision that would save both screen and production time. Its full impact would not be felt until Sam turned in his final cut of the show. Then it would become clear that he hadn't been thinking of production practicalities at all.

Peckinpah completed his sixty-three-page teleplay on September 26, 1966 (a second draft would shear away twelve pages). It was promptly mailed off to Katherine Anne Porter, who had to approve it. If Porter gave it a thumbs-down, the project would be dead in the water.

"Everybody sat around in Melnick's office wondering: is the show going to happen or not going to happen? I'll never forget that," says Reza Badiyi. "And finally she called and gave her approval. She said, 'This is good.' "

Porter followed her phone call with a letter: "I usually pay little attention to theatrical interpretations of my work because I fully understand they will in all probability be destroyed. But, oh, how I wish my novel, *Ship of Fools* [adapted for the big screen a year earlier by Stanley Kramer] had been in Peckinpah's hands."

The production was laid out on a seven-day shooting schedule with a budget of $265,000. Peckinpah would get $15,000 for his services as writer and director. The balance of the cast began to fall quickly into place. Olivia de Havilland was signed for the part of Ellie Thompson, Sam brought in Theodore Bikel to play the bounty hunter, Ben Johnson to play the town sheriff, and L. Q. Jones for a small but critical part as a white-trash neighbor of the Thompsons. Melnick signed Per Oscarsson, who had just won the best-actor award at the Cannes Film Festival for his role in director Henning Carlsen's *Hunger,* to play Olaf Helton.

The "Stage 67" shows were all shot on videotape using state-of-the-art equipment in an attempt to capture a filmlike look. But state of the art in 1966 meant taking huge trailers full of humming electronic equipment and bulky, hard-to-move cameras on location. The episodes were usually shot with three cameras and a switcher so that in the control booth the director could switch from one camera to another as the action unfolded, thus enabling the shows to be shot in a fraction of the time that it would take to film them with a single motion picture camera, as was the practice in feature films. During their first meeting, Melnick asked Peckinpah if he'd ever shot on videotape before, and Sam quickly assured him he had, citing his vast directing experience at KLAC-TV in the early fifties. In reality, of course, this consisted of *Portrait of a Madonna,* which he'd shot on the station's prehistoric Kinescope system, a far cry from the elaborate technology he'd be dealing with on *Noon Wine.* Fortunately a team of ABC's top production personnel would be backing him up, including associate producer James Clark, production supervisor Harry Sherman, and technical supervisor Clair McCoy.

As usual, Sam prepared no elaborate shot lists or storyboards, though he did sketch out rough camera angles for several scenes on his copy of the script, noting where he would need a camera crane for high-angle shots of Robards to heighten the sense of isolation and despair when he stands alone in the courtroom after the trial and tosses in bed the night he kills himself.

Melnick rented a rehearsal hall on Third Street, between La Brea and Fairfax in Los Angeles, so that Sam and the principal cast members could rehearse the script for three whole weeks before shooting began. It was the longest rehearsal period Peckinpah had on any production, and it paid off.

"We rehearsed like we did in the old live-television days; we'd do run-throughs of the whole script, just like you would rehearse a play," says Jason Robards.

By the time rehearsals ended and shooting began, on October 17, the actors had polished their performances and worked out most of their blocking. Melnick could breathe a sigh of relief. Sam seemed in complete command, and it looked like they would have a trouble-free shoot. Obviously all those callers who had warned him about this psychopath were full of shit. But when the company began shooting out on a farm in the San Fernando Valley, near Thousand Oaks, the producer's sense of well-being began to erode.

Instead of using all three television cameras to shoot scenes from multiple angles simultaneously, Sam was shooting most scenes with a single camera only, and devising complicated moves for it, which was time-consuming because of its behemoth size. This completely defeated the purpose of shooting on videotape in the first place, and precious hours were being devoured every day. To Sherman and other veteran members of the ABC crew, this was the mark of an amateur.

But what he was losing in time, Sam was gaining in visual quality. Lighting for a single camera allowed for more subtle gradations of light, color, and shadow, greater depth of field, and more elaborate and carefully composed shots. "Sam wanted a dark look, which was unknown on video at that time," says Reza Badiyi, the award-winning cameraman who functioned as Peckinpah's special assistant on the production. "He wanted the shadows. It was a dark story; he didn't want it to be lit like a gas station."

Badiyi was impressed by Peckinpah's ability to ignore the pressures of the schedule and to keep working on a scene until it came close to perfection. "There's a scene in *Noon Wine* where Olivia and Jason are in bed. It's very near the end of the picture; he goes to hold her and she turns away and there's that realization on Jason's face that he's lost her, that she believes he murdered the man. I remember Sam sitting with Jason and Olivia in a huddle, telling a story, a personal story, and he became so emotionally involved in it as he was talking to them, he was fighting to keep his tears back. I was dying to get closer. I just heard the fragments of it, I didn't want to break that moment. He was talking about witnessing that moment with his parents. He was using that story as an aide for directing the scene. And that's a very, very lovely moment in the show."

Sam was getting extraordinary footage, but by the end of the third day it became clear the production would run two days over schedule unless drastic action was taken immediately. Melnick called Reza Badiyi to his office. Badiyi had a four-person, non-union film crew that did free-lance work, mostly for television commercials (they had done a number for director Robert Altman). Badiyi, Melnick knew, could work fast and still produce high-quality material.

At Melnick's direction, Badiyi came up with a plan for making up the lost time and presented it to Peckinpah. Unhindered by the cumbersome television equipment, his team could get ten shots for every one Sam was completing. In one day, Badiyi explained, he could nail all the missing shots and finish the show on schedule.

"Sam wasn't jumping for joy over the idea," says Badiyi. "He was reacting like, 'Hey, you want to shoot my show?' He was a hair away from punching me out. So I looked him right in the eye and told him, 'Hey, Sam, I'm your friend. I can go out and shoot this shit. You look at it, if you don't want to put it in your show, throw it away. Melnick is putting up the money out of his own pocket. It won't cost that much for me and my crew.' He liked that. He noticed that I wasn't afraid of his anger at that moment, I stood up to him, and I offered him a sweet deal, and I wasn't pushing him to accept it."

Peckinpah laid out all the shots he wanted Badiyi to get. They were long shots or for montage sequences; none required sound, which meant Badiyi could work even faster, and cutting the montages together on film would be much quicker and easier than editing them on video.

"My crew was a non-union crew," says Badiyi. "We had to shoot this on the sly, so we scheduled it for a weekend. Melnick, Harry Sherman, Lois O'Connor, Sam, and a group of about ten people that I got showed up. I had three cameras and my assistants. While I was shooting with one camera, my assistants were setting up the next two shots. As soon as I finished a shot, I ran to the next camera. We didn't use lights, we used reflectors. I did 115 setups for Sam in one day. At the end of the day Sam said to me, 'I never, ever worked as hard in my life as I did today.' And he hugged me. Sam was very, very grateful."

Noon Wine finished five hours over schedule and $35,000 over budget, but Melnick didn't complain; he knew they had a diamond in the rough. Cutting and polishing that diamond provided Peckinpah with a new challenge; he'd never edited videotape before. "It was very time-consuming to edit videotape in those days," says Clair McCoy, technical supervisor on the production. "Editing had not progressed anywhere near the sophistication of today. We'd just gotten out of the stage of cutting videotape with razor blades. We had electronic editing, but it certainly was not computerized; you couldn't just preload all of your edits and then sit back and watch it happen."

Reza Badiyi edited the montages on film, then transferred them to videotape for Sam to insert into the show, which saved a lot of time and money. "I showed the finished sequences to Melnick, and he loved them," Badiyi recalls. "Sam saw them and loved them. Later Sam didn't want to give me any screen credit at all on the show. Melnick insisted that I got a credit." Badiyi's credit on the final show was for title design—ludicrous because the titles were nothing but white lettering rolled over a long shot of the Thompson farm. The proper credit, second unit director, was denied him by Peckinpah. But Badiyi felt little bitterness. "My attitude was: hey, after all this is Sam's vision, his show. I'm glad that I came aboard and that I did something that he liked, even for a day. He was a master. He accepted a thing that I did, he put it in his show, and he put his own name on it. That's higher praise for my work than if he gave me credit."

To do the musical score, Melnick brought in another man who had once been blacklisted by Hollywood. Jerry Fielding was unable to find a job for almost a decade, not because of his personality or working methods, but because of his political beliefs.

Someone had named him as an enemy of the state before the House Un-American Activities Committee. It was only after Otto Preminger had the courage to hire him to compose the score for *Advise and Consent* that the committee's shadow withered and Fielding found his services in demand again.

With a wild mane of black hair, a wiry beard, horn-rimmed glasses and an ever-present cigarette dangling from his mouth, Fielding was cocky, iconoclastic, passionately opinionated about music, movies, and politics, and a fanatical workaholic. He and Sam hit it off immediately. Fielding had been a sickly, unathletic youth, and like Sam was a voracious reader. The two formed a blood-brother bond. Like his friendships with Don Levy and Jim Silke, this was the opposite side of the coin from Sam's hard-drinking, hard-playing and fighting camaraderie with stuntmen and the Walker River Boys. With Fielding there were a lot of quiet evenings spent talking about the novels of Albert Camus and the poetry of W. H. Auden.

Jerry would go on to score five more Peckinpah films and work without screen credit on two more. Sam would stay at Fielding's house in the Hollywood Hills for weeks at a time when he was in between film projects. Jerry, his wife Camille, and their two daughters offered a unified family that Sam could attach himself to during these lulls.

But it was more than personal rapport that brought Fielding into the Peckinpah fold; the man was an exceptionally fine film composer, able to read Sam's cryptic way of talking, and graced with an almost infallible sense of where music was, and, sometimes even more importantly, wasn't needed. Fielding knew how to use music in ironic counterpoint to Sam's explosive visual style, and how to use it to leach out the tender subtext in many of Peckinpah's scenes. His score for *Noon Wine* was a model of subtle restraint, relying mostly on a lone piano and a harmonium to provide an undercurrent of melancholy throughout the piece.

When *Noon Wine* was finally finished, Sam showed it to the cast and key members of the crew at a screening room on Sunset Boulevard. The final product was stunning.

"PBS did another version of *Noon Wine* twenty years after ours," says Jason Robards. "Terrible! It was awful! They didn't catch what Sam caught in it. He caught how this momentary streak of mad violence in a person can change their whole life. Roy Earle Thompson could have lasted his whole life without having to face that if circumstances hadn't brought these events to a head. But in that moment where he felt threatened, it all came apart. Sam caught the essence of that. Now, the PBS show, they didn't get that at all. You couldn't touch what he did."

It was in Thompson's suicide at the end of the show that Peckinpah made his one subtle yet bold departure from Porter's text. Instead of taking his shotgun to the farthest end of the field, Robards crosses the dark barnyard—shot from a long, high angle to emphasize his complete isolation—to the barn. At a rickety wooden table, he pulls out a pencil and sheet of paper and tries one more time to explain that he did not take Hatch's life on purpose. "I've told all this to the judge and jury, and they let me off," Robards' voice says in voice-over as he writes. "But nobody believes it. My wife . . ." He stops and looks off into the shed's dark hollow space, every line eating deep into his face, then scratches out the reference to her and finishes the note, speaking aloud as he writes. "It was Mr. Homer T. Hatch who came to do wrong to a harmless man. He caused all this trouble and deserved to die, but I'm sorry it was me that had to kill him."

He places the note carefully under a lead weight, then picks up the shotgun, pulls back both hammers, and, after a moment's hesitation, brings the barrels to his forehead.

Cut to a long shot of the farm, resting tranquilly in the night. Boom! The report echoes off the nearby hills.

Cut to an extreme close-up of Ellie's face floating in the darkness of the house, her eyes puzzled, forehead crinkled with the first dawning of a terrible realization. Fade out.

The ending drove home the fact that Ellie Thompson had failed her husband as much as he had her. It intensified the drama, in seconds, to a double-edged tragedy: the failure of love.

The screening room on Sunset Boulevard was silent when that last image faded and the harsh house lights came up. All knew they had witnessed something awesome. "The effect of that ending stays with me always," says Reza Badiyi.

Unfortunately, the ratings for "ABC Stage 67" had been dismal. The network had gone after big stars rather than solid scripts and consequently most of the other shows in the series were thoroughly mediocre. So when *Noon Wine* aired on November 23, 1966, it was to a relatively small viewing audience.

But the show caught the eyes of the critics. "The reviews, my God," says Jason Robards, "I've got an envelope full of rave reviews. It really was one of the best things Sam ever did."

John Mahoney of the *Hollywood Reporter* wrote: "Peckinpah's realization emerged as one of the finest hours of many a season, something of a milestone in location color videotape production, and one of the few TV moments which might be termed poetic."

But there was one viewer who did not share the critics' enthusiasm: Fern Peckinpah. Olivia de Havilland's performance—of a pale sickly woman who took refuge from a troubling and confusing world in her flower garden, or in a dark room with a damp cloth over her throbbing head—cut too close to the bone. "Mom did not like that show," says Susan Peckinpah. "She never talked about why, but she *did not* like it." It was the only show of D. Sammy's that Fern ever disapproved of. By and large she was a devoted fan. She would even like *Straw Dogs*, much to her son's dismay.

Noon Wine won Peckinpah a Writers Guild nomination for Best Television Adaptation and a Directors Guild nomination for Best Television Direction. His professional exile had come to an end. "Suddenly," he later recalled, "I was back in business again." Those who had said "The Westerner" and *Ride the High Country* were flukes, the products of ghostwriters or talented assistant directors or luck, had been silenced. *Noon Wine* demonstrated resoundingly that whatever else he might be, Peckinpah was one of the most startling and original talents of his generation.

By the mid-1970s ABC had destroyed all the master tapes for the "Stage 67" series to make room for storage space in its vaults. It is a sad commentary on the state of television that the last attempt at a serious dramatic anthology series was incinerated to make room for more episodes of "Bewitched" and "The Lawrence Welk Show." The medium that had held such promise when Sam went to work as a stagehand at KLAC in 1952 had become "the vast wasteland," polluted with the brain-killing aesthetics of consumer culture. Today it's possible to see mint condition copies of the show, in color, in only three places: the Library of Congress in Washington, D.C., the Museum of Broadcasting in New York City, and Jason Robards' house in Connecticut. (Robards donated copies of his tape to the two archives.)

Noon Wine did more than rehabilitate Sam's career. From his intense scrutiny of Porter's deceptively intricate narrative, he gained a deeper artistic vision. "It [*Noon Wine*] is my favorite piece of work," Sam said shortly after completing the show.

In *The Wild Bunch* and *Straw Dogs* Peckinpah would weave incredibly intricate thematic webs, stitched with ironies, psychological dichotomies, and troubling truths. There would be a new complexity that had not graced his earlier work. *Noon Wine* carried him across the threshold into artistic maturity.

Peckinpah followed *Noon Wine* up with an episode "That Lady Is My Wife"—for another TV anthology series, "Bob Hope's Chrysler Theater." The script was pedestrian, but Sam managed to pack the show with bizarre imagery, tumescent with undercurrents of eroticism, dread, and anxiety. The final product was weird, audacious, and completely mesmerizing—a remarkable achievement considering it had been made in the heart of Hollywood's most rigid assembly line, Universal Studios. Peckinpah had been able to pull it off because the show's producers, Jack Laird and Jeannot Szwarc, were great admirers and willing to cut him some slack.

Shortly after Sam finished the episode, the break he had been waiting for materialized. Ted Richmond, a producer at Paramount, offered him a chance to write a script based on William Douglas Lansford's biography of Pancho Villa. Villa couldn't be the only character, Richmond explained—they'd need a white face in the story, say an American who gets caught up in the revolution. Yul Brynner had already been signed to star as Villa. If Brynner liked Sam's script, Richmond promised, he'd get the green light to direct the film as well.

Sam was given a small office at Paramount, a copy of a treatment that William Douglas Lansford had written for Richmond, a stack of yellow legal pads, a drawer full of pencils, and three months to come up with a screenplay. James Coburn, who was about to star in one of the camp classics of the sixties, *The President's Analyst*, heard Peckinpah was on the lot and decided to look him up.

"Here was Sam sitting in this little fucking office, a little pot belly, sitting there," says Coburn. "He said, 'Hey man, how are you? Sit down and have a drink.' We had a little drink, talked for a little while. My heart just fucking went out to him. I mean, here was this guy who had been this general on *Dundee*, who had now been demoted to like a fucking private in the cavalry who sweeps the horse turds out of the stable . . . working on that script. I felt so badly. I didn't know how to help him out."

If he found his present circumstances humiliating, Sam didn't dwell on it, for this was his chance to get back into the big time. As he ordered more and more books and old newspaper articles from Paramount's research department, the walls of his cramped office fell away and the vast panorama of the Mexican revolution spread out before him.

This was the revolution John Reed wrote about in *Insurgent Mexico*, the revolution Ambrose Bierce charged into, never to return. A time of tremendous turmoil, corrupt warlords, fanatical idealists, hypocritical politicians, and long-suffering peasants finally rising up out of their stoicism to pursue the thin ray of a dream, a desperate vision of a better world. It was China in 1945, America in 1967. It was the whole sad turbulent story of mankind packed into six raging years.

In his script Peckinpah drew Villa not as a cleft-chinned Robin Hood but as a warped idealist who shares disturbing similarities with the brutal regime he's fighting against. A revolutionary motivated at least as much by his love of war as his passion for the lower classes, his cause is noble but his methods savage. Do the ends justify the means? Peckinpah asked the question again and again in the screenplay, but offered no easy answers.

But even more fascinating than the revolution's leader was the material Paramount's research department dug up on the American mercenaries who flocked south by the hundreds to join the civil war. Some were true idealists, like Reed and Bierce; others were professional soldiers in it for the money, or because they simply loved to fight. Mexican warlords and rebel leaders recruited American gunmen throughout South Texas, paid handsomely for weapons and ammunition, and asked no questions about where they came from. El Paso became a hotbed of gunrunning and other forms of smuggling.

Villa had more than a hundred "Yanquis Soldados" riding with him under the command of Sam Drebben, known as "the fighting Jew" to both his friends and enemies. Photos of these American adventurers reveal dark, weathered, slit-eyed faces beneath army field hats, rigidly postured men on horseback, weapons in hand—strikingly similar in appearance to the publicity stills later made for *The Wild Bunch*.

Others who drifted into the various factions of the revolution included outlaws—bank and train robbers forced south by the barbed wire and telegraph and telephone lines that had strangled the American frontier—cowboys looking for a new line of work now that the great trail drives had come to an end, and drifters and misfits from all walks of life. Men with no place else to go, nothing left to lose, men hungry for a little action, any kind of action that would help them forget the wreckage of their lives.

As he read the life stories of these various characters, Sam began to get an image of the American he wanted for his screenplay. A man without direction or ambition, who seldom thinks about the future, a man as disillusioned with just causes and patriotism as America was in 1967. He travels south of the border to sell his services as a mercenary, but after fighting alongside of Villa and his men he ends up a true believer in their dream. Through this mercenary's redemption, Peckinpah suggested that, even in a world that is riddled with corruption, hypocrisy, and injustice, it is still possible to find meaning, a cause worth fighting for, even dying for.

Sam finished the script on April 24, 1967. Bearing the title

Villa Rides it had some vividly drawn scenes, complex characters and themes, but was episodic in structure and at times contrived and unconvincing, particularly in the final pages, when the American makes his conversion from self-centered cynic to fervent Villista. Sam knew that although it was a good start, it fell far short of what he was capable of. He had something really big boiling inside, but hadn't yet managed to get it on paper.

But there was a much bigger problem that he hadn't anticipated: star ego. His multifaceted portrait of Villa did not sit well with Yul Brynner—not at all. In Peckinpah's script, Villa hangs a young boy after he's told the rebel leader everything he wants to know; he watches impassively as one of his lieutenants guns down a corral full of unarmed prisoners; when Villa is captured by General Huerta and placed before a firing squad, he breaks down and cries. Brynner couldn't believe what he read. Those were things that a villain did, not the hero of the movie. His fans would never accept such onscreen behavior.

Sam had sent Brynner a note along with the script in which he humbly solicited his suggestions. But the star had only one suggestion, and that was that producer Richmond replace Sam with another writer. "Brynner said I didn't understand Mexico," Peckinpah later recalled. Just like that he was off the project, out of his tiny office at Paramount, and back on the beach—his comeback project a miscarriage. One of the most exciting eras in the American cinema was now thundering full-speed ahead, but he'd missed his chance to hitch a ride on the train and was left standing behind by the tracks, lost in the coal smoke.

To the gang that gathered at Broad Beach every weekend he seemed to shrug it off and take it philosophically. Only Begonia saw how deeply he'd been wounded. When they were alone he broke down and wept. It shocked her, she didn't know what to say; to her Sam had always been *muy fuerte*. "I'll never get to make another film," he muttered. "They're never going to let me direct again."

Soon afterward he didn't even have Begonia to lean on anymore. Their marriage had been troubled from the beginning. Bego quickly discovered the difficulties of living with an obsessed artist. First there was the editing of *Dundee.* Sam would be gone fifteen, sixteen, eighteen hours a day. When he got fired from *Cincinnati Kid* and began writing at home she thought they might settle into a more normal marriage, but then he would lock himself up in his ground-floor office for the same long hours. If she interrupted him he exploded.

"Sam, dinner's ready."

"Dinner? You're talking to me about dinner and I'm sitting here in the middle of the Mexican revolution! Begonia, come on!"

He took time off on the weekends, but then there was always a crowd of people around, partying late into the night; there was never any time for real intimacy.

He was a very lonely man, she came to realize, but it was a self-inflicted loneliness. He pushed the people who loved him away. He loved her as much as he had ever loved any woman, she knew that, but the deepest, most vital part of him remained out of reach, held in reserve for his one overriding passion: his work.

"Bego tried clinging to Sam too much, and tried to be too close to him all the time," says her uncle, Chalo Gonzalez. "Sam has to have space to think. I think that was one of the main reasons that he started exploding at her."

Begonia found herself stranded on the northernmost tip of Malibu, where the only other Mexicans were cleaning the neighbors' houses. She didn't speak English very well, which made her feel self-conscious and inhibited, and so she developed few friendships. In her own country she'd been a star in nightclubs and the movies, here she was nothing but a housewife, a role she was poorly equipped to play.

Raised under the protective guidance of her strong-willed mother, coddled and catered to as the family prodigy and meal ticket all her life, she was lost in a kitchen, rarely drove a car, and became flustered over the simplest tasks, like making doctor's appointments. Sam enlisted Fern Lea's help, and soon his sister had a full-time job on her hands, running errands for Begonia, even helping to clean the house at Broad Beach and prepare meals for the hordes of weekend guests.

Sam did make an effort to get Begonia work in American movies. "One day Sam and Bego and I went to three studios; he was introducing her to people to get her into films," says novelist Max Evans, who had formed a close friendship with Peckinpah by this time. "My God, his attention to her, his adoration for her, had everybody stunned. Everywhere we'd go these executives, these honchos, these producers were just stunned. They'd never seen him be so attentive, so loving, so caring. It was just as sincere as hell. You know, he could play games with women; I've only seen three or four people in my life who could play games with women's heads as smooth as he could. But this was not a game, and they sensed it, and that's what got to these people, 'cause they'd seen him play every kind of trick on women."

But Sam was having a hard time getting work himself, so his efforts didn't amount to much. Robert Culp got Begonia a small part on an episode of "I Spy," and Sam gave her another on "That Lady Is My Wife." Hollywood wanted bleached-blond Barbie dolls, and Begonia, for all her fiery beauty, just wasn't the product they were buying.

The three miscarriages put a terrific strain on their relationship. "It was very hard for Bego," says Chalo Gonzalez. "She wanted a baby so bad."

"Jesus, the conversations about getting her pregnant were ridiculous!" says Jim Silke. "Going through all kinds of things, trying to get her medically checked to be pregnant. It got very intense."

And then there was Sam's drinking. By now he was going to bed with a bottle of brandy on his night table and reaching for it first thing in the morning. Begonia would plead with him, "Sam, why do you need that when you have me?"

"I need it to relax," he'd answer in a terse tone that indicated the topic was closed to further discussion.

But in the late afternoon and evenings, after he'd been sucking on that bottle all day, the effect was anything but tranquilizing. His eyes would sharpen into a vicious glint and he'd start in on her. "Bego took and took and took," says Lyn Silke. "She was a woman in love, and she wanted to make him happy. And he wanted to be happy with her. But she couldn't do it. He'd test her: can you make me happy? He was testing her all the time. He took her on a camping trip that was really rough. There would be no water. Can you imagine? It was the kind of thing where a man would get annoyed after a while. He really pushed her."

Begonia didn't passively accept the abuse; often she flew right back at Sam with a rage that nearly matched his own. "She was just as tough as he was," says Max Evans. "Absolutely. I do believe that was the first woman that just called his hand any damn way he wanted it called, mentally, physically, or any way. She took no shit and he respected the hell out of that."

"Begonia was real, absolutely real, that's why Sam loved her," says Jim Silke. "She was an honest, emotional person, just as genuine as you can get, which is a rarity in that town. He admired her. She was a passionate, vibrant, happy, vital person. She was a real animal woman; it's the basic thing and so alive. The anger, oh, he loved her anger as much as anything else. They fought a lot, she'd be tough. They'd scream at each other."

But finally the clashes became too severe even for Begonia. She fled back to her mother in Mexico City and divorced him. Within a matter of weeks he flew down, brought her back, and remarried her. But after another explosive fight, Begonia fled to Mexico and divorced him yet again. Sam went to Lyn Silke, distraught. "Bego won't talk to me," he said. "She won't talk to anybody, but I know she'll talk to you. Phone her. I just want to know if she's okay."

So Lyn called Bego's mother's house in Mexico City. "Lyn," Bego said in the middle of their conversation with a strange emphasis, "I broke my arm."

"Oh, I'm sorry to hear that," Lyn replied awkwardly. "Begonia, I know he loves you."

"I love him too, with all my heart." Then she said it again. "Lyn, I broke my arm . . ."

"I *couldn't* bring myself to ask how," Lyn says, her voice still knotting up these many years later, "and I never told Sam she said that."

"He could never tell me he'd really hurt Begonia," says Jim

Silke. "He'd let me know, but he would never really say it; he'd let me know that something really bad and ugly had happened."

Yet when he went down to Mexico after her, she came back with him and they got married a third time. There was a wild, unspoken passion between them that wouldn't die. Their last marriage had been a proper Catholic ceremony; this time around it was a dry civil service down at the Los Angeles courthouse with the Silkes as the only witnesses. Sam almost got kicked out before they had a chance to take their vows; he'd been caught on his knees in the hall shooting craps. "It was wild!" Lyn Silke recalls.

The last catastrophic breakup was not long in coming. They had a fight one night and Sam stormed out of the house. When he returned he discovered that Begonia had locked him out. "Lock me out of my own house, you bitch!" He went berserk, slamming his fist through a plate-glass window on the laundry room door to gain entrance. Begonia fled out another door and ran down the Pacific Coast Highway to a local emergency clinic, where Walter Peter picked her up the next morning.

Deciding someone should check to see if Sam was all right, Fern Lea went over to her brother's house. It looked like a gang of rioters had sacked the place. She found Sam in the kitchen, perched on one of the bar stools, barefoot. He glared at her with bloodshot eyes. "What are you doing here?"

"Oh, I just thought I'd come by," she said, trying to sound casual.

He had gotten a piece of glass in his big toe from the shattered window. Fern Lea searched through the rubble and finally found a safety pin to dig it out with. She took hold of his foot. "I'm going to have to hurt you," she warned.

He looked at her with a strange intensity. "Go ahead, hurt me."

He was drinking brandy and coffee, and offered Fern Lea some. She declined, worrying silently: she'd never seen Sam drinking so early in the morning before. Without warning he picked up the phone and called Jack Curtis, the writer he'd caught kissing Marie seven years before. They hadn't spoken since that terrible night. He gave Curtis hell, called him every four-letter word imaginable, then slammed the receiver down.

"Sam," Fern Lea ventured, "how can you do something like that?"

"Well, he oughtta know better!" her brother growled. Then suddenly he crumpled up, sobbing uncontrollably, like a small child: "I'm never going to make another movie! I'm never gonna get to make another movie!"

Bego was gone for good. A couple of days later, while Sam was out, her brother, Juan José, snuck into the house and packed up all of her possessions, as well as a good many of Sam's. But that wild unspoken thing between them never died. They would have sporadic reunions over the years that followed—intensely passionate, but short in duration. Inevitably a blowup sent Bego packing. It was Bego Sam was going to see on his last flight to Mexico in Christmas of 1984; it was Bego and Fern Lea who were with him at the end.

As he sat on the baking sand at Broad Beach in the Summer of Love—the empty house behind him, the weekend fiestas now forever over—gazing out at the gray, white-capped surface of the Pacific, it seemed as if he had lost everything, even his art. He had nothing left to look forward to but decades of TV hack work and an endless succession of bottles to kill the pain.

Then one day a producer from Warner Bros. showed up at the house, introducing himself as Phil Feldman.

Jack Warner had recently sold his 30 percent ownership in the studio to an independent production company, Seven Arts, leaving Darryl F. Zanuck at 20th Century–Fox as the only old-time mogul left in Hollywood. Owned by Elliot Hyman, Seven Arts specialized in daring, innovative New-Hollywood style pictures like *Lolita,* directed by Stanley Kubrick, *The Heart Is a Lonely Hunter, Reflections in a Golden Eye,* directed by John Huston, and Francis Ford Coppola's directorial debut, *You're a Big Boy Now,* which Feldman himself had produced.

Hyman appointed his thirty-nine-year-old son, Kenneth Hyman, as the new head of production at the studio. A graduate of Columbia and a former marine, Ken Hyman had just produced *The Dirty Dozen*—a box-office smash that slyly appealed to both the reactionary and antimilitary factions in America. Two years earlier Hyman had produced a far subtler and more artful antiestablishment military drama, *The Hill,* directed by Sidney Lumet and starring Sean Connery. The picture premiered at Cannes in 1965. Sam Peckinpah was in France at the time, trying to sign Alain Delon up for *Ready for the Tiger.* After the screening at the festival, Hyman was approached by a small, slender man with strangely penetrating eyes. He spoke in a voice so soft that the young producer had to lean in to catch the words. "That's a hell of a picture you made."

"Thanks very much," Hyman replied. "I'm sorry, I don't know who you are."

"My name's Sam Peckinpah."

Peckinpah mentioned that he'd been a marine and had served in China. Hyman too had done time in the Corps and had deep ambivalence about the experience. The conversation couldn't have lasted more than five minutes, but Peckinpah's coiled intensity got under Hyman's skin. When he returned to his office in London, he looked up Peckinpah's credits, screened *Ride the High Country,* and was totally taken by its original style.

Now in charge of Warner Bros., Hyman was dark-haired, sleekly handsome, studiously casual in attire, well-read, and eager to produce important artistic films—a New-Hollywood producer was now in charge of a major studio. Under Hyman's leadership, Warners would bankroll a series of idiosyncratic films by first-time or offbeat directors: *Rachel, Rachel,* directed by Paul Newman, *I Love You, Alice B. Toklas,* written by Larry Tucker and Paul Mazursky, *Finian's Rainbow,* directed by Francis Ford Coppola, *The Sea Gull,* directed by Sidney Lumet, and *THX-1138* by George Lucas.

"I wasn't a former agent running a studio, like you have in Hollywood today," says Hyman. "I wasn't a deal-maker. I was a hands-on producer, I was a picture maker, and I believed in doing everything I could to support the director, to allow him to make the movie he wanted to make."

Sam Peckinpah had gained quite a reputation as a maverick who flaunted convention in pursuit of a deeply personal vision. He might be the perfect director, Hyman concluded, for *The Diamond Story,* a large-scale adventure movie about a multimillion-dollar robbery in modern Africa that Warner Bros. had recently bought as a possible vehicle for Lee Marvin. In Peckinpah's hands it could become something more than just another caper movie. Hyman sent Phil Feldman—who'd been brought over from First Artists to produce movies at Warners—out to talk with Peckinpah.

Taking a seat in Sam's office at Broad Beach, Feldman sketched out the plot of the picture. Sam sat very still, scrutinizing the man. At first glance Feldman looked like a cartoon caricature of a Hollywood producer: overweight, bald, of pallid complexion, with a huge cigar fixed in the corner of his mouth. But there was more than first met the eye. Feldman held two law degrees, one from Georgetown University and one postgraduate degree from Harvard. As part of a military-intelligence unit during World War II, Feldman helped crack the Japanese radio code and was awarded the Presidential Citation of Merit. He had been a vice president in charge of business affairs at Seven Arts and 20th Century–Fox before becoming a producer, and had a brilliant talent for maneuvering through the financial and political white water of Hollywood. Feldman was reasonably well-read, and played a couple of sets of tennis every day; beneath the Pillsbury Doughboy surface he was, mentally and physically, as cold and hard as polished granite.

Wrapping up his pitch, Feldman explained that he and Hyman wanted Sam to rewrite the script and direct *The Diamond Story*. Sam glared at the producer, eyes sharp as two knobs of barbed wire, and said, "Well, I've heard that shit before."

Feldman shifted uncomfortably. "What do you mean?"

"Everybody comes to me and says they want me to direct. The truth is they want me to rewrite. You're no different than the rest, you just want me to rewrite the story."

But Feldman persisted. They did want him to direct the picture; as a matter of fact, Feldman wanted to take Peckinpah down to San Blas, on the west coast of Mexico, near Santa Cruz. The land there was covered with dense rainforest and might serve as a perfect stand-in for the African coast, where the story took place.

Sam's gaze swiveled away from the producer out the wide

window to the glimmering sand and expanse of ocean beyond. "Well," he said finally, "I guess I gotta take a chance, because I don't think anybody's going to let me direct again anyway . . . What the hell."

No tiny, closet-sized office this time. He was set up in a roomy suite adjacent to Feldman's in the Producers Building on the Warner Bros. lot. When he moved his things in he brought with him a stack of screenplays that he'd written or acquired over the last two years, including *Castaway, The Hi Lo Country,* and *The Ballad of Cable Hogue.* If *The Diamond Story* actually came off, maybe he could talk Warners into financing one of them.

Also buried in the stack was an odd little script, a crudely fashioned western given to him by Roy Sickner, a stuntman pal of Lee Marvin's. Sickner had come up with the story and Walon Green had fleshed it into a screenplay. The plot wasn't much, a loosely strung-together series of shootouts à la spaghetti westerns. The main characters were a band of outlaws in the fading days of the frontier who meet their end, like Ambrose Bierce, in the firestorm of the Mexican Revolution. Marvin had expressed interest in doing it, so if *The Diamond Story* deal began to unravel he might offer it as an alternative. Pretty thin material, but he saw something in it, though he couldn't say what. He just couldn't seem to get that revolution out of his system.

7

The Wild Bunch

While Sam was rewriting *The Diamond Story,* Curtis Kenyon, head of the Warner Bros. story department, delivered a rave report on a script that had just been submitted to the studio by William Goldman. Goldman had written several novels, including *Soldier in the Rain,* and the screenplay for *Harper,* a Paul Newman detective thriller that had been a big hit in 1966. Goldman's new script, *Butch Cassidy and the Sundance Kid,* traced the escapades of the last great western outlaw, who had rustled cattle and robbed banks and trains across Utah, Colorado, and Wyoming at the turn of the century. Cassidy's gang was known throughout the West as "The Wild Bunch," and its members included several murderous psychopaths—such as Harry Tracy and Kid Curry—who took savage delight in putting bullets through bank guards, lawmen, bounty hunters, and occasional innocent bystanders.

Legend had it that Cassidy himself never killed a man, that he believed in honor among thieves, that he never broke his word once he'd given it to another man, and that he was fiercely loyal to his comrades. In exchange for a pardon, Cassidy once promised the governor of Wyoming that he would never commit another crime in that state, and never did, though he pillaged all the neighboring territories. Blue-eyed, blond-haired, with a winning grin and amiable manner, Cassidy, like many western outlaws, enjoyed a popular Robin Hood image with all but the ranchers, banks, and railroads he stole from.

This image smacks of dime-novel romance rather than reality, but even if all of Cassidy's positive attributes were true, it was a fine hair to split since he surrounded himself with vicious triggermen who salivated at the chance to do his dirty work for him. By 1901 barbed wire, telegraph lines, and the Pinkerton detective agency, which used railroad cattle cars to speed posses after the bandits, forced Cassidy and the Sundance Kid to flee to South America, where the Wild West still lingered. There they formed another gang and continued robbing banks until 1911, when they were surrounded by Bolivian soldiers in a small town. After a tremendous shootout that lasted all day and through the night, the *bandidos yanqui* were killed and passed into the realm of myth.

Goldman's script drew upon many real events from Cassidy's career, but he bleached away all of the outlaws' more disturbing colors. The dialogue was glib, the outlaws glamorous and lovable, the plot twists inventive, the action exciting. It played like a Hope and Crosby road picture, slyly satirizing the conventions of the Hollywood western, yet slickly preserving a veneer of romance, adventure, and sentimentality.

Kenyon declared it the best screenplay he'd ever come across. When Feldman read it he agreed and urged Ken Hyman to buy it. But Goldman knew he had a hot property and was holding out for an astronomical price: $400,000, plus a percentage of the gross. Irwin Margulies, vice president in charge of business affairs, thought it an outrageous figure and convinced Hyman to pass on it. Richard Zanuck, then head of 20th Century–Fox, promptly swooped down and snatched up the property. Paul Newman and Robert Redford were cast as the leads, and George Roy Hill was brought in to direct it. "I never mentioned it to

Sam," Feldman recalled, "but had I ended up producing it, I probably would have had Sam direct it."

Instead they were left with *The Diamond Story.* In the fall of 1967, Feldman took Peckinpah, as promised, down to San Blas to scout locations for the film. While there they were caught in a torrential rainstorm that confined them to their hotel for three days. Since they had nothing but time to kill, Sam pulled out a copy of that western written by Sickner and Green—he just happened to have brought it along on the trip—and handed it to Feldman, telling him that Lee Marvin loved it and wanted to play the lead.

Sickner had used the name of Cassidy's gang, the Wild Bunch, for the title, but he and Green had changed the names of the outlaws—Pike Bishop was the leader—and placed them in Sam's favorite fictional territory: along the no-man's-land of the Texas-Mexico border in 1913. Sickner had laid out the story and Green had expanded it into a ninety-six-page screenplay, the basic plot points of which never changed.

After robbing a Texas railroad office, the Bunch flees from a posse into Mexico. There they agree to steal a shipment of rifles from the U.S. Army for a Mexican warlord, General Mapache, who's aligned himself with Huerta in the war against Villa. But one of Pike Bishop's gang, Angel, is himself a Mexican, born in a nearby village that Mapache recently plundered. Angel pleads with Bishop: "Let me have just one case of rifles from the shipment to give it to the people in my village; with guns they will be able to defend themselves." Bishop agrees, Angel's people get their guns, but Mapache finds out about it, captures Angel, and is in the process of slowly torturing him to death when Bishop and the Bunch return to rescue him. It's 250 Mexican soldiers against four gringos. By the time the smoke clears the outlaws are dead, but so is Mapache and most of his army. The region has been liberated from a vile tyrant and the quartet of *bandidos yanqui* have passed into legend.

There was nothing elegant, witty, or slick about the Sickner-Green screenplay. It was stark, ruthless, without a trace of romanticism—as much a polar opposite to *Butch Cassidy and the Sundance*

Kid as Pier Paolo Pasolini's *The Gospel According to St. Matthew* had been to George Stevens' *The Greatest Story Ever Told*.

Feldman saw the potential at once. It drew upon the same Yankees-south-of-the-border theme that had made *Vera Cruz*, *The Magnificent Seven*, and *The Professionals* box-office smashes. There were enough meaty parts for an all-star cast to be assembled around Marvin as had been done with *The Dirty Dozen*, and there were plenty of slam-bang shootouts.

When the rains cleared, Feldman and Peckinpah returned to the U.S. and the producer immediately sent a copy of the script to Ken Hyman. In an enclosed memo, Feldman wrote: "My feeling about *The Wild Bunch* . . . is that it is a 'gasser.' It needs changes that Sam and I have discussed, and I think if you have time to look at it, it will prove to be the kind of picture with Lee Marvin that you would be most sympathetic with. Most importantly, it would seem that if you are available sometime next week for a meeting with Lee, Meyer [Mishkin, Marvin's agent], Sam and myself, there is a possibility that a multiple picture deal with Lee could be made to include *The Wild Bunch*, which he seemingly likes, and *The Diamond Story*, which we like."

The prospect of nailing Marvin down to a multipicture contract was mouth-watering. Having won an Academy Award for *Cat Ballou* and made two back-to-back hits—*The Professionals* and *The Dirty Dozen*—he was at the zenith of his popularity. One of only a handful of bankable leading men in Hollywood at the time, he had his choice of a dozen exciting projects, including *Patton* and *Paint Your Wagon*.

Hyman agreed that *The Wild Bunch* had the makings of another big action blockbuster. What's more, it offered an opportunity to beat *Butch Cassidy* to the theaters with an outlaws-at-the-end-of-the-old-west saga at only a fraction of the cost. Instead of $400,000 plus a piece of the gross, Warners had to shell out only $100,000 for *The Wild Bunch*. Twenty-eight thousand dollars would go to Sickner and some outside investors who'd fronted the money for the Green screenplay; $72,000 would go to Peckinpah for rewriting the script, plus another $100,000 for directing it. Big money for Sam, but bargain-basement prices for Warners.

Everyone agreed that the characters needed filling out. In its present form the script was a slender thread of story on which a series of shootouts had been strung—not much more substantial than your average spaghetti western. But Sam assured Feldman and Hyman that he could spin this flax into gold. "Of all the projects I have ever worked on, this is the closest to me and as you already know, there is no other place in the world I would rather do it than here," Peckinpah wrote in a memo to Hyman in late October 1967.

Sam told Hyman and Feldman that he was going out of town so he could be alone to work on the script, but that was just a cover story. In reality he was taking off for his annual rendezvous with the Walker River Boys in the High Country of Nevada. Not even a hot movie deal could keep him from his yearly deer hunt. But that fall the boys noticed that he seemed distracted, his eyes dull and inward-focused as he stalked through the stands of sugar pine. He made a show of enthusiasm when they hit Bobbie's Buckeye, but it was only a show. Something was eating at him.

For years Sam had dreamed of filming *Castaway* and *Hi Lo Country*. But he hadn't been lying to Hyman; there was something about this crudely fashioned horse opera that had him in a headlock, though he didn't know quite what. There was the Mexican Revolution, of course, the same basic premise as *Villa Rides:* a cynical band of money-hungry American mercenaries plunge into the middle of a civil war they can't hope to understand and, despite their best efforts, wind up converts to Villa's cause. And there was the glittery dark lure of writing about really bad men, killers who go to Mexico.

"The outlaws of the West have always fascinated me," Sam would later explain. "They were people who lived not only by violence, but for it. And the whole underside of our society has always been violence—it will be and still is. It's a reflection of the society itself." The challenge was making the audience care about these human beasts, to make them actually *love* them by the movie's end.

A couple of weeks earlier, Sam had brought Jim Silke in to help him with the rewrite. But Silke was burnt out. He had spent the last two years writing scripts with Peckinpah about Mr. Lecky, Big Boy Matson, and a rogue's gallery of misfits, murderers, and misanthropes. (These included a pilot for a television series called "The Heavies," in which irredeemably evil characters were the stars of the show. Of course it didn't sell; a file folder filled up with rejection letters from dismayed producers.) Silke just couldn't face another journey into the twisted psyches of such characters, but couldn't bring himself to say no when Sam asked for his help. Sam gave him the first ten pages of rewrites that he had done and a week later called Silke to see what he thought of them. "I was just at a point where I couldn't deal with it," says Silke. "Sam started talking about this new character he'd added, Crazy Lee, and how much Lee Marvin had liked it. I tried to bluff him and said, 'Yeah, it's great.' "

But the tightness in his voice gave Silke away.

There was a long, ominous, Peckinpah pause on the other end of the phone before Sam growled, "You lying son of a bitch! You haven't even read it!" He slammed down the receiver.

"He was right," Silke says. "It was the first time I ever lied to him. I'd always told him the truth up until that point, and that had been the basis of our relationship: absolute trust. But I just couldn't bring myself to work on the script. I lied to him, but I never did it again."

Two weeks later in Nevada, Sam was grimly resigned to doing the rewrite himself. The thought of it was about as appealing as laying a hot coal on top of his tongue. All his boasting to Hyman and Feldman, and he didn't have the slightest idea how to rewrite this thing. What had he gotten himself into?

Yet even with all the ample distractions available at Bobbie's Buckeye, he couldn't stop brooding about it. While the rest of the Walker River boys cavorted at the bar or in the back rooms, he snuck off to the pay phone to call Silke back in L.A.—the rift between them was bridged by sheer desperation. "He needed someone to bounce ideas off of," says Silke. Though he never did any writing on the script, in this and subsequent telephone conversations over the next few weeks Silke helped Peckinpah focus on what he wanted to do with the story.

"The whole idea was, who would really do that—rob and kill, steal guns, and yet in the end give the guns away to the peasants and go back for Angel and die for him?" says Silke. "That was the problem, because everybody wrote that story: the outlaw with the heart of gold. It was really an old-fashioned western. Sam said, 'What if we made a film where they really did that? What kind of guys would really do that? Walk in and sacrifice themselves like that?' Every guy that wrote a western wrote that story, but it never works. It's pure romance. So that was the intent from the outset, to make that story work."

In the Sickner-Green screenplay, Pike Bishop's gang is chased into Mexico by a posse hired by the railroad they've robbed and led by a former member of the Wild Bunch, Deke Thornton. Almost nothing was revealed about Thornton's background. There was no hint of what his past association with the Bunch had been, or why he had now agreed to track them down.

Jim Silke recalls: "I said, 'Who is Thornton? We don't know who he is. We don't know what his relationship to Pike was or is. We need that back story.' Sam realized all of that stuff had to be built in, because you have a story of men changing. Thornton is the one who changed; they made him change. It was the whole idea of people changing, and others who refuse to change, and what that does to people."

The key to the characters' humanity, Sam realized, lay in their individual pasts. Slowly the key themes began to emerge. Pike Bishop, like Butch Cassidy, would be a man who refuses to change with the times, a dinosaur who's outlived his day in the sun. Deke Thornton, his nemesis, would be the man who had changed, the wild stallion now broken, saddled, and harnessed by the system; the man who had sacrificed his vitality for the chance to go on living, who would survive physically but spiritually was dead.

But how would he make the climax believable and Bishop's decision to lead the Bunch back to get Angel, and to certain death, convincing? It had to be real. Going back for your partner, the outlaw with a heart of gold who sacrifices himself for a noble cause—Silke was right: it was an old story, as old as the western itself, as old as the legend of Robin Hood. Could such a rusted-out myth shine like new again in 1967? Had it relevancy anymore, could people be made to believe in it again? He knew one thing: the motivation for the Bunch's final sacrifice had to be more than mere tribal unity; it had to be more multifaceted than that.

Over the course of the story Bishop had to be forced to see himself, not as he liked to idealize himself—a man of his word who lives by his own code and therefore a man of true honor and integrity—but as he really was. Little by little he had to be confronted with reality: that his code was a sham, that he had violated it repeatedly whenever circumstances made it convenient to do so, that it had served only as a rationalization to disguise the brutality and moral bankruptcy of his life. "You see them by the end," says Silke, "at least one of them, Pike Bishop, come to a recognition of who he is and what he has done." That final realization would have to come near the end of the picture; it had to propel Bishop and the Bunch into the final bloodbath in which they would ultimately be redeemed.

When Sam returned to Warner Bros. in the first week of November, his eyes burned like those of a fundamentalist zealot, a man possessed. Whirling inside his skull were all the loose threads, characters, themes, scenes, situations—all the elements of that big story he'd always felt burning within. He'd tried to tell it before but failed. Now he could feel it beginning to crystallize. *The Dice of God, Major Dundee, Villa Rides*—"They all became part of *The Wild Bunch*," Sam later said. "So if you lose, you don't really lose: you use it for the next picture. It's a learning process. If you stop learning, you're dead."

Gay Hayden, who would once more type up all of Peckinpah's script revisions, remembers: "Sam told me to go buy him a pencil sharpener. So I came back with the standard hand-crank sharpener and Sam was livid. He made this big scene about how that's not what he had in mind, he wanted an electric pencil sharpener, he wanted a Panasonic pencil sharpener. You could hear him all over that wing of the building. I said, 'Yes, sir,' and came out of the office and Feldman was leaning in the doorjamb, chuckling. Sam used those big brown drafting pencils, you know, the big brown fat drafting pencils. You can only write about three words with them before they're dulled down. So he had this huge jar of these things and he just kept poking them in this pencil sharpener and you'd hear it buzzing away. It drove me nuts!"

But in between the buzzing in that back office, in the margins and on the back of the pages of the Sickner-Green screenplay, Sam was tearing scenes apart and putting them back together again, pushing, pulling, searching for ways to "take it one step further," to make it real, make it personal. The spine of the story was like the Christmas trees he hauled into his high-ceilinged living room at Broad Beach: onto its firm branches he now began hanging his glass balls and ribbons, light bulbs and strands of angel hair. He added, reexamined, added some more here, took some off there, and little by little the story became his.

For the next six months he would be at it. Occasionally the dialogue spilled right out on the page in his chicken scratch: the word choice, the cadence, the imagery—all crystallized effortlessly. More often it was a process of laborious refining. Dialogue was rewritten and rewritten until at last the perfect word choice was found, or sometimes jettisoned completely and the scene started over again from scratch.

Slowly, one scene at a time, Sam was transforming Pike Bishop from a macho stick figure into a tragic character of great complexity: a man haunted by his failures in both the distant and recent past, who fails time and again to live up to the ideals and ethics he has set for himself.

"You're not gettin' rid of anybody! We're gonna stick together, just like it used to be. When you side with a man you stay with him!" Bishop barks at two members of his gang when they want to kill one of their number because of his constant bumbling. "If you can't do that you're like some animal—you're finished—we're finished—all of us!" But Bishop himself repeatedly fails to live up to that tenet of his code. When their robbery of the railroad office at the opening of the film turns out to be a bounty-hunter ambush, Bishop leaves one of the Bunch behind with hostages as a decoy to help facilitate his own escape. As they ride south toward the Mexican border, a wounded gang member falls from his horse, no longer able to ride on his own. Pike coolly pulls out his .45 and finishes the man off. And a flashback, added by Peckinpah, reveals why Thornton has betrayed his former partner: because Bishop betrayed him years ago. When the two were surprised by Pinkertons in a Denver hotel suite, Bishop leapt out a window, leaving the wounded Thornton behind, again to cover his own escape.

Over the course of the story, Peckinpah forced Bishop to face his failures: by letting him discover that young man he left to die in Starbuck was the grandson of his oldest crime partner, Freddie Sykes; through the reappearance of Thornton, which dredges up the memory of his earlier act of cowardice—and, finally, through Angel.

Fleeing south after the robbery at Starbuck, the Bunch arrive at the banks of the Rio Grande, the gateway to Mexico. They come to it as men thoroughly disillusioned with humanity. "We're not *associated* with anybody," one Bunch member will tell General Mapache when they meet him. Bishop will add, "We share very few sentiments with our government."

Only Angel—the sole native among them, the odd man out with a name to match his romantic vision—sees something special when they gaze across the river at the land they are about to enter:

Angel, softly: "*Mexico lindo.*"

"I don't see nothin' so lindo about it," one of the gang sneers.

"Just looks like more Texas, far as I'm concerned," says another.

Angel: "Ah, you have no eyes."

One of Peckinpah's most crucial alterations was to have the entire Bunch visit the village where Angel was born and raised, the village recently pillaged by Mapache's troops. Though it would be layered with authentic details to bring it vividly to life on film, Peckinpah's vision of Mexico was not realistic at all, but mythic. "I don't make documentaries," Sam later said. "The facts about the siege of Troy, of the duel between Hector and Achilles and all the rest of it, are a hell of a lot less interesting to me than what Homer makes of it all. And the mere facts tend to obscure the truth anyway . . . I'm basically a storyteller . . . The western is a universal frame within which it is possible to comment on today . . . There are a great many people who are disturbed because they feel something is going wrong. I am one of them."

The Bunch's cynical disillusionment reflected that of America in 1967, and their ride into Mexico became, though they would not realize it until the very end, a quest for meaning and spiritual rebirth. The south-of-the-border land they entered was not Mexico in 1913, but Peckinpah's dreamscape facsimile, an Old Testament realm offering polarized visions of Eden and Sodom. Mapache's stronghold, Aqua Verde, is a cruel, lacerated landscape of guns and gold, free-flowing liquor and whores; mothers nurse their babies through the straps of ammo belts, and a blood-soaked warlord laughs heartily at the sight of a woman getting shot through the heart.

But in Angel's village the Bunch discover the world as it should be, as all of us desperately wish it to be. In contrast to the sandblasted hellscape of southern Texas and Agua Verde, the village is a shady green oasis where children cavort naked in a cool flowing river, and men and women live in simple harmony, sharing all that they own willingly with one another. The Bunch quickly fall under the spell of Angel's people. The two most murderous psychopaths, the Gorch brothers, follow a teenage girl around like a pair of love-struck teenagers, sitting in the shade and playing cat's cradle with her. Bishop laughs softly at the sight. "Now that I find hard to believe."

"Not so hard," says the village elder. "We all dream of being a child again, even the worst of us—perhaps the worst most of all."

When Bishop and the Bunch later agree to let Angel take a case of rifles from the shipment they steal for Mapache, it is the first time in their lives that they have ever taken a risk for anyone else and for no financial gain. The visit to Angel's village cracks open a door in their consciousness, and Angel's passionate plea on behalf of his people nudges the door open still further.

When Angel is caught and tortured by Mapache, Bishop and

the Bunch at first try to rationalize their way out of rescuing him. "They [Mapache] got guns and two hundred men," says Lyle. "No way . . . no way at all," Pike agrees.

Instead, they go to an Agua Verde whorehouse to get laid and drunk. But to do so they have to pass through the main square where Angel is being dragged along the ground behind Mapache's automobile, his face shredded and bleeding. Even at the whorehouse the image haunts them; it eats at Bishop's gut, and the specter of another moral failure finally proves intolerable. He rises to his feet and shuffles to the next room, where the Gorch brothers are arguing with a whore. The two men fall silent at the sight of him in the doorway. They can read the thoughts behind his hard stare and grim face. "Let's go," Pike says tersely. After a moment of hesitation, Lyle Gorch replies. "Why not?" And they reach for their gunbelts.

And so the Bunch march toward their own apocalypse, in part because they have nowhere else to go and are at the end of their road and know it, in part as penance for all the sins of the past, but also to, for once—as Angel has shown them by sacrificing himself for his people—stand up for something noble, something beyond themselves—a dream of a better world. The fact that Villa's revolution is probably doomed because it too has been fashioned by the corrosive hands of man is irrelevant. The ideal, the hope, the vision alone is worth sacrificing your life for. In death the Bunch find the meaning that eluded them in life. The worst of sinners, they redeem themselves in the final hour, four avenging angels washing clean depraved and debauched Agua Verde in a bath of blood. Like that of Conrad's Lord Jim, Pike Bishop's heroism is propelled by overwhelming guilt and a despairing death wish.

By the time Peckinpah lifted the last dulled drafting pencil from the script in the spring of 1968, he had refashioned a stark spaghetti western into an epic tragedy of Shakespearean dimensions.

Hyman and Feldman read each draft of the script as Sam rewrote and rewrote it, and with each new version their excitement grew. Peckinpah had turned *The Wild Bunch* into an offbeat action-adventure movie packed with vivid characters and high-voltage scenes. They may not have understood the full scope of the story, or its subtler nuances, but they knew it was several cuts above your average western. By December 1967 *The Wild Bunch* was on the front burner. Warners pressured Lee Marvin to sign on to the picture, with *The Diamond Story* as a followup.

Then, disaster struck. Marvin, who had expressed great enthusiasm for the property months earlier, backed away and signed instead with Paramount to star in *Paint Your Wagon* for an incredible $1 million. Marvin's agent, Meyer Mishkin, had been against *The Wild Bunch* from the start, and counseled his client that after two bloody action pictures in a row he needed to broaden his range. The Broadway hit musical-comedy offered the perfect opportunity to do this. Feldman felt Marvin still could have been signed if Hyman would have topped Paramount's offer, but once again tight-fisted Irwin Margulies talked the production chief out of it.

It looked like *Villa Rides* all over again, but this time the producers were in Sam's corner. Hyman liked the *Bunch* script so much that he decided, the hell with Marvin, they'd get another star and make the picture anyway.

It was hard to believe, but Peckinpah seemed to have found a home in Hollywood at last; it was like the old Four Star days again, with producers whom he both respected and was respected by. The blood pumped more quickly as he and Feldman began bouncing around the names and salaries of various stars for the role of Pike Bishop. Burt Lancaster, James Stewart, Charlton Heston, Gregory Peck, Sterling Hayden, Richard Boone, and Robert Mitchum were all sent copies of the script, but it was William Holden they finally settled on.

Now fifty years old, the postwar "Golden Boy," star of *Sunset Boulevard*, *Born Yesterday*, and *The Bridge on the River Kwai* had seen better days. His most recent films—*Alvarez Kelly* and *The Devil's Brigade* (a cheapie clone of *The Dirty Dozen*)—had flopped at the box office. Years of heavy drinking had thickened his Adonis-like physique, curved the weary shoulders inward and fractured the once finely chiseled face. He still had a frayed-at-the-cuffs charisma, but the self-possessed cynicism of his early films had given way to a tired melancholy. Sam thought he was perfect for the part. Pike Bishop was "what Bill Holden is today," Sam said, "fifty, middle-aged, wrinkled, no longer the glamour boy." Holden's established price was $400,000, but due to his declining fortunes they were able to haggle him down to $250,000 and a percentage of the picture's box-office gross (based on a complex formula intelligible only to astrophysicists and studio accountants). Once again Warners saved hundreds of thousands in up-front money.

For Deke Thornton they considered Richard Harris, Arthur Kennedy, Henry Fonda, Ben Johnson, Van Heflin, and Brian Keith. Keith had grown fat grazing at the TV cash trough for the last three years, starring in the brain-dead hit *Family Affair* and turned Sam's offer down.

At Ken Hyman's suggestion they finally cast Robert Ryan, who'd been in *The Dirty Dozen*—one of the most underrated and wasted actors in American films. It turned out to be another brilliant coup; Ryan was ill at the time and his tall, gaunt, graying presence wordlessly conveyed Thornton's spiritual depletion.

For the part of Dutch, Bishop's second in command, Peckinpah had at first been trying to cast a younger man. Steve McQueen, George Peppard, Charles Bronson, James Brown, Alex Cord, Robert Culp, Sammy Davis, Jr., and Richard Jaeckel were among those considered. But Hyman pushed another of his *Dirty Dozen* alumni on Peckinpah: Ernest Borgnine. With visions of "McHale's Navy" dancing in his head, Sam at first resisted. "I was against it," he told Garner Simmons. "At that time I had never worked with Ernie and with this picture I wanted to be sure of everybody. Anyway, Ken talked me out of my reluctance, and Ernie turned out to be just one of the greatest guys I'd ever worked with." Borgnine signed on for $120,000. Sam had to do some rewriting, but it turned out to be worth it.

For the role of Freddie Sykes, the oldest member of the Bunch, Sam first, at Feldman's suggestion, considered Jason Robards. He also thought about Walter Brennan, Lee J. Cobb, Elisha Cook, Jr., William Demarest, Paul Fix, and Andy Clyde. The final selection was Edmond O'Brien, whom he had directed nearly ten years earlier on an episode of "Zane Grey Theater." O'Brien had led a hard life and by 1968, at the age of just fifty-three, looked a good twenty years older than Holden. Plagued with cataracts and a variety of other ailments, he would have to be handled with kid gloves throughout the shooting of the picture, but he responded to Sam's job offer with the enthusiasm of a famished scenery chewer.

For the part of Angel, they initially approached Robert Blake, who'd turned in a stunning performance in *In Cold Blood* just a couple of years earlier. They offered him $75,000, but Blake thought the part was too small; he was looking for starring roles now. So instead they signed—for just $35,000—Jaime Sanchez, a New York stage actor who'd appeared on Broadway in *West Side Story* and made his film debut in Sidney Lumet's *The Pawnbroker.*

For the balance of the cast Sam brought in his stock company. Ben Johnson and Warren Oates would play the Gorch brothers. Oates had been offered a part in *Support Your Local Sheriff,* a Burt Kennedy western that would be shot entirely in Los Angeles. But even after the *Dundee* ordeal, he chose instead to follow Peckinpah once again into the depths of Mexico.

Oates' wife at the time, Teddy, recalls: "I wanted Warren to take *Support Your Local Sheriff* because it was in town. But Warren read the script for *The Wild Bunch* and he really felt Sam could do it justice. Warren had been gone three and a half months on *Major Dundee.* I said, 'This is going to kill our marriage. I didn't get married to be alone!' Blah, blah, blah. I was so stupid. He had done *Return of the Seven* in Mexico; he got hepatitis, plus the revenge, plus something else. They called me at one point, they thought I should go over there because they thought he was going to die. I had already been talking about divorcing him. I said, 'Don't take *The Wild Bunch* because we're pretty rocky here, I don't think we can stand a separation.' But off he went again with Sam. He loved going on location. He loved the adventure of it. He had great admiration for Sam. Sam Peckinpah and Monte Hellman were the two directors Warren would work with anytime anywhere." By the time *The Wild Bunch* reached the theaters, Warren and Teddy would be divorced.

Strother Martin and L. Q. Jones were cast as the two most

reprehensible bounty hunters, Coffer and T.C., and Dub Taylor as the head of the Temperance Union who leads his lambs to slaughter. For the part of Crazy Lee, Sam cast a young actor with only a few television credits on his resume, Bo Hopkins.

For the role of General Mapache the choice was simple: "El Indio," Emilio Fernandez, the gun-toting murderer-movie director who lived in his own castle in Mexico with a harem of fifteen-year-old girls. Fernandez was Mapache incarnate. For his two lieutenants, Sam cast a pair of prominent Mexican actors, Jorge Russek—who had done some still photography for him on *Major Dundee*—and Alfonso Arau, a nightclub and television star famous throughout Latin America. "Peckinpah told me that with my character he wanted to make a homage to Alfonso Bedoya, the Mexican bandit in *The Treasure of the Sierra Madre,*" says Arau, "the one who says, 'We don't have to show you no stinking *baaadges!*' A fantastic scene. Peckinpah said, 'I want to do that.' I loved that film, it's one of my favorites, so immediately we had a connection."

They decided to shoot the entire picture on location in Mexico, which showed impressive nerve on Feldman's part, considering the *Dundee* horror stories that by this time had taken on legendary proportions in Hollywood. "I was not at all concerned about making a picture anywhere in the world with Sam, for two reasons," said Feldman. "The first and most important reason was I had lived up to my word with Sam, that he would be the director of a picture that I did. I knew that that would be a matter of loyalty, almost fealty, in terms of our relationship. And secondly, I was self-confident enough to feel I could control anybody. I've since found that there are people that you can't control, whom I won't mention, but I felt quite confident that I could control Sam."

For a location scout Peckinpah chose not a Warner Bros. staff man but Begonia's uncle, Chalo Gonzalez. The two had become close friends after Sam married Begonia; they shared a consuming passion for pulp westerns and hard liquor, and their friendship survived Sam's three divorces from Chalo's niece.

A native of Mexico, Chalo immediately set off for the

sparsely populated state of Coahuila. In and around the cities of Parras and Torreon—where Pancho Villa defeated the forces of General Huerta in 1913—Chalo found all of the various landscapes required for the picture. Parras was a dusty little town a hundred miles east of Torreon. Founded in the 1600s, it had been a center for the surrounding vineyards and wineries that drew water from nearby lakes, but an earthquake in 1916 dried up the lakes and the vineyards with them. Now Parras was a sleepy desert community with a scattering of large vacation homes owned by wealthy Mexican families. The town square was old and dusty enough to, with some remodeling, serve as the fictional Texas border town of San Rafael (which was named, of course, after Sam's old military academy).

The nearby desert would provide locations for shots of the Bunch fleeing southward; a local country club with a canopy of cottonwood trees could be converted to the green oasis of Angel's village; caves at Dinamita, forty miles outside of Torreon, could serve as one of the gang's hideouts, and the Rio Nazas could substitute for the Rio Grande. For Mapache's stronghold, Agua Verde, Chalo found an abandoned winery, the Hacienda Cienga del Carmen. A forty-five-minute drive from Parras, it had long crumbling buildings, a mammoth wine cellar, a huge outdoor courtyard, and a majestically crumbling aqueduct. All the locations were tightly clustered around the two towns. No exhausting trek across Mexico; this time all energies and resources could be directed toward the making of the film.

Chalo returned to Warners two weeks after he'd been dispatched with a satchel full of photos of all the locations. Sam went wild over them, especially the hacienda.

William Faralla, an old Four Star hand, was brought on board as production manager, and in January 1968 he, Feldman, Peckinpah, and Edward Carrere, a studio veteran who'd been assigned as the art director, went to Mexico to look at the locations themselves. Feldman got the first inkling of what he was in for when Faralla drove him out one blistering afternoon to inspect the ruined hacienda. They turned off the highway and up an unpaved road. Hubcap-deep in dust, they drove and drove for eighteen miles before they reached the hacienda. Yes, the location looked fantastic, but there was no running water, no electricity, no way to haul all the heavy equipment needed to make a movie up to this godforsaken spot.

Returning to Parras, Feldman tried to talk Peckinpah into finding a more practical location. But Sam wouldn't hear of it. If they could plow the dirt road wider and water down the dust, they would make it work. Feldman later recalled: "Sam said, 'I can't get along without that winery, it's the greatest. I've got it all in my head, I know just how I'm going to shoot all the scenes. Here's the row of shacks where all the whores will be, and this will be where their last march will be. I've got that all mapped out.' The truth of the matter was Sam very rarely mapped anything out, as I found out later. He was a directorial genius, but mostly improvisational, which I didn't realize. So I thought: yeah, he's got it all mapped out and choreographed and I'm not going to interfere with that, so let's give him his way on this one."

When the production team returned to Los Angeles, Warner Bros. submitted *The Wild Bunch* screenplay to the MPAA for review. After reading the script, Geoffrey Schurlock wrote back to Ken Hyman: "In its present form this story is so violent and bloody and filled with so many crudities of language that we would hesitate to say that a picture based on this material could be approved under the production code. However, in the knowledge that you will undoubtedly revise and tone down these excessive elements, we feel that under the SUGGESTED FOR MATURE AUDIENCES label, an approvable picture could be made. We are therefore advising Mike Linden, the code director for advertising, who will take up the matter with your New York advertising department so that they will be alerted well in advance of the picture's release."

The MPAA had been steadily losing ground to the New Hollywood producers who challenged it with movies that contained more and more explicit sex and violence. In an effort to maintain some control over the industry, the Association had recently instituted a system for rating movies that all theatrical exchanges had agreed to adhere to: "G" meant a picture was suitable for general audiences, "M" meant suggested for mature audiences, "R" meant no one under seventeen admitted without a parent or guardian, and "X" meant no one under seventeen would be admitted, period. "R" and "X" ratings cut off whole segments of the paying public, so the agency still wielded some clout over content, but with a padded club.

In negotiations with the MPAA before a picture's release, producers were almost always able to avoid an X-rating by making only minor cuts, and if they were willing to cut back a little more, could get an "M" with relative ease. An "M" or "R" could prove a plus: while younger viewers might be lost, the rating tagged it as a hip film, a tantalizing piece of forbidden fruit. In the swinging sixties a G-rating could be the kiss of death, tagging a movie as cornball kiddy fare, which kept adults away in droves.

Thus when Schurlock listed two pages of objections to the rough language, violence, lewd behavior, and nudity in *The Wild Bunch*, Warner Bros. shrugged it off, knowing they'd be able to negotiate a R or M-rating when the finished film was ready for release. Feldman sent Sam a copy of Schurlock's letter along with the following note on February 9, 1968: "I think you can disregard this on the whole. As a matter of fact, I am rather pleased, as I'm sure you are, that he finds it objectionable. The only thing I do suggest is that the word 'goddamned,' wherever it is used—and I think there are about five or six places—should be covered [with a second version of the scene] without the word in it. Not that I am very religious, but I think sacrilege may be the one touchy point. Congratulations on arousing the MPAA." Times had changed since he'd been fired off *The Cincinnati Kid* just three years earlier.

Sam began filling in his key crew members for the picture. Cinematographer Lucien Ballard was coaxed back into the fold; it was the first time they'd worked together since *Ride the High Country*. Ballard and Peckinpah screened all the newsreel footage they could find on the Mexican revolution. Sam was determined that the picture look authentic down to the smallest details. "We were both very taken by the shallow effect of these images [in the newsreel and still pictures of the revolution]," Ballard later recalled. "We selected out [camera] lenses in an attempt to recapture this same kind of visual texture."

Meanwhile, Eddie Carrere had assembled a crew of Mexicans and Americans in Parras and begun refacing all of the buildings in the town square with false fronts. The cobblestones and asphalt of the main street were covered over with dirt, and breakaway windows were installed in some of the storefronts. Day by day, Parras was slowly transformed into a Texas border town circa 1913. Peckinpah was so insistent on detail that signs reading "San Rafael" were put up in some spots and others reading "Starbuck" were hung elsewhere to reflect the confused identity of many Texas border towns just sixty-five years after the United States had seized that land in the Mexican-American War.

As shooting approached, Peckinpah rode Carrere mercilessly: insisting that all buildings be authentically aged, that more windows be added to the railroad office so they could be blown out in the shootout, that the dirt in the street be dug up and pitted and strewn with trash rather than evenly raked, and that the town be denuded of all greenery. The hacienda, already in ruins, had its walls blackened and lightened in random patterns and its plaster sanded away in places to provide visual contrast.

Jim Silke made sketches of the costumes for all the major characters. To build the costumes themselves, Peckinpah hoped to recruit Gordon Dawson again, but here he met resistance. Dawson had grown disenchanted with wardrobe work, feeling he was never more than a "glorified valet" for the stars and directors he worked for. So he had taught himself to write and had been selling scripts to such television series as "Cowboy in Africa" and "Gentle Ben."

Gordon Dawson recalls: "Then Phil Feldman called me and said, 'There's this picture called *The Wild Bunch,* Sam wants you to do the wardrobe on it.' I said, 'Oh, absolutely not, not even in question.' Feldman kept calling me over a period of five or six weeks and they started putting money into it, and then lots of money, twice as much as any wardrobe man had ever been paid. Feldman said, 'Sam refuses to do the picture without you.' I didn't even think Sam would remember my name. Finally I got a call, it was from Sam, he said, 'Well, Dawson, you chickenshit, it's time for guts poker, you up for this or not? Come on, you want to take a walk on the wild side?' So I agreed to go over there and talk to him about it. He told me, 'I've got a motherfucker, I don't know how to do it, it's too fuckin' big, it's all fucked up, if wardrobe goes in the bucket they're going to have my balls. It's my big chance, it's my comeback.' And so I said, 'Well, you know, I'm writing now.' He said, 'Well, we'll write together, man, you and I can write together, don't worry. We'll come out of this, you'll see.' So I agreed to do it."

Dawson had only five weeks to fit all the actors and age their costumes, but he was determined that Peckinpah would never catch him unprepared on this picture. He took 150 wardrobe hampers with him to Mexico and 500 feet of pipe to hang the clothes on; there were seven duplicate costumes for each actor to cover for those that would be ruined during filming. He had every possible contingency covered: hats, boots, neckerchiefs, shirts, pants, army uniforms, and on and on.

"I was very proud on that picture," says Dawson. "Wardrobe was the only department that was never one time in the bucket. Not so for props and special effects. I was walking by the gun man when he was loading up his cases for customs and I saw his ammo. I said, 'You better take some more ammo, I'm telling you.' I was a young kid and he was this old Warner Bros. guy and he said, 'Don't tell me what the fuck to do! I know what I'm doing, I've been in this business longer than you've been alive!' We ran out of ammo the second day of shooting, ran totally fucking out of ammo, and he left and a new gun man came in!"

The Wild Bunch was scheduled for seventy days of principal photography, with a budget of $3,451,420, which included an allotment for 225,000 feet of film. Peckinpah, the cast, crew, and equipment, having ridden southward by truck convoy, converged in Parras in mid-March to begin rehearsals and final preparations for shooting, which began on March 25. For a week the cast gathered each day around a long table at the Hotel Rincon de Montero, where the crew and production office were housed. (Sam, Feldman, and the stars were put up in palatial villas, complete with servants.) The actors read through the script and discussed their characters and the story with Peckinpah.

"Sam inspired the actors without saying hardly anything; he

inspired them to give their lives for him," says Jaime Sanchez. "I thought there was something very special the first day we started rehearsing with this man. I didn't know the man, I didn't know anybody in Hollywood. I realized this guy is going to do something incredible, because you can sense when someone is great. There is an intensity that you see in people like him, like Elia Kazan. They have a fire and you see it in their face when they talk to you, they're almost scary people. Sam instilled an inspiration in all of us; we were all working on this as if it was the movie of all times. He wouldn't really let you know that you're doing well, to make you do more, to keep you on that edge: 'Am I doing good? Am I not doing very good?' Sam made everybody feel that you go for broke. Not to go for broke was an act of dishonor."

There were some tense moments when Sam asked William Holden to wear a thin fake mustache in the movie. "Like hell I will!" Holden belligerently responded at first, explaining that he had never worn a mustache on screen and he wasn't about to start now. But Sam kept working on him with that soft purring voice and those big-pupiled eyes and by the time shooting started Holden was wearing the mustache. It was almost identical to the real one that Sam had, many noticed, but few dared comment on that.

"We did complete read-throughs of the script, which is good because you can talk about things as you go along," says Bo Hopkins. "The crew was there too, the prop man and others, in case there were questions. It was pretty well organized. Eddie O'Brien was just reading his part, no expression, he was practically mumbling. Sam got a little worried. He said, 'Eddie, what are you planning on doing?' Eddie said, 'Oh, you mean how am I going to do the character? Did you want to see that now?' Sam said, 'I'd like to see some of it now.' And O'Brien jumps up and dances around the room cackling: 'They, why they are just plain and fancy they! Heh! Heh! Heh! Haw! Haw!' Sam said, 'Okay, I got you, you got it.' "

"Sam may be very hard to work for," O'Brien told an interviewer, "but he is an enormously creative human being, and that's really what separates the men from the boys. Sam fought *so hard* to make every scene tell it as it is. I was costumed up here [in

Hollywood] and I got down there and Sam just ripped them [the clothes] off me and he said, 'You're gonna wear one suit that was taken off a dead man's body and that's it!' "

"Because of the direction by Peckinpah it was a novelty every day to go to work," Ernest Borgnine later recalled. "I watched him go down the line and show actors different things to do with their costumes that made them even more real. You know, something like that inspires you. I felt a great affinity with him."

"One of the special-effects men interrupted us during a script reading and we went outside," says Howard Kazanjian, a second assistant director on the picture who would go on to produce *Raiders of the Lost Ark* and *Return of the Jedi.* "There was corral there and up against the corral fences they had a cutout of a human being with clothes on it and they were showing us the squibs that would simulate gunshot wounds. I'd never seen squibs before. They went off, blowing holes in the clothing. And Sam said, 'That's not what I want! That's not what I want!' Finally he got a gun and he said, 'This is what I want.' And he went BANG! BANG! BANG! BANG! with a real gun and real bullets, and he said, 'That's the effect I want.' And from there they began testing with bigger squibs loaded with blood and pieces of meat."

Sam insisted on squibbing the actors on the front and the back to achieve the visceral impact of a bullet passing through the body. Small charges were also placed on the actor's stomach so he would be able to react realistically. Sam was chasing a ghost: the haunting image of the first deer he shot in the foothills of Sierra Nevada, its blood blossoming out with the bullet across a patch of white snow.

Peckinpah would have occasional bouts with the bottle over the next four months, but only occasional. After each day's shooting, instead of running out to the local cantinas and whorehouses as he had done too frequently on *Major Dundee,* he was returning to his villa for yet more production meetings with key crew members. On a typical day once shooting started he would be up at four in the morning reading over the scenes he had to direct that day—staging and restaging them in his mind, visualizing them from every conceivable camera angle, but settling on no fixed plan until he was on the set with the actors. Lucien Ballard would pick him up at seven or eight, depending on the call time and location, and they would drive to the set together so they could discuss various ways of shooting that day's scenes. After nine hours of filming Sam would run the latest batch of dailies, then return to his villa for more production meetings and, finally, drop off to sleep somewhere after midnight, usually with the script in his hand. At four A.M. it started all over again.

This was it and he knew it. Everyone around him knew it too. "You see how wonderful God is?" says Jorge Russek, who played a lieutenant to the malevolent General Mapache in the film. "Sam was on the beach for three years without work, and suddenly somebody in this world believed in him, Phil Feldman. Sam was burning to work again."

The white-hot focus he brought to the film would show in the incredible layers of detail that he applied to every scene, details that connected to one another in a vast and intricate web of irony and metaphor.

One detail in particular snapped the whole film into focus, and it came not from Sam but Emilio Fernandez, just before shooting started. Peckinpah told Garner Simmons: "I was sitting there with Don Emilio and six girls, all of them his, and I was supposed to meet this other girl I was seeing for dinner that night. So Don Emilio and I are talking about the script when suddenly he says to me, 'You know, the Wild Bunch, when they go into that town like that, are like when I was a child and we would take a scorpion and drop it on an anthill . . .' And I said, 'What?' And he said, 'Yes, you see, the ants would attack the scorpion . . .' And I said, 'Get me the phone!' And I dialed the producer in California and I said to him, 'I want ants and I want scorpions, and I don't care how you get them down here!' And from that point on, that was the way I saw the whole picture. I began rewriting immediately in order to get this sensational opening down on paper and when the girl I was supposed to be seeing for dinner called to find out where I was, I simply told her that I was sorry but I couldn't be bothered because I was writing. I think she hung up."

The image of laughing children torturing scorpions on an anthill would open the film. The Bunch would ride past and look down on the kids' game with a flash of premonition. As Paul Seydor has pointed out, the image functioned as an epic simile that sent ripples of association across the entire expanse of the film. It established in an instant the cruel self-devouring world that the Bunch were born into, a world devoid of grace. Even the children are tainted, born in original sin.

The scorpions and ants writhing in the children's miniature coliseum also establishes an eerie fatalism that pervades the film, foreshadowing the Bunch's demise in a swarming sea of red. As the Bunch ride out of Starbuck after the opening massacre, they again pass the children, who have covered the ants and scorpions with dry grass and lit them on fire. An extreme close-up of the agonized insects slowly dissolves to the corpse-littered street of Starbuck—bodies splattered with blood, grieving survivors rushing to the moaning and shrieking wounded: a chain of carnivorous violence from young to old with ever-escalating consequences. When the Bunch first enter the inner sanctum of Agua Verde, where they will later die, the bowl-like geography of the open-air cantina with barred windows along its periphery echoes the children's scorpion pit, right down to a fleeting shot of a group of children perched in a high window, legs dangling through the rusty bars as they toss pebbles down on the heads of the Bunch.

Shooting began on March 25, and as usual the shit hit the fan. Peckinpah pushed the accelerator to the floor. Those who couldn't hang on for the ride . . . well, that was just too bad. Twenty-two crew members would be fired over the course of the production. "Sam said, 'We're going to bury *Bonnie and Clyde.*' That was his goal, to do it a thousand times better than that picture," says Gordon Dawson. "No one was prepared for the demands Sam made for that opening shootout. He started saying, 'Give me more people here, I want more people there. Now I'm going to run them here and I want to shoot down this street. Now I want to shoot up there.' The first few days of shooting were very difficult. The first day's call sheet called for sixty-three extras and twenty-three animals; by the time noon rolled around we had 230 people in costume and fifty-six horses on the set. Sam just wanted more and more and more."

The special-effects crew had spent two weeks rigging the main street of Parras with squibs to simulate bullets pounding into the wood and adobe storefronts. After the first couple of takes they had all been detonated and the crew was frantically scrambling to plant new ones. When the squibs on the windows of the railroad office failed to blow the glass out dramatically enough (to simulate the blasts from pump shotguns) Sam ordered the effects crew to rig the windows with dynamite.

By the end of the first day the company was completely out of ammo and fake blood, and a special-effects man and the gunsmith who'd shrugged off Dawson's warning to bring more ammo were "on the bus" back to the States. Feldman coolly flew in replacements the next day, along with more ammunition and blood. In the course of shooting, *The Wild Bunch* would use 239 rifles, shotguns, revolvers, and automatics and over 90,000 rounds of blank ammunition—"More than was used in the entire Mexican revolution!" Warner Bros. publicity would later claim.

Peckinpah was determined that there would be no repeat of the *Major Dundee* catastrophe, and so this time sought to control the editing of *Bunch* from day one. Rudi Fehr began as an editor at Warner Bros. in 1940 and became head of post-production at the studio in 1954. He had survived Jack Warner's departure and was equally determined to defend his sphere of power. For the last fourteen years he, like Margaret Booth at MGM, had assigned the editors to all the Warner Bros. pictures. Up until this time it had been Fehr and Jack Warner who took the movies from rough to final cut. The directors' input had been minimal—a few notes after the public previews that Fehr and Warner would consider before making the final changes themselves. But with Peckinpah's arrival at the studio shortly after Warner's departure, Fehr received a rude awakening: the age of the auteur filmmaker had arrived in Burbank.

"I was a very lucky man, in all my career as an editor, I have never had a director in my cutting room," says Fehr. "Never.

They trusted me. I always made contact with the director when a new picture started, to help him find an editor, make suggestions. So when Mr. Peckinpah first came on the lot I went over to his office. He walked out of his office and wanted to walk over to Feldman's office. I said, 'Mr. Peckinpah, I'm Rudi Fehr, head of post-production, I wanted to meet you and say hello. If you need any help or have any ideas of who you'd like to have edit the picture, please call me.' He said, 'I'll call you, don't worry.' He didn't. He told the head of production [Ken Hyman] to hire Lou Lombardo as the editor for *The Wild Bunch.* And the head of production calls me, he says, 'Peckinpah told me to hire Lombardo. Why don't you do that?' That was our beginning. Already I didn't like him!"

Lombardo had been part of Reza Badiyi's camera crew on *Noon Wine.* He and Peckinpah had a drink together after that last frantic day of shooting and Sam learned that the brawny Italian had also worked as an editor on several filmed television series. Peckinpah filed Lombardo away in the back of his mind, and when *The Wild Bunch* got the green light, requested him. Sam wanted an editor who would be loyal to him, not the studio; a young editor who wasn't bound up in traditional conventions, who was eager to try new approaches. Lombardo fit the bill.

"Sam gave me the picture of all times to cut, and I had never cut a feature," says Lombardo. "He had faith in me, he'd seen my work and he liked it because it was out of the ordinary. I showed him an episode of [the television series] 'Felony Squad' called 'My Mommy Got Lost.' I had done a slow-motion sequence where Joe Don Baker gets shot by all these cops. In television they didn't have the money or the inclination to do anything like that, so I printed every frame five times on an optical printer to get the slow-motion effect. Joe Don Baker comes out with this shotgun and all these cops open up on him. So I intercut the slow motion of him getting hit with the cops firing at him [in normal speed] until he finally lands on the ground. It knocked Sam out. He said, 'Let's try some of that shit when we get down to Mexico!' I said, 'Great! I can cut it, you shoot it.' "

Lombardo's intercutting of slow and fast motion in one continuous sequence had at last provided the key. Peckinpah now knew how he would integrate slow motion into the action sequences. He would film the major shootouts with six cameras, all operating at variable frame rates—24 frames per second, 30 frames per second, 60 frames per second, 90 frames per second, 120 frames per second—so that then when cut together the action would constantly be shifting from slow to fast to slower still to fast again, giving time within the sequences a strange elastic quality. Later, Lombardo would further alter the speed of shots with an optical printer, speeding them up or slowing them down so that just the right rhythms could be achieved.

With his cameras Peckinpah sought to penetrate the primitive heart of the violence, to capture both its seductiveness and its horror. "The point of the film," he would later say, "is to take this façade of movie violence and open it up, get people involved in it so that they are starting to go in the Hollywood television predictable reaction syndrome, and then twist it so that it's not fun anymore, just a wave of sickness in the gut . . . It's ugly, brutalizing, and bloody fucking awful. It's not fun and games and cowboys and Indians. It's a terrible, ugly thing. And yet there's a certain response that you get from it, an excitement because we're all violent people." Peckinpah was not a detached iconoclast, cynically manipulating his audience from his camera crane; Sam himself was deeply ambivalent about the violence he portrayed and the violence within himself. Compelled by his romantic concept of masculinity to provoke barroom brawls with stuntmen, he was also mortified and racked with guilt when his drunken rages scalded loved ones—Marie, Begonia, his kids. He knew he wasn't alone with Vietnam, Watts, and other American cities going up in flames. The whole blood-drenched history and mythology of America graphically illustrated that his personal struggles were a microcosm of those tearing his country apart at the seams.

"The whole underside of our society has always been violence and still is," Peckinpah later said. "Churches, laws—everybody seems to think that man is a noble savage. But he's only an animal, a meat-eating, talking animal. Recognize it. He also has grace, and love, and beauty. But don't say to me we're not violent.

Because we are. It's one of the greatest brainwashes of all times to say we're not . . . I just try to portray what I've experienced and what I've seen without aesthetic distance. Sometimes I do and sometimes I don't. I'm concerned with violence. I see so much of it in myself and in people that I know and love. I'd like to know why and how we can channel it to positive effects."

Sam's cameras were covering the action from a bewildering variety of angles: he shot 25,290 feet of film from 131 camera setups in the first six days of shooting alone.

"Sam's baptism of fire was on the street of Parras, filming that opening shootout," says L. Q. Jones. "He began to realize what he could do with the characters. He watched what Strother and I did with what he had given us and he began to see that the pieces—what he had written, what he had changed, what the people who he was comfortable with were doing with it—and he realized that he could take it a step further than he thought he could. He grew into it."

It was a baptism of fire for the actors as well. William Holden sat beside Peckinpah and the camera and watched him direct the aftermath of the opening massacre. Strother Martin, L. Q. Jones, and the other bounty hunters swooped down off their rooftop like human vultures, to snatch the valuables off the outlaws and innocent bystanders they'd blown holes through.

"Sam wanted absolute intensity," says Jones. "So after the shootout, the instant we come through that door on the run into the street we're gonna pop: go right up to the sky, keep hyper. The only thing Strother and I added was to take it to the point where we were screaming at each other, and then work in a little bit of gay feeling between the characters when I backed off and was almost ready to tear up because he called me a liar. That wounded me. We thought we'd try that to see if it worked. Now, it could have totally destroyed everything we were doing prior to that, you don't know. That's why you need your director as a good audience."

Martin and Jones improvised dialogue in and around Peckinpah's scripted lines, adding even more abrasive edges to their personalities, and at the same time a childlike vulnerability that brought a sympathetic dimension to otherwise repulsive characters. Coffer and T.C. became, in the hands of these two highly skilled actors, a demonic Laurel and Hardy, lovable even in the depths of their depravity.

"Sam said, 'Cut. Ah, that's okay. Let's try it again and see if we can add a little something to it,' " says Jones. "Bill Holden, who had been sitting there watching the whole thing, got up and started to walk away. Sam said, 'Wait a minute, where are you going, Bill?' Bill said, 'I'm going back to my room.' Sam said, 'Well, why are you going back to your room?' Bill said, 'Is that the way you're going to shoot the rest of the picture?' Sam said, 'Yeah.' Bill said, 'I'm going home and studying.' And he walked over and got in his car and we didn't see him until it was time to shoot his first scene. He went back and started working on his script 'cause he saw this was what Sam was gonna do, and this is what the actors that he was working with were prepared to do. So Bill was gonna carry his end of the load. He'd obviously seen the picture slightly different, and then realized: wait a minute, this is what Peckinpah's going to do with the supporting actors, he's going to want the same intensity from me, so I better get my ass in gear. And that's what he did. And when he came out to do his first scene, he was flawless."

As shooting progressed, Holden began, more and more, to resemble Peckinpah. It wasn't just the thin mustache that Sam had insisted he wear; Holden had begun to take on the vocal qualities and mannerisms of his director. Lou Lombardo recalls: "I told Holden one day after dailies, 'I got you figured, you're doing Sam.' He was running that Wild Bunch just like Sam was running the movie. His gestures, his tone of voice, it was all Sam. He picked up on that. I told Sam that. He said, 'Ah, you're full of shit!' I said, 'No, I'm telling you, the guy's got you!' "

The actor was successful. Sam's children got chills when they first saw some of the completed sequences. And Holden caught Pike Bishop's vulnerability as well as his authority. The actor knew only too well what it was like to have once been the best and to now feel yourself diminishing, to slowly, year by year, month by month, lose your grip. Nowhere did he capture Bishop's desperate struggle to hold on to his dignity better than in a scene where Pike's stirrup breaks when he tries to mount his horse. He is thrown to the ground and the impact on an old bullet wound causes him to writhe in momentary agony. Finally he pulls himself together and forces himself to his feet despite the throbbing and the ridicule of the Gorch brothers. Then hoists himself into the saddle and rides on. As his horse shuffled wearily over a desert sand dune, Peckinpah let his camera linger on Holden's weary, hunch-shouldered back in what would become perhaps the most poetic image in all of Sam's work.

When they first screened the scene in dailies, Peckinpah swung his fist at the screen and exclaimed, "Great! Great! Look at that back! That's a lonely back!"

It was a loneliness Sam Peckinpah understood. The parallels between himself and his mythic alter ego came closest in Bishop's interlude with the young prostitute just before he and the rest of the Bunch decide they must go back for Angel, even though it means certain death.

Holden stands, and pulls on his shirt, facing a rough adobe wall where a crucifix hangs on a small wooden altar with a flickering candle. He glances back at the girl, seated at a rickety wooden table. No more than nineteen, with yawning brown-black eyes and dark hair flowing to the middle of her back and a face as smooth and girlish as Holden's is rough and lined. Her frayed white blouse is unbuttoned, half-exposing her large round breasts. He turns away with a fleeting expression of shame, tucks in his shirttail, hoists up his pants, and fastens his belt. She begins to rub her shoulders clean with a damp cloth. He sits on the bed and yanks on his boots. A baby begins to bawl and he turns to look. There it is in a dusty corner of the room, wrapped in a blanket, its tiny curled fingers groping helplessly at the air.

He looks back at the girl; she stares back at him, still dabbing her shoulders and breasts and arms. The lines of guilt deepen on his face and he reaches for an unlabeled bottle there on the bed. He upends it and drains the last of the clear liquid, winces as it burns its way down, stares vacantly into space, then down at the empty bottle in his hand, expression tightening as an intolerable realization takes hold: the spiritual bankruptcy of his existence, all the failures, the love that might have been but now will never be. The realization that this at last is the end of the road, that there is no place else to go on this most weary, unbright cinder . . . except back for Angel.

From the adjoining crib come the voices of the Gorch brothers fighting over money with their whore. Holden tosses the empty bottle away in disgust; the dull thud of its fall starts the baby crying again. He stands, puts on his shoulder holster, and walks across the room, spurs gently chinking, and pulls open the curtain to the Gorchs' room. Ben Johnson lies on the bed, toying with a tiny sparrow on a string. Warren Oates stares at Holden with bleary, weaving eyes. Holden stares back with irises steady and gray-blue. "Let's go."

Oates' sweat-slick face emerges from its drunken oblivion, suddenly clearly focused. "Why not?"

Holden passes back through his girl's room, pausing to toss the gold coins he won't be needing onto her table. She picks them up, sheepishly, sighing, looks up with those eyes so dark and endless, and moves her lips to speak but finds no words.

He stares down at her, his creviced face half in shadow, stares down at what might have been, a look of unspeakable sadness and regret passing over those weathered features as he pulls on his hat and walks out into the sunblast of Agua Verde.

"Johnson with that bird on the string, that was Peckinpah's," says Cliff Coleman, assistant director on the film. "He would do things like that, he would come up with things that guys would do. If you walked on the set and it wasn't what Sam thought the inside of whorehouse would look like, well I tell you what, we spent four hours making it look like a whorehouse that he was in, in Durango or Tijuana or wherever. It would even smell like it! When you were in there shooting you were there."

Peckinpah had indeed visited cribs like that, and drained the last of bottles as he tried to forget all the times he'd failed to measure up: Begonia . . . Marie . . . Melissa's illness. It is without a doubt one of the most tenderly autobiographical scenes in the cinema, and Holden's finest moment as a performer.

"The great thing about Sam Peckinpah as a director," says poet and novelist James Dickey, "was that he could get unexpectedly good performances out of people who were more or less stereotypes. Somebody like Ben Johnson, for example, and Edmond O'Brien—someone who people before *The Wild Bunch* remembered only as the protagonist in *D.O.A.* or as Casca in the [Hollywood] production of *Julius Caesar*."

To appreciate the full magnitude of Peckinpah's achievement, it's instructive to watch Borgnine's scenery-chomping performance in *The Dirty Dozen* two years earlier, or L. Q. Jones' cardboard characterization in *Hang 'Em High* the year before, or Edmond O'Brien's healthy portion of ham in *The Man Who Shot Liberty Valance.* The performances in *The Wild Bunch* are a universe apart. These men are not acting in Peckinpah's film, they've slipped into their characters' skins: Jones in pigtails, face stubbled and creased and twitching with pathological urges as he huddles with his rifle before the opening shootout; O'Brien's gray beard stained orange-brown down the center from a river of drooled whiskey and tobacco juice, teeth like rotted treestumps, shrunken body prancing arthritically as he cackles an unhinged mixture of grief and glee, "*They?* Why, they is just plain and fancy they, that's who they is!"; Warren Oates shrieking like a rabid simian as he fires the machine gun; Borgnine sitting in the dust outside the whorehouse, whittling a stick, listening to the distant laughter of Mapache's men as they torture Angel, exuding with each stroke of his knife a palpable aura of self-disgust, and in the moment after they've killed Mapache urging Pike on with a high manic giggle and eyes that burn like carbon-arc spots, and crying out in his last moments as he staggers toward Holden's bullet-ridden body—"Pike! Pike!"—so shrill, so visceral in his physical pain and sense of emotional loss while he stumbles and bleeds and falls and gasps his last "Pike . . ." that it chills one's marrow.

Though he spent hours going over his script, imagining countless ways he might stage and shoot sequences, Peckinpah did not draw storyboards and diagram every shot the way an Alfred Hitchcock or Martin Scorsese would. The closest he got to nailing anything down before he walked on the set were the crude sketches of possible camera angles that he drew on the reverse side of script pages. Like John Huston, Sam needed to get the actors up and working on the set to see how a scene developed before he could begin placing his cameras.

This improvisatory approach often caused him to completely change the staging and camera setups at the last minute. To deflect blame for these costly delays, he would attack a member of the crew—the wardrobe, makeup, or prop man—for some fictionalized deficiency. The company fell days behind schedule and Bill Faralla and the assistant directors were driven to the brink of nervous breakdown trying to anticipate Peckinpah's next outrageous demand.

But then there were those moments when it all came magically together and Sam's spontaneous intuition opened the door to a transcendent realm where whole sequences materialized out of thin air, unfolding before the cameras in one mad rush.

It was that way with the Bunch's final march to their deaths, which was originally a scant three-line description in the screenplay. The Bunch walked out of the shabby whorehouse. Borgnine, who had been sitting outside, whittling, looked up at Holden with a tight but fierce grin, and they moved to their horses to pull out their shotguns and pistols. "Cut," Sam said softly.

"All right, people!" assistant director Cliff Coleman called out. He began issuing marching orders for the next setup, the Bunch's arrival at Mapache's inner sanctum, but Peckinpah stopped him.

"No, no, Cliff, wait," Sam said softly. "I want to do a walk thing first."

"Fine," Coleman said, nodding nervously. These were the moments he'd learned to dread. "What do you mean, 'a walk thing?' "

Peckinpah growled something unintelligible, then began lining up Holden, Borgnine, Oates, and Johnson to make a long walk through the outlying buildings with their shotguns cradled in their arms. Suddenly the pace accelerated to breakneck speed. Sam set up a group of drunken Mexican soldiers, playing guitars and singing, for the Bunch to walk past. Coleman began layering in other extras in the foreground, background, and at the edges of the frame and giving them action, while Peckinpah moved the camera back and slapped a long lens onto it. "And all of a sudden, Jesus Christ," says Coleman, "the music's going and the camera's rolling and these fucking guys started to walk and everybody's going, 'Wow, it's the real thing!' Nobody knew what Sam was going to do or what he wanted to do. Before you knew it, it built and it built and it built and it built until it became that scene. Very, very, very, very, very, very good. He had those moments, and he could bring those moments out."

The same thing happened when they shot the Bunch riding out of Angel's village. In the script it had been only a couple of lines of description, nothing more than a routine expository shot. But when Sam set the cameras up, once again gold was spun out of thin air.

"Sam liked that song, 'La Golondrina,' " says Coleman. "He knew the feeling of that song and he had it in his heart and he just interpreted it on film. Again, nobody knew what he wanted. All of a sudden we start lining the Bunch up to ride out of the village. Then we added smoke to it. Then Sam sent somebody back to his house to get the record, 'La Golondrina,' and now the music is playing, and now the old man [the village elder] is there waving, and now all of a sudden a girl is coming out of the crowd to hand Warren his hat, and then another to give Borgnine the flower. All developed by stages, no idea in the beginning that he was going to use the song, that he was going to stage this farewell with the people. He had no idea where he was going to shoot, what he was going to shoot, or how he was going to shoot it, but once it started, the stimulus of the activity of the people and the looks and the moments cued him into incorporating the song, the girls, the looks down from the Bunch. Peckinpah created on his feet, but he didn't have the privilege of doing it over a long period of time; he had to do it as quickly as he possibly could."

The ride out of the village became the pivotal moment in the movie, the point at which the Bunch first begin to change, though they aren't consciously aware of it. "I shot that in less than a day," Sam later recalled. "All of a sudden we knew the picture needed it. If you can ride out with them there and feel it, you can die with them and feel it."

But when Peckinpah reached the climactic gun battle at Agua Verde (which was actually filmed in the middle of the shooting schedule), his spontaneous style led him up a blind alley.

The confrontation between the Bunch and Mapache's army had, at Phil Feldman's urging, been shifted from a night sequence to an afternoon one. The producer hoped this would save time—the production was already running four days behind schedule. Sam staged and shot the action all the way up to the point where Mapache slits the throat of Angel. Flesh-colored makeup disguised a perforated tube running across Sanchez's throat. When Emilio Fernandez passed his rubber knife over it, a special-effects man pumped out the movie blood. "Sam used three cameras for that one," Sanchez recalls. "On the first take the blood flew out like a fountain, like the image in *Julius Caesar* when Caesar says, 'She dream'd tonight she saw my statue, which, like a fountain with an hundred spouts, did run pure blood.' "

The Bunch's vengeance for the murder of Angel was swift: all drew their guns and fired on Mapache. Emilio Fernandez, then sixty-four, waved the stuntman off and insisted on being squibbed and taking the fall to his death himself. He won applause from the entire crew.

This was followed by, as Sam later explained, "a strange existentialist little number when they [the Bunch] . . . turn around and everybody has got their hands up and they can get out, and they know it, and they look at each other and they start to laugh because they know this is the end and they want it all." Peckinpah told Holden to deliberately take aim at the Mexicans' German military adviser and fire.

Now the apocalyptic battle was to begin. The crew hovered edgily as Sam sank deep in his director's chair, eyes hidden behind those mirrored lenses. They waited for him to give them the next piece of action, the next camera setup, but the order did not come.

"He didn't have a fucking clue of what he was going to do," says Gordon Dawson. "It was not happening. He cleared the set and he sat there for about three or four hours, and then he brought in the cameraman [Lucien Ballard] and Cliff Coleman. Coleman had already rehearsed all the extras, they were great. But, okay, where do you put the cameras down for this thing? Where do you start? Where do you bring your principals in and what do they do? Where's Borgnine go? Where's Warren [Oates] go? Coleman had set up the attack by Mapache's soldiers, he'd set up what all the extras were going to do. Now Sam had to figure out how to work his actors into them and then adjust the extras as he did that. He had to figure out who got on the machine gun, who was going to die where and how. The script wasn't really very helpful; it's only three pages of written description in the script. It wasn't really there and Sam had to figure that out."

"It was very worrisome," said Phil Feldman. "Sam was stymied, so that weekend he begged to have a meeting. He had a conference with all of the people who were involved, namely the cast, myself, and anybody else that he thought could help. He wasn't sure how to do it. It was a Saturday, after work, and he pleaded for somebody to give him direction. So as a result some collaboration occurred, mainly between him and Lucien Ballard, and Cliff Coleman, and he finally worked it out. But it took many, many more days than we had scheduled for it."

Chalo Gonzalez, who served as an assistant production manager, an actor in the sequence, and Sam's personal driver, recalls: "Once Sam figured out how to do it, we did the master without a hitch. Then Sam started picking up shots from different angles. It was really murder then, Sam was tremendous. All the shooting around the long table there on the porch, people jumping all over, and the prop master trying to straighten things up for the retakes and put them back together. Sam went way beyond what anybody expected he would do with that sequence; he was at his peak. When we'd get home after shooting every night, he'd spend two or three hours with mockups and drawings of the hacienda working out what he would shoot the next day. He had it all up in his mind, then he'd show up on the set and expect wardrobe and props to be ready for what he'd planned and it was almost impossible."

"We took six cameras and faced them toward the porch, side-by-side, shot the entire master with the principals, moved the cameras forward five feet and shot the entire master again, moved them five feet and shot the whole thing again right up to Holden getting shot in the back by the kid and the other soldiers," says Gordon Dawson. "Then we turned the six cameras around and shot all of the Mexicans, that whole half of the battle. Ran the master, then moved the cameras forward five feet, and another five feet. It took twelve days and we called it 'The Battle of Bloody Porch.' Cliff Coleman choreographed all of the background action. Those extras hit their marks time after time after time. You'd look at it in the cutting room and that extra was there no matter what camera you cut to. Cliff is a genius at background action."

"They wired the courtyard with ten thousand squibs," says Howard Kazanjian. "They had a big switchboard for detonating them all. Each charge had to be timed to go off with the actions of the extras. It was painful to get it done right, and Sam was insistent about what he wanted, and rightfully so."

"I only had three-hundred-fifty Mexican soldier uniforms and we blew up six thousand of them," says Gordon Dawson. "I had a uniform-repair factory going right behind the blood hits. They'd come through there after getting shot and get hit with hot water, washed off. We put tape behind the bullet hole and I had a painter that would be painting them khaki. They'd come in bloody, ragged, torn, they'd be taped up, painted over the tape, stuck in front of a heater lamp to dry the paint, a guy would go over the patch with dirty gloves to make it look like aged cloth, and then we'd throw them back in front of the cameras to get blown up again. It was quite an operation."

"There were nights when we'd finished shooting and I'd say, 'My God!' " Ernest Borgnine later recalled. "But I was always back the next morning because I sincerely believed we were achieving something."

"It was such an intense bunch of people," says Chalo Gonzalez. "Their concentration was intense. Something would happen to interrupt them and you would see the flash of anger in their faces. Especially the actors, they were so involved in what they were doing, if anybody said something to them or touched them they jumped down your throat. Sam had them that focused."

"The way Peckinpah staged that massacre, I will never forget it," says Alfonso Arau. "It was so complicated, and he was so precise and disciplined and methodical. I learned a lot from him."

"We felt it there on the set," says Howard Kazanjian. "I remember feeling it. You had worked with these guys on the set, you really loved these guys, and then you saw them die. I got a chill."

After the master shots came the endless close-ups of soldiers and the Bunch taking bullet hits in slow and fast motion. Peckinpah wanted as much material as he could get for the cutting room.

"Sam said, 'We're just down here mining the ore. I don't start making the jewelry till we hit the cutting room,' " Dawson recalls. "You could say that when Sam shot the final battle he overcovered it, but he did it really brilliantly. He may have overcovered out of fear that he wasn't getting it, but he turned that to his advantage in editing. Fear is really a great taskmaster."

Sam was getting great footage, but by this time the production was running five days behind schedule and costs were rising out of sight. Phil Feldman got a sick feeling in his stomach that he was reliving Jerry Bresler's nightmare on *Major Dundee.* Then two telegrams arrived for Sam, one from Ken Hyman and another from Edward Feldman [no relation to Phil], a Warners production executive. They had both seen the dailies back in Hollywood and thought they were fantastic. "We are absolutely thrilled with the wonderful footage we have seen," Edward Feldman wired. "In fact Chasin-Park-Citron [Sam's agent] is negotiating with AIP [American International Pictures, a B-movie company] for a bigger fee for you than Mike Nichols got from Joe Levine. All kidding aside, I think we have a tremendous film. It's nice to see talent express itself."

"Just for the record," wired Hyman, "*The Wild Bunch* will wind up in history as one of the greatest pictures of all time. Thank you, thank you, and thank you again."

"I was kind of angry about that," said Phil Feldman. "I called

Ken and said, 'Mind your own fucking business! We have some problems, you can't do this to me, Ken! You're ruining the guy. I mean, he's doing a fine job, but we have some problems. You give this guy his head and he'll give us worse problems.' "

"I approved Sam's overages because I saw his rushes," says Hyman. "I was delighted, I thought they were extraordinary, so if he wanted a few more rifles and a machine gun, God bless him. Poor Phil got very upset, but Sam thrived on trust. Sam was a strange animal. If you trusted Sam and he trusted you, he'd go out of his way not to hurt you, he really would."

But Hyman was more than 1,000 miles away, not on the set every day at this godforsaken hacienda witnessing this obsessed perfectionist at work. Feldman saw his percentage of the profits running through Sam's cameras at high speed as he continued to film close-up after close-up of soldiers getting shot and blown into the air. Desperate to rein Sam in, Feldman fired off a series of long memos pleading for restraint. Panavision had told Feldman that *The Wild Bunch* was rapidly approaching the world record for equipment requests. "Frank Bogel of Panavision says we have enough equipment to make several pictures and wonders why we need the 800mm and the 100mm and the two fifties, thirty filters, and some other accessories," the producer queried. "Do you need all this equipment?"

When Feldman complained about the slow progress and urged his director to pick up the pace, Sam responded with a litany of production snafus, using his classic strategy of deflecting the blame on his assistant directors and various other department heads. The crew's incompetence, not his perfectionism, was to blame. On May 14, 1968, Feldman wrote a memo to Peckinpah that read, in part: "Dear Partner . . . If you are not out of the hacienda this week you are really whistling in the dark about June 22 [projected as the final day of photography]. By Saturday you will have spent 20 days at the hacienda on a 19-day schedule. Going in we hoped for 17 days, to pick up two, but we lose time every Saturday. If we don't move next Wednesday, we are late for many many things, trains, bridges, etc., etc. . . ."

Two days later Sam blasted back with a memo of his own. He again listed in detail all of the shortcomings and bungling of various department heads and lambasted Feldman and production manager Bill Faralla for not being present on the set during shooting to lend him support. Peckinpah's memo read: "Regarding your memo—for the most part I found it exaggerated, slanted and just plain untrue . . . Phil, 'the facts of life' from where you sit need an open window. Come on the set where the facts of life of how the picture is being shot are evident. And as a gesture, bring your production manager. We need him, and you. All of us need every bit of help we can get. Partner is not a loose term with me, I'm beginning to think it is with you. But while I may be many disreputable things, I have always been a man of total commitment. Partner is not just a word. Come on down and see how it works."

After this exchange the clouds of tension began to thin a bit. Feldman showed up on the set every day, riding herd on all of the departments and improving communication and organization; and Sam, finally satisfied he'd mined all the raw ore he needed for the final gun battle, moved on to the scenes of its aftermath—Robert Ryan and the bounty hunters descending on Agua Verde to pick over the decomposing bodies—the dénouement of the picture.

"I remember when we were finally done with the battle," says Dawson. "Sam said, 'All right, now we're going to bring in Ryan's group. Dawson, change the blood.' I said, 'What?' He says, 'It's all red blood. Make it black.' Because blood blackens as it dries. We had blood running down the walls and on all the bodies. I had to go through and change every ounce of blood to black blood."

Overall they spent nearly a month at the hacienda, six days over the nineteen days scheduled for shooting there, but when it was all over even Feldman had to admit they'd captured something awesome. Peckinpah, for his part, recognized that his producer, despite all his bitching, had in the end backed him up all the way and cut him the slack to "do it right."

"You are my partner," Sam wrote to Feldman on May 30, "and I write to you with love. You are the best producer I have ever worked for (or with) and I look forward to doing many pictures under your guidance . . ."

Secure that he now had an electrifying opening and climax to the picture, Sam made good on his promise to Feldman to pick up time; he worked confidently and at an incredible pace.

"The improvisational scene he did on the train robbery," Feldman recalled, "I could understand how that would have been very difficult to stage. But that didn't stymie him at all. I honestly tell you that he had no idea how he was going to shoot that the night before. He went down to the location that morning, looked at the train, looked at the guys, said, 'Bill [Holden], you start here. Ernie, you start here. You go around the train like this, you uncouple the car here . . .' Now I know he didn't block it out. I know he woke up maybe at six o'clock in the morning, thought about it, and went down and did it. It turned out to be a very simple scene. That would have stymied me a lot more than the shootout at the hacienda. That was one of the best jobs that Sam did, he did it marvelously, with precision and with no hesitation, just a great job. That's one of his signs of directorial genius, his ability to improvise those action scenes. He exquisitely timed the whole sequence, with Jaime Sanchez hiding in the water tower and everything."

For their getaway after the robbery, the Bunch hijacks the locomotive and the flatcar carrying the arms shipment, uncoupling it from the passenger cars in the rear, which hold a troop of green cavalry recruits—and, unbeknownst to the Bunch, Ryan and the bounty hunters. As the Bunch pull away with the front cars of the train, the door to one of the rear boxcars opens and down a ramp come the horses of the posse. This too was based on the history of Butch Cassidy. A similar train-transported posse tracked the real Wild Bunch. But with Holden at the throttle of the locomotive, they quickly outdistance their pursuers and, miles down the track, rendezvous with Ben Johnson and Edmond O'Brien, who are waiting with a buckboard wagon to transport the arms across the border into Mexico.

Warren Oates, who rode on a flatcar in front of the engine with a shotgun across his lap, told Garner Simmons: "When it came time for my part in the action, Sam really let me do what I wanted because by then I really knew my character. After I killed off the two soldiers who were sitting on the front of the flatcar,

Sam wanted this one shot where I'm supposed to be really enjoying the ride. Well, Sam said to do 'something,' so I pretended I was the engineer like a kid might do and, of course, the Mexican engineer always gives a little 'toot' when he's going to move the train—that's the custom—so that's what I did. I just pretended it was my train."

Oates yanked at an imaginary whistle and hooted like a seven-year-old playing choo-choo. It was a beautiful piece of counterpoint—like the Hammonds singing a hymn for brother Billy's wedding march in *Ride the High Country*—that brought out childlike qualities within this cold-blooded killer.

One of the hairiest moments on the shoot occurred when Peckinpah insisted on several retakes of the engine streaking down the tracks, then locking its steel wheels in a screeching, sparking skid to a stop before the waiting buckboard.

"Holden's in the cab of the engine, and it's *hot*," says Howard Kazanjian. "He's bringing the train up and stopping it, and Sam is on a crane with the camera. The train was supposed to come in and stop just about at camera. But Sam was insisting that Bill Holden drive the train himself. There was plenty of room for the real engineer to be aboard and not be seen. Ernie and Jaime Sanchez were on the rear flatcar, and Warren was on the flatcar in front of the engine. About fifty feet beyond where the engine was supposed to stop, on a trestle, was another flatcar with our generator and camera equipment. Underneath the trestle was all of our equipment, hidden so the camera wouldn't see it."

"Holden floor-boarded that train about the fifth take because Sam said it wasn't going fast enough," Oates told Garner Simmons. "Holden got mad and . . . took that lever and went all the way to the hilt, and away we went! It was about a mile and three-quarters run, and we got down there pretty damn quick, and I could see guys diving off the tracks because I'm up there on that flatcar out in front of the damn engine. And suddenly I'm saying to myself, 'Oh-oh, something's wrong!' because the brakes are on and we're sliding and the sparks are flying. And up ahead is this flatcar parked on the tracks . . . I saw it approaching, and it was like slow motion. These two flatcars hit like dominos. Somebody said I looked like I was doing a ballet. I grabbed the railing on the front of the locomotive and stepped up alongside the boiler and watched it happen 'cause it was something to behold!"

"The two flatcars hit in the middle of the goddamned bridge and went up in the air," says Gordon Dawson. "The whole crew was hiding under the bridge at the time and everyone is running because they think the engine is going to blow. We're running like hell up this ravine away from the bridge. I'm a strong young kid at the time, I've already passed women and children, I am way out in front of the explosion, right? And I hear someone gaining on me. Warren had run down the flatcar, across the trestle, down the side into the ravine and up, and he passed me saying, 'I beat it again! I beat it again!' It was a very dicey moment, but the engine didn't blow and no one was hurt."

The last sequence to be shot was the Bunch fleeing with the stolen arms across a bridge over the Rio Grande into Mexico, with the bounty hunters in hot pursuit. The outlaws rig the bridge with dynamite and light the fuses before crossing; it blows just as the bounty hunters reach it, dumping five horses and riders into the river below. It would be one of the most daring stunts in movie history, performed without any photographic tricks or special-effects gimmicks. Peckinpah insisted: it must be the real thing.

Edward Carrere built a balsawood bridge over the Rio Nazas river, its superstructure supported by steel cables hidden from the cameras. The middle span of the bridge was rigged with a dropaway panel that would pitch the horses forward into the river when the charges blew. On the day that the stunt was to be filmed tensions flared, first of all over the setting of the explosives.

Joe Canutt, of the legendary Canutt dynasty of stuntmen, was one of the five men slated to make the drop into the river. He told Garner Simmons, "That was the last time I ever worked for Peckinpah. He had a dynamite man named Bud Hulburd who rigged the bridge. Working with explosives is a risky business. And when I'm gonna be standing on a bridge that blows up under me, I want to have a good look at how much of a charge they're using. Well, Sam had fired the special-effects people over Hulburd for not giving him what he wanted. So this was the first time

Hulburd had really been in charge and he was scared to death of Sam."

Hulburd, it should be noted, had worked in Warner Bros.' special-effects department for more than thirty years. Over the course of his career he developed more than fifty patented special-effects devices, many of which are still in use today.

Canutt told Simmons: "I looked at the rigging and he had enough explosives to blow us clean onto dry land. My mother didn't have any stupid children. I told him if he didn't cut those charges, they'd have to find somebody else to do the stunt. Well, he eventually did, and I rode the stunt. But I told that son of a bitch Peckinpah that I'd never work for him again."

The stuntmen's anxiety was not eased by the fact that Sam delayed the stunt a good part of the day while he shot inserts of the fuses burning along its superstructure. "They couldn't get the camera out of Sam's hands," says Gordon Dawson. "We were screaming and yelling and he was shooting burning inserts to the very last ounce of light."

"Sam was again stalling and stalling and stalling," says Howard Kazanjian, "and I had the five stuntmen on the bridge, sitting there on horseback, nervous. The wind was blowing and we thought we were going to lose the bridge, and the water was raging [at sixteen mph], and Eddie Carrere was going crazy. You had the stuntmen sitting on the bridge for hours, and then coming off and getting back on again, on and off, and the longer they waited the bigger the stunt was becoming in their minds. Finally it was too dark, so we didn't shoot it that day. We came back the next day, which was a Sunday, and shot it then."

Peckinpah's six cameras were placed on barges in the river, on the riverbank, and on a hill overlooking the bridge. "Every angle was covered beautifully," says Fred Gammon, an assistant director on the feature. The stuntmen and horses took their places on the second span and the charges were detonated. Green geysers of smoke, water, and splintered wood shot skyward, the platform dropped out and five men and five horses plunged through twenty-five feet of space into the swift river below.

"The place where a horse is really dangerous is in the water, where he's having to swim," says L. Q. Jones. "The reason he's dangerous is because he can't get his feet onto solid ground, so he will beat you to death with his front feet trying to climb up on you. The stuntmen had crash helmets on under their hats and pads on their bodies, but they didn't know what was going to happen with the horses. The camera barges were controlled from shore by cables and there were three or four boats out there to pick up the stuntmen because the water was running pretty fast. Warren was in a boat with somebody, I was in a boat with somebody. The fall was okay, but Billy Hart was knocked out. He washed downriver and went over one of the raft cables; it caught him around the waist. He couldn't get off of it, he was too weak from the explosion and fall and the current was too strong. My boat was fairly close so we went over. The current was so strong, I had to stand on the cable and lift him off while someone else held me. Once they pulled the pin on that explosion, things stayed busy for the next six or seven minutes."

"We thought we were going to lose two of the horses," says Fred Gammon. "The water was going so fast and there really wasn't any bank and the horses couldn't get up. We had to lasso those things and drag them downriver to where we could get them out."

One of the camera barges broke loose from its cable and careened toward the bank. A low-hanging tree branch swept all its occupants and the camera, an Arriflex, into the water. Miraculously, the camera was the only serious casualty that day; all of the horses and the stuntmen survived. The stuntmen had only a few cuts and bruises and they earned $2,000 each for the "gag." Special-effects man Bud Hulburd bragged, "I've just had the opportunity to hang a Rembrandt! It will probably never happen to me again." In the hotel bar that night, Peckinpah plopped down on a stool next to Strother Martin's wife, who had come down to Mexico to watch the last days of shooting. Sam sighed: "Thank God nobody was hurt!"

There was only one more day of quick pickup shots to be done in Mexico City before principal photography would be finished, nine and a half days over schedule.

"The last hour of the last day as the sun was going down,"

says Dawson, "Sam had Holden and Borgnine and all the other actors up on top of a semi-truck, shooting low-angle close-ups with a sky background. 'Look right! Look left! Look up! Look down!' Just so he had all kinds of looks in all kinds of costumes, just in case he needed them in editing. Sam would shoot a preposterous amount of film in ratio to what he finally used. The thing with Sam was, it was very hard to get him to start a picture when he said he would, and then once he started shooting it was very hard to get the camera out of his hands at the end of the picture. Once he got into it there was always another shot he wanted."

For eighty days he had driven a crew of more than a hundred men and women to the limit of their endurance and finally beyond, had seduced, inspired, and terrorized his actors and crew to give more than they ever thought themselves capable of, and in so doing had driven himself to his highest achievement as a filmmaker. For eighty days they and he had thought of nothing else but the film. Now, suddenly, it was over. When he wrapped that day at Churubusco Studios in Mexico City, he wandered off to an isolated corner of the sound stage and broke down.

Many of *The Wild Bunch* cast and crew would have found it difficult to believe him capable of such emotion; to many he had been one cold, hard son of a bitch. But others saw an inner warmth, even vulnerability beneath Peckinpah's ruthless façade.

"After my last day on the picture, we were in the hotel that night and I saw Sam," says Paul Harper, who played one of the bounty hunters. "I went up to him and said, 'Sam, I just want to tell you how much I appreciate your giving me the opportunity to work with you and to work on this picture. I've really enjoyed it.' He said, 'Well, Paul, you can call yourself a Peckinpah man now, 'cause you're one of my boys. You gave me everything and more that I wanted for the picture.' "

"What happened on *Wild Bunch*," Gordon Dawson told Garner Simmons, "almost never happens: everyone was there, on his toes, job and homework done, eight possibilities in each hand and his mind searching for eight more, on a dead run for eighty days. Everybody gave total, full-bore commitment—or they just weren't there!"

While the crew had been submerged in Peckinpah's Purgatory, Martin Luther King, Jr., and Robert Kennedy had been assassinated, more American cities had been consumed by the flames of riots, and the Democratic presidential convention in Chicago turned into a bloodbath. "We didn't know any of that shit was happening," says Dawson. "We were totally wrapped up in the film." They had missed the mayhem that was tearing the country apart, but Peckinpah returned to America with a film that reflected it.

The cast and crew of *The Wild Bunch* scattered in the last week of June 1968 and raced back to their homes in the states. Except for Sam and Lou Lombardo—they set up editorial offices in Torreon to stay out of reach of Rudi Fehr and the rest of the Warner Bros. brass. The Warners executives had already seen the dailies and loved them, and rumors that *The Wild Bunch* footage looked incredible had spread throughout Hollywood, but Peckinpah wasn't taking any chances. This time he, not the studio, would control the editing—at least until he got the three public previews guaranteed to him by his contract.

Sam had shot 333,000 feet of film with 1,288 camera setups. This was well over the 225,000 Warners had budgeted for the production, and higher than the average for most feature films at the time (250,000 feet), but far lower than the 1.5 million feet of film George Stevens exposed on *Giant*. Considering all the scenes shot at high speed and with multiple cameras, the amount of film Sam exposed was relatively low. This was because he rarely went beyond three or four takes of any given shot. But he printed most of what he exposed so he'd have as much raw material as possible to draw upon in editing.

As a result, most of that 333,000 feet found its way into Lou Lombardo's cutting room. The editor was drowning in celluloid: "I was down in Mexico for *six fucking months!* My daughter was growing up in California. She hardly knew me when I got home. Six fucking months. Sam loved it, he had a villa with servants, he had nothing to come back to America for. I was trying to get the film in one piece, I mean, there was fucking film everywhere, Jesus Christ, there was film! Why did I have to be living in a stinkhole like I was living in? I mean, it was bad enough when everybody else was there, Holden and everybody. We all used to get together and drank and had fun. But when everybody left, all I had was Sam."

To help him with assembling and cutting scenes, Lombardo brought a second television editor, Robert Wolfe, down to Mexico. Wolfe would go on to work on four more Peckinpah films.

An editor's normal procedure is to assemble the footage into chronological order as it is being shot. Though the sequences are crudely cut at first, the idea is to at least get all the film into a coherent form before going back to refine each scene. But halfway through the shooting of *Bunch*, Peckinpah had ordered Lombardo to abandon this approach.

"I had about ten reels assembled and suddenly Sam says, 'I don't want you to cut any more film,' " Lombardo recalls. "I said, 'What?' He says, 'I want you to go back and start polishing, and polishing, and polishing what you already have.' I said, 'But, Sam, I've got all this footage coming in, it'll pile up to the fucking ceiling!' He says, 'Don't worry about it.' I said, 'Okay.' So I started polishing and polishing."

Lombardo returned to the opening shootout and struggled to integrate all of the multispeed footage into one smooth-flowing sequence.

"When I first cut the street fight it was twenty-one minutes long. I'd cut a lot of gunfights, so I cut it like a gunfight. There was so much happening that I would go to this piece of action, then this piece of action and then this one. Sam looked at it and he said, 'Jesus Christ, it's good, it's good, but we can't play it for twenty-one minutes.' I said, 'Well, I'll cut it down.' He said, 'No, don't cut it down. See if you can't mesh it together, I don't care if you use cuts a few frames long, use everything and put it together.' So that's what I did, I intercut all the separate pieces of action. I might start with this guy being hit, then cut to that guy being hit, cut to this guy falling, that guy still falling, then cut to somebody else over there getting hit, to a horse spinning over there, somebody going through a window there, and then back to the first guy just landing on the ground. I meshed it, I took every piece of action and intercut it with another. I said to Sam, 'Maybe we can make it like an explosion, like the audience is right in the middle of an explosion.' He said, 'That's what I want.' "

It was parallel action, first refined by D. W. Griffith, taken to new and dizzying heights. One slow-motion shot of a bounty hunter getting pierced by a bullet and falling off a rooftop, cartwheeling lethargically through space and crunching heavily onto the dirt street, was intercut with fraction-of-a-second images of the Bunch escaping from the railroad office and exchanging gunfire with the other bounty hunters. The dead man's fall was cut away from and back to four times before he finally slammed to earth. The effect was not realistic, as some critics would mistakenly assert, but decidedly surrealistic. Gothic in its horror, poetic in its beauty, it pursued the psychological dynamics of violence, not the clinical details.

When Lombardo had completed his second cut of the sequence, Sam sat down with him to polish it yet again. Phil Feldman later recalled: "Sam would say to Lou Lombardo, 'Give me one more frame on that shot.' Now, very few people do that. But Sam would say, 'I think one frame more.' Or, 'One frame less.' Nobody does that anymore, or did it before. I think that was the most completely edited, most completely dubbed picture of all time. I don't think anybody was as careful with detail as Sam was. He made me careful. I would not have thought of frame cuts; I mean, that didn't mean anything to me before this picture. I didn't know that a sequence was one frame or two frames too long or too short. I learned a lot."

By the time Peckinpah was finished fine-cutting the opening gunfight, it ran just five minutes. Together he and Lombardo had devised the most creative use of montage since Sergei Eisenstein's *Battleship Potemkin*. They had forever changed the way movies would be made.

More than twenty years later Michael Sragow would write in *The New Yorker:* "What *Citizen Kane* was to movie lovers in 1941, *The Wild Bunch* was to cineastes in 1969. Its adrenaline rush of revelations seems to explode the parameters of the screen."

By August Peckinpah could hold Warner Bros. off no longer. Ken Hyman demanded to see some cut footage, so Sam sent him the first ten reels (a hundred minutes), which he and Lombardo had honed sharp as a straight razor. Feldman saw the footage before Hyman and, nervous about the opening image of kids torturing ants and scorpions, wrote a letter to Sam urging that he remove it for the Hyman screening "so that I don't have to explain the symbolism." Feldman then gingerly hinted that Sam might want to remove the scene permanently, for it was certain to alienate large segments of the paying public before the movie got past its opening title sequence.

Sam fired back this response: "Received your letter and comments . . . I found them interesting, provocative, valid and—penny dreadful. I cannot in the name of Jesus Christ understand how my producer, who has sweated through this entire production with his devoted director, can casually or not so casually request the deletions of children—scorpions—children in counterpoint to the Wild Bunch. If this is your feeling, why did you have me direct this film and why are you interested in my doing another film for you? Why not Dick Donner? Or Bill Boudeen? Or Dave Dowell [an assistant director Sam fired from *Bunch*]? . . . Phil, be advised that you are the most dangerous off the top of your head memo writer (and talker) in the world."

The scorpions and the kids stayed in, and Feldman's jitters proved unfounded. "Sam knew what he was doing," says Lombardo. "He knew they were thinking of taking the film away from him. So he showed the Warner execs those first ten reels, which we had really polished, we even had some sound effects in already, and they fucking flipped over it. When it was over they applauded, especially Phil. They could smell a hit. Sam wanted more time and money for editing it. Ken Hyman said, 'Give him anything he wants.' "

While the editors hunched over their moviolas fifteen and sixteen hours a day, putting the gargantuan jigsaw puzzle together piece by piece, Sam kept his promise to Gordon Dawson by guiding him through a rewrite of *The Ballad of Cable Hogue.* In August Sam submitted their new draft to Ken Hyman, who, still flushed with excitement over *The Wild Bunch* screening, gave it a green light for the cameras. With *Hogue* now moving into pre-production, Sam and his editors returned to the Warners lot in September 1968 with a three-hour, forty-five-minute rough cut of *The Wild Bunch*.

Peckinpah went into pre-production on *Hogue*, then off to Nevada to begin shooting it, leaving Feldman behind to work with Lombardo. Over the next three months they cut the picture down to two hours and fifty minutes. "It played well at three hours and forty-five minutes," says Lombardo. "It was very powerful. Every frame we took out was gold." But out those gold frames came, for Warners demanded a two-and-a-half-hour movie. On the weekends, Lombardo would travel to the Valley of Fire in Nevada, where Peckinpah was shooting *Hogue*, to screen reels that he and Feldman had further refined for Sam's approval.

The first public screenings of *The Wild Bunch* took place at the film schools at USC and UCLA, and in Phoenix, Arizona, where Sam was finishing up the shooting of *The Ballad of Cable Hogue*. A local moviehouse was rented and the entire cast and crew of *Hogue* showed up at nine A.M. at the Fox Theater in downtown Phoenix to see the film. There was no musical score yet and many sound effects were still missing, but the impact was awesome. "The crew and all these actors were there in this big box theater," Lombardo recalls. "We ran the whole fucking picture and it was like an explosion. People cheered and applauded and just went crazy."

Gill Dennis, an American Film Institute intern with the *Hogue* company, recalls: "It was *incredible*, incredible. It was *so* powerful. The opening shootout . . . It was *awful*. I remember watching it and crying, and I'd never cried at violence in a movie before. A movie had started, you didn't know who was who, and suddenly all these people were dying and some of them were innocent . . . The woman was dragged by the horse . . . It was incredible, it was something you'd never seen."

Over the next month another twenty minutes would be cut from the film. Lucien Ballard protested that the deletions reduced the picture's scope and majesty, but Peckinpah felt they were necessary, both to tighten the sprawling story and to please Warner Bros., which said it was impossible to market a three-hour western.

To compose the musical score, Peckinpah brought in Jerry Fielding. He explained to Fielding that he wanted a minimalist approach: no over-orchestrated Elmer Bernstein numbers dripping sap out of the theater speakers, just a few guitars strumming Mexican and American folk songs, like on "The Westerner." As much as possible the music should come from natural sources—a mariachi band, a lone guitar player idly strumming a tune. The music had to be authentic, real folk songs sung by real folk singers, not Arthur Freed perversions. He suggested they use Julio Corona, a guitar player Sam had met in a cantina during one of his sojourns in Mexico, to both play for the soundtrack and to suggest a selection of songs and music for various scenes. Chalo Gonzalez was sent south of the border to track the diminutive musician down. He would be gone for a week, combing every cantina and whorehouse in northern Mexico.

Sam was off in Nevada shooting *Cable Hogue* when Fielding first went to work. He began by screening *Bunch* over and over again, and as he did so he started to get ideas of his own. Yes, he agreed, it would be good to use authentic music wherever possible, and he too detested overscored pictures. But the violence and abrasive characters in *Bunch* were in desperate need of counterpoint.

Fielding told Paul Seydor: "Sam's message in that picture, while it was very strongly the depiction of the horrors [of violence] . . . there was a much more important priority . . . as far as I was concerned, which had to do with the relationship between two men [Holden and Ryan] which was actually a right down love affair. Not a dirty one, but a real one. And a love affair on Sam's part with the ambiance of the time and the place—that was what that picture was about. It was not about gunshots and open wounds and children getting shot. Even the battle was a ballet . . . a fucking ballet . . . I did an awful lot of pulling the other way on *Wild Bunch.* If you listened to that score and didn't see the picture, you'd think it was a love story. I prefer to talk about it in this way: there is a poetic element. A writer does it with words, I'm doing it with inarticulate sounds which are a little more ambiguous."

Having developed a strategy, Fielding set about composing

some music and recording it, not with a couple of guitar players but with a six-piece orchestra. Phil Feldman had been resistant to using Fielding at first, but when he heard the session tapes he did an about-face: "I thought it was quite good. It was very beautiful music, and I could see that Jerry had incorporated what Sam wanted in terms of Mexican music, as well as bringing in his own stuff."

Fielding's music was sent to Peckinpah in Nevada to be played with the appropriate scenes from *Bunch*. But the screening facility at the tiny resort where the *Hogue* company was lodged was a converted laundry room. Played over a pair of tinny speakers and echoing off the concrete floor and metal washers, the music sounded abominable. Peckinpah shot off an outraged letter to his composer and friend. "I found your music for *The Wild Bunch*, for the most part, overscored, pretentious and distracting. As I have said before, I am not speaking of melodies or the music you wrote, I'm speaking of the execution. I've spent a great deal of money and a great deal of time explaining to you exactly what this picture means. You're obviously unwilling or incapable of going along with me in any substantial degree. I know that you have worked very hard and your work has been excellent, except that its execution in my opinion is damaging to an extremely serious degree to the film I made. Therefore I would appreciate it if you would do me a favor and just back off . . . I wanted Mexico—what did I get, Vienna?"

Feldman and Camille Fielding both urged the composer to fly down to Phoenix, where Peckinpah had just moved with the *Hogue* company, and have it out with him.

Fielding told Paul Seydor: "So I got up in the morning, I had an ulcer and I drank four cups of black acid coffee, ate no breakfast, got on an airplane, by the time I got to Phoenix I was so fucking mean you wouldn't believe it. Sam was going to look at dailies at the local theater. I walked in that theater, he came in a few minutes later and I was ready for him. He didn't get a chance to open his mouth. I jumped out of the chair and said, 'You fucking two-bit Toscanini, you twerp! How dare you fucking send me that letter, what do you know about anything?' I really lit into him. He never opened his fucking mouth. He sat down in the chair and hid behind his hat."

"Jerry went in there screaming his head off, which Sam did not expect," says Camille Fielding. "Sam was surprised. He didn't expect Jerry to fight back, because Jerry's personality was such a pussycat, he was an intellectual and abhorred violence in any form. He would always discuss, he would never argue. It surprised Sam, but he liked it. He liked that Jerry was not afraid to argue for what he believed in, that he so totally believed that he was right."

Sam agreed to listen to the music again, over a decent sound system this time, and to Fielding's reasoning for the creative choices that he'd made. After careful consideration, he did a turnaround and gave the composer carte blanche to score the rest of the movie.

With the go-ahead from Peckinpah, Fielding's real work began. "He was working all day, all night, around the clock. He used to sleep in fits and starts—two hours here, an hour there," says Camille. "But other than being exhausted, he loved every moment of the experience."

Meanwhile, Chalo Gonzalez had finally located Sam's expert in tequila-sodden cantina songs, Julio Corona, after searching all over Mexico. He brought the guitar player back to Burbank, where Julio found himself sitting in on recording sessions with some of the world's finest musicians.

Jerry Fielding told Paul Seydor: "Julio couldn't read music. He was Sam's troubadour. Sweet little guy. Alcoholic. He played all those Mexican songs, those Rancheros, those cry in your beer things. He knew 'em all. He was, like, born with his fingers on a guitar, nobody ever taught him, he just did it. Julio was 200 percent Mexican and a very sad man. He used to say, 'It's time for gasoline,' and you'd give him some tequila. He couldn't read music and he had hell of a time with the parts on the five guitar sections, but when he played, it was not a studio musician trying to be a Mexican imitation. There's something about the authenticity of the random way he played things."

By the time he was finished, Fielding had scored an hour and ten minutes of music for *The Wild Bunch,* more music than there was in *My Fair Lady.*

Not everyone was thrilled by Peckinpah's mercurial perfectionism; Feldman and the Warner Bros. sound department and the entire staff at Technicolor were frazzled candidates for the laughing academy. "We were in post-production for a year," said Feldman. "The dubbing was enormous, I'm not sure that anybody has used as many dubbing hours as we did—hundreds of dubbing hours. It was because of Sam's attention to detail. I would have been satisfied with less attention to detail. His attention to sound effects, in terms of different gunshots, to the music mix, to the music itself made it all very difficult. We would spend days on reel number one [out of fifteen reels] and then more days on reel number one. Post-production really was a pain in the ass. I could tell that this was what had eliminated Sam from completing his other pictures in post-production. Because I had the patience of Job, I just went with him, I went with him and I went with him."

But there were valid concerns behind Sam's obsessiveness. The first time around, the Warners sound department laid in the same gunshot effects they'd been using since Errol Flynn made *Dodge City* in 1939. Every six-gun and rifle sounded the same. Sam threw a fit, insisting that new gunshots be recorded so that each gun in the picture had its own individual sound. By the time they were finished more than a hundred different gunshots were used on the effects track. "To mesh all of those onto one track and still bring out those individual sounds was a son of a bitch, but it happened, you'll hear it," says Lou Lombardo. "You know when Holden fires, 'cause that forty-five barks, and you know when Strother fires that thirty-ought-six. Sam raised hell over that effects track, but he got them to bring it up to a level of quality that won them the S.M.P.T.E. sound-effects award."

The first fine cut of *The Wild Bunch* ran two hours, thirty-one minutes and had a total of 3,642 cuts in it, more than any other film processed by Technicolor up until that time. (American movies in the late sixties had an average of 600 cuts.)

By May 1969 it was ready for the three public previews that Sam had been guaranteed in his contract. He got them: one in

Kansas City, another in Fresno, and a third in Long Beach, California. The Kansas City preview, of course, was a disaster. One irate audience member wrote her congressman, who in turn wrote to Jack Valenti, head of the MPAA. Valenti defended the picture's violence on the grounds of the First Amendment, but the flap did not set a great tone for Warners' upcoming battle to win an R-rating from the Association instead of an X. In Fresno, a group of nuns settled like a flock of fussy doves into a row of seats just before the movie began, only to fly up the aisle minutes after the opening shootout erupted, habits fluttering like blue flames behind them as they raced out to the street.

The reaction cards filled out by audience members at the three previews were far from reassuring. Sixty percent strongly disliked the film; only 17–18 percent rated it outstanding, and the remaining 22–23 percent fell somewhere in between. But whether audiences praised the film as a masterpiece or condemned it as pornography, the emotional response was passionate. The answers scrawled on the studio's questionnaires were not those of bored patrons hastily fulfilling a tedious obligation. The response sheets were covered from top to bottom with manic handwriting. *The Wild Bunch* definitely struck a chord.

At almost any other time in history such a high percentage of negative responses would have caused the studio brass to hit the panic button, take the film away from the director, drastically recut it, or dump it on the market with little or no publicity. But Ken Hyman was convinced that *The Wild Bunch* was a great film and he stood by it. "Kenny was on our side all the way," says Lou Lombardo. "He didn't care, he loved the movie. He loved making movies."

"I was at the Fresno screening," says Hyman. "Listen, the audience loved it, absolutely loved it. The majority of the preview cards were negative, but that wasn't the audience's reaction. Once they sat down and thought about it and started to fill out the cards, they thought: Christ, what a violent movie! But if you sat in the cinema and you watched the people, how they reacted and how they became involved—I mean, nobody was ambivalent about that movie. The only movies that are a washout, in my opinion, are the ones where people say, 'Eh, I should have stayed home and read a book.' When the lights came up after *The Wild Bunch* was over there was no applause, only a shocked silence. If you had those previews with a major studio today, the executives would go bananas. You see, the difference was we owned the company and we weren't frightened, we did what we believed."

But everyone agreed there was too much blood. If a third of your audience runs out to vomit in the street, you're obviously failing to reach them. Peckinpah later told an interviewer: "I cut several points of violence out of the film . . . I thought that they were excessive for the point that I wanted to make. I not only wanted to talk about violence in this film, but I have a story to tell too and I do not want the violence per se to dominate what's really happening with the people . . . We are not doing the film for five people, we're doing it for an audience . . . I am savage against myself; even though I loved the scenes, I cut them. And now it plays so instead of having thirty-five people walk out we only have ten. Well, that's a good average. I don't mind ten."

And then there was the MPAA, its scissors sharpened by complaints from a United States Congressman. If Sam didn't clean up some of the gore and language, the picture would get slapped with an X-rating, which would guarantee disaster at the box office. So from mid-May to mid-June Peckinpah shaved another six minutes off of the film—more than even Feldman or Hyman thought necessary. Still, it took seven meetings with the MPAA, and after each more frames of spurting blood and lines like, "Lookit here, Lyle, a nipple as long as your thumb!" were snipped out. Finally they won their R-rating.

Months earlier, rough cuts of the film had been screened for Warner Bros.' domestic and foreign distributors, who wielded considerable power over how *The Wild Bunch* would finally be marketed to the public. The European distributors were ecstatic and agreed to sell the picture as a road-show. It would open in a few select theaters in 70mm with a stereo soundtrack (then a rarity) and an intermission, then move into wide release after reviews and word of mouth had built up audience interest.

But the American distribution chief, Ben Kalmenson, balked

at this approach. *Bunch* was a western, a very good western, but a western just the same, and no western merited a 70mm, hard-ticket premiere in select theaters. Kalmenson wanted to release it in 35mm, mono sound, without an intermission. It would open, like all the John Wayne westerns, in mass bookings across Texas and the Southwest—the drive-in circuit—then be brought north with saturation bookings in hundreds of theaters across the country.

Phil Feldman thought the domestic distribution plan myopic and lobbied long and hard against it. *The Wild Bunch* was not just another western, Feldman argued, it was an epic adventure story, a classic, like *Bridge on the River Kwai* and *Lawrence of Arabia.* It should open in a few select theaters in New York, Los Angeles, and a handful of other major cities so that the reviews, which Feldman was sure would be raves, and word of mouth would give the public a chance to discover it. *Midnight Cowboy, Easy Rider, Alice's Restaurant,* and other recent high-brow films had been released that way and done very well. Release it to 400 theaters at once and *The Wild Bunch* would flame out early without reaping its full potential.

Because of Feldman's relentless lobbying, Kalmenson finally agreed to a slight compromise. A 70mm version would be released to a few select theaters—such as New York's Trans Lux—in northern cities in conjunction with the Texas bookings. But these 70mm versions would have no intermission and Kalmenson insisted that the film had to be shortened for the domestic market. To pacify him, Feldman and Peckinpah cut out a flashback that revealed how Pike Bishop had lost the only woman he'd ever loved. That saved a scant minute and twenty-six seconds of screen time, but it enabled them to tell Kalmenson the film had been shortened. When he screened it again, the executive agreed that the picture played "much faster now."

They had had no choice but to make the compromise, but it pained Sam. An important piece of character motivation and dimension had been lost. Important, but not crucial. The film still worked without it and it would be the last compromise—or so Sam thought—and he could live with it. *The Wild Bunch* was 96 percent Peckinpah, and considering the odds, he concluded with a resigned shrug, that wasn't bad at all.

The official world premiere of *The Wild Bunch* came on June 28, in the Bahamas, where Warner Bros. included it in their "International Film Festival" there, which in reality was a giant press junket for their summer releases, but it was Peckinpah's film that struck lightning—provoking bitter condemnation from the low-brow reviewers and glowing raves from the intellectuals.

Warner Bros. launched the nationwide release a week later with a heavy publicity campaign that included two giant billboards on Sunset Boulevard—where the studios tout their most prestigious productions—as well as radio, TV, newspaper, and magazine ads. Warners spent $200,000 on print ads in Texas alone in the first few weeks of the picture's release, which Feldman considered a colossal waste. The money could have been put to better strategic use in the major urban centers and strung out over a longer period of time.

The critics may have been divided, but the impact that *The Wild Bunch* had on an entire generation of filmmakers and film buffs was deep and far-reaching. "I think everyone remembers where they were when they first saw *The Wild Bunch*," says Ann Godoff, a film student at NYU at the time, and now an executive editor at Random House.

One of Godoff's instructors, Martin Scorsese, remembers where he was. He tagged along with Jay Cocks, then a movie critic for *Time*, to a special screening of the film at Warner Bros. "It was just the two of us witnessing this incredible work of art. We were stunned, totally stunned, overwhelmed. *Ride the High Country* was a good indication of a new approach to the western. It was like the beginning of the end, and *The Wild Bunch* was the end. But it was an incredible blaze of glory. The violence was exhilarating, but you felt ashamed for being exhilarated, mainly because it reflected what we were doing in reality in Vietnam, which we would see on the news at six o'clock at night. The exhilaration had to do with the way he used film and the way he used the images with a number of different cameras going at different speeds. You really get a wonderful choreographed effect, it's like dance or like poetry. Jay and I had been expecting something really incredible, but we were still taken aback by it, because it was much more than we expected."

"I saw *The Wild Bunch* about the second or third day after it opened on Hollywood Boulevard," says John Milius, screenwriter of *Jeremiah Johnson* and *Apocalypse Now* and director of such films as *Big Wednesday* and *Conan the Barbarian.* "That was because George Lucas saw it and said, 'This is the best movie ever made! It's better than *The Searchers,* it's better than anything! You all have to go see it!' So we went and saw it. I really liked the movie. There was a side of Peckinpah that was out of control; I liked that. And then you have that wonderful scene where they're sitting there drinking and the old man says, 'We all dream of being a child again, even the worst of us, perhaps the worst most of all.' You will remember that line all of your life, *all of your life!* It's something you take away from that movie and you'll *never* forget. How many movies ever give you that? There are many moments in *Wild Bunch* that are like that."

In England, where the film won almost unanimous raves from the critics, Alex Cox, director of *Sid and Nancy* and *Walker,* was among the first to see it. "I'd never laid eyes on a western like that. It seemed to me to be so much a film about the Vietnam War, a film about guys in military uniforms taking hostages and committing atrocities, going to foreign countries and murdering people, and really not giving a damn for anything except their own little community. They had this tremendous sense of their own heroism and their own importance and their own sense of honor. I thought it was a fantastic film. It was an extraordinary action movie, a great action movie, but it had such a sense of cynicism and brutality as well. It's amazing that he got it made. The cast was so perfectly chosen, Holden, Borgnine, Ryan, all of the performances were so full of passion and sadness. That was the great thing about all of Peckinpah's films, the *sadness* that the characters have inside them."

Ron Shelton, director of *Bull Durham* and *White Men Can't Jump,* was a minor-league ball player scratching out a living on dusty baseball diamonds in the Southwest. "I went to movies every day, basically to kill the afternoon 'cause you didn't have to be to the ball park until four-thirty and the theaters were air-conditioned. Well, in the summer of sixty-nine I went to a movie called *The Wild Bunch* in Little Rock, across the street from the hotel. I was just going to kill another afternoon. It was just a western, but I liked westerns. After it was over I was exhilarated and I didn't know why. I was exhilarated, and I'd just seen a bunch of killers kill a bunch of other killers. I wanted to know why I was exhilarated. I've never fired a gun in my life, I've never held a gun. I think I was exhilarated because of the sense of shifting loyalties and the compiling of irony upon irony without the movie getting bogged in the cerebral. It functioned at an emotional level that narrative art needs to, and compounded and confounded the mythologies and the ironies in a way that never felt self-conscious. The sad thing today is that action movies have degenerated into cartoons. We forget that at their best action movies can be as complex and intelligent as anything in Shakespeare."

After seeing *The Wild Bunch* at a preview on Hollywood Boulevard, Paul Schrader told Peckinpah that he thought the editing was as good as any in Kurosawa's samurai epics. "I think it's better," Sam said. The kid from Fresno had made it, all the way to the top of the highest peak.

The media controversy over *The Wild Bunch* made it one of the most talked and written-about films of 1969, but, as Phil Feldman had feared, Warner Bros.' distribution of the picture had terrible consequences at the box office. It had opened in only one theater in both New York and Los Angeles, playing in prestigious 1,000-seat houses in 70mm with a stereo soundtrack, and in both cities it did smashing business. In L.A., where it played in one of the old movie palaces on Hollywood Boulevard, it was even outgrossing *True Grit,* John Wayne's last great blockbuster, which occupied the premiere showcase, Grauman's Chinese Theater. (By mid-September, *Bunch* would still be outgrossing *True Grit* in L.A., $160,000 in a single week compared to $120,000 for *Grit.*)

But in the twenty-odd theaters in Texas where *Bunch* first opened, it took a steep nosedive. The grosses were terrible. Instead of a "big wind" blowing out of Texas to carry the film to the top of the box-office charts, as Warners had planned, there came only a fitful breeze. By mid-July, two weeks after its initial release, *The Wild Bunch* was rated by the trades as the eighth highest-grossing film in the U.S., pulling in $291,000 in the week of July 16. The highest-grossing film that week, Walt Disney's *The Love Bug,* grossed more than twice that much, $658,000. *True Grit,* rolling up the greenbacks in the South and Midwest, grossed $403,000.

Overall, *Bunch* was doing respectable business but falling far short of the breakaway hit that Warners had hoped for. And by this time Sam had lost his godfather at the studio. As head of production, Ken Hyman had produced some exciting and innovative films, but unfortunately not much in the way of revenue. The studio's net profits plunged from $10,350,000 in 1968 to only $300,000 in 1969. Warner Bros. was sold to Steve Ross in 1969, and Hyman was replaced by a new regime. Ted Ashley took over as the new president and John Calley, who had helped get Peckinpah fired from *The Cincinnati Kid,* became the new head of production just as *The Wild Bunch* was released. Strangely enough, Peckinpah held no bitterness toward Calley—he'd always blamed Ransohoff as the one who sacked him—and the two began discussing a variety of future projects, including *Summer Soldiers,* a screenplay about modern-day mercenaries who get involved in a revolution on an obscure Caribbean island.

But Ashley was strictly a bottom-line man. Under his leadership Warners' profits would soar in 1970 to $27,713,000, thanks largely to the documentary *Woodstock* and another John Wayne western, *Chisum.* Ashley took a look at *Bunch*'s disappointing performance and complaints from exhibitors that the film was too long, and decided that it needed to be cut by at least ten minutes.

Ashley issued an order to Phil Feldman via Ben Kalmenson, head of domestic distribution: cut ten minutes out of *The Wild Bunch* and do it now. Feldman received the message just after Sam had left for Hawaii with his kids to recuperate from the crippling stress of editing one movie and simultaneously shooting another. He had set up editorial offices on Oahu with Lou Lombardo and Frank Santillo to cut *The Ballad of Cable Hogue,* again out of the reach of the studio.

Feldman could have called Peckinpah to see if he wanted to fight Ashley. Or he could have tried to convince Sam that such a battle would be useless and asked him to come back to L.A. to make the cuts himself and that way minimize the damage to the picture. But Feldman did neither. Instead he made the cuts himself without telling Peckinpah, and he went right for the scenes that he had objected to throughout editing: the flashbacks that explained Pike Bishop's past failures and his relationship with Deke Thornton, some crucial campfire dialogue between Holden and Borgnine, a giant battle between Mapache's forces and those of Pancho Villa, and some of the atmospheric scenes at Angel's village. By the time he was finished, Feldman had shorn over eight minutes from the movie, enough to pacify Ashley, without damaging—he believed—the integrity of the picture. In fact, Feldman believed he'd improved it. Near the end of his life, twenty-two years later, he still expressed no regret over his actions.

"I regarded it as out of Sam's province by that time. His picture had been shown in many places, particularly in London, in 70mm with an intermission, in full glory. I thought at that point, where a distributor was suffering and asked that a picture be shortened, I don't think that I felt that that was an artistic decision any longer. I felt that was a salvage operation that we were obligated to do. Now, I'm sure that Sam's feeling was otherwise, because he didn't care about that aspect of it. But my training on the other side of the desk made me understand that there are some things that you have to do." When asked if he'd consulted with Sam before making the cuts, Feldman's eyes dropped to the ground and he muttered vaguely that he couldn't remember.

AFI intern Gill Dennis, who was in Feldman's office at the time, discussing a screenplay that the producer wanted him to write, remembers quite clearly that Feldman did not consult with Peckinpah and went out of his way to keep the truth from him: "I was sitting there when Phil got on the phone with John Calley and started to explain the cuts. Calley said, 'Now wait a minute, Phil, does Sam know about this?' He was obviously reluctant to go ahead with it. Sam calls a little later and Phil says, 'No, no, no, Sam, no one's going to cut anything.' Right in front of me, he says this, knowing, of course, that the next thing I would do would be to get a hold of Sam."

By the time Sam learned the truth, it was too late. Cutting instructions had gone out to Warner Bros. distribution exchanges throughout the country. As prints of the film came back to the regional shipping houses, in transit from one theater to the next, employees hacked out the indicated scenes. Sometimes they followed the instructions properly, sometimes they bungled the job, sometimes they didn't bother to make the cuts at all, sometimes the prints were already so chopped up from poor projecting equipment that it hardly mattered. Within a matter of weeks Peckinpah's version of *The Wild Bunch* could no longer be seen in his own country and floating around the nation's theaters were countless bastardized versions. This helped confuse film scholars for decades, and obscures the truth and fosters exaggerated legends about the "uncut" *Wild Bunch* to this day.

Phil Feldman had pushed *The Wild Bunch* into development and then into production; he had given Peckinpah full leeway throughout shooting and editing and worked miracles to satisfy Sam's impossible demands. He had conquered the logistical nightmares of Parras and Torreon so that Peckinpah was free to immerse himself in the imaginative universe of his film. After all the crises, the pledges of fidelity, honesty and honor between the two men, why did Feldman in the final hour stab his partner in the back? Maybe he was just plain worn out by two years of incredibly long and stressful days and nights, by too little sleep and too many blown-out-of-proportion confrontations. Maybe—knowing the explosive response he'd get on the other end of the phone if he told Sam the truth, and all the traumatic turmoil that would likely follow—he decided to take the easy way out, avoid the Peckinpah hassle, and just make the cuts himself. Certainly he felt the deletions he chose were the right ones, that he had helped and not hurt the picture. "The film was very important to Phil, too," says Gill Dennis. "He knew it was a good film and it was very important to him not to have it bomb."

When Sam learned that all 400 hundred prints of the film were being recut, he sent a cable to Feldman from Hawaii, vehemently arguing that this would destroy the story's intricate tragic framework that he had so painstakingly constructed. Feldman was unmoved. He defended the cuts, claiming they picked up the pace of the movie and made it more commercially viable. Feldman wrote: "You will be interested to know that within two days after we made the lifts the Trans Lux East's [receipts] rose there $200 a day. While it was showing at the Trans Lux West, where we didn't make the lifts until a couple of weeks later, it was dropping $200 a day. So whichever of the lifts helped, and maybe all of them did, it increased business. We have now made the lifts in every print in the country and it doesn't seem to have hurt anything."

At first Sam tried to take it philosophically. If it hadn't been for Feldman there would never have been a *Wild Bunch,* he knew that better than anyone. But the more time passed, the more the cuts festered. When he returned to L.A., journalist Winfred Blevins conducted a joint interview with Peckinpah and Feldman. When Blevins asked about the exact number and the contents of the deletions, Sam deferred to his producer. Blevins later wrote: "[Feldman] began ticking off the shots and sequences one by one. Suddenly a crash came, the dishes on the table rattled. Peckinpah had slammed his fist against the table, and he looked livid with anger. 'You mean *that's* out?' he squeezed out through his apoplexy. 'Yes, Sam,' Feldman said pacifyingly, 'I thought I told you.' "

After all the projects they had talked about doing together, all the promises, the talk of the duty and obligation a man had to his partner, the quoting of lines from the movie back and forth to each other—*I go with you, Jefe. When you side with a man you stick with him*—Feldman's act of betrayal—that's how Sam saw it—became harder and harder to stomach. In later years he would vilify his former partner with terms as withering as those he used on Jerry Bresler and Martin Ransohoff. Rarely mentioned was Ashley, the real decision-maker who had pulled Feldman's strings.

In *Ride the High Country,* Mariette Hartley asks Joel McCrea if he'll go easy on Randolph Scott, testify on his behalf when he's brought to trial for trying to steal the shipment of gold. "No, I won't," McCrea answers reluctantly.

"Why?"

"Because," he says with a mixture of anger and grief, "he was my friend."

Sam managed to get a print of the complete version of *The Wild Bunch* from Warner Bros. as part of a settlement for a lawsuit he had with them over *The Ballad of Cable Hogue.* He would screen it from time to time over the years at colleges where he lectured, or in theaters he rented out for a day, or in the screening rooms of whatever movie studio he happened to be camped at. Aside from these mostly private affairs, the American public has never had the opportunity to see the complete *Wild Bunch* presented in a theater as Peckinpah originally intended.

Bunch beat *Butch Cassidy and the Sundance Kid* to the theaters by a couple of months but did little harm to its competitor. William Goldman's slick, glib western did fantastic business, grossing $46,039,000. The other big winners that year included *Easy Rider*, the relentlessly hip counterculture odyssey that drew in the tie-dyed, leather-clad multitudes and $19,100,000 at the box office. *The Love Bug* grossed $21,000,000; *Midnight Cowboy* $20,325,000; *True Grit* $14,250,000. *The Wild Bunch* grossed $7,503,192 during its first year in release. By 1976 it had raked in $13,099,790 worldwide—$5,241,207 from the domestic market, $6,280,336 from foreign markets.

The film's final negative cost had been $6,224,087, nearly double its original budget, but costs had been inflated by the studio with the specific goal of assuring that profit participants like Peckinpah and Feldman never saw a dime of extra revenue. Creative accounting practices, such as charging the repainting of sound stages to a picture, etc., are standard operating procedure with most Hollywood studios. Feldman challenged some of Warners' cost figures, but to no avail. On top of the negative cost, Warners slapped on a huge interest charge—$1,088,951—for the money it had fronted for the production, plus a 30 percent distribution fee—$2,503,702—and exorbitant charges for producing prints—$643,929—and shipping and advertising—$1,764,065. Thus Warners was able to claim that the production was $5,366,611 in the red after its first year of release.

"It is almost impossible for a film to show a net profit," says Sam's business manager at the time, Robert Schiller, "because of all those extra charges."

And the gross revenue reported by the studio is not the true gross but a distributor's gross, 30 to 40 percent of the true gross already having been siphoned off by the exhibitors.

Kip Dellinger, who took over as Peckinpah's business manager in 1972, observes: "The real box-office gross on *The Wild Bunch* may have been thirty million. In those days it was a known deal that first the theaters stole money, then the distributor stole money, then the studio loaded the production cost with a whole bunch of bullshit expenses. Outright sales to foreign territories could be very distorted too. The distributor might sell the picture outright to an entity in a foreign country that it in fact already owned. There is a buddy-buddy deal, 'We'll sell you *The Wild Bunch* for $300,000, and then we'll sell you *Shit on a Stick* and you give us another $300,000 for an outright sale.' They're really paying $600,000 for *The Wild Bunch,* but *Shit on a Stick* gets credited with half of the *Wild Bunch* money."

So *The Wild Bunch* was $5,366,611 in debt after its first year of release. By 1976 it had grossed another $5,596,598, but according to Warners' bookkeeping it was now $5,826,871 in the red. The more money the movie made, the studio asked its profit participants to believe, the more money it lost. Only after Sam's death would the picture officially show a profit; today his children receive a modest income from the revenue it pulls in from theatrical showings and the home-video market.

Peckinpah liked to give interviewers the impression that he couldn't care less about winning an Academy Award, but in the spring of 1970 nothing could have been further from the truth. Sam might have relished the role of the rebel, the outsider who took on the Hollywood power brokers, but another part of him craved approval from that same community, lusted, despite his best efforts to deny it, for a wink of recognition from the glamorous bitch goddess. Feldman and Peckinpah hired a press agent, Joel Reisner, who mounted a PR campaign—promotional parties, special screenings, press interviews, ads in the trades, and a retrospective of Peckinpah's films at the Los Angeles County Art Museum—designed to win *The Wild Bunch* a bouquet of Oscars. Sam reviewed the ad copy, participated in the selection of theaters for special return engagements of the film, and embarked on publicity tours to heighten awareness of the picture and its director.

But Warner Bros. refused to throw any serious money behind the campaign, guessing correctly that *The Wild Bunch* and its director were too abrasive to win any honors from the Academy. Reisner's efforts couldn't hope to compete with the lavish parties other studios threw for such bloated turkeys as *Anne of the Thousand Days* and *Hello, Dolly!*, parties that softened the voters' brains with bottles of champagne and smothered their integrity with piles of prime rib, sliced ham, chicken breasts, and French pastries. *The Wild Bunch* won only two Academy nominations, one for Jerry Fielding's score and another for the screenplay by Sickner, Green, and Peckinpah: no nomination for editing (only five editors out of the 150 that belonged to the Academy showed up at the screening Reisner set up for them), for directing (though Sam was nominated for best director by the DGA), nor for best picture. The omissions were ludicrous at face value, but given the clubby beauty-contest criteria if not outright bribery on which the awards are based, it was a minor miracle that the enfant terrible got any nominations at all.

The Wild Bunch lost in both categories it was nominated for. Best musical score went to *Butch Cassidy and the Sundance Kid*, and William Goldman took best original screenplay. Best director went to John Schlesinger for *Midnight Cowboy*, which was also pronounced the best picture.

Time, the great equalizer, would correct this injustice, though Sam Peckinpah never lived to see it. *The Wild Bunch* exploded on American movie screens in 1969 like a shrapnel bomb, easily the most controversial picture that season. But it has since risen to the status of a respectable classic. Its violence, though still intensely disturbing, has lost its sensationalism in the wake of the hundreds of high-tech (and truly nihilistic) bloodbaths that have followed it. The depletion of its shock value has cleared the way for a deeper appreciation of its thematic complexity, rich characterizations, textured detail, and its epic and profoundly romantic vision. It now regularly appears on critics' lists of the ten best movies of all time. In a recent article in *The New Yorker,* Michael Sragow wrote that with *The Wild Bunch* Peckinpah "produced a movie that equals or surpasses the best of Kurosawa. *The Wild Bunch* is the Gotterdämmerung of westerns."

Ethan Mordden writes in his recent book, *Medium Cool—The Movies of the 1960's: "The Wild Bunch* was not generally regarded as one of the era's climactic (or even important) films. Of immediately coeval titles, *Easy Rider* seemed more accessibly epochal, *Alice's Restaurant* more chummily countercultural, *Medium Cool* bolder, *They Shoot Horses, Don't They?* more responsible, and *Midnight Cowboy* more artistic. . . . Yet *The Wild Bunch* is an astonishingly unique film virtually frame by frame, Peckinpah's masterpiece and, as aficionados are gradually learning, one of the masterpieces of American cinema."

It has played continuously to packed houses in Paris since its first release twenty-five years ago, and in revival houses and on college campuses, where it has inspired whole courses devoted exclusively to Peckinpah's work.

When home video opened a whole new market up in the early 1980s, *The Wild Bunch* was one of the first twenty films that Warners released. The uncut version was eventually released on videotape as well, though the wide-screen images were cropped for TV, obliterating Peckinpah's original compositions, and the soundtrack was in muddy mono—all those hundreds of hours Sam spent on the dubbing stage were lost.

Will Americans ever get a chance to see one of the greatest films ever produced in their country in the form that its creator intended? In the early 1990s Martin Scorsese, Robert Harris, Garner Simmons, and Paul Seydor began lobbying various Warner Bros. executives for a theatrical release of Peckinpah's version of the film. In February 1993 their efforts appeared to have paid off. Warners announced plans to release a 70mm, fully restored print of the film, complete with its original six-track stereo soundtrack. After premiering at the Cinerama Dome in Los Angeles, the picture would go on to play in fifteen other American cities, including New York, Chicago, San Francisco, and Boston.

Then, like a scene in some black comic nightmare, disaster struck again. Not realizing that Peckinpah's version had already been given an R-rating by the MPAA in 1969, the new generation of Warners executives submitted it to the Association for a rating. To the studio's dismay, the MPAA rerated the film NC-17 (the equivalent of the old X-rating), which rendered the plan to release it commercially unfeasible.

Taken at face value, the MPAA's action was absurd. Dozens of other recent "action" movies starring Arnold Schwarzenegger, Steven Seagal, Sylvester Stallone, and others have been packed with graphic violence that goes far beyond anything in *The Wild Bunch.* Why the double standard? Because it was never the mere explicitness of its violence that made the film disturbing. It was Peckinpah's ability to provoke complex reactions to that violence, to simultaneously arouse excitement and horror in his viewers and cause them to look inward at their own hearts, that gave the film its harrowing power, a power that obviously has not diminished over the last two and a half decades.

Warners promptly canceled its plans to release the restored film "until further notice," and *The Los Angeles Times* Sunday "Calendar" section was filled with letters from outraged fans for two successive weeks afterward. Barry Reardon, vice president of distribution for Warners, vowed that some sort of compromise would be negotiated and that the restored film would eventually make it to American theaters. But given the studio's devotion in the past to its cinematic legacy, nobody's holding their breath.

One can imagine Peckinpah baring that strange grimace-grin and shaking his head. After all these years his work still incites controversy and raging passions. "As long as you provoke a reaction," he told his son Mathew in later years, "you've done your job. If they jump up to their feet and scream for your head, or give you a standing ovation, either way you've succeeded. The only time you've failed is when you get no reaction at all."

8

"Images They Can't Forget"

Sam Peckinpah had chased the holy grail of art and fame for more than twenty years; now he had it in his grasp. He had sacrificed much to get it, perhaps too much, but how it glittered there in the spotlight. *The Wild Bunch* had been only a marginal success at the box office, but *Time*, *Life*, *The New Yorker*, and dozens of highbrow movie critics had declared him one of the greatest filmmakers of his generation, a brilliant artist in an era when art counted in Hollywood as it never had before.

The next three years would pass like an eight-second ride on the back of a Brahma bull. One whirling frenzy of action—thrilling leaps toward the sky, sudden twists, and pounding falls to earth. He managed to hang on through it all, but the jolts took their toll—at first deep inside, where no one could spot the damage, but in time no one would be able to miss it.

Sam's suite of offices at Warner Bros. became a beehive of frantic workers. At times during the production of *The Wild Bunch* and *The Ballad of Cable Hogue* there were four secretaries crammed into the outer offices. Lou Lombardo, Bob Wolfe, and Frank Santillo set up editing rooms on the lot, Jim Silke was in and out on various writing projects, and Gary Weis and Gill Dennis had an office for editing their documentary on the making of *Hogue.* Robert Culp stopped by frequently to talk about their *Summer Soldiers* script, which Sam hoped to direct next, and the rest of the Peckinpah Bunch—L. Q. Jones, Strother Martin, Jason Robards, Frank Kowalski, Jerry Fielding—boisterously barged in and out.

Joel Reisner, who was masterminding *The Wild Bunch* Academy Awards campaign, also had a desk in Peckinpah's suite. About Sam's height with the same slight build, Reisner was highstrung, incredibly well-read, and incredibly enamored of Sam's work. Jean Renoir and Sam Peckinpah, he was fond of saying, were the two greatest filmmakers in the history of the cinema. Determined to win Sam the recognition he deserved, Reisner mounted a PR blitzkrieg.

He put together a retrospective of Peckinpah's work at the Los Angeles County Art Museum. Everything from episodes of "The Westerner" to *Ride the High Country, Major Dundee, Noon Wine,* and *The Wild Bunch* was shown, and Sam participated in audience discussions afterward. Reisner also arranged hundreds of personal and telephone interviews with magazines and newspapers across the country, including interviews with *Sight and Sound,* the British Film Institute's prestigious magazine, *Film Quarterly,* and other highbrow publications. He set up a European tour in which Sam appeared at the Sorrento Film Festival for a screening of *The Ballad of Cable Hogue,* stopped in Paris to do interviews with all the auteurist film critics, and lectured at the British Film Institute and the national film schools in Sweden and Denmark. Reisner put together a ninety-minute radio documentary, "Sam Peckinpah's West," which aired on KPFK in Los Angeles, and got Sam guest slots on the David Frost and Dick Cavett shows. The new hip, intellectual alternatives to the showbiz babble of Johnny Carson's "Tonight Show," Frost and Cavett attracted strong followings in the early seventies.

Under Reisner's guidance, Peckinpah's image as a public figure crystallized. *Major Dundee* and *The Cincinnati Kid,* two major setbacks, were now transformed into inverse triumphs that helped draw the portrait of Peckinpah as the eccentric genius who had seen his best work butchered by Hollywood philistines. Sam was an enthusiastic collaborator in Reisner's revisionism. He began telling journalists that before Jerry Bresler cut it to pieces, *Dundee* had been "possibly the best picture I've made in my life." But when Columbia offered to let him restore the picture to his original version, he turned down the proposal, claiming he no longer had the time. *Dundee* was more useful as a lost masterpiece than a rediscovered failure.

With great enthusiasm, at first, Sam recreated himself for the media. Gone now were all traces of the rich lawyer's son who had always worn fancier clothes than any of his classmates. The uniform was now complete: dirty jeans, a dusty bandanna wrapped around the graying head, and a pair of mirrored sunglasses masking the eyes. To listen to him now one would think he'd spent his entire youth cowboying and hunting at Dunlap's Ranch rather than just his summers, that he'd grown up in some dilapidated log cabin rather than a sprawling ranch house with elaborately landscaped gardens and an exquisite interior decor.

He took up knife-throwing, hurling the steel blades into the doors and walls of his office and home. Jerry Fielding's kitchen cabinets were gashed and splintered by Sam's constant target practice when he visited their house in the Hollywood Hills. If a journalist or studio executive stepped into his office the response was Pavlovian; Sam reached for the knives and fired away.

He spoke freely to reporters of his drinking binges, his whoring and brawling. Far from diminishing his reputation—at least at first—it fueled it, for this was an era that reveled in excess, that celebrated rebels and cheered mavericks. And here, in the heart of the Hollywood machine, a bizarre anomaly had surfaced: a combination of Ernest Hemingway, Hunter S. Thompson, and Wild Bill Hickok who, through sheer will and gall, had taken on the Combine, the System, with both fists swinging wildly, and damn if he didn't seem to be winning! They dubbed him "Bloody Sam," "The Picasso of Violence," and soon he was a bigger star than any of the actors who appeared in his movies.

But fame concealed a deadly double edge. No one seemed to remember anymore that "The Westerner" had been far less violent than its counterparts on television, or recall the naive romantic scenes between Elsa and Heck in *Ride the High Country* or the subtle characterizations of *Noon Wine.* Now all they wanted to write about were his "ballets of blood"; all they wanted Sam to talk about was violence.

"It was all bullshit," says Jim Silke. "I told Joel Reisner one night, 'Do Sam a favor and leave him alone. It's what he does that counts, not what you say about him,' which was a direct quote from Sam. That really got Reisner upset. Jerry Fielding gave me a big hug. He said, 'Somebody had to tell him that.' But you couldn't stop Reisner and Sam would go along with it. Sam never was the kind of guy that was in shape to deal with all of the publicity. That's when he was weak, in my opinion. When things were tough he was great. But when he got all that adulation it was not good for him. He lost his perspective. It's an incredible thing to try and deal with that kind of attention, I don't see how Sam stayed sane . . . I don't think he was very happy, much, after that."

He was drinking heavily again, the restraint observed during the shooting of *Bunch* now abandoned. He'd start with vodka in the afternoon and switch to whiskey or tequila or any other imaginable combination of liquors in the evening, not showing the effects until the small hours of the night. He could still put the work in and his intellect and creative instincts were still razor-sharp, but his mood swings were becoming more radical.

His romantic entanglements had accelerated along with everything else. Never had his sexual liaisons been so plentiful and so unstable. While shooting *Bunch* he had been comforted by the charms of the two most beautiful Mexican actresses on the picture, Yolanda Ponce and Aurora Clavel. Now that he'd returned to L.A., both wrote passionate love letters that inevitably concluded with pleas for money. He never sent them as much as they asked for, but he usually sent something.

Most of his secretaries did double duty as lovers; he had his own harem set up in the suite at Warners with anywhere from two to four women in attendance at any given time.

A great number of beautiful young women were eager for a piece of the man who'd been hailed as a cinematic genius. As Sam traveled across the country and through Europe in 1969, 1970, and 1971, he marked his trail with more than a dozen brief but intense affairs. It took very little persuasion to get most women into the sack, and there were very few—including the wives and girlfriends of his associates—whom he couldn't seduce if he really set his mind to it.

Peckinpah's correspondence files from 1969 to 1972 are jammed with hormone-saturated letters from starry-eyed conquests professing their desperate and unquenchable passion for the maestro. If a secretary, groupie, or other naive prey were not available, there was always the file of hookers' phone numbers that he kept within easy reach at the office. It hadn't been difficult to assemble the list; Hollywood's studio executives, agents, directors, producers, and stars supported a thriving prostitution industry.

But even an enthusiastic whoring partner like Frank Kowalski had begun to notice how Peckinpah's sex drive had become a compulsion fueled by a disturbing undercurrent of hysteria. "We were down in Mexico one time right after we finished *Cable,* and this Mexican nurse came into the hotel room to give Sam a shot for the flu or something. She was a big two-hundred-pound woman, not even remotely attractive, not by any stretch of the imagination. So Sam drops his pants and bends over, and as she's giving him the needle in the ass, he's reaching back trying to fondle her breasts. It was weird! I thought to myself: this is the strangest display of human emotion I've ever seen!"

Occasionally the hysteria broke to the surface. Jason Robards, who was renting a house in Malibu, stopped by Sam's place at Broad Beach frequently, and by the office at Warner Bros. during pre- and post-production of *The Ballad of Cable Hogue.* By this time Robards had fallen in love with Lois O'Connor, the associate producer on *Noon Wine,* and decided to marry her. Sam and Lois had been lovers briefly when both were working for Martin Ransohoff during pre-production for *The Cincinnati Kid.* But Sam's volatility had caused the affair to crash and burn shortly after it took off.

Now Robards wanted Peckinpah to be best man at his wedding. It would be a small civil ceremony officiated by a Superior Court judge at Jason's house, with only a few friends in attendance. Sam showed up the morning of the wedding wearing a white tuxedo with an apple blossom in its lapel, and a gold tie that Robards had given him. He hung around the house all day while the bride and groom prepared for the ceremony. The radio was playing and the theme to *The Wild Bunch* came on. Robards noticed a strange tug-of-war of emotions on Peckinpah's face. Then Lois came down the stairs in her wedding dress. Sam wrote in a letter years later, that he would always remember Lois "coming down the stairs wearing on her head—blossoms cut in the fog and worn in the sun."

They rose before the judge. Sam handed Jason the ring on cue. Bride and groom recited their vows, looked lovingly into each other's eyes, kissed tenderly, and were pronounced man and wife. People came forward to congratulate them. Sam, who'd been standing stiffly, suddenly broke down, crying uncontrollably. Before any of the shocked onlookers could react, he turned and fled the house and didn't return that day.

Peckinpah had bought the rights to *The Ballad of Cable Hogue* back in 1967 while he was still scrambling for TV assignments to make ends meet. John Crawford and Edmund Penney had written the haunting, allegorical screenplay about a stubborn desert rat who discovers a water hole along a stagecoach route at the dawn of the twentieth century. Cable Hogue lays claim to the water and opens a stage stop that services the needs of weary travelers. For a time he prospers, but then the automobile arrives on the Western landscape. In the blink of an eye the stagecoach line and Cable Hogue are obsolete, and both pass into history.

When Ken Hyman gave the project the green light in August 1968, Gordon Dawson and Sam did a minor rewrite, adding comical scenes, tightening up some sequences, and polishing the dialogue of others. The film would be a tribute to Sam's great-uncle, Moses Church, his grandfather, Charlie Peckinpah, and all the other wild and woolly entrepreneurs who carved their own empires out of the great untamed land in the nineteenth century, then faded into obscurity when "progress" eventually passed them by. Peckinpah's team—Dawson, who would function (without credit) as associate producer, cinematographer Lucien Ballard, art director Leroy Coleman, and prop man Bobby Visciglia—cranked pre-production into high gear in December 1968.

Jason Robards would star as Cable Hogue, Stella Stevens as a prostitute, Hildy, whom he falls in love with, and Englishman David Warner would play the Reverend Joshua Duncan Sloane, a lascivious, self-ordained minister to "the church of the wayfaring stranger, a church of my own revelation," who befriends Cable. Strother Martin and L. Q. Jones would revive their demonic Laurel and Hardy act as two former partners of Hogue's who betray him, and whom he then plots vengeance against, and the Peckinpah stock company would fill out the rest of the cast. The picture was to be shot in thirty-six days in the Valley of Fire, just east of Las Vegas, and in Arizona on a slender budget of $880,000.

But when shooting began in January 1969, the simple low-budget picture turned into a financial quagmire. The Valley of Fire became the Valley of Thunderstorms. Heavy rains and technical and logistical problems caused the production to fall ten days behind schedule in its first month of shooting. Peckinpah took his frustrations out on the crew. He fired thirty-six people from the production, an average of one a day. The dismissals grew so frequent that a car was kept on location for the express purpose of carting the fallen from the set, and a shuttle service transported casualties to the Las Vegas airport and fresh fodder out to the valley. Sam terminated camera mechanics, assistant directors, caterers, drivers, an animal handler, a set dresser, a projectionist, a gaffer, grips, a makeup man, and production manager Dink Templeton.

Sam had hired Sharon and her boyfriend, Gary Weis—a talented still photographer—to shoot a 16mm documentary on the making of the film. But far from being fascinated by the assignment, Sharon was disgusted by the way her father treated the crew and outraged by the use of small animals in many of the scenes.

The screenplay for *Cable Hogue* dictated that as Hogue

scratched out an existence from the barren desert he would kill lizards and rattlesnakes, rabbits and birds for stew meat. Sam insisted that live animals be used, and that some of them be killed on camera.

When Gary Weis learned that Sam intended to squib a live lizard for one shot and blow it up in slow motion to simulate the reptile's being shot by a rifle, he mounted a "Save the Lizard!" campaign. "I started leaving these phantom notes around, on Sam's car, on the bulletin board at the hotel where all the production notices were posted," says Weis. "They'd say things like, 'To kill a lizard on Thursday is bad luck for a hundred years—Akira Kurosawa.' I always signed the names of Sam's idols on them."

Weis' efforts were in vain. Sam blew the lizard up anyway.

Sharon was horrified. Looking at all those rabbits trapped in their tiny wire cages, knowing they would be slaughtered for a scene in a movie, was unbearable. It was Simbo's puppies all over again; it was the way she, her sisters and brother, everybody and everything came second to his films that infuriated Sharon, and she told him so. Sam shot back at her, "Who do you think is paying for your education?" and ridiculed her as naive. But it was bluster—Sharon's verbal darts were drawing blood.

"She and Gary really got to him," says Gill Dennis, an AFI intern on the production who ended up codirecting the documentary. "They were making him feel *so guilty*. Every time Bobby Visciglia took a rabbit off to kill it for a shot, Gary would film it and *zoom* in with the camera, you know?"

The final confrontation came when Sam summoned Sharon and Gary to his hotel room one night. He launched into a tirade against his eldest daughter, accusing her of disloyalty. Did she have any idea how stressful it was to direct a movie? Under such high pressure he needed all the emotional support he could get, but instead she had betrayed him.

Sharon's anger matched his own. She told him she didn't believe in what he was doing. "Do you think making a dumb movie is going to be worth hurting so many people? All the people you've fired, all the people you've humiliated and degraded, do you ever think about that?"

Suddenly, Sam burst into tears. "You've got to get out of here," he cried.

"I'm out of here!" Sharon said, rushing to the door.

"That was a weird moment, it made me choke up a little," says Gary Weis. "It was weird, he broke down, he *cried,* tears, sobbed. It was off-putting. It made me feel sad."

Cable Hogue finished principal photography on April 1, 1969, nineteen days behind schedule; when finished with post-production it would rack up a final negative cost of $3,716,946, almost $3 million over its original budget—much to Phil Feldman's displeasure. Feldman thought it was a nice little picture, but at a price tag of nearly $4 million, he saw little chance of it ever turning a profit.

After wrapping the picture, Peckinpah returned to L.A. and finished post-production on *The Wild Bunch.* Then, as that picture went into release, he left for Hawaii in July, where he would do the bulk of the editing on *Cable Hogue* with Frank Santillo, that master of montage who had cut *Ride the High Country.* When Lou Lombardo had put the finishing touches on *Bunch,* he also joined the team.

In the fall Peckinpah returned to Warner Bros. for the final phases of post-production: looping, scoring, and dubbing the picture. By this time the Ted Ashley–John Calley regime had taken hold of the reins at Warner Bros. Because the picture had been green-lighted by Ken Hyman, they had no vested interest in it. If it laid an egg at the box office they could simply chalk it up as another of Hyman's failures and claim a hefty tax write-off.

And when a two-and-a-half-hour rough cut of the film was shown, without Sam's knowledge, to Warner Bros. distributors in August, they were convinced that an egg was exactly what they had. The movie was funny in parts, but disjointed, too long, and the ending a real downer. Sam was horrified that it had been screened in such a rough form. "This was not a fine cut," he explained to Garner Simmons, "it was a rough cut without the final soundtrack or music track."

Sam and Phil Feldman were barely on speaking terms, but they put up a united front in an attempt to save *Cable Hogue.* Feldman explained to the Warners brass that another half-hour would be cut from the picture. He urged them to hold their judgment until they saw the final product. But the executives were not moved by this appeal. A few suggested reshooting the ending. Instead of having Cable Hogue die in the end, why not have him run off to New Orleans with Hildy, the whore with a heart of gold, and live happily ever after? Even Feldman was appalled by this suggestion, which subverted the entire concept of the movie. When he backed up Sam's refusal to compromise, the executives shrugged it off. They gave Peckinpah a free hand to finish the film his own way, not out of respect for his artistic talent, but out of apathy. The picture was simply not worth the hassle of another battle with Peckinpah.

Feldman was hoping the previews would save them. If audiences liked the picture, certainly the Warners brass would have to change its attitude. With its running time now hovering at about two hours, *Cable Hogue* previewed at theaters in Long Beach and New York at the end of January and beginning of February. Seventy percent of the reaction cards rated it from good to excellent. But this was not enough to change Warners' attitude about the picture. *The Ballad of Cable Hogue* was dumped into second-rate theaters across the country with barely a ripple of publicity—one billboard on Sunset Boulevard, an ad in the trades, only quarter-page ads in newspapers, and no radio or TV advertising at all. "Warner Bros. didn't release it," says Stella Stevens, "they flushed it."

Though some critics found its allegorical style heavy-handed and pretentious, the film won many raves that were every bit as good as those for *The Wild Bunch.*

But the reviews were not enough to save *Cable Hogue.* After a couple of weeks in second-run theaters it sank to the bottom half of double bills on the drive-in and grind-house circuit, then disappeared altogether. By 1973 it had grossed a grand total of $2,445,863.

Devastated and enraged, Peckinpah denounced Warner Bros. at press conferences and in interviews and sued the studio for damaging his professional reputation. The suit had no legal grounds to stand on and Warner Bros. eventually had it thrown out of court.

In later years, when he appeared on college campuses and at

film festivals, the movie Sam Peckinpah most urgently wanted audiences to see was *The Ballad of Cable Hogue.* He frequently referred to it as his favorite film, and it's easy to see why, for it exposes the tender inner core of this turbulent, often misunderstood artist.

Today, over twenty years after its release, it plays as a startlingly unique and stylized film, but flawed in one of its most central elements: the love story between Cable and Hildy. The relationship between the two is strangely (by Peckinpah standards) underdeveloped. The "Butterfly Mornings" montage in which Robards and Stevens sing to each other, bathe each other, pick flowers together, and serve each other breakfast in bed, are disturbingly absent of genuine feeling—as empty as the "Raindrops Keep Falling on My Head" sequence in *Butch Cassidy and the Sundance Kid.* If *The Wild Bunch* displays the incredible range and depth of Peckinpah's artistic vision, *Cable Hogue* reveals its limitations.

Those limitations are not of craftsmanship or creativity—*Hogue* is brilliantly crafted; its audacious staging and luminescent imagery confirm Peckinpah as one of the great originals of the American cinema. The limits are defined by the psychological scar tissue of the artist himself. Peckinpah had been many times more powerful, convincing, and insightful when depicting the failure of love in *Noon Wine,* and would be again in his next film. It's no accident that the most genuinely moving moment between Robards and Stevens occurs in the dinner scene, where Cable's vindictive jealously drives Hildy away. Sam knew that moment very well.

But the love scenes themselves, which Sam intended as an "affirmation of life," remain as flat and facile as a Hallmark valentine card. The calendar-girl image of Hildy reveals an innate flaw in his vision of women. They are adored as beautiful objects, longed for from afar, they are to be fought for and possessed, but they are never really understood as human beings in their own right. (The exception to this is older women, such as Olivia De Havilland in *Noon Wine* or Ida Lupino in *Junior Bonner.* When they are no longer ripe for sexual conquest, Peckinpah has an easier time discovering their humanity.)

But when *Cable Hogue* shifts its focus to the allegorical tale of a Wild West entrepreneur who found water where it wasn't, it works superbly. At its core, the film is yet one more act of mourning for the death of the Old West. Nowhere before or after did Peckinpah dramatize its demise with such self-conscious stylization. The film's dream imagery—passionate, bizarre, and warmly sentimental—matches the best of Fellini.

Sam was still taking off for the the mountains of eastern Nevada every fall on his annual hunting expeditions with the Walker River Boys. But now even the crisp snowy air of the High Country bore the unmistakable whiff of Hollywood hysteria.

He wasn't quite finished editing *Cable Hogue* when he left for a week in the Shell Creek Mountains in November 1969. The next day Lou Lombardo received a call in his editing room at Warner Bros. It was Sam, phoning from his hotel room in Ely. He'd had a sudden inspiration about the film and needed to talk to Lou immediately. "Get your ass up here, Lombardo, right now!" One couldn't fly into Ely, so Lombardo and Frank Kowalski got a plane to Las Vegas, rented a brand-new 1969 Thunderbird, loaded it up with cases of beer and Jack Daniels, and headed northward into the night.

"We're drinkin' whiskey, flyin' down the fuckin' road, nobody on it," says Lombardo. "We get to Ely the next day, to this hotel, and we just missed Sam. He'd left for the campsite up in the mountains. What is Ely but a hunting town with a lot of brothels? We don't go to bed. We missed him, we'll go in the morning, so we sat down at the blackjack tables and played all night and I won eighteen hundred dollars, and in those days, on a thirty-dollar-limit table, that's hard to do. Frank Kowalski will try to tell you he won all the money, but he's lying. Frank was too drunk to even read the cards. I was the one who won it."

"Did Lou tell you he won all the money?" Kowalski demands with an angry gleam in his eye when the subject of the trip is brought up. "He's a liar. He wouldn't know how to win eighteen hundred dollars at blackjack if his life depended on it. I won the money. I played all night; they kept switching dealers on me, but it was one of those lucky streaks. I just couldn't lose and I knew it, so I just kept playing and winning."

Finally, at 6:30 in the morning, they checked into a room and got a couple of hours of sleep. When they awoke, refreshed and ready to hit the road again, Kowalski counted up the money bulging in his jeans and had a sudden inspiration: "Let's buy out the brothels in town and take the girls up to the camp!"

They went to three different brothels, rented six girls, stuffed them in the Thunderbird, and roared up into the mountains. Following the directions Sam had left for them, they got up to the general area of the hunting camp but couldn't find the dirt road they were to turn off on. They sped back and forth along the same stretch of highway, twice passing a group of cowboys loading cattle into a trailer truck. The cowboys' leathery heads swiveled as the T-bird and its glittery cargo rocketed by. On the third pass one of them signaled for Lombardo to stop. "You must be lookin' for Peckinpah."

"Yeah, where's he at?"

"Go up that dirt road there about five miles through the trees; when you come out the other side they're camped up there. But be careful, you can't go up that road with a Jeep more than five miles an hour."

"Well," says Lombardo, "now I'm flyin' up this fuckin' road and there are rocks comin' up through the floorboard of this new Thunderbird. Boom! Bam! Bong! It's dusk and we burst into camp. They're all sitting there around the campfire and here we come screaming into this campsite, girls are falling out of the car and they're screaming at me, and I walk over to Sam, and he says, 'What kept you?' "

The next morning Sam asked to borrow his older brother's camper so that he and Kowalski could return the girls to their various establishments in Ely. "Okay," Denny said, "but have it back here by four o'clock this afternoon."

"No problem," Sam said, and took the keys. And off they went down the mountain and into town. One thing led to another, and Sam and Frank didn't start back for camp until nine o'clock the next morning. All the way up the mountain Sam gripped the wheel white-knuckle tight and muttered anxiously about how angry Denny would be and what he might do.

When they pulled into camp it was deserted. Everybody had gone hunting—except Denny. He was sitting by the fire, leathery face focused on the pale flames, as if he hadn't noticed the prodigal's return.

Sam and Frank hopped out and called to him with false cheer. "Hi, Denny!" Denny gave no response. The air was stinging cold and they stepped up to the fire opposite him to warm themselves. There was a long, incredibly uncomfortable silence, then Denny got up and walked around the fire toward his younger brother with all the righteous bearing of Steve Judd himself. He stopped beside Sam, eyes burning, and said softly, "You lied to me."

"Sam was white, absolutely white," Kowalski recalls. "I'd never seen him like that before. He didn't say a word to Denny, he couldn't even look at him."

Denny pivoted slowly away from Sam and shifted his gaze to Kowalski, saying just as softly, "And you lied to me too." Then he turned from the fire and walked away.

With the release (or flushing) of *The Ballad of Cable Hogue,* the wild and heady days at Warner Bros. came to a close. Had the film been a hit, Sam Peckinpah might have had a much different career. But *Hogue*'s failure solidified the Hollywood power brokers' perception that Peckinpah was an "action" director, a high-toned version of Andrew McLaglen or Michael Winner. With only one splendid exception, the projects Sam managed to find financing for after this were riddled with gunfire, high-speed car chases, and spurting blood. He would have to snatch fragments of poetry and meaning between the falling bodies before the characters slapped another clip in their weapons and opened fire again.

Peckinpah's lawsuit and public attacks on the new regime at Warner Bros. ended his relationship with the studio. Warners had announced plans to produce another Peckinpah film, *Summer Soldiers,* but it abruptly canceled the picture. And Sam lost out on two other juicy projects, John Milius' *Crow Killer,* which eventually became *Jeremiah Johnson,* and an adaptation of James Dickey's harrowing novel, *Deliverance.* In both cases the writers lobbied hard for Peckinpah to be signed as the director, but Warners refused.

Dickey met personally with Sam to discuss how he would go about adapting *Deliverance* to the big screen and to see if there was any way to get Warners to reconsider. "I wanted Peckinpah because I thought he was the best action director there's ever been in movies, and I liked his work very much," says Dickey. "We talked for the better part of a whole day. When we shook hands to say good-bye, he said, 'Well, you know, if they don't let me do this movie, we'll do something later on. But always remember this, you and I are doing the same thing, me with my images up on the screen and you with your words on the page. We're trying to give them images that they can't forget.' I said, 'I go with that, you bet.' " But Dickey's efforts were in vain; Warners wanted nothing more to do with Peckinpah.

Now a free agent, Sam made the rounds of various studios and independent producers, trying to find financing for *Castaway, The Hi Lo Country,* and adaptations of two other Max Evans books, *One-Eyed Sky* and *My Pardner.* But producers considered these properties either too weird or too "soft." Where were all those famous Peckinpah ballets of blood?

There were two other novels that Sam was eager to turn into movies: Joan Didion's scathing behind-the-scenes vision of Hollywood, *Play It As It Lays,* and Ken Kesey's awesome masterpiece, *Sometimes a Great Notion,* which told the story of an Oregon logging family that bore striking similarities to the Peckinpahs. But producers wouldn't even consider Sam because they assumed that the psychological subtleties of both books were beyond his grasp.

Daniel Melnick was eager to break into features, so Peckinpah took *Castaway* to him, but like Feldman, Hyman, and almost every other producer Sam ever showed it to, Melnick didn't know what to make of the weird nightmare piece. He was certain, though, that he didn't want to make a movie out of it.

But Melnick owned the rights to a novel, *The Siege at Trencher's Farm*, by a Scottish writer, Gordon M. Williams. He had shown it to Martin Baum, the head of the newly formed ABC Pictures, a division of the television network. (The fees that networks were having to pay to air theatrical features had begun to skyrocket, so ABC decided to cut out the middleman by producing its own movies.) Baum agreed with Melnick: *Siege* had the makings of a strong "action" picture. It told the story of an American college professor who moves with his wife and daughter to a cottage in the English countryside, where he hopes to find peace and quiet and time to finish writing a book. But the family is terrorized by a group of local hooligans who, by the climax of the novel, lay siege to the American's farmhouse. The college professor is forced to defend his family, and with his back against the wall does so savagely and successfully.

It was pure exploitation melodrama with a plot as old as movies: the meek bookworm is finally pushed to the brink, his passive façade is cracked, and he turns on his tormentors with the wrath of a wild cat and emerges victorious. The story had been used in hundreds of western, gangster, and boxing pictures, even by comedians like Buster Keaton, Harold Lloyd, and Harry Langdon. Moviegoers had seen it over and over again, but, like salted peanuts, they could never get enough of it.

Melnick thought the tissue-thin narrative and characters could be turned into something of substance. He saw possibilities in a story about an East Coast liberal-pacifist who is thrust into a violent inferno, forced to fight for his life, and thus to confront his own repressed barbarity. If anyone could make an important film out of it, Peckinpah could.

Martin Baum, who'd seen and loved *The Wild Bunch*, agreed. Melnick had already commissioned a screenplay from David Zelag Goodman, who had written *Lovers and Other Strangers* and the adaptation for Jack Schaefer's classic western novel, *Monte Walsh*. But Baum didn't like Goodman's script, so ABC offered Sam $200,000 to rewrite it with Goodman and to direct the picture.

Once again Sam was being asked to spin flax into gold, and Baum and Melnick had promised to give him a free hand. He respected and trusted Melnick, but it was not without a twinge of bitterness that he accepted this assignment; he had told the press on several occasions that he would never make another bloodbath like *The Wild Bunch.* Trapped in the Hollywood high-stakes game by his own financial and psychological needs, he felt he had no choice. One night in late May 1970, shortly before he left for London, Sam sat up drinking in the Malibu Colony house that he had been renting since wrapping *Cable Hogue.* With him was Joe Bernhard—his pal from Fresno grade school who had abandoned the Hollywood rat race and now lived, like Hogue, in a ramshackle cabin in the grassy hills of Madera County. Sam affectionately called Joe "Orr," after the one flier who escaped the insanity of World War II in *Catch-22.* "All right," Sam said to Bernhard when the bottle between them was nearly empty. "They want to see brains flying out? I'll give them brains flying out!"

He rented a tastefully furnished two-story flat at Eaton Mews, smack in the heart of London; his $500-a-week tax-free per diem made it easily affordable. Ken Hyman had set up a production company in London and was operating out of Universal's headquarters at Piccadilly and Hyde Park. He got Sam a suite in the same building and introduced him to the city's movie-making elite. Everyone was eager to shake hands with the big-time Hollywood director who'd come to London to make his first European film—Peckinpah was even more revered in England than at home.

The nights were filled with exciting new adventures; no city swung like London in the late sixties and early seventies. But Sam's days were consumed by an all-too-familiar horror: writing.

Martin Baum was right; David Goodman's script needed a lot of work. But Goodman was a solid craftsman and he had given Sam what was so essential: a solid structure and the basic components of the characters and their dramatic conflicts.

What was it about this story, Sam asked himself as he thumbed through Goodman's script a second and third time—why did American audiences hunger to see it again and again?

A decent, peace-loving man is besieged by evil forces rushing at him from all directions. Finally the mild-mannered hero is pushed to the brink and transformed—like Jesus at Armageddon—from pacifist to righteous warrior. It was a fantasy of potency for middle-class men—men besieged by bill collectors, domineering bosses, marriages gone cold for reasons too convoluted to comprehend, and inner demons that gnawed at their self-esteem. Gathered together in the cloaked darkness of the theater, audiences could revel in the spectacle of a heroic alter-ego laying waste to surrogate enemies, conquering life instead of being conquered by it.

That hidden rage seemed to be racing up through the fissures of the American landscape and spewing out everywhere: the Manson Family, Charles Whitman—the former altar boy and Eagle Scout, an architecture honor student who climbed to the top of a twenty-seven-story tower on the University of Texas campus and proceeded to methodically shoot forty-five of his fellow students, killing twelve. ("Boy there was an honor student, the good guy, the Boy Scout leader who was kind to his mother and small animals," Sam later said. "Whether he enjoyed shooting all those people isn't the issue. The issue is that he did it. He had all that violence in him and he went up into the tower and let it out.")

And then came My Lai, the massacre of 567 innocent Vietnamese villagers by a platoon of American soldiers led by Lieutenant William Calley. The American soldier was no longer a broad-shouldered, straight-talking, benevolent warrior dispensing goodwill, cigarettes, bubble gum, and justice from the barrel of his Thompson submachine gun; he was a mad-dog killer, Charlie Manson in uniform.

Meanwhile, from New York to California students were taking over college administration buildings and shutting down classes to protest the war. On May 18, 1970, National Guardsmen at Kent State fired into a group of students who had been hurling rocks at them: four were killed and eight wounded. The civil rights movement had also turned bloody. Twenty-eight Black Panthers had been killed in the last two years in shootouts with police, and in 1969 alone there had been over 2,000 bomb scares in New York City and eight actual bombings of such stalwart capitalist institutions as the RCA Building, Rockefeller Center, the General Motors Building, and Chase Manhattan Bank.

"Everybody was fighting against the violence," Peckinpah

later observed, "fighting against this, fighting against that. Everybody had it in them."

Peckinpah had recently read two books by a playwright and self-taught anthropologist, Robert Ardrey: *African Genesis* and *The Territorial Imperative.* Marshaling an impressive armada of evidence gathered by paleontologists, biologists, and anthropologists, Ardrey argued that man's voracious appetite for violence is not the product of a negative socioeconomic environment, as Karl Marx and other sociologists believed, nor the product of traumatic childhood experiences, as Freud contended, but was caused instead by powerful instinctual drives.

Man was a carnivore, argued Ardrey, a murderous ape who had learned over the centuries to fashion ever more sophisticated weaponry with which he bludgeoned and hacked his way to the top of the food chain—a killer with a natural love of slaughter and an instinctive impulse to fight for the control of a sphere of territory, for himself, his family, his tribe, his nation. This, explained Ardrey, was why the history of man was written in blood, why it was marked by the bleached headstones of war after war after war. It was a good fight, the exquisite pleasure of murder that man lusted after more than sex, Ardrey explained—it was the control of territory, not women, that most men battled for.

The eroticism and horror of violence and man's fascination with it had been just one theme among many in the epic tragedy of *The Wild Bunch,* but in *Siege* it would become the focal point. To engage his audience on an emotional level, to force it to confront its own conflicted feelings about violence, Peckinpah would have to reach down into his own guts and yank up a fistful of entrails. When it came to his own demons, in life Sam Peckinpah was secretive, evasive, desperately self-deceptive; but in his art, with the mask of characters and a story to hide behind, he plunged into his soul's darkest regions with ruthless courage. In the many interviews that followed the release of this film he cited Ardrey's theories and talked about man's innate violence and the need to come to terms with it. But never once did he talk about how deeply personal the movie was, how he had infused the material with his own torment, except to admit ambiguously that "every one of my films is autobiographical."

But anyone familiar with the details of his parents' marriage, and his own to Marie and Begonia, could see what he drew up out his own past and siphoned into the finished film. The tortuous process began with the script. Once again he rewrote it scene by scene. The copies of the drafts survive in his files, the pages stained by coffee and cigarette ashes spilled as he scribbled new dialogue and scenes in margins and on the reverse sides. Some of the sequences sprang forth fully formed and would survive, barely altered, in the finished film; others would go through numerous rewrites by Sam, and later Goodman, Dustin Hoffman, and the other actors.

Peckinpah shifted his protagonist's inner conflict from that of a worn-out liberal struggling to overcome a sense of moral impotency to that of an apolitical intellectual who struggles to repress his passions, most particularly his incredible rage, which he tries desperately to hide from others and himself. Sam grounded that rage not only in hidden primitive instincts, but also in the accumulated resentments of a bad marriage.

Peckinpah eliminated the couple's daughter and made them both younger. The wife would now be barely twenty and beautiful—a native of the village who had gone to college in America. The script implied that she had been the professor's student there and married him in the heat of mad crush. Now she's brought him back with her to England and the bloom is wilting quickly from the rose. When the couple make love or express affection in Sam's rewritten scenes, it is with the flirtatiousness of high school kids. This interaction is charming at first, but as it keeps recurring the lack of depth builds a disquieting tension. The young professor, David Sumner, tries to contain the relationship emotionally, to keep it within a safe, compartmentalized box that will fit neatly into his labeled and filed life. Yet subconsciously he senses the shallowness of his marriage and resents it, even though he is the one who set it up. Again and again he sticks blades of sarcasm into his wife, Amy, subtly ridiculing her for her lack of intellect.

For her part, Amy is stung by David's patronizing attitude and craves attention, her only source of self-esteem. When she doesn't get it she, like Fern Peckinpah, finds manipulative ways of striking back at her husband. She sneaks into his study when he is absent and alters the convoluted equation on his blackboard (he's an astrophysicist), changing a plus sign to a minus. Several mis-spent hours later he will discover her little "joke." She walks outside to where the burly workmen from the local village are erecting a garage for them and begins flirting, knowing that David is watching from inside the house. She interrupts his work constantly with requests that he perform minor chores, or by barging into his study to flirt, then acting hurt when he kicks her out.

The dynamics match precisely those between Sam and Begonia at Broad Beach, when he would lock himself up in his office to write for hours on end, leaving her adrift in the alien Malibu landscape.

Amy's flirtations with the village workmen open a Pandora's box. Already envious of the American professor because of his money and his beautiful wife, the workmen begin to subtly, then not so subtly taunt and humiliate him. Then, one night, David finds their pet cat strangled by the light chain in his bedroom closet. Amy claims the villagers did it to prove they could get into his bedroom and presses David to confront them, but he refuses. "Listen, I'm not going to accuse them . . ." he protests. Instead he tries to win their friendship. They appear to warm to him and invite him to go hunting in the woods the next day.

When the finished film was released many critics would attack it under the assumption that David Sumner reflected Sam's contempt for introverted intellectuals, but if David Sumner represented anyone it was Sam Peckinpah. Not the knife-throwing wildman of the countless magazine profiles, but the inner Sam, the one who hid behind the mirrored sunglasses, the bandannas and barbed one-liners, the tag along runt of the litter at Dunlap's Ranch, dwarfed by the Peckinpah men who towered all around him, who craved their approval but was often ridiculed instead for being a shy, self-conscious bookworm.

Following Charlie Venner, Norman Scutt, and the other men of the village into the woods, David Sumner is handed a shotgun almost longer and heavier than he is and shown how to load it. He handles the gun awkwardly and the other men snicker, but as Sam notes on one script, "he grins with them, just happy to be a part of it." They take him out to a remote forest meadow and leave him there, literally holding the bag, telling him they will drive the birds to him. "We'll be spread about—iffen need us, call," says one villager, Cawsey. David nods resolutely, determined to earn his place among men, and answers, "I'll be here."

Then, of course, they ditch him. David waits there for hours before realizing he's been had.

Meanwhile, back at the farmhouse, Amy's former lover Charlie Venner arrives at her front door. He invites himself in; there is some bittersweet banter about the old days, then he forces himself on her. She resists, he slaps her around, she gives in, reluctantly at first, then passionately—all the pent-up frustrations, anger, and unmet passions of her soured marriage released in a frenzied coupling. It starts out as a rape scene, turns into a sad and tender love scene, then veers hideously back into rape when a second villager, Norman Scutt, shows up on the scene with a shotgun in hand. Venner's loyalties shift in an instant from his old girlfriend to his tribal comrade. He helps hold Amy down while Scutt brutally rapes her. Amy doesn't enjoy it this time, not at all.

And through it all David Sumner stands in a lonely field, holding an empty bag. It was a clip right out of Sam's worst anxiety-attack dreams, the nightmare of the cuckold; Sam knew how David Sumner felt at that moment. But he knew also that the cuckold is rarely an innocent victim, but often as guilty as his betrayer. Peckinpah later explained: "[David] set it up . . . There are eighteen different places in that film, if you look, at it, where he could have stopped the whole thing. He didn't. He let it go on . . . As so often in life, we let things happen to us because we want it to . . . I've had to lecture twice now, really, about the film to psychiatrists . . . They say, 'How did you find out about this?' Well, I got married a few times."

The trauma and all the sordid imagery it conjured haunted and fascinated him. He couldn't stop playing and replaying it in his mind. And each time it took on greater malevolence, pathos, and erotic power. It was no longer a real event, but a recurring nightmare that he'd never be free of.

Having no knowledge of its roots in Sam's personal life,

many critics attacked the scene as the ugliest of male-chauvinist fantasies. It would earn Sam Peckinpah a foremost place in the feminist hall of infamy, and become a prime illustration in women's studies courses in universities across the country of Hollywood's debasing of women as wanton sex objects who enjoy nothing better than a good rape.

The story came to a climax when David Sumner accidentally hits the village idiot, Henry Niles, while driving home one foggy evening. The simpleton is cut up and bruised, but not seriously hurt. David takes him home and calls the town pub. Unbeknownst to him, earlier that evening Niles accidentally strangled a young girl from the village, and now the villagers are looking for the missing girl and Niles, who was spotted walking away from a church social with her.

Sumner's phone call alerts them to the retarded man's whereabouts, and soon a group of drunken vigilantes are pounding on the door of the American's isolated farmhouse, demanding he hand Niles over to them. Included in their number are Venner and Scutt. Sumner refuses to hand Niles over to a mob: "They'll beat him to death," he explains to Amy. His last stand begins on solid principles, but soon more primitive instincts take over: "This is my house! This is where I live! . . . This is mine! Me! I will not allow violence against my house!" And as the battle escalates to orgiastic heights, David Sumner descends into a murderous rage more frightening and effective than that of all of his attackers combined.

"Violence usually begins with a reason, with some principle to be defended," Sam told one interviewer. "The real motivation, however, is a primitive thirst for blood, and as the fighting continues reasons or principles are forgotten and men fight for the sake of fighting." But clearly David's pump has been primed from a wellspring of disillusionment and despair. Whatever fantasies he still harbors about saving his marriage are shattered when, in the middle of the siege, Amy attempts to abandon him for Charlie Venner.

It's the moment where David Sumner gets the blindfold pulled off, where he finally sees Amy and his marriage for what it really is. "In marriage so often," Sam later said, "especially if the man is lonely, he will clothe her [his wife] in the vestments of his own needs—and if she's very young she'll do the same thing to him. They don't really look at what the other person is, but at what they want that person to be. All of a sudden the illusion wears off and they really see each other."

It's this intolerable realization that causes David Sumner to explode. Afterward, when his living room is littered with bodies, he exclaims, elated, "Jesus Christ . . . I got them all!" By perfecting his skills as a killer and smothering his more vulnerable emotions—as D. Sammy had by becoming an expert hunter and an equal at last in the eyes of the Peckinpah men—David Sumner has passed a bloody rite into manhood. But at what cost? For Sam Peckinpah personally the price had been a stiff one, and he was still making payments on it.

When the finished film hit the theaters more than a year later, many critics would attack it as a fascist celebration of the joys of combat; just as many would defend it as an antiviolent statement that cautioned us against our own innate savagery. Peckinpah himself switched from the first interpretation to the second from one interview to the next. Sometimes he seemed to embrace both interpretations in the same interview, even in the same breath.

He told William Murray of *Playboy:* "He [David Sumner] didn't know who he was and what he was all about. We all intellectualize about why we should do things, but it's our purely animal instincts that are driving us to do them, all the time. David found out he had all those instincts and it made him sick, sick unto death, and at the same time he had guts enough to stand up and do what he had to do . . . True pacifism is manly. In fact, it's the finest form of manliness. But if a man comes up to you and cuts your hand off, you don't offer him the other one. Not if you want to go on playing the piano, you don't. I'm not saying that violence is what makes a man a man. I'm saying when violence comes you can't run from it. You have to recognize its true nature in yourself as well as in others and stand up to it. If you run, you're dead, or you ought to be."

David Sumner, Peckinpah seems to be saying, is horrifying

yet admirable, both hero and a villain. This dichotomy lies at the heart of the film. The movie is not a simplistic statement about violence being "good" or "bad." Instead Sam uses the story as a vehicle for probing his own profound ambivalences about violence. "Why do we hunger to see such bloody tales over and over again," he is asking his audience, and himself. "Why are our heroes all killers? What does this say about us?"

This would not be an antiseptic thesis film, but a profoundly personal exploration by a man who told one person that his boyhood years spent learning to hunt in the Sierra Nevada had been the best in his life, then told another friend they had been his worst; who had spent a lifetime passionately pursuing a mythical Wild West fantasy life but now was just beginning to perceive its corrosive effects on him.

It would remain an open-ended film, without answers, for he himself had none. "I always thought that what he was doing was putting things on film that he did not understand," says Gill Dennis. "You know? I thought he was saying, 'Here, look at this. How does this fit into your scheme of things?' " Sam later told an interviewer: "I'm defining my own problems. Obviously, I'm up on the screen."

Peckinpah turned in his first rewrite of the screenplay in late August 1970. Martin Baum and Dan Melnick loved it, though it would continue to go through rewrites for the next four months with Sam, Goodman, and Melnick all making contributions.

Baum also insisted that the title had to be changed. A demographic study (which was just emerging as a powerful marketing tool in Hollywood) told ABC that most people thought *The Siege at Trencher's Farm* sounded like a western. Sam came up with *Straw Dogs.* He'd gotten it from a passage in *The Book of 5,000 Characters,* by the Chinese philosopher Lao Tzu, that read, "Heaven and Earth are ruthless, and treat the myriad of creatures as straw dogs: the sage is ruthless and treats the people as straw dogs . . . Is not the space between Heaven and Earth like a bellows?"

Baum couldn't make heads or tails out of this Chinese mumbo-jumbo, but *Straw Dogs* had an intriguing ring to it—enigmatic, allegorical, it suggested hidden depths of meaning without spelling anything out. Instead of ordering another demographic study to test its marketability, Baum went with his instinct—*Straw Dogs* it would be.

Now they were ready to go after a star. After batting several names around—Beau Bridges, Stacy Keach, Sidney Poitier, Jack Nicholson, Donald Sutherland—they finally decided on Dustin Hoffman. Hoffman read the script, screened some of Sam's films, and signed on for $600,000. Before he was brought on board, ABC had envisioned *Straw Dogs* as a leanly budgeted "little" picture. Now it had suddenly become the company's most important production. The budget was doubled from $1,070,221 to $2,117,263, and the film was given a sixty-one-day shooting schedule, quite generous considering it required only one location and a few interiors. The adrenaline began to pump both in ABC's Hollywood offices and in London, where Melnick and Peckinpah cranked into pre-production.

It took a very special breed of secretary to cope with Sam's around-the-clock madness. He burned through a half-dozen in London before Katy Haber walked into his life. A voluptuous twenty-six-year-old with a rich mane of coffee-colored hair and sharp, intelligent eyes, Haber was a lightning-fast typist with brilliant management skills and a computer-like mind for detail. She would become the primary organizational force in Sam Peckinpah's life for the next seven years, and one of his most complex dark and twisted romantic entanglements.

Haber had seen plenty of darkness before meeting Peckinpah. Her parents were Jewish refugees from Czechoslovakia; they had escaped just three days after the Nazis marched into Prague. "They were the only members of my family to get out," says Haber. "They lost everybody." A poster-sized picture of one of her aunts, who was burned in a death-camp oven, now hangs in a Czech museum that documents the horrors of the Holocaust.

Katy was born in London in 1944 and sent away to boarding school when she was twelve because her parents feared they would spoil their only child and the last blood relative they had left in the world. When Katy was eighteen, her mother fell ill. Her father was convinced she had cancer. Unable to face the loss of another loved one, he committed suicide. It turned out Katy's mother did not have cancer. She recovered, but Katy didn't. The shadow of her father's death—all the guilt, the intense fear of abandonment—hangs over her to this very day.

She scuttled plans to enter a university, went to secretarial college instead, and then went to work as a production secretary on a series of undistinguished comedies and horror pictures.

Just a few months before meeting Peckinpah, Haber was offered a job by an English producer who was doing a picture in Hollywood, but she turned it down because it would have meant leaving her mother alone in London.

Then James Swann, the associate producer for *Straw Dogs*, called Katy up and asked if she'd be interested in working for this big American director who'd come to London to make his first movie in Europe. It sounded interesting, so Katy agreed to go in and meet him. When she walked into the office she found a graying but handsome man with a neat mustache sitting behind a cluttered desk in a pair of beige jeans and an Italian leather jacket. "Katy, this is Sam Peckinpah," Swann said.

Two huge hot hazel eyes swiveled up at her. "Well, are you ready?" he said abruptly.

"What are you talking about?" Katy's face felt warm.

"I've been through about six women. None of them can read my writing."

"He'd hired these girls and they wanted lunch breaks and wanted to be out by six," says Haber. "With Sam that doesn't exist—lunch, tea breaks, having your hair done and having dates, being with other people—it just doesn't exist. If you're with him you don't have another life and that's it."

"Sit down and start typing," Swann said, gesturing toward a desk with a typewriter and a disheveled pile of stained pages covered with Sam's chicken scratch.

Katy complied. They were Sam's script revisions and the very first thing she typed up was the rape scene. *Jesus, who am I working for, Jack the Ripper?* she wondered. It was tough following the circuitous path of his scribbling up and down margins and around onto the backs of pages. But she liked it. The script was bleak as a moonless moor, but riveting. She worked till midnight, much to Sam's amazement. "He was overwhelmed," says Haber. "You know, here was someone who could finally do it all."

She worked straight through till Sunday for him, typing away while Sam was on the phone to Jason Robards, Dan Melnick, and Marty Baum. He began taking her out to dinner with him after work; she met Jerry and Camille Fielding and Frank Kowalski, who were in London at the time. (Kowalski was on Peckinpah's payroll, writing the treatment for *Bring Me the Head of Alfredo Garcia.*) "It was very exciting for a nice little Jewish girl who was supposed to marry a doctor, move to the suburbs, and have babies," says Haber. "Then one night while we were working late, Sam said, 'When I'm working with somebody it always becomes a very close relationship.' I knew what he was intimating and I said, 'I never mix work with pleasure, Mr. Peckinpah.' He laughed. He had these eyes, they were so loaded with emotion; they were so powerful, they drew you in, but at the same time they made you want to turn away."

It didn't take them long to draw her in. "I fell in love with Sam very quickly," says Haber. "I'd never experienced anyone like him before. He seemed so sophisticated compared to the boys my own age whom I'd been going out with. I'd been in love before, but never like this. At first it had been something that I didn't want to get into, but it was stronger than I was. I had intended to keep it on an even keel. Then one thing led to another. He was a very charismatic man. He didn't force himself on me, he was just very entertaining, larger-than-life, and I fell for it. He knew how to pour it on thick with the roses, the notes, the phone calls. He told me, 'I can't live without you, you're everything I've ever dreamed of in a woman. You've got everything I ever would want. You make me feel fulfilled.' It's awful hard not to be seduced by that."

But Katy quickly discovered that Sam had two sides. One night they went out to dinner with Dan Melnick. It was a pleasant evening filled with exciting talk about the picture. Sam was drinking heavily, beginning to slur his words, and almost knocking glasses over when he swung his hands to emphasize remarks.

Katy had a lot of work waiting for her back at their apartment and decided to leave early. She got up, said good night to Melnick, then Sam, and left. Sam was still not back when she went to bed around midnight. A couple of hours later she awoke to the sound of screaming. It was Sam, standing over her, spewing a stream of curses. He yanked her out of bed, struck her across the face, and began picking things up—the alarm clock, a water glass, a table lamp—and smashing them against the walls. Finally, he wheeled on her, bellowing his first coherent sentence, "What the hell is going on between you and Dan Melnick?"

"It was all because I had said good night to Melnick first before leaving the restaurant," says Haber. "He was convinced we were having an affair. I told him that was ridiculous, that I wasn't the least bit interested in Melnick, that I was just being courteous."

The next morning Sam was apologetic, obviously mortified, but avoided full responsibility for his actions by claiming he'd been drunk and couldn't really remember what he had done—which may have been true; more and more frequently he was experiencing alcoholic blackouts. "He never fully admitted his guilt for things like that," says Haber. "He would offer a roundabout apology. But I know he felt terrible, you could see it in his eyes. After every one of those incidents he took on a little more guilt, and because he could never really talk about it it just accumulated."

She quickly learned to handle Sam's jealousy by devoting her attention exclusively to him when other men were present. If another man in the room started to pay too much attention to her, she would immediately go and sit or stand beside Sam, direct her attention to him, and distance herself from the others so there could be no doubt where her loyalty lay.

Katy quickly assumed control of all the day-to-day details of Sam's life. He definitely needed a steady hand on the tiller, and Katy provided it. She kept track of all his phone calls, his appointments—both business and personal—paid his bills, bought gifts for his kids, relatives, and friends, made all his travel arrangements, kept copious notes during all his meetings, and during filming kept track of all the shots he needed to get on a given day and the myriad production details that he needed to attend to.

Sam would often praise Katy to others, both in her presence and when she was absent, admitting that he couldn't have gotten past this or that obstacle without her. But just as often he would turn on her, snarling invectives with an entire movie crew looking on until Katy finally fled in tears. Many felt sorry for Katy and disgusted by Sam's sadistic treatment of her.

But others in the inner circle noticed that Katy often seemed to provoke the attacks with manipulative behavior. Says one former member of the Peckinpah Bunch: "Nobody deserves to get hit, there's absolutely no excuse for it. But Katy would egg Sam on. She was with him for seven years, she must have known what would trigger him. On one movie we worked on she brought up a conversation she'd had with the producer, who Sam hated and was at war with. The producer had complained to Katy and now she was going over their conversation word-for-word in front of Sam. Finally, Sam said, 'Okay, I don't want to hear any more.' He kept trying to change the subject and she kept coming back to it until finally he exploded and shoved her. It was as if she had gotten what she wanted. She could then play off his guilt for having done it and play the martyr."

Meanwhile, unbeknownst to Haber, Sam was also having an affair with Ken Hyman's secretary, Joie Gould, a slender but shapely blonde in her mid-twenties, with big eyes, a sharp wit, and a vivacious personality. Sam started seeing her shortly after his arrival in England. "It was amazing, physically, when you first met him, after you'd heard so much about him," says Gould. "You imagined he would be this great big tall John Wayne–type guy, but he wasn't big at all, he was very slender, and in his eyes, he was *so* vulnerable. Our courtship went on for months. For the first few weeks we met for lunch; I only saw him during the day."

Then they started going out to dinner together. Sam would dress very elegantly, but always with a pair of cowboy boots beneath his slacks. He reminded her of James Garner in "Maverick": the gentleman cowboy, handsome, smooth tongued, utterly charming. During the eight months they dated before *Straw Dogs* started filming she never once saw him drunk, never once saw him have more than a couple of martinis with a meal. "He hid that side of himself from me."

People kept warning her: "He's not for you. Don't get involved with him." She'd heard the stories about his drinking and brawling. "But I never saw any of that behavior. He was the most courtly, gentle man you could imagine. I never saw him angry. We never so much as had a disagreement."

He was so thoughtful, so attentive. He was always buying her funny little gifts, sending her breathtaking flower arrangements and little cards with touching endearments on them. He was obviously brilliant, incredibly well read, and loved to spontaneously make up poems and haikus. She could easily picture him teaching a literature course in a quiet little college somewhere.

The warnings only increased his allure. She knew there had to be some truth in them, but believed their blooming love had had a calming effect on him. She'd brought him the peace and contentment he'd always yearned for; she, at last, had made his life whole—he told her all this, and she believed him. She was going to be the one to change him.

By this time Katy was aware of their relationship but did not know that they had become lovers. "He told me that he was having dinner with her and stuff," says Haber, "and that it was rather serious, but I thought they were just friends."

It was when *Straw Dogs* went into pre-production that Joie noticed the first disquieting changes in Sam. He told her, "I've really got to do my homework on this thing because I'm working with Hoffman." He grew tense, restless.

"When he got ready to shoot a film it was as if he was going away to war," says Gould. "He expected the producers to betray him at every turn, that the film would be taken away from him. The creative concentration took every ounce of his strength. Dealing with all the elements—the actors, the producers, the crew—and all the conflicts, it took a tremendous toll on him. That's when the heavy drinking began."

He gave her the script to read and the characterization of

Amy left her aghast. "What a horrible woman!" she told him. "She has no redeeming qualities, not a single one! Why is David married to her?"

Sam shrugged. "Well, maybe you should rewrite some of her scenes. See if you can make her more sympathetic." She did just that, but when he read her pages he rejected them as "too sentimental."

By now Joie had begun to see the deep insecurities behind Sam's self-assured façade, and how *Straw Dogs* was his Rorschach inkblot. "He'd tell me how young and beautiful and smart I was. He said I could have any man I wanted, and he couldn't understand why I'd picked him."

He began interrogating her, his voice softly encouraging intimate disclosure, but ominously persistent; his eyes probed hers for the slightest flicker of insincerity. If the timing had been different, he insisted, she could easily have fallen in love with someone else. "How about Dustin Hoffman, do you think you could have fallen in love with him if you'd met him before you met me?"

"No, Sam, look, I love you!"

"Come on, you can at least admit to the possibility, can't you?"

"He was always playing that game," says Gould, "always testing your loyalty."

Take away all the artifice—the cowboy boots, mirrored glasses, and throwing knives—and, Joie realized, Sam didn't really believe he was that interesting. Beneath it all he saw himself as David Sumner: small, inadequate, dull. "If a woman fell in love with him, he couldn't understand it. He never really believed me when I told him that I loved him. It was very sad."

But he wanted to believe her, very badly. On the back of one of his scripts Sam one day penciled: "Joie says, 'Who you are, what you feel, and who you love are totally different in each person. If you can't see the love in my eyes you'll never see it anywhere.' " He tried to see it there; in his own warped way he was looking for it, but all he found in her gaze was his own doubt.

Joie's attempt to rewrite Amy gave Sam a sudden inspiration: "You could play the part! I'll cast you! You'll bring all of your natural sweetness to Amy, you'll make her sympathetic simply by being yourself!" An alarm went off inside Joie's head, and not because she'd never acted before. But she couldn't pinpoint the exact cause of her anxiety. Sam's enthusiasm overcame her doubts. She did a screen test with other actors and met with the costume designer to discuss possible wardrobe. When they ran her test in the projection room the response was very positive from all but Sam, who brooded. She had definite star potential, the others were saying. Dan Melnick suggested she get a nose job.

"The positive reaction from everybody made Sam very anxious," says Gould. "I don't think he ever seriously thought I'd play the part, and when it became a real possibility he was very alarmed. I said, 'Well, you started it all.' He said, 'Yeah, but I didn't expect anyone to like you.' I said, 'Well, thanks a lot!' Finally he said, 'You've got to choose between me or a career as an actress!' That was fine with me, I never wanted to be an actress to begin with."

What was going on here? The costumes used for Amy in the final film bore a striking resemblance to Joie's own wardrobe, and Dustin Hoffman wore many items that could have been pulled out of Sam's closet. (Peckinpah was dressing—coincidentally or purposely—more preppily than he had in the States.)

Peckinpah was not only using his own past as raw material for the film, but manipulating his present, himself and the people around him, to help feed the psychodrama. A dangerous game, as Joie would learn the hard way.

Meanwhile the search for the real Amy continued. Among the actresses considered were Judy Geeson, Jacqueline Bisset, Diana Rigg, Helen Mirren, Carol White, and Charlotte Rampling. One of the most intriguing candidates was Hayley Mills, the impish blond child star of such squeaky-clean Disney flicks as *Pollyanna* and *The Parent Trap*. Then twenty-four, Mills was trying to make the tricky transition into adult roles. And what a transition it would have been, but Sam realized that despite the possibilities the choice would have been too camp.

Finally, a twenty-year-old actress named Susan George walked through his office door. George had been acting in television since age four and had recently appeared in sex-kitten roles in such British features as *Lola, The Strange Affair,* and *The Sorcerers.* Her performances demonstrated no shining talent; like so many movie starlets, she skated by on her stunning looks (which were strikingly similar to Joie's): blonde, olive-skinned, with bright hazel eyes, full round lips, and a body that could have been sculpted by a Greek master. Certainly all that got Sam Peckinpah's immediate attention, but it wouldn't have been enough to win George the part. As soon as she walked into the room he felt it: a palpable sensuality and, just beneath it, the claws of a wildcat.

"From our very first meeting I think he gleaned the idea that I was bright," says George. " 'You're smart, kid!' he'd say with *loathing,* he couldn't bear it! This was the great love-hate relationship that I had with Sam, it really was love-hate from beginning to end. He knew I was smart and a thinker, and he knew I was wicked, and all of it was attractive to him, and yet he would have loved to rip it all away from me so that I would have to go and claim it back. I thought: God, who is this person, he's frightening the life out of me! But I stood up to him, I stood up to him from the beginning, and he absolutely loved that in me. I never let him know what he was doing to me."

Sam had found his Amy. George was signed for twelve weeks' work at $10,000 a week.

On January 22, the cast and crew moved down to the rolling countryside of the Cornwall peninsula on the very southwest tip of England. Here all of the exteriors for the picture would be shot in the village of St. Buryan, and at a nearby farmhouse that would serve as the Sumners' residence. Dustin Hoffman and Susan George spent days wandering around the village doing Actor's-Studio-style improvisations to develop a relationship that paralleled the characters in the film. David Goodman followed them, scribbling down their exchanges, some of which were incorporated into the film.

For the actors who would play the villagers who lay siege to the Sumners' farmhouse—Peter Vaughan, Del Henney, Ken Hutchison, and Jim Norton—Peckinpah orchestrated slightly less gentle "improvisations" to get them into character, namely a series of drunken parties that often ended in brawls. T. P. McKenna broke his arm at one of these improvs and was forced to wear it in a sling throughout the shooting of the movie. Ken Hutchison responded to this approach with great gusto, and one "Indian-wrestling" match between the young actor and his director left both with swollen and bleeding faces. Sam threw an affectionate arm around Hutchison after they'd fought to a draw and dubbed him his "Dog Brother."

"It was all very calculated on Sam's part," says Hutchison. "He was setting the tone for the movie and our characters. It was a very dark, violent piece. I mean, we weren't making *Mary Poppins.*"

"There was a definite self-destruct mechanism in Sam, no question about it," says Susan George. "But he found his match on that movie with Ken Hutchison. Ken was his soulmate. Ken was as stupid at times and volatile and as frightening as Sam was. Hoffman and I came back to the hotel one night after being out together all day and this fight was going on in the middle of the dining hall. I thought: oh God, no, not another one! Because we were always coming back to these barroom brawls. I said to Sam, 'Oh, please, don't do it! Please, don't be so stupid!' And it was going on and on, eventually they smashed into some glasses on a table and Ken cut his arm. I had to take Ken to the hospital. But I was always the one who could talk to Sam when this was going on. When he hurt Ken I was furious with him. I stopped them from fighting. It troubled me greatly. Sam would listen to me; he hated to hurt me. He treated me as if he was my boyfriend and my father."

Peckinpah kept drinking heavily, day and night, throughout rehearsals and even after shooting started, much to Dan Melnick's alarm. "Whenever I walked by Sam on the set," Melnick recalls, "he'd say, 'Would you like some coffee?' To prove that it was just coffee, not coffee and brandy. And I knew that as soon as I walked away Katy Haber gave him the coffee from the other thermos, which had the brandy in it."

Two weeks into shooting, Peckinpah's around-the-clock carousing pushed his body to the breaking point. It was 3:30 in the morning. Ken Hutchison had gone to bed early for once; he had several tough scenes to do the next day. Suddenly his hotel-room door blasted open. There stood Peckinpah in a Mexican poncho and Indian headband with a bottle of tequila in his hand. "Dog Brother," he croaked, "let's go see the sea."

Hutchison looked out his window. A winter storm was hurling rain down out of a tar-black sky. He said, "Sam, it's raining. It's 3:30 in the morning."

"Let's go anyway."

"Anyone else in the world, I'd have gone ape," says Hutchison. "We went down to the car park and got in my car and drove fifteen minutes through the storm to Land's End. This is the furthermost southern tip of Britain, surrounded on three sides by the English, French, and Irish seas. We got out of the car, walked to the point in the dark. The wind and rain was coming in every direction. We sat down, listened to the sea, drank the tequila, and he taught me the lyrics of a song called 'Butterfly Mornings.' I found out later that it was from *The Ballad of Cable Hogue.* Pissed as two farts, wet, cold, in the middle of winter—never been so happy in all my life."

The next morning Sam showed up on the set, red-eyed, flushed, and coughing badly. His behavior became erratic, and his direction chaotic. The next day, the fifteenth of principal photography, Sam's cough and coherency were even worse. In those two days of shooting the company had fallen a day behind schedule.

Both Melnick and Dustin Hoffman were deeply concerned. The producer had to make one of the toughest decisions of his career. "I closed the picture down because Sam was getting really out of control. I told him that I would close the picture down for good or replace him if he went on drinking."

A doctor was called in to examine Peckinpah. He diagnosed walking pneumonia and said Sam had to be hospitalized immediately. After wrapping the seventeenth day of shooting, with the company now four days behind schedule, Sam left by train for the London Clinic.

Melnick placed a call to Martin Baum in Los Angeles. There was no doubt in his mind, he told the studio head, that Sam's boozing had triggered the illness. Sam's contract was suspended "until further notice," and Baum got on a plane to London.

Upon arriving he looked at the dailies. They were terrible, chaotic. Hoffman had had enough. He wanted Peckinpah replaced and suggested Peter Yates. Melnick said he would go along with whatever decision Baum made. The production head decided to pay a personal visit to Peckinpah at the clinic.

"I spoke to Sam," says Baum. "He was in a drunken haze. I said, 'Sam, you're sick. If I fire you, you're never going to work again. If I keep you, I've *got* to have your absolute promise that you will be sober and steadfast and responsible for the remainder of the picture. Sam, forget me, don't do it for me. If you're fired and replaced on this movie, who's gonna hire you?' I think the honesty with which that was stated won his respect. There was no bullshitting him, it would be out of my control, I couldn't justify continuing with a man who was going to behave the way he had behaved. He knew what was at stake. He gave me a hug and promised me that he would do the best he could to make it a brilliant film. And he did, he straightened himself out. That built a tie of mutual respect between us."

Peckinpah was in the London Clinic for five days. The downtime cost ABC over $85,000, but most of the loss would be picked up by the production's insurance coverage. Sam's treatments included injections of vitamin B12, which helped restore the nutrients that all the alcohol had burned out of his system. He was so impressed by the injections' restorative powers that he took a supply of syringes and needles back to Cornwall with him and had Katy give him a vitamin shot every day. It became a ritual that continued for the next seven years. Many a writer, producer, and editor would be startled by the sight of Peckinpah nonchalantly dropping his pants in mid-conversation so that Haber could jam a needle into his butt. Afterward he'd pull up his trousers and continue the conversation as if nothing unusual had occurred.

When the company resumed shooting again on February 22, Sam had not quit drinking, but he had reduced his intake considerably. There would be no more late-night expeditions to Land's End. One more time he picked himself up off the barroom floor and returned to the fight. All the fears, the self-doubt, the reluctance to paddle out upon the film's cold dark waters dropped away now. In Martin Baum he had a new father figure to prove himself to. "I have bet on people all my life," Baum cabled Sam after he was back on his feet. "Some, like Sidney Poitier, Cliff Robertson, Red Buttons, and Gig Young have thanked me publicly as they picked up their Oscars. Others have thanked me privately for their hits. Now I bet my last chips on Sam Peckinpah. I believe in your talent and courage and your total dedication. Good luck."

Once again Sam summoned up that fierce intensity, that all-consuming commitment and total focus. All the company felt it, emanating from him like a force field. Sam arrived on the set at 8:30 A.M. his first day back, completed his first setup by 9:55, and by the end of the day had seven minutes and forty-five seconds of printed film in the can. The tension between him and Hoffman melted away as everyone put their shoulder to the wheel and really went to work.

"It was a tough experience," Hoffman would later say. "But I liked working with him [Peckinpah]. He had the spontaneity of a child. Suddenly he would come up with things that were very exciting."

By the time they started shooting the exterior night scenes of the siege at the farmhouse on March 1, they were moving in high gear. Sam was in his element. "It was a very hard shoot, physically," says Peter Vaughan. "There was a lot of camaraderie between the whole unit and Sam. It was a very happy, but hard shoot. The hours were long, it was cold. The roles were quite demanding, physically: breaking up the house, firing guns, getting my foot shot off. Sam would say, 'Go through there!' And you went through the window. The fact that the curtains were on fire didn't make any difference; if Sam said you go, you go. We actually did break that farmhouse apart; it was an extremely violent couple of nights' work. It moved very fast, Sam shot with great speed. It was an extraordinary thing to do, from the acting point of view. We were really hyped up. You just don't stroll casually through a window which was on fire. There were stuntmen, but the definition of what a stuntman does and what an actor does gets a little blurred when these things get exciting."

Once the hysteria started to flow, Peckinpah found it difficult to shut off the valve, and now it washed over his personal life like a flash flood.

He wasn't staying at the hotel anymore. Production supervisor Derek Kavanagh had rented a house for him nearby. Shortly after moving into it, he called Joie in London and asked her to come down and stay with him. Joie—already uneasy because of the dark waters she'd seen stirring before he left—said no. "He wasn't used to people defying him," she says. "He blew up, got very angry, and hung up the phone. But then he called back the next day, very contrite and very gentle. 'Why don't you come down next weekend? I really need to see you.' He kept working on me that way until I said yes."

Katy Haber, incredibly, still didn't know that Sam's relationship with Gould was romantic, nor about his other liaisons. She believed she was the only woman in Sam's life, his one true love. But that illusion was shattered when Joie arrived in Cornwall.

"I went to pick Sam up one morning to take him to the location, and there's Joie in bed with him," says Haber. "I was devastated, I was in total shock. I had to sit there and wait for Sam to get dressed and all the while she's just lying there in bed completely oblivious to me. Can you imagine how I felt? She had no respect for my feelings, what it did to me. The unspoken message was, 'I'm here now and you're out.' "

Katy became hysterical. Sam said, "Look, don't you understand, we can't be involved sexually while I'm shooting a picture. We can't have both a working relationship and a sexual relationship and the picture has to come first. Don't you understand that the work is more important? If you can't cope with it emotionally, then you'd better leave."

And so she did. She didn't quit the picture, but instead went back to Twickenham Studios in London to work in the production office. "I wasn't going to quit altogether," Haber explains. "I was learning more about making movies than if I'd gone to the British Film Institute for two years."

But Joie had won no great prize. She was shocked to discover the change in Sam since he'd left London. He was still drinking heavily in the evenings and on weekends. Around the actors and crew she, like Haber, learned to be on her guard. It was dangerous to pay attention to anyone else besides Sam, especially Del Henney or Ken Hutchison—the two who would rape Amy in the film. The slightest smile or exchange of pleasantries with another male would throw Sam into a fit of jealousy.

By the time they returned to the house in the evenings his eyes were two red pulsing sores and his mood swings were rapid and unpredictable. He flew into a rage at the slightest provocation. And the abuse wasn't just verbal anymore.

"Sam had been working all night, and drinking," says Joie. "We were sitting upstairs talking and suddenly he got up and started wrecking the entire room. He took a lamp and broke all of the windows in this room. And then he started beating on me. It had come out of nowhere. I was scared, I had never been hit by a man before, it was so shocking to me. It was so dramatic. It was very very dark, it was the middle of the night. I had watched him shoot the last of the siege that night and now the exact same thing was taking place, only now it was real! It was really weird. I ran downstairs and out of the house."

The cast and crew had been having a party that night to celebrate the end of shooting in Cornwall. Driving home from it, Del Henney came upon Joie, bruised and disheveled, wandering along the side of the road. He picked her up, took her into town, and let her sleep in his hotel room. Henney didn't stay, he doubled up with someone else that night so Joie could have the room to herself. "Later Sam found out about it and assumed I'd slept with him," says Gould. "The poor guy, he got in the middle of this and he was just trying to be so helpful. He was so nice, he never asked any questions. Everyone left the next day to go back to London. I was so embarrassed. People knew that I was there, obviously, because the news must have gone around, but not one person came in to see if I was okay. I remember watching everyone leave the hotel. I left on my own the next day when everyone had left."

When the rift with Joie opened up, Katy Haber rushed in to fill the gap. But she soon discovered that Joie was only the first in a long line of betrayals: "Sam had this amazing ability to seduce women," says Haber. "It was unbelievable. A female reporter would show up. 'Hello, I'm so-and-so with *The L.A. Times,* I'm here to interview Mr. Peckinpah.' I'd take her back to see Sam, then go off about my business. I'd go back a half-hour later to see how it was going and there the two of them would be in bed together! Actresses, socialites, women from all walks of life, women you'd never in a million years expect would be susceptible would leap right into bed with him."

But Katy endured all the women who came and went over the next seven years, for in the end Sam always came back to her, or rather, called her back to him. "He was with me longer than any other woman, outside of Marie," says Haber. "He relied on me one hundred percent to run his life, yet emotionally, he expected me to take anything he dished out. I know for a fact, without lauding myself, that I was one of the most important people in his life. And yet it was very difficult for him to accept. He didn't want women to have control of his life, he didn't want *anyone* to have control of his life. The fact that he relied on me on so many different levels was something very difficult for him to cope with. A lot of his lashing out at me was just for that reason. 'I don't need you!' But at the same time he realized that he did, which was real tough for him."

"After the affair with Joie, Dad treated Katy more like a servant than a girlfriend. She was an emotional stand-by," says Melissa Peckinpah. "If he had done that to me I would have gotten as far away from him as possible. But Katy came back, she always came back. I always thought she was a leech. Dad felt suffocated by Katy's intense attachment to him, so he'd do something really cruel to push her away. Then Katy would develop some independence and start to stand up on her own two feet and Dad would get attracted to that and pull her back. It was one of the most dysfunctional relationships I've ever seen."

But it wasn't all bad, Katy told herself. There were times, many times, when Sam could be wonderful—warm, funny, incredibly generous. He taught her the film business inside and out—writing, producing, and directing. She sat in on all the conferences where the most important creative decisions were made both on and off the set. Today she is a producer herself, something that never would have happened without Sam Peckinpah. "He expanded my whole life. One of the most generous things he ever did for me, he bought my mother her apartment. That was ten thousand dollars. I was going to buy it. There was an apartment that came up to be purchased and then he said that he wanted to buy it for her."

But twenty years later, after many hours of therapy, Katy realizes there were deeper reasons why she clung so desperately to Sam's coattails. "I think it had to do with my father's suicide. I had never looked at what it meant to me, how I felt about it. My therapist says I put up with all that abuse from Sam because he was a father figure to me, and I didn't want to lose my father's love again. My father abandoned me, and I was willing to put up with anything not to be abandoned again."

After completing the exteriors for the picture, the company moved to Twickenham Studios in London to shoot all the interiors of the Sumner farmhouse: the early scenes that established the conflicted dynamics of the couple's marriage, the siege from the Sumners' point of view, and the rape sequence.

"During the early part of the film," recalls Dan Melnick, "where Susan George was the princess come back to the village with her husband, Sam and Dustin and everyone was loving to her. Then, as the conflicts in the marriage progressed, they started behaving toward her in a mean way. She was being totally manipulated. I was very upset about it and spoke to Sam a couple of times. I said, 'Listen, you cannot treat this young woman this way.' But that's what he did."

"Sam and Dustin fed Susan off-camera lines that had nothing to do with the script," says Ken Hutchison. "It was to get reactions. I mean, some of the words that were used to get some of the reactions were pretty unbelievable."

"Wait till your parents get a load of this rape scene we're gonna shoot, baby," Sam would murmur from beneath hooded eyes. "How do you think they're gonna react, think they'll be proud of their precious girl then? . . . Roll it, please!"

"I dreaded that rape scene," says George. "Sam kept saying

he was going to shoot the greatest rape scene ever put on film. He went on and on about it and he'd be very visual in his descriptions of the things he was expecting, physical things that he was going to film. He kept talking about it and it was getting bigger and bigger in my mind, quite out of proportion. It had started out as a small scene and now it was becoming a trilogy, and I was getting scared."

Finally she went to Melnick and said, "Look, I need to sit down with someone and talk about this. I want to know, on paper, what we're expecting of me in this scene, I really do! Because I'm not sure what Sam's expecting, it's getting larger by the day. I'm not sure if it's just me thinking it or whether it's him thinking it. So I need to get a few things straight."

Melnick smiled warmly, patted her on the shoulder, and cooed in his FM-disc-jockey voice, "I think the best thing for you to do is sit down with Sam and talk to him about it."

So she went to see him one day after shooting, in his office. As usual he was throwing knives. He hurled three of them into the wooden door not two feet from her head. "Are you finished?" she asked, lips drawn tight around her teeth.

"Yeah, sit down, kid."

She took a seat opposite his. "Look, I want to talk about the rape scene."

"What do you want to talk about?"

She shifted uncomfortably in her chair. "I really need to talk about it, exactly what we're going to do."

"What do you mean, what we're going to do? What, do you want it written down?"

"Yes, actually, I would love it written down. I know that sounds funny, Sam, but I would love it written down. Then I could take it home and go over it and make perfectly sure that I can do all the things that you require me to do."

"I'm not writing it down."

"But if you don't write it down and I don't know what you're expecting, it's becoming an insurmountable problem for me and it's bothering me. If we could talk about it from A to Z I'd be really thrilled."

He leaned forward, pointing a forefinger at her. "Listen to me, when you took this picture, did you or did you not agree to do this rape scene?"

"Yes, I did."

"You said you'd do it."

"Yes, I did, but I lied."

"You what?"

"I lied. I lied because I wanted to get the role and the rape scene was in the picture, and now I'm not sure if I can do it."

Suddenly he was on his feet; a knife flew, quivering into the wood-paneled wall. "What do you mean you don't think you can do it?"

"I just don't think I can do it."

"Well, you'll have to do it! I'm gonna make you do it!"

She was trembling as she rose to her feet as well. "All right, Sam, find yourself another Amy." Then she stormed out of his office and ran across the parking lot in floods of tears. Melnick appeared, as if popping up out of the asphalt, and stopped her. "What happened, what happened, what happened? Have you spoken to Sam about the scene?"

"Yes, and I've just walked off the picture!"

"You *what?*"

"I've walked off the picture."

"Don't be ridiculous. That's ridiculous, child, you can't do this! Go back and see Sam."

"I'm not going back into that room, he's positively livid with me. He's ranting and raving and screaming and throwing bowie knives. I'm not going back up there. I've just told him to find himself another Amy."

"You can't do this. You'll be sued by the production company, your career will go down the tubes!"

She walked anyway. The next day Melnick made several frantic phone calls to the actress and her agent, John Redway, who finally coaxed George into going back for another meeting with Peckinpah. "I was terrified," she says. "I walked into Sam's office and he was very quiet, *very* cold."

"You want to see me?" he demanded.

"Yes, I do. I need to see you because I think this is silly, really, because I've walked off the picture and I don't think you want me to walk off, and it's all because I'm frightened. You won't help me with that fear that I have, and I'm only asking you to tell me what you want me to do. That will help me not to be so frightened."

Peckinpah's face thawed a few degrees. "All right, I'll tell you what I want to shoot."

"He wrote down everything on a piece of paper," says George, "and it was awful, horrendous! I wish he hadn't written it down. It was ghastly, worse on paper than when he'd told me about it."

"I can't do that," she said, "I just can't do these things."

"Well, how else do you propose to show me these emotions?"

"Well, I propose to do it through my eyes. If I'm the kind of actress that you think I am, and the kind of person that you think I am, I think I can tell you everything with my eyes. If you focus on my eyes and my body movements, I promise you I will lead you down the road you wish to be led down. I will make you believe every bloody moment of it."

She could see the gears whirring behind his eyes. The sequence was important to him, very important, she knew that. "I want to shoot the best rape scene that's ever been shot," he said again.

"You will! And I will do it for you. If you let me do it my way, I can give you the most provocative, beautiful, and telling rape scene you'll ever see! I can pull it off without showing pubic hair. I know I can."

He thought for a moment longer, then his face relaxed. "Okay, I'll make a deal with you. I'll do it your way, and if, when we've done it your way, I'm not satisfied . . . then we have to do some things my way."

"I understand."

They had a deal.

"So we shot it," says George. "For a week we shot the rape scene. On the first day I arrived absolutely petrified. Sam came in to work that day, and he sat with his legs crossed, in a little ball on the floor in front of the couch where I was raped, and he never moved and he never said a word to me for five days. He did talk to Del Henney and gave him a terribly hard time. He started saying things like what a dreadful lover he was. He provoked Del terribly, but he never said a word to me. When Del was on top of me he would be saying things like, 'Christ almighty! Is this it?' It was really unbelievable. I used to try not to listen to that, but he never said one word to me, just smiled at me from time to time. And he did what I begged him to do, which was focus on my eyes and upper body and let me tell the story. Sam was so volatile and lethal on the one hand, and so quiet and kind and loving on the other, that's what was fascinating about him."

"It was a difficult scene to shoot," says Henney. "It was rather harrowing, actually. But you just have to do it. Halfway into it, it turns into a sort of love scene, a tender scene. There were two forces working in the character I was playing, one of them pushing him forward and the other pulling him back. The one was pushing him to transcend his background, to be more humane. He was brighter than the others, but the other force, the peer pressure from his mates, pulled him back. That's why he ends up holding Amy down so Scutt can rape her."

"After we finished it Sam wouldn't let me go in to see the rushes," says George. "He had let me see rushes throughout shooting, but now he refused to let me in. He went to rushes alone and I went home and fretted all weekend, wondering what the consequences were going to be, whether I'd managed to pull it off or not, and just how angry he was going to be if I hadn't. I wasn't shooting that Monday, but I went in anyway at about eleven A.M. Sam had just been to see rushes and I caught him coming out of the screening room and I thought: Christ! What do I do, turn and run? Get out of the way, get back in the car, what do I do? I was standing there and he walked all the way across the tarmac toward me, stony-faced, and when he got right up close to me he put his hand out and said, 'You've got it, kid.' And he held my hand, and that was the conclusion of the rape scene."

She had captured Amy in all her conflicted, tortured passion.

It was a stunning performance, easily matching Hoffman's finest moments in the picture, and when Peckinpah was through cutting it, it would become one of the most perversely erotic sequences in cinema history.

"My character started out strong and by the end of the movie she's completely stripped, emotionally," says George. "When I shot that scene with Del Henney, Dustin Hoffman came to the studio that day. He didn't come on the set, he just came to the studio and knew it was going on inside the sound stage. And the next day he treated me as if I'd been unfaithful to him. And after that, this relationship between he and I, which had been fabulous up until then, deteriorated. It was as if I'd hurt him. I was absolutely distraught because by the end of the movie Hoffman had really cut himself off from me and become terribly distant. From a very kind and humorous and loving friendship, he had become extremely aloof. I was really hurt. I didn't see him again for years and years and years. Mind games, incredible mind games, coming from both Dustin and Sam. But that's the way they worked, and I believe to this day and always will that Peckinpah was a genius, likewise Hoffman, so I was willing to take anything and everything they had to give."

Straw Dogs finished its sixty-sixth and final day of photography on April 29, 1971, five days over schedule. Peckinpah had shot 261,195 feet of film, only a little above average for a feature at that time. But once again the footage was broken up into a staggering number of setups, and Sam printed almost all of it.

To carve the mountain of raw footage into a finished film, Peckinpah hired a stable of editors—Tony Lawson, Paul Davies, Roger Spottiswoode, and Bob Wolfe—and walked from editing room to editing room to supervise their work on the various sequences. Sam had covered each scene from a multitude of angles with little regard for matching action; often actors played scenes completely differently in the close-ups from the way they did in the long shots. The violation of continuity was intentional. Peckinpah used the close-ups as an opportunity to explore the nuances of a scene and pull out details of characterization and interaction that hadn't existed in the long shot. To a conventional editor it looked like madness, but those who grasped the possibilities found whole new vistas opening up before them.

"Sam's films were discovered in his editing rooms," says Garth Craven, who worked as a sound editor on *Dogs*, and as an editor on four subsequent Peckinpah features. "Sam didn't want you to cut a sequence the way he'd envisioned it, he wanted you to come up with ideas he hadn't thought of, and he would either reject them or be thankful for them. I remember Bob Wolfe saying to me, 'This is an editor's dream. You've got all this footage and it's unshaped and you get to shape it.' "

The most brilliant member of the team, all admitted, was Bob Wolfe, who would work on a total of five Peckinpah features. "There would be these enormously complicated sequences with thousands of feet of film and all these elements," says Roger Spottiswoode, "like the church-social scene, where Amy is having flashbacks to the rape. Bob could conceive of that scene as a finished piece, and would cut a version of it which would almost be a fine cut. If you looked at the footage he started with it was a remarkable act of imagination. That was his brilliance, he understood the inner dynamics of the scene. He was inside of what Sam was doing, more than any of us, he was able to conceive of it that way."

In June Peckinpah's editors followed him to Hollywood, where they completed post-production while Sam prepared for his next feature, *Junior Bonner*. By the fall *Straw Dogs* was ready for its first public preview at the North Point Theater in San Francisco. "We had no idea how powerful it was because we never showed it to anybody, and we'd become desensitized to it," says Roger Spottiswoode.

When the opening credits flashed on the screen, they featured not the producer's name above the title, but a new credit reflecting the rise of the auteur theory in Hollywood and the fact that Sam Peckinpah was one of its leading practitioners: SAM PECKINPAH'S STRAW DOGS. The theater was packed, and the reaction was every bit as volatile as it had been to *The Wild Bunch*.

A third of the audience walked out before the picture ended, yelling comments like "This is obscene!" as they marched up the aisles. Many of those who remained cheered Dustin Hoffman on to each escalating act of brutality. "There was this blood thirst that was horrifying," says one member of the production team who was present. "I think we were all shocked to have provoked that, we had no idea that it would have such a visceral effect on an audience."

Afterward, Peckinpah and Melnick were standing in the lobby when a small man walked up to them and asked, "Who's responsible for this film?"

Melnick straightened up proudly and purred, "Well, I'm the producer. How can I help you?"

The man began to vibrate, his face turning purple and the veins on his forehead popping out like surgical tubing: "You filthy rotten pornographer!" he began screaming. "You fucking horrible dreadful monster, how could you think of doing this to the American public! What do you mean by—"

Without missing a beat, Melnick pivoted smoothly toward Sam. "Well, as the producer I'm not responsible for contents of the picture. I think you should address your comments to the director . . ."

The little man whirled and sighted in on his new target. Sam took off across the lobby. Slaloming through the exiting crowd, he disappeared into the theater, the little bulldog still snapping ferociously at his heels.

Melnick rushed out to the stretch limo waiting in front of the theater and ordered the driver to race around to the back alley, where they screeched to a halt just as the rear exit door smashed open. Out came Peckinpah, running full-tilt. Melnick threw open the door, Sam dove in, and the car screeched off into the night, leaving the outraged pacifist panting and empty-handed.

"That was a different era in filmmaking," says Spottiswoode. "They made more chancy films then because they did less market research and they weren't scared. That was the only preview we had for the film, and I don't think we changed anything. We might have taken a minute out of it. The general consensus was we had an extraordinary, strange film and there was nothing you could do with it. There was a lot of discussion about changing the title, but they didn't do that; nobody had a better title. Today it's become automatic that you preview and you change your film according to the preview. The idea that films are tailored to the marketplace has become an accepted and dreadful fact."

ABC was much more savvy than Warner Bros. when it came to promoting a Peckinpah picture. The print ads and billboards designed for *Straw Dogs'* release in December 1971 featured a close-up of Dustin Hoffman in the wire-framed glasses he wore in the film, with the right lens shattered and the glass fragments scattered across his face. It was accompanied by captions like THE KNOCK AT THE DOOR MEANT THE BIRTH OF A MAN AND DEATH OF SEVEN OTHERS! The studio also produced some very slick thirty-second television commercials, two-minute theatrical trailers, and sixty-second radio spots that echoed the same theme.

The publicity campaign had both a good and bad effect. It certainly provoked interest in *Straw Dogs,* but the ad slogans and the commercials, which reflected the studio's interpretation of the movie's "message" but certainly not Sam's, caused many reviewers to jump to the conclusion that the film was an elated celebration of physical conflict.

Across the nation the movie incited even more polarized reviews than *The Wild Bunch* had. *Time* and *Newsweek* pronounced the film brilliant; *The Atlantic, Variety, The New York Times, Life,* and *The New Yorker* denounced it as depraved, misogynistic, and fascist.

William S. Pechter wrote in *Commentary:* "Surely, whatever his conscious attitudes toward the violence of his films, no one can stage scenes of violence with the kind of controlled frenzy Peckinpah brings to them without being susceptible to the frenzy despite his controlling it; without in some sense enjoying what he does, and it is this investment of himself, an attempted exorcism of his devils in his work, perhaps even more than his film-making genius, that makes Peckinpah at once so hard to take and so impossible to turn away from. [Stanley] Kubrick coldly lectures us that we are living in a hell of our own making; Peckinpah writhes in the flames with us, burning."

But much more disturbing to Sam than the response of critics was that of an old acquaintance from Fresno—Fern Peckinpah. "Strangely enough, my mother not only saw it, but wanted to go back and see it again," Sam wrote to a friend.

The final negative cost for *Straw Dogs* was $3,251,794, more than a million dollars over its original budget. Despite the controversy about its graphic sex and violence, the picture did only modestly at the box office. By the end of 1973 it had grossed $7,980,902 worldwide, $11,148,828 by 1983. After Peckinpah sicced a team of lawyers and accountants on the studio, the production showed a profit of $503,405, and Sam received his first share of the proceeds: $21,505.

The public furor that *Straw Dogs* provoked made Peckinpah's name the most widely recognized of any director since Alfred Hitchcock. He even became a target for the English comedy troupe Monty Python, then at its zenith of popularity on the BBC. The group did a sketch—"Sam Peckinpah's Version of *Salad Days*"—in which a genteel English lawn party turns into an absurdly grotesque, slow-motion bloodbath.

His fame had contributed at least as much if not more than Dustin Hoffman's to the success of *Straw Dogs.* His services were more in demand than ever before, but the mold they had forced him into was hardening.

He did his best to break through. By the time the film hit the theaters he was hard at work on his next, *Junior Bonner.* The script, by Jeb Rosebrook, had not a single gunshot in it, and the body count was zero. It told the story of an aging rodeo champion, Junior Bonner, who returns to his hometown of Prescott, Arizona, to find that times are changing. His brother, Curly, is converting the family's ranch into a mobile-home park. He offers Junior a chance to cash in with him by selling off the acreage in little postage-stamp lots, but Junior clings stubbornly to the life of a rodeo cowboy, a life his body will be able to endure for only a few more punishing years.

Marty Baum had sent the screenplay to Peckinpah in London in the spring of 1971 while he was still cutting *Straw Dogs.* Steve McQueen, eager to take on something more substantial than his usual action fare, had already been signed to star.

Sam sat down to read the script in his flat in Richmond. He knew by page six—when Curly's bulldozers flatten the family's old ranch house—that he wanted to do the picture. It was a page right out of his own life; he couldn't have written it better himself. And the script only improved with each page he turned. Rosebrook's screenplay unfolded with the graceful prose of a novel. The story reverberated with Peckinpah's own experiences: its depiction of a frontier family cut off from its roots, fragmented, its individual members filled with love and rage and wounded wariness for one another—longing to be reunited, yet recognizing the impossibility of that.

He agreed immediately to make the picture.

Throughout the final weeks of shooting and the first month of editing *Straw Dogs*, Katy Haber functioned as Peckinpah's right arm during the day and his lover at night. But now, as he left for the States, Sam said good-bye. He promised he would return to London and they'd work together again soon. It was not at all what she had been hoping to hear, but she affected a casual acceptance.

Katy didn't know that Sam was seeing Joie Gould again and that he was taking her with him to California. After that terrible night in Cornwall, Joie had vowed she would never see Sam again. "I mean, I had never had a man lay a hand on me before." But while he was finishing up at Twickenham Studios he had called her. His voice sounded so small and frightened on the other end of the line. He said she had to come see him, he really needed to speak to her *today.* Joie agreed to meet him in Richmond Park.

"I probably by this time was really very much in love with him," says Gould, "but I really don't know why I went down to meet him that day, because I really didn't want to. I was really scared of him and I was very confused."

They walked through the park together and Sam apologized for what had happened, his voice strangled with genuine anguish. It would never happen again, he promised. It was the siege, he explained—it had gotten under his skin and he just exploded. But he was through with making those kinds of movies. It had nothing to do with Joie, she just happened to be in the wrong place at the wrong time, and he couldn't be more sorry. It would never happen again, she had to believe him.

But she held firm that day. She told him she couldn't see him again, said good-bye, and drove home. He phoned her that night and begged her to have dinner with him. "Sam was very charming when he wanted to be. He would recite poetry, things like that. As a twenty-five-year-old girl listening to him . . . suddenly I found myself sitting in a restaurant with him, this charming, gentle man."

And so the courtship began all over again, and slowly but surely he swept her off her feet. "He was manipulating you all the time and you didn't know it," she says. He sent her flowers with haikus written on the attached cards. She began writing notes in return, with little poems in them that expressed her growing feelings for him. Sam loved them and praised her sensitivity and insight.

"He was madly romantic, and very elegant," says Gould. "I could imagine him in Paris in the twenties with Hemingway and that lot. You look back on it and you say, 'Why did I do that? Why didn't I walk away?' But you're so involved in this whole thing by that time, somehow you don't think. I don't remember ever thinking straight during the whole time I was involved with Sam. I justified all this *terrible* behavior, always justified it: 'Oh, he's just caught up in the movie. He had too much to drink and he was so tired.' I mean, you don't rationalize that kind of behavior. It's not suddenly all right because you've come up with these rationalizations. It doesn't make any sense. But I was *very* young. I was twenty-five, but a very young twenty-five. I saw everything as nice. I also liked intense, interesting people. I thought: 'Here's this very intense man who just wants to be happy. He needs someone who really loves him, who really makes him feel secure.' You think that if you do all the right things this person is going to be happy—that great misguided fantasy."

So when Sam returned to America, Joie came with him. But they were only in L.A. a few weeks when he provoked a terrible argument, then took off for Arizona to begin shooting *Junior Bonner,* leaving Joie stranded in a strange, sprawling, smog-smothered city. She couldn't go back to London, not after having told all her friends she'd be gone for six months. She couldn't face the staring faces, the subtle I-told-you-so's. So she stayed in L.A. and picked up secretarial work at the various studios through her friends in the business. "But Sam kept tabs on me that whole summer," says Gould. "I had a number of temporary jobs in Hollywood and he knew every person that I worked for. I guess he just didn't want to be involved with me while he had a movie to shoot, and I was still very much in love with him."

After Sam left London, three eternal weeks passed before Katy heard from him again. Living and working with Sam had often been a nightmare, but she missed the thrills of the roller-coaster ride. Everything seemed so mundane, so pointless now that he was gone, and she missed the dire sense of purpose that a Peckinpah production provided. The prospect of working on an ordinary movie again made her spirits sink. Then came the phone call. He barked, without so much as a hello: "Get your ass over here!" He'd already gone through a couple of secretaries; no one could handle him. He needed her.

Before she met Sam Peckinpah she'd turned down a job in the States because she didn't want to leave her mother alone in London. Now one phone call and she was packing her things in a frantic rush, hurrying to join a man her mother thought insane and dangerous. A leaden feeling of guilt came over her when she boarded the plane at Heathrow, an image of her mother all alone in that tiny flat, but it was quickly submerged in the excitement of rejoining Sam on another picture. She was hooked, unable to stop herself and ask why.

Peckinpah began shooting *Junior Bonner* on June 30, 1971, in Prescott, Arizona. Robert Preston and Ida Lupino had been cast as Junior Bonner's mother and father, with whom he is reunited when he returns to his hometown, and Joe Don Baker played his brother Curly. Much of the action was shot in and around the real Frontier Days Rodeo held in Prescott every year, which writer Jeb Rosebrook had often attended as a teenager. Peckinpah managed to keep tight control over his drinking throughout shooting. Most days he didn't start hitting the booze until after five o'clock. Then he'd drink steadily throughout the evening production meetings and the screening of dailies. By ten P.M. he'd be bombed, but he was back on the set on time the next morning—red-eyed and pale—on all but a few occasions.

The picture wrapped on August 17, one day over schedule but $1 million over its $2.5 million budget. The overrun was caused by a lack of pre-production time (Peckinpah had only five weeks to prepare from the time he landed on American soil till the first day of shooting, which had to start with the rodeo in Prescott) and by the high labor and equipment costs of maintaining up to nine camera crews for shooting the rodeo sequences.

Bonner was in post-production for ten months, but the time and money lavished on it paid off. The final product—which was edited by Bob Wolfe and Frank Santillo, and scored by Jerry Fielding—was a small but glittering jewel. The understated performances were as truthfully rendered, the characters as sharply observed, and the directing as quietly assured as they had been in *Noon Wine.*

ABC had expertly exploited *Straw Dogs* as a thinking man's *Dirty Harry,* but when the studio released *Bonner* in June 1972 it made the same mistake that Warner Bros. made with *The Wild Bunch.* A subtle and subdued character study, the film should have been released to a few select theaters in major cities to give it time to find an audience. But the studio treated it as just another Steve McQueen action vehicle, mass-releasing it to hundreds of theaters across the country simultaneously. McQueen himself argued strenuously against this approach, but his pleas fell on deaf ears.

But *Junior Bonner* may have had a tough time finding a large audience no matter how it was distributed. The response of critics was far from overwhelming. Both *Time* and *Newsweek,* which had raved about *Straw Dogs,* gave it a thumbs-down. Vincent Canby of *The New York Times* praised the film as a beautifully crafted slice-of-life drama, as did *The New York Post* and the *Daily News.* But most of the critics who'd marched forth to condemn Peckinpah's bloodfests in *The Wild Bunch* and *Straw Dogs* were conspicuously silent on the subject of *Junior Bonner.* The picture received scant attention from the media.

One of the most positive and insightful reviews came from William S. Pechter of *Commentary.* "Nothing much happens except that some people, the place they inhabit, and the quality of their lives are brought vividly before us," Pechter wrote, "which is to say that everything happens. At the end, as in a good novel, one feels one has known and lived with some people through a time in their lives, the moments of which crystallize into a definition of who and what they are. . . . But what is distinctively Peckinpah's own (beyond the look and feel and texture of the film, and its orchestration of first-rate performances which have been drawn even from such an actor as Steve McQueen whom I've rarely liked before) is the way it's been put together. That one can probably see the film without even being conscious of its editing is to some extent a measure of Peckinpah's achievement. For what Peckinpah has done is to create a profusely edited style in which, despite the shimmering mosaic effect, there's no sense of narrative fragmentation. . . . *Junior Bonner* provokes me to wonder whether anyone making narrative films has ever edited film more beautifully than Peckinpah. Yet I wouldn't want to isolate this accomplishment or artificially draw distinctions about my unified sense of *Junior Bonner* as being at once beautifully made and beautifully felt: rowdy and sad, a film which lives, breathes and richly fills a space."

In its first year in distribution, *Junior Bonner* grossed $2,306,120 worldwide. By 1977 that figure had more than doubled, to $4,647,876. Officially it was still $3,497,909 in the red, but, taking into account the larcenous bookkeeping of movie studios, it probably turned a small profit. (Martin Baum says, in a moment of either memory lapse or candor: "*Junior Bonner* cost so little to make, it showed a very nice profit. Absolutely, a profitable film.")

But it didn't make enough to convince the Hollywood power brokers that Peckinpah was capable of directing delicate dramas about the subtleties of human relationships. The fact was that, with seven feature films under his belt, Sam Peckinpah had made not a single commercial hit. His most renowned movies—*Ride the High Country, The Wild Bunch,* and *Straw Dogs*—had been only moderately successful at the box office. Only a runaway success would give him the leverage to pick his own material. And suddenly the opportunity for a hit presented itself.

Steve McQueen loved *Junior Bonner* despite its disappointing financial return. He was eager to work with Peckinpah again and had a property he'd been developing for First Artists, the production company he'd formed with Barbra Streisand, Sidney Poitier, and Paul Newman. Following the example of Charlie Chaplin, Douglas Fairbanks, Mary Pickford, and D. W. Griffith in the twenties, the biggest box-office stars of the seventies hoped that by forming their own company they could actually see some net profits from the films they appeared in.

The property McQueen had was *The Getaway*, a crime thriller by novelist Jim Thompson, who had won a cult following every bit as fervent as Peckinpah's. *The Getaway* told the story of Doc McCoy, a mastermind bank robber, and his lovely but deadly wife Carol, who embark on one last dangerous score. Thompson's book unfolded in a bleak landscape: the scummy back alleys and sleazy hotel rooms of a hopelessly corrupt society inhabited by a wide variety of human sharks who fed off one another without a glimmer of guilt. The vision was as dark as a black hole in space, but a young screenwriter, Walter Hill, had scrubbed away all the shadows and polished the story into a slick action vehicle. It had the potential of becoming another *Bullitt*, which had grossed $19,000,000. McQueen offered Peckinpah $225,000 plus 10 percent of the profits to direct it. Sam accepted without hesitation.

Since returning to the U.S., Sam had been living in motel rooms, Jerry Fielding's house, and in his office at Goldwyn Studios, where a small cot was set up. Most of his possessions were still packed away in boxes at Fielding's and in a storage garage in L.A. When shooting on *Junior Bonner* was completed, he sent Katy Haber to move his belongings into an apartment in Studio City that Bob Schiller had rented for him. Sam had to stay in Prescott for a couple more weeks, he told Haber, to oversee the closing down of the production.

Schiller had found Peckinpah a beautiful two-story townhouse on Acama Street, just a stone's throw from the old Four Star Studio. Haber had all Sam's possessions shipped to the new place and began unpacking. The project turned into a nightmare.

"None of the boxes were labeled. Whoever had packed the stuff up had just emptied all of Sam's things into boxes in no order whatsoever. It was as if they'd taken the coffee table and just tilted it so that everything slid into a box, and taken drawers and simply upended them. There were ashtrays with the cigarette butts still in them. It took me three solid days to get everything unpacked and the place in some sort of order."

But her labor was lightened by the fantasy that this would be the home that she and Sam would share; she was building a nest for herself as well as him. At the end of three days she stood back and surveyed the interior with a glow of pride. It wasn't much—Sam's furniture was a mishmash of unmatched pieces, and his idea of decor was some rusty branding irons and a haphazard collection of pre-Columbian art—but it was a start. Sam would be proud of her, and she imagined herself basking in his praise.

Then the phone rang—it was Sam. He said, without even a hello, "Are you finished yet?" She started to answer, but he went on, "Joie and I have been here at the Santa Ynez Inn in Malibu for two days waiting for you to finish. When can we move in?"

Her head reeled—it was worse than from any physical blow he ever dealt her—her stomach heaved, she wanted to be sick. All through the making of *Junior Bonner* he had assured her that it was all over between him and Joie, that Joie was a part of the past. Now here she was again, suddenly materialized in America like some hideous specter. Her eyes blurry and wet, she started screaming into the phone, unable to follow her own words.

When she'd finally screamed herself out of breath, Sam's voice murmured calmly in the earpiece, "Obviously you can't cope with this."

"Fuck you and everything you stand for!" She slammed down the receiver, checked into a motel in Studio City, and a couple of days later was on a plane back to London.

On the flight home guilt closed in on her. She had abandoned her mother, the only relative she had in the world, maybe the only person that really loved her in the world, and had left her alone in that tiny flat for what? To be abused, to give everything and get nothing but cruelty in return?

But three weeks later, as *The Getaway* was gearing up for pre-production, she received a phone call from Sam. "Have you got your head straight?" he said to her. "Whether you like it or not, Joie and I are living together. But we've got a picture to make. Either you want to work or you don't. Do you want to work? Are you on board or not?" The next thing she knew, she was on a flight back to Los Angeles.

Both Katy and Joie would travel with Sam to Texas for the shooting of *The Getaway*, and both would work as production secretaries there. He slept with Joie, but Katy was always at his side on the set, organizing his life for him—an arrangement that only Sam Peckinpah could slip comfortably into.

Twenty-five thousand dollars of Sam's up-front fee for *The Getaway* was to pay for whatever rewriting he did. On *Ride the High Country*, *The Wild Bunch*, and *Straw Dogs* Peckinpah had, through a painstaking process of rewriting, transformed simplistic commercial properties into profound and complex works of art. But this time was different. He suffered no illusions about the kind of movie McQueen wanted—in fact, needed, since the star had not had a hit since *Bullitt* some four years earlier, and his personal production company, Solar Productions, was now in perilous financial straits. For McQueen as well as Peckinpah, *The Getaway* offered a chance for big bucks. If it went through the roof, both would be able to exert some control over the films they made in the future; if it went into the toilet, they'd both be at the mercy of the studios.

"We're not doing *War and Peace*, Tolstoy is not writing this thing," Sam would tell Gordy Dawson the night before shooting started. "We're here to be pros—get it on, get it over with, get the fuck out. It's not *War and Peace*, it's not Dustin Hoffman, it's not Brian Keith either. It's a flick. We'll make a good one, it's going to be a good flick—people are good in it, but Steve is marvelous—he can mate with it and he knows it." For the first time, Sam did not fight to add dimension to the characters or substance to the high octane action. He'd given Jim Silke a copy of the script, and when he finished reading it Peckinpah's longtime collaborator shook his head. "The first thing I told Sam was, 'There's no second act in this script.' He said, 'Fuck you! We're not going to have a second act in this show! We're making a genre movie.' Where's the second act?—we worried about that on every script we ever worked on. But now he couldn't bother, he had to go shoot. That's where he was, he kind of gave up on that stuff. He'd get in with those movie stars. Steve McQueen was a total asshole in my opinion."

To maximize profit potential, Hill updated the story from the 1950s to contemporary southern Texas, and the picture was laid out on a lean sixty-two-day shooting schedule with a budget of $2,826,954. For the part of Carol McCoy, McQueen and the film's producer, David Foster (a former publicity man for the star), wanted supermodel-turned-actress Ali MacGraw. MacGraw had the acting range of a department-store mannequin, but her last picture, *Love Story*, had grossed fifty million dollars, so Sam readily accepted their selection. An excellent ensemble of character actors was created to support the two stars, including Ben Johnson, Sally Struthers, Al Lettieri, Slim Pickens, Richard Bright, Jack Dodson, Dub Taylor, and Bo Hopkins.

The crew was almost the same as it had been on *Junior Bonner:* cinematographer Lucien Ballard, art director Ted Haworth, property master Bobby Visciglia, editors Bob Wolfe and Roger Spottiswoode, and Gordy Dawson returning to the fold as associate producer and second unit director.

They had eight weeks to prepare from the time the production got the green light from First Artists to the first day of shooting, February 23, 1972—that was three more weeks than on *Junior Bonner*, but in this case the logistics were much more complex. The company would be constantly on the move as they followed the McCoys on their flight across Texas, from Huntsville to San Marcos to San Antonio, then west to El Paso and the Mexican border. Yet Peckinpah and his team of hardened veterans would pull it off. *The Getaway* was shot in sixty-six days, just four over schedule.

Peckinpah was at the height of his powers despite the fact that the tenuous control he'd maintained over his drinking on *Junior Bonner* was slipping away. "I'd go to pick him up to take him to the set," says Chalo Gonzalez, "and his hands had started to shake in the morning. He'd want a drink to stop them. He'd take a vodka and tonic, something light, then he'd hold up his hand and it would be steady. He'd say, 'See? Okay, now we can go.' So he'd have one or two drinks in the morning to get going."

After his first couple of eye-openers he would try to make it through the afternoon without booze. But the rule of no drinking until five o'clock was broken more often than it was kept.

"Chalo, bring me a drink!"

"But, Sam, it's not five o'clock."

Peckinpah would slouch deep into the canvas sling of his director's chair for a moment, then ask, "What time is it in New York?"

"Five-thirty."

"Then bring me a goddamned drink!"

And if Chalo wasn't close at hand, there was always Katy Haber or the short, dark-haired prop man, Bobby Visciglia, Sam's gregarious court jester and partner in crime. (The two were forever hatching new schemes for embezzling thousands from the production company. Visciglia ran his prop department as a lucrative entrepreneurial enterprise.) "I had one of those peanut-hawker trays that they use to sell peanuts out of at football stadiums," says Visciglia. "I wore it to work on the set. I had it loaded with a bucket of ice, bottles of vodka, Campari, scotch, soda, and everything else. Sam would say, 'Bobby!' I'd say, 'Yeah?' I'd be propping on the set, but I'd have this goddamned tray. He'd say, 'Well, let's try, let's see, some soda, some Campari, and a splash of vodka.' I'd say, 'Okay, Sam.' I'd fix him his drink, bring it over to his chair, and I'd fix myself a drink, the same thing. Every time he'd have one, I'd have one. All day long."

"Sam had this fucking tumbler of booze in this holder on his director's chair all through the picture," says producer David Foster. "And Bobby kept refilling it. He shouldn't have done that. It was dumb. He loved Sam, and yet he helped destroy him. I don't know where his head was at."

Yet Peckinpah still managed to put in a full day's work, and though it took him longer and longer to rev up to speed in the mornings, once he did his mind was as alert and creatively agile as ever. *Getaway* was a solidly crafted mixture of comedy, thrills, horror, and subtle subtext, balanced on a hair. Peckinpah delivered the action-picture goods and at the same time subverted them with sly undercurrents of black humor.

Sam returned to Goldwyn Studios in Hollywood in mid-May to supervise the editing of the picture by Bob Wolfe and Roger Spottiswoode. Wolfe cut the eight-minute opening sequence of McQueen cracking under the pressures of prison life, sculpting it out of the mountain of footage Peckinpah and Dawson had shot at Huntsville Penitentiary. It was the most brilliant passage in the film. "Sam wanted the sequence to build to a great climax," says Mike Klein, Wolfe's assistant on the picture. "It was Sam's concept, Bob carried it out."

Instead of following a chronological structure built out of a conventional series of scenes, the sequence jumped back and forth in time in a breathless rush of images. The soundtrack too was a montage of elements—the voices of guards urging the prisoners to work harder, the teletype pounding of the textile machines—synched not literally to the images on the screen, but to the inner reality of Doc McCoy as he reached the breaking point. And intercut throughout the sequence were flashes of McQueen and MacGraw in bed together, making love—painful strobes of memory impinging on Doc's intolerable present. The collage of images and sounds accelerated to breakneck pace as Doc's stress peaked and finally snapped, causing him to crumble a matchstick bridge that he had painstakingly constructed to fill the idle hours into a thousand pieces.

A bravura demonstration that Peckinpah was still at the peak of his craft, able to crawl inside a character's head with his camera and let us experience life through his eyes, it was also a quintessential piece of early-seventies filmmaking. The experimentation in Hollywood movies that began in the mid-sixties had now reached its apex. Two other films released around the same time—*Catch-22,* directed by Mike Nichols, and *Slaughterhouse-Five,* directed by George Roy Hill—also fragmented and molded "real" time in profound explorations of the psychological stream of consciousness of their characters.

Peckinpah's highly refined use of parallel action made the various subplots and chase sequences in *The Getaway* move like greased lightning. Though character development had been sacrificed for pace, no other Peckinpah film, before or after it, moved with such velocity.

In and around the action Sam wove a rich subtext of comic nightmare images: banks of television monitors, surveillance cameras, automated prison gates, hammering textile machines, and carnivorous garbage trucks—a labyrinth of malevolent machinery through which the McCoys have to flee.

The media, which had been indifferent to *Junior Bonner,* showed keen interest in *The Getaway* when word got out that it would be packed with Steve McQueen car chases and Sam Peckinpah "ballets of blood." *Rolling Stone* ran a cover story featuring a picture of Sally Struthers and the caption, WHY DID SAM PECKINPAH TELL STEVE MCQUEEN TO BELT THIS ACTRESS IN THE FACE? There was another feature in *Life,* with a generous spread of photos by John Bryson, as well as articles in *Esquire* ("Working with Peckinpah"), *The Los Angeles Times,* and other newspapers across the country. Almost all of these stories focused on Peckinpah—not McQueen, not MacGraw—as the central dramatic figure behind the making of the movie. (This so incensed McQueen that he fired the unit publicist from the picture.)

In August 1972, four months before the film was released, *Playboy* published William Murray's interview with Peckinpah. *Playboy* was at the height of its popularity, and its long and thoughtful celebrity interviews—Marlon Brando, Dustin Hoffman, and so on—had become one of the most prestigious plums in the world of slick magazines. Peckinpah had reached his height as a public personality. The interview was widely read and debated, since Peckinpah jousted volatilely throughout it, alternating between honest and insightful responses and answers that baited Murray and seemed calculated to further outrage Sam's detractors. It made for great copy, but comments like, "There are two kinds of women. There are women and then there's pussy," helped solidify his image as a flamboyant caricature of machismo.

After reading it, Lee Marvin, an expert provoker in his own

right, told Grover Lewis of *Rolling Stone:* "Christ, he [Peckinpah] only used the word cunt maybe two or three times in *Playboy,* for Christ's sake. There was a chance to really get it on and agitate his audience and he didn't do it."

Steve McQueen and Ali MacGraw had fallen in love during the shoot, and when MacGraw left her husband, Paramount production head Robert Evans, newspapers and magazines headlined the story from coast to coast, which provided the picture with a windfall of free publicity. First Artists promoted the stars as "the hot new love team!" and designed posters and newspaper ads with huge black copy that read simply, "McQueen . . . MacGraw," and featured wanted posters of the stars on a table-top with a .45 and bullets strewn over them. Inset into this image was a smaller picture of McQueen blowing apart a cop car with a shotgun.

Theater exhibitors crawled over one another to book the film. David Foster wrote in a memo to Peckinpah: "We are getting all the best houses throughout the country and the world, and the most lucrative terms available. Example: one Paris exhibitor has already agreed to give us a $200,000 guarantee, sight unseen. And that pattern is developing all over the place." First Artists was able to line up $7 million in such guarantees before *The Getaway* opened.

The picture's final negative cost was $3,352,254, almost $500,000 over its original budget—a substantial overrun, but Peckinpah's smallest since *High Country.* The overage was reduced by $300,000 when Ali MacGraw agreed to defer her salary in exchange for 7.5 percent of the picture's net profits. Unlike Charlton Heston on *Major Dundee,* MacGraw made the right move, since with advanced bookings of more than double its negative cost *The Getaway* made money before it even opened, and this time First Artists would be in charge of the books.

The film was released over the Christmas holidays. Judith Crist and Rex Reed, two critics Sam detested, loved it. Both had deplored the violence in the *The Wild Bunch,* but voiced no objection this time around because the bloodletting was all in good fun. Kevin Thomas of *The Los Angeles Times* also gave it a thumbs-up.

But other critics who had supported Peckinpah in the past, like Jay Cocks of *Time* and Pauline Kael of *The New Yorker*, were disturbed to see him squandering his talent on such light material.

William S. Pechter wrote in *Commentary*: ". . . the action sequences are directed with a cold brilliance, though it is somewhat dismaying to see the violence in a Peckinpah film relieved of its power to disturb and used to no other purpose than melodramatic excitement, as in *Dirty Harry* (with, naturally, the film then lauded by just those reviewers who raised the most sanctimonious outcry against the violence in Peckinpah's previous work). . . . Well, *Junior Bonner* flopped and *The Getaway* is a big hit. I only hope Peckinpah is fully conscious in this instance of just how much of a whore he has been."

Peckinpah shrugged and told interviewers that the critics had taken the movie "too seriously." He wrote to Ali MacGraw: "Anyway, the film is doing well, and what it is supposed to do, which is make over $20 million."

For the first time in his career Sam Peckinpah had a film that went to the top of *Variety*'s box-office chart. It grossed $874,000 in thirty-nine theaters across the country in the week of January 10, 1973, beating Irwin Allen's all-star disaster behemoth *The Poseidon Adventure,* John Boorman's *Deliverance,* and a Charles Bronson gangster picture, *The Valachi Papers.* During its first year of release *The Getaway* grossed $18,943,592.02—almost as much as *Bullitt* had made, and more than double what either *The Wild Bunch* or *Straw Dogs* had grossed in their first year. Because of past experience, Peckinpah was convinced he'd never see a penny from his 10 percent of the net profits, even if First Artists was keeping the books, so his eyes popped out of their sockets when the first check for $70,255.04 arrived just six months after the picture had been released. Over the next ten years *The Getaway* would gross $26,987,155, and Peckinpah would earn over $500,000 from his percentage of the profits—roughly the same amount Doc and Carol McCoy made off to Mexico with.

McQueen would earn well over $1 million, MacGraw over $400,000. Sam gave away one point of his profits to Lucien Ballard and another to Gordon Dawson.

Peckinpah's combined earnings from *Junior Bonner* and *The Getaway,* both released in 1972, would approach $1 million—mere pocket change to the whiz-kid directors who would soon storm the industry (Steven Spielberg's earnings in 1991 totaled $57 million), but in the early seventies it was enough to rank Peckinpah among the highest-paid directors in Hollywood. *The Wild Bunch* had taken him to the top of his profession artistically; *The Getaway* took him there commercially. Now he was a bankable name. His signature on a contract, like McQueen's and those of a handful of other Hollywood talents, was enough to guarantee the financing of a picture.

Considering the progression of his alcoholism and the emotional chaos that both fed and was fed by it, Peckinpah's output of five feature films over four years had been nothing short of phenomenal. He had not only been making films back-to-back, but frequently two at a time. True, he had not done anything that approached the stature of *The Wild Bunch,* but *The Ballad of Cable Hogue, Straw Dogs,* and *Junior Bonner* were impeccably crafted pictures, each startlingly original, provocative, and different from the last. And *The Getaway* demonstrated that he was still operating at the peak of his abilities. No other American director had matched him during these years.

His major rivals—Stanley Kubrick, Arthur Penn, and Mike Nichols—had much smaller outputs during roughly the same period. Kubrick directed two films, *2001: A Space Odyssey* and *A Clockwork Orange;* Penn made three, *Bonnie and Clyde, Alice's Restaurant,* and *Little Big Man;* and Nichols three, *The Graduate, Carnal Knowledge,* and *Catch-22.* Robert Altman had burst into prominence with *M*A*S*H,* but his brilliance as a satirist would prove erratic, soaring and taking nosedives from one picture to the next.

But suddenly these directors had become the older generation, a part of the Hollywood establishment they had challenged just a decade earlier. Now arriving in force was a new breed of young turks: the film-school directors. They had flocked to university cinema schools—NYU, USC, UCLA—in the sixties, where they learned the dogma of the auteur theory and watched hundreds upon hundreds of movies, burning the scenes, the lighting, the camera moves, and bits of business and dialogue into their memories.

They'd broken in to Hollywood as screenwriters, assistant directors, production assistants, film critics, wearing T-shirts that read: "But What I Really Want to Do Is Direct!" And now they were. Francis Ford Coppola had just completed *The Godfather*, which, like *The Wild Bunch*, took a played-out Hollywood genre to new Shakespearean heights. Peter Bogdanovich had established himself as a contender with *The Last Picture Show*, and Martin Scorsese was warming up in the bull pen for *Mean Streets*.

The field was getting crowded, the competition heating up, but at forty-seven Sam Peckinpah was still one of the leaders of the pack and from every indication likely to remain so for many years to come.

And now, like Doc McCoy, he had not only the money and professional accomplishment, but also the girl. On April 13, 1972, while he was still shooting *The Getaway* in Texas, a column item had appeared in the trades. It read: "Sam Peckinpah snuck off to Juarez Sunday to marry English-born Joie Gould, his steady of sixteen months. The newlyweds surprised the cast of *The Getaway*, which Sam is shooting in El Paso with Ali MacGraw and Steve McQueen."

At the end of *The Getaway*, Doc McCoy drives off into the shimmering horizon of happy-ever-after land with Carol and the money securely beside him. Life isn't like the movies; the emotions and actions of real people are much harder to manipulate than actors on a set—nobody was more painfully aware of that than Sam Peckinpah. He was fond of complaining that once he stepped out of his director's chair his life always seemed to run at least "three frames out of synch." But this time, maybe it would work out.

9

Caught in the Spotlight

I've seen you standing there stunned in the spotlight,
I've seen the sweat streak the pain on your face,
'Cause you're caught like a clown in a circle of strangers,
Who do you screw to get out of this place?
It's one for the money, and too far to go,
Three fingers of whiskey, just for the soul.
That lady you're pleasin' is hungry and cold.
Don't look in her eyes, you'll see what you've sold.
Too many bodies and too many bars,
Too many feelings of falling behind,
'Cause you're easy to fool when you're lost in the stars.
Shoot out that spotlight before you go blind . . .

written by Kris Kristofferson
on the set of *Pat Garrett and Billy the Kid*

When Garner Simmons asked Sam Peckinpah why he had married Joie Gould, he replied: "We had gotten into an argument, and I slapped her with my open hand. I really felt bad about it. So in a moment of remorse I agreed to marry her—in Mexico, where I knew that I could get a one-day divorce."

But Joie's memories of how it all came about differ sharply. "Before Sam started shooting *The Getaway* he had to go to Europe because Dustin Hoffman was making a film in Rome and Sam had to loop some of his lines for *Straw Dogs.* I went to meet him in London, just for the weekend. Then we flew back to Los Angeles together and he proposed to me on the plane and put this ring on my finger. I was so shocked. To be someone's fiancée, after the sixties no one ever got engaged. It was *so* romantic. I remember the sun streaming down in through the airplane windows as we were taking off. He went through this whole thing, it was almost corny. He gave me this little box—you know, like they do in old movies—and had me open it. He had bought me an engagement ring from Cartier. He put it on my finger and said he hoped I'd be his wife."

The second honeymoon continued throughout the shooting of *The Getaway.* Sam wanted to get married in May or June, after he finished the picture. But one day during shooting he said suddenly, "Let's get married on Saturday. I'm gonna organize it all."

"He arranged everything," says Gould. "It was the most fantastic, beautiful Mexican wedding at the Camino Real, with mariachis and everything. Sam had our whole hotel room filled with yellow roses and he got French champagne, from God knows where in the middle of Mexico. He made all of these preparations on his own in three days. It was the side of Sam Peckinpah that not many people know about. That was the poet that I suppose all us wives fell in love with. That dearness about him was so real, but it was hard for him to expose it."

To the men on his crew he put on a different face. "I didn't even know they were gonna get married," says Chalo Gonzalez. "The next day Sam comes over to me and says, 'Where the hell were you?' I said, 'What?' He said, 'When I needed you you weren't there!' I said, 'What the hell happened?' He said, 'I got married to Joie and you weren't there to talk me out of it!' "

The marriage meant banishment for Katy Haber. "The night

before the wedding Katy was in this little honky-tonk in Fabens, Texas, where we were shooting," says Gordon Dawson. "She was feeding quarters into the jukebox, playing old, sad, sad cowboy love songs. Boy, it was really sad for Katy."

When *Getaway* wrapped, Katy left for Spain to work on a Sam Fuller western, *Reata,* and Sam and Joie returned to their apartment in Studio City, now as man and wife. He tried to integrate her into his inner circle, but most of his friends were baffled by the marriage and greeted the young bride with frigid smiles.

"Joie was a very, very nice person," says Fern Lea, "and she absolutely did not go with Sam. She seemed stylish. Sam had never really gone with stylish women before. She wanted terribly to have Sam be a certain way, and not the angry person he was. She wanted him without his anger, which wasn't gonna happen. What she was looking for and what she got were worlds apart."

"I thought I could change him, of course," says Joie, "that was part of the attraction. I was the one, it would be different with me . . ." The thing she most wanted to change was his drinking. His daily intake of alcohol on *The Getaway* shocked her: "That he could stand up straight every day was extraordinary. He had an extraordinary constitution. I was terrified the whole time we were married that he would suddenly drop dead. He stayed up around the clock, he'd sleep for a few hours, but he'd wake up at five and start right in drinking again."

When she tried to talk to him about his drinking he would say that he wasn't an alcoholic, that he could quit any time he wanted. And then he would, cold turkey; wouldn't touch a drop for three weeks. During these periods he was calm and retiring. He'd spend hours reading, would go out to dinner and the movies; the violent mood swings, the explosions of rage receded almost completely. "He became a normal person," says Gould. But sooner or later—usually sooner—he'd fall off the wagon again.

"I can't direct when I'm sober," he became fond of saying, conveniently forgetting that he'd directed *The Wild Bunch* without a drink in his hand.

On the set the crew would fawn all over him, cater to his every whim. Chalo or Bobby or Katy kept the drinks coming, but when he got home at night, Joie refused to cooperate. And so they had fights, terrible fights. Once the deadly mixture of booze and repressed rage was ignited, there was no putting out the flames until somebody got badly scorched, usually Joie.

"We were staying at the Fieldings' home once. Sam had gone to bed and I was sitting in one of the rooms, reading. I just didn't go to sleep. I can't remember the circumstances of the evening, what upset Sam so much, usually it was nothing. He came in the room and out of the clear blue—I mean, we weren't even having an argument—just started walloping me. He really knocked me around. It was really weird. I ran, I was so scared, and they took me to the bedroom upstairs and they put Sam back down in his bedroom."

"What set it off? Who knows?" says Camille Fielding. "The booze made him mean and the reasons for the blowups were nonexistent, it came out of nowhere. Anyway, he suddenly reached out and hit her, right in the face. I threw him out of the house."

The next day Joie was going to leave to stay at a friend's house. "I was really scared. Sam wanted to see me and I told the Fieldings that I didn't want to see him, and everyone made me go speak to him."

"You can't just leave him," they told Joie. "You have to go in and tell him you're leaving."

He was sitting alone in the den, like a lost and frightened little boy. He was sorry, he told her, his eyes welling up and voice quivering—he would never do it again, *never.* "It was a heartrending performance," says Gould. "I felt so badly for him. He was so sad and vulnerable. He was so hurt by what he had done, you felt you couldn't hurt him any more. I, and everybody else did too, rationalized his behavior. It was the alcohol. When he drank he was out of control."

After four months, Joie had had enough. She filed for divorce. "This girl was on the verge of a nervous breakdown," says Bob Schiller. "I don't know if this was brought on by Sam, or if her life had led to that. Her eyes were constantly shifting, her hands were shaking. She looked like a person who was very tightly strung, as tightly strung as Sam and maybe even more so."

Sam later told Garner Simmons: "When things fell apart it took me a year to get the divorce and it cost me my shirt, my pants, and my embroidered jockstrap. But some you win and some you lose. She took all the money I got on *Getaway* and took a trip around the world at my expense."

That was not quite the truth—Joie's settlement amounted to $25,000, and she got not a cent of Sam's profits from *The Getaway*. "I don't think Joie was terribly interested in getting a big settlement," says Kip Dellinger, who had recently taken over from Bob Schiller as Peckinpah's business manager. "I think she wanted to put the whole thing behind her. The case could have gone on forever; it wasn't that clear that she had a legitimate interest in *The Getaway* profits."

As a bonus Sam gave Joie his Porsche. He'd stopped driving it anyway after getting a DUI charge. For the next six years drivers—Chalo Gonzalez, Stacy Newton, Jim Davis, and a succession of others—would chauffeur him to and from film sets, meetings with studio executives, and social events, as well as do his shopping and run miscellaneous errands.

The apartment in Studio City was vacated. When they were married, Sam had bought a plot of land north of Broad Beach. He had planned to build a home for Joie and himself there. After the divorce, he held on to the property for a while, then sold it, along with his ranch outside of Ely. Instead he rented a tiny patch of land in Paradise Cove, an inlet with a fishing pier and restaurant where most of the beach-party movies and a thousand other Hollywood films had been shot. Sam bought a twelve-by-fifty-six-foot mobile home not much larger than the ones he used on locations, stuck it up on a bluff overlooking the cove, and moved in. It would be his base of operations, the closest thing he would have to a home for the last twelve years of his life. "I'm a goddamned nomad, I live out of suitcases. My home is wherever I make a picture," he told William Murray of *Playboy*.

The loss of Joie hurt more than he wanted anyone to know. However misguided the marriage, he had loved her and he had a hard time letting her go. Shortly after the divorce, Frank Kowalski received a phone call at four in the morning. It was Sam. "Listen, partner, I need you. I want you to drive by Joie's apartment and see if she has any company."

Frank sighed wearily. "No, Sam, I don't do that. I would never do anything like that."

"You no-good fuckin' bunch quitter!" Sam shouted, then slammed down the receiver.

"I did a lot of things for Sam," Kowalski says. "You get sucked into that whole thing of being part of the inner circle, it was tremendously attractive—that opportunity to be in the center of all the action, privy to all the high-level creative decisions. You were willing to subject yourself to many things just for a taste of that. Sam knew that and exploited it, and if you didn't watch it he'd draw you by degrees into becoming nothing more than a servant for him. But I drew the line at doing anything really demeaning, like doing Sam's laundry or spying on his women. I just wouldn't do that."

Bobby Visciglia had fewer inhibitions. "I was peeking in windows and tracking her down and seeing where she was going. I spent many a night parked in a car outside of her apartment—and I'm married, trying to raise three kids. Then she went to work over at 20th Century–Fox and I had to call people to find out who she was going out with, where she ate for lunch."

Finally Sam accepted that the relationship was over; the surveillance missions were dropped. But he kept inviting Joie to screenings of his movies; they had a few lunches together, and she tried to maintain a friendship with him. But it was always strained.

"He was obviously quite upset, seeing me again," says Joie. The encounters stirred up a mixture of feelings in her as well: anger, love, pity, frustration. "He had every opportunity to change, yet he didn't. He had gone to a psychologist, Dr. Wahl, for therapy, but when it got too close to the things that were really troubling him he stopped. He had plenty of intelligent people around him who loved him and would have helped him if he had just let them, but he wouldn't."

After his third marriage burst into flames, Sam went into a tailspin from which he couldn't, or wouldn't, pull out. In the past he would have plunged into his next picture, *Pat Garrett and Billy the Kid,* with savage fury, but now he found it harder and harder to get it up anymore. Fame had proved to be sweet-tasting junk food devoid of any real nutritional value. Art had failed to purge him of his demons; their grip on him was now a slowly tightening strangle hold. Was this all there was left for him? Another movie, and then another and another and another?

In the midst of a long, drunken interview with Jon Tuska in 1975, Sam would make a very curious statement: "Since my home burned down, I don't have any place to live anymore." The only home that he ever lost to fire was the Quonset hut almost twenty years earlier. He'd lost a whole world there, along with Simbo's puppies, and he'd never get it back. "I'm the greatest stupid romantic in the world," he said in another interview. "Really stupid. I'm an outsider, and I think being an outsider is a lonely, losing job. I would love to be married and live in a split-level house. I love all that shit, but I don't do it. I get in too many problems. I drink too much and I get in too many fights. Next year I'll be fifty years old and I've got to quit. Three knuckles have been broken; it's gone, right there, right there, and right there. You can see it . . ."

He abandoned even token efforts to control his drinking. From the moment he opened his eyes each morning—racked by the shakes and vomiting, sometimes blood—until the small hours of the night when he finally blacked out, he was knocking back shots of vodka, whiskey, Campari, tequila, brandy, and deadly mixtures of some or all of the above. He was spending more and more time in bed—sometimes whole days, if he didn't have a set or meetings to go to. It became a kind of rumpled throne from which he held court; secretaries, crew, and other members of his entourage gathered around its perimeter, hanging on each half-whispered word. He took most of his phone calls and held production meetings from under his sheets, a bottle always within easy reach on the nightstand.

In an article published in *New York* magazine in 1974, Sam's long, drunken monologues circled back again and again to the memory of his father: "He had great hands. I have good hands, but he had great hands, to hold somebody and tell them it's okay. He was all right." It was a subtle cry for help. He was, of course, romanticizing the memory of his father, but the longing for a strong authoritative force to take control of his life was heartfelt.

"I don't think Sam would have destroyed himself the way he did," says Fern Lea, "if my father had lived. Dad wouldn't have let him." But David Peckinpah was long in the ground and no other Steve Judds appeared on the horizon. Most of his entourage cheerfully reinforced his drinking and many got drunk right along with him; for them, locations became one long party and the increasingly outrageous and erratic behavior of "Yosemite Sam" a cause for merriment rather than alarm. "He'd wake up in the morning with the DTs and people laughed about it," says Walter Kelley, who worked as a dialogue director and actor on most of the later features. "They made jokes about it . . . It was sick." As long as his pilot fish could keep the living legend upright and shuffling through his paces, the paychecks would keep rolling in.

By the time Sam's marriage to Joie ended, Katy Haber had finished the western in Spain and went back to England. She too had been wrenched by an unlucky affair. She'd fallen in love with a member of the crew, a married man who returned to his wife and family after the picture wrapped, torn between his loyalty to them and his new passion for Katy. Katy returned to her apartment, where the phone was ringing. She picked it up.

"I hear you're back from your picture." It was Sam.

"Yeah."

"Well, do you want to come to Mexico? We've got another picture to make."

"What happened to Joie?"

"She's gone."

A few days later she was on a flight. Before she left, she told her lover, "When you make your decision, let me know, because I promise I'll come back to you." All through the making of *Pat Garrett and Billy the Kid*, she received letters from him in which he wrote, "I'm dying of a breaking heart. I don't know what to do. I'm torn between my child and you." One day the letters stopped coming. The picture wrapped, the crew returned to L.A., and Katy called the London studio where he worked, only to be told that her lover had died of a heart attack two weeks earlier. He was thirty.

"I was devastated," says Haber. When Sam found out about it he was very solicitous. Soon they were sleeping together again and the tortuous pattern of their relationship resumed—she obsessed with him, willing to do anything to please him, he handing out vicious punishment to her for having the bad taste to love him.

Gordon Carroll was one of the hip young New Hollywood producers to rise up through the ranks of the fragmented movie industry in the 1960s. Tall, good-looking, genteel, a graduate of Princeton, he had produced a couple of mediocre Jack Lemmon comedies—*How to Murder Your Wife* and *The April Fools*—and one of the milestone antiestablishment flicks of the era, *Cool Hand Luke.* In the early seventies Carroll was looking for another project when he suddenly came up with the idea of making another movie about Billy the Kid. (Forty-five of them had already been made.)

Carroll's inspiration for putting a new "topspin" on the played-out legend was to draw conscious parallels between the saga of Billy the Kid and the modern living legends of rock and roll. Maybe Billy and his gang could even be played by rock stars. "The story that I wanted to do, the story that most clearly defined a young person who is a prisoner of his own legend, was Billy the Kid and Pat Garrett," Carroll told Paul Seydor. "That was the story that could tell what it must be like to live all of your life in one incandescent span. Then, what is it like when that short period of time is over? Your incandescence is over. You're alive and you're twenty-four and you've got all of the rest of your life to be somebody that you used to be."

To write the script, Carroll hired Rudolph Wurlitzer, a young novelist who'd just completed a screenplay for *Two-Lane Blacktop* that had been hailed in a cover story by *Esquire* as one of the most brilliant and idiosyncratic scripts ever to come out of Hollywood. The movie, directed by Monte Hellman, became an instant cult classic and one of Sam Peckinpah's favorites.

Wurlitzer was also fascinated with the Billy the Kid legend, and had already done a lot of research on his own. He produced a screenplay that piqued the interest of MGM, but the studio wanted a big-name director attached to the project before they'd commit to it. Carroll sent the screenplay to Peckinpah, who read it in his office at Goldwyn Studios, where he was preparing to shoot *The Getaway*. By the time he reached the last page he knew he had to make the movie. It was another crack at *The Authentic Death of Hendry Jones*, the novel by Charles Neider that he had adapted for his second screenplay fifteen years earlier.

Wurlitzer's script was beautifully written. Like Neider, he had stripped away all the layers of legend to render a harsh, realistic portrait of the last days of Billy the Kid. Wurlitzer's Billy was no noble Robin Hood, no misunderstood neurotic driven to a tragic end by a cold and corrupt society. He was simply the product of a crude and brutal time and place: New Mexico in the late 1870s. As a wild and fearless youth he had recklessly won a reputation in the Lincoln County War—a fierce battle between rival commercial interests for control of commerce in the region, in which both sides hired armies of professional gunfighters. But Wurlitzer began his story at the tail end of Billy's outlaw career, opening with the Kid's escape from the Lincoln County Jail and following him during the last three months of his life as he tries to elude Pat Garrett and is eventually shot down.

Wurlitzer portrayed Pat Garrett as a former friend and fellow bandit who tracks Billy down and kills him; as an aging gunman clutching at the coattails of the political machine that has taken control of the territory, a small-minded man troubled by few scruples and little guilt when he finally guns down the Kid. It was a stark, unglamorized portrait, probably very close to the real Garrett.

Wurlitzer's western dialogue was every bit as rich as Peckinpah's: it was filled with the idiosyncratic rhythms, colloquialisms, and unvarnished poetry of the American Southwest. The script was episodic in structure—a loosely strung series of vignettes that occurred as the Kid first flees toward Mexico with Garrett in pursuit, then changes his mind and returns to Lincoln County to meet his fate.

The script offered Peckinpah an opportunity to explore yet again the themes that obsessed him: two former partners who are forced by age and changing times onto opposite sides of the law; the ambiguous nature of that law, which is manipulated by huge and faceless economic interests that are slicing up the rolling grasslands for a fast buck, and the tragic consequences this inflicts on individual lives. Sam didn't have to think twice; he gave Carroll an immediate yes.

Within eighteen hours, MGM's head of production, James Aubrey, came back with a pay-or-play (a contract that guaranteed to pay Peckinpah his full salary even if the production was eventually canceled) offer of $228,000 to direct the film—$3,000 more than he got for *The Getaway*—plus a percentage of the profits based on a convoluted formula concocted by the studio. Wurlitzer would get $98,130 for the screenplay and Carroll $95,721 for producing.

When he finished post-production of *The Getaway* eight months later, Sam moved into one of the big luxurious dressing rooms on the MGM lot and sat down to read Wurlitzer's screenplay again. When he did, his enthusiasm soured. The script didn't work. For all its impressive qualities, by the final page it left him feeling nothing—nothing for the Kid, nothing for Garrett.

"The script was elegiac and beautiful, but it was a tone poem," says Roger Spottiswoode, who would work as one of the editors on the picture. "There was very beautiful writing, Ruby's a wonderful writer, there was a beautiful quality to the text. But it was a deceptive script. Whenever the script cut to Billy, he was never doing anything except hanging out with his buddies, and everyone's drinking. I suspect the deal gathered steam too fast. Rudy was hot, the project was hot, and all of a sudden Sam reads it one night a couple of months before he's supposed to start shooting and he realizes: this doesn't work."

As he did whenever he was caught in the throes of a creative crisis, Sam picked up the phone and called Jim Silke. Silke was sent a copy of the screenplay, then met with Peckinpah at MGM. Sam threw up his hands. "What the hell am I gonna do with this thing? Maybe this is the way it really happened in Lincoln County in 1881, maybe this is really the way these men were, but who gives a damn?"

"What are we gonna do, Sam?" Silke responded Socratically. "Are we gonna do the real Billy the Kid, or are we gonna do the legend?" Peckinpah sat there for twenty minutes without answering. Silke simply waited. Finally, Sam said, "Let's do the legend."

His vision of what the film could be snapped suddenly into focus. He read Wurlitzer's script again, and a major structural weakness that was initially camouflaged by the dazzling dialogue and stark poetic prose leapt out at him. Wurlitzer opened with Billy's escape from the Lincoln jail, then cross-cut between him and Garrett as one reluctantly fled and the other even more reluctantly pursued. The two characters never appeared in a scene together until the climax, when Garrett shot the Kid in Pete Maxwell's darkened farmhouse at Fort Sumner.

The writer had made this choice quite consciously, as he later explained to Jan Aghed in *Sight and Sound:* "I wanted to eliminate all the usual historical cliches . . . I was very interested in not having them meet until the end; that seemed to be a more dangerous thing to do, more interesting, creating a subtler tension."

It was an unconventional approach, even daring. But the problem was that it gave one nothing about Garrett's relationship with the Kid—its history, what they had meant to each other, and how they felt about each other now. Nearly every living American knew the basic plot points of the Billy the Kid legend, but the interpretation of the characters, their actions, and motivations had changed constantly over the ninety years since the Kid's death. From one newspaper account to the next, from biography to biography and movie to movie—as the society changed, it remolded the myth to suit its current emotional needs. (And the historical facts were quite different from the myths. All reliable evidence suggests that Garrett and the Kid were acquaintances before the older man put on the sheriff's badge, but never close friends, as virtually every version of the legend, including Peckinpah's, insists. For it is this crucial fiction that has given the tale potency, decade after decade.) So one couldn't simply assume the audience would know the background story of Garrett and the Kid and therefore leave it out; you had to reinterpret it for them once again—that's what kept the myth alive.

Not letting Garrett and the Kid meet until the climactic scene was a clever but empty device, Sam concluded. They had, he decided, to portray Garrett and Billy together at the opening of the story, before Garrett becomes sheriff, so they could show what their relationship was, and how it changes when he puts on the badge.

The other major problem was the characterization of the Kid. Wurlitzer told Jan Aghed: "You can say that Billy at some point made a fascinating existential choice. Everyone told him to leave New Mexico. The governor of the territory, Lew Wallace, said: 'Look, we're settling this territory and trying to attract money from the East. The country is changing and there just isn't room for outlaws anymore, and it's gone past the point where you can disappear because you're too famous.' So he was given that choice. They said, 'Go to Mexico and we'll forget it. Or California or wherever. But just get out.' And what interested me was his decision not to get out. In other words, he chose to be Billy the Kid. If he had gone to Mexico he would have become just another gringo. But this choice made him become a hero. Because in choosing to be who he was, he also chose his death. He knew he was going to get killed. So there's that kind of fatalism, which really intrigued me . . ."

But such philosophical concepts were abstractions forced onto the characters by the writer; they didn't rise out of the characters themselves. Billy's actions, Peckinpah insisted, had to be motivated by his character.

In a series of story conferences with Carroll and Wurlitzer in September and October 1972 Sam outlined a radical restructuring of the script. Just as he had done in his adaptation of *Hendry Jones* fifteen years earlier, Sam tenaciously pushed this slice-of-life western into the realm of epic tragedy. Many of Wurlitzer's supporting characters and much of his dialogue would remain unaltered; Peckinpah retained the screenplay's wealth of realistic detail to make his own mythic vision convincing.

Two new sequences were added on to the beginning of the

screenplay. The first, written by Peckinpah, took place at Fort Sumner just five days before Pat Garrett officially became sheriff of Lincoln County. Garrett rides into Fort Sumner to tell the Kid that he has to clear out of the territory. The two share a bottle of whiskey in a dusty saloon for old times' sake. The sequence established with precision the characters' past history, their affection for each other, and the social forces now pressing them onto a collision course.

After this sequence, Peckinpah had Wurlitzer add another taking place some five weeks later. A cabin that the Kid is using as a base for cattle rustling with two of his gang is surrounded by Garrett and his posse. Billy's companions are killed in the shootout that follows and he is captured and taken back to the jail at Lincoln to await hanging.

Next came the sequence that had originally opened the screenplay: Billy's incarceration and eventual escape. Garrett had been absent from these scenes, but Sam inserted him into the action to further develop the relationship between him and Billy, and he rewrote the dialogue of Garrett's deputy, Bob Ollinger, to transform him into yet another of the psychopathic preachers who wander through Sam Peckinpah's fictional universe toting a Bible and a shotgun.

In this sequence and throughout the rest of the script Sam sprinkled in bits of dialogue from *Hendry Jones* and some new material of his own. The screenplay improved dramatically, but still something was missing; it didn't come together with the impact he was looking for. Why, he asked himself, even bother to film this well-worn legend for the forty-sixth time? What possible relevance did the story have in 1972, nearly a century after the Kid's corpse had grown cold?

He needed to look no farther than his morning paper for the answer. That summer, at the height of the presidential campaign, five men had been arrested for breaking into Democratic headquarters at the Watergate Hotel in Washington, D.C. Richard Nixon would win the election by a landslide that fall, but within months his administration would unravel.

The scandal didn't surprise Peckinpah; he had despised

Nixon with a passion ever since he had won a seat in the U.S. Congress in 1947. It was the Republican president's boys-will-be-boys attitude toward the My Lai massacre that really galled Sam. "Nixon's pardoning Calley was so distasteful to me that it makes me really want to puke," he told Anthony Macklin. To Peckinpah, Nixon personified the dark side of America: the smoke-filled back rooms where big business and sleazy politicians conspired to murder, rob, rape, and pillage the land under the banners of law and order, patriotism, and "progress."

By the time the Watergate scandal reached its traumatic conclusion, it would disillusion both Republicans and Democrats and both sides of the generation gap. It was the final jolt in a decade of shocks that had left the country on the verge of a nervous breakdown. The outrage and exhilaration of the 1960s was sliding into the generalized alienation, apathy, and exhaustion of the seventies. The more Sam worked on *Pat Garrett,* the more the story became for him an allegory not only of Watergate but of the entire greed-ravaged expanse of the American experience.

The killing of William Bonney did not make Pat Garrett a popular man in Lincoln County. He was voted out of office soon afterward and lived on as a little-loved ghost from an era that died with the Kid. Twenty-seven years after he put a bullet into Billy, Garrett became embroiled in a bitter property dispute and was shot in the back while urinating on his own land.

Peckinpah told Jan Aghed: "The inevitability of Billy and Garrett's final conflict fascinates me. Also the inevitability of Billy's death. The . . . irony is the so-called Santa Fe Ring, which was controlled by a group of people represented by Albert Fall and involved in a lot of land-grabbing and shady financial dealings, and Billy and the people around him resented that. Albert Fall later defended the murderers of Pat Garrett and got them off. You see, the same people who had hired Garrett to kill Billy years later had him assassinated, because as a police officer he was getting too close to their operation . . . Albert Fall later became United States Secretary for the Interior, which may be some comment on today's government."

Peckinpah was well on his way to spinning yet another version of the myth, half-based on fact. Albert Fall did indeed defend the alleged murderer of Pat Garrett and was aligned with local ranching interests that Garrett had antagonized for the reasons that Peckinpah cited. And Fall did go on to become Secretary of the Interior, and the prime villain in the Harding Administration's Teapot Dome scandal. Both Garrett and the Kid were victims of the factionalized range wars that plagued New Mexico throughout the last two decades of the nineteenth century. But they were killed by different coalitions of business and political interests, not by one all-controlling entity, as Peckinpah insisted. Here he was taking artistic—or paranoid—license, allowing the mythical Santa Fe Ring to stand for all the powerful unseen economic and political forces that manipulate the fate of individual American lives.

Discussions along these lines in the story conferences gave Gordon Carroll an inspiration: why not add a prologue to the film? Open the picture in 1908, when Garrett—an old, embittered man, warped by twenty-seven years of guilt after killing the Kid—is himself gunned down by agents of the Santa Fe Ring? Then dissolve into the main story in 1881; then, after the climactic scene of Garrett killing the Kid, dissolve back to 1908 again, when Garrett himself lies dying. Peckinpah loved it.

Sam wrote the prologue into the script immediately and explicitly described how it was to be intercut with the first scene in the main body of the film, which takes place in 1881. In that scene Billy and his gang are engaging in a little target practice at Fort Sumner: blowing the heads off live chickens buried up to their necks in the sand. Sam planned to intercut this with Garrett getting ripped open by assassins' bullets in 1908 so that Billy would appear to be taking part in his murder—thus the deaths of the two men would be linked in a strange, fatalistic way.

After the epilogue, in which Garrett dies, a title card would be superimposed over the frozen image of his fallen body. It would summarize the circumstances of his murder, the involvement of Albert Fall and his role in the Teapot Dome scandal, and would be followed by the title: "So what else is new?" and the Sam Peckinpah brand.

Like gluing on one piece of a huge mosaic at a time, Sam

added an extra dimension here, a nuance of character or theme there, until he had in Garrett a complex and tragic character, a man in conflict with himself, every bit as mythic yet profoundly human as Pike Bishop in *The Wild Bunch*.

Unfortunately, the other half of the story's equation—Billy the Kid—never developed a comparable level of sophistication. In response to Peckinpah's urging that Kid's character needed more development, Wurlitzer had added some formulaic "motivation." He inserted a Mexican sheep farmer, Paco, into the story. Paco attempts to flee the war zone of Lincoln County for his native land, but to do so he must cross over some of John Chisum's open range. A trio of Chisum's cowboys capture him and torture him to death. Billy, also fleeing for Mexico, comes upon the scene just as Paco is dying. He kills the cowboys; then, after listening to Paco's long, rambling last words, decides he has to go back to Fort Sumner, rally his gang, and seek frontier justice against Chisum and the rest of the ring's henchmen.

When forced to abandon his idiosyncratic style, Wurlitzer's writing became as contrived and stilted as an old TV hack's. The Paco scenes were as phony as Monopoly money because they were motivated not by the psychology of the characters but by the author's need to plug a gap in the story. In contrast to the excellent dialogue throughout most of the script, Paco's dying soliloquy was hideously bad.

The most disturbing thing is that Peckinpah accepted this material without requesting more rewrites. Perhaps there simply wasn't time. MGM had scheduled the first day of shooting for November 6, which gave him only about six weeks for pre-production, and the studio insisted on a tight budget and shooting schedule. Carroll, Wurlitzer, and the studio brass were already irritated with the amount of rewriting Sam had demanded. So maybe he took the path of least resistance and shrugged it off with the famous last words of many a movie director: don't worry, we'll fix it during shooting.

But the other factor that cannot be denied is that Sam's alcoholism was finally beginning to affect his creative judgment. His incredibly acute vision was beginning to blur.

In the finished film, the image of Billy the Kid would veer indecisively from that of a charming psychopath in one scene to a romantic anarchist in the next. Peckinpah had brilliantly dramatized the dichotomies of the human animal in the past—through Pike Bishop, David Sumner, Roy Earle Thompson—but in this portrait of Billy the Kid the mixture failed to cohere.

While Wurlitzer was revising the screenplay, Sam proceeded with casting. For the part of Billy, folk singer Kris Kristofferson was signed. A Rhodes Scholar who had won Atlantic Monthly Awards for short stories he'd written in college, Kristofferson had recently skyrocketed to stardom with a pair of hit songs, "Help Me Make It Through the Night," and "Me and Bobby McGee," and had segued into acting with supporting roles in *Cisco Pike* and *Blume in Love.* For the part of Pat Garrett Sam cast *Dundee* veteran James Coburn.

To fill the gallery of small parts in Wurlitzer's string of brilliant vignettes, Sam assembled a roll call of nearly all the great western character actors alive at the time—an entire generation of men who collectively had appeared in thousands of westerns. Many, like Peckinpah, had grown up on cattle ranches and farms, or in the small rural towns of the American Southwest. They would parade through the movie, trailing with them the associative memories of all the roles they had played in the past, in everything from classic "adult" westerns to cheap B-programmers: Katy Jurado, L. Q. Jones, Slim Pickens, Chill Wills, R. G. Armstrong, Richard Jaeckel, Dub Taylor, Luke Askew, Matt Clark, Richard Bright, Jack Dodson, Jack Elam, Barry Sullivan, Paul Harper, Emilio Fernandez, Jorge Russek, Gene Evans, Jason Robards, and Paul Fix (in his first part for Peckinpah since Sam created his role on "The Rifleman" some fifteen years before).

As the picture geared up for pre-production, the first rumblings of trouble between Peckinpah and the management of MGM began. The president of the studio at the time was James Aubrey. A graduate of Princeton, Aubrey had moved up through the ranks at CBS in the late 1950s to become president of the network in 1959. There, he earned a reputation as an insufferable autocrat who made erratic creative decisions. Writers and directors began calling him "the smiling cobra," and even Phil Feldman would say, "Jim Aubrey is about as cold as you can get without being declared a corpse."

Aubrey was put in charge of MGM by hotel and airline financier Kirk Kerkorian. Kerkorian had gained control of the company in 1969. He promptly announced plans to build a glitzy MGM Grand Hotel in Las Vegas and stuff the gambling palace with studio memorabilia. Aubrey's main achievement during the four years that followed was the dismantling of what had once been Hollywood's mightiest movie factory. One by one, the company's assets were sold off. The annual stockholder reports had less to say about the studio's production of films and more and more to say about the new hotel, into which $120 million had now been poured.

James Coburn had just completed a film, *The Carey Treatment*, at MGM, and had watched how Aubrey nearly destroyed the director, Blake Edwards. In the middle of shooting the production head suddenly decided to cut fifteen days out of the schedule, forcing Edwards to drop several major sequences and scramble to fill the gaps by rewriting as he shot the rest. "What an evil motherfucker this Aubrey was," says Coburn. "Blake refused to edit the film. He left. He was broken up by the end. Aubrey would hire big-time directors and top writers and stars, and then step in and fucking destroy the film. He was totally irrational."

When Peckinpah came to him with *Pat Garrett and Billy the Kid*, Coburn tried to warn him: "Jesus, are you sure you want to make this film here? Aubrey will fuck you up, man, he's gonna go for you. He screws everybody."

A grin crossed Peckinpah's face. "Don't worry about a thing. I bought one share of MGM stock, and if anything happens I'm gonna call a stockholders' meeting and I'm gonna fuck him!"

"Aubrey was a challenge to Sam," says Coburn. "And Aubrey saw Sam as a challenge too. Sam was a bad boy. He did a lot of things that grated the Hollywood production community, and yet they all wanted to take on the challenge of being the one who could 'handle' Sam. 'I can make him heel, I'll be the one!' Instead of being the producer who could support his work."

Sam may have perversely relished the challenge of taking on Aubrey, but he also wanted desperately to make the film. It was a project too close to his heart to pass up. Besides, there were some good people working under Aubrey. Dan Melnick was vice president in charge of production, and Lew Rachmil the studio's production supervisor. Melnick, of course, had saved Sam's career with *Noon Wine.* Sam had worked with both men on *Straw Dogs* and Rachmil again on *Junior Bonner.* He respected their creative judgment and believed their assurances that they could protect him from Aubrey. And with *The Getaway* completed, Sam would be riding the wave of his first runaway hit. At the height of his career, both artistically and commercially, surely he had the clout at last to prevent another *Major Dundee.*

His contract guaranteed him two public previews of his cut before the studio could step in and make changes in the film. Today it is a standard clause in the Directors Guild basic agreement, but in the early seventies it was rare for a director to get even that concession from a studio. Surely this was an indication of MGM's good will.

Wrong. He began to see the terrible mistake he'd made when they laid out the shooting schedule and budget. MGM wanted the picture shot in fifty days for just $3 million. Sam hoped to make a film that approached the power and epic sweep of *The Wild Bunch,* but the studio expected him to do it with thirty fewer shooting days and at under half the cost. After intense lobbying he finally got the schedule extended to fifty-three days, but the studio's penny-pinching continued. MGM refused at first to hire many of Peckinpah's regular crew members because, executives argued, their salaries were too high. Sam claimed that without his regular team he could never bring the picture in on time. Finally, after much debate, the brass gave in.

But on another crucial issue the studio refused to compromise. The picture would be shot in Durango, Mexico, and Sam knew from past experience that the fine silicone sand of the Durango desert could wreak havoc on camera equipment and cause lengthy and costly delays. For this reason, he requested that a camera mechanic be brought down to Durango to service the three Panavision cameras throughout the shoot. Too expensive, MGM management concluded. Absolutely not. Sam boarded a flight to Durango in the first week of November with clenched teeth.

The studio had rented him a huge four-bedroom house in Durango, with a walled-in garden and a swimming pool. A ghost from Peckinpah's past reappeared upon his arrival: Begonia—her Castilian features as smoothly drawn as the last time he laid eyes on her, her dancer's body still firm and richly curved. Sam decided that he wanted her to play the part of Garrett's wife. Once again he was crossing the wires of his real and fictional life to strike sparks, for the dialogue between Pat and Ida Garrett bore a striking resemblance to the fights he and Bego had had when she found herself left alone at Broad Beach for hours and days while he was off writing or directing.

"You might say that you are glad to see me," Ida says resentfully as Pat Garrett sits down at her dinner table. "It's been over a week since you've been gone."

He looks up at her but cannot hold her gaze. "I'm sorry." He pushes his chair back and suddenly walks away from the table toward the front door. "I've got to go down to the saloon, there's a drunk down there causing a lot of trouble, goes by the name of Alamosa Bill . . ."

She follows him to the door. "Will you be blessing this house with your presence for dinner?"

"Oh, looks like it's going to be a long night." He grabs his hat off the rack.

Her voice breaks. "It's been a long year."

"Not now," he says quietly, eyes averted.

"My people don't talk to me. They say you are getting to be too much of a gringo since you've been sheriff, that you make deals with Chisum, that you don't touch me . . . that you are dead inside. I wish you had never put on that badge."

"Not now!" he shouts.

"*Sí, ahora!*" she shouts in return, "or I won't be here when you get back!"

He wheels on her, grabs and rips the heavy velvet curtains

that frame the dining room door right off their rod. For a moment it seems he might lunge and strike her; then he pulls back, wrestling his voice to a subdued monotone: "We'll deal with this when it's over."

Sam and Bego fell into bed together immediately. In the first flushed hours of their reunion, they called Jim and Lyn Silke in California and babbled about "old times" like a couple of lovestruck teenagers. The Silkes were thrilled. Of all Sam's women, Bego had always been their favorite; with Bego Sam was at his best.

But in a few days it went up in flames again; another terrible fight erupted. "Sam threw Begonia out," says Chalo Gonzalez. "He told me, 'Get her the hell out of here! I don't care how, put her on a plane to Mexico City, I don't want to see her!' "

Begonia got one thing out of their brief reconciliation: the child she had never been able to have during their marriage. Nine months later she would give birth to a little wisp of a girl—Lupita. To his entourage Sam would growl, "I wonder who the real father is." But he would make regular payments for the child's support over the remaining decade of his life, and during brief reunions with Bego was attentive and affectionate to his youngest daughter. Lupita would never be burned by his fury like his other kids, mainly because he never saw her for more than a few consecutive days at a time.

As for Ida Garrett, Aurora Clavell—who had become Sam's icon of the woman left behind or betrayed—would play the part.

Shooting was to begin on the sixth of November, but Sam immediately came into conflict with the production manager, Frank Beetson, who had worked on *True Grit* and other westerns for director Henry Hathaway. Sam had, as usual, thrown the company into chaos by changing production plans and vetoing costume and location selections he'd previously approved. He was drinking heavily, and Beetson made the mistake of questioning his judgment.

"Frank was a tough old guy," says Gordon Dawson. "He and Sam got into it pretty good. Beetson was one of the few honest people who said, 'Sam, you're drinking this picture into the toilet! You're ruining yourself. You're a better director than this!' "

Peckinpah fired Beetson and replaced him with a new production manager, Jim Henderling. Shooting was pushed back a week while Sam walked the streets of the Fort Sumner and Lincoln locations with art director Ted Haworth and cinematographer Johnny Coquillon, making modifications and discussing how various sequences would be shot. He also finished casting the Mexican parts, reviewed the wardrobe, and tested various special effects.

James Coburn arrived a few days before shooting began. Kristofferson was there too, as well as the other principal cast members. For three days they all assembled at the long wooden table in Sam's dining room to read over the script, the rehearsals inevitably sliding into marathon drinking sessions.

At this point another performer joined the company. His role would be minor, but his presence on the set and the screen enormous. Gordon Carroll had sent a copy of the script to Bob Dylan, who was a friend of Kristofferson's and had expressed some interest in playing a small part in the film. Dylan read the script, screened *The Wild Bunch* in New York, and signed on to the picture.

"I talked to Bob after he had just finished screening *Wild Bunch,*" says Kris Kristofferson. "He was totally knocked out by it, and was so excited about the idea of *Pat Garrett and Billy the Kid* that he had already written a song about Billy the Kid, which I loved."

Carroll was ecstatic. The producer's reverence for the skinny, curly-headed folk singer put Peckinpah on edge, but when he heard Dylan's ballad about Billy the Kid he fell in love with it and had it put on tape so he could play and replay it over the course of the production. The folk singer was cast in a minor part as Alias, a member of Billy's gang, but Peckinpah had Wurlitzer expand the role from a nondescript outlaw to an enigmatic newspaper reporter who discards his printer's apron to follow the Kid. The implication was that Alias would weave the outlaw's legend in the years that followed his death.

When shooting began on November 13, the conflict between Sam and MGM quickly escalated. The first of an unending series of crises struck when a mounting flange on a 40mm Panavision lens was bent and went undetected. As a result, in the shots made with this lens (almost all of them masters because it had a short focal length) the entire right half of the screen was out of focus. The film had to be shipped back to MGM in Culver City for development, then back to Durango, so Peckinpah and his crew did not discover the problem until a week later. By that time they had filmed a dozen scenes with the defective lens.

"We started watching the first night's dailies and the shit's out of focus," says Gordon Dawson. "Sam says, 'Can't I expect fucking focus?' And the second shot was out of focus, and the third shot was out of focus. Sam got so mad he took out a folding chair and he stood up, he almost fell off of it because it was gonna fold, and he took his cock out and he pissed on the screen with this big S. And he walked out of the fucking room."

"Bob Dylan and I were sitting in the screening room when he did that," Kris Kristofferson recalls. "I remember Bob turning and looking at me with the most perfect reaction, you know: what the hell have we gotten ourselves into?"

"From then on," says Dawson, "every night we watched dailies with this S-shaped piss stain on the screen."

If the studio had given Peckinpah the camera mechanic he'd asked for they never would have had the problem. Now he demanded one be sent to Durango immediately. But MGM still refused. The camera crew still hadn't discovered the source of the problem, and so the company continued to shoot for another two weeks, checking and rechecking its equipment until the bent lens flange was finally discovered. By that time dozens more out-of-focus shots had been made, the footage completely unusable. Finally, a month into shooting, Aubrey relented and sent a camera mechanic to Durango.

Peckinpah wanted to reshoot the fuzzy footage, but Aubrey forbade it even though the cost would be covered by the studio's insurance.

"All of the masters were out of focus," says James Coburn. "We couldn't use any of the masters. And Aubrey kept saying, 'Nah, nah, nah, the people will never know.' He didn't really give a shit, he didn't care. He had no respect at all for the public.

'They'll take whatever we give 'em!' His trip during that time was to sabotage films. Evidently he hated people with talent."

Peckinpah was aghast at Aubrey's insanity, then enraged by it, and the war was on. Sam reshot most of the ruined footage anyway, stealing the needed shots here and there while shooting other scenes, or sending Gordon Dawson and dialogue director Walter Kelley out to shoot them with the second unit. Dawson and Kelley were constantly conferring with the editors to figure out exactly what was required to fill the gaps in various sequences.

"Aubrey didn't know we were reshooting the stuff till he saw it in the rushes back in L.A.," says James Coburn. "Then this big edict would come down, 'You can't shoot anymore retakes! No reshooting at all. *None!* Cut the fucking scene out, forget about it.' Well, we reshot everything that was necessary. But we had to reshoot it within the context of shooting the new scenes. We were reshooting scenes at lunchtime, we were reshooting at the end of the day, we were reshooting whenever we could. But that's exciting moviemaking. Fuck it, why not? You've got to go for it as long as you're into it."

It was exciting but chaotic, and the disorganization and constant infighting pulled Peckinpah's focus off the quality of the work. It became a monumental effort just to get the scenes on film at all; there was little time or energy left over for worrying about if they were any good. And the scenes reshot by Dawson and Kelley lacked the vitality and precision of Peckinpah's. Many lay flat as a fallen cake on the screen.

Not only did he forbid any retakes but Aubrey began sending telegrams complaining about the number of camera setups Sam used in the scenes, the amount of coverage, and the time it was taking to shoot them. He gave explicit instructions on how certain sequences were to be shot, but again Peckinpah ignored him.

Caught in the middle between Peckinpah and Aubrey was Gordon Carroll. "In the beginning," says Gordon Dawson, "Carroll was on Sam's side. He had this ridiculous assumption that he would be able to handle Sam, and that Sam was going to be a pussycat and this was gonna be wonderful, and he was going to catch lightning in a bottle with this picture. But he just never could control Sam, and he became a turncoat once shooting started."

"I would not say that the picture was anything but a battleground," Carroll himself told Paul Seydor. At Sam's instruction, Gordy Dawson tapped his telephone and routinely taped all of his conversations with production personnel. "Are you taping this conversation?" suspicious parties would query.

"No," Dawson would coolly coo, time after time. "Trust me. I would have, but I just ran out of tape."

That he was engaging in just the sort of behavior that he had condemned Richard Nixon for completely escaped Peckinpah. "On that film Sam created an atmosphere that was so poisonous," says one former crew member.

Even Dawson, Peckinpah's most loyal and fervent foot soldier, was becoming disenchanted. As the second unit director, Dawson shot some of the most beautiful footage in the picture, like the exquisite sunset silhouette of Billy riding past a high desert lake. But he also shot the most repulsive: the scene in which Billy and his gang took target practice on the heads of live chickens. Dawson wired the chickens with squibs and methodically popped their skulls off for his camera. "That was one of the worst things I ever did for him," says Dawson. "Anything for the picture though, right? . . . That's what I used to think. Sam drilled that into me: anything for the picture. The end justifies any means. I really believed that for a long, long time. But Sam had changed. He'd become very paranoid. Everyone was out to ruin his picture. He'd accuse Wurlitzer of trying to ruin his picture; shit, half the time he'd accuse me of trying to ruin his picture. Everyone's out to ruin his picture, you know? He got *very* paranoid."

Hours were consumed in petty debates between Peckinpah and Carroll over minor logistical problems. Sam became obsessed with getting back at the studio every way he could. Actors were flown in to Durango for scenes that could have been shot in a couple of days, but Peckinpah kept them waiting around on the set or in their hotel rooms for weeks—on salary—while he shot other scenes instead. As on *Dundee*, he was getting back at the studio by squandering its money.

Costs skyrocketed. Sam was getting a $500 a week per diem, but that didn't stop him from billing MGM for the cost of furnishing his house, for the salaries of his gardener, maids, and pool man; for the mariachi bands he hired to entertain at weekend parties, the flowers he bought for Katy Haber, and the over $2,000 worth of "refreshments" that poured forth from his bar. It was the same vindictive game he'd played on *Major Dundee,* and it was a losing game. He more than anyone should have known that, but once the pump had been primed he couldn't reverse the flow.

By mid-December, after thirty days of shooting, they were nine days behind schedule. Weather bore some of the blame—rain and wind had shut filming down for hours at a time—and an epidemic of influenza took its toll; almost every member of the company would be stricken and miss work days over the course of the shoot. The topsoil of Durango was permeated with animal manure that dried up, blew around with the fine silicone dust, and lodged in people's lungs, causing chronic pulmonary infections.

"Everybody got very sick," says Coburn. "Sam and I got so sick that we shot a scene that neither one of us remembered shooting. We didn't think we'd shot it. It was the scene with Richard Jaeckel in the saloon, after the scene where I'd been with all the whores upstairs and was really drunk. I was asking Jaeckel to help me go get the Kid. It was a particularly tenuous scene for Garrett, because he was wiped out and fucked up and fearful. It was really cold and damp, there was wind and a thousand years of horseshit floating around in the air, and that stuff really gets potent as hell."

On December 8 Sam was vomiting too frequently to work and the company had to shut down for three days. He went back to work on the twelfth, but remained weak, both physically and mentally, for the rest of the picture.

Of course, his drinking didn't help. He began every day with a big tumbler of vodka to stop the shakes and get himself upright, dressed, and out the door. Most days he arrived a half-hour to forty-five minutes late on the set; the crew rarely completed the first shot before ten A.M., and often not before eleven. "Every morning on the set, Sam would start off with a great big tall glass of grenadine and water," says James Coburn. "As the day wore on it would get redder and redder and redder, until it was almost pure grenadine. And then it would start getting lighter and lighter and lighter again because he had started mixing it with vodka, or gin. He was a totally indiscriminate drinker. What it did for him, I guess, was close out all of the shit going on around him, all problems and chaos, so he could just focus on the scene."

In the late morning he reached a state of alcoholic equilibrium, appeared sober, and worked with clarity until the mid-afternoon, when he began slurring his words and swaying on his feet.

"After about four hours, Sam was gone," says Coburn. "He was a genius for about four hours, then it was all downhill . . . He didn't want to shoot sometimes. He'd be sitting there in the trailer waiting for them to light a scene and they'd call him to the set and he wouldn't come out of the fucking trailer. We'd all be sitting around waiting for him, and I'd have to go into the fucking trailer and say, 'Sam, what's happening? Why don't we go shoot this fucking scene? What's the matter?' He'd say, almost in a whisper, 'I don't know, I don't know what I'm doing—' I'd say, 'That's bullshit!' And finally he'd go out there and—boom!—plug right into it. It was like a writer not wanting to sit down and face the typewriter."

When L. Q. Jones arrived in Durango he was shocked by Peckinpah's appearance: "This apparition came around the side of the building. It was Sam. My first impulse was to say, 'My God, Sam, I didn't realize you'd died.' He had the sickest, weakest look I'd ever seen in my life. It was so bad that I would not have been the slightest bit surprised if after I'd gone back to the hotel that day the company told me Sam had dropped dead. That's how bad he looked. He wasn't coherent. He'd tune out in the middle of a conversation and be someplace else. Probably it was a combination of the drinking and the flu."

"It was the classic alcoholic syndrome," says one former crew member. "He was surrounded by enablers. Katy and Bobby Visciglia would bring him drinks. Everybody would say, 'Sam's having a bad day.' The cronies made it impossible to get to Sam. You'd go through all these acrimonious and painful things to try and tell an alcoholic the truth and then there'd be these fucking enablers who'd slap him on the back and give him a drink."

When word got around in Hollywood that Peckinpah was drinking on the set and falling behind schedule, Sam took out a full-page ad in the *Hollywood Reporter* that showed him flat on his back on a hospital gurney, receiving a bottle of Johnny Walker intravenously. A caption read: "Dear sirs: With reference to the rumors that seem to be spreading around Hollywood that on numerous occasions Sam Peckinpah has been carried off the set, taken with drink. This is to inform you that those rumors are totally unfounded. However, there have been mornings . . ." It was meant as a hilarious sendup, an up-yours to Aubrey and the rest of the MGM brass. Instead, the image was absolutely chilling. Peckinpah, a gray, withered scarecrow, was surrounded by the frostbitten grins of his entourage, all egging him on, Katy Haber gripping the bottle that fed the scotch down the coil of surgical tubing.

The half-dozen men in Hollywood who had the power to green-light a movie were not amused. To them the image said only one thing: Peckinpah's out of control. If he could keep turning out money machines like *The Getaway* they would tolerate such behavior, but let him stumble a few times and it would be a much different story.

There was something else wrong with the dailies besides the focus, something far more disturbing. For the first time one could see the mark of all that alcohol. *Pat Garrett,* and all the films that came after it, would be plagued by gaps in continuity, sudden lurches in tone, and scenes that were sloppily staged, overwritten, overacted, and sometimes embarrassingly bad. There would still be scenes and sequences of great brilliance as well, but the motor had begun to sputter; the grip on the throttle had slackened. One can almost graph out the sequences shot during Sam's four good hours of each day and those filmed when that tall glass of grenadine and water had turned deep red.

A self-consciousness had crept into his work. The dialogue had become bloated and awkward at times, overstuffed with "meaning." When the Kid is captured by Garrett, Kristofferson holds his arms out in the position of Christ on the cross. In *The Wild Bunch* Angel evokes the same icon, but in that film it is so well integrated into the action of the scene that the symbolism registers subliminally. In *Pat Garrett* it leaps out like a neon sign. There are shots of kids swinging playfully on the gallows that wait to hang the Kid in Lincoln, with an American flag all-too-carefully framed in the background. Such touches had the impact of a lightningbolt in *The Wild Bunch;* now they seemed stale, the contrivances of an artist running on fumes. He'd read too many of the reviews that raved about "the Peckinpah touch," and the "recurring themes" in his work, and now took the path of least resistance, feeding the critics an easy-to-read schematic of the movie's "message."

But then there were those days when Peckinpah pulled himself together and really came on, and the old magic began to happen and everybody was galvanized again.

There were the jailhouse scenes in which R. G. Armstrong played Bob Ollinger, Garrett's Bible-obsessed deputy with his peculiar interpretation of Christian mercy. "Repent, you son of a bitch!" he bellowed as he held a double-barreled shotgun to the Kid's head. It would be Armstrong's last incarnation of this character in Peckinpah's work, and his finest. And there was the sequence in which Garrett enlisted Slim Pickens, a small-town sheriff, for a raid on a faction of the Kid's gang. Pickens took a bullet in the belly and staggered to the edge of the Pecos River to gaze upon the silver-green water for the last time. It was one of the most poetic sequences Peckinpah ever committed to film. And there were a half-dozen other brilliant character vignettes that together, like dots in a pointillist painting, formed a vast panorama of life on the frontier as the first strands of barbed wire began to subdivide the open plains.

Because the production was running sixteen days behind schedule, Aubrey ordered Peckinpah to cut most of these vignettes from the script to make up for lost time. Sam defied him and shot all the scenes despite vehement protests by Gordon Carroll, who was present on the set. When the vignettes showed up in dailies back at MGM, Aubrey went through the roof.

Peckinpah's out of control and Carroll can't handle him, the production chief concluded. Something had to be done to rein this director in or they'd have a runaway production on their hands. And so, as on *Dundee,* a parade of executives in Tony Loma boots,

Neiman-Marcus Stetsons and Gucci leather goods began materializing in Durango, where paranoia and horseshit swirled thickly in the air.

"I went down to Mexico two or three times, trying to get Sam to dry out," says Dan Melnick. "I got a call from Jason Robards, who played a small part as Governor Wallace in the picture. He called me after he got back and said, 'Sam's in real trouble, you've got to go down there.' So I go down. And he greets me with open arms, the tenderness of a brother, and three drinks later he's slurring his words and saying, 'Go fuck yourself! Don't tell me not to drink, I'll do whatever I want. Go on home! I don't need you!' I went through that a few times and came away with a terrible sense that I couldn't make a difference."

"I went to dinner with Sam and Rachmil and [MGM's vice president of operations, Lindsley] Parsons and Melnick," says Gordon Dawson. "They were trying to tell us how we could shoot the film cheaper and faster. And we were saying, 'Bullshit, we're out here making a first-class movie.' "

MGM couldn't fire Peckinpah; the studio was in too deep. He knew that and it knew that. If the studio tried to remove him the entire cast and crew—which were loyal to Sam, not MGM—would have walked, leaving it with a three-million-dollar loss and an unfinished picture. Besides, Peckinpah was the movie's major box-office draw, the name on posters and ads that would, with luck, sell enough tickets to recoup MGM's investment. Now it was Peckinpah who had Aubrey by the short hairs. All the studio chief could do was keep the pressure on and hope Peckinpah stayed upright long enough to wrap the picture.

Shooting continued right through Thanksgiving, Christmas, and New Year's. John Wayne's BATJAC company sent its cast and crew home for the holidays, but MGM refused to do the same, so they gathered at various houses on the different days and made the best of it. Bobby Visciglia had saved six of the wild turkeys used in the scene where Kristofferson and Dylan chase them, and fattened them up for Thanksgiving. The cast converged on actor John Beck's house and cooked them, but the birds were as tough as a set of radial tires.

Sam's kids came down for Christmas. He sent a mariachi

band out to greet them as they got off the plane at the Durango airport, and the driver had a box of candy for each of them. On Christmas Day they all received beautiful Mexican ponchos from their father, but Sharon couldn't help noting that they were all exactly the same—a generic gift. He'd probably sent Katy Haber out to buy them.

Mathew, almost eleven then, had the worst time of it. His father rode him mercilessly. "Mathew had dyslexia, and some of the same learning problems that Sam had as a kid," says Walter Kelley. "When Sam would get together with him he would then, I think, be like his father was to him. Which was mean and physical. He was really mean to Mathew, and in fact would like to break his spirit. That seemed to be playing out something that had happened to Sam as a kid."

Peckinpah threw massive parties at his house on both Christmas and New Years, complete with mariachi bands and pits in the backyard filled with glowing-hot rocks and roasting pigs, turkeys, and rabbits wrapped in banana leaves. So much tequila and mescal was consumed that the two events blend liquidly together in the memories of the survivors.

Sam was having alcoholic blackouts almost every evening now, and it was during these that his behavior became wildly erratic and, too often, violent. Knife throwing had lost some of its shock value over the last couple of years. Most of his co-workers and even the press had grown used to his hobby, so he took up a new one, inspired by Emilio Fernandez and the patrons of Durango's dance halls and whorehouses: pistol shooting. He carried a loaded gun around with him much of the time and, without warning, would whip it out and fire off a round into the air, into walls, and into ceilings.

"He was just happy, it's a common thing to do in Mexico," says Chalo Gonzalez.

But the American and English crew members often failed to appreciate the fun. Several were summoned to Peckinpah's house on weekends. They found him upstairs in bed with a half-empty bottle of vodka between his legs and a revolver in his hand, taking shots at a mirror on the opposite wall. "I'd never been that close to a gun before," says one former crew member. "I was only a few feet away when he fired it. The shot from a gun is huge as the bullet goes by you. Then I look, and I see that Sam's shooting his own image in the mirror."

Peckinpah began filming the picture's climactic sequence on January 26. In it Pat Garrett stalks through the dark streets of Fort Sumner, a maze of crumbling adobe, drawing closer and closer to his final rendezvous with the Kid at Pete Maxwell's house.

Shooting up the mirror in his bedroom had been more than drunken theatrics; even in an alcoholic haze Sam constantly manipulated the film to reflect his life and his life to reflect the film. As shooting progressed he had grown more and more interested in Garrett and less and less in the Kid. Kristofferson's scenes often seem rushed and perfunctory, as if Peckinpah simply wanted to get them over with so he could get back to Garrett. The Kid remained little more than a blurry symbol of his own youth, now lost. But Garrett was a character of truly tragic dimensions, a man caught at the crossroads of a moral dilemma. For Garrett to become more than a facile symbol of America's moral corruption in the era of Watergate, for him to become a living, breathing human being, he would need a transfusion from Sam's own veins. And the only way to do that was to open one and let it bleed. Garrett sells out to Chisum, Governor Wallace, and the Santa Fe Ring, and kills a part of himself, perhaps the best part, in the bargain. What had Sam Peckinpah sold out?—he asked himself as he lay in bed holding a loaded gun on the withered image in the mirror. Sharon, Kristen, Melissa . . . Mathew. Mathew, that blond, skinny, shy, uncertain, lost boy who he could hardly look at without vomiting rage. That awkward, vulnerable kid he'd had to murder in himself so long ago in the hills of Dunlap's Ranch in exchange for a curt nod of approval from the Peckinpah men. Joie, Begonia . . . Marie. Lying on the bed with her in that airy apartment on Rimpau Boulevard, pressing his palm against the swell of her belly to feel Sharon's first stirrings. Where was that apartment now, was it still there, could he find his way back to it again? Lost, so many years, so many things lost. And he'd sold it all for what? Magazine profiles of a fictional identity he'd created, film festival awards, a mountain of money, the cold hungry clutching bodies of star fuckers, a circle of back-slapping, puppet-grinning strangers offering him another drink, who knew the image but not him, loved his celebrity but not him . . . It hadn't turned out the way he thought it would . . . not even close.

In the sequence, Garrett stalks through the darkness, like an iron filing pulled irresistibly toward the magnet of Pete Maxwell's and the Kid, he pauses for a moment at the shack of a coffin maker who is working late—another of Wurlitzer's character vignettes. Sam had now expanded the dialogue and cast a new actor in the role . . . himself.

Coburn wades through the night. Ahead lies Pete Maxwell's dimly illuminated farmhouse; to his right is a small pool of gold light, where a thin figure hunches over an unfinished coffin. A small coffin, a child's. "Hello, Will," Coburn utters softly.

The graying head tilts up with eyes fierce and piercing. "Hello, Sheriff," Will replies tensely. Coburn offers him a drink from the ever-present flask. Peckinpah waves it off and continues to stare at his fictional creation with those bottomless eyes. "You finally figured it out, huh? I thought you'd be out pickin' shit with the chickens, cuttin' yourself a tin bill."

Coburn takes a giant swallow of whiskey, his face puckering. He repockets the flask and stares at the waiting farmhouse.

"Go on," Peckinpah purrs, "get it over with."

Coburn can't move, but can't take his eyes off his fate.

Peckinpah moves his hands over the raw-wood frame of the tiny coffin. "You know what I'm gonna do? I'm gonna put everything I own right here, and I'm gonna bury it in this ground, and I'm gonna leave the territory."

Like a sleepwalker Coburn starts toward the farmhouse; his face is that of a dead man as his spurs lightly ching upon the ground. Peckinpah calls after him, "When are you gonna learn you can't trust anybody, not even yourself, Garrett?" It is the filmmaker in dialogue with his fictional alter ego, documenting his own spiritual crisis on film.

When Garrett had gone to visit his wife in the beginning of the film, he stopped before her house: a huge, two-story white

Victorian with a picket fence surrounding a neatly kept yard, it juts out of the earth, towering above the other colorless adobe structures of Lincoln, a hallucinatory icon of hearth and home embodying all the allure and horror of domesticity that American men run toward and away from. Garrett himself fled shortly after entering its claustrophobic confines, then later had sought to fill the terrible vacuum within himself by hopping into a bed full of prostitutes.

Now, approaching the shadowy farmhouse of Pete Maxwell, Garrett comes upon another picket fence, weathered and warped from many years of neglect. He pauses before the gate and considers it; then, as if in some recurring dream, he swings it open with the same deliberate motion he'd used when entering his wife's home. Creeping up onto the porch, hand on the butt of his gun, he peers through a window from which he hears the sound of soft moaning and a breathless voice crying, "Jesus! Jesus!" It's the Kid, making love to his girl with a passion that is only a memory to Garrett. Garrett backs away from the window and collapses into a porch swing and waits for the Kid to finish.

When he does, Billy pads out onto the porch, barefoot and shirtless, to dig a midnight snack out of the cooler. Garrett creeps around back, enters the dark house, and moves silently to Pete Maxwell's bedroom, just inside the door from where the Kid stands.

"When we were rehearsing it I saw the mirror there by the door," says James Coburn. "I saw myself in it and I said to Sam, 'After I shoot the Kid, I want to shoot myself in the mirror.' Sam said, 'No, no! No, no, no, no!' I said, 'Yes, goddamn it, I want to do that! Fuck you, man! That's what I'm gonna do, I'm gonna do that! Now set that fucker up!' We were yelling at each other and he was adamant, he wasn't going to do that, didn't want that to happen! . . . And then, somehow, we rehearsed all that night, but we didn't shoot. We came back the next night. I said to Sam, 'Are we gonna shoot the mirror?' He said, 'Fuck yes, you're gonna shoot the mirror! That's what you want to do, isn't it?' That's the way he was. Of course I knew about him shooting himself in the mirror at his house. It was just another kind of thing . . . shooting the ghost."

The Kid backs in through the open door of Maxwell's bedroom, his bare shoulders and spine exposed to Garrett sitting on the bed. The Kid turns, gun in hand. "Hey, Pete, who's that out there?" Then he sees Garrett sitting there. He doesn't raise his gun, but instead smiles beatifically at Garrett, opens his arms, and offers his naked chest to him. Garrett—jaw set, eyes burning—raises his gun and fires. Like a stroke of lightning, the flash from the barrel illuminates the room. The Kid is punched backward, flying through space, lyrically floating through air, torso curved in on itself, face twisted. Then it descends toward earth, and Garrett rises and sees his own image fill the mirror before him. He grimaces and fires, the glass shattering and sprinkling, his image fragmenting just as the Kid's body completes its fall, thumping softly to rest on the wood planks of the porch just outside of the doorway. His face still has that beatific smile. Garrett steps closer to the mirror, staring at the fissured, broken image of himself with a gaping black hole in the center.

Seeing that the Kid is safely dead, Garrett's deputy, Poe, pulls out his pocket knife, opens it, and starts across the porch. Before he can get to the body Garrett steps into the doorway and looks down at the Kid, at the chest perforated by one neat bullet-hole, the face smiling up at him. Garrett stares with wide, unbelieving eyes. "I shot him," he mutters softly, then steps over the body onto the porch. "I killed the Kid."

It was a sequence of astonishing power. When Jim Silke saw it, he thought: *damn, he finally did it!* Sam had finally caught on film what he had been after in *Castaway:* the moment when Mr. Lecky kills the monster, turns over the bloody corpse, and discovers it to be himself.

"*Pat Garrett and Billy the Kid* is, for me, the masterpiece," says Lyn Silke. "It's more complete than *The Wild Bunch.* The man was in there all the way, it's all of him, it's his whole story. There's a feeling afterward of completion, the world has been born and created and died. It's a wonderful, fulfilling feeling."

The film finished twenty-one days behind schedule. Peckinpah had shot 367,440 feet of film in 803 camera setups (more footage than he'd shot on *Wild Bunch* by over 30,000 feet, but with 400 fewer setups). He had defied MGM and gotten every scene he wanted in the can. Some scenes were weak, many things in the picture didn't work, but much of the footage was stunning. Despite its many flaws, he knew he had a picture of incredible power. He had won the battle—but, back in Culver City, the smiling cobra was coiled and ready to strike.

Roger Spottiswoode, Garth Craven, and a team of Mexican editors had been cutting sequences together in Durango as Peckinpah shot them. When Sam returned with them to MGM in February 1973 he had a rough cut of the picture that ran three and a half hours. It needed a lot of work, but he hoped he could find ways in the cutting room of minimizing the weaknesses and carving out a great movie.

Then Aubrey dropped the bombshell. He wanted to release the film at the end of May, on Memorial Day weekend. The studio had sunk all of its reserves into the MGM Grand Hotel and was desperate to develop some cash flow in time for its stockholders' meeting in July, so Aubrey was rushing as many pictures into theaters as possible despite the fact that the haste might cripple their box-office potential. *The Wild Bunch* had been in post-production for a year, and most of Peckinpah's subsequent pictures for six months. *Pat Garrett* would have just two and a half months to become a finished product. Aubrey's deadline was insane, but Gordon Carroll agreed to it on the condition that they would be able to add more editors to the team and thus work around the clock. Peckinpah had no choice but to go along with this plan—it was either cooperate or turn the film over to Aubrey—but he knew it obliterated his chances of shaping *Pat Garrett* into a great film.

Six editors—Roger Spottiswoode, Bob Wolfe, Garth Craven, Richard Halsey, David Berlatsky, and Tony de Zarraga—plus a stable full of assistants worked on the movie. "We had so many people working on the film," says Bob Wolfe's assistant, Mike Klein, "it was like the right hand didn't know what the left hand was doing."

Peckinpah had worked with a large team of editors on *Straw Dogs*. By walking from cutting room to cutting room he'd been able to bring a unified vision to the film. He used the same approach on *Pat Garrett*, but by now he only functioned well for about four hours a day. Sometimes he never even showed up for the screenings of the various rough cuts; sometimes he'd stagger in halfway through the movie, collapse in a chair, and pass out. Just when Sam needed to be in peak form, he was dropping the ball.

Yet somehow they managed to produce a fine cut of the picture by March 13, which they screened for the MGM brass. "Hell of a first cut," James Aubrey said when the lights came up. To the editors' surprise (Peckinpah was not present) the production chief seemed to like the film. But Aubrey harbored the illusion that this was only a rough cut, and that Peckinpah would greatly reduce its length. When he discovered shortly afterward that Sam considered it his final cut, he blew his top. The picture was too long, Aubrey insisted. Westerns, like comedies, should never run longer than ninety minutes. He hated all the strange character vignettes that gave the picture its epic scope—they slowed down the action, got in the way of the plot—and he thought the prologue and epilogue were too confusing and beyond the comprehension of the general public.

Peckinpah's editors urged him to appease Aubrey with some concessions, to give away a few sequences to save the most critical ones, but Sam refused. "He could charm the birds out of the trees if he wanted to," says Katy Haber. "He could manipulate the biggest and most difficult stars in Hollywood until they were eating out of his hand, but he refused to do that with Aubrey. It was almost as if he was asking Aubrey to destroy the film."

Aubrey had Peckinpah right where he wanted him. Sam's contract guaranteed him two public screenings of his cut of the film before MGM could take it away from him. But instead of setting the previews up in Kansas City or at least San Francisco, the studio informed Peckinpah that the previews would be held right there on the lot in MGM's screening rooms. Furthermore, Sam would be permitted to invite no more than sixteen personal guests to each of the screenings. "[Sam] wanted people with some influence in the industry to see the film—Henry Fonda, Marty Baum," Katy Haber told Garner Simmons. "We sent the list to MGM and they removed all the names they felt were influential. So that left only Sam's family and a couple of people [that] I was able to sneak in under assumed names as boyfriends of Sam's daughters—three newspaper reviewers."

A few days before the first preview, Sam managed to smuggle three other outsiders into one of his own editorial screenings: Jay Cocks of *Time* magazine, Martin Scorsese, and Pauline Kael.

"I thought it was a masterpiece," says Scorsese. "*Pat Garrett and Billy the Kid* was the only other Peckinpah film that came close to *The Wild Bunch.* It came very close."

Dan Melnick was still hoping to broker some sort of compromise between Peckinpah and Aubrey, and so anxiously awaited the results of the first preview. Members of the general public were being bused into the studio for the screening; Melnick hoped their response would hit Sam like a pail of cold water and cause him to loosen his position. But when the lights dimmed in the MGM theater at eight P.M. on May 3, Sam had yet to show up. He still hadn't materialized by the time the lights came up again, two hours and three minutes later.

"After the preview Sam got us on the phone and told us we could shorten one shot by about twelve seconds," says Roger Spottiswoode. "That was it. Then Melnick called us and said, 'What are Sam's changes?' We told him that Sam hadn't come to the preview. Melnick said, 'What's he going to do, is he going to make some changes?' We said, 'Well, he called us and told us to shorten this one shot, we can take fifteen feet out of it.' It outraged Melnick that Sam didn't go to his own preview. Dan was one of the few people who could talk to Sam and understood the movie, but he knew it was suicidal as far as Aubrey was concerned."

"Sometimes things happen to us because we want them to," Peckinpah had told a journalist a year earlier. In the film, Garrett destroys himself through killing the Kid; now his creator seemed bent on living out a parallel scenario.

When Melnick reported the results of the first preview, Aubrey wasted no time. Memorial Day was looming on the horizon. He would get his ninety-minute western one way or another.

Just days after the first preview, editor Mike Klein noticed something funny when he reported to work in the morning. "I said to Sam, 'Something strange is going on.' He said, 'What do you mean?' I said, 'Well, our film is put up on the racks in a certain way. When we finish up at night I know how everything is sitting up there. After everybody leaves, something happens to that film. They're sitting up there differently than the way they were left. I notice our trim boxes are put back differently, because I always keep everything very neat.' Well, we found out that MGM was grabbing reels of film and making black-and-white dirty dupes of them. They had their own crew recutting the show without us knowing about it."

"Sam was going to get his two previews," says Roger Spottiswoode, "but that wasn't the film they were going to release."

Aubrey had given the orders to dupe and recut the film, but only one man could implement them: the head of production, Dan Melnick. "Melnick was the hatchet man for Aubrey," Bob Wolfe told Paul Seydor. The man who had saved Peckinpah from professional oblivion with *Noon Wine* had now betrayed him—though, of course, Sam refused or could not see how he had forced his former partner's hand.

At the second screening, also held at MGM, Sam's guests were mostly family members and close friends. Fern Lea and Walter Peter were there, as well as Sam's nephew David Peckinpah, the Silkes, and Gordon Dawson. "Sam wanted the people who he cared about to see his film, the film he wanted to make," says David Peckinpah. "After the screening everybody went up to Sam's office. Everyone was very quiet. Sam said, 'They've taken it away from me. They're recutting the film right now.' Everyone was crowding around him; it had a very wakelike atmosphere, it was strange. I could see it in his face, he was broken."

"After the preview Roger and I went back up to the cutting room," says Garth Craven, "and the studio people had already moved in. They were already there working. The body wasn't even cold." After giving every waking hour of his life to the film for four months, after all the trauma and heartache and frustration, Spottiswoode snapped, cursing as he kicked and smashed one of the moviolas around the room.

It was a dark night for Peckinpah and his bunch, but fortunately for film history MGM had not managed to completely crush their spirit. "That night I suddenly realized that our preview print was still up in the projection booth of the screening room," says Garth Craven. "So I corralled Smiley [editor Sergio Ortega, who looked remarkably similar to Alfonso Bedoya, the bandit chief in *The Treasure of the Sierra Madre*], and Smiley got a studio bike [used by messengers] with a rack on the front and brought it to the back door of the screening room. I loaded the film into the basket and Smiley pedaled it across the studio and threw it in the back of Chalo Gonzalez's car, and off it went. Of course, a few days later the studio's looking all over for it. I said, 'I don't know where it went. Don't you have any security in those screening rooms?' "

"The preview print disappeared, but the soundtrack didn't," says Roger Spottiswoode. "Somebody called Sam and said, 'Sam, there's been an extremely stupid theft. Somebody has stolen the picture but forgotten to steal the sound that went with it. We're hoping the thief comes back and gets the sound tonight because once the studio finds out it's going to be very difficult to take. So if the thief has got any smarts at all he'll move fast.' "

Chalo Gonzalez recalls: "I parked my car close to the editing rooms and left my trunk open and Smiley would come and drop the reels in there. Then when I took Sam home at night I drove them off the lot. It took us three days, but we got it all. We took it all out to Sam's trailer in Malibu, then later moved it to a film vault."

James Aubrey wasn't finished with Sam Peckinpah. Butchering his film wasn't enough; he wanted to make that bandanna-headed prick bleed and bleed and bleed, so he struck at another major artery, one close to the director's heart: his team, his precious bunch.

Just days after the second preview, Aubrey called Bob Wolfe to an MGM screening room and had the projectionist run a ninety-six-minute version of *Pat Garrett* that had been prepared by the studio's editors. "It was a disaster," Wolfe later told Paul Seydor: the epic scope of the picture and much of the character development had been yanked out, roots and all. What was left was a plotless series of shootouts in which characters appeared without introduction then disappeared as abruptly and never returned. The actions of the Kid and Garrett often lacked motivation, even coherence.

"Go back and tell your colleagues," Aubrey said to Wolfe, "that we're going to release this version unless they cooperate. If they help us, we're willing to meet you halfway. We'll only cut twenty minutes out instead of a half-hour."

Wolfe went back and told the other editors. Garth Craven refused to cooperate, but Wolfe and Spottiswoode decided they would. "We should not have made the deal," says Spottiswoode. "I hold myself responsible, responsible for my own actions anyway. I did not want the most brutalized version to go out to theaters. We had put a huge amount of ourselves into the film and it had been a very painful and unpleasant experience. We wanted as much of it to be saved as possible. I always felt that if Sam had been willing to negotiate with them he might have saved even more of the film. However, I must admit, as I go on now as a director, I sympathize with Sam. After you've been fucked over a few times you begin to think, 'I won't make any deals.' "

Wolfe and Spottiswoode junked the studio's cut completely and over the next twelve days worked with Aubrey and Melnick to bring Peckinpah's version down from 124 to 106 minutes. The prologue and epilogue were removed—Aubrey wouldn't even consider leaving them in. Several vivid vignettes were dropped and the dialogue and pace tightened throughout the rest of the scenes. The editors fought hard to save what they could.

Roger Spottiswoode told Paul Seydor: "Aubrey was ordering scenes cut out for no other reason except that he knew Sam didn't want them cut. There were literal bartering sessions in which we traded away some scenes to save others. We had these screenings with Aubrey in which he became absolutely incoherent and obscene and terrible. We lost most of Walter Kelley's scene in the brothel near the end, with Walter Kelley leaning on the bar. Aubrey hated Walter Kelley and knew he was Sam's friend and wanted it out. Well, in the final negotiations the raft scene was kept in; Kelley went out. It was a trade. That's the way it went. That way we were able to keep in certain scenes that Aubrey really despised. But we lost a lot of them. The things that got cut were the nuances, the beats between the action. Sam's scene [as the coffin maker] with Garrett was very good, a lovely, melancholy Kafkaesque scene. Aubrey took three-quarters of the last half of it out. The epilogue was removed and Garrett's ride out of Fort Sumner now dissolved into a freeze-frame of Garrett and Billy laughing together. That was Aubrey's idea and it was appalling, just appalling."

And after Spottiswoode and Wolfe delivered the compromise version, the cuts continued. As Spottiswoode walked past the cutting room one day he heard the soundtrack for one of the scenes playing on a speaker box. He stormed in to find an editor he'd never laid eyes on before hunched over a reel of film on the workbench. "What the hell's going on?" Spottiswoode demanded. "That's my reel, I cut that!"

The other editors looked up sheepishly. "It's nothing to do with us, sorry. Orders from Mr. Aubrey—we're taking out two minutes here." It was two minutes of film that Spottiswoode had fought for and won, or so he thought, the right to keep in by agreeing to take out another scene.

By the time Aubrey was finished, *Pat Garrett*, one of Peckinpah's most audacious and elaborate films, had been shrunk into an ordinary western. But Wolfe and Spottiswoode had preserved some of the most powerful sequences, including the climactic murder of Billy. Peckinpah's vision, though fragmented, was still there, and the film still resonated with strong emotions. Though the movie's chain of events now seemed haphazard and confused, it was at least possible to sense what had been lost, what the film had once been before Aubrey took a meat cleaver to it.

"The MGM cut really blew my mind, it was really fucking terrible," says James Coburn. "It made me sick, after all the anguish making the fucking thing. I kept asking Sam, 'Where's this one share of MGM stock that you told me that you were prepared to go to war with, huh?' He didn't want to fucking talk about it."

Of course, what hurt Peckinpah almost as much as the butchery was the fact that his own editors had helped Aubrey perform it. Sam still had an office on the MGM lot and was coming in every day while the recutting was being done, but he'd been frozen out of the process and was helpless to stop it. "We had recut Sam's film and he was angry," says Roger Spottiswoode.

One evening shortly after the recutting had been completed Spottiswoode ran into Bob Wolfe while crossing the studio lot. The soft-spoken, gray-haired editor's face was ashen, his eyes watery. "What's wrong?" Spottiswoode asked.

"I've just been up to see Sam," Wolfe muttered, his eyes dropping to the ground. Sam was angry, very angry, he hesitantly explained. When Bob had stopped in the office just a few minutes earlier, Peckinpah had gone for his jugular. "You know, I like to have one really third-rate person on a show, and you're it, and you always have been," Sam had said in his lethal whisper. "That's why I have you on my films, because you're sort of a dummy. You're quite good at editing, but you're kind of a dummy and it's just a good reminder of where one could go if one wasn't careful. You're it. You're the dummy." And from there Peckinpah went systematically through every film they had worked on together—*The Wild Bunch, Straw Dogs, Junior Bonner, The Getaway*—and gave vivid examples that illustrated Wolfe's mediocrity.

Wolfe was a gentle, softspoken man. He had always tried to see the good side of Sam Peckinpah, and screen out the bad. When other editors condemned Peckinpah for some abusive act, Wolfe always made excuses for him. Now Sam had turned around and savaged him. Bob looked like a small, wounded animal—devastated, completely destroyed.

Enraged, Spottiswoode took off for Peckinpah's office at a full run. He burst through the door with clenched fists. Peckinpah started out belligerent, but when Roger came around the desk after him, shouting, "You fucking asshole!" Sam held up his hands and started apologizing.

"What can I do?" Sam pleaded, suddenly desperate for forgiveness. "I'll give you anything!" Spottiswoode turned his back on him and walked out. Halfway across the MGM lot Katy Haber caught up to him. "You have to come back," she pleaded. He let himself be led back to Peckinpah's office.

Sam was sitting behind his desk, crying. "I've known you too long, you can't leave me, you can't leave me! You can't . . . I'm sorry! I'll say I'm sorry to Bob."

"No, you cannot fix it," said Spottiswoode. "You can't take those words back, and you do this a lot. You do things that you can never take back, and that is one of them."

Bob Wolfe had been a major creative force on five of Peckinpah's films. Four years later, Sam would admit to Paul Seydor that out of all the editors that ever worked for him, "Wolfe was the best." But now Wolfe was gone and he wouldn't be coming back. Spottiswoode was gone too, out of the country and back to England. He would eventually return to pursue a directing career of his own, but he and Peckinpah never worked together again.

Despite the mad rush in post-production, *Pat Garrett and Billy the Kid* did not make its Memorial Day release date, but instead opened in Los Angeles six weeks later, in July 1973, to mixed reviews. Many critics complained that the film was incoherent. Some blamed MGM's hatchet job, others fingered Peckinpah.

Paul D. Zimmerman wrote in *Newsweek:* "This new film is a casualty of a prolonged shootout between director Sam Peckinpah and MGM president James Aubrey. The battle ended with Aubrey taking away Peckinpah's 'final cut' . . . And the question remains: did the studio ruin an interesting film, or did it merely try to salvage a hopelessly muddled one? Whatever the case, the movie is a misshapen mess."

But others recognized that the picture had a warped greatness. Jay Cocks wrote in *Time:* "Even in the maimed state in which it has been released, *Pat Garrett and Billy the Kid* is the richest, most exciting American film so far this year. There are moments and whole sequences here that stand among the very best Peckinpah has ever achieved . . ." Cocks would later number the film among the ten best of 1973.

Jim Hamilton, who would be one of the screenwriters on *Cross of Iron,* saw *Pat Garrett* in a movie theater in San Francisco: "That's the movie where, if you studied Sam's work, you knew that the game was over and that the fatigue and melancholy had set in. It's one of the most fatigue-ridden movies ever made, you can feel it running off of the screen. But what Sam does is make all these wonderful images for the last time, like the wonderful death scene with Slim Pickens. Sam must have known: 'This is all I've got left.' He was finished with that genre."

Pat Garrett's negative cost came to $4,638,783—more than $1,600,000 over the original budget. During its first year of release it grossed $4,652,724; by 1976 that figure had crept up to $5,367,980. So the picture probably turned a small profit, but not enough of one to save MGM. In October 1973 James Aubrey announced the studio's complete withdrawal from theatrical distribution. MGM sold its entire library of films to United Artists and Aubrey resigned. "Mr. Aubrey is now unemployed," Peckinpah told an audience at the San Francisco Film Festival in 1974. "So maybe I've done something good for the world."

The preview print that the Peckinpah Bunch stole from MGM was shuffled over the years from film vaults to office refrigerators to Kristen's apartment in Silver Lake.

In April 1986, not quite a year and a half after Sam Peckinpah's death, a screening of that print was quietly arranged at USC. A few handbills were stapled to bulletin boards in the cinema and drama departments, and the word spread like wildfire. The night of the screening, the plush Norris Auditorium was packed. Scattered among the crowd were such Peckinpah veterans as James Coburn, Roger Spottiswoode, Alfonso Arau, and Richard Bright. The next day an article appeared in *Variety* entitled "Restored Version of Peckinpah's *Garrett* Surfaces." MGM immediately made inquiries about the print, which it wanted to repossess. But the film had already disappeared into another hiding place.

Two and a half years after the USC screening Jerry Harvey—vice president of programming for Z Channel, an adventurous Los Angeles cable station that specialized in showing cult movies, obscure American classics, and foreign films—convinced Ted Turner, who now owned the MGM film library, to put up the money for a full restoration of the film. The picture and sound quality of the restoration were first-class, but for some inexplicable reason the newly struck prints did not include the crucial scene between Garrett and his wife. Nevertheless, a screening of the Z-Channel version drew another packed house at the Directors Guild of America theater on Sunset Boulevard, and the subsequent airings in revival houses across the country and on television sparked a serious reevaluation of the film.

Today, twenty years after it was made, the movie's scathing vision of the American frontier slowly strangling to death in the grip of big business, corrupt politicians, and their hired henchmen is more relevant than ever. As in *The Wild Bunch,* Peckinpah injected his own spiritual crisis and personal despair into a larger mythological framework that addressed the spiritual crisis and despair of a nation. It is for this reason that *Pat Garrett and Billy the Kid,* for all its shortcomings, remains a work of awesome power and penetrating vision.

"I felt very gut-shot about the movie when MGM first released it," says journalist and critic Grover Lewis. "I mean, it was impossible to defend the film. It had some pretty scenes in it, but you couldn't even tell what was going on. Then, years later, I saw the Z-Channel version and I was in tears by the end of it. That's the darkest film I've ever seen."

Many other critics have come to agree. *Pat Garrett* now regularly appears on their lists of the ten best westerns ever made, and is widely regarded, along with *Ride the High Country* and *The Wild Bunch,* as one of Sam Peckinpah's masterpieces.

10

Into the Abyss

In the fall of 1972 Sam Peckinpah's clout reached its peak. First Artists had launched its promotional blitzkrieg for *The Getaway* and the consensus in Hollywood was that it would gross as much as *Bullitt*, if not more. *Pat Garrett* was about to go before the cameras and had all the earmarks of another *Wild Bunch.* After twenty years of struggling, Sam was finally in the position to acquire financing for any movie he wanted to make. He chose not *Castaway*, nor *Hi Lo Country*, nor *My Pardner*, but a bleak, repulsive nightmare entitled *Bring Me the Head of Alfredo Garcia*.

The story had originally come from Frank Kowalski. "So, you got any ideas for a movie?" Sam had asked Frank in January 1969.

"Funny you should ask . . ." Kowalski drawled, and then laid out the story he'd been working on. "You've got this bartender. He's over forty, got a drinking problem. He lives in some shithole apartment, and he realizes he's headed up a blind alley, that he's wasted his life. What would a man like that being willing to do for one last chance at the brass ring? What if he were given the choice of doing something absolutely repugnant, reprehensible, a crime against humanity, against God. Would he do it? Suppose a mafia don is looking for a guy, wants him dead in the worst way and is offering *big* money for whoever gets the job done. Suppose our bartender knows the guy he's looking for, knows the guy is already dead, and knows where he's buried. Suppose he goes out one night to the graveyard, digs up the body, and takes something off it to prove he killed the man and claim the reward."

"Like what?" Sam asked.

"His head. He cuts off the guy's head, for proof, and has to take it cross-country to the mafia don to cash it in."

"Jesus Christ, that's fantastic!" For a man who had once rigged up a bloody corpse for his mother's tea party, the appeal must have been irresistible.

Over the next two years the screenplay slowly took shape. Kowalski and Peckinpah wrote a twenty-nine-page treatment, which Sam passed on to Walter Kelley. Kelley wrote the first half of a screenplay, then ran out of gas, so Gordon Dawson and Peckinpah pulled it together in a 105-page screenplay. They changed the locale to Mexico, and the mafia don to a South American crime baron—El Jefe—who offers one million dollars for the head of a former foot soldier who has impregnated his daughter out of wedlock.

Bennie, the bartender, takes off with his lover—Elita, a high-class whore with a heart of gold—to bring in the quarry. It'll be easy pickings, he reassures her. All they have to do is sneak into the bone yard under cover of darkness, dig up the stiff, snip off *la cabeza*, and they will have their ticket to happy-ever-after land.

But when he sneaks into the cemetery to perform the deed, Bennie is ambushed by two of El Jefe's henchmen who have followed him there. They kill Elita, smash Bennie over the head with a shovel, leave him for dead, and take off with Alfredo's head. Bennie comes to later and discovers Elita's body. Convulsed with grief, rage, and self-hatred, he embarks on a spree of vengeance.

Bennie recaptures the head and murders his way up the chain of hitmen and crime bosses, following the trail of blood and money all the way back to El Jefe's South American stronghold. El Jefe pushes a suitcase filled with a million dollars in cash across a wide polished desk into Bennie's hands—payment in full for the "merchandise." Bennie is rich beyond his wildest dreams, but has lost all his dreams in the bargain. In a surge of rage, he pulls his gun and kills El Jefe. In the original screenplay Bennie then grabs the money and the fly-covered cranium and shoots his way out of the stronghold, but when Sam actually shot the sequence he decided that Benny had to die for his sins.

Peckinpah submitted the script to Martin Baum, who'd formed his own production company with financing from United Artists. UA agreed to put the picture into production after Sam finished *Pat Garrett*, provided Baum and Peckinpah shot it in Mexico in forty-six days on a budget of $1.5 million.

Warren Oates was signed to play Bennie; Mexico's hottest sex goddess, Isela Vega, was to play Elita, and Emilio Fernandez El Jefe. Shooting began in the fall of 1973 and the production proceeded smoothly, but a blanket of melancholy settled over the company. It wasn't like the old days. Something had happened to Sam; the flame in those hazel eyes had flickered out.

"*Pat Garrett* broke his back," says Gordon Dawson. "He really lost it on *Alfredo.* He was into a lot of weird doctors. Every time you wanted to get him out of his trailer he was hooked up to an IV of some sort. He wouldn't talk to anyone on the crew but me. It was really tough to read what he wanted." When Sam arrived on the set, he was listless. He didn't even seem to care if the action matched from one shot to the next. *Garrett* broke Peckinpah, but *Alfredo* broke Dawson. Sam had been his idol, his mentor; Gordy couldn't stand to watch his disintegration. "It tore my heart right out . . . so disappointing." They had worked on six pictures together, but *Alfredo* would be Dawson's last. "I had him up there on the pedestal. My fault for putting him up there, you know, that's a tough place to be, but he sure fell off on that picture, and I couldn't put Humpty Dumpty back together again in my mind."

Dawson went back to writing for television. Over the years that followed, Peckinpah called him up several times and tried to lure him onto films that he was directing. "Come on, Dawson, take a walk on the wild side!"

But the old pitch rang empty now. "Sorry, Sam, I can't do it. I'm writing a 'Rockford Files.' "

"I wish he had loved himself as much as I loved him," says Dawson. "I really did love him. It started out as fear and became respect and admiration. There was so much to respect. He had the greatest eye of any director I've ever seen, and before it all came apart he really applied it."

When completed, *Alfredo Garcia* would lack the great visceral force and stunning filmmaking virtuosity that had characterized every Peckinpah film since *The Wild Bunch.* Even the shootouts lacked energy, the precision of the shots and the editing had gone slack, the intercutting of slow and fast motion was a stale imitation of the glory days.

And yet the film would have an undeniable power, a disturbing emotional effect despite its anemic execution. Something happened to this strange little morality play as Sam shot it in and around Mexico City and Cuernavaca. The scenes grew even weirder, warped by the psychological obsessions that emanated from both Peckinpah and Mexico itself. The imagery, the characters, and the plot twists began unfolding like the distorted visions of a mescal-drenched fever dream.

As a filmmaker, Sam Peckinpah had never been a slice-of-life realist. In the TV shows and movies that he directed he offered a mythic, sometimes even surrealistic vision of the world, but never before had his imagery been so bizarrely stylized, the shifts in tone from cartoon comedy to gothic horror to pastoral idealism so abrupt. As in a dream, the people, objects, landscape, and events in *Alfredo Garcia* were constantly transmogrifying, taking wild and improbable leaps in continuity and logic. Never before had the narrative been so tenuous, as if the filmmaker had little or no interest in fashioning a believable story, but had intentionally thrown coherency to the wind as he bounced from one subconscious association to the next.

There were two public previews of *Alfredo Garcia* in July 1974, both disasters. "By the time the lights went up at the end of the movie there may have been ten people left in the audience," says Martin Baum. "They hated the picture. Hated it! They wouldn't sit still to watch it."

The tide had turned against the director. In 1969 Sam Peckinpah had injected his deepest personal conflicts into the framework of the western, and with *The Wild Bunch* addressed a collective spiritual crisis. His psyche had been perfectly attuned to those of his countrymen, but by 1974 he had fallen out of synch. Times had changed. The Vietnam War was winding down to a bleak conclusion, as senseless and frustrating and tragic in its end as it had been in its beginning. In another month Richard Nixon would resign from office. Americans would try to shake off the memory of his disgrace, and along with it so many other traumatic memories from the most troubled decade since that of the War Between the States. It was time to heal, time to forget. Collective amnesia was the order of the day.

American Graffiti, directed by a film-school whiz-kid named George Lucas, had been released the year before and racked up a staggering $55 million at the box office. It struck paydirt by applying a pair of electrodes to the long-dead utopian vision of fifties America—of smalltown suburbia with its malt shops, letterman jackets, pleated skirts, high school proms, apolitical feel-good rock and roll, and squeaky-clean values. The movie was followed a year later by a copycat television series, "Happy Days," which shot to the top of the Nielsen ratings and ran on prime time for another ten years.

People wanted to forget the incandescent dream of the Summer of Love, for it had concealed beneath its bouquets of romantic illusions a deadly straight razor. The highway that Sal Paradise and Dean Moriarty had roared down at the dawn of the sixties on a desperate-ecstatic search for higher highs and wild adventure had ended for too many as it did for Bennie in *Alfredo Garcia*—in an exhausted fit of self destruction.

Most critics were as repulsed by *Alfredo* as the preview audiences had been. There were a few defenders. Jay Cocks of *Time* interpreted the film as a black comic sendup craftily designed to provoke those who had attacked Peckinpah as a purveyor of mindless violence and crude macho fantasies. Roger Ebert of *The*

Chicago Sun-Times proclaimed the picture a "strange, weird masterpiece that will turn off a lot of people but will be remembered for a long time . . . It's a definitive Peckinpah work."

United Artists dumped *Alfredo Garcia* into second-run theaters, supporting it with only quarter-page ads in newspapers. In sharp contrast to its fate in America, the picture received rave reviews in England (four critics with *Sight and Sound* included it in their lists of the ten best pictures of the year), but it proved so disturbing to authorities in Germany, Argentina, and Sweden that it was banned. By 1977 the picture had grossed $2,168,998.25, with more than half that money coming from overseas markets. Even after allowing for the studio's creative accounting, there could be no doubt that *Alfredo* lost money.

Peckinpah's 5 percent cut of the gross brought him an extra $100,000, so he wound up making almost as much as he had on *Pat Garrett*. But the damage to his reputation as a filmmaker was cataclysmic. Vincent Canby wrote in *The New York Times*: "Sam Peckinpah. The agonizing reappraisal award given each year to the director whose earlier career seems in urgent need of critical rethinking in light of his recent string of disasters (*Bring Me the Head of Alfredo Garcia, Pat Garrett and Billy the Kid*). How could the same man have also made *The Wild Bunch* and *Cable Hogue*, or were they as good as we originally thought?"

From this point on, not only would each new Peckinpah film be regarded as just another mindless bloodbath, but in the memory of the public and critics alike the common perception became that that was all Peckinpah had ever made. The triumphs of *Ride the High Country, Noon Wine, The Wild Bunch,* and *Junior Bonner* faded like images on decomposing celluloid.

Some of Peckinpah's acquaintances suspected he used the studio butcheries of his pictures as an excuse for his own failures as a filmmaker. He could always lay the finger of blame on the moneymen. But to the end of his life, drunk or sober, he stood up and took full responsibility for *Bring Me the Head of Alfredo Garcia.* "I did *Alfredo Garcia,*" he would say time and time again, "and I did exactly what I wanted to, good or bad, like it or not. That was my film."

Roger Ebert was right; *Alfredo Garcia* has not been forgotten.

In the years since the director's death it has attracted a small but passionate following—a cult of its own within the much larger Peckinpah cult. In 1991 UCLA's film school organized a series of screenings of great but forgotten American movies, and included the film in the program.

"*Alfredo Garcia* is the grimmest, the bleakest, the funniest, and the most horrifying of his films," says Paul Seydor. "There are places Peckinpah went in that movie that he went noplace else. Fifty or a hundred years from now people will be looking back on that film the way we look back on Faulkner today. Professors used to get fired or be denied tenure for arguing that Faulkner was a great writer; today he's recognized as one of the greatest American writers. People will look back on us and wonder how we failed to understand *Alfredo Garcia*."

After the back-to-back catastrophes of *Pat Garrett* and *Alfredo Garcia*, Sam Peckinpah needed another hit like *The Getaway* to put his career on solid footing again. He thought he had it in *The Insurance Company*, a fast-paced thriller that he agreed to do for 20th Century–Fox for $325,000. But the picture fell through when Peckinpah was unable to attract a bankable star. "Twentieth gave the script to Charles Bronson," says Kip Dellinger, "and Bronson said, 'I won't work with a drunk.' "

It was the first movie to get canceled on Sam since he'd catapulted back into the big time with *The Wild Bunch*, and the thought of another long stretch of unemployment threw him into a panic. So when Martin Baum came to him with an offer to direct *The Killer Elite*—an espionage potboiler with an abundance of shoot-outs, a high body count, and minimal character development—he grabbed it. United Artists provided the financing again. After the studio took a bath on *Alfredo*, UA's head of production, Mike Medavoy, was determined to pull in the reins. He stipulated that Peckinpah was to do no rewriting of the screenplay.

Caught in the studio's straitjacket, Peckinpah reverted to the same guerrilla tactics he'd deployed on his very first feature, *Deadly Companions*. He ridiculed the movie his producers were forcing him to make. When they began shooting the picture in San

Francisco, Sam had his actors ad-lib sophomoric asides that undercut the drama and encouraged the audience to jeer at the movie they'd paid good money to see.

Marty Baum was not amused. Once he had trusted Peckinpah's dramatic instincts, but now they had become erratic, and Baum knew damn well why: cocaine.

The drug could be found on the set of almost every Hollywood production in the late seventies. Directors and stars snorted lines before they shot scenes, writers tooted before story conferences, agents before pitching a client to an important producer, actors before auditioning for a part. Coke helped you get it up for your performance before or behind the cameras.

According to several former *Killer Elite* crew members, the star of the picture, James Caan, and his entourage were major users. One of the star's flunkies served as his supplier, but didn't stop there. Caan's dealer aggressively marketed his product to every member of the cast and crew, including Peckinpah. Sam, a compulsive addict, never had a chance.

"Sam said there was a kind of immediate high that it gave him," says Garner Simmons, "a rush that he felt provided certain insights into the material [of the movie], that it really lifted him and it was worth doing for that. His phrase at the time was, 'It sharpens the senses.' "

"Initially cocaine probably did sharpen Sam's mind," says Kip Dellinger. "But what eventually occurred was that he would use cocaine to counteract the booze, and then the booze to counteract the cocaine, and all he ended up doing was more of both."

"Sam certainly had his demons," says Katy Haber. "That's why he drank, to try and escape those demons. When he did do something bad, he was always full of remorse. But when he started doing cocaine the remorse just turned into anger. Cocaine changed him so much that I could no longer say, 'Oh, well, he didn't really mean it.' The niceness was going and paranoia and the nastiness was dominating; the balance between the two was disappearing."

And of course it affected his work. "I couldn't believe it was happening to Sam," says Whitey Hughes, stunt coordinator on the picture. "On *Killer Elite* he would forget conversations that he had with you. You'd set up a stunt, you'd discuss it with him and he'd approve it, then he'd come out of his trailer and we'd do a take and he'd completely reverse himself and say that's not what he'd asked for at all. That kind of thing began happening all the time."

The old rigorous dedication to detail crumbled. Sometimes he even sent assistants out to direct the scenes so he could stay in his trailer, drinking and snorting. But because he wasn't pushing to make a really substantial film, he did manage to shoot it swiftly. The picture wrapped on June 18, 1975, just one day behind schedule.

The Killer Elite opened to bad reviews and fantastic business in December 1975. In the last week of that month Sam Peckinpah had, for the second and last time in his career, a picture at the top of *Variety*'s box-office chart. The film grossed $849,000 that week, just $25,000 less than *Getaway* had done during its first week in release. But when the Christmas holidays ended, ticket sales took a nosedive. Word of mouth, critical to any sustained success at the box office, failed to support the picture. By the last week in January, *Killer Elite*'s receipts had dropped to just $266,923.

In contrast, another film released that year, *Jaws*, grossed an incredible $133,429,000. Its director was twenty-eight-year-old Steven Spielberg, who had made only one other theatrical feature. Like George Lucas, Spielberg was a baby boomer, the product of a comfortable, middle-class suburban childhood. He'd grown up with a television in his living room and had soaked up thousands of hours of old movies and Saturday afternoon kids' shows like "Johnny Quest," "Fireball XL-5," "The Twilight Zone," and "The Outer Limits."

Technically speaking they were brilliant, this new generation: fascinated by special effects, able to access the thousands of movies and TV shows inputted into their brains and recombine them into new and highly marketable products. Psychologically they were arrested in adolescence, in those glorious "Man from U.N.C.L.E.," "Lost in Space" days of their youth. When they talked about expanding the parameters of the cinema, they were thinking of innovations in the computerized motion control of cameras and animated models, of animatronic robots controlled by radio signals and powered by hydraulics—not bold experimentation with narrative structure or attempts to penetrate the inner world of complex characters. Their mission was to entertain, to make the movies that the Hollywood dream factories had rolled off their assembly lines in the thirties and forties, the kind of movies Hollywood hadn't made for fifteen years or more, ever since Sam Peckinpah's generation had risen to dominance.

And the studio heads quickly discovered that these adolescent men made adolescent movies that drew millions of real-live adolescents like flies to sugared water. *Jaws* grossed $50 million more than previous chart-toppers—*The Godfather, The Sting, The Exorcist*—because teenagers flocked to see it not just once, but five and six times. Those repeat admissions created a whole new genre of movie: the special-effects blockbuster.

Compared to *Jaws, The Getaway* looked like an art-house cult film. The studios now realized it was possible to turn a fantastic annual profit based on the revenue from a single film. Producers, directors, writers, and stars discovered they could make a fortune with a single hit. Blockbuster fever swept through the town as everyone scrambled to lay their sweaty hands on the next high-concept spectacular that would make them multimillionaires.

And so the curtain began to lower on the greatest decade in the American cinema since the 1920s. Who cared about revolutionizing the language of film or creating a lasting work of art when you might score $10 million off your gross points in a single picture?

Sam Peckinpah, Arthur Penn, Hal Ashby, Robert Altman, Mike Nichols, John Schlesinger, Nicolas Roeg, and Stanley Kubrick were still important names, but they, like the generation before them, now found themselves being elbowed toward the periphery of the spotlight by an impertinent horde of young turks with a radically different set of values.

But Peckinpah collaborated with the forces that caused his professional decline. The coke and the drinking sparked a number of public explosions that further eroded his reputation. There was the AFI Life Achievement Award banquet for James Cagney at the Century Plaza Hotel. Peckinpah arrived in a slick black tuxedo with a bright red bandanna wrapped around his gray head, his face flushed and eyes bloodshot. When Jack Lemmon, also quite sloshed, took the podium and embarked on a long and rambling monologue, Sam bolted to his feet and roared: "We didn't come here to hear you talk about yourself! We came here to honor Cagney! Get off the stage!"

And then there was the altercation at Los Angeles International Airport. Peckinpah got in an argument with a ticket agent, sucker-punched him, and was subsequently booked for assault and battery.

Both incidents were reported in the national media, and they inspired comedian John Belushi to perform a running sketch on "Saturday Night Live" called "Sam Peckinpah Directs." In it Belushi caricatured Peckinpah directing Gilda Radner on a movie set. Every time Radner blew a line Belushi would softly call "Cut," saunter over to her, and casually punch her in the face. The demolition of Sam's reputation as a serious artist was nearly complete.

At around the same time another mishap occurred that received no publicity but was much more disturbing to those who were close to Peckinpah.

When Sam got tired of sleeping in his office on the Goldwyn lot or his tiny trailer in Malibu, he would check in to the Beverly Hilton and luxuriate for a few days. One night, after drinking heavily for hours, Sam plunged into the hotel pool with all his clothes on to swim a few laps and refresh himself. Instead, he sank straight to the bottom and stayed there. Ron Wright, who had worked as an assistant director on *The Getaway* and *Killer Elite* and had become a good friend—happened to be there. He dove in and fished Sam out while his wife, Bitsy, called the paramedics.

Peckinpah was taken to UCLA Medical Center. Fortunately there was no serious damage to his brain or vital organs, but unfortunately the incident failed to scare him into sobriety. "Bitsy and I went to visit him the next day," says Ron Wright, "and he was sitting up in bed, firing people right and left because they wouldn't bring him any booze or cigarettes."

Two years earlier, Jason Robards had nearly killed himself after a marathon drinking session at Tommy Runyon's saloon up in the hills above Malibu. Driving home, Robards lost control of his car and careened down a steep embankment. The near-fatality sobered Robards up, literally. He went on the wagon and stayed on it, which put a strain on his relationship with his old drinking buddy. When Robards learned of Sam's accident, he called him at the hospital. "Don't bother to come and visit me," Sam barked, "unless you bring a fucking bottle of vodka with you!"

"Well, okay then," Robards said softly, "then I guess I'm not coming."

The two men would remain friends for the rest of Peckinpah's life, but the old camaraderie dissipated, the letters and phone calls grew few and far between, and their conversations tense and awkward because so much was left unsaid.

But to Ron Wright, who'd saved his life, he displayed a mellower side. "Sam said to me, 'A life for a life,' " Wright recalls. "And he sponsored a child through Save the Children in our names, Bitsy and I. He bought a twelve-year sponsorship; it was a twelve-year-old kid and the sponsorship supported her until she became an adult. We got letters from her all the time. That incident was a real epiphany for me, because it made me realize just how much I cared for Sam . . . He was a scared little guy in a great big world. Why was he so magnetic? Because he was so incredibly vulnerable, and yet he wouldn't let anybody comfort him. And so you kept on chasing after this urchin. He was like everybody's bad child. He was the kid that you saw potential in and you wanted to spur that on, but he wouldn't let you. He was still going to be naughty."

Like the gold nugget plucked from California's American River in 1848, *Jaws* spurred a greedy stampede. Producers trampled over one another in the rush to grab hold of the next special-effects spectacular. The formula was simple: plenty of eye-popping cinematic tricks, thrill-a-minute action, and ankle-deep good-guys-versus-bad-guys plots. Comic books were a good prototype for these new movies; in fact many of them would be based on comic books.

This did not necessarily spell doom for Sam Peckinpah and his generation. If they were willing to change with the times and adapt their skills to the new trend in the marketplace, there were plenty of assignments and a mountain of money to be made. Sam was given two opportunities to hitch a ride on the gravy train, both on the same day. In the winter of 1975 he met with two of Hollywood's most successful independent producers, Dino De Laurentiis and Ilya Salkind. De Laurentiis asked him to direct his megabudget remake of *King Kong,* which would feature a forty-foot, six-and-a-half-ton hydraulic-powered robot gorilla, and Salkind offered him *Superman,* which would take full advantage of a new computer-controlled, hyperreflective front-projection system that gave a 3-D effect to Superman's flying sequences.

Sam thought hard about it, very hard. If either picture approached the gross of *Jaws* he would make millions. But, finally, he turned down both movies. He needed a project he could sink his teeth into, a story, characters, and a human dilemma he cared deeply about.

This led him to a producer who was a far cry indeed from flashy freewheeling entrepreneurs like De Laurentiis and Salkind. Wolf Hartwig, a German purveyor of softcore pornography films, yearned to break into legitimate features. He sent Peckinpah a copy of *The Cross of Iron,* a novel about a platoon of German soldiers caught in the Battle of Krymskay in 1943 as Hitler's Russian front, and his thousand-year Reich, teetered on the verge of complete collapse.

From his very first screenplay, *The Dice of God,* through *Major Dundee, Villa Rides,* and *The Wild Bunch,* Peckinpah had explored the psychological landscape of the professional fighting man. Here for the first time was an opportunity to deal with the subject in the context of a modern war, of Nazi Germany, where the male madness of fervid nationalism led the human race to the brink of self-annihilation. Sam agreed to do the film for $300,000, plus another $100,000 after the movie broke even, and 10 percent of the net profits.

Hartwig had hired Julius Epstein—who had worked on the screenplays for *Casablanca, The Strawberry Blonde, Yankee Doodle Dandy,* and dozens of other Hollywood films in the forties and fifties—to write the script. But his 161 pages of convoluted melodrama regurgitated every worn-out war-movie cliche in Pat Hobby's screenwriting handbook. Fortunately Hartwig was willing to give Peckinpah complete creative control, so Sam hired Jim Hamilton, a San Francisco writer whom he had met through Lucien Ballard, to write a whole new draft.

A hard-drinking ex-marine who had survived vicious trench fighting along the 17th Parallel in the Korean War, Hamilton knew how professional soldiers lived and died. He pounded out a 167-page script in just twenty-nine days. The dialogue was stilted in many of the scenes, but the structure was solid and the images and action were as vivid and hideous as a veteran's nightmares. When Peckinpah left for Munich to begin pre-production in December 1975, he took Walter Kelley—who also had had extensive combat experience in the South Pacific in World War II—with him to collaborate on the rewrites. Katy Haber also accompanied him; James Coburn, who'd been signed to play Corporal Steiner, the leader of the German platoon, rendezvoused with them in Munich.

After some meetings with Hartwig, Peckinpah, Coburn, and Kelley traveled to the German film archives in Koblenz, where they screened dozens of Nazi documentaries made during the war. Then they moved on to London to look at every foot of celluloid they could find in the British archives. Slowly the themes for their own film began to emerge.

"We'd see this German newsreel film that was shot during the war of some battle," says Coburn. "Then when we got to London we saw the same footage edited completely differently for a propaganda film for the Russians. It was like there was this independent film unit out there shooting the war and selling the footage to both sides! Two totally different ideologies were editing it for their own purposes. So what we realized—and this really hit Sam—was that they were both liars."

Over the next four months Peckinpah and Kelley wrote in parallel to each other, revising Hamilton's scenes and adding new ones, with Sam acting as the final editor, cutting, pasting, and rearranging the scenes again and again and again.

Peckinpah's name still held enough prestige to attract a first-class cast of actors, and for *Cross of Iron* he put together one of his finest: Maximilian Schell as the glory-mad Captain Stransky; James Mason as Colonel Brandt, one of Steiner's sympathetic superiors; David Warner as Brandt's dysentery-drained adjutant, Captain Kiesel; and Senta Berger as a nurse that Steiner has a brief affair with while in a rehab hospital.

Hartwig was financing *Cross of Iron* with cash from his porno movies and advance money from a number of distributors. Officially, the picture's budget was $4 million, but the German had only scraped together a fraction of this money before shooting began. To reap the maximum yield from his limited capital, they would shoot the picture in northern Yugoslavia, between Zagreb and Trieste, Italy. The costs of labor, building materials, studio space, etc., would be only a fraction of what they would be in Western Europe.

"Wolf Hartwig, the poor man was in over his head," says Murray Jordan, one of the editors on the picture. "He had no idea how to produce a film of that scope." This became apparent to Peckinpah when he and his cast and crew converged on Zagreb in the first week of April to begin shooting. None of the locations was ready because Hartwig had failed to produce the money needed to secure any, or to hire enough skilled craftsmen to have the sets and wardrobe ready in time.

For the battle sequences, Hartwig had promised to rent fifteen World War II tanks that the Russian army still had in Yugoslavia and several vintage airplanes. But when it came time to shoot, he produced no planes and only three decrepit tanks. By the end of the production, Peckinpah had sunk $90,000 of his own money into the picture to pay for the salaries of several of his key crew members.

It was money well spent. Despite the many obstacles, they were getting stunning footage in the battle sequences. Peckinpah and second unit directors Walter Kelley, Ron Wright, and Murray Jordan skillfully chose their camera angles to make three tanks look like a hundred and 300 extras look like thousands.

But the myriad budget and logistical problems were compounded by Peckinpah's drinking. Cocaine was unavailable in

Yugoslavia, so instead he was guzzling 180-proof slivovitz. His intake seesawed. For two- and three-week periods he would manage to keep it somewhat under control and work steadily and with a fair amount of clarity. But then he'd spiral off on a terrible bender and his direction would become erratic and confused. Sometimes he'd have blackouts for days at a time and forget that he had already shot scenes, even entire sequences. This is evident in the finished film, which oscillates between passages of breathtaking radiance and embarrassing mediocrity.

Sam's kids all came to visit him during the making of the picture. Melissa and Kristen's stays were mostly pleasant and trauma-free. Sharon, as was becoming the common pattern, soon locked horns with her father and ended up leaving abruptly for the States.

But for Mathew it was even worse. He stayed in Yugoslavia for several weeks in a house that his father had rented in Porto Roz. During that time Sam continued to cruelly ridicule his son's reading and writing deficiencies. One night Sam put the soundtrack to *The Wild Bunch* on the stereo. Holding up the album cover, he said to Mathew, "Maybe, if you're lucky, you'll do something great like this too someday." His voice was not warm and encouraging, but hard and challenging. For Mathew the unspoken message was, you'll never measure up.

Then fourteen, Mathew was no longer a little boy. He had shot up like a weed; standing five-foot-ten, he was already taller than the old man. He was skinny and gangly as a colt, but limber, well-coordinated, and deceptively strong. And in the hazel eyes that quickly averted whenever his father stared him down there burned a flame, steady and hot, ready at the twist of a knob to ignite.

Like his father had with Fern Peckinpah years ago, Mathew found crafty, passive-aggressive outlets for some of his anger. He found he could drive his father into a mouth-foaming rage by continuing to mispronounce Rommel's name, even after Sam had corrected him several times. Mispronouncing Cable Hogue's so it sounded like "Cable Hog" worked even better. Then he discovered a way to make the phone ring in the Porto Roz house. That was good for hours of fun. He'd sit downstairs and listen to his father up in the bedroom yelling into the receiver, "Hello . . . Hello? Goddamn it, who is this?"

But one Sunday morning Mathew's rage burst out of its hiding place, surprising no one more than Mathew himself. His father was hungover, as usual, and pissed off because he had to get up to check out some possible locations that day. "He was nervous because he had a lot to do," says Mathew.

Sam stumbled around the house, pulling clothes on from the pile beside his bed, lighting a cigarette, looking at the clipboard Katy had given him with the day's itinerary on it, downing a cup of brandy-laced coffee. Then he started in on Mathew. "It was something very trivial that set him off," says Katy Haber, who was present. "It always was. Mathew hadn't washed his clothes, or shut the door to his room, or had turned the music on the radio up too loud. I can't remember what it was because it was so bloody trivial."

Mathew had been getting ready to go out to the locations with them when Sam started in on his tirade. Mathew felt his face grow hot under the barrage of barbed words. Sam jabbed a thick index finger at his chest and said, "You're not going with us today, you're staying here!"

"Fine, whatever," Mathew replied, shrugging sullenly. "I don't want to go."

Sam's lips drew tight. "And you're gonna stay here, in the house. You're not setting foot outside this door today!"

Before Mathew knew it, the words jumped out of his mouth: "No I'm not! I'll go out if I want! I'll walk around, I'm gonna do whatever I want!"

Sam froze for a second, in shock. Then he lunged. He grabbed Mathew by his long blond hair, but a thin white forearm flew up and knocked loose his grip.

Sam's left hand swung out in a wide circle. Mathew watched it sail in, his breath grunting out as it hit him, the side of his face prickling electrically. Then Sam was swinging with both hands. Mathew back-pedaled, blocking most of the blows with his forearms. Katy screamed something and tried to get in between them, but Sam shoved her back with his elbow and forced Mathew into a corner by the window, his face stinging as more of the blows connected. But it was the eyes that hurt most, the way his father's eyes were looking at him. Like he was nothing, just an object to hate, to break.

And then his own anger rose up from inside him. His hand flew out to Sam's chest and shoved him back a few staggering steps, but he leapt forward again, swinging wildly. "He was ready to hold me down," says Mathew. "He was hitting me; I was like a rat in a corner."

Mathew's fists flew like those of a crazy cartoon character, knuckles thudding against the hard bones of Sam's skull hard enough to jerk his head back, and then into the soft spill of his stomach. And then it was Sam raising his arms to block the blows, Sam back-pedaling, Sam with eyes wide and frightened.

Then everything stopped and they just stood there facing each other, gulping air, tears drooling down from the corners of Mathew's eyes. He turned and ran for the door. His father shouted something but he didn't listen, he didn't look back. He just kept running.

"Sam was very quiet afterward," says Katy Haber. "He was stunned. He didn't discuss it. It made him realize who he was and what he was doing, it just killed him, but after a day or two he found a way to justify it, to rationalize it away."

"He didn't want to talk to me at all," says Mathew. "I moved out of the house and into the Metropol Hotel. I felt horrible, like it was my fault, I guess. I kept on asking Katy, 'Would he want to see me?' She said, 'No, no, no.' I didn't pursue him. I just laid low for a week, I felt like a leper, then I went back to California. Before I left I said good-bye to him. He kind of shrugged. He couldn't really look at me. He said something like, 'Yeah, I had it out with my old man once.' Like it was something all fathers and sons go through. That was it, that's the only time we talked about it."

Later, Sam said to Walter Kelley, "If I had killed Mathew, I would have killed myself"—explaining, perhaps, both the motive for the outburst as well as what stopped it. "It had nothing to do with Mathew, it had to do with himself," says Walter Kelley. "That's the sad part of it."

Sam couldn't find the courage to express his guilt and regret to his son, and so, as always, put it on the screen instead. Mathew Peckinpah had appeared in five of his father's films. Often he stood at the center or on the periphery of some act of brutality perpetrated by the adults stampeding past him. Like the boyhood image of D. Sammy himself bearing witness to the casual brutality on Dunlap's Ranch, the image of innocence destroyed.

The image recurs again in *Cross of Iron.* This time Slavko Stimac would stand in as the blond-haired, big-eyed twin of Mathew, playing a captured Russian soldier whom Steiner tries to save. (They have been ordered to shoot all Russian prisoners.) Steiner hides this boy of no more than fourteen in his bunker; then, during a lull in the fighting, sets him free in the nearby woods. Their farewell is marred by a terribly pretentious soliloquy by James Coburn—easily the most embarrassing moment in the film—but before and after Coburn's monologue the wordless glances between him and the boy are permeated with terrible unspoken sadness and regret.

Ironically, Coburn's act of mercy turns out to be a death sentence. The advance guard of a Russian assault snakes through the woods into which the boy flees. Mistaking him for a German, they machine-gun him. Coburn turns away from the sight of it with a strangled, animal scream.

On July 6, 1976, the eighty-ninth day of photography, Peckinpah was ready to shoot the climactic sequence for *Cross of Iron.* In it, Steiner and Captain Stransky, who had been in conflict throughout the picture, were to put aside their differences and turn to face together the Russian troops advancing on their crumbling defenses. Both had come to realize that the masculine mythology of glorious conquest and grace under pressure was a sham, that in the end there are no victories, moral or otherwise; there is only the ignoble grasp at survival. Moving off together, the two figures were to recede into the vast panorama of the battlefield.

The schedule gave them three days to shoot the sequence in an abandoned trainyard. Special-effects man Sass Bedig had already stacked piles of tires in the yard's empty railroad cars and set them aflame. Smoke billowed out of the broken windows, making it look as if the whole yard was on fire.

But before they could begin shooting, Wolf Hartwig and his co-producer, Alex Winitsky, arrived with bleak news. The picture had been budgeted for $4 million, they had already spent $6 million, and now they were finally out of money and had to pull the plug.

Winitsky passed out script pages for a new ending that no one had seen before, a wretched Stanley Kramer–style dialogue scene between Stransky and Steiner. "You're going to shoot this instead, then wrap it up. The picture's over."

Coburn and Peckinpah turned away and walked off together across the railroad tracks. "Sam and I were looking at all these fucking old trains," says Coburn. "It would have been a wonderful place to shoot, the visuals would have been just great. And all of a sudden, Sam started crying. He started sobbing, 'They're taking the fucking film away from me!' I couldn't fucking believe it, man, here was Sam Peckinpah crying as we're walking down the railroad tracks. He was so pissed off, tears were coming down his face. This enraged me, that these fuckers could bring about that kind of reaction out of this man that I loved and respected. So I put my arm around him and I said, 'Come, on Sam. Sam, goddamn it!' "

Peckinpah pulled himself together and they climbed to the top of an old wooden guard tower. Looking out across the tracks, they saw Hartwig and Winitsky walking toward them. "Well, here they come," Sam said through his teeth.

"Fuck 'em!" Coburn cursed. He flew down the steps, ran out across the tracks to the approaching producers, grabbed Winitsky, and shoved him backward. Winitsky stumbled, then regained his footing. Coburn spat at Hartwig, "Get this fucker off the set! We're gonna do this fucking thing! We're gonna do it right! We're not going to shoot that scene, we're gonna shoot what Sam wants to shoot! Now get the fuck off the set!"

Flustered and white-faced, Hartwig and Winitsky hustled back across the tracks to their cars. Coburn turned and looked up at the guard tower to find Peckinpah doubled over with laughter. Then Sam stood up straight and called out in a voice strong and steady, "Okay, Sass, set it up!"

Suddenly, for the last time, he was the old Sam Peckinpah again, standing tall against the sky on the wooden platform, firing orders, catalyzing the cast and crew as they hustled to set three cameras up to film Coburn and Maximilian Schell running down the railroad tracks, exchanging fire with pursuing Russians.

Instead of taking three days to shoot the ending, they did it in four hours and wrapped the picture that afternoon. Peckinpah flew to London, where he would spend the next seven months editing the film with Tony Lawson, Murray Jordan, and Michael Ellis at Elstree Studios. "We had an army of people working on the picture—music editors, sound-effects editors," says Murray Jordan. "We thought we were the hot shots. 'We're making a Sam Peckinpah film at EMI!' I remember introducing myself to a woman a few cutting rooms away. I said, 'Hi, I'm Murray Jordan.' She said, 'Hi, I'm Marcia Lucas.' I said, 'What are you editing?' She said, 'Oh, we're making this movie called *Star Wars.*' I thought: 'Ah, science-fiction bullshit. Hey, we're making a Peckinpah movie!' "

Peckinpah started snorting coke again and continued to drink heavily throughout post-production. Yet he still managed to stay on his feet and coherent for four to five hours every day, and his editorial eye and instincts were still sharp. The use of montage in the opening documentary footage and the battle sequences in *Cross of Iron* equaled and even surpassed *The Wild Bunch* with their complexity, visceral impact, and terrible beauty.

When *Cross of Iron* was released in Europe in the spring of 1977 it received rave reviews. It became the biggest-grossing picture in Germany and Austria since *The Sound of Music* and won a Bambi, one of Germany's most prestigious performing-arts awards.

The reception in America was the polar opposite. The public wasn't interested in a World War II movie that cast the Germans in a sympathetic light and ended on such a bleak and nihilistic note, and most critics had already written Peckinpah off as little more than a hack with a flair for action sequences. Most reviews were either dismissive or hostile. Avco-Embassy, which distributed the picture in the U.S. and the U.K., dumped it into second-run theaters with barely a whisper of publicity. It grossed a dismal $635,620 in those markets. Meanwhile, that same year *Star Wars,* the flick that had been edited down the hall from the Peckinpah crew at Elstree, grossed $175,849,013. And *Superman,* which Sam had turned down, raked in $81,000,000.

But there was at least one American who liked *Cross of Iron.* Sometime after its release, Orson Welles sent Peckinpah a telegram praising it as the finest antiwar movie he'd ever seen.

Thirteen years later, in the summer of 1990, UCLA hosted a film series at the Melnitz Theater on its campus in Westwood. The series featured forgotten classics selected by Los Angeles critics. Steven Gaydos, programming chairman of the Los Angeles Film Critics Association and an associate editor at the *Hollywood Reporter,* chose *Cross of Iron.* "I wanted to prove the point that this may be the most overlooked of Peckinpah's movies."

But when Gaydos went looking for a print of the movie, he had trouble finding one. Hartwig had sold the distribution rights to a company that later went bankrupt; the rights were then passed on to several other companies, all now out of business. Though there were plenty of copies on video, a theatrical print no longer seemed to exist. "It's a perfect example of how many films we are losing because of neglect," says Gaydos.

Gaydos finally did find a print, in America. Vestron Video had a pristine 35mm print that had been run through a projector only once or twice for videotape transfers. "We ran that print at Melnitz and it looked incredible," says Gaydos. "We had a packed house the night we showed it and the movie blew people away. People's jaws were dropping. They were saying, 'How come we've never heard of this film?' People were outraged, they were saying, 'Well, why can't we get this movie rereleased?' We tried to explain that's not the way the business works. You get your shot and if it doesn't perform in the first week of its release, you're history. But I took great pleasure in dispelling the myth that this movie was a piece of garbage. It's a great movie."

Despite the booze and drugs and the escalating chaos they brought to his life, Sam Peckinpah had managed to turn out four films in the last five years—a more than respectable pace. Three of the four had turned a profit, but just barely. Their revenue was not nearly enough to offset his reputation as a producer's worst nightmare. His artistic standing had so eroded that few in Hollywood were eager to subject themselves to the ordeal of making a picture with him. But executives at EMI, a British production company, were impressed by *Cross of Iron*'s performance in Europe, and felt that Peckinpah had another *Getaway* in him if given the right vehicle and kept on a straight and narrow path.

EMI had bought the screen rights to a cornball country-western song, "Convoy," by C. W. McCall. Its lyrics told the story of a convoy of semi trucks that blasts past the fifty-five mph limit and an armada of police cars that try to enforce it. B. W. L. Norton wrote a script to go with the song's lyrics and jammed it full of moronic slapstick. The characters had as much dimension as Saturday-morning cartoons and the action came fast and furious.

Peckinpah read the *Convoy* script through a fog of coke and booze. The similarly imbecilic *Smokey and the Bandit* had grossed $61 million just a year earlier. Here was a chance to make a box-office smash that would put him right back on top again. Sam signed for $350,000 plus a $2,000-a-week per diem and 10 percent of the gross after the picture broke even.

Those close to Peckinpah were dismayed by his decision, but he didn't feel he had the luxury of turning down the picture. With hundreds of thousands of dollars tied up in real estate and art investments and Latigo Production's pension fund, and the rest of his earnings hemorrhaged away on Porsches, yachts, oceanfront apartments, hotel suites, booze, and coke, he was having cash-flow problems. "At that point in time Sam would have taken almost anything," says Katy Haber. "He didn't have any other offers."

Peckinpah had agreed to make a comic-book movie, but as he began going over the script during pre-production he decided he couldn't leave it at that. This was going to be a Sam Peckinpah film, and he felt compelled to turn it into something more substantial. Brain bobbing in a sea of chemicals, he was incapable of rewriting the script himself, so nothing happened until the cast and crew converged in Albuquerque, New Mexico, in late April. When shooting began, Peckinpah threw the script aside and encouraged his actors—Kris Kristofferson, Ali MacGraw, and Ernest Borgnine—to rewrite and even ad-lib their own dialogue. But the characters that they had to work with were flimsy cardboard façades and the scenes phony and contrived. The actors floundered. Simple, straightforward scenes in the script turned into amorphous, convoluted, and often incomprehensible improvisations on the set.

Out on the highways, the chase and stunt sequences with the hundred-truck convoy were filmed with five cameras. Peckinpah, riding with a camera in a helicopter high above the action, attempted to coordinate the movement of the vehicles below via radio. But the logistics overwhelmed him. Stoned out of his mind, he contradicted himself constantly. The coke-fed paranoia so overwhelmed him that he spent more and more time hiding in his trailer. The entire cast and crew, the trucks with all their teamster drivers, and the extras would stand around for hours in the hot sun waiting for Peckinpah to emerge and give the order to roll the cameras. Finally they got tired of waiting.

"Sam had brought James Coburn onto the picture as a second unit director," says Katy Haber, "because Jimmy wanted to get his DGA card. Jimmy ended up directing scenes with the principal actors; so did Walter Kelley, and so did I. We had to because Sam was dropping the ball."

One by one the hardened veterans of Peckinpah's Bunch, who had fought the battles with him on picture after picture, began to desert the sinking ship: assistant director Newt Arnold, stuntman Whitey Hughes, script supervisor Frank Kowalski—and finally, Katy Haber.

The straw that cracked Katy's back was Marcy Blueher, an attractive middle-aged widow. Sam met her while looking for a house to rent in Albuquerque. Soon they were living together.

"Marcy was a wonderful, sweet, family woman," says Ron Wright. "She'd been married to a dentist who passed away. She had two kids. She was a normal person. She took care of Sam, she was so supportive. When Sam was with them, that was probably the gentlest I'd ever seen him be, and the most loving and caring."

Katy's heart was far from warmed by Sam's latest paramour. Yet she might have endured even Marcy—after all, she'd survived far worse in the past—but what she couldn't stomach was Sam's disintegration as a filmmaker. Her idol was crumbling, and that sickened her. "I was tired of making excuses for him," says Haber. "He was no longer the man that I was proud to be beside. That's when I knew I had to leave. He was destroying himself and I wasn't ready to go down with him."

Katy began an affair with one of the camera operators, something she'd never dared to do before. Not long afterward she went to get some socks out of the bureau drawer in her hotel room, and as she did she discovered a small radio microphone hidden among her clothing. "And then I suddenly realized what was going on. I had been paying all of Sam's bills. Not only was I paying the rent on his house and for his room at the hotel, but I was paying for another room for a Mr. Richardson, and the room was next door to mine. I later discovered that next door to me was Bob Gray [a Hollywood chiropractor, one of the new species of pilot fish that had begun to hover around Peckinpah] with a radio transmitter, listening to everything that was going on in my room."

The next morning, as usual, she picked Sam up and drove him out to the set. Halfway there he suddenly said, "I have to go back to your office." He meant her hotel room, which doubled as Haber's work station.

"What do you mean, you have to go back to my office?" she asked.

"There's something I have to do in your room."

Katy pulled the tiny microphone out of her bag and dangled it before Peckinpah's horrified eyes. "Is this what you're going to go back for?"

"Oh, shit!" he gasped.

"Why did you do it, Sam?"

He squirmed in his seat, awkwardly attempting to recover the situation. "Damn it, I wanted to put a note with it! It's a joke, it isn't a real microphone." She gave him a long, cold stare and he withered into silence, looking out the window, pretending to be fascinated by the endless expanse of sand and tumbleweeds.

A few days later Sam sent Katy on a bogus errand to Los Angeles and, when she arrived there, fired her for the last time. After seven knotted, bruised, and bleeding years it was over. "I never spoke to him again after that, ever," says Haber. *Convoy*'s executive producer, Michael Deeley, offered Haber a job in EMI's Los Angeles office, and she took it. Whenever Peckinpah came there during post-production, she left the building to make certain she'd never have to see him.

"She's gone over to the other side!" Peckinpah would growl whenever Katy's name came up in the years that followed.

"I knew that I had to cut the umbilical cord," says Haber. "I had to. If I was to see him or talk to him I would fall back into it and I'd be lost."

Convoy finally wrapped on September 27, 1977. Garth Craven, who was editing the film with Tony Lawson, was on the set that day. At one point Peckinpah stepped up beside him, stared off into space, and said, "I haven't done one good day's work on this picture—not one day that I really felt I'd put it all together."

He had shot over 800,000 feet of film—almost half a million feet more than he'd exposed on *The Wild Bunch.* The picture finished eleven days behind schedule at a cost of $11 million—more than $5 million over budget. And they hadn't even started post-production.

Peckinpah returned to L.A. and set up editing rooms with Lawson and Craven in a small suite of offices just off the Pacific Coast Highway in Malibu. Post-production lurched along in the same haphazard manner that shooting had. Peckinpah's contract gave him three months to deliver his director's cut for two public previews; EMI allowed him five, but by March 1978 the film was still nowhere near a final cut. It still ran three and a half hours long and had no musical score other than the three-minute title song. *Convoy* was slated for release at the end of June; if the picture had any chance at all of making its money back it would be in the summer, when audiences flocked by the millions to see action pictures and comedies. EMI had no trouble deciding what to do. It could remove Sam and still market *Convoy* with his name prominently featured in advertisements and promotional copy.

For the first time in his career, Sam Peckinpah let a studio take a film away from him without putting up a fight. When a *Los Angeles Times* reporter heard that he'd been fired and called him for a quote, Sam refused to take the call.

EMI's 110-minute version of *Convoy* went into mass release at the end of June 1978. Amidst the rubble of the final product it was possible, if one looked hard enough, to spot the glittering fragments of a once-great talent; the old poetry still sang forth here and there in the images of the big rigs thundering across the vast expanse of the American West.

But only briefly. Throughout much of the movie Peckinpah was all too willing to steal from his earlier work, regurgitating old themes, sequences, set pieces, and dialogue in a vain attempt to raise a pulse in the stillborn movie.

Convoy was greeted by overwhelmingly negative reviews. Many major critics no longer even bothered with Peckinpah; the picture received its licks on the back pages, the whip snapped by second-string critics who reviewed most of the summer's other throwaway exploitation movies.

The final irony of the *Convoy* debacle was that it turned out to be Peckinpah's highest-grossing picture, the biggest box-office hit of his career. It did outstanding business along the drive-in circuit in the Midwest and South, and in Europe and Japan, grossing $46.5 million worldwide ($35 million of that came from overseas markets). As had been done with *The Getaway*, *Convoy* was presold to foreign exhibitors on the strength of its "concept" and the names of Peckinpah, Kristofferson, and MacGraw. The picture turned a profit for EMI before it ever played in a theater.

Unfortunately, *Convoy*'s financial success was not enough to save Sam Peckinpah's career. The picture's final negative cost was $12 million, more than double its original budget. For all its overblown glamour, Hollywood is a small town where gossip travels fast. Those who returned from the *Convoy* location quickly spread word of Peckinpah's white-powder madness. Few studios or independent producers were interested in putting another multimillion dollar picture in the hands of an addict.

For the first time in nine years, Sam Peckinpah finished a picture and found himself without another to grab on to.

Call him "Mike Corey." Matinee-idol handsome, a terrific athlete with a sharp analytical mind, Corey broke into the business at Four Star in the late fifties when Sam Peckinpah was writing and directing his first episodes of "The Rifleman." He quickly rose through the ranks from assistant director to production manager to producer. By 1978 he had accumulated a long and impressive list of credits and was widely regarded as one of the most accomplished producers in television.

Though the two never worked together again after Sam left Four Star, Corey became a regular member of the bunch that gathered at Peckinpah's various beach houses throughout the sixties and seventies. "Sam was easily the most seductive human being I've ever met," says Corey. "He loved to challenge you, but he did it in a very flattering way. He'd say, 'Jesus, Mike, you are *strong!*' Then he'd get this glint in his eye; he'd smile a little and say, 'Almost as strong as me.' Then he'd challenge you to an arm-wrestling match, or something like that. I loved Sam. I guess I was drawn to him because I was the exact opposite in many ways. I'd been much more conservative with my career."

The television shows Corey worked on rarely required out-of-town locations. He was home in time for dinner most week nights, and rarely worked on weekends. Peckinpah, on the other hand, led his movie crews off to the most primitive and miserable locations he could find—loving every minute of it.

"Sam liked to court disaster, he liked the intensity of that," says Corey. "He was wild, unpredictable and crazy, but I found that exciting. You never knew what was going to happen when you were around Sam, there was that sense of danger, adventure. I went to Mexico with him a couple of times. You'd end up in these bars, surrounded by these guys who looked like they'd stepped right out of *The Treasure of the Sierra Madre*. Sam would provoke fights with these guys; one night a Mexican pulled a knife on him on the beach in Baja—Christ! But I always came home at the end of the weekend and went back to work on Monday morning. Sam thought I played it too safe, in my career and in my life. He'd be out there on the edge of the abyss and he'd try to lure me out there too. 'Come on out here, Mike, you'll like it out here.' I'd crawl out to the edge and peer over, but I never jumped in with him."

Shortly after he was fired from *Convoy,* Peckinpah called Corey up and said, with that familiar tension in his voice, "Mike, I have a project I think you'll be interested in. Why don't you come over to my office. We'll talk about it." Another sly challenge, a contest of some kind. Corey couldn't resist.

He drove over to Goldwyn Studios, where Peckinpah still had an office. Sam handed him a copy of *Snowblind,* a recently published biography of a cocaine trafficker that took the reader on a rogues' gallery tour of the drug underworld, from the cocaine factories of Colombia to the New York high-society end users. "This is going to be my next picture. I've already bought the rights to it and lined up the financing, and I want you to produce it. We fly down to Colombia next week to meet with the investors and scout locations." Peckinpah stared across the desk at Mike with a serpent's grin.

"Of course I knew why he wanted to make a picture in Colombia, I wasn't stupid," says Corey. "He wanted to establish his own cocaine connection. That was at least as important as the movie deal. I could see that the potential for trouble was unlimited, but Sam had that look in his eye. The subtext was: 'Do you have the balls to come with me?' "

Corey had a TV movie in development, but it would be at least two weeks before it got a green light. "I had this window of free time, and the adventure of it excited me," he says. "I figured I had nothing to lose. If Sam's deal didn't come together, I could always bail out and come back to my other project in L.A. See, I'd go on these things with him, but I always had my escape hatch."

And the way Sam was acting, he might well need it. There was a television set in the office, tuned to a vacant channel. The speaker blasted static throughout their conversation. Every fifteen minutes or so Peckinpah got up and walked to the minikitchen at the back of the office to snort one of the lines of coke laid out on the top of the stove.

Returning from the stovetop yet again, Sam sniffled and ran a finger beneath his nose, his eyes bright. He named a prominent character actor, whom we'll call "Peter Martin." Martin had lined up the financing in exchange for a percentage of the profits and a juicy role in the picture. "Peter will be going with us to Colombia," Peckinpah explained. "There are a couple of entrepreneurs in Bogotá, a pair of brothers. They're putting up the money for the picture, he's set up a meeting with them."

"Sam," Mike interjected, "why do you have the TV on like that?"

"Shhhh!" Peckinpah raised an index finger to his lips in alarm, then mouthed the words, "The office is bugged." Then he continued in a normal voice. "Anyway, Mike, expenses are not going to be a problem on this trip." He leaned back, opened a desk drawer, pulled out a paper bag, and handed it over to Corey, who looked inside.

"It was filled with money, large bills," Corey says. "There must have been at least ten thousand dollars in cash in there."

On the day that Peckinpah, Corey, and Martin were to depart for Bogotá, Sam called Corey up to tell him there'd been a slight change of plans. Sam had to go to Mexico City on urgent business, and so would fly from there to Colombia and meet Corey and Martin at the Bogotá Hilton.

It wasn't unusual for Peckinpah to make such last-minute changes, so Mike shrugged it off and took the flight with Martin, his pockets stuffed with wads of cash from Sam's paper bag. When they arrived at the Bogotá airport they were met by a lawyer for the Colombian brothers, who led them through customs. The officers waved Mike through without even asking him to open his bag, and he walked out through the glass doors to the street, where cabs idled for passengers. He stood there and waited and waited and waited, but Martin and the lawyer did not follow him. Finally he turned and walked back into customs and found the place in an uproar. A group of customs officers, including one of high rank, now surrounded Martin and the lawyer. They had popped open Martin's huge Samsonite suitcase. It was packed with hundred-dollar bills—$500,000 in cash, one of the officers reported after they finished counting it. Martin appeared unperturbed by their discovery, "We're bringing this money in to finance a movie," he coolly explained.

The officers confiscated the cash, but told the Americans and the Colombian lawyer that they were free to go. On the car ride to the Hilton, the lawyer cursed and explained, "The guy we bribed wasn't there today. He was supposed to be, but he didn't show up." Corey thought it best not to press him with any follow-up questions.

They checked into the Hilton, where they had a three-bedroom suite that Peckinpah had already moved into. When they got there Sam pulled Mike aside and whispered, "I had no idea Peter was acting as a donkey for these people! I can't believe he did that, that's insane!"

The next night Peckinpah and Corey met in their suite with the two Colombian brothers who were to invest in the movie. The brothers were well groomed and dressed like Creative Artists agents except for the fact that they wore sidearms. Martin was nowhere to be seen. "I never could figure out what Peter's role was," says Corey. "He was always coming and going with great secrecy; he seemed to be pursuing his own agenda with these people, which may or may not have been connected to our movie deal. I never got a straight answer from either him or Sam on that."

They did a few lines of coke before getting down to business. Finally one of the brothers said, "So tell us about the great Sam Peckinpah movie that you want to make."

Sam's head swiveled toward Corey. "Tell 'em the story, Mike."

Feeling a bit on the spot, Corey cleared his throat and launched in, synopsizing the basic plot to *Snowblind.* "Well," Corey recalls, "these guys had no idea Sam wanted to make a movie about the cocaine trade. Somehow they'd gotten the impression that it was going to be a movie about the oppressed peasants of Colombia rising up against the ruling class, one of those Marxist manifesto numbers. When they found out that we wanted to make a movie about coke dealers, they went ape shit!"

"That's fucking crazy!" the oldest brother bellowed. "Absolutely no way will you make this movie! Understand? No way!"

The meeting broke up at dawn with all participants coked to the gills, and Peckinpah trying to reassure his investors: "We'll begin organizing exactly what kind of movie we're going to make. I'll make a movie about love and hate and lust and greed and man's inhumanity to man. We're going to need transportation to look for locations."

The next day the brothers reappeared. "You cannot stay here, it is not safe," the eldest said cryptically. "All of the rooms in the Hilton are bugged. You're coming with us!"

Peckinpah and Corey loaded their luggage into the brothers' waiting car and were driven out of town. "Way the fuck out in the middle of nowhere, they take us," says Corey, "to this country club type place with a golf course and hotel rooms. They put us up there in adjoining rooms."

The brothers had arranged for a lavish banquet in Sam's honor. The affair had been set up before Peckinpah arrived in Colombia, before the brothers discovered exactly what kind of movie he intended to make. It would be embarrassing to cancel it now, so Sam was instructed that his attendance that evening was mandatory. Held in the sprawling mansion of one of Bogotá's elite, the champagne, roast beef, and roast chicken were consumed by a crowd of politicians, wealthy landowners, businessmen, and military officers festooned with colorful medals and regalia.

At the conclusion of the party, the brothers and a phalanx of gunmen ushered Peckinpah and Corey to a waiting car and drove them off to another house owned by the younger brother. "The place was crawling with guys all carrying guns," says Corey. Once there the oldest brother began arguing with Peckinpah again: "You will under no circumstances make a movie about cocaine, *comprende?*"

"Sam's trying to play macho with him," says Corey. "A press conference had been set up for the next day; it had been set up before we even arrived, and Sam was supposed to announce his plans to make a movie in Colombia. So now he's saying to this guy, 'I'm going to that press conference tomorrow and tell them what kind of movie I'm going to make, and I'll tell them whatever the hell I want!' "

"No, we tell you what you're going to say and do!" said the oldest brother.

"It seemed like Sam was pushing this guy's buttons on purpose," says Corey, "to see if he could goad him into actually killing him."

The quarrel degenerated into a screaming match, and finally the gunmen split Peckinpah and Corey up. Each was ushered into a separate bedroom and Mike found himself alone with the younger brother, a gunman, and the brothers' lawyer. "The lawyer was more moderate, he was like the good cop and the brother was the bad cop. They get in an argument. It's in Spanish, so I miss most of it, but I catch enough to realize that they're arguing about the movie, the suitcase at the airport, and what they should do with me—whether they should knock me off or not. I could tell that the lawyer was arguing for moderation, saying that I wasn't part of it, that I didn't know anything."

Finally, without any explanation, they hustled him out of the room again, just as gunmen brought Sam out of another. The two were escorted out of the house through the predawn air to a waiting car. Peckinpah slid into the front seat between two triggermen, and Mike into the back between two more. "I looked in Sam's eyes and I could see he was finally scared, he wasn't trying to act macho anymore, the game was over," says Corey. "I felt totally powerless, like you did when you were a small child and completely at the mercy of adults—that same hellish feeling of helplessness. When the car drove off into the night, it felt like I was riding on this huge wave of adrenaline. I was totally convinced that they were taking me off to some jungle to blow my brains out."

But to his amazement, the gunsels drove them back to the country club and dropped them off without explanation. Back in their adjoining rooms, Corey paced frantically while Peckinpah did more coke. "Sam went into this long coked-out monologue, this stream-of-consciousness confessional sort of thing. At one point he suddenly said to me, 'You know, Mike, I'm impotent. I have been for years.' It was a strangely moving moment. After all the years of trying to out macho each other, for him to expose that vulnerability to me when we were so close to death . . . It sounds weird to say, but I never felt closer to him than right then."

But the shadows of Colombian triggermen loomed large, and there was little time for self exploration. "Sam," Corey said, "we've got to get the hell out of here! We've got to get out of this country now!"

"I can't," Peckinpah murmured, "they took my passport away."

"They what? Oh, shit!" They hadn't taken Corey's. Why? "Sam, what in the hell are we doing here? Why the hell did we come down here? What the hell is this all about?"

"Mike"—Peckinpah looked at him steadily and spoke with calm deliberation—"I don't want to go out like Roman Polanski, getting busted for screwing a twelve-year-old. I want to go out in flames."

"Welcome to my suicide—that's what it was all about," says Corey. "The only problem was I didn't want to go down with him. I had other plans. I really felt torn. I mean, I loved Sam, I really *loved* him—but I wasn't ready to die with him in that fucking place!"

Peckinpah listened to Corey's pleas for another alternative, then finally said calmly, "Mike, there's only one thing you can do: Make a run for it."

"But I can't leave you here!"

"You've got to." Sam produced the phone numbers of his lawyer, Norma Fink, and a couple of other associates in Los Angeles. "If you make it back, call them. They might be able to get me out of this."

"I had a wad of cash left in my pockets," says Corey, "so I called a cab, got my luggage, and headed straight for the airport. It's six in the morning, the sun's up, and I'm scared to death I'm gonna get stopped, that someone's gonna murder me or bust me, but I got to the airport. I got there and caught the first plane smoking. I didn't care where, I just wanted to get out!"

Corey made it to Miami, then caught another flight to L.A. For weeks afterward as he drove around Hollywood and Beverly Hills, Corey imagined he was being followed. He carried his .357

magnum with him everywhere he went and slept with it under his pillow. "I called Fink and the other numbers Sam gave me," says Corey. "I don't know what they did or didn't do to help him, but ten days later he made it back to L.A., and so did Martin. The next time I saw Sam he acted as if the whole thing had never happened. Later I found out he didn't even own the rights to *Snowblind.* Some other production company had already optioned it. It was the most hellish experience of my life. But you know something, it was also the most exciting. That time, Sam pulled me over the edge with him. He was crazy, out of control, but so *alive!* Most people spend their entire lives in a comfortable rut. You could accuse Sam Peckinpah of almost anything but that."

After he returned from Colombia, Peckinpah closed up his office at Goldwyn's and the trailer at Malibu, and moved north, out of L.A. and into the High Country of Montana. Warren Oates had built a cabin on 700 acres of land outside of Livingston, and one sodden night Sam negotiated a serpentine deal to buy a chunk of it: 25 acres, plus another 600 which he would co-own with Oates. He hired local contractors to build a massive cabin for him at the highest point (6,970 feet) of the property, in a canyon below the jutting peaks of the Absaroka Mountains, which tower at the back end of Yellowstone National Park.

It was a spectacular structure, yet strangely hollow inside, the furniture lost in its dark and cavernous interior. It served as a metaphor for Sam Peckinpah's life. "The contractor talked him into building it that way," says Joe Swindlehurst, a Livingston attorney who became Peckinpah's lawyer and close friend in the Montana years. "Sam was drunk most of the time when they were building it—too much drinking and not enough thinking. He never came out and said it, but I think Sam felt very bad about that cabin. I bet he didn't spend more than a couple of weeks total in the place."

Most of his time was spent at the Yellowstone Lodge in Livingston, and then later in seven rooms he rented at the top of the Murray Hotel, where he set up his "production offices."

He had taken Marcy Blueher—the Albuquerque widow—

and her children with him and made her the fourth Mrs. Peckinpah. "I think it was a new start for Sam," says Ron Wright, "a chance for him to have a ready-made family, a very stable trio of people . . . it just didn't work." Within a matter of months Marcy, like Marie and Bego and Joie before her, was driven away by Sam's drinking and drug use, his rages and his increasingly irrational behavior.

He still had an entourage that hovered at his bedside, catering to his every whim. But the species was now considerably lower on the food chain. "Sam pushed all of his old friends away," says Kip Dellinger. "He was paranoid, he didn't trust them, he thought they were trying to steal his money. The only people he trusted at that time were his drug friends, and they, ironically, were the ones who really were interested in stealing his money."

On May 18, 1979, Joe Swindlehurst's secretary tried to call Peckinpah, but his phone was busy. The hotel operator promised to get through as soon as the line cleared. When she did, a few minutes later, she could tell by Peckinpah's slurred response that he was in serious trouble.

The paramedics were called. Sam had had a major heart attack. They rushed him to the local hospital, where the doctors managed to stabilize him. After a series of tests they decided that Sam needed a pacemaker to regulate his erratic heartbeat and rushed him into the operating room. "That went on all day," says Swindlehurst. "They put three separate pacemakers in him and he was completely wild, he thrashed around so much, he kept yanking out the pacemaker wires. They lost his pulse I don't know how many times, and the nurse was yelling at him to come back. Finally they got the third pacemaker to take and he stabilized. Then word of what had happened got out and people started arriving from out of town. Half of Hollywood showed up."

Jim Silke was one of those who flew up from L.A., along with Kristen, Sharon, Denny, and David Peckinpah. At one point Silke found himself sitting in Peckinpah's room with Paul Peterson, a frequent companion of Sam's during this period, and Peterson's girlfriend, Patty. Sam begged them to get him some cocaine, then spewed a jet of hot curses at his former co-writer: "Fucking Silke! He'll never do anything, he won't get me anything! The fucker's no good!"

"I just sat there and listened," Silke recalls. "Finally Paul and Patty left. I stood up and walked over. He looked at me. It was all an act. He started to cry. We hugged each other. He knew I knew. That was always the relationship. He knew he could never lie to me, and I could never lie to him. It was an understanding. He was so ashamed. He didn't want to die. At other times I thought he did, but this time he didn't, he really didn't."

Peckinpah stayed in the clinic for two weeks. Finally the DTs passed and his heartbeat and the rest of his vital signs returned to normal. By that time the circus of well-wishers had departed. Sam checked out on a Sunday morning; Joe Swindlehurst and his wife, Carolyn, came to pick him up. "He didn't really have anybody," says Swindlehurst. "Carolyn and I were about as close to family as he had. We went and got Sam and put him in the car. The doctor had been lecturing him for days: no cigarettes, no vodka, no this and that. We said, 'Where do you want to go? We'll take you home to our house, you can stay with us.' No, he wanted to go back to the hotel."

When they arrived at the hotel, Peckinpah stepped into the lobby, made a sharp right, and went right into the bar. The place was just opening up; a houseman was vacuuming the cigarette-littered carpet. Sam took a seat on one of the high stools at the bar and Swindlehurst and his wife sat down beside him. "Get the bartender," Sam barked at the houseman.

The bartender arrived and asked them what they wanted to drink. "Orange juice," Swindlehurst and his wife chirped meekly.

"Bullshit," growled Peckinpah, "we're having Ramos Fizzes!"

"Well, the bartender doesn't know how to make a Ramos Fizz," says Swindlehurst. "Sam explains that it's a lot of gin. So he fills up a planter's punch glass with gin and eggwhite, etc. Sam drinks this puppy down and licks the eggwhite off of his mustache, then he goes 'Augghhh!' and grabs his chest, and the son of bitch goes right off the back of the bar stool. He's lying there on the barroom floor. We thought he'd died. My wife started to cry and we're looking at the son of a bitch. I mean, we can't believe it. And all of sudden he can't help it anymore and he starts to laugh."

11

"It Ain't Like It Used to Be, But . . . It'll Do"

Mathew Peckinpah was now eighteen years old and lost. His shaggy blond hair flowed over his ears, he'd dropped out of high school and had no idea what he wanted to do with his life. Consumed by the self-loathing his father had passed on to him, Mathew numbed himself with clouds of marijuana smoke, his hazel eyes remote and inward, his face and voice a monotone mask.

The boy's directionless apathy enraged Sam, and his sarcastic asides to him grew even more vicious than they had been in the past. "What you need is a few years in the Corps," he growled at Mathew. "A few weeks on Parris Island would straighten your ass out!"

One day Mathew decided his father was right. He was tired of drifting, of not knowing who he was or what he wanted. He desperately wanted some structure in his life, a solid foundation, to belong somewhere, to gain respect in his father's eyes.

So he called a Marine Corps recruiter in Butte. The recruiter agreed to drive down to Livingston, pick Mathew up, and take him to Butte for a presentation on the Corps. When Mathew told his father about it, Sam suddenly became flustered and anxious. "Well, just listen to what they have to say; whatever you do, don't enlist until you've had time to think about it."

But after hearing the presentation, Mathew knew what he wanted to do. He called his father from Butte. "Well, I did it, I signed up," he said excitedly. "I'm a marine."

The other end of the line fell silent for a long moment. "Well, all right," Sam finally said, sounding tired and sad.

After he hung up, Sam dictated a letter to his son that read, in part: "This day, September 9th, is probably the most important day in my life—I know it is in yours. For, from this day on, both our lives have changed. I am proud of you and I am proud to be your father. . . . Sometimes homesickness, loneliness, will become almost unbearable. But know, as I did, that your Dad is right there with you."

Mathew shipped off for San Diego a month later to enter boot camp. The words in Sam's letter were almost comically out of synch with his behavior over the last several years—Sam had been anything but a sturdy father figure—but when Mathew took hold of his own life and pulled himself out of his psychological quagmire, Sam followed his lead.

He left Montana, moved back to his trailer in Malibu, and began picking up the pieces of his career. He would continue to drink and snort coke over the next couple of years, but now made a concerted effort to reduce his intake. The deranged excess of the Montana years receded. There would be periodic binges, lost weekends, but in between these he managed to limit his consumption of booze and cocaine so that he remained upright and coherent, if never quite cold sober.

He set up a production company with Ted Post, the director of *Go Tell the Spartans* and *Magnum Force* and a friend dating back to Sam's "Gunsmoke" days. They rented offices at MGM, but they never managed to assemble financing for any of their projects. By this time Martin Baum had grown tired of the blood-vessel-popping frustrations of movie producing and had become an agent again, joining Creative Artists, which was rapidly becoming the most powerful talent agency in Hollywood. Disenchanted with his current agent, Herman Citron, who had represented him for years, Peckinpah went to Baum, hat in hand, and asked if he would represent him. The animosities of *Killer Elite* melted away and Baum agreed at once to take Sam on as a client. It was quite a coup for Peckinpah to sign on with the most prestigious agency in Hollywood, but the uplift lasted only a brief time.

Baum soon discovered that Peckinpah was a hard sell, a very hard sell. Sam's erratic behavior on *Convoy* had not been forgotten. Nobody wanted to put a multimillion dollar production in his hands. Baum's sales pitch gradually worked its way down the ladder from big-budget features to shoestring independent productions. Peckinpah had to land an assignment, any kind of an assignment, to prove that he'd pulled himself together and could bring a picture in on time and on budget. Finally, Baum turned to episodic television, which Sam hadn't worked in for fifteen years, but still he found no takers.

Peckinpah's career had bottomed out. But professional catastrophe had its consolations, he discovered. Now that the spotlight of fame had passed him by, his vision cleared and he saw, for the first time in decades, the things that really mattered to him. Like his kids.

After Mathew graduated from boot camp he stayed on at Camp Pendleton to undergo additional training, and his father began driving down to San Diego on weekends to visit him. For the first time ever, Sam was going to Mathew instead of Mathew coming to him.

On Sam's fiftieth birthday, in 1975, all Hollywood had convened on Jerry Fielding's house to help him celebrate it. His kids, as always, had found themselves shoved into the background by a horde of celebrities and syncophants. In February 1982, Sam drove down to San Diego by himself in his cream-colored Lincoln, to spend his fifty-seventh birthday with his son.

At the time Mathew was undergoing intensive training for a special rifle squad. He'd been screwing up and the pressure was pushing him toward the breaking point. On Sunday he met his father at a hotel in San Diego. Begonia's brother, Juan José Palacios, was also there, and together the three drove across the border into Tijuana to have lunch. Sam had several margaritas with his meal and asked Mathew to drive them back to the hotel. Mathew climbed nervously behind the wheel of his father's aircraft-carrier-sized Lincoln and drove stiffly toward the exit of the parking lot. *I hope Dad doesn't start riding me about my driving,* he thought.

As he passed through the exit he noticed the parking-lot attendant waving urgently. *Oh, shit, forgot to pay,* Mathew realized. He stopped the car and threw it into reverse.

"No!" Sam cried from the backseat, "no, don't back up!"

POOOOSH! The Lincoln's rear radial tires deflated in an instant, their now-flabby rubber impaled on the exit spikes. Mathew leapt out of the car, slamming the door behind him. Sobs clawed their way up his throat despite his best efforts to contain them. He heard the rear door open. Sam stepped out.

"I turned to look at him," Mathew recalls, "and he was laughing, but not in a hostile way. He was very warm. I just felt like shit. He thought it was funny, but at the same time he could tell that I had all this built-up stress from the training and all this negative shit. He just took me in his arms and he understood what I was feeling. He didn't wonder why I was crying, he *knew.* He was supportive and there for me, but also he was still light and jested about it."

Sharon had married an actor, Richard Marcus, and in February 1981 they had their first child, a boy, Theo. Sam Peckinpah was a grandfather. When news of Sharon's pregnancy had first reached him, Sam wrote a letter to her husband, Richard, that read in part: "To become a father is an enlightening, terrifying, and rewarding experience—it was to me—I'm sure it will be to you—but—after my initial elation over the knowledge that I was to become a grandfather, I began to and still do wonder about my obligations, privileges, and role, so to speak. . . . I await with fear and trepidation, delight, anticipation and joy the birth of your child, my daughter's child."

Sam visited Sharon's house regularly after Theo's birth, and his eldest daughter tried to set her limits with him: "I don't want you showing up here with an entourage, and I don't want you showing up drunk." He came by himself, or occasionally with Walter Kelley; one time he'd be bombed out of his skull, and the next time cold sober.

Kristen would go out to visit him at his trailer in Malibu. Sometimes he'd be drunk and angry, but many times now he'd be sober and relaxed and they'd just sit and talk calmly about everyday things. Sometimes these tranquil moods would last for weeks, far longer than she'd ever experienced with her father before.

Kristen lived with Gill Dennis in an apartment in Silver Lake during the time that the Hillside Strangler was plying his trade. One night after visiting with her father at the trailer, Kristen got in her car to go home. Gill was out of town, so Dad said, "You call me when you get there. Call me and let me know you're all right." On the drive back to Silver Lake, Kristen tried not to think about the Strangler, but hairy psychopaths kept lunging into her thoughts, so when she got home she conducted a fearful search of the entire apartment—the closets, the space under the bed, the shower—to assure herself that no mad-dog killer lay in ambush. In the midst of this she forgot all about Dad—until the phone rang. "You said you'd call! Are you all right?"

"He wasn't mad," says Kristen, "he was relieved to know I was safe. It was a nice feeling, knowing someone was that concerned about you."

Sam Peckinpah desperately needed to prove to Hollywood that he'd licked his demons, that if given the chance to direct again he would behave responsibly and was still capable of doing good work. The opportunity came in the summer of 1981 from the man who'd given Sam his first big break in the business, Don Siegel. Siegel was in the middle of shooting *Jinxed,* a comedy-melodrama starring Bette Midler and Rip Torn. He asked Peckinpah if he would be interested in coming in to direct twelve days of second unit work, which would include many incidental scenes with the stars and one major stunt in which a truck and trailer careen off a remote highway and down the side of a cliff. The salary was generous for a second unit director, but a fraction of what Peckinpah had once commanded: $25,000. Sam didn't have to call his agent; he said yes immediately.

Walter Kelley, who had worked as a dialogue or second unit director on four Peckinpah features, also went on salary as Sam's assistant. Together they laid out a detailed storyboard of the shots for the big stunt sequence—something Sam had rarely done for his own films. "God," Siegel exclaimed when they presented it to him, "this is the most detailed storyboard I've ever seen!"

"Sam wanted to prove himself to Siegel," says Walter Kelley. "He was almost sick to his stomach the first day on the set. The night before they shot the big stunt sequence in the San Gabriel Mountains Sam couldn't sleep, so he went out to the location early in the morning before any of the crew arrived to look the place over and think about how he wanted to shoot the sequence."

Peckinpah used three cameras set at different speeds to film the stunt. He staged and shot it and the rest of the assigned scenes with the swift assurance of an accomplished craftsman. "Peckinpah helped Siegel out as much as Siegel helped Peckinpah," says Reza Badiyi. "Sam helped him finish the picture; it was a collaboration. By doing it, Sam proved that he wanted to work, and that he could."

Suddenly he was back in the game again. Peter Davis and William Panzer—bottom feeders in the Hollywood food chain who specialized in low-budget exploitation pictures—offered him the chance to direct an adaptation of a Robert Ludlum espionage potboiler, *The Osterman Weekend.* Alan Sharp, author of *Night Moves* and *Ulzana's Raid,* had written the screenplay. It was incredibly convoluted, barely coherent, but action-packed and better than the slimy drive-in movies Peckinpah had recently been offered. And the money was decent, $450,000, though only a fraction of what the top directors in the business now commanded. Baum told him he had to take the assignment to prove that he could deliver a picture on schedule and on budget. If he wanted a crack at another major feature, there really was no other choice.

When he moved into his spacious office in the musty old Columbia Studios on Gower Street in Hollywood, Peckinpah talked

Panzer and Davis into giving him a shot at a rewrite. But when he turned in his first twenty pages, the producers took one look at them and forbade him to touch another word.

Panzer and Davis not only forbade him from any rewriting, they also vetoed the hiring of many of his old bunch for the cast and crew. He wanted James Coburn to play an upper-echelon CIA agent and Lou Lombardo to cut the picture; the produces refused to hire either, fearing Peckinpah would build a power base from which he could wage war against them.

He was at least able to get his old cinematographer, Johnny Coquillon, who had shot *Straw Dogs, Pat Garrett,* and *Cross of Iron,* and to assemble a first-rate cast that his producers approved of. John Hurt, Craig T. Nelson, Dennis Hopper, Meg Foster, and Burt Lancaster all signed on, most for significantly less than their usual salaries—many actors were still eager for the chance to work with Peckinpah. For the lead, Panzer and Davis insisted on hiring Rutger Hauer, a Dutch actor who usually played heavies but was hovering on the edge of stardom in the wake of *Blade Runner* and the sprawling TV miniseries, "Inside the Third Reich." The production was laid out on a fifty-four-day shooting schedule with a budget of $6,699,192. A non-union crew would be used and the movie would be shot in and around Los Angeles to cut costs.

In the old days Peckinpah would have mobilized his cast and crew into an all-out war against the producers. But, as Baum continued to remind him, he needed to bring this picture in on time, needed to prove to Hollywood that he was not impossible to work with. So he gritted his teeth and sometimes turned and stalked away cursing, but he held back his anger time and time again. The picture wrapped on January 17, 1983—on time and on budget.

Over the next eight months Peckinpah worked closely with editor David Rawlins to produce his cut of the film; together they searched for ways to breathe a little life and style into the pedestrian material. Unfortunately Rawlins was a heavy cocaine user, and under the deadline pressure Peckinpah's discipline crumbled. "Sam and Rawlins were both doing coke and fighting with the producers, making it an impossible situation," says Walter Kelley, who worked as the dialogue director on the picture. "You know, people in this town talk, and word got around that Sam was using again, which ruined his chances of getting another film after *Osterman*."

Yet he still managed to deliver a fine cut for the one public preview guaranteed to him under his contract. In his version, Peckinpah once again resorted to the same guerrilla tactic he'd employed on *Killer Elite:* subtly ridiculing the movie his producers had forced him to make. In the climactic shootout Hauer's wife, played by Meg Foster, shoots an assassin with a crossbow. The action is brilliantly edited and for one brief spurt the old magic comes to life again. But otherwise one had to squint hard to spot the traces of a once-great talent.

Panzer and Davis recut the picture, removing most of Peckinpah's satirical edges; the finished product was a pretentious, hopelessly muddled potboiler with a few nice performances and fitfully energetic action sequences. Released in November 1983, it received a few sympathetic reviews from sentimental critics who remembered the glory days and hoped that, with encouragement, Peckinpah would get a shot at one last great film. *Weekend* grossed over $6 million domestically during its first year of release and did extremely well in Europe and on the home-video market that had just exploded onto the American scene. It made the top-ten chart in video rentals and stayed on the list for a number of weeks, and so probably turned a substantial profit for the producers.

Realizing that future employment depended on the picture's performance, Peckinpah agreed to go on a promotional tour of Europe, and took his attorney, Joe Swindlehurst, along with him. Sam fell off the wagon and the trip turned into another long, drunken nightmare. Swindlehurst found himself by turns doubled over with laughter, enraged, and depressed by his friend's alcoholic hysteria.

But it was Sam's last bender. When he returned to the States he quit drinking, for good this time. For the last year of his life he touched not a drop. He did continue to take Seconal to calm his anxiety and help him sleep at night, and still snorted coke, though the blinding blizzard of the late seventies now slowed to occasional light flurries.

The early 1980s brought a string of staggering losses. Bill Holden, Robert Ryan, Warren Oates, Jerry Fielding, and Strother Martin died. And then there was that final death in 1983, the one he never talked about, not even with his closest family members and friends—Fern Peckinpah's. Her last years had not been pleasant. Her grip on reality had always been tenuous, but creeping senility and a Darvon habit—her psychiatrist had given her a prescription—caused her to lose it altogether in the late seventies. The symptoms were small at first—she became absentminded, her thoughts and conversation wandered—but they quickly gathered momentum. Once she left the phone off the hook for days. When a repairman came to check on it because of complaints, she pulled a gun on him. Then neighbors noticed her walking her property line at two in the morning with a loaded shotgun.

Finally she had to be committed to a nursing home, where she spent the last seven years of her life. Once there, she quickly drifted off into a foggy dreamworld; her mumblings revealed a mind that danced through the long-lost landscape of her youth.

Sam was living in Montana at the time. "He used to agonize about her," says Joe Swindlehurst. "He would announce, out of nowhere, that he was not going to see her. Well, if somebody announces that he's not going to see his mother that means he's deeply troubled because he hasn't. So I said if it was eating him up like that he ought to go see her, maybe he'd feel better. He'd think about that, and then he'd announce even more emphatically that he was not going to see his mother."

But finally he did go, with Fern Lea. They found her lashed in a chair so she could sit upright, her once-thick curls of brown hair shorn to a white stubble, her skin pale and slack, eyes glassy as she babbled incoherently. Fern Lea couldn't handle it; she turned and fled the room in tears. But Sam sat there calmly beside his mother, nodding his head as if he understood her every word, murmuring in response. "Yes, Mother, of course. I know you do . . ." Like their heart-to-heart talks of the old days. To the very end, in her presence, he played the dutiful and attentive son and kept his anger locked out of sight.

She died shortly after that. There was a small graveside service. He stood by the hole in the earth that waited to take his mother and listened to the eulogy without expression. He did not piss on her grave as he had so often vowed he would, but neither did he shed any tears over it. After the service was over he returned immediately to Los Angeles. If any feelings boiled within, he concealed them entirely.

Sam had come to resemble one of the characters in his westerns—Steve Judd, Pike Bishop, Cable Hogue—a man who'd outlived his time, who carried upon his weary shoulders the burden of a reputation recklessly earned and now impossible to shake off. Yet he didn't give up. "By God, he was a scrappy little guy," says Joe Swindlehurst. "The man was a fighter."

And so he made the rounds. Meeting after meeting with development executives who were younger than his own kids, who'd never heard of H. L. Mencken or B. Traven or even Michael Curtiz and Raoul Walsh. They listened politely to his earnest pitches for *Hi Lo Country*, *Castaway*, and *My Pardner* because they'd been told by the few old-timers left at the studios that Peckinpah had once been a big name in the business.

"He'd outlived his era," says L. Q. Jones. "Sam knew it would happen to him eventually, right from the beginning he knew. It happens to all of us." To friends Sam muttered morosely, "I wonder if there's a place for me anymore in this world."

But if the Hollywood establishment had forgotten him, film scholars had not. His reputation among critics began to climb again, even as his job prospects plummeted. In the early 1980s he received a Golden Boot Award, and another trophy from the Cowboy Hall of Fame for his contributions to the western film genre. USC, the Seattle Film Society, and Rice University in Texas all put on retrospectives of his work. The theaters were packed and Peckinpah stayed after the screenings to answer questions from the audience. At the end of these sessions dozens of fervent Peckinpah-heads rushed forward with posters and stills from his films for him to autograph, and he graciously accommodated all of them.

Four full-length books on his work were published in the late seventies and early eighties, including Paul Seydor's *Peckinpah—*

The Western Films (the most authoritative critical examination ever done) and Garner Simmons' *Peckinpah—A Portrait in Montage* (which still gives the fullest documentation of the making of each of his films). "It's very gratifying," Peckinpah said of his resurging reputation, the barest trace of a smile curving up beneath his white mustache.

The most fulfilling validation in the last year of Sam's life came from a Malibu hairdresser named Carol O'Connor. He first met her when he moved back to the beach from Montana. Walter Kelley, who also lived in Malibu, had been getting haircuts from her and when Sam asked him to recommend a barber, Kelley took him over to the hair salon O'Connor worked at on the Pacific Coast Highway. A shapely thirty-three-year-old blonde, O'Connor was not the typical airhead beautician. Well-read, intelligent, even-tempered and independent, she supported herself and her thirteen-year-old son with her practice.

He did not pounce on her; he didn't even court her at first. In the beginning his advances were tentative. For the first three years they knew each other they remained friends, seeing each other only when Sam came over to her place for a haircut or called her to come out to wherever he was working to give him one there. They talked about books; both read voraciously and began to trade their latest finds.

When he was directing *Osterman Weekend* Sam called and asked if she'd like to work in it as an extra for a few days. It sounded like fun, so she agreed. While they were standing together chatting on the set, Burt Lancaster came up to her and said, "You know, this man has a serious crush on you."

After the picture wrapped they started dating. They went out to dinner together, to movies—it was a formal courtship, something Sam hadn't done in years. "I really liked him," says O'Connor. "He was so intelligent and so insightful and so unhurried. He cared about what you thought. He was a very strong, intelligent man, and yet he was also childlike at the same time."

He'd quit drinking; she never saw him touch a drop. "He said that if I ever saw him drunk I would walk out the door, that he was an ugly drunk. He looked wonderful. He not only didn't drink, he didn't have the craving to drink."

Sometimes, if he was out of town working on a project or a deal for one, he would invite her to come join him for a few days. When she arrived at his hotel suite on these occasions she would find that he had filled it with baskets of flowers, bottles of champagne on ice, and little gifts distributed throughout the rooms like Easter eggs. He would lead her around to discover each of them, as delighted as a kid on Christmas morning.

"Sam said to me at one point, which was always a great treasure to me, that I gave him the happiest year of his life," says O'Connor. "And he gave me the happiest year of my life."

In 1984 Charisma Records decided to make an hour-long documentary about Julian Lennon to promote his first album, which he was recording for them. The documentary would follow Lennon through rehearsals, recording sessions, and concerts. It would be aired on MTV, the rock-and-roll upstart that had risen to prominence with the proliferation of cable TV. The purpose was to solidify a public identity for Julian separate and apart from his father, John.

Martin Lewis, the brash young producer assigned to the project, wanted to hire a major film director. "I didn't want one of these young whiz-kids out of film school, I didn't want a slick music-video director," says Lewis. "I wanted to find somebody who would bring something to it, I didn't know what, but it had to be some texture, some perspective."

He approached Alan Rudolph and Robert Altman, but neither was available. When a friend—Dennis Delrogh, a film critic for *L.A. Weekly*—suggested Sam Peckinpah, Lewis cringed. "Are you kidding me? I can just imagine what he'd do, open the film with a slow-motion recreation of John Lennon's murder."

"No, no, Martin, you're thinking of the clichéd image of him," Delrogh persisted. "You're not thinking of Sam Peckinpah's work and what he's capable of doing. He will at the very least do something very filmic, and he will probably find themes that will be quite interesting."

Lewis sat back and thought for a moment. *The Ballad of Cable Hogue* was one of Martin's favorite films—poetic, melancholy, filled with heart. Then, recalls Lewis, "I realized Dennis was right, I had been thinking of the clichéd image of Peckinpah."

Lewis contacted Peckinpah, and to his surprise Sam expressed great enthusiasm for the project. The documentary deal eventually fell through due to Lennon's reluctance to be filmed playing before a live audience, so Lewis came to Peckinpah with another proposal. He wanted Sam to shoot a pair of music videos for the two hottest singles on Lennon's now completed album: "Valotte" and "Too Late for Goodbyes." They would be shot over three days in a small studio in upstate New York. Peckinpah would be paid $10,000. Lewis wanted to keep the videos simple—no phony avant-garde pyrotechnics, just Julian in a recording studio playing his songs. Peckinpah's challenge would be to draw the introverted young singer's personality out and capture it on film.

Disenchanted with the way Lennon had scuttled the documentary but desperate to get behind a camera again, Sam accepted the assignment with more than a little ambivalence. "Sam had never seen MTV," says Carol O'Connor. "He thought the idea of making a two-minute film was ridiculous, but I could tell he was a little bit intrigued by it."

"Sam called me up," says Lou Lombardo. "He was in New York to do the music videos for Lennon. They were supposed to shoot the next day and he was blue as hell. He said, 'Shit, man, I hate it back here and I don't know what the fuck I'm doing.' I said, 'Listen, Sam, you invented that shit. Remember the still-frame montages you did in *The Losers*? The first time I saw that I fell off my chair. Just go out and do it. Just do what you invented.' "

Once Sam stepped out on to the studio floor like a bullfighter into the ring, the fear left him and the old instincts kicked in. This was work, this he knew, this he could do. The old concentration flooded back for the last time, and over the next three days he worked steadily, all the way till three A.M. the last evening.

"When we were shooting 'Too Late for Goodbyes' Sam found a doorway behind the band at back of the stage that he thought would be interesting," says Lewis. "He had the door removed, had a light put behind it, like heavenly light, bright. He had Moses Pendleton, an excellent modern dancer and close friend of Julian's, get in the doorway. He did a whole series of short shots, which in editing he interspersed in the video, of Moses dancing in and out of the doorway. Moses did his own moves, with Sam making suggestions: 'Can you do something that's funny?' 'Can you do something that's sad?' It was a combination of mime and dancing. Then Sam shot Julian reacting off of him, which brought Julian to life."

No one noticed that Pendleton bore a striking resemblance to John Lennon until Peckinpah cut the video together in a Manhattan studio; then nobody could miss it. Peckinpah added whole layers of associative meaning to the lyrics of the song by the way he juxtaposed the close-ups of Lennon with those of Pendleton. "It gave the video a very dreamlike quality," says Lewis. "It took it to a whole other level."

Sam cut both videos in three days; the 35mm film had been transferred to videotape to take advantage of the new computerized editing equipment that many directors now used. The technology had come light years since Peckinpah made his first crude Kinescope, *Portrait of a Madonna.* The new machinery didn't intimidate him, it filled him with excitement. Lewis remembers Sam dancing a little jig as he moved from one editing booth to the next, supervising the cutting of both videos simultaneously.

Lewis took the finished product to Charisma's London offices in mid-October. The reception was ecstatic. The videos hit the airwaves just as Lennon's album went into the stores, and the record flew to the top of the charts. Lewis called Martin Baum with the news. "Sam ought to be really proud, the music videos are all over British and American television, people are going ape shit! Julian's career has taken off!"

They weren't a *Ride the High Country* or *Wild Bunch* or *Ballad of Cable Hogue,* but the videos exhibited a quiet lyricism and subtle eye for nuance that his critics would never have thought him capable of. But they weren't enough for Sam. The big screen, the large canvas—that's where he longed to be. He couldn't get past the front gates of Hollywood studios anymore, so he was forced to chase after deals with foreign and independent producers—wannabe movie moguls who ninety-nine times out of a hundred failed to come up with the money when it came time to rev up for preproduction.

But Sam finally found a group of independent producers in San Francisco who at least had the money ($25,000) to pay him for a rewrite of a screenplay that they also wanted him to direct. It was called *On the Rocks*. The product of multiple hey-gang-let's-make-a-movie authors, it was a convoluted melodrama about rival street gangs who fight for control of Alcatraz Island, which they are using for drugrunning and a variety of other nefarious enterprises. Peckinpah tried desperately to turn it into something. "He worked himself to death on that script," says Carol O'Connor. "He'd work till two in the morning, and he had me helping him. He needed someone to bounce ideas off of, to make suggestions."

Under the stress and intense intimacy of their collaboration, the dark shadows emerged from Peckinpah's psyche for the first time in their relationship. Suddenly he would become agitated, pacing the floor as he admitted that he never expected to fall this deeply in love at his age. He had lost his desire to sleep with other women; she had made him monogamous. "You're turning me into a monk!" He flashed a grin, but he picked up a magazine and threw it across the room as he said it.

"You don't have to get angry about it, you should be happy. That's what happens in a mature relationship."

He didn't answer her. Instead he started talking about the other women in his life, how they'd all betrayed him and how eventually she would do the same thing. He started grilling her on hypothetical situations. "If I went out of town on a movie for three months, and you met a very attractive man do you think you would be tempted to—"

"Sam, come on . . ."

The tempo of his pacing picked up. "If you start seeing someone else, I don't want to know about it."

"I told him I had no desire to see anyone but him," says

O'Connor, "that he was being ridiculous, that I was very much in love with him. But that wasn't good enough. It had nothing to do with me, it was his past."

O'Connor was beginning to lose clients at her hairstyling practice because she was taking so many days off to help Sam rewrite *On the Rocks*. He urged her to give up her practice altogether and come to work for him as his assistant. He would match her weekly income at the salon—$600. "Look, you're already working for me. Why not get paid for it? Do you want to become a writer or cut hair for the rest of your life? I'm offering you an opportunity." She kept turning him down; she didn't want to become dependent on him, but finally she gave in and went to work for him full-time.

Then she fell ill. Female troubles. He came out to visit her at her Beverly Hills apartment in a big white limo, brought her a beautiful scarf, and stayed for a couple of days, tenderly nursing her back to health. They stayed up late one night talking, and suddenly he veered off into the darkness. He started in on another litany of all his shattered romances. As he dragged each skeleton out of the closet, his anger escalated. He paced around, slamming doors, throwing things. She'd never seen him like that. All the betrayals, he said, all the ways women had hurt and used him, it made him sick. Liars, they're all liars! Suddenly he wheeled on her with the eyes of a lunging rottweiler: "You're no better than the rest of them! You're a whore like the rest! You should never have taken that first check! I never thought you'd do that!"

A shudder ran through her. He knew she didn't like being dependent on him, knew her deep ambivalence about having quit her job. She couldn't believe he'd strike such a low blow. "You're leaving!" she shouted, the level of her own rage surprising her.

His eyes widened. "You can't do that to me," he said. His words carried a double edge. *You're on the payroll now.*

"Get out!"

"You're not throwing me out."

"You're leaving. Now!" She went into the kitchen and called a taxi. "A cab will pick you up at the front door," she said, gathering up his belongings and piling them in the entryway.

They made up two weeks later. He was so sorry, he told her.

He hadn't meant any of the things he said. It had been his demons talking. She had to forgive him. He admitted that her anger had actually frightened him: "I never want to see you that angry again," he said.

"Then don't ever talk to me like that again," she replied.

They spent the weekend of December 5 together in Malibu, and planned a trip to Palm Springs on the fourteenth. But he called her up a few days later and canceled.

"Sam, don't do this. We need to go away."

"No, I can't," he said coldly. Then he dropped the bomb. "Bonnie's coming back to work with me"—referring to Bonnie Engels, a former secretary who had been a lover. It crushed her. A week later he called her again, apologetic this time. "I love you," he said.

"I love you too, but you hurt me, Sam."

His voice dropped almost to a whisper. "I love you, and I'm going to leave you alone."

"Those were the last words that he said to me," says O'Connor.

When Kristen opened up her father's briefcase after his death, she found all of Carol's letters, every phone message left for him at a hotel or office, every card she ever sent with flowers.

Sam had lost his lover and his collaborator, so he picked up the phone and called his oldest writing partner. "Come on out," he told Silke, "I want you to help me write this script, *On the Rocks.*"

"He gave me this thing," Silke recalls, "and one of the principal characters is named Silke—an old army vet who acts as the ringleader for one of the street gangs. I couldn't say no."

So Jim made that drive again, from Northridge up over the Santa Monica Mountains to Malibu, to that tiny banged-up trailer. As soon as he stepped in the door Sam said, "Let's go shopping."

Oh Christ! Silke thought as he followed him out to the cream-colored Lincoln. "We never mentioned it," says Silke, "but we did exactly what we always did when we first started writing together. We drove to Point Dume and went to the market. I got the white bread and the peanut butter and the coffee and the filters, he got the meats, and we argued about what kind of ice cream to get. We never once blinked an eye at what we were doing. I went back, put the supplies on the shelf, and made the coffee, and then we sat down and talked for two hours. I told him what was wrong with the script and he listened for the first time, the only time, ever. I left and during my drive home he called my wife, Lyn, and talked to her for forty-five minutes about the old days."

The will was still there to dive in and grope for his demons and to wrestle them onto a page, to write and rewrite, to push and pull and take it "one step further," to find the truth, his truth, and tell it no matter how distorted and distasteful it might appear, to devote himself fully to the one thing he still held sacred. The will was there, but not the wherewithal. The little body that had stood up to decades of abuse finally began to give out on him.

That Thanksgiving, Fern Lea invited him up to her house. A lot of the old gang would be there—Joe Bernhard, Max Evans, Gill Dennis, and Kristen. But he turned down the offer, not because he was drunk or pissed off; he just didn't have the energy. Max Evans went down to the trailer, spent a couple of hours with Sam, and for the last time offered one of his elaborate horse trades for the screen rights to *Hi Lo Country* and several of his other novels. (Sam's option on *Hi Lo* had lapsed.)

"I remember his eyes the last moment I saw him," says Evans. "We had been talking for a couple of hours about all kinds of things, little things, like how our kids were doing, which are really the most important things, but we always lose sight of that. As I left, I opened the door and I turned and looked back straight into those old eyes. He was standing in the middle of the trailer, all alone. It was like two old boys who were going into battle and they absolutely knew they would die, but they had to go anyway. It was a heart-wrenching son-of-a-bitch of a moment. In the little distance between us, just seven or eight steps, I saw and felt everything that had ever been in that man. I felt all his suffering, all his lost loves, his yearning for those loves, his yearning for a solidity that his tormented soul would never let him have, the special torment of his creative soul—I saw all that and felt all that. That moment seemed like hours, yet it was briefer than a sigh."

Sam's relationship with Mathew had changed dramatically in the last year. Now out of the Marines, Mathew was taking a full load of classes at Santa Monica College, plus special classes to help him conquer his dyslexia. More and more often on the weekends he could be found at the trailer in Malibu, hanging out with his father. "For the first time in the ten years that I'd known them," says Garner Simmons, "Sam and Mathew had a real relationship. They related to each other as human beings, not as projections of their own fears or expectations. The change was remarkable."

"It seemed like we really came to terms, in a lot of ways," says Mathew. "We were able to deal with each other more honestly than we had. He was proud of me for going back to school. He was trying hard not to be a crazy renegade, the wild son of a bitch that he'd been in the past. He'd call me up in the middle of the night sometimes and say, 'You remember that time up in the cabin in Montana, when I said so-and-so?' It was something he'd said years ago when he'd gotten pissed off. I hardly remembered it. He said, 'I just want you to know I didn't mean it. I'm sorry I said it.' He did that several times."

As Christmas approached that year, Peckinpah sank into his usual funk. Having torpedoed the relationship with Carol, he decided to fly down to Mexico City to spend the holidays with Begonia and Lupita. "He was always going back to Bego," says Jim Silke.

Mathew was going to fly up to San Francisco to join his mother, Melissa, and his cousins. He called his father at the trailer in Malibu a few days before they both left. Sam started in on one of his I'm-so-depressed-I-hate-fucking-Christmas monologues, but the pain in his voice carried an even sharper edge than it had in the past. All the unspoken regrets, the countless losses and desperate yearnings were present though not articulated in his words. Finally, Mathew gently interjected, "Well, hell, if we decide we're going to be here and continue on in this life, we've got to accept where we are and go forward."

Sam fell silent for a moment, then said softly, "That's right. That's what my father always used to say."

So Mathew headed north and his father headed south, back

to Mexico City and Bego. But he never got there. He stopped in Puerto Vallarta first to see Bego's brother, Juan José, and was suddenly stricken with massive chest pains. Bego flew immediately to Puerto Vallarta to join him and a flight was chartered to bring him back to Los Angeles, where he was rushed into intensive care at Centinela Hospital.

Fern Lea and Walter Peter arrived shortly after Sam was admitted. The doctors in the ICU told them that they weren't sure what was wrong with him. They wanted to do some tests but didn't think he could stand the stress, so for the moment they were just trying to stabilize him. "He's not being cooperative," the doctor said. "We need his cooperation if we're to help him. Can you have a talk with him?"

Fern Lea walked into the room and found her brother lying in bed, the sheets down around his waist and EKG wires attached to his chest. Beneath the sheets his legs were moving as if working the pedals of a bicycle—pedaling, pedaling, pedaling, but going nowhere. He seemed unaware of them. "He was bewildered and scared," says Fern Lea. "He didn't understand what was happening. He looked at me and said, 'I don't feel well.' "

"Sam, the doctor says you're not being cooperative," she said.

He gave her one of his astonished, innocent boy looks. "I'll do anything they want," he replied.

"Well, you're going to have to, because they want to make some tests."

"They can do anything they want." Then he turned to Begonia, who'd been at his side since they left Puerto Vallarta. "I can't sleep, I want to go to sleep, get the Seconal, it's in my briefcase."

Fern Lea shot a glare of warning at Bego, who caught it and played dumb. "Uh, I don't know where is your briefcase, Sam. I have to look for it."

"I told him that I loved him and we left," says Fern Lea. "He looked at me with this puzzled expression. He was scared, really frightened. I left fully thinking that I would see him in the morning. The hospital called me at home at seven A.M. and said, 'He's had a major heart attack, but we've stabilized him.' "

When she stepped into the ICU waiting room an hour later,

Begonia stood up from one of the chairs and burst into tears. "I don't understand. Samuel *es muy fuerte!* Why he is not going to make it?"

The hairs stood up on the back of Fern Lea's neck. "What are you saying?"

"The doctor say he's not going to live!"

"I wish I had turned around and gone into the ICU to be with him," says Fern Lea. "I don't know if they would have let me in. But he died alone . . . I ran out to call Walter at his office. He says I wasn't very coherent, but I said, 'Get here! He's not going to make it!' And I went back and he was gone. They said that they would clean him up and then I could go in and see him."

She and Bego went into his room a few minutes later, and Bego erupted with hysterical shrieks. Fern Lea, raised in a clan that preached emotional control as a sign of good character, was appalled by the display. She looked down at the body lying so still and shrunken on the white sheets. *He's not dead,* she recalls thinking. *He's going to sit up and say, "Fern Lea, get me the fuck out of here!"*

But he didn't sit up, and she saw how the color had drained out of his face, how the mouth lay slackly open, weirdly hollow, and knew that he would never sit up again. She heard herself saying, "Now no more torment. You're at peace."

His personal belongings had been laid out on the bed. Fern Lea picked up the grubby white suede jacket that he'd worn almost constantly in the last few years. She fished through the pockets and found twenty dollars and a half a roll of Certs.

Bobby Visciglia answered his phone at home at about ten o'clock on the morning of December 28. It was Walter Kelley. "Sam died this morning," he said in a broken voice.

The receiver froze to the side of Bobby's face. *How fuckin' dare he,* he thought. He hung up, and found his mind leaping back through the years to the last day of shooting on *Cross of Iron,* a sad day on any picture because the strange family of actors and grips and makeup and wardrobe and camera people splits up and scatters, never to re-form again. "I hate that," says Visciglia. "I hate wrap parties; I never go to them because they're always like a goddamned wake. Once a picture finishes everything dies. You never see those people again."

They had just finished the movie's last sequence, the one in which James Coburn and Maximilian Schell flee across a ruined trainyard past a row of burning freight cars. Black-gray smoke hung heavy in the air, the sky above darkening into dusk. The grips loaded the cameras and lights into the trucks, and actors and crew members hustled across the rusty tracks with their bags, hurrying to catch rides to the airport, their voices echoing off the twisted steel rails as if over water: "Well, what plane are you taking?" "Are you gonna stop off in Paris, or are you gonna go on to London?"

A hundred yards down the tracks, near the smoking boxcars, Peckinpah and Visciglia sat on a steel rail, each taking pulls from a bottle of slivovitz. Faces smudged from the smoke, clothes rust-stained, hair tousled, they looked like they'd just returned from the Russian Front themselves. Not a word passed between them while the footfalls and shouts behind them grew fainter and the sun sank beneath the distant hills. Finally, Peckinpah set his bottle down, turned to his prop man and said, "Now, tomorrow, for my first shot, I want to get two cameras, one set up there with a long lens, and another over there. I want to . . ." On and on he went with his description of a vast battle sequence that would never be.

"That's what I thought about when I got Kelley's phone call," Visciglia says, his normally brassy voice dropping to a soft contemplative murmur. "You see, it never ended for Sam, the picture never ended. You had to fight to get the camera away from him."

A memorial was held at the Directors Guild Theater on Sunset Boulevard. Television crews and 350 fans and survivors—actors, writers, editors, prop men, even a few producers—converged there, one last gathering of a clan as wild and loyal and dangerous as the Hammond Brothers. Don Siegel, L. Q. Jones, Brian Keith, Lee Marvin, Jason Robards, Mariette Hartley, Walter Peter, and Kris Kristofferson all got up on the stage to tell Peckinpah stories, to read poetry or sing songs about a man they had all loved. Denny Peckinpah couldn't face the high emotions and stayed out back in the parking lot throughout the service, nursing off a bottle of whiskey.

"I think the miracle of Sam was that he got any of them [the movies] done at all, given the odds against a creative force—and he was a force of nature, there's no other explanation—that was constantly and diametrically opposed to the establishment," Robert Culp said when he took the podium. "It's amazing that there is a *Wild Bunch* and all the other pieces. Absolutely astonishing that they were done at all. I think we ought to hold on to that, as opposed to: 'Gee, I wish he'd done one more, or two more,' or whatever. Let's just thank him, and thank that incredible, savage, iron, burning will that he got them, and that we knew him."

A week earlier another, more private service had been held. Fern Lea, Kristen, Gill Dennis, Melissa, and Sharon and her family stood on the sandy shore of Paradise Cove early one overcast morning and watched as Mathew and Walter Peter paddled a rowboat out beyond the breakers. Over waters that Sam had scuba-dived in, sailed and surfed upon, they paddled. A quarter of a mile out beyond the green undulating kelp beds they pulled in their oars and glided to a stop. Mathew uncapped the urn and emptied the ashes onto a rolling swell. Then together they spread loose flower petals upon the water's surface, and some long-stemmed yellow roses that had been sent by Joie Gould.

Notes

Unfortunately, space does not permit a complete itemization of all the information sources drawn upon for this book. The following is a brief summary of only the most important ones.

Prologue

Sources for the description of *The Wild Bunch* previews in Kansas City and the Bahamas include production files from the Sam Peckinpah Collection at the Margaret Herrick Library; interviews conducted by the author with Lou Lombardo, Phil Feldman, and Roger Ebert; "Sam Peckinpah Breaks a Bottle" by Chris Hodenfield, *Rolling Stone,* May 31, 1971; "Man Was a Killer Long Before He Served a God" by Aljean Harmetz, *The New York Times,* August 31, 1969; "Peckinpah Gets Nonviolent (Offscreen)" by Jeff Milan, *Los Angeles Times,* May 21, 1972; *Daily Variety,* May 7, 1969.

Sources for comments on Peckinpah's importance as an American filmmaker include interviews conducted by the author with Paul Schrader, Martin Scorsese, Gill Dennis, and Ken Kesey; "Sam Peckinpah: No Bleeding Heart" by Kathleen Murphy, *Film Comment,* 1985; "Sam Peckinpah Going to Mexico" by Paul Schrader, *Cinema,* 5, no. 3, 1969; a review of *Straw Dogs* by Stephen Farber, *Cinema,* 1971; "Peckinpah's Progress: From Blood and Killing in the Old West to Siege and Rape in Rural Cornwall," by Dan Yergin, *The New York Times Magazine,* October 31, 1971.

Chapter One

Sources for the history of the Peckinpah and Church families and Sam Peckinpah's childhood include the letters and diaries of Louise and Denver Church, David and Fern Peckinpah, Sam and Fern Lea Peckinpah; research materials and correspondence in the Sam Peckinpah Collection at the Margaret Herrick Library; interviews that the author conducted with Denver Peckinpah, Bob Peckinpah, Fern Lea Peter, Susan Peckinpah, Kristen Peckinpah, David Peckinpah, Betty Peckinpah, Camille Fielding, Joe Bernhard, Don Levy, Doris Roullard, Earlene Heafey, Tom Mullins, Marie Selland, Walter Harpain, and Ed Klippert; "Playboy Interview: Sam Peckinpah," by William Murray, *Playboy,* 19, no. 8, August 1972.

For Peckinpah's years at San Rafael Military Academy the sources include interviews conducted by the author with John Breed, Fern Lea Peter, Marie Selland, and the letters and diaries of Fern and David Peckinpah.

For Peckinpah's years in the Marine Corps, the sources include the diaries and letters of Fern, David, and Sam Peckinpah; interviews the author conducted with Denver Peckinpah, Fern Lea Peter, Susan Peckinpah, Craig Carter, James Weddle, Leo Cardarelli, Mike Fitzgerald, Mike Zownir, Tom Dowlearn, and Marie Selland; "What Price Violence," by P. F. Kluge, *Life,* August 11, 1972; "Sam Peckinpah: Hawk of American Directors," by Joyce Haber, *Los Angeles Times,* 1972.

Chapter Two

Sources for Peckinpah's years at Fresno State College include the letters and diaries of David, Fern, and Sam Peckinpah; the Cal State

Fresno University Archives; interviews that the author conducted with Denver Peckinpah, Fern Lea Peter, Marie Selland, Susan Peckinpah, Marian Dysinger, Vern Selland, Howard Campbell, Dick Lewis, George Zenovich, Dave Parker, William Walsh, Wanda Dove, Jim Baker, Merlyn Burris, and Don Levy. "Playboy Interview: Sam Peckinpah," by William Murray, *Playboy*, 19, no. 8, August 1972; "The Wild Bunch in New York," by John Bryson, *New York* magazine, August 19, 1974.

For Peckinpah's years at USC and the Huntington Park Civic Theater the sources include the letters and diaries of Fern, David, and Sam Peckinpah, and Marie Selland; interviews that the author conducted with Fern Lea Peter, Marie Selland, Don Levy, George Pappas, Rory Guy, Marvin Kaplan, Adele Cook, Don Stoutenborough, Lola Owensby, and Nanette Flynn; an interview conducted by Paul Seydor with James Butler.

For Peckinpah's years at KLAC-TV, the sources include the letters of Sam Peckinpah and Marie Selland; interviews conducted by the author with Marie Selland, Rudy Behlmer, Jerry Tamblyn, Don Forbes, Jim Hobson, Jim Baker, John Langdon, Don Levy, William C. White, Don Stoutenborough, Walter Peter, Denver Peckinpah; an interview conducted by Paul Seydor with James Butler.

Chapter Three

Sources for the section on the loss of Dunlap's Ranch include the diaries and letters of Denver and Louise Church; interviews conducted by the author with Ed Klippert, Susan Peckinpah, Fern Lea Peter, Marie Selland; an interview with Sam Peckinpah conducted by John Bryson in 1972.

Sources for the section on Peckinpah's years at Allied Artists include the letters of Sam Peckinpah and Marie Selland; interviews conducted by the author with Marie Selland, Fern Lea Peter, and Charles Marquis Warren; Don Siegel's eulogy at the Memorial Service for Sam Peckinpah in January of 1985; "Shoot! Sam Peckinpah Talks to John Cutts," *Films and Filmmaking*, 16, no. 1, October 1969.

Sources for life at the Quonset hut include interviews conducted by the author with Marie Selland, Kristen Peckinpah, Walter and Fern Lea Peter, Jeanette Gariss, Nancy Galloway, Frank Kowalski, Rudy Behlmer, John Langdon, and George Zenovich.

Sources for Peckinpah's early years as a television writer and director include the Sam Peckinpah Collection at the Margaret Herrick Library; interviews that the author conducted with Marie Selland, Nancy Galloway, Charles Marquis Warren, Adele Cook, Gay Hayden, Michael Ansara, John Lupton, Jules Levy, Arthur Gardner, Arnold Laven, Joe Mazzuca, Robert Heverly, Chuck Connors, Don Levy, Jack Curtis, and Mike Klein; "Shoot! Sam Peckinpah Talks to John Cutts," *Films and Filmmaking,* 16, no. 1, October 1969; "Playboy Interview: Sam Peckinpah," by William Murray, *Playboy,* 19, no. 8, August 1972.

Sources for the section on life at the Malibu Colony include interviews conducted by the author with Marie Selland, Kristen and Melissa Peckinpah, Walter and Fern Lea Peter, Frank Kowalski, Robert Culp, Brian Keith, Paul Stader, Norman Powell, Nancy Galloway, and Denver Peckinpah.

Chapter Four

Sources for Peckinpah's years as a writer-director for "The Rifleman" and "The Westerner" include the Sam Peckinpah Collection at the Margaret Herrick Library; interviews conducted by the author with Jules Levy, Arthur Gardner, Arnold Laven, Frank Baur, Brian Keith, David Levy, Jack Curtis, Robert Heverly, Norman Powell, Jim Silke, and L. Q. Jones; Sam Peckinpah's interview before an audience at the Seattle Film Society on July 19, 1978; "Talking with Peckinpah" by Richard Whitehall, *Sight and Sound,* 38, no. 4, Autumn 1969.

Sources for the section on the disintegration of Peckinpah's marriage to Marie Selland include the letters and diaries of David, Fern, and Sam Peckinpah, interviews that the author conducted with Marie Selland, Fern Lea and Walter Peter, Kristen, and Melissa Peckinpah, Brian Keith, Robert Heverly, Joe Bernhard, Bob Peckinpah, Chalo Gonzalez, Joie Gould; "What Price Violence," by P. F. Kluge, *Life,* August 11, 1972.

Sources for the section on *Deadly Companions* and *Ride the High Country* include the Sam Peckinpah Collection at the Margaret Herrick Library; interviews that the author conducted with Brian Keith, Maureen O'Hara, Charles FitzSimons, Gay Hayden, Mariette Hartley, Hal Polaire, L. Q. Jones, R. G. Armstrong, Peter McCrea, Cleo Anton, James Drury; "Sam Peckinpah's West," a documentary produced by Joel Reisner for KPFK radio; "Playboy Interview: Sam Peckinpah," by William Murray, *Playboy,* 19, no. 8, August 1972; "Talking with Peckinpah" by Richard

Whitehall, *Sight and Sound*, 38, no. 4, Autumn 1969; "Sam Peckinpah Going to Mexico," by Paul Schrader, *Cinema*, 5, No. 3, 1970.

Chapter Five

Sources for the section on Peckinpah's years at the Bird View house include the Sam Peckinpah Collection at the Margaret Herrick Library; interviews that the author conducted with Walter and Fern Lea Peter, Jim and Lyn Silke, Max Evans, Begonia Palacios, Kristen, and Melissa Peckinpah, Joe Bernhard, and Suzanne Peter.

Sources for the making of *Major Dundee* include the Sam Peckinpah Collection at the Margaret Herrick Library; interviews that the author conducted with Charlton Heston, John Veitch, John Dutton, Jim Silke, Oscar Saul, R. G. Armstrong, James Coburn, Ben Johnson, L. Q. Jones, Gordon Stulberg, Gordon Dawson, Senta Berger, Forrest Wood, Whitey Hughes, Hal Needham, Begonia Palacios, and Howard Kunin; *The Actor's Life: Journals 1956–1976* by Charlton Heston; "Sam Peckinpah's West," a documentary produced by Joel Reisner for KPFK radio; "Talking with Peckinpah" by Richard Whitehall, *Sight and Sound*, 38, no. 4, Autumn 1969; "Peckinpah's Return," by Stephen Farber, *Film Quarterly*, 23, no. 1, Fall 1969.

Sources for the making of *The Cincinnati Kid* include the Sam Peckinpah Collection at the Margaret Herrick Library; interviews conducted by the author with Martin Ransohoff, John Calley, Ring Lardner, Jr., Jim Silke, L. Q. Jones, Philip Lathrop, E. Jack Neuman, Austen Jewell, Robert Schiller, and John Veitch.

Chapter Six

Sources for Peckinpah's years at Broad Beach include the Sam Peckinpah Collection at the Margaret Herrick Library; interviews conducted by the author with Martin Baum, Elliot Silverstein, Reza Badiyi, L. Q. Jones, Begonia Palacios, Kristen, Melissa, and Mathew Peckinpah, Jim and Lyn Silke, Walter and Fern Lea Peter, Marie Selland, and Norman Powell.

Sources for the making of *Noon Wine, That Lady Is My Wife*, and *Villa Rides!* include the Sam Peckinpah Collection at the Margaret Herrick Library; interviews that the author conducted with Daniel Melnick, Reza Badiyi, Jason Robards, Harry Sherman, Clair McCoy, Camille Fielding, Susan Peckinpah, Jeannot Szwarc, Begonia Palacios, and James Coburn; "Sam Peckinpah's *West*," a documentary produced by Joel Reisner for KPFK radio.

Sources for the breakup of Peckinpah's marriage to Begonia Palacios include interviews that the author conducted with Begonia Palacios, Walter and Fern Lea Peter, Chalo Gonzalez, Kristen, Melissa, and Mathew Peckinpah, Max Evans, Jim and Lyn Silke, Robert Schiller, Phil Feldman, and Ken Hyman.

Chapter Seven

Sources include the Sam Peckinpah Collection at the Margaret Herrick Library; interviews that the author conducted with Ken Hyman, Phil Feldman, Jim Silke, Gay Hayden, Jaime Sanchez, Ben Johnson, Teddy Oates, L. Q. Jones, Bo Hopkins, Jorge Russek, Alfonso Arau, Chalo Gonzalez, Gordon Dawson, Howard Kazanjian, Rudi Fehr, Lou Lombardo, Cliff Coleman, James Dickey, Fred Gammon, Helen Martin, Paul Harper, Gill Dennis, Camille Fielding, Ann Godoff, Martin Scorsese, John Milius, Alex Cox, Ron Shelton, Robert Schiller, and Kip Dellinger; an interview that Paul Seydor conducted with Jerry Fielding in 1977; "Playboy Interview: Sam Peckinpah," by William Murray, *Playboy,* 19, no. 8, August 1972; "Sam Peckinpah Breaks a Bottle" by Chris Hodenfield, *Rolling Stone,* May 31, 1971; "Man Was a Killer Long Before He Served a God" by Aljean Harmetz, *The New York Times,* August 31, 1969; "Peckinpah's Progress: From Blood and Killing in the Old West to Siege and Rape in Rural Cornwall," by Dan Yergin, *The New York Times Magazine,* October 31, 1971; "Peckinpah's Return," by Stephen Farber, *Film Quarterly,* 23, no. 1, Fall 1969; "Sam Peckinpah Going to Mexico," by Paul Schrader, *Cinema,* 5, no. 3, 1970; "Sam Peckinpah's West," a documentary produced by Joel Reisner for KPFK radio; Sam Peckinpah's interview before an audience at the Seattle Film Society on July 19, 1978.

Chapter Eight

Sources for Peckinpah's years at Warner Bros. and the making of *The Ballad of Cable Hogue* include the Sam Peckinpah Collection at the

Margaret Herrick Library; interviews that the author conducted with Nancy Galloway, Gay Hayden, Terra Waters, Frank Kowalski, Gill Dennis, Jim Silke, Jason Robards, John Crawford, Edmund Penney, Bobby Visciglia, L. Q. Jones, Gordon Dawson, Gary Weis, Stella Stevens, Lou Lombardo, and Walter Peter.

Sources for the making of *Straw Dogs* include the Sam Peckinpah Collection at the Margaret Herrick Library; interviews that the author conducted with James Dickey, John Milius, Daniel Melnick, Martin Baum, Joe Bernhard, Gill Dennis, Walter Kelley, Katy Haber, James Swann, Joie Gould, Susan George, Peter Vaughan, Del Henney, Ken Hutchison, Kristen Peckinpah, Tony Lawson, Paul Davies, Roger Spottiswoode, Garth Craven; "Playboy Interview: Sam Peckinpah," by William Murray, *Playboy*, 19, no. 8, August 1972; "The Ballet of Death in Sam Peckinpah," by Ray Loynd, *Los Angeles Herald-Examiner*, April 11, 1974; an interview with Peckinpah conducted by F. Anthony Macklin in 1975; "Peckinpah's Progress: From Blood and Killing in the Old West to Siege and Rape in Rural Cornwall," by Dan Yergin, *The New York Times Magazine*, October 31, 1971; *Cahiers du Cinéma*, 1982; *Dustin Hoffman* by Jeff Lenburg, St. Martin's Press, 1983.

Sources for the making of *Junior Bonner* and *The Getaway* include the Sam Peckinpah Collection at the Margaret Herrick Library; interviews that the author conducted with Jeb Rosebrook, Martin Baum, Katy Haber, Joie Gould, Frank Baur, James Pratt, Camille Fielding, Chalo Gonzalez, Bobby Visciglia, Robert Schiller, Kip Dellinger, Gordon Dawson, Jim Silke, David Foster, Ben Johnson, Bo Hopkins, Mike Klein, Roger Spottiswoode, and Grover Lewis.

Chapter Nine

Sources include the Sam Peckinpah Collection at the Margaret Herrick Library; interviews that the author conducted with Kris Kristofferson, Joie Gould, Katy Haber, Chalo Gonzalez, Gordon Dawson, Fern Lea Peter, Camille Fielding, Bobby Visciglia, Kip Dellinger, Frank Kowalski, James Coburn, Walter Kelley, Roger Spottiswoode, Garth Craven, Jim Silke, R. G. Armstrong, L. Q. Jones, Jorge Russek, Dan Melnick, Paul Harper, Lindsley Parsons, Lyn Silke, Mike Klein, Martin Scorsese, David Peckinpah, Jim Hamilton, and Grover Lewis; interviews that Paul Seydor conducted with Gordon Carroll, Bob Wolfe, and Roger Spottiswoode in 1977; an interview given by Peckinpah before an audience at the San Francisco Film Festival in 1974; *Encounters with Filmmakers: Eight Career Studies,* by Jon Tuska, Greenwood Press, 1991; "Pat Garrett and Billy the Kid," by Jan Aghed, *Sight and Sound,* 42, no. 2, Spring 1973; "The Wild Bunch in New York," by John Bryson, *New York* magazine, August 19, 1974.

Chapter Ten

Sources for the making of *Bring Me the Head of Alfredo Garcia* and *The Killer Elite* include the Sam Peckinpah Collection at the Margaret Herrick Library; interviews that the author conducted with Gordon Dawson, Chalo Gonzalez, Jorge Russek, Martin Baum, Frank Kowalski, Walter Kelley, Garth Craven, Katy Haber, Kris Kristofferson, Don Levy, Roger Ebert, Paul Seydor, Kip Dellinger, Garner Simmons, Ron Wright, and Whitey Hughes.

Sources for Peckinpah's altercations at the AFI tribute to James Cagney and the Los Angeles International Airport, and his near-drowning in the pool of the Beverly Hilton Hotel, include the Sam Peckinpah Collection at the Margaret Herrick Library; interviews that the author conducted with Ray Bradbury, Jim and Lyn Silke, Jason Robards, Bobby Visciglia, Katy Haber, and Ron Wright.

Sources for the making of *Cross of Iron* and *Convoy* include the Sam Peckinpah Collection at the Margaret Herrick Library; interviews that the author conducted with Katy Haber, Ron Wright, Frank Kowalski, Walter Kelley, Jim Hamilton, Kip Dellinger, James Coburn, David Warner, Senta Berger, Murray Jordan, Bobby Visciglia, Kristen, Melissa, and Mathew Peckinpah, Tony Lawson, Steven Gaydos, Kris Kristofferson, Michael Deeley, Whitey Hughes, and Garth Craven.

Sources for Peckinpah's Montana years include the Sam Peckinpah Collection at the Margaret Herrick Library; interviews that the author conducted with Joe Swindlehurst, Kristen and Mathew Peckinpah, Gill Dennis, Ron Wright, Kip Dellinger, David Peckinpah, and Jim Silke.

Chapter Eleven

Sources for Peckinpah's life in Malibu in the 1980s include the Sam Peckinpah Collection at the Margaret Herrick Library; interviews that the author conducted with Mathew, Kristen, and Melissa Peckinpah, Ted Post, Martin Baum, Jeb Rosebrook, Garner Simmons, Gill Dennis, Walter Kelley, Fern Lea and Walter Peter, L. Q. Jones, Don Hyde, and Carol O'Connor.

Sources for the making of *The Osterman Weekend* and the Julian Lennon rock videos include the Sam Peckinpah Collection at the Margaret Herrick Library; interviews that the author conducted with Alan Sharp, Kristen Peckinpah, Gill Dennis, Walter Kelley, Jim Hamilton, Lou Lombardo, David Rawlins, Martin Lewis, and Martin Baum.

Sources for Peckinpah's last days, his death, and its aftermath include the Sam Peckinpah Collection at the Margaret Herrick Library; interviews that the author conducted with Carol O'Connor, Jim and Lyn Silke, Kristen, Melissa, and Mathew Peckinpah, Fern Lea and Walter Peter, Gill Dennis, Garner Simmons, Bobby Visciglia, Walter Kelley, Joie Gould, and the tape-recording of the memorial service held for Peckinpah at the Directors Guild Theater on Sunset Boulevard.

Index